TWO CENTURIES
TO FREEDOM

The True Story of One Family's Two-Century Migration from Lucca, Italy, to New Mexico and Other American States

TWO CENTURIES
TO FREEDOM

*The True Story of One Family's Two-Century Migration
from Lucca, Italy, to New Mexico and Other American States*

❧

DAVID F. MENICUCCI

SUNSTONE
PRESS
SANTA FE

Sunstone books may be purchased for educational, business, or sales promotional use.
For information please write: Special Markets Department, Sunstone Press,
P.O. Box 2321, Santa Fe, New Mexico 87504-2321.
Printed on acid-free paper
∞
eBook: 978-1-61139-766-6

Library of Congress Cataloging-in-Publication Data

Names: Menicucci, David F. author
Title: Two centuries to freedom : the true story of one family's
    two-century migration from Lucca, Italy, to New Mexico and other
    American states / David F. Menicucci.
Description: Santa Fe : Sunstone Press, 2025. | Includes index. | Summary:
    "The true story of one family's two-century migration from Lucca, Italy
    to New Mexico and other American states"-- Provided by publisher.
Identifiers: LCCN 2025007962 | ISBN 9781632937506 hardback | ISBN
    9781632937490 paperback | ISBN 9781611397666 epub
Subjects: LCSH: Menicucci family | Italian Americans--New Mexico--History |
    Italian Americans--West (U.S.)--History | Lucca (Italy)--Emigration and
    immigration--History | LCGFT: Family histories
Classification: LCC CS71.M54274 2025 | DDC 929.20973--dc23/eng/20250501
LC record available at https://lccn.loc.gov/2025007962

WWW.SUNSTONEPRESS.COM
SUNSTONE PRESS / POST OFFICE BOX 2321 / SANTA FE, NM 87504-2321 /USA
(505) 988-4418

DEDICATION

This work is dedicated to my mother, Emma Dalle Menicucci, who encouraged me to write it, provided a rich source of historical material and has anxiously awaited its arrival for over a decade.

CONTENTS

PREFACE

This work aims to provide an in-depth, comprehensive view of early Twentieth Century Italian immigration as seen through the eyes of the Menicucci family, which began its quest for American economic freedom around 1780.[1] This true story chronicles the two-hundred-year migration of the Menicucci family from Lucca, Italy, to America's western states, with special emphasis on Albuquerque, New Mexico. It presents hundreds of new historical details about the Italian immigration experience in Michigan, Illinois, California, Nevada, Idaho, Montana, and Albuquerque, New Mexico. The story is based on official records, published reports and firsthand accounts.

The story begins in the late 1700s in Lucca, Italy, at the foothills of the Apennines, where the Menicucci family had lived for countless generations. It tells of the first pioneering Menicucci members who migrated to western states of America, where many of their descendants reside. The bulk of the book discusses the actions of Julio and Amerigo Menicucci, who chose to settle in Albuquerque, where they prospered under America's free-market capitalist system.

Julio and Amerigo Menicucci, my grandfather and his brother, who immigrated around 1910, were among the early Twentieth Century wave of Lucca Province Italians who migrated to the United States, starting around 1890 and petering out by 1920. The book describes the acts and works of these men and women as they labored in America and explains the historical context that drove their decisions. Doing so can help avoid presentism, a tendency to judge historic actions based on current norms or standards that often leads to pernicious conclusions.

I present events realistically, rather than the heavily cliched tales carried through the generations as lore, many of which are distorted by a natural tendency to emphasize positive memories and to summarize away details. For example, my father, Charlie, said about my grandfather, "One day, he decided he should give America a try, so he did." While fundamentally true, Italian peasant families living on the outskirts of Lucca in 1908 focused on day-to-day survival in a stultifying economic environment. Scooting off to another continent on a whim was never on the agenda. Such an endeavor was an enormous decision of monumental financial importance, as we shall see.

But an audacious new nation named after a great Italian explorer was brandishing a reputation for economic freedom in a land where families grew and prospered based on their merits rather than their birth-assigned societal status. It beaconed for intrepid people to come to its shores. Economically stagnant at the lowest rung of Italian society, a rare generational opportunity lay before the Menicuccis, one worthy of the greatest investment in family memory and one that would consume nearly all of the family's resources. For generations, the Menicuccis believed that God presented special events at various times in people's lives to provide new and potentially fruitful opportunities.

The story tells of setbacks, triumphs, clever business maneuvers and embarrassing blunders. Attitudes and beliefs about the Menicuccis emerge in the story as they wrangle with life's many experiences, illness, injury, financial losses and humiliations. Their attitudes toward race, sexual practice and mental health—some of which would be condemned based on modern standards—become rational when viewed in a historical theater.

Many strangers played pivotal roles in guiding the Menicucci family to Albuquerque. The interaction between immigrants and these people helps define their personalities, beliefs and traits. Finally, the story exemplifies the families' religious beliefs and the defining role of Catholicism in their lives and many other Albuquerqueans.

Throughout the book, I describe the events as I concluded them. Some conclusions are firmly based on facts, such as birth records. Others are logically derived based on credible evidence, such as newspaper reports, audio recordings, or personal letters. Still, other conclusions are based on my experiences living in an Italian family in Albuquerque's Italian colony.

All chapters after the second one are presented chronologically, beginning in the late 1700s and continuing to the deaths of the four original family immigrants in the late 1980s. Each chapter's title contains the approximate historical dates to which the discussion applies. At the end of each chapter are notes and references.

A discussion about the Italian boundaries along with maps are presented in the notes.[2]

RESEARCH BASIS

This book is the culmination of over twelve years of research, including two years of writing. Much of the information about the Menicucci is based on my knowledge of Julio and Amerigo and their wives, the original New Mexico Menicucci patriarchs. Since I grew up only a half city block from my grandfather, Julio, I spent much time with him. He was retired when I was young and it was only a thirty second bike ride to his home. I had an open invitation to visit, and I did so frequently. With Julio being close to his brother Amerigo, I learned much about him also. I was often invited to join Julio, Amerigo and their friend Victorio Bachechi on fishing, hunting and mushroom-gathering trips in the Jemez Mountains in Northern New Mexico. As a young preteen lad, I listened as the men discussed one subject after another, mainly business, politics and the church, but the story of their immigration was often interspersed. Much of the conversations were in Italian, which, by necessity, I understood reasonably well. I estimate I spent over three hundred hours with them on various outings.

In the late 1970s, my wife and I bought a home just three residential properties from Julio. During that time, there were three generations of Menicuccis on San Carlos Road in Albuquerque's Huning Castle Addition—my father, Charlie and Julio—just a few properties apart. For years, nearly every night, Charlie walked to his folk's home to sip wine and chat for a couple of hours. I was invited to join and visit a few evenings a week. I estimate that I spent fifteen hundred hours listening and learning during those evening talks.

Other sources included official civil records in the U.S. and Italy, historical directories, newspaper articles, interviews with immigrant families, church records, published historical documents and some internet-published genealogical family trees. I liberally integrated information from the dissertations and theses of University of New Mexico scholars Frederick Bohme, Nicholas Ciotola, Judith DeMark and Michigan Technology University scholar Christina Menghini, all of whom investigated early Italian immigration. I extracted information from dozens of books, articles and academic theses, along with vital records from the Italian Civil Registry, which around 1866 began recording births, deaths and marriages in all Italian provinces. I viewed over a hundred thousand Italian civil records, translating and studying dozens of them. In addition, I utilized the resources of the Albuquerque Public Library Genealogy Center, which has archived historical local directories, newspapers and church records.

Additionally, I listened to dozens of hours of interviews with early Italian immigrants that Nicholas Ciotola conducted as part of the University of New Mexico Oral History Project, which the University of New Mexico Center for Southwest Research curates. I also recorded hours of personal interviews with family members and family friends, producing additional verbal history. I provide partial family trees that are pertinent to the discussion.

NOTES FOR EACH CHAPTER

At the end of each chapter are notes. Each note provides additional information for a topic under discussion. In most cases, the note references other publications. In other cases, it provides detail that is too extensive for the main text.

ACCURACY

Research for this book involved the assimilation of diverse sets of information, each possessing varying degrees of value. I started with family lore, which I assumed was accurate, especially when it was based on recorded interviews with or written documents from immigrants or first-generation direct descendants. Records, such as official civil documents, labeled and dated media reports, or publications, especially scholarly ones, provide proof. Such documents trump lore. This vetting process either qualifies lore as history or refutes it. Family trees are rampant in many common genealogical search platforms, but most are questionably reliable because they tend to be based solely on lore and have few factual citations. The standard of proof I applied is described in the notes.[3]

In other cases, suspicions may be all that are available. For example, even without a death record, I might suspect that an individual died in America within a specific period based on his or her sudden disappearance from a city directory and no reappearance elsewhere. I can deduce a certain action by an individual based on my knowledge of the person's personality.

GENERAL GUIDANCE

Numerous anecdotes are presented in the text. Stories told by witnesses contain both quoted and unquoted dialogue. Quoted dialog represents the speaker's actual words. An unquoted dialog represents my summary of the unclear parts of the story. Over time, as witnesses recanted stories, the wording changed, sometimes substantially. The stories I present are my best attempt to reconcile these differences and present an accurate rendition. I only quote those who are deceased or from whom I have permission.

The first time an Italian word appears in the book, I place an adjacent English translation in parenthesis. Proper nouns are printed exactly as they exist. Many Italians Americanized or changed their given name. For example, Johnny Giannini was born Austutillo Giannini. Others adopted nicknames, such as Cherubino Domenici, known as Chopo. Still others modified the spelling of their surname to ease pronunciation. For example, Giacopetti became Jacopetti.[4] In the text, I used a person's given Italian name until it was altered; after that, I used the changed version.

When required for clarity, especially in the genealogical discussions in the initial chapters, I refer to individuals by their complete names, which includes the given name, the names of the father and mother and the given name of grandfather(s) followed by provenience. For example, my grandfather is Julio, son of Raffaello and Teresa Rondina, son of Pasquale, son of Paolo, son of Bartolomeo Menicucci from Lucca. Similarly, I refer to a woman by her given name, maiden surname, her father's and mother's names, followed by provenience. Later in the book, I dispense with these descriptors as the characters are fully identified and the discussion pivots from Italian familial lineages to modern historical information about the families in America.

For the convenience of the expected predominantly American readers, measurements of any kind are presented in English units, even though the Italians used the metric system. Also, all dollar amounts noted in text always have an accompanying conversion to 2024 dollars. I computed the conversions manually using an average discount (i.e., inflation) rate for the intervening years computed from published inflation rates per year.[5]

COMPANION MATERIALS

Six appendices provide relevant Supplemental information.

Appendix I: Immigrant Italians and the Economic Development of Jemez Mountain Communities
Appendix II: Comprehensive list of all Italian surnamed families in Albuquerque in 1900, 1925 and 1950.
Appendix III: Verified family trees relevant to the period of discussion.
Appendix IV: Guidance and suggestions for genealogical searching, including accessing and searching the Italian civil records.
Appendix V: The story of the emigration of Pat Scanlon, son of Mariangela Menicucci, and his family to Italy.
Appendix VI: Scandalo (Scandal) in Italian Culture.

FINAL SPECULATIONS

The book concludes with the author's essay on how the original four Menicucci immigrants might judge the family's progress relative to the family's original immigration goals.

Notes

1. American freedom was almost unimaginable for the Italians living in the backwoods of Lucca province. The idea that a man and woman could grow and thrive based on personal merits was a powerful draw because they had been held hostage to the Mezzadria system for many generations. All Italians, especially the Lucchese, believed they could compete with anyone in the world in a fair and free market. *Foner* describes the American freedom that they sought.

2. Italian political boundaries are confusing. Lucca is both a province and a comune (community or city). Lucca province is an area within the Tuscany region. There are no exact parallels between Italy's political boundaries and those in America, but a region in Italy is roughly equivalent to an American state. A region's provinces are roughly analogous to counties in an American state. Within each comune are cities and hamlets called frazione (villages). Unlike America, where boundaries, public and private, are carefully delineated to within inches of accuracy,

Italian boundaries evolved over centuries and the exact locations of historical boundary landmarks are long gone. Regions and provinces both retain specific boundaries. For comune and fraziones, the locals decide, more or less, their boundaries.

On the west side of the Lucca province lay the Lucca Comune, the walled city. The Capannori Comune lay east of Lucca. The principal characters in the book hail from Capannori fraziones of Lammari, Segromigno in Piano (lower plane) and Segromigno in Monte, all located northeast of Lucca comune, the walled city. None of these areas have specific boundaries. (See maps below) It was common for Italian immigrants to list their birthplace as Lucca or Capannori when they all might have been born in Segromigno. Or vice versa. Sometimes, in a ship manifest, an immigrant declared his Italian hometown as different from his declaration on a previous voyage, e.g., Segromigno instead of Lucca. Those subtle differences were unimportant then but provided valuable details in this investigation.

Italy showing the location of Lucca province.

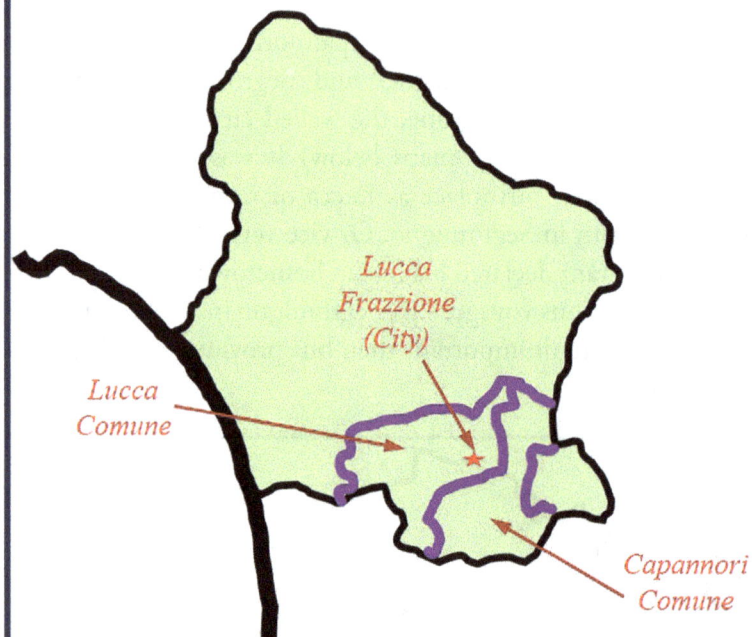

Lucca Province

Lucca Frazzione (City)

Lucca Comune

Capannori Comune

Close up of Lucca province showing the comune of Capannori.

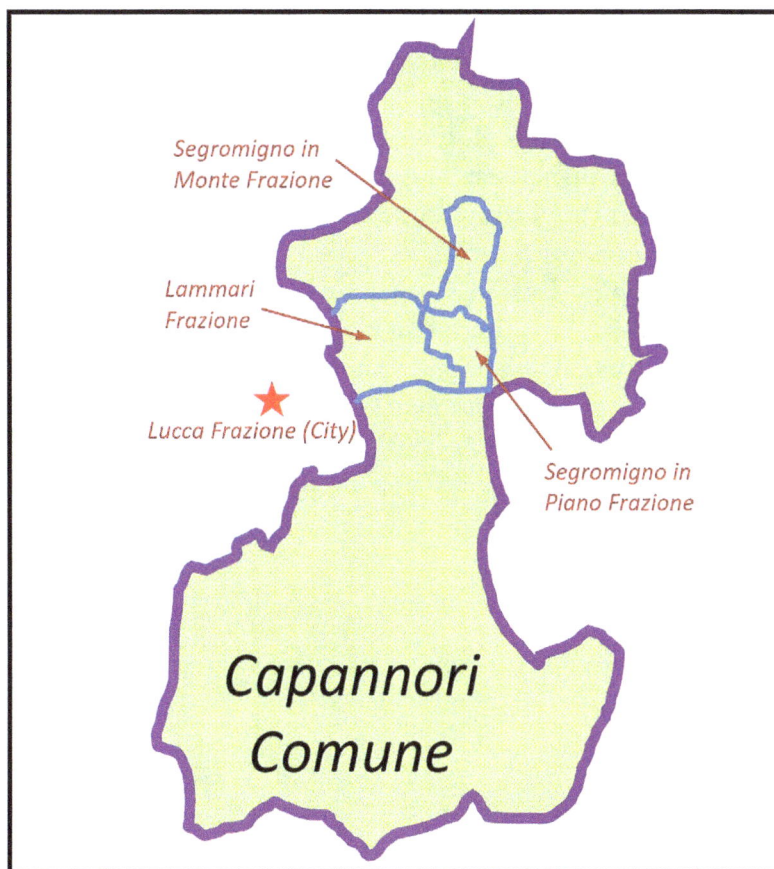

Close up of Capannori comune showing the principal fraziones of interest in the story.

3. I have endeavored to meet the Genealogical Standard of Proof so that this work can serve as the basis for further investigations. *Stahle* (*Understanding the Genealogical Proof Standard*) presents a description of this standard which consists of five elements, all of which must be satisfied to constitute proof of a conclusion:

Reasonably exhaustive research has been completed.

Each statement of fact has a complete and accurate source citation.

The evidence is reliable and has been skillfully correlated and interpreted.

Any contradictory evidence has been resolved.

The conclusion has been soundly reasoned and coherently written.

Noel Stevenson (*Genealogical Evidence, A guide to the Standard of Proof Relating to the Ancestry, Heirship and Family History*) also provides a guidebook on how to meet the standard of proof. The work is somewhat dated because it was published well before digital searching methods via internet had emerged. However, many of the principles for proving claims can still be applied.

4. The typical English speaker stumbles over Italian names that begin with "Giu" or "Gia," uncertain how the letter combinations should be pronounced. An English speaker phonetically pronouncing Jacopetti, produces the correct pronunciation of Giacopetti. The letter J is not part of the Italian alphabet.

5. Investopedia's inflation rates are published at its website: www.investopedia.com.

ACKNOWLEDGMENTS

Many people have advised and assisted me with this project. I thank Barbara, my wife for fifty-two years, who provided support, comfort and tolerance for my quirkiness in this effort. She is a Catholic school teacher with forty years of experience at St. Charles Borromeo School, including administration, and was a primary reviewer of the document. I deeply appreciate her love, consideration, and consequential comments and suggestions.

Many family members and friends assisted. I thank my mother, Emma Dalle Menicucci, a reviewer, who provided ongoing consultation throughout the effort. Similarly, Theresa Domenici Menicucci contributed much historical information about the Domenici family, including many annotated photos. Adele Morelli Davis provided outstanding support, contributions and encouragement. All three of these ladies were/all first-generation Italian immigrants. Despite their advanced ages, all displayed remarkable recall clarity and provided many unique historical details. I appreciate my immediate family members for excusing me from many normal functions so that I could complete this book.

David Morelli, my cousin, served as a reviewer, consultant and principal advisor. He produced critical information that directed the early course of the research. Ed Matteucci, served as a reviewer and was the principal consultant concerning the Matteucci family. I credit my cousins Laura Menicucci Miller, John Menicucci, Mark Menicucci, Gemma Menicucci Morris, Ann Menicucci, Giuli Scanlon Doyle, Pat Scanlon, Marie Mongomery Schwaner, and my sister Kathy Menicucci Meadows for their contributions, suggestions and assistance. All live in Albuquerque except for Guili Doyle, in Phoenix, Arizona, and Pat Scanlon, in Viterbo, Italy. Ioli Giomi's publications of the Il Giornalino in the 1970s provided much accurate historical information for the book.

Amanda Lewis of the Jemez Springs Public Library assisted in collecting information about Jemez. Anne Van Arsdall, PhD, English, of North Carolina, provided advice and consulting about grammar, structure and style. Lisa Kindrick, head genealogical librarian at the Albuquerque Public Library, supplied outstanding technical support and guidance in locating historical documents. I appreciate the ecclesiastical expertise and advice of Father Jerome Mueller (retired) of Jemez Springs, New Mexico. I value the cooperation and help from the University of New Mexico Center for Southwest Research for providing convenient access to the many Italian interviews in the Italian Oral History Project. I appreciate the many historical pictures provided by Jill Hartke at the Albuquerque Museum.

Finally, in producing the book, I recognize my cousin Steve Scanlon, president of Rewire, Inc., West Linn, Oregon, who provided guidance and assistance in the publication process. I also appreciate Rose Marie Kern, president of Southwest Writers and RMK publications, Albuquerque, New Mexico, who assisted with excellent advice regarding book publications. John Druga, in Ohio, provided key advice at the outset and helped edit various drafts.

Thank you to all others I failed to mention.

FOREWORD

While the book focuses on the Menicucci family, one could pen a similar story in equivalent detail for every Italian immigrant who landed in Albuquerque in the first half of the Twentieth Century. Each family's story is unique, but many similarities are rooted in Italian culture. The Menicuccis represented a typical middle-class family in Albuquerque's Italian colony.

1

INTRODUCTION

SUBCLASS LIFE

"Colono" is how Raffaello Menicucci described his profession on his April 8, 1888, Italian marriage license application in Lucca, Italy. Colono literally means settler, but at the time, it defined an occupation—a Lucca-province sharecropper—and a specific career path. There was little that Raffaello could aspire to professionally other than perhaps to be a fine Colono farmer. Similarly, his wife, Teresa, was predestined to a specific job in the home, whether or not she desired it.

This sharecropper system in Italy in the late 18th Century developed over many centuries, evolving from the Middle Ages. Called the Mezzadria (sharecropping), the land owners—the Padrone—allowed the Mezzadria (sharecroppers) to farm the land. The crops were split roughly in half. The Mezzadria and their families lived on a Padrone's land rent-free as long as they farmed the lands and shared the crops. This system was sometimes dubbed the Latifando (estate). Theoretically, it is workable and productive. Colono was the lowest social class within the Mezzadria community, on par with dirt peasants.[1]

The Franchini family in front of their home in Molina Nuevo, Lucca Province, circa 1911. This shows a multi-generational Mezzadria family housed under a single roof. Courtesy Lynne Franchini Peckinpaugh.

The system certainly worked for the Padrone because it was subtly but significantly biased against the sharecropper. It was not that the Padrone were moralistically deviant, but they had a prime advantage in negotiations: they owned the property and facilities the Mezzadria needed to live. Even though the Latifando laws were intended to ensure Padrone-Mezzadria parity, the Padrone typically had personal acquaintances, family members and business partners in the local government who could easily circumvent the law whenever it was convenient. Further, there was little bureaucracy to adjudicate any Mezzadria claims of injustice, even if they found the money to hire legal counsel.

Often, the Mezzadria were subjected to overtly oppressive practices, such as requiring a Colono tenant farmer to provide a constant annual supply of crops to the Padrone regardless of the amount of harvest. The Mezzadria families could be short of food in lean years, while the Padrone had plenty. In other cases, the padrono (boss) might be less obviously biased, e.g., insisting on having a first selection of the crops for his portion of the harvest. The practices were not unlawful but certainly did not build a fellowship with Mezzadria families.

The Padrone business community was small relative to the population but outsized in community influence. Each typically oversaw farming operations, including multiple Mezzadria families spread over the various properties. So, a small group controlled most of the land and resources. Although the Padrone were politically powerful relative to the Mezzadria, they wisely refrained from overt subjugation because it risked sparking unrest and protests, especially organized ones that could disrupt their pleasant lifestyle. There was also enough competition between the Padrone families for Mezzadria workers that the normal market forces moderated any significant excesses; the Mezzadria still had the freedom to choose where they wanted to live and for whom they wished to work. The Padrone understood that their situation was sustainable only if the Mezzadria had little money left over from the annual operations, effectively tying them to the land and discouraging them from becoming landowners. More landowner competition could imperil their situation. This fact was always in the Padrone's mind as they negotiated contracts with the Mezzadria families.

Even after Italy was unified in 1861, the government was poorly organized and dealt with strife and violence in all peninsula regions, especially the south. There were few national resources and even less collective political will to address a sharecropper system that worked for the Padrone but left the Mezzadria with no personal flexibility and few growth opportunities. With little national government intervention, the local governing officials did as they had for decades: let it be. And they let it be until the middle of the twentieth century.

The Padrone class comprised competent business people with the economic upper hand in the Mezzadria system and used it in negotiations. Colono farmers fared poorly because they possessed the fewest resources and were the least educated. For people in the lower class, the goal was to find the least disadvantageous situation to ensure family survival from one year to the next.

Giulio Menicucci and his brother, Amerigo, were born in the depths of Italian economic malaise in the late 1800s. They were typical boys, but boyhood was brief in Italy during that era. Prior to starting school at the age of seven, they worked around the farm and home under the guidance of their mother, Teresa. As stated on the wedding certificate, her profession was Alta a Casa (Head of Household), which meant that she controlled the home, including the children's affairs, until they attained working age. She managed all household inhabitants' diet, health and welfare regardless of age or relationship, including boarders.[2]

The Apennine Mountains, looking north from Reggio Emilia, about thirty miles north of Segromigno in Monte. This picture typifies the countryside of Italy in the Lucca province. Courtesy Wikimedia Commons, in the public domain via https://commons.wikimedia.org, 2023.

Wedding picture of Teresa Rondina and Raffaello Menicucci, circa 1888. Courtesy author's collection.

EDUCATING THE MASSES

The Casati Act of 1859 mandated public education. Comunes managed primary schools, and the provinces handled secondary education. Regions managed universities. The Capannori community where the Menicuccis lived is located just east of the ancient walled city of Lucca.[3] It maintained several elementary schools, grades one through eight.

Mezzadria children received three years of primary education at the local community-run primary school, the minimum mandated by law. Although higher grades were available, three years were more than ample for Colono life. Even though the government provided education at no cost, the actual cost to the Colono peasants was the loss of a productive family member from the farming crew. It was a strong incentive to remove a child from school at the earliest possible moment.

Elementary school pupils spent about twelve hours daily with school work, including walking time between home and classroom. School education was fixated on reading, cursive writing and arithmetic, with some Italian history and political propaganda thrown in as sidenotes. School days included Saturdays and Sundays for pupils who fell behind in their studies. By the age of eleven or twelve, young boys were expected to be fully educated and physically able to become productive members of their family's Mezzadria endeavors. Of course, the wealthier families, including most Padrone, could retain their children in school for many more years, many proceeding to higher education and professional work.

Religious education was managed by the Catholic church, the dominant religious power in the country, which was independent of the government. The province of Lucca, which contained Capannori, was replete with Catholic churches, at roughly twice the density of Catholics per church as in the United States. The local pastor of each church was responsible for religious education on Sundays. He focused on teaching women the best religious practices for their children. Although they did not operate a formal Sunday School, the homilies and other counseling centered on developing and maintaining a God-fearing parishioner community. Girls were expected to perform their duties as wives, heads of households and mothers. Similarly, men were expected to supply resources for their families and direct the family's business activities, including guiding youngsters as they joined the workforce. This was the way for millions of Italian families for countless generations and the way it was for Raffaello's family.

Home of the Morelli family in Ponte a Moriano circa 1911. It is located about three miles west of Capannori Comune and is typical of a Frazzone in Lucca province. Courtesy David Morelli.

DREAM OVER THE HORIZON

While Italy struggled with a stagnant economy at the turn of the 19th Century, the United States was rapidly developing as a new nation, full of opportunity and economic freedom for anyone to pursue dreams. It was a unique political structure—a country without a king. It was a difficult concept for the Italians because it was foreign to their life experiences. But even in the early 1800s, just a few years after the American Revolution, the news about the United States' economic potential spread around the globe. America was fascinating to impoverished Italians. As a few of the Menicucci neighbors ventured to America and then returned, they reported that America was no fluke; it was a free and open land of opportunity replete with natural resources. Even common laborers in America reported making triple or quadruple the wages they could garner in Italy for the same work. The news uplifted many of the Mezzadria, especially a Colono such as Raffaello, who had seen his family struggle in an entrenched system with no realistic hope for an exit.

There was an obstacle to acquiring those high-paying jobs: getting to America. Most Colono families had limited savings and often lived hand-to-mouth, especially if the family was dealing with an injury or the loss of a significant family member. Raffaello operated at a loss for most of the year and returned to even after the fall harvests. A bad harvest or an unexpected adversarial incident could leave the family in the red for several years. Colono families were perpetually broke. As we shall see, Raffaello's family was among the most impoverished of all of Pasquale's seven children, and there were virtually no government assistance programs. The church and neighbors helped families to survive crises.

Pasquale and his sons, including Raffaello, sensed that America represented a multigenerational economic opportunity for the family, which could finally help them escape the bondage of a Colono career. Saving money was difficult. Streamliner passage for one to America typically cost about what a healthy Mezzadria family might save in a couple of good farming years. It was nearly out of reach for Raffaello.

By the early 1900s, many early Italian immigrants from Lucca, including some family members, sent back to Italy ample amounts of money that they had earned from American jobs. As the American nation grew, it needed a constant supply of raw materials, such as metals. Gold, discovered in California in the mid-1800s, became the buzz in the Italian peasant communities. There were dazzling tales of men who rode off to the hills in California in the morning and returned with bags of gold in the evening. Gold was glamorous, but the U.S. industry desperately needed construction metals such as copper, aluminum and steel. Demands also grew for fuel to produce electricity and for heating and cooking. Coal was the primary energy source for most Americans in the early 1900s. Those materials came from extraction mining, which depended on a constant supply of young, strong men eager to work in harsh, dangerous underground conditions. The wave of youthful immigrants from Ireland, Italy, and the Scandinavian countries fit the bill perfectly.

The Italian government was slow to catch on to America's allure. In the early 1800s, the Italian government prohibited emigration for all except landowners or those with high financial means. Later, the government removed restrictions as the revenues from immigrants flowing back to

Italy became an important revenue stream. The government eliminated passports for emigration as long as the receiving country did not require them. In 1888, Prime Minister Francesco Crispi's administration removed nearly all the emigration restrictions and authorized vettore, persons legally appointed by the shipping companies to recruit Italian laborers for work in America. The door was opened to the Mezzadria, but the Italian government offered no direct assistance to emigrants as they left.[4]

The Padrone jumped on the vettore law, and many quickly became employment brokers matching immigrant Italian men to mining jobs. Potential immigrants paid a padrono (boss) to bring them to the American job. Several neighboring families, especially the poorer ones, had used the padrono's service and recommended it. Padrone constantly canvassed the areas around Lucca, looking for eligible men of sufficient physical size and strength for rigorous work in a mine.

The padrono's fees for job placement in America were less than the cost of an individual paying outright for the voyage. More importantly, he guaranteed a job, which was uncertain for a young, penniless, ignorant Colono peasant traveling alone. There was no magic in the Padrone's discount. He offered lower travel prices because, as part of the vettore process, he negotiated bulk travel fees for the ship and train travel. Therefore, he could provide a discount for the emigrant and still have plenty of profit margin after taking his fee from the mine operators.

The vettore system helped to stem the tide of Padrone miscreants who had plagued the system for years, swindling one unsuspecting Italian immigrant after another. The Padrone system was unregulated and uncontrolled outside of Italy, creating a breeding ground for graft and outright thievery. These corrupt men often took up-front fees for service, abandoned their clients en route, and departed to another area where they were unknown to repeat the process. In the initial years of the great Italian migration to America in the late 1800s, Padrone thievery flourished as most wannabe immigrants were keen to emigrate but were ignorant of the dangers. Many young immigrants were stranded on docks in France, New York, or other distant places. As time passed, the reputations of these unscrupulous men spread, and by the mid-1900s, most of the populace had taken precautions in dealing with them. The first safeguard was ensuring the padrono was qualified as a vettore. The most crucial requisite was personal knowledge of the padrono; preferably, he was a neighbor or one well-vetted by friends.

One local vettore, a Tuscan, was known in the area and respected for his honesty. He was the best bet for young Italian boys to find productive and lucrative American jobs. He had been working in Lucca and had escorted many young men to the copper mines in Hancock, Michigan. Typically, he gathered a group of men from Lucca, escorted them to Michigan, and collected his fee from the mining operators. He then spent a few weeks working in the mines, collecting money before returning to Italy and starting the process anew.

He had contacted Raffaello about sending his boys to mining jobs in America once they attained the correct physical size. The mining operators were indifferent to a man's age as long as he had the physical stature to perform mining duties, which typically involved loading thousands of pounds of rock daily. The Padrone knew the size requirement well, for if an undersized man were delivered to the mines, the operator rejected the man and denied the padrono his fee. This local padrono was Raffaello's only option, and he agreed to the deal. It reduced the required money for the trip. It still was not cheap because he had to pay the upfront, nonrefundable fee for the Padrono's service. It was all set except for the date of departure.

To Amerigo and Giulio, two young teens, these were all incidental and unimportant details interspersed with the regular chores of manually running a farm. But their expectations faded as weeks of waiting for news of the trip morphed into months. Giulio was increasingly cynical while waiting for the call, even as his brother remained upbeat and enthused. Giulio was a young and cantankerous youngster, full of energy, ideas and impatience. Amerigo was developing into a more reflective man, employing caution about important decisions. As is typical of teenagers with limited understanding of the world, the magnitude of the situation had not quite sunk in with either of them. A pivotal event in early 1908 changed their views.

See notes 5, 6, 7, 8, 9, 10.

Notes

1. The word Mezzadria is associated colloquially with a sharecropper. It is a variation of the Italian work mezzo, meaning half. The idea was that the land operations were to be divided equally between the property owners and the farmers.

2. *Felice & Vecchi* present an overview of Italy's gross domestic product from 1861 to 2011, showing the effect of the great Italian emigration around the turn of the 19th Century.

3. The walls encircling Lucca were constructed in the 1500s as a defensive measure. They are about two and a half miles in circumference and forty feet high.

4. *Menghini* discusses Italian laws.

5. Two factors engendered the early Twentieth Century emigration from Italy: pervasive unfavorable economic and geopolitical conditions that stymied Italian growth and the American calls for laborers to build a new nation. Six authors present information on the economic and political situation in Italy that created the incentives to immigrate:

La Sorte briefly describes Italy just before the waves of emigration that began in the late 1800s. He presents the material through the eyes of actual immigrants.

Gilmore documents the history of Italy from early in the First Century to the Twenty-First. He presents a detailed description of how the Italian peninsula became splintered into many smaller, unincorporated communities with no national identity. His account of the political conditions and military skirmishes that led to unification is particularly informative. He devotes over half of his four-hundred-page thesis to the history of Italy prior to unification.

Moreno provides a broad overview of Italian immigration to America.

Mangione and *Morreale*, sons of Italian immigrants, discuss the Italian experience in the New World, starting with Columbus. They describe the conditions in Italy that drove many to the new land. Their accounts of some of the personal experiences of Mezzadria families, including copies of letters and detailed interviews that vividly enlighten the reader regarding the rigors of Italian life at that time. They present an extensive review of the Padrone system, including the different types of services they offered to emigrant hopefuls. They discuss various stories about the corruption of the Padrone system, including typical scams played on ignorant peasants. Throughout their book, they explain how immigrants thousands of miles from their homeland and decades after unification slowly came to view Italy as a single nation. To many immigrants who had never strayed from their homes, thousands of miles of distance masked the differences among the people from different regions of Italy. Giulio Menicucci once said that by the time he and his brother came to Albuquerque, they viewed all Italians, north and south, to be paesani (countrymen), a stark change from his early years where I remember him and Amerigo arguing about whether a family was Lucchese or Siciliani, clearly differentiating the two. Later, they did business with an Italian southerner and were good friends; distance from their homeland mitigated regional prejudices.

Langer summarizes, in encyclopedic format, the historical events in the history of Italian unification, including detailed references and other bibliographic material suitable for research applications.

6. *Menghini* describes the economic conditions in Northern Italy that drove immigrants to mining jobs in America. She points out that the Italians at the time had no concept of a country, so they aligned with their villages for identification. And the alignment extended from the province to the tiny villages that comprised the comunes within the provinces. The folks in Lucca, for example, aligned first with Lucca, bypassing Tuscany and its region and subsequently positioning with their home villages. Lucchese, as they called themselves, was the calling card for any citizen within the province of Lucca.

7. Newspaper reports from the newspapers in Michigan's Copper Country were helpful in piecing the story together.

8. *Tucciarone* and *Laurino* present discussions of the common methods used by some Padrone to swindle commoners seeking work in America.

9. Padrone is a word that describes the upper class of professional people. The padrone involved with landownership and those engaged as vettore are from the same group. Analogously, in America the padrone class would include CEOs, medical and technical professionals, lawyers, etc.

10. Some materials have been developed for teaching the history of Italian immigration:

> *Parker* presents a book for children in early grammar school.
> *Rapczynski*, a teacher, outlined a complete lesson plan for an 11th-grade class investigating Italian immigration from 1870 to 1920. *Menicucci (Barbara)* examined the lesson plan and

found it complete except for an evaluation component.

La Bella documents in simple terms the conditions leading up to the Risorgimento and the events that followed. The book is suitable for middle school.

Ciongoli and Parini present a version of the story of Italian immigration that is suitable reading for middle and high school students.

2

A MAN IS BORN (1908)

UNTIMELY INTRUSION

Even at sixteen, Giulio had come to expect the unexpected in his Colono life. It was a foggy morning in late summer in an olive grove in Lucca, Italy, when he heard some commotion at his Colono home, about two hundred yards away. The sun had just broken above the horizon, and its rays scattered through the fog, enveloping him in a white cloud that limited his vision to a dozen yards. He kept harvesting olives, figuring someone would come for him if it were important.

Giulio had been laboring for nearly thirty minutes in the two-acre orchard, one of many smaller plots that were part of the Padrone's (bosses') agricultural properties. He heard Amerigo, his younger fifteen-year-old brother, huffing as he ran towards him. As he met Giulio, Amerigo paused to catch his breath and then said haltingly that there was a new plan for the day. Giulio groaned because he knew they were already behind on the fall harvesting and pruning, and did not need interruptions. Amerigo reported that birds were overrunning their uncle Geocondo's barn and his one-acre wheat field.

Wheat attracts birds, mainly pigeons and doves, ranging in size from about a half to a pound each. They fed in the field but favored the barn's large supply of fresh grain, which was always available. Geocondo's plot was too small to support a family fully but was an important part of their revenue. The feathery raiders were literally stealing food from Geocondo's family. Worse, their droppings contaminated other produce, such as eggs, and disturbed the animals. He had a large chicken coup in his barn and the birds roosted on top of the cages, soiling the eggs and drastically reducing their value. Eggs were one of the family's prime sources of revenue. The Menicuccis and every other Colono family considered the birds to be pests.

However, the birds provided a chance for meat, which was in short supply on Colono dinner plates. He and Amerigo had been longing for a meal of meat. Nevertheless, it interrupted normal activities, which were paid for in future extra labor. Sure, they were going to Uncle Geocondo's and harvesting birds, solving his problem, but it left them further behind schedule. And papa had been increasingly agitated about the schedule.

The boys gathered up the olives that Giulio had harvested and the branches he had trimmed. He baled the branches to sell them to a paper mill near Lucca. Giulio wondered aloud why Papa wasted time and effort on branches for so little return. He could not understand why Papa was always scrounging for money.

Amerigo continually fantasized about America, dreaming about the glorious day when they arrived in the United States. To both boys, America was magical and captivating. But Giulio was growing more cynical each day. Many months passed since the padrono had visited. No letter was delivered. No word was sent. Nothing happened except unabated Colono work, full of interruptions.

Amerigo could see agitation growing in Giulio, and he constantly encouraged, sometimes even badgered, him to pray to the Madonna for help.[1] Logical and pragmatic, Giulio was not swayed to religion. As time passed, Giulio's frustration grew as he perceived the Lord's inaction. All the Madonna hype sounded like fairylike thinking. That morning, when Amerigo asked if he had been praying, he struck out at the Madonna, telling Amerigo to order her to do something because they could not wait forever. Amerigo was incredulous. She is the Lord's mother, after all. Italian mothers' influence on their sons is part of a long-standing Italian tradition: a mother is respected by her children and is especially revered by her sons. There are multitudes of stories of Italian men, even those in powerful positions, acquiescing to their mothers' requests.

But he was not going to argue with his older brother. At that age, the sixteen-month difference between the boys was large. Giulio graduated from school a year before Amerigo. A single year of experience is significant to boys who have only worked for a couple of years. Besides, Giulio was the oldest male, which gave him seniority and authority. Giulio did not seek debate about the Madonna and wondered aloud how the harvested birds would taste for dinner. Aside from America, food was the other subject that commanded Amerigo's attention. Amerigo took the bait and reminisced about the delicious variations that his Aunt Elena employed to prepare game birds. They had been promised more than half of the birds as compensation for their help. As many male family members had immigrated to America, the family had drawn together to help one another.[2]

Sistine depiction of the Madonna, circa 1900. Courtesy United States Library of Congress.

The immigrants working mining jobs in America were economically advanced compared to their relatives in Italy. Most sent a majority of their earnings back home. The Menicucci family members still living in Italy witnessed the struggles of Raffaello's improvised family, and shared those incoming resources whenever possible. They knew Giulio and Amerigo were primed to emigrate, and Raffaello had few resources.

Giulio took charge and told Amerigo that he needed to quickly repair their chicken coop, which foxes had invaded the previous night. If the screen were left breached, they would lose more chickens while away for the day. Chickens were popular farmstock as egg producers, but as soon as production dropped, the bird became a valuable piece of meat, good for bartering, sale, or food.

As the two boys split up, Giulio reminded Amerigo to check the hooves of Bello, their mule that was their main beast of burden for farming chores and hauling goods. Like machines and humans, parts fail, and damaged hooves were typically the first sign of a declining animal. But they were determined to make him last as long as possible because they did not have money to replace him.

Amerigo trotted off back to the family home and as he approached the kitchen he heard his mother, Teresa, call to him to load the side bags on Bello. She would chock them full of utensils for gutting, cleaning and salting the birds for future consumption or sales. She was not joining the family at Geocondo's because she had to care for her toddler, two-year-old Aledino. He was a late arrival to the family and suffered from congenital mental and physical handicaps. There was virtually no medical treatment in that part of Italy, so they accepted the situation. They expected Aledino to be unproductive and die at an early age.

While Teresa was packing the mule, she sent Amerigo out to spur Giulio, who was struggling to secure the chicken coop against the marauding foxes, a perpetual problem for Colono farmers. This coop was a dilapidated structure with a few standing posts and cross members, with chicken screens draped over them, tacked, and tied down in places. It was built against a shed near the home. The screen was buried deeply along the perimeter to discourage critters from burrowing underneath it. Eventually, the foxes figure out how to breach it by digging and pulling up the buried screen along the perimeter, leaving a hole for entry and exit with their feathery booty. The coop door was a square frame with some chicken screen nailed to it. The Menicuccis knew how to build a better coop, but their philosophy was that it stayed in service if it could be repaired. Giulio, as usual, was thinking that they always had time to make repeated repairs but never enough time for permanent fixes. It was the Colono way of life.

Giovanni, Geocondo's oldest son, was in charge of the bird abatement and had procured a large sack of shot (small, lead pellets), four horns of powder, some borrowed guns, and the remaining implements for the harvesting. Thousands of the marauding birds hanging around Geocondo's barn were the targets.

They used muzzleloading shotguns in that era, which required both the gunpowder and the shot to be loaded from the end of the barrel, the muzzle. It is an intricate procedure that must be followed precisely because a mistake could lead to anything from a misfire to an explosion. Typically, Colono boys learned to load and fire muzzleloaders around the age of five.

When Giulio and Amerigo arrived home, Teresa was packing the mule's side bags. After the mule was fully loaded, they packaged more equipment and materials to carry manually. Giulio improvised a carrying system comprising a pole suspended between his shoulder and his brother's. The payload was suspended from the pole and swung freely between the two boys.

Amerigo and Giulio hoisted the ninety-pound payload on their shoulder and placed some rags underneath the poles as pads for their shoulders. They made off with a brisk, no-nonsense walk to Geocondo's home in Segromigno in Piano, about a mile away. Their big German Shepherd, Alto, walked alongside because he had an important role in the harvest. Every member of the Menicucci household worked.

HARVEST TIME

When they were in earshot of Geocondo's home, Raffaello directed them to eat lunch and go to the barn for the shoot. It was already well past noon, birds were gathering nearby, and the shooters had to prepare for the afternoon harvest. The barn was about fifty feet by thirty feet in size. It was old, with stone siding and an unfinished, faded, leaky tile roof. There were two large doors on each end of the barn, with a window above each one. Each of the other two sides had several large openable windows. The barn stored grain for the animals and the families. It also housed beasts of burden and production, such as mules, cows, rabbits and chickens.

Giocondo briefed all on the plan. Giovanni would allow birds into the barn to feed, close the doors, and then panic them by beating a drum. He would open a window briefly, allowing out a manageable number for the men to harvest using one shot each. He would repeat the process until all the birds fled. Then, he would reopen the barn and let the birds regather inside to repeat the process. Each cycle required about ten minutes. During the break, the boys ferried the dead birds to the women at Giocondo's home for processing. Harvesting resumed when all returned to their positions near the barn.

Shooters surrounded the side of the barn where the birds would exit. Giulio and Amerigo worked as a pair: Giulio shot and Amerigo loaded. As birds were downed, Alto and Geocondo's dogs were ready to retrieve carcasses and chase down wounded ones. Raffaello clarified that Geocondo would shout out the time to begin coordinated shooting. Shooting out of sequence would be disruptive and could reduce their take of birds. It was similar to a military operation where discipline is essential for mission success.

ELENA'S REALM

Meanwhile, Geocondo's wife, Elena, prepared for the bird processing and the evening meal. Nutritious meals were a foundation of Italian life at all levels of society and they were a high priority for the heads of households, the women. They believed that delectable meals encouraged all to eat plentifully, contributing to good health. This day's event was important because they had a chance to secure a load of meat and eliminate pesky birds simultaneously. She believed bird feces contaminated eggs, making them unsavory to eat and thus difficult to sell, even if the visible stains were washed away. She never threw out soiled eggs but served them with a scowl.

The women's role in the harvest was to clean and salt the birds for storage. Every family member had a duty to support the harvesting because it provided food for the family. The youngsters viewed it as an opportunity to train for when they had their own homes and families. About twenty newly harvested birds would be dinner that night. Nonna (grandmother) Amelia Morelli Menicucci, mother to Geocondo and Raffaello, attended a large pot of simmering herbed tomato sauce. She planned to braise the birds in the sauce. Despite severe arthritis in her legs and spine brought on by seventy-five years of hard life, Amelia continued contributing her culinary skills. She had lived with Geocondo since her husband, Pasquale, died in 1875. There were no nursing facilities in Italy at the time. Caring for older folks fell upon members of the family.

While Amelia cooked, Elena was busy with the normal chores, cleaning the house, feeding and watering the chickens and donkeys, and directing the preparation of the other parts of the meal. The escarole had to be cut and boiled with onions and carrots. The polenta had to be cooked and ready for the dinner. The wine bottles had to be filled. And the table had to be set for extra family members. Despite the special activity, the regular farming chores still needed to be completed. With the polenta, birds, and greens comprising the main course, it portended to be a fitting Italian feast after a harvest of meat for the family.

Later that afternoon, with the men harvesting hundreds of birds, the women would be plucking, drawing, salting and packing them. The family harvested the entire bird, including feathers, intestines, feet and heads. Elena set up a processing line that resembled a factory line, with young women laboring intensely alongside their elders. As birds arrived from the field, the first station in the line plucked off all the feathers, including the wings and feet. The clean birds resembled game hens commonly found in markets. They separated the down feathers from the larger ones so they could sell them to the local pillow and bed-cover makers. The large feathers were composted.

Next, the birds were drawn, recovering the guts and giblets—the heart, lungs and gizzard. They sliced open each gizzard and pinched out the tough, leathery internal sack and saved the muscular part for consumption. The gizzard sack, intestines and feet went to the dogs. Next, they cut each bird along the backbone and washed and dried the two halves. They laid the halves on a bed of salt in the barrel. Once a layer of birds filled the bottom of the barrel, they liberally sprinkled salt on them, and the process continued. The salt barrels stood around two feet tall and eighteen inches wide with a rough-sealed removable wooden lid. The giblets were also salted but placed in a separate container.

AWAKENING

In the field near the barn, the men huddled in their blinds and waited for Giovanni to begin the harvest. Birds were flowing into the barn in their normal manner. Impatient as always, Giulio mounted his muzzleloader to his shoulder in mock action, declaring how many birds he would knock down. Eager to shoot, he spotted birds lighting on a nearby tree. He forgot about the plan and told his brother to be ready for him to knock down several with one shot. Papa would be proud, he said, because he likes efficient shooting. Amerigo reminded him to wait for a word, but he shot anyway, knocking two of the three birds to the ground. The blast from his shotgun alarmed the birds already in the barn, and they scattered before the other shooters were ready.

It was a mistake. Raffaello shouted from about thirty feet away, demanding to know why he shot. Giulio explained his logic of taking multiple birds with one shot, but Raffaello had no interest. He walked up to Giulio, grabbed him by the collar put his face in his. He let loose with a tirade never before seen. Papa had been in a rotten mood for months, and Giulio thought he was taking it out on him. But there was a message. Raffaello asked if he wanted to be Colono forever and do this same thing for life. He reminded him that America had good jobs and the family had a rare chance to escape their domestic conundrum. Everyone had to do their jobs to get to America. But there was more, and it was grim. The family did not have the money for America. Aledino greatly complicated the situation. He was handicapped and unable to work. He was another mouth to feed but produced nothing. Then he said the key words: If the padrono came tomorrow, they could send nobody to America. He reminded him that as the oldest boy, he had a special responsibility to the family. He would carry the Menicucci blood to America. Both boys were left with mouths agape and droplets of spittle randomly scattered about Giulio's face.

With that, Raffaello walked away in frustration, but Giulio now understood the situation, and it was unlike what he had imagined. Raffaello's words rattled in his brain: They could not afford America. It hit Giulio hard. Not only was he dressed down by Papa in front of his younger brother, but as the oldest son, the magnitude of his duty sank in. He was now responsible for the future of the family. Those were indeed high stakes, and he knew he had to lead. A new determination replaced his glumness. It was the first of several critical moments in Giulio's life that set the tone for many decades.

Raffaello had been suffering from health problems, mostly depression related. Aledino's birth and his degenerative condition weighed on him. From almost any perspective, the family's outlook was bleak, and each day he sank deeper into an emotional funk of anger, guilt and sadness.

Later in life, Giulio succinctly summarized the family's situation: "Nothing discourages a man more than being poor and having no hope."

THE HARVEST

Meanwhile, birds were again flocking into the barn for their usual evening meal. The men were ready, and Giovanni put his plan into action. When birds flew from the barn window, Geocondo shouted to the fire. Giulio stood and shot into the group of birds streaming out of the barn. Raffaello's and Geocondo's guns fired simultaneously. They took about ten birds in each round of shooting, repeating the process for hours until they could no longer see in the day's dwindling light.

Geocondo called a cease-fire and ordered everyone to dinner. Those words hit home with all, and the boys jumped out of their blinds, rapidly stashed the guns and equipment into the barn, and headed off for the kitchen. Their mouths watered as they envisioned eating bowl after bowl of polenta with birds swimming in Nonna's tomato sauce. Even without birds, polenta topped with sauce was a treat to dream about. They might be poor Colono farmers in the Mezzadria system but when it came to food, they dined like kings, thanks to the women.

The boys were first to arrive at Geocondo's home. Elena directed them to the rain barrel to wash for dinner. She also encouraged a trip to the outhouse, which they called the il piccolo puzzolente (little stinker). Like many things on a Colono farm, the little stinker was a rickety building over a hole in the ground with a makeshift toilet seat. This one was reeking because it was overfull, and they had no time to dig a new one. It was a typical complication of Mezzadria life.

When the men arrived at the home, their first question was: "How many?" Elena reported that around 600 were salted and packed, with about a dozen beaten so badly that they were good only for dogs—a greater harvest than anticipated.

A WELL-DESERVED FEAST

Elena's kitchen was modest, typical for Mezzadria families. The activity centered on the wood- and coal-stove used for frying, boiling and baking food. Above the stove were two long shelves attached to the wall, each loaded with plates and bowls of different sizes and shapes that had accumulated over the generations. An open wooden box on the bottom shelf stored eating utensils, forks, spoons and knives. Pots, all cast iron, lay on the shelves or hung from hooks on the wall. It was the minimum set of cooking utensils, containing nothing elaborate. They used knives until the blades had been essentially honed away to a sliver. Pots and pans were ancient. Over the years, they scrounged to replace broken plates or cups, resulting in a hodgepodge of mismatched dinnerware. In the Mezzadria system, the Menicuccis leased a farm based on what they could afford, typically not much more than subsistence. They paid their padrono rent, a fixed cost, regardless of farm revenues. So, every investment in utensils and kitchen tools was carefully considered with the same seriousness as garden implements.

Under the lowest shelf and just above the stove hung her knives, cleavers and other large tools, including four mezzalunas of different sizes. A sharpening stone lay nearby to keep them razor-sharp. An adjacent pantry cabinet near the stove stood five feet tall and about three feet wide. It had two doors in front and shelves storing many dried spices, herbs, and other products used to prepare the daily nutritious meals the family enjoyed. A cabinet on the other side of the stove served a double purpose. It stood about three feet tall, three feet deep and three feet wide. Inside its tightly fitting doors were sacks of flour, cornmeal, oatmeal and other staples of the day. Mice and rats eat grain, so this cabinet remained tightly sealed. The top was constructed from hard maple, which was two inches thick, providing a platform for chopping, cutting, dicing, carving, and processing meat and vegetables.

The large, wooden kitchen table could seat twelve adults comfortably. It had been in the family so long that nobody could confidently say who built it or when. It was so old that depressions in the middle of the tabletop were ground over time by the repeated placements of large, hot bowls. The table had sat in its exact location for generations as one family passed to another. It was not unusual for a multi-generational family to have lived in a house so long that they could not pinpoint the exact date of the family's first occupation.

Two olive oil lamps, which had been used for generations, lit the kitchen. A single candle glowed in the middle of the kitchen table. As the men streamed in for a meal, they were overwhelmed by the aroma of Nonna's sauce and the birds braising inside it. On the stove was a huge pot of bubbling Polenta, which was close to the consistency of oatmeal.

Elena prepared an antipasto of thick-sliced toasted bread painted with olive oil, crushed garlic and salt. As the men waited for the main meal, they munched bread and sipped wine. They bantered about the experiences of the day. It was a typical Italian social gathering that brought many ideas and suggestions for efficiency improvements.

Elena served every meal "family style" by placing large bowls of food in a central location on the table, allowing each to take a portion from it. Elena sprinkled the polenta with olive oil and a generous dusting of parmesan cheese. She laid out loaves of bread on towels, along with a bread knife. Geocondo cut it into serving-sized pieces, sending them around the table. Polenta and bread, both high in carbohydrates and low in cost, were meal staples. Teresa prepared a large bowl of steaming escarole, which had been boiled and sauteed with garlic, herbs and wine.

Everyone knew the seating arrangement at the table. Geocondo, the oldest male and family leader, sat at the head of the table, flanked by his brother Raffaello and son Giovanni. The boys lined up along one side according to age, with the oldest nearest to Geocondo. The women sat on the side facing the cooking area to access the kitchen area easily. Nonna Amelia sat at the opposite end of the table from Geocondo, an honorary position for the aging matriarch.

Geocondo popped the cork from a three-quarter-gallon bottle of wine and placed it on the table.[3] Six hundred birds were worth celebrating. Raffaello filled the glasses, including the children's, who drank it diluted with water. Usually, they mixed wine with water for meals to extend it and mask the rancid taste of the well water. Some believed it sanitized.[4] For special occasions, they drank pure wine.[5]

She then put two empty bowls on the table for the bones, which the dogs ate. She called out a warning as she placed the steaming boiling pot of birds and sauce on the table. When she pulled off the lid, a mushroom cloud of steamy flavor burst towards the ceiling, where it ricocheted and rolled back down, enveloping the dinner gathering. All salivated with delight; their hunger had their glands in high gear. Next, she put a large bowl of vegetables dressed with fresh olive oil, a handful of chopped parsley and a healthy dusting of their locally produced parmesan cheese. The wonderfully rich perfume of these basic fresh vegetables perfectly complemented Nonna's sauce.

Elena stood by and surveyed the table. Satisfied that dinner was ready, she gave the word to pray. Geocondo led in the traditional Catholic way, "In the name of the Father, the Son and the Holy Ghost. Bless us, oh Lord and these thy gifts that we are about to receive, from thy bounty, through Christ, our Lord. Amen." Geocondo added his own prayer, a plea to the Madonna to speak to the Lord about Giulio's and Amerigo's quest for America.

Geocondo kicked off the dinner with a healthy swig of wine, which swirled in his mouth, and he swallowed it with a shake of his head. He quipped about the competence of Luigi Pucci as a vintner, noting that even his cheaper wines, ones that had not been aged, were excellent. At best, the wine was aged only a few weeks, as it was a table wine meant for heavy consumption, not sipping.

Each took turns filling their plates with the polenta, topped by a couple of birds and vegetables. She implored all to clean every bone without wasting a scrap of meat. When all were served, both women sat down to eat. Seeing all enjoy their culinary craft with such fervor delighted them.

As people finished the main meal, Elena stood at the table with a bowl of dried apples, figs and raisins on which she dribbled about an ounce of Pucci's grappa. She gave the bowl to Nonna to serve herself and started it around the table. No food was left. Every plate was wiped clean with bread. The wine bottles were dry. And the boys and men stretched back in their chairs like beached whales. They might be Colono families, but their food was majestic.

During the meal, the conversations ranged over many topics. Most were interested in tales of southern Italians migrating into the area. Giovanni was in the Lucca walled city and learned that drunk Sicilians instigated a fight over a bar tab that injured several people. That kicked off a discussion with harsh words of warning for the southerners if they dared to disrupt the Menicucci's home areas. The violence that the Southerners often brought disturbed the Lucchese, who preferred battles of wits to battles of fists. The story rekindled talk of Nonno (grandfather) Pasquale's death, which had been lurking in family lore for years. He was rumored to have died of the plague after a trip to Naples. Not likely, but it did not take much to engender hatred and fear of the Southerners.[6]

PLAY IT AGAIN

The euphoria did not last long. Giulio and Amerigo were expecting a relaxing night's sleep in the barn, as they had done on previous work projects. Raffaello informed them that they had to go home and rise before dawn to shoot the foxes that had targeted the chicken coop. They had the borrowed guns to knock off yet another pest competing for their food. The boys were downtrodden, another disappointment typical of Colono life. They knew Papa was right. They had been under siege from the foxes for weeks.

The dinner gathering broke up, and Raffaello directed traffic to walk back home. They packed up Bosso and their carrying poles to haul back the equipment and the salted birds. As they prepared to leave, the boys bid farewell to family members, especially thanking Nonna Amelia. They trudged along the dimly moonlit path in weary silence, with only a few incidental comments about the stars, a comment about one of the neighbor's fruit trees, or the fireflies that were flirting with them. Giulio was uncharacteristically silent, with Papa's chilling words about America still ringing in his head. Upon arrival at home, Raffaello turned to the boys, directing them to water Bello and prepare for bed. He wanted them to be ready at three o'clock in the morning. He knew the foxes operated then, so he planned to ambush them.

FRUSTRATED CONTEMPLATION

As Teresa greeted the returning men, she saw despondency in Raffaello. She had noticed his increasingly short temper coupled with bouts of depression. He had been reticent about discussing his concerns, but the weight had become too much, and he vented some of his frustrations. Raffaello looked up and lamented. How could they go forward? They were broken. The future was bleak.

Teresa tried to console him, suggesting that the Padrone would bring news for the boys. She had confidence because the Madonna was the Lord's mother and she talked to the Lord. But it only inflamed him, complaining that with all the praying to the Madonna, nothing had happened. Teresa reminded him that the padrono was a Tuscano, growing up only about five miles from their home. He had helped many other Lucchese, as Lucca province residents were called, to America. And he promised. A promise from a Paesano (countryman) was considered a social bond. But Raffaello lashed out, claiming that Padrone of all types, whether from Tuscany, Rome, or Sicily, were thieves. They take money and buy wine, he said. He felt foolish, and there was little she could do but pray for a better tomorrow and hope money would be available when the padrono arrived.

The boys shared a bedroom, a place so small that the only way to accommodate two beds was to bunk them. Aledino slept with Raffaello and Teresa. The beds were simple one-mattress systems, each lying on planks of hardwood supported on a simple, unfinished frame. The mattresses, made of bird down, sagged severely in the middle as they had logged thousands of hours of use. Each had a worn set of sheets and woolen blankets fraying badly along the edges. But they were good enough for the boys who were so tired they could have slept on rocks.

Amerigo dreamed aloud whether the Madonna would bring the padrono tomorrow. It will be glorious, he thought, joining so many other Lucchese in America. Then he thought about the meat they might have for many meals over the next few weeks. He was fifteen years old, and the situation had not yet sunk in, which is typical for a boy with less than a fully developed brain.

Giulio was more than a year older than his brother and had a more mature brain. The seriousness of supporting a handicapped person was sinking in. They were already poor, and now this. It was depressingly logical. America appeared to be a longshot for the family, but any chance they had depended on him. It was much to comprehend for a skinny 16-year-old with only a third-grade education, but these kinds of events mature children quickly. He did, however, understand why Papa was always scrounging for money.

"That day, I was a man," Giulio said.

See notes 7, 8.

Notes

1. Young males in the extended Menicucci family were in increasingly short supply, and by 1908, many had already immigrated to the Americas, most to North America. Emilio and Letizia, Raffaello's brother and sister, had transferred their families to the United States. Luigi, Pasquale's oldest son, was in Idaho. Another Pasquale daughter, Adelina, had married and planned for their youngest daughter, Arduina, to live with Geocondo while she and her husband built a home in Albuquerque, New Mexico. In 1908, more than half of Pasquale's family had emigrated from Lucca.

2. Madonna is a contraction of the Italian words mia (my) and donna (lady). In this context, it is highly respectful. Madonna is frequently used outside Catholic circles, most often in reference to the Blessed Virgin. In later chapters, I discuss the masculine form of this term, mio uomo (my man).

3. The wine consumed at this dinner was likely greater than normal because it was a celebration. Three quarter gallons equals twelve cups, about one and three-quarter cups for the seven adults. Normally, an adult male consumed about a half to full cup of wine with both lunch and dinner, and another at bedtime. Some, might add a splash of Grappa as part of dessert. Men tended to consume more than women. Many of these same consumption habits were carried to America by the immigrants.

4. Some bacteria are killed by alcohol. However, wine sours, which means two things: some bacteria are not killed even by undiluted wine with thirteen percent alcohol by volume; second, diluting the wine with water will not improve its already weak antibacterial properties.

5. In northern Italian tradition, especially among country dwellers, water and wine were mixed for various reasons. First, mixing water with wine is a tradition from the Catholic Mass, where the two are combined and consecrated as the blood of Christ. Second, it masks the taste of poor-quality water available at the time. Third, they believed that the alcohol in the wine sanitized the water. Most wells were shallow and easily contaminated with bacteria. Surface water posed the same hazard. Fourth, it was a method to control the amount of alcohol. Many Italians enjoy large glasses of water with just a small amount of wine after rigorous activity where the goal is to rehydrate the body. Thus, they could consume larger amounts of liquid without inebriation. At other times, such as a family wedding, the goal might be to induce intoxication, and the ratio of water to wine swung heavily toward pure wine. Some families introduced water and wine to children as young as a few years old to help the child develop a taste for wine. Last, it was economical. Mixing wine with water extends the supply. There was a constant fear among families about running short of wine as the harvest season approached. Mixing the two liquids allowed the family to ration the wine without severely impacting its taste sensation, which is one of the staples for an Italian meal. Wine is an integral part of the culinary experience in Italian cooking and dining.

Not all of the Italians acquired a taste for wine. Mariangela Menicucci Scanlon, daughter to Giulio, told the story: "Everyone in the family drank wine. Mama drank at least a cup of it straight at the table noon and night. Charlie and Teresa loved it. I didn't like it. It made me sneeze. But I still had to take my turn with the other kids getting a jug from the basement for the family meals. I just drank water."

Most Italian peasants preferred dry, red wine. Chianti is the trademark wine of Italy, but the Mezzadria rarely bought it or any other commercial wine. They fermented their own. Red grapes were grown widely in Lucca province. They were the primary source of what the Italians called "table wine," characterized by a deeply red or purple color with a powerful, aromatic bouquet and slight bitterness with a strong bite but a pleasing aftertaste. Some sweet red and white wines were produced by expert vintners, such as the Puccis, typically for personal consumption. There was little demand for them among the peasants. In Albuquerque after prohibition, red wine was essentially the only wine the Italian liquor stores stocked on their shelves.

6. Sicily's economic and health conditions were some of the worst in Europe. They had suffered a number of infectious plagues that had been introduced from northern Africa. Extended periods of drought had decreased food production, and there was significant political distrust among the leaders of the unification government, most of whom hail from the northern regions. No love was lost between the northerners and those from the south, especially when the southerners consistently stirred up trouble. Plagues of various types hit southern Italy in the late 1800s and into the Twentieth Century. Droughts and pestilence were more severe and frequent in the South than in the Northern states. Corruption and organized crime flourished in this environment, especially the Mafia, which had taken control of some southern towns. The Southerners also appeared different. The southerners tended to be shorter, with pronounced facial features and generally aggressive personalities engendered by decades of deprivation. The Menicuccis' disdain for the Southerners often burst forth as they recalled dozens of stories of trouble and insults the Sicilians were causing in the area. Dire economic conditions and social disruption were the primary drivers of emigration from southern Italy to the north and to America. Southerners eventually composed the largest group of Italian American immigrants in the United States. *De Sluca* describes Sicily in detail.

7. This story originates entirely in family lore taken directly from the original immigrants. I had unique opportunities to spend time with all

of the original immigrants. I frequently joined Giulio, Amerigo and Victor Bachechi on fishing or mushroom-hunting trips. Most of these trips were in the Jemez mountains, but they also fished the irrigation ditches around Albuquerque, and I was frequently invited to come along. Victor owned a Chevy Suburban Carryall with positive traction rear differential, a luxury for folks in the late 1950s. (A positive traction differential puts power to the rear wheel that has the best traction.) Victor was always the driver at outdoor events, and Giulio sat in the shotgun seat on the front right. Amerigo sat in the back but scooted over to the middle of the bench seat to lean his head forward between the two of the two men in front. I was left with about one-eighth of a seat near the window. They generally talked as if I were not there, but occasionally, one asked me a question about what they were discussing to play with me. My response often led to some discussion about family. They spoke Italian except to me. I understood the Italian well, but I could not speak it. I learned much about Italian history and culture during those many one-day outings.

I obtained significant historical lore at family events, such as holidays, birthdays, etc., where after a few glasses, people are bubbling with discussions, much about family. Stories and perspectives often emerged at events. I remember one July 4th in the 1960s when Giulio told the whole story of America from his perspective. "If those American farmers had not beaten the English king's army," he said, "we wouldn't be sitting here in our home drinking wine and good food. We would be in Italy with nothing and working for nothing." That is why, he emphasized, America is the greatest country in the world. It was like a parable. Easy to understand, right to the point and transfers the message quickly. He was correct, of course, and his version of American history was a testament to his strong belief in the country and its unique concept of freedom.

The 1908 story is stitched together from snippets of lore meshed with historical facts. It is impossible to know, for example, the exact year of the event. I deduced the date based on my memory of Amerigo or Giulio saying that Aledino was a little boy in diapers at that time. Aledino was two years old in 1908. He was born on May 7, 1906 (Record #81, posted May 10, 1906) as Giovanni Pietro Aladino. Teresa was in her middle forties at the time of his birth. It is well known that birth defects become increasingly common as a mother's age advances. Aladino suffered from a birth defect, which rendered him dependent on his family for his life. The medical community at that time had scant knowledge about congenital conditions. They sent the victims home with little or no medication and left their care to the families. Aladino's birth was witnessed by Giuseppe Lencioni, who, as we shall see, was likely related to Lorenzo Lencioni, the padrono who accompanied Giulio on his initial trip to America.

The details about the muzzleloaders are based on my recollections of Victor Bachechi discussing hunting in Italy. Birds were known to be pests in the area, especially during the later summer harvest season. Shooting them was the only practical solution, especially as shotguns became more affordable. Thinning the bird population also produced food, a substantial benefit in those days.

8. The birth records for the two Menicucci brothers are managed through the *Portale Antenanti*. They are stored in the "Italian Civil Records, Tuscan Region, Lucca Province, Capannori Comune, Birth Records."

Every record contains the precise time of birth, the complete names of the father and mother, the names and signatures of at least two citizen witnesses, and a confirming signature from the consigliere, the official advisor for the Comune of Capannori. Below are the birth records of the two Menicucci brothers.

Giulio: Record #7, posted on January 15, 1892. Giulio was born on July 14, 1892. His mother, Teresa Morelli, son to Luigi and his father, Raffaello, son to Pasquale, are explicitly mentioned as was his birth location in Segromigno in Monte in Lucca.

Amerigo: Record #175, posted December 2, 1893. Similarly, Amerigo's birth record is populated with details. He was born on November 28, 1893, and named Francesco Americo. Amerigo spelled his name with a "g" throughout his life, even though his birth record clearly shows a "c." He was enamored with Amerigo Vespucci, the famous Italian explorer and usurped the name for his own. Of course, it was a close spelling, but Amerigo believed the "g" added elegance to the name.

3

FIRST INKLINGS
(~1780–1869)

A SHOT

The struggles of the Raffaello Menicucci family in 1908 represent an intermediate chapter in the Menicucci's long struggle to migrate to America. By the end of the first decade of the Twentieth Century, more than half of all Capannori families had members who either migrated to the new world or worked there temporarily. Roughly half of Pasquale's family had immigrated. But the Menicucci family's quest for economic relief commenced one hundred and twenty-five years earlier, at the end of the 18th Century.

Bartolomeo, my paternal fourth-great-grandfather, was the first Menicucci who heard the Shot Heard Round the World. It was the faint and distant metaphorical sound of the first shot in the American Revolution, initiating one of the greatest political gambits in world history. In 1775 in Italy, that American rifle shot was drowned out by the gunshots they constantly heard around Tuscany, which killed Italians and disrupted daily life. While the US Constitution was being ratified, George Washington was elected president, and Americans debated the Bill of Rights, it was America's discoverers who captured Menicuccis' interest.

The western Continents were dubbed America based on the voyages of Amerigo Vespucci, who grew up in Florence, about thirty miles east of the Menicucci home. A German cartographer examined the historical records and labeled the North and South American Continents the "Americas" on his world map, which was widely published. He had concluded that Vespucci was principally responsible for discovering the lands. Columbus, of course, was the initial Italian explorer, but it was Vespucci who was hailed by the populace as the greatest world explorer, and that is why his namesake was etched into Western history. These two explorers were sources of pride for the people in a land largely devoid of it. Italian pride played a tiny but non-insignificant role in the lives of Colono peasants in Italy, who were overwhelmed by the day-to-day rigors of surviving in a moribund economy with never-ending conflict.

When Paolo, son of Bartolomeo, married in the early 1800s, the American Revolution had concluded, and business enterprises flourished in the new land, including trade. America was still a novelty to the peasant community in Segromigno in Monte, the Menicucci's home in Lucca, but of growing interest. More importantly, a few Italians, mainly from the Padrone class who had money to invest, embarked on exploratory trips to North America, which was wide open land and rapidly expanding. Word filtered back to Italy that America's defining characteristic was its unique form of government, one without a king. It was a foreign concept for most peasants because their entire experience was based on the idea of governing by a central, controlling leader, such as a monarch. They had figured that a king-like figure must lead all systems. After all, wolves had leaders of packs, ants had queens, and armies had generals. Their astonishment grew as they learned how America's self-governance and personal freedoms promoted new businesses, leading to individual economic wealth.[1]

The era of the early 1800s was the beginning of the global diminution of monarchical rule. Besides the Americans, the French Revolution disposed of the traditional French monarchy. Brazil and Spain were experiencing growing public protests against the monarchs. All this made little sense to the Mezzadria. France may not have had a king, but as Emperor of the northern Italian regions, Napolean ruled like one. To the simple farmers like the Menicuccis, he was a king with a different title. More important, he was waging war in northern Italy near their homes.

NAPOLEON

In 1792, Napoleon invaded northern Italy and took control before the occupying Austrians could react in defense. In 1799, he attacked the Papal States that constituted the Holy Roman Empire, which had existed since medieval times, forcing Pope Pius VI into exile. In 1805, Napoleon declared himself King of Italy, fulfilling the suspicion of many Italians about his intentions. His treatment of the Pope outraged the populace, which was primarily Catholic. The Napoleonic governors engendered distrust and resentment by imposing rules, regulations, and taxes on the citizens based on French law with no recognition of local culture or needs. Life was miserable enough without the Napoleonic tumult, and these new measures fomented more desperation among the masses to skedaddle. Napoleon was not the answer for them. America was waiting.

In 1815, Napoleon was defeated for the last time and exiled to the island of St. Helens near Africa. The northern Italian regions that the French held were subsequently returned to their previous positions, with Austria in command of much of northern Italy. After Napoleon, relative peace returned to the peninsula for a couple of decades, but instead of a war inflicting misery, a deep economic recession ensued for years, weighing heavily on the Colono peasants. Then, an economic calamity was triggered in 1816 by Mount Tambora, a volcano in what is now Indonesia, that spewed so much ash into the air that the planet cooled precipitously, producing widespread grain shortages. As crop failures mounted across Europe, including in Italy, Paolo and his family shivered through a year without a summer, as it was called, and was likely among the millions short of food. Crops failed throughout Italy, and the cost of grain on the market inflated hundreds of percent, unaffordable to peasant families. The famine caused widespread illness and other conditions, such as Pellagra, which results from poorly balanced meals, producing dramatically rising death rates. Pellagra is a systemic, potentially fatal disease caused by a severe deficiency of Niacin. The famine lingered for several years until the planet recovered and temperatures returned to normal.[1, 2]

For as long as he could remember, Paolo's family lived in one of the three frazziones (village) of Capannori: Segromigno in Monte, located about five miles northeast of the walled city of Lucca on the foothills of the Apennines; Segromigno in Piano directly south of it, and Lammari, just west of Lucca comune. To add a geographical perspective, the Lucca Province contains about six hundred eighty-five square miles of land surface, about half the size of Rhode Island. The Capannori comune within Lucca province is sixty square miles, about the same as Staten Island, New York. Segromigno (including Monte and Piano) encompasses approximately six hundred acres, the perimeter of which could be walked in about an hour.

The Menicucci family was generally impoverished, but the economic conditions varied among members. A few, such as Geocondo Menicucci, owned small parcels of land, but all were either subsistence farmers or sharecroppers wholly committed to working the lands of the

Padrone. In class-conscious Italy, there was a societal hierarchy among the peasants. Those in the lowest class, Colono, were pure sharecroppers with virtually no other resources. They comprised about half of the peasants. The remainder were agrilatore (farmers) who did subsistence farming. They rented a padrono home but had more overall income than the colonos. A small piece of land could not move them up to the Padrone class, but it was above Colono. For Mezzadria peasants, lifetimes were short, medical care was virtually nonexistent, and the outlook for change was bleak. Their long-term economic potential was nil.

In 1829, Paulo produced a new son, Pasquale. Little information about Pasquale is known, but like his father and grandfather, he was destined for farming and consigned to work the land in Segromigno for life. Around 1841, he married Amelia Morelli, Luigi's daughter. It was the first known connection of the blood relationship between the Menicucci and Morelli families. The Menicuccis and Morellis had farmed in the frazzione of Capannori for generations and knew each other well. It was not unexpected that they intermarried.

As Pasquale's first children began appearing in the late1840s, the tales of American opulence spread. A few Italians, those with resources for investment, ventured to America and started earning significant amounts of money relative to Italian standards. If one could get to the country, America was a land of economic opportunity and easy to tap. The Italian political and economic situation created a sense of urgency to immigrate, and America was the endgame. Still, relatively few Lucchese (folks from Lucca province) were in America, and interest remained minimal.[3]

ITALIAN GOLD BUG

That quiescence changed after 1849 when gold was discovered in California. Exaggerated rumors spread among the peasants about miners in California becoming wildly rich overnight by scooping gold out of a stream or digging it out of the hills. Gold has historically attracted people with aggressive personalities and bold ambitions to grow rich by disgorging something from within the earth. This was the quest of multitudes of Europeans, notably Coronado, who in the 16th Century spent years in Mexico and the American Southwest vainly searching for El Dorado gold. The farming families in Capannori were fascinated by the prospects of digging in the dirt and finding gold instead of carrots. To those people,

American gold captured their attention. Even as the California gold rush ran its course, gold was discovered in Montana and Nevada in 1862 and 1872, respectively, maintaining high levels of interest among the Italian peasantry.[4]

Among the few Capannori men who did venture to America, they returned with tall tales and much money. Dollars flowing from the early immigrants back to their families in Capannori also enhanced America's allure. Ironically, that allure was shared by the Italian government. The newfound source of wealth—American money—was a welcomed addition to the country's flagging economy. In fact, by the middle of the great Italian migration (1880-1920), the revenue from Mezzadria families in America became the principal means of income for many of their Italian relatives in Italy. By 1910, American money was the leading source of income in Capannori. When the mayor of Capannori was asked about the population of his town, he responded with a number and then added that the other half of them lived in America.

The money flow from America trumped all of the rumors that had been floating about. It was true that gold did not line American roads, but the wages in the new land were much higher than anything they could garner in Italy for similar work. America was growing—and it was not just talk. There were genuine economic opportunities in the new land, and as more information rolled into Lucca, the Menicuccis quickly discovered that American mining jobs paid especially well. Mining looked like a long-sought-out answer for the family's plight. Mezzadria at that time were wholly impoverished, completely ignorant about international travel, spoke no foreign languages, and had no worldly experience working in a new land with a unique form of government. However, they could perform physical labor, a primary need in American mines. The Padrone were quick to fill that need.

UNIFICATION'S EFFECT

As Pasquale's family was maturing, Italian unification began to unfold. The Risorgimento (resurrection) was philosophically founded on the same republican principles as the French and American revolutions, highlighting free thought and enlightened expression. These ideas fanned the burgeoning winds of revolution based on the concept of ordinary citizens participating in the workings of the government. Various governmental structures were debated. Some pushed for a parliamentary system modeled after the new French system. Some traditionalists proposed to organize the peninsula under the Pope, but that did not sit well with many people who felt a papal government essentially created a monarchy, which was philosophically incompatible with the Risorgimento. Endless debate prevailed with little progress until 1848 when Italy and most of Europe revolted against central governments. By 1848, Italy was divided into three regions: the northwest Piedmont up to about Milan on the east and the island of Sardinia, both governed by the Kingdom of Sardinia. The Pope controlled the Papal States in the middle. The island of Sicily and the Italian peninsula south of the Papal states were ruled by the Kingdom of Two Sicilies, employing the philosophy of the House of Bourbon. The Austrians controlled the regions northeast of Milan.

The years 1848–1849 are sometimes called the First Italian War of Independence because it was the initial effort by people from all areas of the peninsula to rise for reform. Milan hosted the initial battle when a rag-tag group of residents routed a small garrison of Austrians. The Piedmont, sensing weakness and seeking complete control of the northern areas of Italy to Austria border, declared war on Austria. The ensuing battles did not go well for the Piedmontese, even after allying with the Papal states. Following the loss of several strategic battles, the movement was quashed. The only noteworthy—or better yet fateful—event was Victor Emmanuel II's ascension to the throne of Sardinia after his father abdicated, setting him up for a major role in the Italian unification.

The Sardinians and the Austrians each controlled a portion of the northern part of Italy, and they continually skirmished until 1859, when Austria declared war on the Piedmont. The Austrians were repulsed by an allied force of Sardinians and the French army, leaving the entire northern third of Italy under the solid control of Victor Emmanuel, the King. Sensing an opportunity, he authorized his General Garibaldi to attack Sicily, which had been reeling due to various insurrections and violent protests over House of Bourbon rule. In lightning fashion over six months, Garibaldi solidified control of Sicily and the entire bottom half of the Italian peninsula.

The Papal States were in the middle and vulnerable to a pincer attack from its north and south flanks. It happened. Count Cavour attacked the Papal States from the north while Garibaldi advanced from the south. Once the pincer was complete, the peninsula was united under a single controlling entity for the first time since the Roman Empire. On March 17, 1861, Victor Emmanuel declared himself King of a united Italy. Italy had been fractured for so many centuries that it would be many decades before Italians experienced a sense of nationality. Thus, the concept of a paisano, a countryman, was not well-developed until the early Twentieth Century. The populace clung to the ancient practice of identifying with localities rather than a nation. This regionalization was one reason the northern and southern Italians often conflicted; they both considered the other to be from a different country.

These events meant little to Paolo's family, which focused on survival. However, the turmoil was unnerving and consistently produced an incentive to seek better living conditions. Every day, more news came from neighbors and relatives in America who were thriving and sending money back to Italy. So much money was coming back that some families could move themselves up socially by buying parcels of land. Geocondo, one of Pasquale's sons, purchased his small wheat field using money that his boys in America sent back to the family. That extra income was theirs alone and provided resources Geocondo used to pay for his travels to and from America. It was solid evidence that the new nation was the answer to their prayers for an improved life.

Notes

1. *Gilmore, La Sorte,* and *Mangione & Morreale* present detailed accounts of Italian life then. *Morris (Barry)* and *Langer* present in encyclopedic form a chronological rendition of the world and American events at the time.

2. *Gregory* presents a detailed account of how the Italians reacted to Napoleon's rule.

3. Few details about the Menicucci family in the early 1800s are known. No civil records were kept in Lucca until new laws demanded them around 1866. Churches kept records, but electronic photocopies are not yet available. Most familial lineages were determined by studying civil records containing lineage information. For more information, see Appendix IV.

4. *Craig & Rimstidt* provide an overview of the development of gold mining in the Southwest United States.

4

MENICUCCIS IN WESTERN AMERICA (1870–1910)

BEACON OF HOPE

Many Menicuccis living in the western United States, particularly New Mexico, Idaho and Montana, can trace their origins to Paolo Menicucci's family. Before Paolo, few immigrants traveled to the United States because the country was in its infancy. The first great Italian emigration to America began around 1870, as reconstruction following the U.S. Civil War increased manufacturing, becoming the foundation for the burgeoning economy. Paolo's children were the first of the Menicucci family to seriously consider emigrating, although there is scant evidence that any did. The same cannot be said of Paolo's grandchildren, such as Pasquale, who were coming of age just as the first wave of migration was developing.

Paolo married Margherita Santori and he had a large family, which was customary at that time to maintain the family's human resources. The family was the first line of defense against hazards of any kind, such as epidemics. The more children in the family the greater the chances that some survive to care for the older generation. More children meant more revenue and security. The Catholic church understood the need, and weekly homilies at the Masses often touted the benefits of large families. Most Italians were devout Catholics and the church was influential.

In keeping with the tradition, Pasquale and Amelia Morelli produced seven children: Letizia (1848), Luigi (1849), Carmelinda (1851), Raffaello (1859), Geocondo (1861), Adelina (1862) and Emilio (1863). Many Menicuccis now living in Albuquerque, Pocatello, Idaho and Anaconda, Montana, likely descended from Pasquale and Amelia.

All were born in Capannori, spread among the hamlets of Segromigno--Monte and Piano—and Lammari, and were Colono farmers by profession. As these children matured, America became an increasingly interesting topic of discussion as word about the new country spread around the Italian countryside. Interest was piqued by a constant stream of letters from Paesani (countrymen) living in the new country. In Italy, their letters were passed around friends and relatives like gems, dazzling and wooing their countrymen with romantic accounts of American life. Vespucci and Columbus had done very well discovering America, many thought.

INTREPID YOUNG ITALIANS

Oreste Bachechi was born in 1860 in the Lucca province and immigrated to Albuquerque in 1885. The Bachechi family was a successful and respected business and property owner in Italy. Oreste's skills worked well in the small desert town tucked in southwest United States. He opened a saloon in 1885 and was earning more money than he had ever imagined possible. Considering the relatively high status of his Italian family, it was all the more impressive that he found America fruitful. Of course, a little exaggeration was often sprinkled into the letters to accentuate the new country's allure and the immigrant's wisdom. In Oreste's case, no exaggeration was needed. America presented a ground-breaking economic opportunity for Italians.

Oreste adored American free-market capitalism and frequently sent letters to his family and friends, exhorting them to immigrate. His letters repeatedly made one point that caught the interest of the Colono farmers in the area: the ease of creating and operating a business. There were no taxes, little regulation and relative freedom to create whatever business was desired. Better still, Albuquerque was a growing community that produced a steadily increasing customer base. He reported that profits from his saloon were flowing in at a rate about seven times what Colono farmers could produce. It was American capitalism that Oreste described, something the Menicuccis had no knowledge of, but it sounded appealing.

This was all fine, but there was a huge impediment for the Menicuccis—one that Oreste did not have—the cost of travel to America. The Bachechi family had sufficient resources to send members directly to America. Oreste originally traveled to Brazil and into Middle America before finding Albuquerque. Other early immigrants, such as the

Matteuccis, did similarly by immigrating to other western states before alighting in Albuquerque. All were thriving in the city. These successful Italians took their business skills and resources to the United States, where they flourished in a free market.

The Menicucci Colono family could barely make their budgets work. They had little money left from their farming operations, and for most of the year they operated in loss, recovering only when the crops were harvested and sold in the fall. It was a conundrum that bedeviled all of Pasquale's children. But the prospect of the fruits of America was attractive and a potential escape from the centuries-long grip of the Mezzadria. In addition, there was growing concern about conscription in the Italian army. If boys were drafted, they earned even less than farming and probably died in the effort. They carefully watched the postings of the government's Liste de Leva postings, a list of the young men eligible to be drafted. A name on the list was not automatic enlistment, but he was a candidate to be called at the government's discretion.

These fears were fanned by worrisome developments with the Italian Army, including incompetence. Italy, like many other European countries, was waging war in colonial Africa. In 1895, the Ethiopians defeated the Italians at Amba Alagi, where the Italians lost a third of their three thousand-troop force. To save face, Prime Minister Crispi ordered General Baratieri to attack Adua. Astonishingly, Baratieiri lost all twenty-five thousand of his soldiers in a little more than a day, with half killed and the remainder captured. It was the worst colonial defeat for a European country in history. Amba Alagi and Adua were losses that could bring on the draft. All of this information was dribbling down to the countryside, agitating the populace and discouraging youthful interest in the army. Not surprisingly, after the world-class debacle in Ethiopia, Crispi's government fell and was replaced by the Marquis di Rudini.

The Mezzadria class, including the Menicuccis, could barely pronounce the names of the African countries where their countrymen were dying, much less find motivation for military service in the Italian Army. It did the opposite. Ten percent of Italian men bolted the country specifically to avoid the draft. It did not make sense to peasants to work in the army that paid only average wages and end up dead in a place as far away as the moon. These wars were useless to Colono families in their daily struggle for survival.

Meanwhile, adverse weather and bad political policies hammered the Italian economy, which led to a rapid and dramatic reduction in wheat production, producing bread shortages in the late 1890s. The public discontent was wide and deep, involving everyone from the local civil authorities to the Mezzadria. On May 3, 1898, a bread riot broke out in Milan, a city of over half a million just one hundred and sixty miles north of the Menicucci home. Martial law was proclaimed, and over a hundred citizens died at the hands of the army; Thousands were injured, and dozens were jailed with heavy sentences. Riots and protests were occurring throughout Italy, but the bloodiness of Milan reverberated through Lucca. It was dubbed the Fatti di Maggio (i.e., the Facts of May) and was used as a rallying cry against the government, forcing Prime Minister Antonio Starabba to resign and be replaced by Luigi Pelloux. The country might be officially united, but the Italian minister position looked like a party of musical chairs, turning over frequently, projecting instability and ineptitude. The Menicuccis, like their neighbors, fretted that the political unrest and riots could come to Lucca and surrounding areas, engulfing their homes. The worsening economic and political situation reinforced the desire of peasants to leave the country, especially with America's beacon of economic hope summoning them.

IDAHO GOLD

Each of Pasquale's children had unique personalities. Emilio was a rambunctious and energetic youngster who was fearless. He was intrigued by America, especially the gold mining opportunities. In 1888, in Italy, he married Artemisa Manioli. But he was destined to work in American precious metal mines. Emilio's had two daughters, both born in Segromigno; Maria, (1890) and Argene (1892).[1]

Emilio saved money even with the responsibility of caring for his family. In 1896, he had cobbled together enough for a journey and headed to San Francisco, hoping to cash in on gold. In 1848, James Marshall discovered a large amount of gold in placer deposits near Sutter's Mill on the South Fork American River banks in Coloma, California, about thirty miles northeast of Sacramento. Placer deposits naturally form when small flecks of gold are weathered out of the rock by river-water action and are washed downstream, eventually accumulating in certain areas of the river banks. Placer miners scour these deposits using pans to separate the gold from the river debris and sand. It is intensely laborious because the gold flakes are small, around one-eighth inch in diameter. The initial placer miners did well, scarfing up the easily accessible rich gold deposits.

Placer mines were especially intriguing to the Italian peasants, who were already enamored with the idea of digging precious metals out of the ground. In placer mining, all that is needed is a pan and the willingness to stand in cold water for hours scooping up sand and sifting out the tiny gold nuggets. Italian peasants were not alone in wild enthusiasm for the gold prospects. Tens of thousands of people seeking their fortune descended on the California mining areas during the Gold Rush of 1849.

In those days, it took much time for news to pass from one part of the world to another, even news as important as gold. Emilio, in the late 1800s, was beginning to hear about the discovery of gold in California. He envisioned gathering gold from the natural deposits along California's river banks. Paesani (countrymen) were there, and the Caselli family was known to the Menicuccis in Italy. He originally planned to work temporarily in American mines, returning to Italy when he had made his fortune.

When Emilio arrived in California in 1896, the rush was well over and the gold placer deposits had been picked clean of easy catches. Mining continued underground, operated by large companies. By this time, though, the gold bug was deeply embedded in his soul, and he followed the metal as it was popping up in several America's mountain states. He wanted to cash in on early rushes, especially placer fields. Precious metal mining had developed in Nevada, and in the early 1900s, he moved to Carlin, home of the Carlin Trend, one of the world's richest gold deposits. The operators of these underground mines were desperate for workers. There were few placer deposits but plenty of well-paying jobs underground. He immediately found work, could send money home, and save enough to bring his family to America. Before he could do so, his wife Artemisa died in Italy, and his two daughters moved in with his brother, Geocondo. Emilio subsequently moved to Pocatello, Idaho, where many mining jobs were available.

The abundance of high-paying American mining jobs and Emilio's early success caught the attention of his Segromigno family. Emilio's brother, Luigi, immigrated in 1898. He was married to Carmelia Bertilacchi, but traveled alone to Great Falls, Montana. At the age of forty-nine he likely worked in the copper mines as a smelter, a person who manages the machines that heat the ore to melt and extract precious metals. It was about the only mining job that an older man could do. Luigi's movements in Montana are murky due to a paucity of records about him. He later appears in the 1913 directory as the proprietor of a confectionary shop specializing in tobacco products. Luigi might have had a son, Joseph, but no records confirm it. He likely moved to Pocatello earlier, probably in the middle of the first decade of the century, as the grueling smelting job wore the aging man down.

Pasquale, son of Geocondo, joined his uncles in Pocatello in 1906. Pasquale worked in the mines, which had the highest-paying jobs. Unfortunately, as was the case with many miners, Pasquale was crushed to death in a mining accident in 1908 when he was twenty-three years old. Tales of men being mangled in the ore processing facility were gruesome, some reporting men being swept into the huge open gear works. Workers watched in horror as a victim was slowly dismembered and shredded by the huge rotating gears. Typically, nothing but splattered blood, piles of flesh, and scraps of clothing were left of the unfortunate victims. When these accidents happened, the operation was halted for a day to give workers time to gather the remains and hand them to the grieving family. Work resumed the following day after a few obligatory words of remorse by the bosses. Miners were considered tools of the trade that were occasionally lost. To miners, it was a hazard of the job, which they were personally responsible for avoiding.

Geocondo was a forceful and deliberate man. He had emerged as the de facto head of Pasquale's family and had been exploring American mines for employment potential, stopping long enough to work at each one until he had the travel money to venture to the next destination. Of course, he returned all that was possible to his family in Italy. In 1905, he traveled to Hancock, Michigan, where large, underground copper deposits were being commercially developed. Italians were well represented in the northern Michigan mining community, including many whom Geocondo knew, such as the Giannins, Pireronis, and my maternal great-grandfather Achille Barsanti. Geocondo labored in a copper smelting operation for a year. The smelter, which melts the ore in a mill located on the surface, paid less than an extraction job but was less arduous work. Alas, even that was beyond the capabilities of an aging forty-four-year-old man. Geocondo moved back to Idaho to work with his brother Luigi in his confectionary business for a couple of years, sending money to his family in Italy. After his son died in 1908, he returned to Italy and had a second son, who was named Pasquale.[2]

In 1911, Geocondo returned to Idaho, accompanied by his wife Elena and Argene, Emilio's eighteen-year-old daughter. They delivered Argene to Emilio, reuniting her with her father for the first time in years. Geocondo worked a few menial jobs before he and Elena returned to Italy the following year. This visit was the last time that the brothers celebrated as anything resembling a family unit. Emilio was naturalized in Pocatello in 1910 and died of Pneumonia in 1918.[3] Many of his descendants remain in various western states, most notably Montana.[4]

MONTANA COPPER

Idaho was not the only western U.S. state featuring attractive mining jobs. By 1910, the Amalgamated Copper Company in Anaconda, Montana was rapidly developing into the principal copper producer in the United States.[5] In the early years of the Twentieth Century, the United States was characterized by vigorous economic growth, not unlike what the world witnessed with China from 1990 to 2020. America's new system of railroads provided travel and trade from coast to coast. As the westward movement expanded, communities grew along the rail tracks and the West Coast.

Construction materials, metals and lumber became high-value items. Coal, too, was demanded for fuel for trains, factories, mines and homes throughout the country. The United States was blessed with extraordinary natural wealth, and these materials were rapidly consumed to fuel economic growth and prosperity. Mining operators were eager to meet the demands of a growing country, as expected in a capitalist society. Copper and iron were the metals in greatest demand; iron was used for the machines needed for mining, transportation, and construction, and copper was used for water pipes and electrical products, including wire for electric motors, which were becoming ubiquitous in the industry, including mines. Electric motors provided power to lift buckets of ore from the depths and to move rail cars. Hand-held machines, such as power drills, appeared. These machines assisted humans in the most difficult jobs: drilling horizontal holes into rock faces for dynamite charges. Coal supplied the heat to smelt the ore into salable products and to run the large steam engines. Coal and other fossil fuels were increasingly used in the maritime industry as steam engines replaced sails.

Mining is arduous and dangerous but was especially so before the introduction of power equipment in the early 1900s. Miners labored in perilous conditions with little protective equipment, such as face masks or eye protection. Mining operators' primary need was raw labor: young and vigorous young men. The labor needs did not abate with machinery; they were diverted. Mining operations became more productive because the new tools allowed miners to extract more ore with the same labor, but the amount of labor and the danger remained steady.

Luigi, son of Geocondo, immigrated in 1915 to Anaconda, Montana. A few years later, he was joined in Montana by his brother, Alberto, the second. Luigi was naturalized in Montana in 1921, and he was buried in Anaconda in 1972. Alberto, another son of Geocondo, married Ida Unti of Anaconda in 1924, but he died in 1931 at age thirty-three. He and Ida had one daughter, Albertina. Many of the Menicuccis living in Montana today are descended from Luigi and Alberto, both sons of Geocondo. Much of the information about them was deduced.[6,7]

THE GREAT BUGOUT

The strange case of Raffaello Menicucci, son of Pasquale, has floated in Menicucci family lore for decades. This man is of interest because all his descendants immigrated to Albuquerque. However, his history is murky and laden with uncomplimentary lore. Teresa Menicucci Clark and Mariangela Menicucci Scanlon, both daughters of Giulio, provide the lion's share of information. They said that Raffaello had traveled to San Francisco in the early 1890s and remained there for at least seven years. He was reported to have sent little money to the family and communicated with them infrequently, with lapses so long that the family considered him to be dead.

What irked Teresa and Mariangela was their belief that Raffaello abandoned the family, one of the worst sins that an Italian man of that time could commit. They expressed their opinions both in private conversations with me as well in recordings, some of which are in the public domain. Mariangela believed that he was a victim of depression, a genetic trait that, unfortunately, had surfaced in some of Pasquale's descendants in New Mexico, including some of her own children. Teresa agreed, and added the fact that Raffaello and his wife Teresa waited four years before producing children. At that time in Italy, marriage was intended to produce a family, and children typically appeared about a year after marriage. She suspects that some systemic problem existed in the family, perhaps related to poverty or Raffaello's mental health, which delayed children for so long after marriage. Mariangela believed that he probably sank into a bout of depression following the stress of married life and his first child, Giulio. She believed he did what many depression victims do—bugout, either physically and/or mentally, from the stressor, which in this case was the family itself. Raffaello apparently chose physical separation as his remedy. What especially disturbed Teresa Menicucci Clark was that "Rafaello left Teresa with two small children and provided no support when he was gone," she said. Mariangela added that Teresa, Raffaello's wife, raised Giulio and Amerigo alone. Both women insist that he had no heroic role in the Menicucci migration and was, instead, a deserter. Interestingly, neither Giulio nor Amerigo discussed their father, although they gave glowing reviews about their mother. Their silence on the history is telling, perhaps shrouding their shame and embarrassment of their father.

UNDERSTANDABLE OUTRAGE

Mariangela's and Teresa's bitterness towards their grandfather is no wonder. They were Italian women in the traditional sense, providers of comfort, care, nurturing and affection to the family, while the men focused on authority as family head and the provider of resources. They sympathized with Teresa's situation of losing her husband during a critical time for the family, just as babies were born.

Unlike his siblings, there are virtually no immigration records, ship manifests, or employment records for Raffaello in America. Very few facts corroborate or refute the tale of lore. The only evidence of his appearance in America is in the city directory in 1893 and it is not certain it was he, although Raffaello is not a common name and it is unlikely that another Raffaello Menicucci would be in San Francisco in 1893, just as Teresa Clark and Mariangela Scanlon reported.

Amerigo's birth in November of 1893 implies that Raffaello left immediately after he impregnated Teresa with Amerigo so that he could be in San Francisco in time to be recorded in the 1893 directory. This scenario was doable given that Amerigo was born in November 1893 and Raffaello could have left in February, allowing plenty of time to arrive in

San Francisco early in the year. Raffaello lived at 320 Clark Street, about two miles south of San Francisco on the east shore of San Francisco Bay. He was probably boarding with friends or relatives.

Aside from lore and the single San Francisco record, Raffaello's movements remain a mystery. It is possible that in his depressed state, he could have stowed away on a ship and later taken a job as a sailor. Stowaways were not uncommon in those days, and the Padrone were readily available to help. Padrone had connections with the ship owners who could be bribed to board people secretly. They could also arrange for sailing jobs. The Padrone had provided stowaway services for many of the young Italian men seeking to avoid the military draft, so they knew the ropes and they were successful. Naturally, the service came with a hefty fee. So, if Raffaello had taken this course of action, he must have scrounged the money, probably borrowing from relatives and raiding whatever savings they had, subsequently handing it to a padrono to move him out. Raffaello might have arranged for a stowaway and a simultaneous job on a ship, with the sailor's wages docked to cover the padrono's fee. The stowaway theory meets all known facts, but few testable hypotheses have emerged that can lead to verification.[8]

Although Raffaello's exact whereabouts for years are unknown, his absence from the family undoubtedly produced significant hardship for the family. First, it removed a working, productive member from the family. Second, it left Teresa to fend for herself. At that time in Italy, almost any official act, such as buying or selling property of any kind or signing contracts, was handled by men, and in Teresa's case, by Raffaello. When a husband abandoned the family, the remaining wife had to appeal to the Italian courts to allow her access to family assets and to assume the role of head of the family. Third, it retarded the family's ability to save money and send their children to America, as other Menicuccis had done. Mostly, it served to further impoverish Raffaello's family. While others in Pasquale's family regularly traveled to and from America, Teresa was saddled with two small children, no husband, steadily increasing debt and little means of support.

Teresa did not file for legal control of the properties but turned to family for help, possibly to Geocondo, who was emerging as the Menicucci family leader, or more likely to her own Morelli family, such as her sister Amabele Rondina, who was married to Francesco Morelli. Another family member could legally proxy for Raffaello in his absence, especially if his abandonment were disguised as a temporary absence. A husband's abandonment was a serious scandal, creating a blight on the family that could not be easily expunged. Victims, such as his wife, Teresa, were keen to keep their plight secret from the authorities who could expose the situation to the public.

In the early 1900s, Raffaello returned. Teresa Menicucci Clark said it was a tense and awkward reunion, but the family needed him back. His reintroduction to the family likely evolved over a few years. Few facts are known, but an event in 1906 is clear. At forty-five years of age, Teresa produced a son, Aladino. It was likely an unplanned birth, and the situation worsened as the baby's intellectual development stalled in infancy. Raffaello cobbled enough money to bring him to a physician in Lucca, the walled city with some health care facilities. The diagnosis was sobering. Aladino had a congenital condition, probably Cystic Fibrosis, that impaired his ability to live normally. He was expected to live about thirty years at most. He would need constant living assistance. That was a depressing prognosis for an already impoverished family. The news likely spun Raffaello into another bout of depression.[9]

Raffaello's disappearance is credible and founded in corroborated lore. However, his movements over seven years cannot be traced via the available civil or other official records, such as ship manifests. Given the many records that typically follow immigrants as they integrate into American societies, I believe it is impossible for Raffaello to work in America for seven years without producing traces of his existence in various communities. Alas, while the stowaway theory conveniently fits the facts, there is little direct evidence to support it. Additional research is needed to solve this mystery.

FATEFUL GIANNINI MARRIAGE

In 1882, Adelina, daughter to Pasquale, married Maruizzo Giannini. The marriage is significant for two reasons. First, the proposed marriage kicked off an investigation into the couple's financial situation. The Italian state declared them, as a couple, indigent. The implications are unclear, but primarily, it probably relieved them from the marriage and other civil fees associated with it and allowed Maruizzo access to certain services and considerations for assistance. Few, if any, state-sponsored welfare systems existed in Italy at the time, but the Catholic Church operated social assistance programs. The church used the declaration to prioritize those most needing their assistance. In any case, this poverty declaration was an exclamation point on the overall economic condition of the Menicucci family at the time. They were inarguably dirt-poor peasants.[10]

Second, the marriage connects the Menicuccis to the Gianninis, a relationship that extended to the United States. Adelina and Maruizzo produced two children, Austutillo and Arduina, born in 1898 and 1905, respectively. Maurizo, by the time he came to America, had dropped his first name and used only his second given name, Giuseppe. He and his family, including his wife Adelina and son Austutillo, immigrated directly to Albuquerque, where they set up a homestead. There is much more to be revealed about Austutillo, as we shall see, including his outsized influence on the Menicucci family and the early community of Albuquerque.[11]

Notes

1. Emilio was the youngest of Pasquale's children, born around 1864, before the onset of regular civil record keeping. His birth date is given on his naturalization record. He arrived in America in 1896. The deduced birth date is based on the travel date and his stated age indicates a birth in 1862. This date differs by two years from his naturalization record, but this discrepancy is common. Birth dates are complicated by number truncation and transcription errors. In a census or on manifests, ages are presented in whole years, with fractions of years truncated to the beginning of the year. For example, using this method, a person born on Jan 1, 1958, and one born on Dec 1, 1958, would be recorded with the same age, even though there is nearly a year difference between them. Similarly, the error could occur in reverse, showing an age difference that does not exist. Thus, errors of at least a year may occur when computing dates based on other events, such as using a marriage record to estimate a person's birthdate based on the reported age at the time of marriage. Human error is a further complication, particularly at the ports of entry. The entire immigration process was a rushed procedure and dates and other facts are often misstated. Given these complications, I have seen errors of up to two years when estimating event dates. Emilio's Italian marriage record is #38, posted on February 26, 1890, located in the Italian civil records for Lucca province, Capannori comune.

2. In 1909, Geocondo and Elena, both in their middle 40s,

produced a son they named Pasquale, replacing their first Pasquale, who died in 1908. Both parents had grieved over the death, which left them longing for a replacement. Late-age births and the associated birth defects were common in Italy at that time, but they proceeded. The new Pasquale grew up in Italy and immigrated to Brazil as a single man; it is unknown if he produced descendants there. Renaming a newborn after his deceased brother was not the first time the couple renamed a son. Alberto, son of Geocondo, was born in 1896 but died in 1898, the same year his younger brother was born. The new baby was given the name Alberto, replacing his diseased brother.

3. In Idaho at that time of the reunion were Geocondo and his brothers Luigi and Emilio, along with Elena, Geocondo's wife and Argene, the first time they had been together in a decade. They had been separated for so long, and by long distances, they barely knew each other. Given the mobility of these early gold-smitten immigrants, family reunions were rare. Geocondo and Elena visited for about a year and then returned to Italy, where the couple lived out their lives managing the Menicucci family affairs, including properties that they had accumulated from the revenue garnered from his family's forays in America. Emilio, his daughter, Geni, and brother, Luigi, lived together at 710 Pocatello Ave in Idaho.

4. In the middle 1910s, Argene's sister Maria immigrated to Idaho to join her uncles. There, she married Edward Dalpino, a maintenance mechanic for an automotive organization. His salary produced fine living conditions for the family, and his trade skills eventually brought them to Antioch, California, around 1950 where high-paying jobs were abundant. In Idaho, they produced at least two children, Silvan and Leonard.

In 1915, Argene, daughter to Emilio and nicknamed Geni (later called Jennie and later Argentina), married Valentino Chelini in Butte, Montana, where they set down roots. Chelini hailed from Lucca and worked as a railroad carpenter; a trade that produced a comfortable lifestyle not tied to dangerous mining. A newspaper report about Argene's death lists her ten children as George, Emil, Chester and John of Butte, Angelo of Indian Springs, Nevada, Mike of Weiser, Idaho, Amelia, Anna Chelini Lasetich of Anaconda and Jenny Chelini Winkler of Anaconda, Montana.

Valentino Chelini died in 1964, widowing Argene. Mourning and lonely, she subsequently moved to Antioch to join her sister and husband, Edward. Argene died in Antioch, California, in 1979, and her body was returned to Butte for burial. Argene's legacy in Montana is long-standing due to her many children, many of whom bore descendants of the Chelini family who likely still reside in the states of Idaho, Montana, and Nevada.

5. Amalgamated Copper eventually became Anaconda Copper Mining Company, which was one of the largest copper mine operators in the world in the first half of the Twentieth Century.

6. Luigi, the oldest male in the family, was born in 1849. In 1887 he wed Carmelia Bertilacchi, daughter of Giuseppe and Stella Matteucci. Luigi's supplemental marriage record is found in the Allegati Matrimoni records, 1886-1888. It is the only known familial relationship with the Matteucci family. Whether Stella Matteucci is in the family line of the Matteuccis in Albuquerque is unknown. As we shall see, the Menicucci and Matteucci families in Albuquerque have long enjoyed and continue to enjoy strong friendships and working relationships to this day.

Luigi was among the early Menicucci emigrants from Segromigno who ventured to America. He arrived on July 21, 1898. The ship manifest shows that he was traveling to Great Falls, Montana, to see his unnamed cousin, who could be the son of his uncle or aunt, possibly a Morelli. Several Morellis resided in Montana at that time, but there is no evidence that they were closely related to the family. No other Menicuccis are known to have lived in that area at the time.

7. As an example of the deductive process in genealogical searches, consider the marriage record for Giovanni Menicucci to Maria Checchini in November 1871, record #83. The record shows a testimonial letter regarding baptisms, and in the second paragraph, it states, "Giuseppe, figlio (son) di Domenico di Paolo di Bartolomeo Menicucci di Segromigno." I deduce that Giuseppe's father, Domenico, was a brother to Pasquale di Paolo di Bartolomeo, all living in Segromigno. Many of Giovanni's children immigrated to America and they likely interacted with Pasquale's family, but tracing the complete extended family is beyond the scope of this book and is an area of additional research. The records are located in the Italian civil records, Lucca Region, Lucca Province, Capannori Comune

Carmelinda, the second daughter to Pasquale and her husband Asalone Ricconini, never emigrated from Italy, although their son, Francisco, immigrated to Montana in 1913 to work in the mines. He died there in 1928 as a single man. A great deal of additional genealogical information can be drawn from the records.

8. The *Gjenvick-Gjønvik Archives* reported on stowaways in 1911. *Irving* published an article about the stowaway issue.

9. Aladino died in 1934 at the age of 28 as a single man still living at Raffaello's home. Thresa Domenici Menicucci and her husband Mario, son of Amerigo Menicucci, visited the family shortly before his death and verified that he had been infirm for a long period. His death record declares that he was a carpenter. Giulio later said he only "carved a few small pieces from wood" and did no construction or any work that required strength, stamina and a well-functioning mind. In those days, a carpenter was one who worked with wood, whether it be carving a small bird out of a lump of oak or cutting and installing wood beams in a commercial building. His medical condition and cause of death are unknown.

10. The marriage record for Letizia, daughter of Pasquale Menicucci, is found in the Registro Dei Matimoni Allegatti, 1871, Record #98. It can be found in the Italian Supplemental records. On the first page, in the bottom paragraph, and continuing on the following page, it reads that she is di "Pasquale di Paolo Menicucci e Maria di Luigi Morelli." This establishes her as part of Pasquale's family because he was verified as Maria Morelli's spouse. It also references her grandfather Paolo. On the fourth page of the record, it reads in reference to Letizia, "Letizia Cristina figlia de Pasquale di Paolo de Bartolomeo Menicucci di Segromigno, e di Maria di Luigi Morelli…" (Letizia Cristina, daughter of Pasquale, son of Paolo, son of Bartolomeo Menicucci of Segromigno and of Maria, daughter of Luigi Morelli.) This statement establishes the familial relationship of the Menicucci men from Pasquale through Paolo to Bartolomeo. The record clearly states that the couple was indigent.

11. *Puelo, Raczynski and Roberts* provide summaries of Italian immigration in America. The *Ellis Island* article provides a description of immigrant passage through Ellis Island. *Lord, et. al.,* present a detailed summary of Italian immigration from the middle 1800s to around 1905.

5

CALL THE PADRONO (BOSS) (1909–1910)

DESPERATION TIME

By 1907, Raffaello was among the last of Pasquale's children without offspring in America. With the possible exception of Adelina's, Raffaello's was the most impoverished Menicucci family, mostly as a result of his multi-year hiatus. Raffaello had no reasonable means to self-fund family members traveling to America. If he could find the money, he could directly send his boys to Idaho or Montana, as his brothers had done. The obstacle for Raffaello was always money. A padrono was the only answer, although not an ideal one. By this time, the Padrone had developed a bad reputation as swindlers, preying on ignorant immigrants. A few were honest and provided quality service, but they were outnumbered. The trick was finding an honest one.

The Padrone operated as employment brokers, like an employment agency. They earned their money by matching men to jobs. Mining jobs brought the highest fee to the Padrone when they delivered a qualified worker, a young man with the physical build to do hard labor in a mine. The Padrone knew the qualifications—a man must be at least one hundred and fifty pounds, and free of defects that could encumber his ability to work. Children were eschewed for mining work not because of child labor laws, which largely did not exist in America, but because they were physically small. A padrono usually specialized in certain geographical areas of Italy and specific job classes in America. Most of the Padrone were affiliated with American mining operators because they continually needed new laborers and paid hefty finder's fees.

Lorenzo Lencioni, a padrono, worked in the Lucca province during the early 1900s and knew the young men in various families. He visited these families regularly to assess the growth of the boys and the family's interest in America. When the boys came of size, he offered them a mining job. The deal was he paid for the entire trip, including any expenses incurred along the way, and the immigrant was guaranteed a mining job. Of course, there was an upfront fee for this service, but it amounted to only about a third of the normal cost of passage to America. The Padrone produced so much travel business and delivered so many laborers that they often obtained travel deals. Padrone bought passengers in bulk, typically bringing traveling groups of up to thirty young men. The railroad operators were delighted to dedicate entire train cars to the Padrone. The ship operators likewise provided perks, such as complimentary second-class passage. A typical padrono made a dozen trips across the Atlantic in a year. Both the rail and steamship owners provided them with substantial bulk-travel discounts, reducing their costs and allowing them to offer attractive deals to immigrants.[1]

PADRONE VIRTUE

An honest padrono, operating legally as a vettore, not only earned a fine living but served the emigrants as well, especially the exceptionally poor ones, such as the Menicuccis. Padrone were often the only means for Colono peasants to access America. Further, the Padrone understood the societal importance of maintaining family and neighborhood kinship in the new land. They made efforts to ensure that family members remained unified on their first jobs. The employers cooperated because it worked for them. The Padrone were keen to understand both the needs of prospective immigrants and American employers and specialized in matching the two.

Padrone typically worked in family teams, with some in Italy and others in America. They had their own communication system between the continents—they put mail directly onto rail cars and/or ocean liners to be picked up by their partners at the arriving dock. Using this method, a padrono in America could contact his partner in Italy in less than two weeks instead of a month or more for regular mail delivery. They also had modern equipment, such as mule-drawn carts, that allowed them to traverse the rural areas of Italy quickly. Further, an occasional, expensive cablegram between Padrone on different continents was written off as a cost of doing business. The shipping and rail companies cooperated with the Padrone because they provided paying customers. For all the infamy of the Padrone—mostly well deserved—the ones authorized as vettore provided a desperately needed service to Italian peasants. And it was a lifeline for the Menicuccis.

THE PADRONO DELIVERS

Lorenzo Lencioni grew up in Lucca, was an authorized vettore and was under contract to the Michigan mine operators to deliver Italian laborers. He had been working in the Capannori area for several years. He had assisted Geocondo in America, which helped his credibility; Italians preferred to deal with other Italians in their home province. He knew every family in the Lucca province, including the boys' names and ages. Each day he surveyed his list of potential young immigrants and then visited the farms to recruit.

By 1907, Lencioni had his sights on Giulio, who was about five feet eight inches tall and about one hundred and fifty pounds, the minimum for mining laborers. Amerigo was smaller but growing rapidly. Lencioni had previously talked to Raffaello about the boys and there was interest, so he posited a deal, which he scribbled on a sheet of paper. The terms were detailed in longhand script: He would deliver his boys to the Franklin Mine in Hancock, Michigan, for about a third of the cost to self-fund the trip. The mining job paid roughly six times what the boys earned in Italy. Lencioni would accompany the boys from Europe to America, guarantee passage through Ellis Island, escort them by rail to the Michigan mine, and set them up in a boarding home and a copper mining job. It was an all-inclusive deal and Raffaello agreed, scrounging and borrowing the money to pay half of the padrono's upfront fee, the other half to be paid when he collected the boys for the journey. Lencioni said he would contact him.

With the actual contact in place, family optimism soared for the first time in ages. Finally, things might be moving in a productive direction. Time quickly attenuated that enthusiasm as 1908 passed without a word. As the silence dragged into spring and into summer, suspicions grew of nefarious intent. The family talked to neighbors who had had their own experiences with Lencioni, hoping to confirm that the decision to contract him was correct. Most corroborated his veracity. The fundamental problem was that he was incommunicado. He constantly moved about the province making deals. But what they did not understand is that he was highly motivated to get Giulio to the mines because that is where he made his big fee; the upfront fee that Raffaello paid was a pittance in comparison. Still, Raffaello's somber state deepened as one quiescent day led to another. Regardless of what happened—accident or nefarious act--it was he who signed the contract and borrowed the money. If there was ever a man who felt more deserving of the label snakebit, Raffaello was he.

In his despondency, Raffaello frequently lashed out at various family members. He was realizing defeat and that he had imperiled his family's finances for nothing. Even Amerigo, with all his enthusiasm and faith, was losing hope. But Teresa was steadfast and used her standing in the kitchen during meals to ask the men to call on the Madonna. Teresa explained that she speaks to the Lord; he listens to his mama, she argued. Giulio and Raffaello went along, but they were not convinced. In contrast, Amerigo had developed a deep faith in the Lord and believed that the Madonna had real power. Teresa had no intention of immigrating to America, but she knew the new land was essential for the future economic security of the family. She understood that with her boys working in America and sending money back home, the family's life in Italy would improve dramatically. With Aladino's medical condition dragging on, the family needed all the help it could get.

THE CALL

In May of 1909, Giulio and Amerigo were laboring in the fields a few hundred yards from their home when they noticed Lencioni riding his mule on the road that passed by their homes. The road dead-ended just past the home so it meant that he might be coming to visit. He was still well off, so Giulio dismissed it because he was depressed and had abandoned hope. Besides, he had seen it before and he always stopped at a neighboring home below theirs and then turned around. But this time, Amerigo watched as he proceeded towards their home. Now Giulio was interested. He and Amerigo gazed from afar as Lencioni stopped at the house to talk to Teresa. Both of their hearts accelerated. Could it be, they both queried. They had been disappointed so many times that they had become calloused to positive signs.

This was different. After just a moment, Teresa shouted out for

Raffaello and the boys. Amerigo led the charge as the two boys sprinted back home. When they arrived, Raffaello was talking privately to Lencioni. They discussed an employment contract for the Franklin mine. The only problem was that it was for only one person, Giulio. Amerigo, at about five feet four inches and one hundred and thirty-five pounds, was too small. The deal was very simple: Giulio could go to Michigan alone or remain in Lucca, and Raffaello could relinquish his deposit. It was not a difficult decision. Lencioni could not lose and Raffaello could lose plenty.

Lencioni took the second part of his upfront fee from Raffaello at that time. He gave Raffaello a slip of paper with a date and time, specifically stating when Giulio should be at the Lucca train station with his bags of personal belongings to travel to America. That was the extent of the guidance he provided. The departure date was a week off. Lencioni added that as soon as Amerigo was of sufficient size, he would arrange a job for him at the same Franklin mine.

NOT AS ADVERTISED

After Lencioni left, Raffaello broke the news to Amerigo, who reacted with anger and disappointment. He asked why only one. He thought the deal was for two, he and his brother. Now there was just one. This was not as advertised. This was not the deal. He was only 16 at the time, but he could smell a double cross. His anger was bursting forth like Vesuvius, the volcano that leveled Pompeii. There had to be a mistake, he conjured. But there was no mistake. Only one of the boys was going and he knew that was not him. He was nearly violent, but Raffaello took command and told him to run and inform Geocondo because it required all the family's mental resources to know what to do next. Besides Raffaello, Geocondo was the only one of the Pasquale sons still in Italy.

When Geocondo arrived, the two men huddled. They questioned a possible breach of contract with Lencioni. It certainly appeared that they had been swindled because the deal was for two boys to go and he paid for two boys, at least that is what he thought. After they read the contract, they found that it never stated the number of men included in the deal. Besides, there was no way to adjudicate a claim, even if they could hire a lawyer. After rationalizing, they realized it was unclear and perhaps there was a misunderstanding. This was typical with the Padrone; even the honest ones pushed the envelope of virtuous action. It was good enough to salve their egos, but they could do nothing to change the situation. On the positive side, finally one of Raffaello's kids was in America.

Amerigo, 16 at the time, had been itching to go to America with his brother. They were a team and lived as such. Breaking them up was never in Amerigo's cadre of possible outcomes. The turn of events left him heartbroken and angry. He was incredulous and he carried on for days. How could this happen, he asked repeatedly. After all, he was the one praying to the Madonna. He should be the one rewarded with travel. For some brief moments he resented his brother, but nobody listened, as all were preparing Giulio for travel and managing the turmoil of losing a major laborer. Still, he moped and fussed for days.

Raffaello called the family to the kitchen, where he set the boys—mostly Amerigo--straight: Giulio will go to America and Amerigo will follow. He said the family had a foothold in the new world, and the opportunity must be seized. Amerigo continued whining until Giulio turned to him and, sternly, said, "Mio Uomo (my man), I will save money and send for you. You stay here and help Papa." Amerigo calmed because he knew what those two words meant. Mio Uomo is a special term in Italian culture, reserved for men extraordinarily close to one another, usually brothers. The older man typically used it to address the younger, but never the reverse. It conveyed the ultimate trust and admiration between two males. Giulio was seventeen years old and now the de facto leader of the Menicucci family in America. In spite of his disappointment, Amerigo and his mother used the moment to crow about the power of the Madonna. She had come through, just as predicted. Giulio, still skeptical, was coming around to their belief, but he needed a more intense lesson that was on tap.

ST. CHRISTOPHER ON CALL

In late June 1909, Giulio stood outside their home in Segromignio in Monte with a small bag of clothes. Tereasa, Raffaello, Aladino and Amerigo sent him off. She told him to be careful, and then she prayed to St. Christopher, the patron saint of travelers, to protect her boy, repeating repeatedly: "Please take care of my son." Giulio repeated his promise to send for Amerigo as soon as possible. They had no idea how long before they could reunite. He trudged off on foot to Lucca as the family watched him until he was out of view.

Lucca's train station is outside the walls on the city's south side. Built in 1846 as part of the Viareggio to Florence rail path, it sported a several-hundred-foot frontal façade comprising multiple arches, each outlined with bright yellow paint. A small pitched roof sat in the middle, and in the gable-end was a large clock, the official timepiece for the train schedule. There were two rail tracks and four loading platforms, all with roof covers to protect waiting passengers. From its inception, the station was the pride of Lucca, declaring to all of Italy that it had joined the modern world.

After a two-hour walk, Giulio arrived at the station early and mingled with some of the many travelers. Many young Lucchese were immigrating to America and were awaiting trains to take them to their seaport of departure. He had plenty of countrymen on the trip. A typical bubbly teen, Giulio talked up his plans to become a miner, make lots of money and send for his brother to join him. All the others had similar plans to realize the American dream, including some traveling to Michigan. Giulio noticed two neighbors, Pietro Martinelli and Giovanni Matteucci, milling around. He struck up a conversation and discovered that both were destined for Hancock, all under the same padrono, Lencioni. Giulio felt good that he had close friends for the entire journey.

When Lencioni arrived and gathered his dozen recruits, he directed them to the platform for boarding the train and pointed to the car they should board, one designated for use by Padrone and their customers. Lencioni warned them that any deviation from his directions would result in abandonment wherever they were, a fearsome prospect. All the young men were highly motivated and eagerly complied with every detailed instruction. This padrono and his family had been operating their employment brokerage for about ten years and were successful. Some men Lencioni was escorting dropped off along the way, some in New York, others in Chicago, and still others in Michigan, which was the end of the line. Lencioni's partner, a brother, worked a flip-flop schedule with him. As he was escorting men to America, his brother was returning to Italy to collect more laborers for America.

Naturally, the immigrants rode in third class, but the ride from Lucca to Havre was fast, about a day of travel. After all were boarded and seated on the hard, immovable wooden benches, wooden backboards, and headrests, Lencioni restated the travel plans and his warnings to follow his directions. Most third-class passengers brought their own seat cushions. Giulio used some of the clothes in his bag as a seating pad. Once at Havre, they boarded the La Savoie, the steamship to carry them on a six-day voyage to New York City, their second of three stops on the journey to Hancock, Michigan. Padrone rode in second class, of course.

The trip to Favre was uneventful, except that Giulio met some other future miners. Giulio's experience with mining was limited to digging a hole for an outhouse. Everything he heard was exciting and new. But the money was the clincher. This job would produce steady, high income, something he could build a future on, just as so many of his neighbors did. His priority was to save enough money for Amerigo, a goal that hounded him constantly.

Giulio had hardly traveled outside of Segromigno. He had never been on a train or seen an ocean liner. To him, a toilet was a fancy, unique device, and he had to be told how to use it. He had never ordered food or slept sitting up. He and his two buddies stuck close to Lencioni.

ABOARD TO AMERICA

Once they had disembarked in Havre, Lencioni gathered the men and directed them to some benches where they waited to board the French-built steamship La Savoie, which had been in service for less than a decade. She was a majestic piece of engineering that ranged from one hundred and ninety yards from bow to stern and twenty yards from port to starboard. She carried about eleven hundred passengers, with about half in third class, or steerage.

They waited overnight at the port and ate some crackers that Lencioni supplied, but he was stingy because any expense he incurred along the trip cut into his profits. Giulio and others had brought snacks. Teresa had prepared a food package for Giulio, including bread, cookies, dried fruit and vegetables, which he rationed so they lasted for the trip. Many Italians, especially southern ones, brought ample supplies of Mustasole, a type of dried bread that resisted molding because it was so hard, almost impossible to consume without a beverage to hydrate it. It was ideal for an ocean voyage because the moist air softened the cookies for eating.

After waiting about eighteen hours on the dock alongside the La Savoie, the ship's crew arranged the walking planks, placing them at a right angle between the ship's deck and the dock. The planks had stair steps and rope handrails. Passengers boarded by walking up the plank in a single file line, each carrying their belongings and children. Single men, such as

Giulio, helped families as needed. Lencioni broke his group of a couple dozen men into four smaller groups, assigning one in each group to be its leader. That leader, he explained, gathered food from the ship's cafeteria for the others in the group. The food hall was small, congested, and incapable of handling a rush of steerage passengers at meal times. Most of those in steerage had similar schemes for meals. Lencioni had none of these problems in second class as he ate in the dining lounge.

The steamship La Savoie coming into port at Havre, France. Courtesy Bruno Corpet's scan of a postcard, annotated for verification, in the public domain, https://commons.wikimedia.org, 2023

STINKY TRAVEL

Steerage was a miserable way to spend a week on a steamship. It is located in the bilge with the steam engines driving the ship. Engine noise was constant, along with the rumble of the huge spinning gears and screws propelling the huge vessel. When the engines were laboring hard, heat could build in steerage to uncomfortable levels, especially in summer when Giulio traveled. Ventilation was poor, and the stench of fuel mingled throughout the lower parts of the ship. At the ship's lowest point, the bilge naturally collected water and debris.

Typically, whole families voyaged in steerage, including babies and small children, with their myriad needs. Fresh water and regular meals were available, but many passengers brought much of their own food for the five-day sea voyage. And, of course, many passengers, especially first-timers, suffered sea sickness. Some passengers were nauseous for the entire trip and it was common to see passengers leaning over and vomiting into the sea. Others vomited on the deck, and gravity and rain steered the rancid material into steerage class.

Illness was also a problem. Others could quickly infect healthy people who boarded the ship in the close quarters of steerage class. Medical facilities were limited, and some succumbed to illness before they arrived in New York. Steerage passengers slept in relatively open rooms, offering little respect for privacy. Most passengers never disrobed for bed; they removed hats and shoes and slept in their day clothing. There were toilets aboard, but expectedly, they were heavily used, soiled and unsanitary.

First and second-class passengers were boarded first, taking about sixty minutes. As steerage passengers arrived aboard, they scrambled to carve out a personal space until they arrived in New York. Steerage boarding consumed ninety minutes. Giulio stuck with his group and his friends. They stashed their bags in a storage bin and found seating on a bench. The kitchen and sleeping areas shared that same large open place in the belly of the giant vessel. Each morning, the ship's crew transformed the space from sleeping to eating by laying out tables, unfolding chairs and firing up the ovens for heating meals. They returned later to convert the space back into a dormitory. They placed a box of eating utensils and napkins on each table. The bustle of the crew arranging for breakfast roused the passengers at six o'clock, who emerged from their bunks, most of them in the public space, and subsequently lined up for one of the sixteen toilets in steerage, eight each for men and women. In the toilet rooms were wash basins, one for each toilet. While the upper classes of the ship had access to ample onboard bathtubs, steerage passengers had only a few shower stalls, which were rarely used. It was easiest for most to sponge-bathe over the five-day journey if they bathed at all.

Meal times in steerage could be compared to modern rush hour on the New York subway. Dozens of people pushed shoulder-to-shoulder through tight corridors, toting anything from babies to dinner plates while balancing loads of food and drinks. Lencioni had organized his group of Italian young men into teams. Each team leader managed food for the others in the group. Each passenger was responsible for cleaning up for themselves, and every other day the quartermaster ordered the steerage area floor to be pressure washed. Despite the efforts, the steerage class was perpetually dirty, with many bits of discarded and decaying food that attracted rats and mice, pests that enjoyed multigenerational lives aboard the steamers.

As the ship made its way west, it passed into the upper part of the Bay of Biscay, with its reputation of rough seas for passenger vessels. For most people seasickness came on after about a half day of rocking and rolling in the Bay. Fortunately, when Giulio was traveling, early summer was the least violent season in that part of the ocean. Even still, it was sufficiently agitating to infirm about a quarter of the passengers. Once the ship had cleared the Bay and sailed on the open seas of the Atlantic, stability improved, and many recovered, but some were plagued with dry heaves from port to port. Generally, there was plenty of vomiting to augment all the other odors and produce a lingering musk similar to municipal sewer gas. It was so potent at times that it could induce nausea even for those unaffected by the rocking ship. Lencioni visited his men several times daily, but he needed to do little else. He enjoyed the trips, but it was easy to enjoy luxurious travel.

Food aboard the ship was nutritious but bland. Excellent cuisine was available for the first- and second-class passengers. For steerage dwellers, mostly Italian Mezzadria peasants who were accustomed to spicy dishes, the boiled Herring, potatoes, beans, stale bread and water offered no gastronomical stimulation, but few complained because they expected difficult living conditions. Besides, most rationalized, it took less than a week to get the land of plenty.[2]

NEW YORK WELCOME

After about five days, the passengers became restless as they neared New York Harbor. Hundreds huddled on deck to get a first glimpse of the Statue of Liberty, the face of America. The ship slowed as it approached the city. It headed south until it could get into the sea lane used by passenger ships, and then it turned sharply north into New York Bay. When the ship passed into the Verrazzono Narrows, it settled into an incoming sea lane along the bay's east side. The passengers could see the communities of Brooklyn on the right and, in the distance, those of the Staten Island borough. But their steely gazes were in the direction of the lady of liberty. As the ship churned slowly north past Governor's Island, silence descended on the passengers as they studied, some with binoculars, the shoreline on the left. Finally, one shouted, "There she is," and passengers packed themselves along the deck rail to see the statue. It was the torch they saw first, emerging above the skyline. Once she was in full view, the passengers cheered, whooped and hollered. They had made it to America. Giulio was delighted. His dream was about to be realized. All of the weight of his family responsibilities faded away in a reverie.

The ship stopped just north of Governor's Island to bring on the pilot, a port worker who guides the ship into a specific dock. Medical officials also boarded to briefly pre-screen the passengers for obvious disease or deformity. These men rowed to the ship in a small craft and boarded via rope ladders. The inspection was cursory for first- and second-class passengers. They examined the steerage passengers more closely. They pinned a card with a large red T to his shirt if they discovered something remarkable, such as an obvious disease. Anyone with a marked card among the steerage class passengers was isolated on board until the others disembarked. Then, these detainees were transferred by barge directly to the quarantine area of the Ellis Island Infirmary, where a detailed physical exam was used to determine the seriousness of the condition and whether any should be sent back. After this brief on-board inspection, the ship proceeded to a dock at the lower end of Manhattan, the final stop before the steerage passengers were barged to Ellis Island.

The La Savoie was recorded in the dock on June 26, 1910. First- and second-class customers disembarked first, consuming about thirty minutes. They had already been inspected, so they could begin their expedited process through customs as soon as they disembarked. The theory held that these passengers were of a high societal class and thus less likely to be indigent, infected, or criminalistic. Very few immigrants traveled in first- or second-class, but gaining admittance to the United States was fast-tracked for those who did.

Immigrants in steerage were treated differently. Many American authorities considered them to be uneducated, perpetually unclean, always in tattered clothing, ignorant, impoverished, and of questionable moral character. Any immigrant who limped or had a missing limb or other deformity was immediately rejected. Immigrants who could not state their intended source of income were rejected for fear of them becoming wards of the state, which was anathema in America's capitalist system with a strong belief in individual responsibility without government handouts. They rejected deviants, such as polygamists, gypsies and others considered ill-suited to American culture. The padrono knew the rules and carefully prepared his clients so they were easily admitted.

Lencioni briefed his men as they gathered up their belongings to disembark. He advised them to stay together and follow his instructions to the letter. He gave each of them a ten-dollar bill, the minimum typically required of immigrants entering the U.S.; he expected the money back when they cleared the immigration office in Ellis Island. He also advised them to report that their fathers had paid for their journey, not wanting to divulge to authorities that he had brokered the deal. Even though his work was legal under the vettore rules in Italy, the American authorities remained suspect of the Padrone. The Padrone system was under political attack by U.S. authorities due to their corruption and exploitation of immigrants. The government was increasing pressure on port authorities to dissolve the brokering system in the U.S., and any immigrant discovered to be operating under a padrono contract might be returned home.

As immigrants came ashore, they were shuttled onto barges that carried them to Ellis Island for processing. Each one had an arrival card pinned to their shirt containing the arrival date and the ship's name. Only the number of passengers who could be crammed onto a barge were released from the ship. Remain passengers for the barge to make the round trip to Ellis Island and back. They repeated the process over several hours until all steerage passengers were properly tagged and safely rested in the Ellis Island holding bins.

Barge passengers were treated to an excellent view of the Statue of Liberty as they approached the Ellis Island facility. The U.S. Congress created Ellis Island with the 1891 Immigration Act, which federalized the immigration process. The federal government chose the island as the main immigrant processing unit in the country, although other ports of entry included Boston, Philadelphia, Savannah, New Orleans and San Francisco. The original federal building on the island burned to the ground in 1897. A new and fire-proof building immediately replaced it. The building, from afar, resembled a cathedral with four towers on each corner of a pitched roof building. In front was a large, rectangular building with a great open room used at the registry and inspection stations. A mammoth American flag waved dramatically over the facility to remind the immigrants where they were.[3]

Immigrants were escorted from the barges to holding bins. Lencioni met with his men in the holding area and collected the money he had loaned to them. Then, the immigrants waited to be called for inspections, sometimes for hours. Immigrants were not required to have passports or other papers at the time. This situation generated the derogatory term used for Italian immigrants, WOPs, or Without Papers. Lencioni had been through this many times and assured them they would make it if they followed his orders. Very few of his customers were denied entry. Any waste of laborers at this point negatively impacted Lencioni's potential income.

When a group was called, they were formed into two lines, one for men older than fifteen and the other for women and children. The lines led to the medical examination room in Registry Hall, a two-hundred-foot by one-hundred-foot open room with a fifty-six-foot ceiling in the middle of the Ellis Island building. The medical exams consumed about twenty seconds each. The physicians in attendance were experts at spotting diseased individuals with a glance. The examinations focused on various ailments, especially Trachoma, a contagious eye disease. Most of the immigrants were passed through. Some were flagged as problematic with a code letter scribbled on the immigrant's clothing with chalk. A T was for Trachoma, B for back problems, M for someone suspected of intellectual handicaps and so on. They were immediately directed to a different holding bin to wait for the barge to the Statin Island quarantine facility, where physicians examined them more closely. Many of these immigrants eventually were treated and admitted, but a few unlucky ones were sent back to Italy in specially designated ships. Those returning to Italy might wait many days for a sufficient number of them to fill out a ship's manifest. The delay was agonizing for these poor souls who were not only diseased but had invested time and money to reach America. Now, they waited for a tortuous voyage back home with nothing.

The next step in the process was the official interview. Using the ship manifest as a guide, each immigrant was called forward. Translators were available. They queried each person about their intent in the United States, the same questions asked on the manifest form, which was completed at the departing dock. The officials compared their verbal answers with those on the manifest form. Any deviations could result in suspicion and additional interviews and scrutiny. The screening process identified undesirables, such as prostitutes, those with no job prospects and similar problems. Lencioni had prepared his men well, and all were passed into the country.

About ninety-eighty percent of immigrants passed through Ellis Island into the United States, but it usually consumed at least a day and sometimes longer. The United States desperately needed labor, and immigrants filled the bill, so the authorities were inclined to allow entry rather than incur the costs of returning a passenger due to a medical condition.[4]

RIDING THE RAILS TO COPPER COUNTRY

After his men were admitted to the country, Lencioni gathered them and separated them into groups with common destinations. Except for his clients whose final destination was New York, they were all headed to the train station. He had already purchased tickets on the appropriate trains for the men. Lencioni contracted with the rail company to use a designated rail car for his men. Other Padrone shared the use of the car for their customers. The end of the line for Lencioni was Hancock, the home of many copper mining operations in the state. Over the years, he supplied the mines with many Lucchese.

The Central Railroad of Jersey rail station was near the Ellis Island facility, and Lencioni directed the men to the platform where they boarded the train to their final destinations. He gathered the men destined for New York and handed them off to the employers on the dock, pocketing his fee as he did so. He accompanied the remainder of the immigrants to other states, dropping them off and collecting his fees.

There were two rail legs on the Journey to Michigan. One was from New York to Chicago, and a second was from Chicago to the Houghton, Michigan, rail station. Hancock was located north of the station on the southern end of the Keweenaw Peninsula. It was a relatively new community developed and platted by the Quincy Mining Company in 1850. They named the town after John Hancock, a signatory of the Declaration of Independence.

The rail trip to Hancock consumed three to four days, depending on weather and mechanical delays. The conditions on board were similar to the train from Lucca to Havre, but the scenery differed. Several Italians were on board heading for the Michigan mines, including his friends

Martinelli and Matteucci. They chatted frequently throughout the trip, centered on the money they would earn.

Giulio had never seen a metropolitan area larger than Lucca, and New York stunned him. He was especially impressed with the civil development along the way to Michigan, including the roadways, expansive bridges and towering buildings. It was unique in his world of subsidence farming in the hinterlands of Lucca. One American city seemed to lead to yet another city. It was not until the train traveled the countryside west of New Jersey that the open country appeared more like Italy. Along the journey, he ate little. He still carried food that Mama had prepared and he rationed it along the way. He had no money to buy food aboard the train. As they approached Chicago, his eyes were greeted with similarly large buildings as in New York, although not as geographically sprawling. In Chicago, Lencioni escorted his Chicago-bound men off, charged his fee, and then gathered all his men and a few new ones and marched them to the connecting train to the end of the line at Hancock.[5]

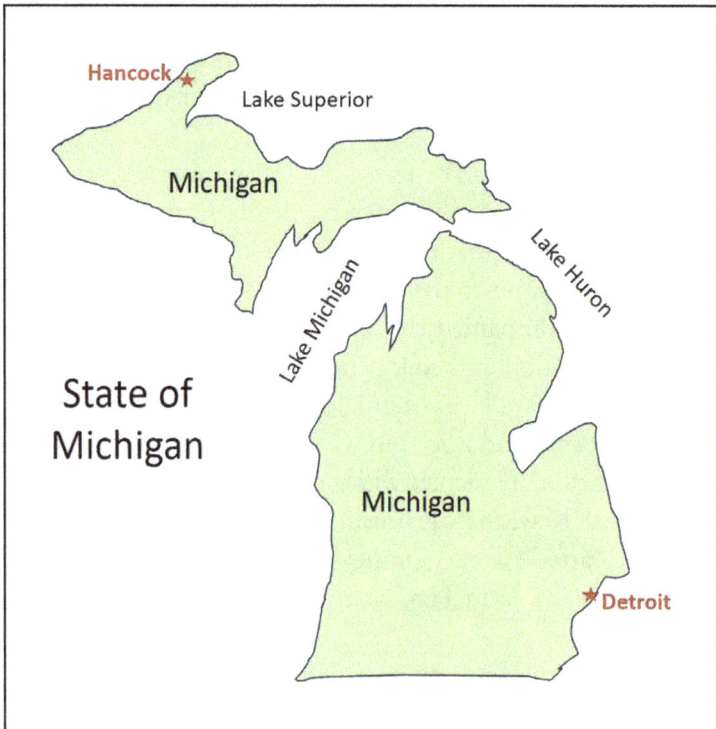

Map showing the location of Hancock, Michigan in the heart of copper country in the early 1900s. Detroit is shown for reference. Map by D. Menicucci.

COMPANY TOWN

The train pulled into the Houghton rail station in the early morning hours in the middle of July 1909. It was not much of a station, a small structure that looked like home with a pitched roof and a tattered US flag flying near the entrance. Nearly all people in the two-passenger cars were associated with the copper mines just across the lake in Hancock. Almost everyone in the area was also connected to copper mining, which drove the community and was why it existed. Every few days the train arrived with new, energetic men going to work in the mines. The train boarded tired or wounded workers returning to their home countries or taking other jobs. Turnover in the mines was high, almost fifty percent per year. Mining accidents and deaths induced about half of the departures, while harsh labor conditions discouraged most of the other half. There were plenty of replacements in Europe; the operators ordered them and the Padrone delivered.

Lencioni was the first to exit the train. He was greeted immediately by another man, an Italian in heavy denim work clothes, a foreman. As the men slowly exited the train, Lencioni talked to the man, exchanged some papers and money, identified the men he had delivered and then quickly departed the scene to his brother's home. Lencioni returned to Italy, where he initiated a new recruitment effort.

When Giulio took his first breath of fresh Houghton air, he thought the conditions were similar to those in Lucca. The climates were similar, at least in the summer. The winter is a different story, as all the new men discovered when blizzards and ten-foot-deep snow drifts frequently buried the Michigan mining country.

The foreman greeted the men and then called roll so he could determine where each of the men was assigned. He went down the list of the eleven men individually, giving each a slip of paper on which he wrote the name of the boarding house and mine shaft they would be working. Giulio, Martinelli and Matteucci were assigned to the Franklin Jr. mine and boarding with the Pietro Fredianelli family. Franklin operated two shafts at its Franklin Jr. mining operation located about five miles north of Hancock, near the intersection of Boston Road and Boston Location Road. Franklin Jr. mine was the second one that Franklin operated in the area, and the Jr. designation provided differentiation.

The Franklin mine, circa 1914 showing the main shaft house in the background with the large smokestack standing in front. The other buildings are storage or housing facilities. Courtesy Unted States Library of Congress, photo by John Vachon, located in the FSA/OWI Collection.

     Franklin Jr. mine operators at the time hired only men of Finnish or Italian origins. Various ethnic groups traditionally conflicted, especially the Italians and Irish, both with penchants towards drinking, the Italians with wine and the Irish with beer. Grievances that developed among the opposing ethnic men in the mines erupted into brawls in the saloon and vice versa. The mine owners discovered that Italians and Finns seemed ambivalent toward one another, at least as much as people of different cultures could be. The Italians seemed content to perform some of the most difficult physical tasks and submit to the Finns, who, because of their experience, were generally in leadership positions.

     All of the new men lived in the company town, which is a kind of micro village dedicated to the needs of the miners and their families. Each small town associated with a specific mine contained several facilities, including a general store that provided most of the staples needed by families, a livery stable for livestock, a school for children—usually one classroom for all grades—a chapel for any religious denomination and housing. These company towns were quickly constructed near the mine shafts and were of marginal quality. Typically, a family rented a large home and used it for their families and boarders. Italian boarders were usually matched with Italian boarding-house proprietors. Like most immigrants, the mining operators knew Italians felt most comfortable living with people who understood their culture and language. They figured that employees would work harder and longer if they were comfortable. Boarding was a good investment for the mine operators and was a good deal for the boarding home proprietor who received rental income.

The foreman quickly added that the workers should be at the mine at six o'clock to begin their shift. The final point was pay, which was calculated by the amount of time they worked based on their time cards. He added that it was important to complete the card accurately, and any mistruths would be met with dismissal. Normal work days were Monday through Saturday, day shift from six o'clock to four-thirty in the afternoon, with a half hour for lunch. The graveyard shift started at six o'clock and extended to four-thirty in the afternoon. The timbermen used the times between shifts to inspect the timbers supporting the mine and make repairs.

Each laborer delivered by a padrono had his pay docked over the initial six months to recover unspecified "employment initiation fees." The operators were covertly recovering their transportation costs for bringing the men to the mines, essentially the padrono's (boss') fee. There was nothing immigrants could do, so they accepted the deal. Each new man had to purchase appropriate clothing along with candles (and plenty of matches) for personal illumination. The candles sat in holders positioned atop each mining helmet. The shape of the helmet, coupled with the candle on top, gave the miners a look of unicorns. Carbide lamps, a relatively new lighting device, used water and carbide to create acetylene gas that burns cleanly and brightly. All the bosses and a few foremen used them, but candles were their lights for common miners. The general store had plenty of used equipment they purchased from departing employees. They resold them to new employees at a discount but left the store with a profit.

Giulio was drowning with new information and his sensory system was in disarray. He knew he had a job starting at six o'clock the following day, and even after the docking of his pay, he was earning twice what he could in Italy. The foreman escorted the men and their meager belongings onto the back of a horse-drawn cart that took them up to the Franklin Jr.

Mine Company town. They headed slowly west along the southern shore of Portage Lake to a bridge that crossed north into Hancock. From there it was a straight shot three miles north to the mining town. As they traveled, the men marveled at the structures they saw along the way, such as the giant shaft houses built over the mines and large earth-moving equipment needed to load copper ore on rail cars. Large millworks they passed along the way belched out smoke and steam. Nothing like these existed in Lucca. As they approached the Franklin Jr. mine, they saw its shaft house, best described as about five residential homes roughly stacked on each other. They were the most unusual structures the young men had seen, but they had not seen much yet.

Slowly, the cart stopped by each boarding home and dropped off passengers. The foreman had just five parting words for each: Don't be late for work. The day was early, but in July, the horizon began to brighten at about four o'clock. (America did not use Daylight Savings Time.) As the driver approached Pietro Fredianelli's boarding home, he called out the names of Giulio Menicucci, Giovanni Matteucci and Pietro Martinelli. Even at an early hour, well before sunrise, the two young men could already see the glow of oil lamps lighting the Fredianelli home, indicating that the family and borders were up and preparing for a work day. The men jumped off the cart, respectfully thanked the driver and walked to the front door.

Mary Fredianelli, the head of the household, greeted them. She welcomed them in Italian fashion with a hug and an invitation to breakfast. All the men noticed the aroma of the home, which was typical of an Italian woman's operation. Not only was it an Italian home, but Giulio knew Maria's family, the Vellutinis because they lived near his Italian home. He also knew the Fredianellis because Pietro was a native of Segromigno. Giulio felt at home as he stashed his bags in the room he shared with his friend, Martinelli.

For Giovanni Matteucci, it was truly a family reunion. His wife, Emma Vellutini, whom he married in Italy, was Mary Fredianelli's sister, making him in-laws with Pietro and Mary Fredianelli. The Fredianellis were married in Segromigno in 1891 and had four small children ranging from infant to five. Pietro was a veteran of the Michigan mines, having immigrated to the area a decade earlier. In addition to Giulio, Matteucci and Martinelli, there was a boarder named Lorenzo Serafini. He was Mary's nephew and had immigrated in 1906. The Fredianelli home was an enclave of Lucca.[6]

The Lucchese clan eagerly ate their breakfast, all the while bubblingly discussions about the old country lifted spirits. Mary's cooking helped them feel at home. She had prepared fried polenta with meat and roasted vegetables topped with olive oil, toasted buttered bread, and as much coffee as they wanted. It was a filling meal and perfect for providing the high energy requirements of mining. Full of pride, the Lucchese team was ready for action.

See notes 7, 8, 9.

Notes

1. Lencioni was noted as a non-resident alien on the ship's manifests, meaning he made repeated trips across the Atlantic without intending to immigrate. He had made many trips to the American mines, typical of Padrone, who were brokering jobs. Albert Lencioni lived in Albuquerque in the early Twentieth Century, but his relationship with Lorenzo is unknown.

2. *Roos* describes steerage travel and the efforts to improve it. *Solem*, *Haskin*, *Durland*, *Dupont* and *NY Times* provide various accounts of steerage travel in the early Twentieth Century.

3. *Allen* describes the allure of the stature of liberty.

4. The length of time needed to process immigrants varied widely, depending on the conditions of the immigrants and the people who ran the processing program at Ellis Island. Most sources of information indicated the process consumed at least a half day. *Ellis Island* and *Kennedy* present details on the immigration process.

5. *Erkkila* discusses the role of rail travel in dispersing immigrants throughout the United States.

6. Information about the Fredianelli household members and their relationship to Pietro, the head of the family, is contained in the 1910 Census for Houghton County, Franklin Township, Michigan. Recorded in Supervisor's District Number 12, Enumeration District Number 115.

7. *Mangione & Morreale*, *La Sorte* and *Laurino* provide overview descriptions of Italian immigrant experience in America in the early Twentieth Century, including many personal accounts. Both authors discuss the problem of the Padrone. *Bruno* presents information about how Italian immigrants were viewed and treated by Americans. *Tucciarone & Laricia* present detailed accounts of how Italian immigrants were swindled.

The *New York Times* article discusses how women were often abused in steerage class travel.

8. *La Bella, Moreno* and *Ciongoli & Parini* produced books suitable for educational settings, particularly middle and high school. They both describe Italian immigration in fundamental terms with many accompanying pictures.

9. The story is well supported in lore with information recorded directly from the immigrants.

6

TUMULT IN THE STOPE
(1910–1915)

MINING SPIRIT

Pietro was the head miner on a six-man team, which included him. He led his men on the short walk to the mine shaft every morning. But this first morning, Pietro left home early, leading his new team members to the general store where they incurred their first debt, credit for used mining clothing, candles and matches. The new miners also bought helmets, gloves and heavy denim work clothes, including a relatively heavy jacket for protection against physical hazards and cold. Mines are usually cool. Noticeably missing, certainly by Twenty-First Century standards, was personal protective equipment, such as safety glasses and dust masks. The company store had the authority to collect employee debts on paydays, deducting money from each man's paycheck before distribution. From there, they proceeded to the mine, arriving about on time to begin work. They were working the coveted day shift because of Pietro's seniority.

Training for the rookie miners was brief. First, Fredianelli said, always follow his lead and do exactly what he said. Second, if there is a problem, especially involving the mine itself, such as a collapse of one of the shafts, drop down and crawl along the ground where the air might be cleaner, extinguish candles, move slowly and cover noses and mouths with a handkerchief. The main fear was being entrapped sufficiently long and dying of either thirst or hunger if they did not first die of asphyxiation from lack of air. The training lasted about five minutes, but there was little time to waste as the team had quotas to meet each day, and they incurred penalties—loss of income—if they failed.

As a relatively new mine, having operated only a few years, Franklin Jr.'s ore prospects were excellent and they expected profitable operation for several years. It was an underground operation with two main shafts, several hundred feet deep at its lowest. The shafts ran from the surface to the lowest part of the mine and sloped down at an angle of about thirty degrees. At various levels below the earth, horizontal shafts, called adits, ran from the main shafts to the stopes, the open areas at the end of the adits where the ore extraction occurred.

The mine's main mining shafts were fitted with rails for a skip, a box-like container used to ferry ore from the stopes deep in the mine to the shaft house, where it was sorted for further processing. The skip was tethered by cable to an electric motor pully that raised loaded cars where they were dumped and lowered empty ones back down to the mining area. The skip was fitted with handles that men used during their ride down in the morning and up in the evening; it was their only way in and out of the mine. The adits had no rails and were big enough for human passage only.

The Hazelton Coal mine showing a skip carrying miners down the main shaft to the stope where extraction took place. It was typical of underground mining operations in the early Twentieth Century. Courtesy B.L. Singley, Keystone View Company, in the public domain, via Wikimedia Commons, https://commons.wikimedia.org, 2023.

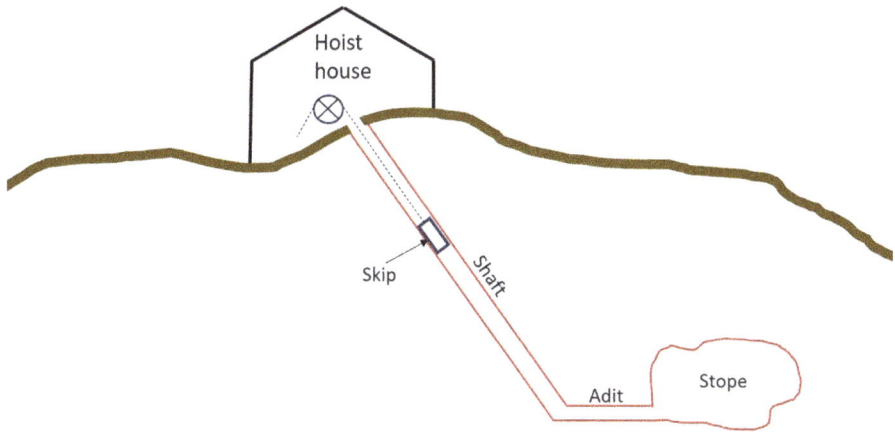

Cross section diagram of a typical copper mine. Diagram by author.

Two other shafts ran from the surface to the depths: the air shaft and the pump-piping shaft. The air shaft provided breathing air and a compressed air line provided the power to run the drills. At Franklin Jr., a large coal stove was built over the air shaft opening inside the shaft house. It was configured to draw combustion air from the mine shaft, creating a suction that drew fresh air into the underground mining operations. The pump-piping shaft contained the piping used to suck water out of the mine. Mines typically contain water because they are usually below the water table. Without a sump pump, the mine quickly flooded. These electric pumps ran constantly. Besides asphyxiation, drowning was one of the principal fears of trapped miners.

Ore that was sufficiently rich in copper went directly from the skip to the smelter. Other ore had to be stamped, a motorized process of smashing the ore between two huge steel plates, helping to expose the copper in the stone. The ore was processed in the shaft house, where it was sorted into quality ore that went to the smelters and the waste that went to tailings pile. Fredianelli and Serafini were classified as miners, a specific designation that described their work of selecting, placing and igniting dynamite charges. The others were called trammers. These men gathered the ore that the miners had blasted from the side walls of the mine and loaded it into the skip using wheelbarrows and buckets that they dragged along adit to the waiting skip in the shaft. A trammer team was expected to load at least several tons of ore daily, but an efficient team with strong trammers could move fifty percent more.

A timberman had an important job building and maintaining the timber posts and beams to reinforce the mine and prevent collapse. The timbermen had their own teams and regularly moved from one part of the mine to another to shore the ceilings of new stopes and adits. Unfortunately, these men were not engineers, nor had they any professional training other than common sense and whatever experience they had gathered over the years. Their work was often questionable.

SKIPPING DOWN

On Giulio's first day, Fredianelli showed the new men how to board and travel in a skip. The skip typically carried two teams at a time. Giulio was crammed into the skip with eleven other men and told to hang on as it proceeded into the depths. The first thing Giulio noticed was the blackness during the three-minute ride. One team was let loose at one level and then proceeded to the lower level where Pietro's team worked. Once stopped, Fredianelli ordered helmet-candles lit and those placed around the stope to provide ambient lighting. He organized his team, assigning shovels to the four trammers, which included three raw rookies, Giulio, Martinelli and Matteucci.[1]

Fredianelli inspected the water and air lines to ensure proper operation. He had the men set up a two-gallon bucket and poured in some disinfectant. It was their outhouse for the day. Each man carried his lunch, one prepared by Mary for each of them. Fredianelli supplied a gallon-sized glass jug of water for each team member to drink and wash. Given the nature of the work, one might expect the miners to need more water. The mine was cold—in the low 50Fs—so the men needed much less water than doing the same task in the summer heat.

Once all was set, Fredianelli identified the drill locations and places for dynamite sticks. The power drill, an innovation, used a diamond-tipped bit that could easily bore a two-inch diameter hole several feet deep in solid rock. Just a few years previous, miners drilled holes by hand, with one miner holding a bit and two others alternately pounding on it. The new drill cut the time by a factor of five and reduced drilling labor from three men to two, but one man could handle it alone if needed.

Miners drilled holes in the direction of the ore body. The objective was to blast out a long, linear section of ore. One miner drilled and the other seated the dynamite sticks in the holes, leaving the fuses sticking straight out. The foreman handled the fusing jobs, especially joining the individual fuses into a single main fuse, which served as the single ignition point. Not only was it a dangerous task, but it had to be done properly to ensure that the dynamite sticks detonated simultaneously, which was the most efficient way to use a dynamite charge to dislodge loadable ore. Every team strove for the highest efficiency possible because it affected their pay. They had minimal quotas to meet. Missing them resulted in a pay cut. Exceeding them resulted in a pay raise.

Fredianelli had become an expert fuser. It was the main reason his team was a top performer. Once the fuses were ready for ignition, he hustled his men back into the adit for safety. He lit the main fuse and sprinted to the adit with the team. The explosion shook the area, jarring small rocks and dinging off the men's helmets. It reminded all of the inherent hazards. But it was also a prime time for a breather. It took several minutes for the air in the stope to clear enough for work. The team returned to the stope and the entire process was repeated endlessly through the day, day after day.[2]

SPIRT OF LUCCA

Giulio was awed. Every bit of this activity was well outside his cadre of real or imagined experiences. He could do little more than follow along and work hard as they cleared the stope littered with chunks of ore, both large and small, that had been blasted from the walls. The miners used picks on the wall near the explosions to release more ore. The trammers picked up the ore with shovels and placed it in buckets, which they manually transported through the adit to the main shaft, where they dumped it into a waiting skip. Once the skip was full, the team sounded a bell that signaled the operator to raise and empty the skip. Once empty, the operator rang the bell and returned it to the trammers.

They had no official work breaks other than lunch, although each man took occasional short breathers, a few minutes to catch his breath or use the chamber pot. Sometimes, an experienced trammer was called to assist the miners, such as helping to hold the drill in an awkward position. It was a way for the trammers to gain the experience needed for their promotion to miner, which boosted pay and respect.

Lunch was a half hour, taken at the discretion of the foreman. Lunch usually consisted of bread, dried meats, fish and vegetables and a little wine to wash it down. They ate in the mine, and usually the team was back working in less than thirty minutes. Production was equivalent to money in their pockets, and little was produced sitting around. Fredianelli was an experienced leader and his proud and young Lucchese team was out to prove its mettle. His team typically was among the most productive, a prideful accomplishment embodying the spirit of their Lucchese homeland.

Giulio set goals for himself. He strove to be the best trammer by showing he could load the most ore. He was eager for promotion. On this first day, his quest focused on hard work while observing and learning. Toward the end of the day, his enthusiasm caught Fredianelli's eye, who complimented Giulio for his efforts. At four-thirty, the bell rang, signaling the end of his shift. The men gathered in the adit and waited for the empty skip laden with ore dust to take them to the surface. At five-thirty, Giulio was back at his new home. Like Mama, Mary directed the men to wash for dinner and served up a big plate of pasta and steamed vegetables, all topped with parmesan cheese and a small glass of wine and water to finish up. It was a feast more than comparable to his mama's. But the meal was fast. They were usually sleeping before eight o'clock. Tomorrow was another day of the same thing.

Giulio was typically the first man to bed and rise in the morning. His thoughts frequently turned to his brother, whom he increasingly missed with each day of separation. Over months, he talked with the other miners about his brother, telling them that Amerigo was big and strong and that he would make an excellent miner. Fredianelli knew the Menicucci family in Italy had a reputation for hard workers, and Giulio was living proof of it. He had little doubt that Amerigo would fit in just fine.

Giulio labored for about six months when he was surprised to learn of his promotion to miner, working side-by-side with Fredianelli, who had recommended him for promotion. Serafini got his own team and another new Italian man joined Fredianelli's team. Simultaneously, the six-month wage-docking period expired and Giulio's pay doubled. Plus, the promotion added another twenty percent. He was shocked at the money flowing his way; he accumulated more in a month than the family typically saved over years. He had been sending most of his earnings back to the family for their survival, especially to cover the loss of his labor. Now, he could not only increase his contribution to the family, he could save for his brother's trip. For the first time, he used the special small safe that the Fredianellis made available to boarders for their prized possessions. No banks of any kind were available to the miners at the Franklin Jr. mine.

Over time, Giulio talked with enough miners and local folks to understand the situation more clearly. He learned that men who came to work at the mine on their own, with no Padrone sponsor, obtained full pay immediately because there were no finder's fees involved. In other words, eliminating the padrono eliminated the docked pay. Giulio was finished with the Padrone and he had the money to make it happen.

MIO UOMO (MY MAN) ARRIVES

By April of 1910, near his first anniversary at the mine, Giulio sent a letter to Amerigo informing him that he would send the money for travel via the Italian Bank, which had a small branch office in Hancock to serve the large Italian population in the area. It was four miles from the mining towns and used only for important events, such as sending money overseas. The bank specialized in serving immigrants. Giulio used the bank to send the bulk of his savings to Raffaello for Amerigo's trip.

When Amerigo received the letter, he was in ecstasy. Finally, he was going to America. Giulio had come through, but he never doubted it. The preparation for Amerigo's travel was less stressful than Guilio's due to the family's previous experiences in America. Most importantly, this time they had money. And a warning to Amerigo: Avoid the Padrone. Plus, advice: Travel in a group. Travel companions were easy to find because Lucca was an excellent source of labor for America. Many young Lucchese were heading west.

In late May 1910, he was set to leave for America with two other Lucchese, Francisco Lombardi and Bencenzo Dal Porto. Amerigo wrote to Giulio informing him of the travel dates so they could be ready for them. Fredianelli arranged for a foreman to meet Amerigo as he did when Giulio arrived. There was only one train serving Houghton and it was typically full of immigrants, mostly Italians. The mining operators sent a man to greet the new employees each day as they disembarked. Amerigo's name was listed as an employee and boarder with the Fredianellis.

Amerigo left his Segromigno home in late May, following the same path as Giulio's but without the padrono. Raffaello wished him good luck. Teresa advised him to pray to the Madonna to watch over his brother in times of difficulty. She repeated it with emphasis, "Take care of your brother."

It had been less than a year since Giulio arrived in Hancock, and Amerigo was now stepping off the train. He was transported to the Fredianellis and knocked on the door early in the morning. Nobody knew the exact date he would arrive, so there was a surprise when he did. Once Giulio and Amerigo saw each other, they broke into wild glee. A small party erupted as Mary welcomed him with a hug and an invitation to breakfast. Amerigo shook hands with the other men, laughing and joking in the familiar Lucchese manner. Giulio and Amerigo spilled stories about their lives, which each had missed due to their separation. There was plenty of news to go around. Amerigo told of the continuing struggle with Aledino and the latest family members who had immigrated to America. Of Pasquale's six children, only Geocondo, Carmalinda and Raffaello remained in Lucca. Giulio's uncles, aunts, and cousins worked in the precious metal mines in the western U.S. Raffaello continued to struggle with depression, but the money coming from America buoyed his spirits. Amerigo's first day was filled with thrills, as was typical. He was a trammer on Fredianelli's team, whereas Giulio was a miner. Like Giulio, Amerigo worked with the fervor of an opportunistic young man intent on building his future. More important, he was lifted by his brother's companionship.[3]

By the spring of 1912, Giulio was all in for America. In April, he walked to Houghton and submitted his declaration to become an American citizen. A declaration is the first step in the naturalization process. Amerigo could not declare because he had not been in America long enough. In 1912, this procedure included a signed affidavit that the immigrant had established residency and committed to becoming a citizen.[4]

By early 1913, Giulio led a team. Fredianelli had been promoted to the position of foreman of miners on one of the main shafts. Giulio's team consisted of him and Giovanni Matteucci, the miners, Amerigo, and three new Lucchese for the trammer team. Giulio was becoming adept with dynamite, selecting the correct places for the detonations to produce the maximum amount of ore. He was also safety aware, pointing the timbermen to various problem areas. They often ignored him and much of their work was slipshod.

STRIKE AND TRAGEDY

The copper market was volatile, straining the operators. In tough times, they cut corners. Deferring maintenance was an easy way for management to improve its bottom line immediately, and its negative effects would be realized sometime in the future. Deferred maintenance slowly produced an increasing stream of mining deaths and injuries. Groups of miners rose to demand improvements. It opened the door to the Western Federation of Miners, founded in Butte, Montana in 1893. Union representatives had been in Houghton County since 1904 but had few members. The union saw a growth opportunity and promoted mine safety, but initially, employees ignored them. But as accidents accumulated, more signed up. Some became activists within the union.

Giulio and Amerigo, with great reluctance, joined the union. They disliked their tactics; they reminded them of the Padrone. They bristled at the idea of union strikes because it negatively affected their pay by preventing them from working. They understood the safety concerns but needed money regularly to fund their family and for their own use. They were there to earn money, not sit outside protesting. They went along because everyone was going along. But they did not say much and were unhappy.

By 1913, the union presented their demands to the mining operators with the threat of a strike if they were refused. By then, the union had signed up nearly all the workers, so they initially appeared to be in a strong position. The mining authorities ignored the request, refusing to recognize the union. Without any collective bargaining laws, the owners had no obligation or incentive to cooperate. In July, a general strike was called. Most of the mines in the County participated. Almost immediately, violence erupted as some men refused to join the strike and attempted to cross the picket lines. They were ruthlessly denied entry. Widespread violence erupted around the mining towns. Militant union members shot up the homes of mining officials. The mining operators responded by bringing in new miners, but these scabs, as they were called, clashed with the strikers, producing a trend of escalating violence with no end in sight. The union tapped into striker's fund, which they had on hand to compensate the striking workers, but the compensation was nowhere near as much as the miners were earning on their jobs.

The violence grew into a cadre of small riots. On July 27th, the governor called in the Michigan National Guard, and twenty-six hundred heavily armed soldiers appeared along with seventeen hundred local deputies, about seventy five percent of whom were hastily deputized. Together, they forcefully suppressed the violence with Marshall Law. After it was lifted, the strike rolled on. Tragically, it sapped the employees' and their families' energy and enthusiasm. Giulio and Amerigo had no interest in picketing. For weeks, they were couped together at Fredianelli's home. They did odd jobs around the house and helped a few neighbors with chores, but the weather was turning cold and upper Michigan winters brought outdoor activity to a halt. The men unnerved one another as the temperatures dropped and the days wore on. To exacerbate the situation, the union was running short of money, so they compensated the miners with promissory notes for future purchases in the country store. This agitated Amerigo, who argued it was unfair to expect miners to sacrifice earnings and be paid with worthless pieces of paper. The Menicuccis bought almost nothing from the store. Their entire existence comprised mining and boarding. Discount coupons were worthless.

The union's resolve was already eroding when an event on Christmas day ensured its demise. The strikers' wives organized a children's entertainment event on Christmas day. The Italian Hall in Calumet was the only building large enough for the holiday celebration. Hundreds of children and their parents attended. The audience had just been seated in the auditorium to view the Christmas pageant when a disguised man yelled fire. He repeated the call many times, starting a panic. There was no smoke and no fire, but that made no difference. By the evening, according to the local news reports, sixty-two children and eleven adults had been trampled to death in a melee of human beasts fleeing the building. Some victims at the bottom of the human mounds were mangled beyond recognition, a historic horror scene.

The entire peninsula of Calumet was bifurcated politically between the union and the owners. The mining families were sure that the man with the faux fire warning was an agent of the mining companies. The union would not kill their own, so they were not suspected of accessories. The perpetrator, likely someone associated with the owners, should have been an easy find, but law enforcement and the press were aligned with the owners. Although the authorities claimed they conducted a lengthy investigation, they never arrested a suspect, further alienating the working families.

The mining operators were publicly embarrassed and apologetic that the situation had spiraled out of control. They made several offerings of help, including free access to the clinics for any injuries incurred in the panic and some financial compensation for the deaths. They also offered condolences in the local papers and other amenities for the funerals, including transportation for the coffins. So many had died in the worst mining tragedy in the history of Michigan that funerals were conducted in groups that were arranged according to nationalities. Several large group funerals were conducted on December 27.

The event made national news and it depressed union members and leaders, who were portrayed in the media as extremists. It was all over. By April, the union capitulated. Members voted to return to work under the original employment conditions. Then they chucked the union; each returning miner signed a contract promising never to join a union nor participate in a strike. Considering all their financial losses, concessions and deaths, the miners were left with less than when they started.

Giovanni Matteucci had enough of the violence, so he moved to Kankakee, Illinois, to work in the burgeoning auto industry. Like Giulio and Amerigo, he was there to work, not strike and end up with losses. The mining money was not enough to retain him. Giovanni was not unusual. Many men had neither the mental nor physical stamina to cope with a hazardous job and labor strife. The outflow of laborers created a continual demand for fresh workers.

Giulio and Amerigo welcomed the opportunity to return to work. They had no affection for the union. They were especially peeved that they lost time and money in the strike and returned with no gain. They were there to work and the strike was a bad investment. Mining was tough work and the strike so disturbed the two brothers that they were getting itchy, constantly considering their job options. Matteucci's departure stoked their interest in other types of work. In the letters with their folks in Italy, they mentioned the mining difficulties, the strike and the violence. The return letters suggested a Lucchese family in Illinois might help them if needed.

Giving up their current jobs was difficult. After all, Amerigo and Giulio were now providing most of the income for their Italian-based family and their own needs. They also had growing savings for discretionary expenses and investments. They loved living with the Fredianellis and worshiped Mary like a mother. They called her Zia (Aunt) out of respect.[5] It was very much like home in Lucca. As expected, both Giulio and Amerigo had been promoted. Plus, the strike had been settled and peace had returned to the region. The mining accidents, which seemed to be occurring more frequently, bothered the brothers. They had encountered minor injuries, such as cuts and bruises, but Mary cared for them. There had been many rumors of deaths in the mines, but details were difficult to obtain. An event in 1914 provided more than enough details for the two brothers.

CALL THE MADONNA

Most serious accidents involved dynamite directly or indirectly. Cave-ins were most feared because they typically claimed large groups of men. Giulio had been inspecting the timbers supporting the adit and stope for some time. He spent his lunchtime walking up the adit examining posts and beams. One in particular caught his interest. He regularly inserted his finger into one of its cracks in the beam holding up the roof of the adit. Amerigo asked him what he was doing. Giulio pointed to an eight-inch by eight-inch fir beam that ran horizontally across the ceiling of the adit. It supported the ceiling, he stated. When he first examined that timber, the crack was so small that he could not fit his pinkie finger inside it. Only a week later, the crack was wide enough for two thumbs. That, he said, indicated that the timber was stretching and giving way. It was a remarkable engineering observation from a man with only a third-grade education. He had complained to the timberman bosses, but they ignored him. They could only pray the timber held until they could finish mining their stope and move to another. With each explosion of dynamite in the stope, Giulio worried that the ground vibrations might trigger a failure of the adit's support system.[6]

His concern hit home in late summer of that year. While they were working their stope, they suddenly heard an explosion nearby followed by another explosion a little farther away. Dust and debris belched out of the adit like a volcano, engulfing the stope in a few seconds. Giulio took command and ordered all candles out, mouths and noses covered with bandanas and to get down near the ground. It took a couple of minutes for the dust to settle so that Giulio could re-light his candle and examine the damage. The adit ceiling had collapsed, trapping the men in the stope.

Giulio checked the airline. It was blocked, so their only air was already in the stope. The water line was not sucking either, which meant the mine could flood. In a few seconds, the stope was host to a life-death situation. Giulio projected calm. He blew out his candle and ordered the five men to lie in total darkness, coughing up dusty mucus in deathly black silence. Giulio kept his ear to the ground to check on rescue operations, but he heard none. As many hours passed, breathing became noticeably more difficult; they were running out of oxygen. Water was accumulating in the stope, introducing a new worry about drowning. The blackness worsened the terror. Light deprivation for extended periods can produce hallucinations. Some of the men shouted as visions in their brains menaced their thoughts. Giulio tried to silence them, but the outbursts and wailing worsened as time passed, and his commands were ignored.[7]

Amerigo interceded with a loud voice. "Holy Mary, Mother of God, pray for us sinners now and at the hour of our death. Holy Mary, Mother of God, pray for us sinners now and at the hour of our death. Holy Mary, Mother of God, pray...." Giulio interrupted him. "What are you doing. Be quiet." Amerigo responded, "I am calling on the Madonna to help us like Mama said." Then he went on chanting.[8] The use of this part of the Hail Mary is a long-standing tradition for Italians on their deathbeds.[9]

Without a response, Giulio joined the prayer chants. Immediately, all were praying in unison. Amerigo had taken command of the situation and settled the men. As Giulio chanted aloud with his team, his mind negotiated with the Madonna. He apologized for doubting her but promised that if she could get them out of this mess, all doubt about her would be permanently eviscerated and that he and Amerigo would never go back in a mine again. At this point, he believed he was asking for a lifetime of favors in this one instance. She might be unhappy if she is called for the same problem in the future. He hoped that it was enough to sway her.

With all the men lying flat on the ground, they chanted to Mother Mary for hours. One of the men called out that water was moving up towards them. That added a new existential threat. But Amerigo kept praying and increased the volume to regain attention to the prayers. Time passed slowly. Finally, Giulio said, "I hear something. Rescuers. Yes." The men immediately talked about it. Amerigo knew they were not yet rescued, and he again prayed in a raised voice until all were calm and praying. He knew that there was nothing they could do from the inside to help the rescuers. They could barely move, much less work. The men continued their repetitive prayer to the Madonna as they awaited the arrival of help.

After thirty minutes, the rescue team broke through. One rescuer, a miner, entered the stope to help the men, all too weak to stand. The men had been in the darkness so long that even the light from the rescuer's candle blinded them, forcing them to shield their eyes. Their entrapment had lasted for over eight hours, and the first breaths of fresh air uplifted bodies and souls. Amerigo once told me that it was "like breathing honey air." Giulio described it as "angels coming out of the earth." As fresh air flooded the stope, candles were lit. After fifteen minutes of recovery, Giulio rose with the help of the rescuer and then both helped the others. One by one, the men were escorted out of the stope and through the rescue hole in the adit. Amerigo helped the men through the adit and into the rescue ship that took them to the surface. Giulio waited until all of his men were out before he squeezed through. He took one last look around. If he had anything to do with things in the future, this is the last he and his brother would see of stopes, adits, or mines of any kind. Giulio was back in charge of his team, but he had learned a valuable lesson that had served him for a lifetime. The Madonna was real and his younger brother had become a full partner in their developing enterprise.[10]

As the evacuated men squeezed through the adit and into the skip, many found themselves short of breath with violent coughing spasms. They had inhaled large amounts of dust over a long period.[11] As Giulio crawled along the adit with the aid of his rescuer, he examined the debris piles. There were two failures. One beam failed and allowed the ceiling to collapse. Its collapse shook loose some of the posts holding up other ceiling beams, causing a second collapse. Rescuers had to tunnel through two debris piles, shoring the ceiling with new beams as they progressed toward the stope.

RENEWAL

As the men stumbled out of the mine, their families and friends greeted them. Mary Fredianelli was there with other women as the rescuers pulled the bedraggled victims out of the hole. The men were filthy, exhausted and still quacking with fear. Upon reaching the surface, most fell to their knees in prayers of thanks as friends and relatives comforted them. Some sobbed, overwhelmed by their near-death event. Mary was on the spot with hot coffee and some blankets for her men. One by one, she gathered her boys, as she called them, and comforted each one individually. The shaft foreman, a Finnish man, gave all of the men the remainder of the day off to recover, without pay, of course. Mary escorted her men home. Once there, she nursed each one, sending them one by one for a five-minute bath. Once cleaned, she settled the men into the kitchen, where she had a pot of simmering coffee that she made by dumping crushed coffee beans directly into the water. The beans settle to the bottom, leaving coffee on top. She ladled the steaming brew into mugs, serving them to each man with soup and crackers. She had seen this before with other miners. Her husband, Pietro, had been in a similar incident, albeit nothing as serious. As the men ate and slowly regained strength, she examined each for injuries, noting and bandaging a few cuts and scrapes. Mary was a traditional Italian housewife and was proud of her important role in the family to provide nurturing and affection to her family.

After the men were refreshed, they all visited the chapel to thank the Madonna for the good fortune she sent them while in peril. No priest or chaplain presided, but the Lord was there and that was good enough for them. Tears welled in many eyes as they prayed in thanks. Giulio, somber beyond description, knelt in prayer and humility as he thanked the Madonna for being alive. Amerigo was content knowing that faith was solidly entrenched in his brother. He had done as Mama had instructed—he took care of his brother when he needed it most, at the time of his death. They remained in the chapel for hours, hunger finally driving them back to Mary's comfort, but all had been permanently changed. Staring face-to-face with the Grim Reaper for eight hours can do that to men.

NOW WHAT?

All the men, except Serafini, Mary's cousin, planned to leave the job immediately. Giulio and Amerigo were done, but where to go next? Mary was supportive. She had seen men come and go as they either burned out from a back-breaking job or scared off with fear, as was the case with the Menicucci brothers. She advised them to take some time to reflect and pray, which they did.

Once reasonably recovered over the next day, Giulio and Amerigo planned their departure. Amerigo pulled out some old letters they had received from Italy. One had the name of a Lucchese man from Ghivizzano, about eight miles north of Lucca, and a good family friend. He was living in Kankakee, Illinois. John Cardosi immigrated in 1887 and opened a fruit and vegetable business in town. He married Angelina Perrini in 1897 and had three boys. Cardosi's mother lived with them.

Cardosi had corresponded regularly with the family in Italy. He and Angelina kept abreast of Houghton's problems and were horrified at the Christmas tragedy. Cardosi knew the Menicucci boys were in the middle of the union scuffle and had repeatedly offered succor to the men if needed. They had room in their home for boarders, and plenty of manufacturing jobs were available in Kankakee, a burgeoning Midwest manufacturing community serving the booming auto industry. Matteucci had left the team and was working in Kankakee. Both of the boys agreed Cardosi's succor was needed.

They immediately penned a letter to Cardosi explaining the situation and asking for his help, specifically boarding and assistance finding work. The next day, fully recovered, the boys met with the Finnish mining foreman and resigned. They were paid what they were due up to the time of the accident and walked out of the mining office for the last time with no regrets. Their next stop was the post office in Hancock, where they mailed an express letter to Cardosi. They returned to their boarding house.

While Giulio dealt with Cardosi, Amerigo kept the family back home informed. They were on edge, waiting for letters and news from the boys. Amerigo had already written several letters during the strike and the Italian hall disaster. His latest letter reported their plan to move to Kankakee, if Cardosi would have them. Now, they waited for Cardosi's reply. Fredianelli was an old timer in the community and assured them that even though the boarding house was for employees only, they could stay sufficiently long to find other work. Fredianellis had seen boarders come and go, and Fredianelli knew how to stretch the rules to accommodate the men, who he treated like brothers.

After a few days, the boys made the daily two-hour, one-way walk to Hancock to check on a posting from Cardosi. Normally, mail was delivered to the mining communities when sufficient supplies of postings warranted the cost of the post office to deliver them. They did not want any delays in getting the news about their escape. While they impatiently waited for Cardosi's letter, the Franklin Jr. mine operators reduced the work week to four days and reduced pay by fifteen percent, all due to low copper prices, they said. The Menicuccis were smug. Their exit was impeccably timed.

Seven days later, an express letter was posted for Giulio. In it was the invitation for him and Amerigo to move to Kankakee to live with the Cardosi family. Cardosi specified the train lines to board and the walking directions to his home at 320 N. Rosemond. They had prepared a room for them and stated a boarding charge substantially less than they paid for the company home in Hancock. It was a day of joy and they celebrated by purchasing a couple of bottles of wine in Hancock for their last supper at the Fredianellis.

After a decade with the Franklin Mining Company, Mary Fredianelli had seen this act. The Menicucci's were departing, but more Lucchese would follow. She prepared an Italian feast of antipasti, grilled cheese, vegetables and pasta with pesto, followed by bananas topped with grappa for dessert. The wine was plentiful. The following morning the next chapter of the Menicucci's odyssey opened.

UNION RECONSIDERED

While waiting for Cardosi's letter, Giulio and Amerigo reflected on the union. The failed beam was a good example of the kind of situation that the union was trying to address. The union contended that the mine operators ignored employee pleas regarding safety and that better communication and cooperation were needed. Giulio was a case in point. He had often identified the faulty timber to the timberman and foreman, but he was ignored. And they nearly died as a result. The union also claimed that maintenance lagged in the mine, especially regarding safety equipment. The accident was due to pure negligence; the failing timber was readily apparent to the timbermen. The union contended that the mining operators should supply candles, matches, wicks, and dynamite rather than the miners. These costs particularly irritated the men because it made no sense for workers to pay for articles integral to the mining work. Finally, the union contended that the miner's compensation was eroded by delays in exiting the mine at the end of each shift, sometimes adding over an hour a day on the job sitting in a stalled skip without pay. These were all valid claims, and certainly, the accident that nearly killed Amerigo and Giulio would have been less likely had a union contract been in place.

The mine owners arrogantly rejected all the union claims and demands. The copper industry was in chaos as copper prices fluctuated and the world marched toward war. Controlling costs became a major operational challenge for the owners, and they did not want additional labor costs to add to their financial misery. Besides, they had little incentive to accommodate the workers because they were relatively easy to replace. The Menicucci brothers realized that although they were satisfied with their pay, at least compared to Italy, by an American standard, they probably should have been paid more. The owners were in an extraordinarily strong position because the local law enforcement and political authorities sided with them on every issue. Without any collective bargaining laws to compel negotiations with a union, it had no bargaining power and, as a result, often resorted to violence. The union had a nasty reputation coming into the community and they did not disappoint.

Mines produced valuable products for a growing nation, including copper, aluminum and steel. It was also one of the most difficult industries in the world. Mining was arduous, dirty and time-consuming, involving many laborers. Importantly, a mine is always a temporary resource, only valuable as long as ore is available to extract. There are expensive up-front investments to extract ore productively. The vein has to be discovered, the ore quality assessed, its size determined, and its economic potential estimated. If it is of sufficient size and quality, the operators can drill a shaft, install the machinery and deploy the men to extract it. This expensive discovery and development process had to be completed prior to any extraction. It was a significant risk and many mines failed because the ore body was too limited in volume or of inferior quality to produce a profit before it was exhausted. The engineering term, premature resource depletion, was an operational risk for mining operators that created a need to discover new ore veins constantly.

Labor was one of the major costs in a mining operation and directly affected profits. It was also one of the few costs the operators could control. The operators' labor concerns set them in direct opposition to the union, which was proposing pay increases. In modern-day American society, labor laws and organized labor work to ensure worker protection while operators are afforded sufficient latitude to reap reasonable profits. At the Hancock mines, the operators had no inducement to address workers' concerns and no laws to compel them. The operators were captivated by their owners, the shareholders, who expected dividends on their stock holdings. The shareholders controlled the destiny of the company. A sudden sell-off of a mining company's stock reduces its market value, imperiling its operation.

What is more, the copper market was as choppy as the North Sea; copper prices careened wildly in response to gyrating geopolitical conditions as the world was marching steadily to war. The operators were constantly challenged to operate profitably.

The treatment of employees following the strike was a testament to their operators' disdain for the miners, who were all immigrants. The Menicuccis saw it and resented it. The operators viewed the men more as tools than humans. In 1914, the mining country of Houghton County was ruled by an oligopoly of owners supported by a biased press and miners laboring virtual indentured servants. Without free-market competition, free press investigations, or government regulations, capitalism had run amuck. The Menicucci brothers realized that the mining owners acted like the Padrone, not the union. In this situation, though, they had a path out. They were in the land of plentiful jobs and would find new ones.

Giulio and Amerigo learned valuable lessons about America. It was a land of opportunity but also one of worker exploitation, which the mine owners demonstrated. Both young men pledged to treat their employees with dignity and respect when they owned a business. They also surmised that if employees are treated properly, they would never form a union to force management to maintain the safe working environment they deserve.

See notes 12, 13.

Notes

1. More trammers than miners were needed to prevent backups. Ore was rapidly blasted out with dynamite but loaded into skips by hand. A six-man team usually contained two miners and four trammers. Seniority counted within those ranks. Among the miners, the most experienced man led the mining work, i.e., dynamiting, and was also a team foreman. His companion miner was next in line for the job. The trammers were similarly organized, with the lead trammer in line for mining.

2. Setting the explosive charges required both skill and daring. Dynamite is a volatile, dangerous product responsible for many mining casualties and is tricky to use. Sometimes, the sticks do not explode properly, and faulty fuses or other problems can delay some explosions. Dynamite sticks are relatively stable and safe if handled properly and do not freeze. Freezing sticks exude nitroglycerin, which is naturally unstable and can easily detonate. Dynamite was stored near the shaft house in a

warm, protected container, and one of the most important cold-weather jobs was to keep the container warm. Inadequate lighting adds to the list of hazards for dynamite. Light is needed to set the charges properly, but the open candle flames in miners' hats sometimes cause an unplanned explosion with catastrophic consequences. The situation is analogous to a person smoking a cigarette while pumping gas in a vehicle. Worse, the miners were not educated about the hazards of the tools they used or the materials they handled. They learned on the job from other workers. In some ways, the mining operations were accidents waiting for opportunities.

3. The arrival records for both Giulio and Amerigo Menicucci are available on the Ellis Island website. Gulio arrived on the La Savoie on July 3, 1909, traveling from Le Havre, France. Amerigo arrived on the La Savoie on June 11, 1910, traveling from Le Havre, France.

4. The residency requirements for immigrants changed over time, often depending on the political party in power. Giulio completed his declaration with barely two years of residency. Using that fact as a guide, when Giulio declared Amerigo was not qualified,

5. The use of Zia (Aunt) for those other than genuine aunts is a means to honor a specific woman while she is living.

6. A dynamite explosion in a mine produces two physical effects. First, the blast removes material from the wall, which is its intent. The wall is part of the structural support for the ceiling of the stope. Removing any part of the wall weakens it in some fashion, albeit small. Over time, careful extraction followed by shoring of the ceiling allows the wall to be gradually removed as ore is extracted. But if too much ore material is suddenly removed, the ceiling may collapse.

Second, each blast produces pressure waves that flow through the ground, shaking it. In effect, each blast creates a micro-earthquake in the mining area. The continual shuddering and shaking also adversely affect supporting structures, such as posts and beams, especially any damaged or improperly installed. Often, a beam failed because it was not secured to its supporting post, and after continual shocks over time, it would work its way off its supporting post, producing a cave-in.

7. *Comer* and *Heaven & Buxton* discuss the effects of sensory deprivation, such as darkness, on humans.

8. The second part of the Hail Mary produces the rhythm of a chant: Holy Mary, Mother of God, pray for us sinners now and at the hour

of our death. (Santa Maria, Madre di Dio, prega per noi peccatori, adesso e nell'ora della nostra morte.)

9. I visited my uncle Dante Menicucci, son of Giulio, as he lay dying. He chanted similarly and asked me to join him. It was the way that many Italians prepared to meet their Lord.

10. This story is one of the most enduring in family lore. The story is well-known to the Menicucci family and many other Italian families. Many of the story's details never deviated over decades of retelling. The quotations attributed to each of the Menicucci brothers as they were being rescued from the stope never varied regardless of which man was quoting. Both brothers acknowledged that the event was the most consequential one of their lives, setting them on a course heading straight to Albuquerque, New Mexico.

11. Miners only donned bandanas or kerchiefs over their noses and mouths in an emergency—they normally donned no breathing, vision, or hearing protection. These crude coverings were marginally effective in the best conditions but virtually valueless in heavily polluted environments. The lack of proper breathing protection exposed the miners to various hazards. While they had no health insurance, they had limited access to the company clinic, which was little more than a first aid station. They collected no pay while convalescing.

12. Background information about mining in the Michigan Copper country is provided by *Rakestraw*, *Courter*, and *Lankton*.

Menghini presents a detailed summary of Italians in the Michigan mines. In her thesis, she lists all miners who worked in the Houghton area copper mines in the early 1900s. Her thesis is available in PDF format, which is fully indexed, meaning that the names of individuals can be easily located in the document.

LeDuc provides additional detail about the ethnic composition of the mining teams.

Simons writes about the Copper mining strike that ended in the tragic death of dozens of people.

13. Newspaper articles published in and around Hancock, Michigan, were useful in providing details about the economic value of the mining activities, the union, and the disastrous strike.

7

AUTO INDUSTRY BECKONS (1914–1917)

GO SOUTH, YOUNG MEN

Giulio and Amerigo rose early on a cold morning in the fall of 1914. They had breakfast with their team and packaged up their belongings, which could be placed in a single burlap sack slung over a shoulder. They put their money in various locations on their bodies—their shoes, money belts, and some sewn into some of their clothes, including their hats. They knew the swindlers, including some Padrone that still prowled the area. They bid farewell to the team with many handshakes and a loving embrace of Mary, their pseudo-mother. The walk to the train depot in Houghton, across the river south of Hancock, consumed about ninety minutes. As they walked, they discussed their prospects. They had no firm employment, but John Cardosi assured them that jobs in the auto industry were abundant and well-paying.

As the two young men ambled south, they verbalized an epilogue to the first chapter of their great American adventure. They realized they had done something impossible in Italy—leave a job and take another in a different career area. For countless generations, the father's business passed on to his sons and grandchildren without end. Their family had always been Colono, so it was cast for the two of them. They realized that America was more than a faraway place to make extra money for the family; it was a land with a unique kind of freedom that allowed men to compete in a fair system that rewarded personal achievement. Giulio once said that it does not matter where you start in America because your actions determine the outcome. In Italy, your actions did not matter because in the end, you ended up where you started. Despite its rough edges at Franklin Jr. mine, they were beginning to appreciate capitalism and to view America as their home. As they crossed the bridge from Hancock to Houghton, nostalgia welled within them as they said farewell to their first home away from Italy.

FLUNKING ENGLISH

These feelings were fleeting as they spied the train station and realized that they were closing the first phase of their great American odyssey. At the station, they approached the ticket office. The attendant asked them what they needed. The boys, puzzled at the language he was speaking, responded in Italian. Fortunately, the clerk knew Italian and sold them the passage tickets. As they waited for the train, they milled around the station. They could hear that same strange language being spoken by many people. Amerigo had infrequently ventured outside of the Franklin Jr mining town. Giulio only had a few visits to the Hancock post office, where the clerks spoke Italian.

They could not understand the situation. They were fluent in English; they had learned it in the mines as the bosses spoke English. As they mingled, they encountered a group of Italian men waiting for the same train and speaking Italian. They broke into the group conversation to ask them about the strange language. Giulio explained that they knew English but many people spoke another strange language. What was that language, he asked them. One of the men asked the boys in English to state their names and destination. Giulio and Amerigo looked at each other and shrugged; they were clueless. So, they asked Giulio in Italian to ask them a question in English. Giulio responded immediately. The men broke out in roaring laughter. "You are speaking Finnish," one of the men said as he choked out the words among chuckles. Naturally, the boys were confused. They had learned English. How could it be Finnish? Then reality struck. The mining bosses were all Finnish and spoke their native tongue. Only two languages were spoken in the Franklin Jr mine—Finnish and Italian. They had assumed that the Finnish men spoke English, and they learned it. Now, they felt like fools and it showed on their faces. The men settled their laughter and advised the brothers that they would easily learn English while working in Illinois. The comment was heartbreaking because the brothers thought they were set for a new job and had the language skills to advance quickly. Now, they were back to square one. Their shock faded and their disposition turned back to optimism. They were, after all, surviving veterans of a nearly fatal mining disaster. This problem paled in comparison but they knew they would learn English just as they learned Finnish.[1]

Interestingly, the Fredianelli home was sandwiched between a Finnish home on one side and an English home on the other. The Menicuccis had been so consumed by their mining jobs that neighborly conversations, which might have enlightened them, were rare. So isolated were the two men at Franklin Jr mine that they were unaware that my maternal great-grandfather, Achille Barsanti, lived on the mining peninsula with his family simultaneously with the Menicuccis. Achille worked at the mine in Osceola, about ten miles north of Franklin Jr. Ten miles is a long walk, and there were no phones. Miners did not have time for recreational outings after laboring hard for sixty hours a week. Their only free time was Sunday afternoons; weekly Mass consumed the mornings. The best use of Sunday afternoon was to rest and recover so they could do it again on Monday. On holidays, they stayed home with their pseudo-family, just as they did in the old country. Even if they had known Achille was there, they had neither time nor inclination to visit.

The trip to Chicago was uneventful, but the boys still bantered about the language situation. As they approached the big city, their attention turned to the magnificence of Chicago. As the train slowly pulled into Grand Central Station downtown, they could see the many factory furnaces in the distance, with their looming towers belching out the smoke of industrial production. In 1825, the new Erie Canal connected Lake Erie to the Hudson River, effectively connecting Chicago ports to the Atlantic shipping routes. With the abundant natural resources in the area, including rich farm land and mining of precious metals, Chicago was becoming the commercial capital of Midwest America. The automobile industry was flourishing in Michigan, especially after Henry Ford developed his assembly line process of manufacturing. The other automobile manufacturers, General Motors and Chrysler, soon followed suit, and the race was on to flood America with vehicles, a key element that fueled the booming economic growth of the new nation. The Menicuccis had no idea of the work they would be doing in Kankakee, but from the looks of it, there was plenty to do, and best of all, it was not mining.

They boarded a train run by the Illinois Central Railroad, which operated several routes from Chicago to the suburban areas where many automobile contractors were. The young men wriggled their way through the crowded station, stumbling over language and fumbling their way to the train that would take them to Kankakee. The three-hour trip to Kankakee was smooth, and the industrial production in the area was evident along the way. Smoke towers loomed near and far, a testament to America's growing industrial might.

ILLINOIS ITALIAN OASIS

As they approached Kankakee, Giulio took out John Cardosi's letter with the directions to his home. Upon arriving, the brothers oriented themselves for the five-minute walk to the Cardosi's home. When they arrived, John and his sons were working at their jobs in town, but Angelina, John's wife, greeted them. She was a typical Italian woman, born in Lucca, trained by her mother and focused on her job to nurture and attend to her family. The greetings were a relief to the young men, who were pleased at being able to communicate in Italian. Angelina brought them into the home and showed them their boarding arrangement, a bunk bed, and a chest of drawers for their belongings. It was a room that was recently vacated by John Cardosi's mother, who had died the previous year. They even had indoor plumbing, including a bathroom with a toilet. No more wandering to an outhouse in a blizzard for personal relief. She then escorted them through the home and ended the five-minute tour in the kitchen, where she placed ample food on the table. Typical Italian fare it was, and it warmed their hearts to be back under the care of an Italian woman. They loved Angelina immediately as she reminded them of their mother.

As they munched on cheeses, cold cuts, bread and wine, they discussed their past adventures, especially the mine cave-in that nearly killed them. Their primary concern was the language. They worried that their employment chances were compromised. Angelina was upbeat. First, she said, many Italian immigrants with no English language skills were gainfully employed. Second, she said she would teach them English. She assured them they would quickly pick up the language, just as they did Finnish. It was a comfort, certainly, but both men were still smarting from the embarrassment of learning the wrong language.

She set the scene for learning by declaring that conversations in the home were in English only. John had imposed that rule earlier to help the family integrate into American society. Then, she spoke English, with some translations from time to time, to assist in understanding. New languages are most readily learned by immersion in the language. She then ordered the young men—in English with some hand signs—to rest and wait for John to return. They had escaped the rigors of the mine and had once again found an Italian enclave in America with a woman who knew how to care for them.

Not long after, John Cardosi and his sons returned home from work. His sons, Victor (sixteen), Joseph (fourteen) and John (ten), were in school, but as was typical in those days, they worked after school to save money for their future education in whatever field of endeavor they chose. They all came wandering in as the sun sank into the late-fall horizon. Again, the greetings were exceptionally Italian-spirited, with warm and welcoming comments and embraces. John ordered the opening of some wine to celebrate. All were gifted a glass full while they discussed the situation before dinner. John operated a fruit stand with his brother Paul and was doing well selling primarily to factory workers. They knew many of the businessmen in the area and had helped other Italian immigrants find work, especially those in the metal foundries that were flourishing in the area.[2]

THE AROMA OF INDUSTRY

In 1913, Henry Ford implemented two important manufacturing decisions when he produced the company's first great line-manufactured vehicle, the famous Model T Ford. One of them affected Kankakee's manufacturing fortunes. Ford's most important decision was his assembly line, which was the first such application to automobile manufacturing and resulted in increased efficiency, a substantial reduction in costs, and increased production of low-cost autos that could be purchased by middle-class Americans, such as his factory workers.

Another innovation was to control the manufacturing of all the components in the vehicle. Before Ford, auto manufacturers constructed vehicles using independently manufactured parts and components available on the market. In Ford's new system, the company either manufactured the auto's components in-house (themselves) or contracted the effort to specialty manufacturers, all Ford-certified manufacturing plants that produced products according to Ford's design specifications. Ford engaged a cadre of private contractors that produced components such as tire rims, gears and engine blocks. Kankakee was home to two of the biggest of these contractors, the Atlas Foundry and the David Bradley Manufacturing Works, which Sears Roebuck Company owned. Both of these foundries, along with a handful of other ones, supplied various metal parts for Ford's Model T automobile.[3]

John Cardosi had already lined up work for the Menicucci's in the Bradley facility. Cardosi was doubly motivated in this brokering role. He received a finder's fee for the referral and helped a paesano find lucrative employment. Several other neighboring families worked at the foundry. Both big foundries in Kankakee were constantly on the lookout for new laborers. The foundry operators especially sought mine workers because they had the experience and disposition to work with raw materials in dangerous industrial settings. Best of all, the remuneration for these jobs was substantially greater than what the Menicuccis made as miners but with less risk. With the success of his new manufacturing systems, Ford doubled the wages of its workers and those wage increases filtered down to the contractors. Cardosi said the Menicuccis should report to the Bradley organization in the morning to begin their new careers.

While they talked at Cardosi's dinner table in his kitchen, they all marveled at what America had given them, most notably freedom. Freedom to access opportunities that allowed for personal economic development without interference from the government and independence to seek a job change to enhance a career. Cardosi pointed out that the Menicuccis had exercised a benefit that was void in their old county—the freedom to seek a job of one's choice. It was one of the aspects of American life that most astonished immigrants.

Angelina had been planning for the Menicuccis' arrival by preparing Italian delicacies, including big plates of meats, fresh and boiled vegetables, pickled giardiniera, various kinds of cheese, Lucca Olive Oil, warm loaf of Italian bread, fruit with Grappa and enough Chianti wine mixed with water for bountiful swilling.[4] The Menicuccis were right at home, except perhaps for the language barrier. But the Cardosi plan to immerse the Menicuccis in English was already at work at dinner, as both young men struggled like stark immigrants to converse in English when they requested foodstuffs to be passed to them. Alas, hunger is a powerful motivator and by the end of the evening the brothers were speaking a few simple English sentences. Angelina could see the kind of students she had. Smart and eager to learn, the ideal time to imbue solid, Italian-American family values in them.

Angelina was a stickler for etiquette at the table. All had to be physically clean and neat, pray silently over the food, sit over plates when eating, politely request food to be passed and, above all, not curse. Not only were the Menicuccis learning English, but they were also being schooled to become gentlemen. It was a far cry from the atmosphere in Fredianelli's home, which was a constant beehive of activity of rough and tumble youngsters dedicated to mining. The only times the activity in that home stopped long enough for the occupants to dine together were the few holidays throughout the year—and, of course, during the disastrous strike. In Cardosi's home, they sat fully relaxed before what looked like a special feast. John Cardosi quickly corrected this perception, proclaiming that this night was typical of the feast Angelina prepared daily. It was her job as an Italian wife and she was proud to do it.

Following dinner, John Cardosi reviewed the room and board details in English and Italian. Previous letters fixed the rental price, and Giulio pulled money from his shoe to pay for the first month. John asked how much money they had, and the Menicuccis counted what they had in various places on their persons—their life savings of more than one hundred dollars (about twenty six hundred in 2024 dollars). When John saw this, he suggested they store the bulk of their money in his brother's safe, located at his home a few homes away. The brothers agreed that a safe was more secure than hiding it in clothing while at work. Finally, John gave the young men a slip of paper with the name of an Italian immigrant who was a recruiter for the David Bradley organization. John said the man would be waiting for them to arrive and they should be dressed in work clothes.

Angelina said they would eat lunch away from home if they worked at Bradley. They only had half an hour for lunch, insufficient time to make the round trip to Cardosis. She packed lunches for the men every morning. Although John worked his fruit stand seven days a week, he closed early on Sunday afternoons to enjoy family time, Giulio and Amerigo included. Mass was at seven o'clock in the morning on Sunday, and each wore their best outfit. This religious ritual might have bugged Giulio a few years ago, but he had no hesitations now. The Madonna had come through in astonishing fashion following their nearly lethal accident. The Lord indeed listens to his mama. This was no time to skimp on prayers or worship of the Lord, and certainly worthy of the best dress available.

The Menicuccis were early to bed and rose at four-thirty to a hearty breakfast, one fitting for heavy laboring in a foundry. Morning shifts at most local foundries and factories typically commenced at six o'clock, with a swing shift at three in the afternoon. In the morning, Giulio and Amerigo had a large breakfast of eggs, rolls, fried ham and plenty of coffee. They walked a couple of blocks and boarded the trolley from downtown Kankakee up to Bradley, the area with the foundry by the same name.[5] The young men had never dreamt of anything like mass transportation, and they needed a tutorial by the Cardosis on how to purchase tickets and where to enter and exit a trolly car.

As they arrived at their stop, they walked another couple of blocks to the Bradley foundry. It was an enormous spread of industrial production rising out of the Midwest farmland. One of the two defining features of the Bradley plant were the smokestacks, some belching steam, others white smoke, and still others emitting coal-black, billowing effluents. One red-brick smokestack, situated in about the middle of the compound, towered over the others. Giulio said that they "made the smell of Kankakee."

A second striking feature was its huge, rectangular-shaped, two- and four-story buildings, replete with high bays, where the foundry processes were conducted. Each building had a footprint of around two-hundred feet by one thousand feet and was lined up in the rank-and-file style of an army formation. The façades of the buildings encompassed an array of rectangularly shaped windows spaced as tightly to one another as structurally allowed. The openable windows allowed for natural ventilation but gave the building a prison look. The Bradley plant consumed around one hundred acres of land.

Artist rendering of the Bradley factory in Kankakee, Illinois, circa 1920. Courtesy Eastern Illinois University, copy of postcard image.

The Menicuccis had little interest in architecture or towering buildings because they had no idea where to go or what to do, only to ask for that certain Italian recruiter. Giulio clutched the note Cardosi had given him with the recruiter's name. The Menicuccis noticed dozens of people, mostly men carrying lunch pails, streaming into the main entrance, a large foyer between adjacent 4-story buildings. They got in line with the others and proceeded through a gate where each person accessed their timecard and used it to gain passage into the plant. The brothers had no timecard, and their confused look caught the eye of the private security guards who stopped them for questioning. Once the guards saw the name on the slip of paper, the pair was directed to the employment office.

Arriving there, they saw several other young men inside, talking to agents or lined up to talk to one. Once inside themselves, they quickly entered a line and connected with the recruiter. He was a native Italian who had immigrated before 1900, working his way up from a laborer to his present professional position. He welcomed the Menicuccis in Italian, asked about their home in Italy, and traded a few Italian stories but quickly hired the men.

He asked the brothers about their skills. Giulio was a miner, so he touted his skills with explosives and big tools. Amerigo was skilled as a stone mason, a trade he learned in the year he spent in Italy without Giulio. He assigned both men to an all-Italian team of molders, who produced large cast iron gears, pullies, and brass bushings. Molder is a hot, difficult and dangerous job, but the brothers were fearless. Not only had they escaped death but they also knew that Madonna was available to help. They signed employment papers that specified the work days, hours and pay. The foreman also noted that a local school, funded by the foundry, provided after-hour training for employees to develop new skills. With new skills they could advance and earn additional money. For now, they were paid the introductory wage for untrained foundry workers.

They were given protective clothing, a full-length leather bib and head covering, a large full-face shield and heavy gloves. They needed this protection to prevent serious burns from splattering molten metal as it was poured into the molds. The Menicuccis had never used personal protective equipment and needed instruction about donning it. Initially, their work was not unlike that of a trammer, loading raw materials into a wagon and moving it somewhere else, cleaning up debris, and assisting in maintenance activities. This was certainly a change from the mines, where employees had no protective gear unless they purchased it themselves. As was their custom, the two brothers jumped in with enthusiasm and immediately discussed ways to progress, including attending night school.

One of the lessons the brothers learned and continued to learn is that, in contrast to Italy, hard work in America produces permanent personal economic growth. They worked with passion and pride to exhibit the dynamic spirit of Lucchese workers. Within a few months, after the brothers had gained reasonably mastered English, they enrolled in the local trade school, which certified technicians for specific foundry jobs. Within a year, flush with technical certifications and excellent job performance, they were promoted to apprentice molders, each assigned to work under a journeyman molder for on-the-job instruction. Along with the promotion was a commensurate increase in remuneration.

Each Sunday at Mass, the young men prayed diligently to the Lord, thanking him for the good fortune he had provided. They also thanked the Madonna and routinely purchased and lit votive candles in the church to honor her. At evening meal prayers, John Cardosi regularly reminded the family of their good fortune to live in America and thanked the Lord for the food. July 4th at the Cardosi's was a bastion of American patriotism, with an importance that riveled Catholic Church holy days.

For the first time, the brothers enjoyed the full fruits of American labor, including free time. They only worked their shifts six days per week, with Sundays off and a short, six-hour day on Saturday. In contrast to the mines, which consumed ten hours per day, six days a week, the extra free time was a luxury. Angelina taught them how to read and interpret the news, especially political events. John and Paul Cardosi showed them how a business is run and how to deal with associated legalities. The two men soaked it up like water on a damp sponge. Giulio was attracted to a mandolin that Cardosi had on hand. With natural talent and a burning desire to learn, he quickly acquainted himself with the instruments and, in a year, was playing some simple tunes. Both men concentrated on learning trade skills, such as carpentry, welding and masonry, which were useful in the foundry.

ODOR OF WAR

As the Menicuccis were busily molding metal gears, metal swords rattled on the European continent as the world was slipping into the largest global military conflict in history. By late 1914, Germany had declared war on Russia and England. Subsequently, U.S. President Wilson, in a national speech, declared neutrality.

That changed on May 7, 1915, when the Germans sank the Lusitania, a British transatlantic steamship off of the Irish coast. The defenseless ship was torpedoed without warning, resulting in nearly twelve hundred deaths, including one hundred and twenty-four Americans. This act initiated widespread American disgust for the German war leaders. Americans who had been transfixed on the border skirmishes with Mexico now witnessed the genesis of a global war. In spite of Wilson's declarations, it was obvious that the U.S. would not avoid the conflict. In Kankakee, the Cardosis took the local newspaper, and they kept abreast of the war because they had three sons, all of military draft age. So, too, were the Menicuccis. A military draft might leave only John and Angelina in Cardosi's large home. All they could do was continue working and pray for the best.

The Menicuccis experienced for the first time another feature of American society that was foreign to them: a free press bringing news from lands near and far. A newspaper arrived each day in front of the Cardosi's home with stories from Europe and the possible repercussions of war on the local population. In Italy, most news passed by word of mouth and personal letters. A few Lucca newspapers were published, but the Mezzadria class rarely subscribed to them. American newspapers were ubiquitous in the country. The brothers read the newspaper daily, learning about the war and the English language simultaneously.

Over the next year, the Menicuccis advanced in the Bradley foundry, both being promoted to molders, one of the highest trade positions. Giulio's innate construction and engineering expertise was noticed. He suggested several production improvements to the management to reduce errors and improve quality. In addition to his technical skills, Giulio had just been naturalized as a citizen, which gave him an inside track for promotions. In the eyes of most businessmen, American citizens were preferred for leadership positions rather than aliens who might leave to return to their home countries.

In late 1916, Giulio was promoted to foreman of one of the molding crews. In Giulio's new position, he had wider authority to make decisions on the floor and to direct process changes. Naturally, Amerigo was his right-hand man, and he worked closely with him, especially regarding the organization of the men on his team. Amerigo was developing excellent organizational skills that would serve the brothers' future business ventures. Amerigo, having witnessed Giulio's promotion and developing his passion for America, submitted his declaration to become a citizen on April 4, 1917. It committed him to America and its defense. The brothers believed that if they lived in America, they fought for America.

By the accounts in the newspapers, a multi-country European land war was about to envelop America. Most Americans held strong patriotic beliefs, including the duty to fight if needed. For the Menicuccis, there was no concern about patriotic conflict of interest because Italy was a member of the European "Allied Powers" and America was an "Associated Power," essentially a non-member-nation ally.

The year 1917 was pivotal for America's inclusion in the Great War. In spite of Wilson's fleeting peace proposals over the previous year, the maritime conflict with German submarines escalated. In March 1916, in what has been dubbed the Sussex Affair, Germany agreed to U.S. demands to cease the attacks on unarmed passenger vessels. Predictably, the Germans violated the treaty in early 1917 by sinking the USS Housatonic, a passenger ship. Wilson responded by terminating diplomatic relations with Germany and requested Congressional approval for the Selective Service Act, which he signed into law on 18 May 1917. The new law required all eligible males between the ages of twenty one and forty five to register for the draft regardless of their immigration status. Alien draftees had the opportunity for instant naturalization upon induction. Most immigrants availed themselves of the opportunity. Those rejected for service or refused to serve were deported and permanently prohibited from applying for American citizenship. The fundamental American message to immigrants was clear: If you are here enjoying the nation's benefits, then you are obligated to fight for her in time of need. If not, then the United States might not be the best fit for you. Most Americans agreed with this concept, especially the Italian immigrants who firmly believed in the ethical principle of self-responsibility and patriotic duty.

Although the president continued to declare American neutrality in the conflict, his resolve was fading in private. By March of 1917, the seafaring toll became unbearable. In the first two months of the year, five allied and American merchant ships were torpedoed, including the Laconia (British), Algonquin, City of Memphis, Vigilancia and the Healdton, which particularly peeved Wilson and his cabinet because it was steaming in what had been mutually declared a "safe zone." The cabinet quickly decided on war, and Wilson formally asked Congress for a declaration with the goal of making the world "safe for democracy." On April 6, 1917, the president signed the declaration, and the country immediately assumed a wartime economic footing. Changes were afoot for the brothers, even beyond the prospect of dying in a foreign conflict.

See notes 6, 7, 8.

Notes

1. This story is well corroborated in lore. The details vary over time, but what is presented is what was most consistently verbalized by the two Menicucci brothers.

2. *Bateman & Selby* tell the story of Kankakee County and its industries.

3. *Wells* describes the detailed history of the Bradley Company.

4. Italians had been mixing wine into water for decades as a way to improve bad taste and sanitize. Although not needed in America, many Italian-Americans continued to mix wine into water.

5. The township of Bradley, just north of Kankakee, was named after David Bradley whose foundry was located in that area.

6. *Strachan* and *Story* describe the history of World War I. *Langer* and *Morris (Barry)* provide in an encyclopedic format the general history of the world in that period.

7. Newspaper reports, particularly from the Calumet News provide historical, real-time reports about the Michigan mining, the European war and the political responses.

8. Census and city directories provided detailed information about the Cardosi family and others in Kankakee. Information about the Cardosis is found in the 1910 and 1920 censuses for Kankakee City, Kankakee County in Illinois.

8

IMMIGRANTS AT WAR
(1918–1919)

FIRST MENICUCCI INVENTOR

All the foundry employees were naturally tense following the war declaration, but there was only one noticeable change for the Menicuccis—the shrinking number of workers due to calls for military service. Some, such as National Guard Reservists, received orders to active duty just days following the war declaration, and their absence in the foundry was immediately felt in the high-bay work areas. However, operational changes were in the offing.

The foundry crews were restructuring their manufacturing lines to meet new demands for wartime materiel and vehicles. At the threshold of World War I, America was evolving into a military manufacturing giant. Automobile manufacturers were on the front line of American war production because they were best positioned to retool to produce war-fighting vehicles and other equipment. As the manufacturers received lucrative new government contracts for military gear, they demanded new components from the various contractors who served the auto industry, including the Bradley facility.

New molded iron products required new molds, many of which were larger and more intricate than they used for standard automobiles. The upsizing caused operational problems; unforeseen failures beset the teams attempting to meet the government's specifications. One intractable molding problem-plagued Giulio's team. To create a gear, they constructed a mold from tightly packed sand formed into the shape of a desired object. Hot, liquid metal was poured into the mold. Once the metal solidified, the mold was broken and the cast object was removed. Workers then sanded and polished the object for delivery to Ford Motor Company to the customer. The foundry was adept at producing these products for automobiles but not those for tanks and other war vehicles three times their size.

The larger object they were attempting to mold frequently fractured as it cooled in the mold. A fracture is costly because the metal has to be cooled, fully reclaimed and re-smelted for a new mold. It wasted time and money. The situation led to accidents, such as burns, and drove up production costs. Giulio was intent on solving the problem and experimented with solutions. The solution was carefully controlling the cooling process using special cooling fins. Giulio, with Amerigo at his side, designed and built a prototype mold and tested it. It greatly reduced failures. It was another remarkable engineering insight that characterized Giulio's technical skills.

The men worked overtime implementing the new system on the line. Until then, management had paid little attention to Giulio's team, as they were not accustomed to ideas emanating from the high bays. That changed when Giulio's team ramped up production with few failures. Cost reductions tend to catch management's attention. They quickly implemented the new mold design throughout the plant. It was a novel concept worthy of a patent because it revolutionized the molding process for large metal wheel rims, gears and other round objects.

Giulio discussed his new system with the Cardosi family and the management's reaction. Giulio was excited, but he was unsure how to capitalize on it. John's brother, Paul, owned an oil distributorship, and he understood American business practices. He could smell a rat in the mix and advised Giulio that his invention had value and that he should claim it and ask for compensation. This was America, where people were recompensed for inventions. Giulio did not have to ask because the Bradley operators already knew the value of the invention and offered Giulio seven hundred fifty dollars (about nineteen thousand in 2024 dollars) for the exclusive rights to the invention. The invention was worth much more but Giulio gleefully accepted the largest bounty he had ever imagined. Bradley patented the process and used it until the 1980s. Some might argue that this situation was unfair to Giulio; after all, he should have been named on the patent and received royalty payments. A patent would have been irrefutable proof that he had invented something, logging him as the first

Menicucci to have earned one. It was incidental to Giulio; he had the biggest pile of money he had ever imagined, which was good enough for him and his brother. However, as military induction notices infiltrated the workforce, a new change was afoot for them.[1]

GRAND PLANNING

The Menicuccis learned how to use the American newspapers as a source of information for making decisions. In 1916 and 1917, with maritime losses in the North Sea making regular front-page news, both men were piqued. They had limited knowledge of geography and no understanding of the nuances of the ground war, but the sea lanes were different. Both had been on a ship in the North Sea and it was rough. The thought of being in the steerage hull of a huge ocean liner with water rushing in from a torpedo attack terrified them. They had a phobia of suffocating to death in cramped places. Franklin Jr. mine haunted them.

It was now late 1917 and Giulio, with his brother's help, had spent nearly a year developing the new molding technique. However, the threat of induction was ever present as they witnessed many of their co-workers disappear daily. There was talk about hiring women to replace the departed men, figuring that even though they lacked the physical strength, they could do many foundry jobs.

Military inductees from the plant were ordered to report to different training camps throughout the country. There was a chance that the Menicucci brothers could even be split up, a prospect they desperately wanted to avoid. They went through a heated period of information gathering, not only by reading the newspapers but also through letters and reports from their workmates who were in military training.

They did what they always did in time of need—turn to family and close family friends for advice and help. They had personal friends and relatives in Albuquerque who all emigrated from Lucca province. Their cousin Austutillo Giannini lived there, although he was still too young to be drafted. Their close friends were also there: the three Matteucci brothers, Amedeo, Alessandro, and Johnny. The Matteucci family all hailed from Lammari, near the homes of some of Pasquale Menicucci's family, who also lived in Lammari. Giulio and Johnny were near the same age and were close friends. Johnny was born Giovanni (John) but immediately employed the English version of the name after he arrived in America in 1906. He loved the ring of Johnny with Matteucci, and it became his namesake for business purposes and among friends. But, his family called him John. Johnny and Austutillo did well in business and urged the Menicuccis to move to Albuquerque. But, until the Army decided otherwise, there was no reason for the Menicuccis to leave Kankakee.[2]

After exchanging a few letters, a reason to exit Kankakee arose. Based on reports, men from Albuquerque reported for Army training at Camp Cody, near Deming, New Mexico. The Albuquerque area was a small town at the time and groups of men were often drafted together. If the brothers could get to Albuquerque and establish residency, they would likely be trained together. But there was still a problem: what if their draft notices arrived at different times? Then, they might still be split up. Johnny had the answer. They would wait in Albuquerque for one of them to be called and then the other two travel with him to the enlistment office at Camp Cody. Men could walk into the camp and enlist. As Johnny hatched it, they planned to travel to Camp Cody and enter the war simultaneously.

It did not take a lot of thought for the brothers. If they had to go to war, it was best to go with friends and family. Cardosis agreed and assisted them in obtaining rail tickets to Albuquerque. The brothers notified the Bradley management and took their final cash payments. Both had impressed the management, and they were verbally guaranteed that their jobs would await them after the war. Importantly, their aunt, Amabele Morelli, lived in Albuquerque and had a place for them to stay. She was sister to the Menicucci's mother and had immigrated about ten years earlier. Her husband, Francesco, widowed her a few years earlier in Italy, and she moved her family to Albuquerque shortly afterward. She had plenty of room at her home at 714 Tijeras Street, just a half block from the Matteucci's Champion Grocery Store where Johnny worked. Before leaving Kankakee, the brothers changed their mailing address to their aunt's Albuquerque address, an important step in establishing residency in Albuquerque. They left their savings in the Kankakee safe because they expected to return following the war.

In February of 1918, the two brothers traveled by rail north to Chicago and, from there, boarded the Atchison, Topeka & Santa Fe railcar that brought them directly to Albuquerque. They walked the eight blocks from the rail depot to their Aunt Amabele's home. As they passed through the door, it was like a trip back home to Italy. The aroma reminded them of their mother. Plus, Amabele and Teresa had similar physical features. She was blood family, the first they had encountered in a decade. That evening Amabele cooked a typical Italian meal for the men, including plenty of wine. They were safe for now, and a relaxing night's sleep followed.

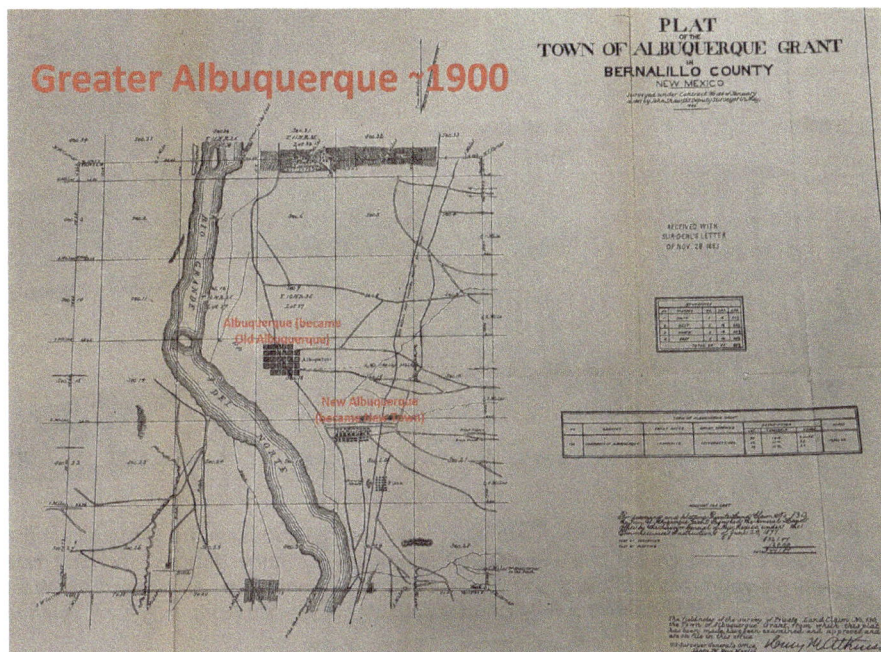

Map of the Albuquerque Area around 1900. The town of Albuquerque, the dominant one in the area, would soon to be dwarfed by the spectacular growth of New Albuquerque. The distance between the two communities—only a few miles—was perceptively large due to limited transportation. The majority of Italian immigrants at that time lived in New Albuquerque. Courtesy Albuquerque Public Library, Plat of Private Land Claim number 130, the Town of Albuquerque, located in the map collection in the Genealogical Center.

The following day, they met with Johnny Matteucci at Champion Grocery. Johnny was the youngest of the Matteuccis and the only one eligible for military service; brothers Amedeo and Alessandro were already too old at forty and forty-six years old, respectively. Alessandro offered the Menicuccis temporary work at Champion Grocery but the Morellis had already secured work for them at the railroad yards, the largest employer in the city. By the time the Menicucci brothers arrived in Albuquerque, the Matteucci family had been in business for years. In February of 1918, they worked as apprentice railcar mechanics. Importantly, Immaculate Conception church was nearby to serve the community.

The Porto Rico Saloon in Old Town Albuquerque circa 1890. Alessandro Matteucci is the Italian owner in the center (with mustache) behind bar. Johnny (farthest to right) was Alessandro's youngest brother. It was one of the first saloons in the area near 1842 West Railroad Avenue (aka Central Ave.). Courtesy Albuquerque Museum, a gift of Yolanda Matteucci Marianetti.

In 1910, Champion Grocery located at 7th and Tijeras streets in Albuqueque was about eight years old and was one of the largest Italian owned retail grocery stores in Albuqueque. The horse drawn cart was used for deliveries. The identities of the people are not precisely known, but the men from left to right were likely Alessandro Matteucci, his brother Amedeo, relatives Pio Lommori and Felice Barsanti (with wide brim hat). The women were likely wives of the men. Immaculate Conception church lay directly in back of the store on the opposite corner of the block.

Inside Champion Grocery around 1910. Alessandro Matteucci is standing in the middle, just to the left of the woman in light dress. Felice Barsanti is at far right. The others are not identified, but likely included Pio Lommari. Courtesy Albuquerque Museum, a gift from Yolanda Matteucci.

Immaculate Conception Church, ca. 1891, Courtesy Albuquerque Museum, a gift of Walter C. Haussamen. This church was rebuilt after the depression and was a key component of Italian life.

TOGETHERNESS

They worked for several months before Johnny Matteucci was called to service. In late June 1917, following their plan, the three men boarded a southbound train for Camp Cody. This military camp was built in the mid-1800s as an Army fortress to bolster American defenses of its southern border following the Mexican-American war. Although the Americans easily defeated the Mexicans in the mid-1800s military adventure, taking Mexico City by force in eighteen months, the Treaty of Guadalupe-Hidalgo that ended the conflict never set well with the Mexicans. They lost much land area and all of the disputed territory of Texas, leaving the U.S. as the controlling entity for the western half of the North American continent. As a result, border skirmishes were normal, and the Army often intervened to re-establish order. The poor relations with its southern neighbor left the Americans worried that Mexico might use the European war as a distractive opportunity to reclaim territory. What was more, reports of an encrypted message dubbed the Zimmerman Memo indicated that the Germans had been negotiating an alliance with the Mexicans. The rumor was that the Mexicans sought to reverse the Guadalupe-Hidalgo accord. This alarmed the Army and further justified the Camp.

Camp Cody, 1917. Individuals unidentified.
Courtesy Albuquerque Museum, a gift of Jane L. Banes-Trujillo.

As the nation entered the war in Europe, US military leaders projected that the resources needed for a global military campaign required an Army many times its size of two hundred thousand men, eventually millions. Training facilities were rapidly built to meet the need. Camp Cody was one of them. Before the war, it was envisioned to train the National Guard and military reservists, but it was quickly converted to handle tens of thousands of inductees, most of whom were deployed to France. The camp was the newest and the most advanced training facility in the Army, with excellent provisions for the men. Some of the first men to arrive at the war front in France in late summer were National Guardsmen stationed at Camp Cody when war was declared.

Johnny and the Menicuccis arrived at the parched, dusty and feverish military facility late on June 27, 1918. They were quickly hustled off to the orientation area, where they took their initial briefing, collected their issued supplies, found their bunks, and met their drill sergeant who would train them. As the men were processed, they recorded Giulio's name as Julius because it was a name that sounded like Giulio. So, he was to the Army Julius Menicucci. At that point, he assumed the Americanized version of Julio and retained it for the remainder of his life. Amerigo had no problems with his name because it was similar to America. Johnny was a common American name.

A quick physical exam qualified each man for the rigors of training and warfighting. Once cleared by the physicians, they initiated the metamorphosis from citizens to fighting men. The rare man who failed the physical was sent back home. Six weeks of training with rifles and other military equipment was standard preparation for deployment to the American Expeditionary Force in France, commanded by General John Pershing. Pershing insisted that all American servicemen and women arrive fully trained and battle-ready regardless of rank or job specialty. This order aimed to prevent high losses when green, untrained soldiers were placed directly into battle and expected to learn on the job. His second concern was maintaining control of his troops under AEF command.

The Allied powers were eager for American equipment and troops but viewed Americans as lacking proper training and organization. They argued that Americans should be placed under Allied command. Many commanders had suggested dividing the Americans among the various Allied Power commanders, essentially using them to replace the losses they had sustained in a stalemated contest. Pershing rejected all of this. Certainly, the Americans had no combat experience in a European ground war, but they had performed well in Mexico, albeit against a rag-tag opponent. Pershing correctly reasoned that if he could demonstrate well-trained and well-organized battle groups, he could justify keeping his units together and under American command. For this, he had President Wilson's ear and his support. Throughout the remainder of the war, Pershing's commanders led American troops in various battles supporting the Allied war effort. Little did Pershing know that his AEF command structure was the prototype for America's future intervention in an even greater conflict with the same European agitator.

At Camp Cody, each recruit completed various aptitude tests, which the Army used as a guide to match individual skills to assignments. The Army understood that men perform better when they enjoy what they do, and they had a huge variety of work to do. It also understood that soldiers with poor English language skills put fighting units at risk. So, all immigrants, regardless of naturalization status, were schooled in reading and writing proper English and American society's ethical norms. Immigrant aliens, which included Johnny and Amerigo, were put on a fast track to naturalization. Both were naturalized in Deming, New Mexico, a few weeks after enlisting. (Julio was already naturalized.) This fundamental civic education of immigrants aided the war effort and created knowledgeable, patriotic citizens. For the Menicuccis, the Army continued Angelina Cardosi's instruction.

Italian immigrants at Camp Cody after induction. From left:
Johnny Matteucci, Amerigo Menicucci, and Giulio Menicucci.
Courtesy author's collection.

BRICKS, MUSIC AND GUNS

Due to his masonry skills, Amerigo was identified as a tradesman and classified as a brick mason who assisted Army engineers in construction. He was permanently assigned as a first-class private to the utilities division at Camp Cody, where he spent his entire enlistment of seven months. He excelled at constructing and modifying buildings on the fort and, in a short period, received two field promotions to Sergeant first class, producing the first non-commissioned military officer in known family history.

Julio was singled out as a musician because he was proficient with the mandolin. He had no formal training in music but had natural musical abilities. At that time, musicians were in demand, and few men came into service with musical skills. He was immediately classified as a third-class musician and assigned to the 109th Engineer Regiment of the 24th Infantry Division of the AEF in Chaumont, France, about sixty miles west of the stalemated battlefront.

Johnny possessed no particular skills or trades; he was a shopkeeper in his brothers' grocery store. He was selected for gunnery training and was assigned to Company D of the 128th Machine Gun Battalion, 24th Division, subsequently deployed to France in September. A gunner's job was especially hazardous because the flames spewing from the barrel when fired became a blazoned target for return fire. Fortunately, Johnny was issued the new Browning Model 1917 machine gun, the most advanced in the world. It was a reliable, water-cooled gun that fired a 30-06 round. Water allowed the weapon to fire tens of thousands of rounds continuously without cooling periods, a tremendous advantage because it kept the enemy pinned down with few breaks to allow it to identify the gunner's position and return fire. Pinning the enemy with fire allowed the infantry to move successfully against entrenched German positions. The gun weighed only about forty pounds, about a third of the German equivalent, and could be handled by a single man instead of two. However, the M1917 gunning team required two soldiers, the gunner and an ammo man. Browning's new gun improved battlefield performance and was a factor in the success of the Muese-Argonne operation, which was the first global demonstration of American military might. A gunner was a perilous assignment regardless of weapon. Many soldiers often quipped that a gunner's life expectancy on the line was one minute after he commenced firing.[3]

During Johnny's assignment, the Allied Powers were executing the Sept 26th Meuse-Argonne offensive. The objective was to cut a major German supply line, divide the German army, and starve it of materiel. Pershing applied every available American division in the effort, about one million two hundred thousand men. It was not the typical trench warfare that had characterized the war for years, as the eager, young Americans with plentiful weaponry overwhelmed and routed the beleaguered Germans. By November, the German war machine was in tatters, the Kaiser snuck out of Germany like a scared rat, and a new German regime headed by Maximilian of Baden petitioned for an armistice.

The timing was Johnny's good luck because he joined the offensive as the Germans were on the brink of defeat and often quickly surrendered positions to the rapidly invading Allied forces. A gunner in an advancing army is not risk-free, but it is less hazardous to shoot at a retreating enemy than one fighting back.

Julio's musical assignment may sound to many as a cupcake job, often portrayed as a serviceman playing the flute while his compatriots were dying in the trenches. Pershing believed that music was the key to a successful army endeavor. He thought music elevated the men's fighting spirit and patriotic levels, allowing him to create the proper atmosphere for battle. He believed music was of comfort and refreshment to the men following battles. He frequently pointed out that the Romans, commanders of some of the greatest armies in history, used music as a key element of army life. Shortly after taking command of the AEF in France, he persuaded Congress to authorize more bands and to build an Army bandmaster and a musician's school at AEF headquarters in Chaumont. Simultaneously, the training camps were put on notice for musicians.

The principal work of an Army band was to provide music for the pomp and circumstances of ceremonies, such as for meritorious awards, holiday festivities, marching in formations, and playing special concerts for wounded soldiers. In sum, their job was to augment important military events with music. Certainly, playing a musical instrument in marching formation was less hazardous than a machine gunner in the field, but it was not risk-free. Musicians were often dispatched throughout the theater of operations, including near the battlefront. These soldiers were permanently on temporary duty, moving from one place to another and playing with different company members at any given time. It was not unusual for a band unit to be enveloped in an enemy surprise attack, forcing them to trade musical instruments for rifles. Some army musicians, especially the lower-ranked ones, were occasionally assigned to assist in evacuating wounded from the field, one of the most dangerous jobs in the Army. Musicians sometimes filled in losses on the line before replacements could be secured. Generally, though an Army musician had an important role in the war effort, he had a much better chance to survive than an infantryman manning a machine gun on the front. Such are the vicissitudes of Army assignments.[4]

SMOKEY CALLING CARD

Julio was proud to serve as an American serviceman. He knew that many of his countrymen also served under the AEF command. In the evening in late fall of 1918, Julio found out how close some of those countrymen were. He was part of a military detail on temporary duty near the southern part of the front in France. His detachment was preparing to provide music for a troop- and command-rotation ceremony the following day. While walking among the barracks one evening, he sniffed a familiar aroma. Tobacco smoke. It reminded him of Italy, especially his neighbors in Lucca. The aroma was distinctively pipe tobacco with its thick, sweet billows of whitish clouds swirling and mixing in the air. Then it hit him. It was Johnny Matteucci's pipe. He had to find the source, so he followed the plume of smoke, sniffing along like a bird dog. He tracked the smoke and saw it slipping around the corner of a building like a sheet of silk flowing in the wind. When he crept up and looked around the corner, he could see a man smoking a pipe—it was Johnny puffing away on his characteristic bent pipe.[5]

On a path as a tobacco aficionado, Johnny sampled some French tobacco he bought at a local market. Johnny smoked at an early age and was enamored by the variety of tobaccos and their various flavors and effects. He often explained how the pipe's wood could alter tobacco's flavor. In pipe smoking, taste and aroma are the defining characteristics. Johnny's pipes always had distinctive aromas as he frequently experimented with different types of tobacco. Before the war, he helped his brothers manage tobacco products in Champion Grocery. My wife and I lived next to Johnny and Teresa for fifteen years before his death, and his pipes and select tobaccos had remarkably distinctive and delightful aromas. One of Johnny's most distinctive personal attributes was centered on his pipe, which he always seemed to be cleaning, packing with tobacco, or smoking.

1917
John Matteucci
Duck Hunting
with Luigi Del Frate

Johnny Matteucci and Luigi Del Frate hunting ducks near Old Albuquerque before they were drafted into military service in WWI in 1917. Johnny is smoking his bent pipe, as he did almost constantly. Courtesy John Matteucci.

That evening, Johnny was outside his hut enjoying some free time before deploying with his machine gun the following day. Pipe smoking was ubiquitous among the soldiers in the trenches and barracks because loose tobacco and matches were included with personal rations; cigarettes were not yet invented. The war was deadly, and the prolonged trench fighting produced a steady stream of casualties ranging from bullet wounds to grossly contorted bodies of those who died agonizing deaths from poison gas. Death was a continual threat and tobacco helped to calm nerves. Pershing believed it helped to develop courage when doubt threatened.

The two men reacted like rediscovered long-lost brothers as they reminisced for an hour about their experiences since leaving Camp Cody just a few months earlier. Johnny had received special instruction on machine gunning and field battle techniques. He was trained to fight in the trenches and fire on the enemy. He would be in battle in the coming days. Julio bragged that he was now playing the accordion, bass and mandolin but had not yet seen action. The men left with a prayer to the Madonna for Johnny and a special request for the Lord to bring them together in Albuquerque after the war.

Julio played in the rotation ceremony for Johnny's division the following day and then returned to his unit at headquarters. Johnny served on the line until the end of the war. This experience between Julio and

Johnny, one of the types that servicemen often muse about, galvanized the already close and long-standing relationship between the Menicucci and Matteucci families, which has prevailed to this day.

Ironically, Julio, who had already demonstrated engineering, design and construction skills, found his way to an engineer regiment as a musician, a non-technical job. Amerigo, who had also demonstrated some technical skills, was identified as a brick mason and assigned to a technical job with the engineers at Camp Cody. Unsurprisingly, Johnny, with no technical skills, became a gunner.[6]

AMERICA TURNS THE TIDE

The American contribution to the war effort was huge, rapid and effective. In less than a year, starting with only 200,000 men in service, the country enlisted, trained and deployed over four million men under arms, with about half of them serving at the front in France. In a year, America produced and shipped over five million tons of cargo to France. The Americans lost more than one hundred ten thousand men, half of them cut down by the Spanish Flu, which by the end of the war had become a major pandemic. Statistically, the flu was as deadly as the Germans.[7]

NAVAL POWER

The influence of the American Navy in determining the war's outcome is often overshadowed by the sheer numbers of Army ground soldiers in the effort. The Navy had a small but critical role in controlling the German submarine menace in the North Sea. At the war's outset, the U.S. Navy's sailors outnumbered Army soldiers by three hundred thousand. Few countries had a larger Navy than the Army. Relative to the Army, the Navy's war-fighting equipment was advanced, some parts even world-class. The government had been building the Navy, expecting battles against Germans along the American east coast.

The battle turned out to be further east. German submarines had for several years wreaked havoc with the shipping lanes in and around the coasts of the North Sea, with huge losses of Allied war materials and personnel. Admiral William Sims, commanding the AEF naval forces, knew that the German menace had to be controlled to safeguard American war materials and soldiers heading to the war front. Almost simultaneously with the war declaration, Sims ordered American military convoys for all of the Allied shipping through the North Sea lanes. Within weeks, he secured a naval operational alliance with the British Navy. Within six months, the two navies, with American might leading, shattered the long-standing German sea blockade around Britain by chasing them south and destroying much of their fleet. It was a significant setback for the Germans.

As soon as the northern sea lanes were secured, American materiel gushed into France and England like water through a broken dam, and the tide was about to turn against the Kaiser's forces. From June 1917 until November 1918, the Americans transferred over four million tons of war cargo, and equipped, trained, mobilized and deployed millions of soldiers to France, of which over a million served on the front lines. Only a few months after America entered the war, her industries had retooled and were cranking out war materials at an astonishing rate, as measured against world standards. American economic strength swung the Allies to victory, capturing the growing admiration and respect of the world. Global history had never seen such a massive national mobilization and it set the stage for the country's true blossoming that was to come. After three years of stalemate, the American contribution could be metaphorically described as pouring fuel in an empty tank; it ignited the Allied Powers and quickly led to German capitulation, followed by a punishing set of post-war conditions from the Treaty of Versailles. The Treaty of Versailles was based on the 14-point plan proposed by President Wilson in January, 1918, in an address to Congress. Paradoxically, this "War to end all wars," as World War I was often dubbed, set the conditions for an even more dreadful conflict to come.[8]

WARRIORS RETURN

Immediately following the war, Camp Cody was on a fast track to closure due to Congressional pressure to control war costs. The threat on the southern border had abated and the camp's training mission was vacated. Those servicemen assigned to the camp were among the first to be released. Amerigo was honorably discharged on January 20, 1919, at the rank of sergeant, a non-commissioned officer, just seven months after enlisting. Additionally, he could legitimately claim to be a qualified professional mason, which in those days was a valuable skill that could produce a comfortable living anywhere in America.

Julio remained in France as the war theater dissipated and troops returned to American shores. With the emergency over, the hectic pace of transport between Europe and America has ground down to normal, meaning that going home consumed more time than getting there. Pershing disbanded units in a planned manner so as not to overwhelm the transportation systems. Generally, when all things were equal, commanders discharged combat soldiers based on their time in service. Thus, the most experienced American veteran soldiers fighting under the AEF were the first to be discharged. Johnny Matteucci, who enlisted on the same day as Julio and saw combat, departed the Army on May 5, 1919. Julio, who had no combat role and played in musical ceremonies for departing troops, was not discharged until July 2, 1919.

Amerigo and Julio had been corresponding via letter to coordinate their reunion, where they would decide on their next move. Johnny Matteucci suggested that they meet in Albuquerque, where work was available. Amerigo moved back to Albuquerque to wait for Julio and Johnny. However, Amerigo would not sit idly while waiting for his brother. He believed strongly in the Christian ethic that the Lord placed people on earth to do good for others in society and wasting time did no good. Amerigo found an apartment in downtown Albuquerque, about three blocks from the Matteuccis' Campion grocery store, where he worked until Julio and Johnny arrived.

Johnny was back home in Albuquerque in May, and in late July Julio arrived. Amerigo had rented a room for him at the Bachechi Apartments on Second Street, where the Albuquerque Convention Center currently sits. Amerigo's apartment, about three blocks away, was too small for two men. Besides, the brothers had plenty of money and were certain they would not remain in Albuquerque for long. Amerigo had done especially well monetarily in the Army as his masonry skills awarded him ten dollars a shift, over twice what Julio made. (Ten dollars equals about two hundred twenty-five 2024 dollars). As a frugal pair, the brothers saved most of their earned during the war. It was easy because the Army issued all they needed to live and work, and they took full advantage of every bit of what they considered a windfall. These war savings, coupled with Julio's bounty from the molding invention, afforded them the financial flexibility to determine and implement the next phase of their future.

CAN'T LIVE WITHOUT THEM

When the three men finally met and discussed their situations, they agreed it was time for wives and families. Julio was twenty-seven and Amerigo was a year younger. Johnny Matteucci was twenty-nine. Austutillo Giannini, who was nineteen years old and a superb salesman, made a compelling case for the Menicuccis to remain in Albuquerque. His idea was to jointly build a business focused on the burgeoning auto industry. All those cars will need gas and tires, he argued. What was more, there were many available Italian women in Albuquerque. The Menicuccis were captivated by the thought of actually owning a business, a proposition that was unimaginable a decade earlier. All three men liked Giannini's plan but concluded that Italy had an even greater supply of women. Besides, all of them had not seen their families for years. They decided to return to Italy, marry and then consider settling in Albuquerque. Johnny Matteucci, of course, had long before settled on Albuquerque as his home. At the time, another Giannini family was headed by Luigi. Luigi's family and Austutillo's were not closely related.[9]

In letter correspondence over the ensuing few weeks, the Cardosis urged the brothers to settle in Kankakee. John Cardosi reported that the Bradley factory, for whom both men worked before the war, was busy retooling for domestic automobile parts production and was hiring experienced men at premium wages. Angelina wrote most letters in the same comforting tone as in person. John Cardosi added business-related excerpts to Angelina's texts to help the Menicuccis understand the job potential in Kankakee. They were acting as typical Italian parents in typical Italian roles.

The Menicuccis were not interested in jobs at Bradley. Like most healthy young men of their age, natural inclinations toward family life were compelling them to a specific objective. They said their appropriate farewells to the Matteuccis, their aunt Amabele Morelli and the Gianninis. Austutillo had made an impression, and they remained piqued about entering the automobile service business. Johnny Matteucci made plans to return to Italy to marry, and the men pledged to reunite in Lucca soon thereafter.

A few days later in late 1919, the Menicucci brothers were in the familiar environs of the Kankakee home. As customary, the reunion between the Menicuccis and their pseudo-family was as warm as when they had first arrived five years earlier. John enthusiastically welcomed them with a raised glass of wine, declaring them, along with his sons, as war heroes. He filled glasses liberally as the men regaled the family with stories of their adventures in the American army, especially the tale of Julio sniffing out Johnny Matteucci. Paul, John's brother, arrived and announced that he had arranged for them to take back their old jobs at Bradley if they wanted them. The two men were overwhelmed with love and respect for the Cardosi family and spoke of them frequently throughout their lives. Certainly, the brothers felt blessed to be serving on a winning national team after witnessing the continuing series of Italian military blunders in its colonial wars and beyond. To the brothers, America was more than a place to invest; it was growing into an economic goliath and an ideal place to raise a family.

There was one problem, though, prohibition. The Temperance Movement had grown steadily leading up to the war and, when it ended, was in a commanding political position. Congress passed the 18th Amendment for ratification on December 18, 1917. In January, America ratified the law prohibiting alcohol products from commercial enterprises. Forty-six states voted in favor of the amendment, with two objectors, Connecticut and Rhode Island. The amendment itself did not specify enforcement details, which meant it needed to enable legislation from Congress to be enforced. Andrew Volstead, a Republican Congressional representative from Wisconsin, was johnny-on-the-spot with such legislation, which passed both houses with big margins. President Wilson vetoed it but was far short of the needed votes to squash it. Volstead was the enabling legislation that put enforcement in effect. And it was troubling to the Menicuccis and their hosts because they greatly enjoyed a healthy glass or two of wine with meals. Plus, wine was a favorite additive in Italian sauces and desserts. To the Menicuccis, this was a negative aspect of the country that needed to be rectified, especially when they were wooing Italian women who also enjoyed wine.

Advice was Cardosi's most important contribution. John and his brother Paul had been following the political developments. They pointed out that citizens could legally ferment and brew alcoholic beverages for personal use. Italians generally knew how to make wine, they argued. From that perspective, the 18th Amendment might not be a potential show-stopper for them after all. Certainly, a local liquor store is a valued convenience, but they had planned to ferment their wine anyway. The prohibition concern passed quickly, and in March of 1920, the men applied for passports to return to Italy. Their singular goal was to marry and return to the U.S. quickly. Julio and Amerigo saw unlimited economic prospects for themselves in America. They had no intention of living elsewhere.

As the Menicuccis departed Cardosi's home, waves of nostalgia enveloped them just as it did when they departed the Fredianellis. From the time immigrants arrived on American soil, Italian-American families had provided comfort and assistance when they were lost and confused. They talked fondly of the Fredianellis, but their memories were clouded by the mine accident that nearly killed all of them. Most of all, though, they loved and respected the Cardosis, especially Angelina, for all that she taught them: the English language, proper dress and the ways of polite American behavior. The brothers were treated like family in Michigan and Illinois, the Italian way among countrymen. Most of all, they loved America and prayed often, thanking the Madonna and the Lord for their good fortune, a practice of faith that was embedded deeply and permanently in their souls. They would need divine graces as a critical phase of their lives lay directly in their path.

See note 10.

Notes

1. Newspaper reports, particularly from the *Chicago Tribune* and *Kankakee Gazette*, provide historical, real-time reports about the impact of the war on manufacturers in the Midwest U.S.

2. *Giomi* (Ioli) presents a description of the early Matteucci family. Published in August, 1977, Volume IV, Number 7.

3. *Segel* describes the novel Browning Model 1917 Water Cooled Machine Gun that was issued to American soldiers.

4. *Villanueva* describes the Army bands in WWI.

5. A bent pipe is one with a cross-section shape like a checkmark. It extends from the smoker's lips, turns down and then bends up, allowing the bowl to be well below the mouth and out of the field of view. Hunters, particularly, preferred bent pipe while hunting.

6. *Laskin* discusses ethnicity in the United States Army in WWI

7. *Erkoreka* discusses the Spanish Flu pandemic from a medical perspective. *Barry* offers a complete history of the pandemic.

8. *Langer* and *Morris (Barry)* present in encyclopedic form an

overview of the world events at the time. The Treaty of Versailles is discussed in detail by *Story* and *Strachan*.

9. While both families harkened from the Lucca province, their homes were about 25 miles apart, a very long distance in the late 19th Century. People tended to marry others in their locality. Second, Giannini is one of the most popular surnames in Lucca, so having the same surname is weak evidence of a familial relationship.

10. Much of the story is based on corroborated lore.

9

LOVELY WOMEN (1920–1922)

RELOADING FOR A LIFE

When Julio and Amerigo left Italy late in the 1910s, they were nothing but a couple of short, skinny ragamuffins donning worn, baggy clothes littered with holes and mismatched shoes. They were penniless, virtually uneducated and ignorant of the world. In May of 1920, they arrived in Lucca standing tall as Italian Signore (gentlemen). They had survived a mining disaster, they were United States citizens and American Army War Veterans, they could read, write and speak three languages; one was a certified technician, the other had invented a manufacturing process that directly aided the war effort, they had supplied nearly all of the financial support for their Italian families for the past decade and they had ample supplies of money in their pockets. These two men had accomplished more in ten years than most people do in lifetimes.

Each Menicucci had gained considerable weight, filling their frames into robust figures. Julio stood about five feet eleven inches and weighed about one hundred eighty-five pounds. Amerigo clocked in at six feet one and two hundred pounds. Both men were strikingly handsome with muscular shoulders and arms, smooth, clean-shaven facial features, thick heads of dark hair and confident demeanors, surefire requisites for attracting women. But their professional business prospects were the real attractions. Most young Italian women of that day would conclude that these men were excellent spousal prospects. The brothers' new social status allowed them to court women of a higher class than Colono. The family had been in the Colono trap for so long that they had no record of any family member attempting to marry above it.

When they exited the train car in Lucca, they headed into the walled city to collect gifts for their family reunion at their Segromigno home. They bought wine, new clothes and shoes befitting Signore, along with gifts for Mama. They proudly made their presence known in their community to announce their arrival and hopefully attract the interest of some young Italian women.

Raffaello and Teresa were expecting the men, but their exact arrival date was unknown. The men could have sent a cablegram to them with the ship's departure date but considered it an unnecessary expense. As they approached the home, they could see the familiar buildings and Teresa hanging up clothes to dry in the sun. When she noticed them, she screamed out in joy. Raffaello and Adelino came running to greet the men. As they approached, Teresa sank to her knees, hands folded in prayer with tears streaming down her cheeks as she thanked St. Christopher aloud for answering her prayers for her sons' safety. She rose and warmly embraced each of them. Congratulations abounded. It was a glorious day for the family as these men had finally broken the bondage of the multi-generational oppression of the Mezzadria.

Teresa immediately changed her plans for dinner. It was a grand celebration, of course. Thanks to Julio and Amerigo, the family was in much better financial condition than a decade earlier. The resources from the brothers had elevated the family from the impoverished living conditions that prevailed when they left. Aladino was well cared for and had money for discretionary expenses, such as new clothes, better food and modern farming tools. While the family was still considered lower class by Italian standards, their lifestyle had dramatically improved due to the fortunes of the two newly minted Americans. This dinner was a lavish affair of fine Italian foods and wines, perfectly appropriate for the greatest heroes in family history. Raffaello, too, was immensely grateful, as the costs of his seven-year disappearance were finally fading in light of the brothers' successes. This Menicucci family was blissful and optimistic for the first time in living memory.

That evening was the most exhilarating and satisfying in the brothers' lives. Teresa cooked a huge meal of pasta, meatballs, salad, vegetables, cheeses, fresh bread, Italian cold cuts, figs and plenty of the finest wines that Luigi Pucci had brewed. They talked for hours about their adventures, filling in details from their letters. They spoke of their mining accident and the Madonna. Teresa sat smugly as both her boys, especially

Julio, finally realized the real role of religious faith in their lives.

It was certainly good to have one of Mama's home-cooked meals, and they spent hours at the table following dinner sipping wine and catching up on all of the family happenings during their absence.

The brothers talked enthusiastically about the wonders of America, the unique governance, the abundant natural resources and especially the economic freedom to build and run a business in a rapidly growing community with little government interference. In other words, they reported that what you make in America is yours to keep—very little went to the government. They were also impressed with America's political stability; government officials came and went from political offices by a vote of the people, and power was transferred from one party to another without fanfare. From the brothers' perspectives, it was the opposite of the stream of dysfunctional governments that had plagued Italy since unification, with prime ministers and government coming and going like hotel guests, creating a perpetual wake of governmental misdirection. They also spoke of the military might of the United States, contrasting it with Italy's history of military misadventures. In sum, they relished serving on a winning team and walking away with something of value. The glory was short-lived. The next day, they began their search for a woman to marry and return with them to a new home in America. It was a generational decision of the greatest proportions, so they moved with dispatch, steely caution and the guidance of prayer.

COURTSHIP, IMMIGRANT STYLE

Marriage in those times and among people of that Italian class was more a matter of function than an idyllic vision of love. Certainly, young folks desired to marry someone with whom they were compatible, but the woman's abilities in running a household and the man's ability to support the family were more important than love at the point of courtship. Undoubtedly, the youth of that time experienced the normal excitement for the opposite sex, providing an initial attraction that can lead to the altar. Marriage was a monumental decision because of its finality. In Italy, divorce was virtually non-existent, especially among the peasant classes. There were two reasons. They could not afford it. It took a man and a wife for a successful household. More important, it was a mortal sin, which unless rectified with confession before death, dooms the person's soul to hellfire and damnation for eternity. In that society, compatibility between the man and woman was paramount because raising a family is difficult and requires a well-functioning marital team to thrive. The prevailing wisdom was that true love grew between married couples as they lived and worked together, following the church's guidance and sharing the common fruits of their labors—their children and their families.

Julio and Amerigo knew what they wanted. An ideal wife understood home economics and desired a family in America. As days passed, word spread among the community that the Menicucci men had returned, and for several days various neighbors stopped in to talk with and congratulate them. The brothers always made it known that they were interested in marriage. Young, eligible women in the area heard of these two desirable suitors.

The two men took some time to relax while they searched for women. Mushroom foraging, bird hunting and fishing consumed some of their time during the first week of their return. Both men immensely enjoyed the outdoor activities, especially angling. Their respite did not last long. The clock was ticking as their income had ceased, and they were now drawing off their savings. They knew they had to find work in Italy until they could return to America with their brides. Amerigo was a qualified, professional mason, a trade that paid reasonably well in Italy. He found work quickly. Julio worked on one or another of the family farms. So many of Pasquale male family members had immigrated to America, there were few farm laborers left. Julio's help was well appreciated wherever and whenever he was available. Naturally, the men sought opportunities for social gatherings where single women were present. Parties, sporting events, public gatherings, church services and the like were places where marriages could be spawned.[1]

The brothers continuously communicated by letter with the Cardosis and their relatives in Albuquerque to keep abreast of the situation. Cardosis noted that Bradley was experiencing a slowdown due to an economic recession that developed immediately following the war. A brief, half-year recession developed because the nation's manufacturing plants were transitioning from war goods to civilian products, which required time and money. Furthermore, it took time for the servicemen to return home and resume work. John Cardosi was certain that business would improve and claimed that Kankakee was the place for them to settle.

Meanwhile, in letters to the Menicuccis in Italy, Austutillo Giannini continued to tout his plan for the automotive service and supply business in Albuquerque. He made the argument that not only was Albuquerque a rapidly growing market, half the people in Albuquerque spoke Spanish, a language that was so similar to Italian that could learn it in just a few days. Speaking the customer's language was a business advantage, he claimed. They also heard from their aunt Amabile Morelli; she reported that the Matteucci brothers were running a thriving business at their Champion Grocery Store on the ground floor below her home. She urged the men to settle in Albuquerque. For Johnny Matteucci, there was no doubt that Albuquerque was his final destination as soon as he found a wife.

Amerigo and Julio held fast to a simple philosophy of life. The Lord God created them for a single purpose: to grow and care for a family. Julio once explained that "when a person is born as a man, he has an obligation to be a man and to take care of his family." The same applied to women. A woman's job was to nurture and care for her husband and family. There was no ambiguity involved. They also believed that while the Catholic Church provided guidance for practicing Christianity, each individual was responsible to the Lord for his or her actions in life. In other words, they believed that everyone should, at a minimum, carry their own weight in the world and eschew dependence on others for support.

A CHEF, TOO

Amerigo had been attending various events, including one in Lucca late in the Fall of 1920, the Winter Festival in Lucca. This annual, multi-day grand event in November celebrated the harvest. Music, dancing, food and drink were on tap, and Amerigo took advantage of the opportunity to meet young women.

Davina Allesandri, a young woman from Lucca, attracted him. He knew the family, as he did most people living in the neighboring area. Her father, David, was the maggiordomo (caretaker) of a large villa in the area. The villa comprised about twenty acres of land with three large villa homes, each containing about forty rooms, numerous halls, dining areas, outdoor recreational fields and other amenities to delight high-class Italian guests. A maggiordomo managed the affairs of the villa at the direction of the owners. This included maintaining the facilities and organizing dinners and other events. He was constantly busy with one task or another and naturally brought his family members in to help. It was a fine job, and his family was comfortable, certainly of a higher class than Colono. Davina worked in the kitchen, assisting professional chefs in preparing meals. She chopped vegetables, stirred polenta, tossed salads, and did other tasks. But she learned about cooking, which she took to heart, and she became an excellent cook. She also assisted in other household duties, such as washing and pressing clothing. She received the equivalent of advanced training in home economics.

Davina immediately took a liking to Amerigo and they talked. She later recalled "how handsome this man was." She noted his large hands and powerful upper body and was impressed at his tales of America and his adventures. Without the American experience on his resume, he likely would have had no hope of marrying such a woman. Plus, she was immediately sold on America. That evening, she talked about Amerigo with her father and mother. They knew the family, and Amerigo's reputation preceded him to the festival. David reported that Amerigo was "a good man" and that Davina would do well with him in life. Some Allesandris had already immigrated to San Francisco and were doing well. The family encouraged her to pursue Amerigo with confidence.

Amerigo called on her a few days later, and they spent some time talking in the Villa and discussing their goals in life. Davina was eager to live in America and was moved by Amerigo's description of how that country differed from Italy. Economic opportunity, he reported, was the main attraction. They left the visit with a promise to meet again.

Davina's mother, Armida Ferroni Allesandri, suggested inviting Amerigo to dinner, which she prepared as a personal gift to him. If anything will sway a man in her favor, Armida claimed, a fine meal with plenty of wine will do it. Davina posted a note to Amerigo inviting him to dinner. When Amerigo received the note, he was ecstatic. He liked Davina and would now experience her cooking, a sign of a capable family woman. He quickly responded with an affirmative message and prepared for the dinner. As the date approached, he groomed himself carefully, shaving and trimming his hair. He put on his best formal clothes and hiked to Davina's home.

Davina, meanwhile, was busy working with Armida to prepare the dinner. She prepared her best dish, white-wine-brazed pigeons with polenta. She also prepared various side dishes of vegetables and a huge fresh salad. For dessert, she made Zuppa Inglese. Dinner commenced with cocktails, which David prepared as he did for villa events.

When Amerigo arrived, he was greeted by David, who welcomed him warmly as a likely future son-in-law. He took Amerigo into the living area, where Armida and other family members sat. David announced that Davina was busy preparing the meal, which she had prepared completely on her own, a signal to Amerigo. The parents used the time to get to know Amerigo in more detail, hearing about his plans for America and his prospects for work. Amerigo entertained the family with stories of his adventures in America. They were mesmerizing. This man was a local hero indeed. David said little, carefully assessing whether this man was worthy of his daughter and her dowry. In contrast to Colono families, David had been saving for his daughters' dowries. He had fifty dollars available (about eight hundred eighty in 2024 dollars) for Amerigo on the wedding day. He saw the entire affair as an investment in the Menicucci family.

The meal lasted for hours as Davina regularly delivered course after course from the kitchen and placed the aromatic plates on the table. David had provided some fine Chianti, the type he regularly purchased for Villa dinners. Amerigo ate heartily, enjoying both the company and the exceptional Italian cuisine. As they finished the meal, David sent his other daughters to clean up the table so that Davina could spend time with the group. They discussed family issues and philosophy over coffee and biscotti, which Davina had prepared. By the time dinner ended, David and Armida were convinced that Amerigo was the right man for Davina. Amerigo said his goodbyes with ample praise for Davina's work.

When Amerigo arrived back home, the family was awaiting his report. He described the meal, the discussions and his conclusion to the family. "If this kind of food is what I will get for a whole life, then it's good for me," he quipped. He was going to marry Davina. Raffaello and Teresa were pleased. Amerigo sent a note to Davina the following day asking if he could visit her. She agreed and expected a marriage proposal or an end to the courtship. She had no worries. As soon after Amerigo arrived at her home, he proposed they marry and relocate to the United States to make their home. She happily agreed and quickly announced the upcoming marriage to her father. David was delighted and congratulated Amerigo, welcoming him to the family. He would be losing a daughter in more than just through the marriage; she would be physically thousands of miles away. He informed Amerigo that he would receive her dowry after the ceremony and wished him the grace of the Lord.

Davina and Armida wed on February 19, 1921. It was a typical

Catholic church wedding, hosting many guests with the marriage at Davina's church in Lucca. Interestingly, Emmanual Menicucci witnessed the wedding, but he was not part of the Menicucci family in Lucca. Likely, he was related, probably a descendant from Paolo Menicucci's family, making him a cousin. Julio certainly attended the ceremony but is not listed on the marriage record. The newly married couple enjoyed a short honeymoon in Northern Italy. In those days and among people of that class, a honeymoon was not the wispy romantic experience prevalent in Twenty-First Century America. It was more of a time of acquaintance and adjustment and, of course, the first sexual encounter. I am certain there was a fair amount of romance among couples, even the peasants; they were Italians, after all. A honeymoon was an exciting time for the couple because the church forbade premarital sexual contact of any kind, and the rule was strictly enforced by fathers of daughters. The honeymoon was the deliverance of one of life's greatest pleasures.[2]

The couple returned to Lucca to live with Davina's parents until they could leave for America. Amerigo talked with Julio about his plans and decided to return to Kankakee to work while waiting for Julio to join him. He contacted the Cardosis and learned that while jobs were still somewhat scarce due to the recession, he encouraged them to return. Given what they had previously contributed, Bradley was proud to hire any Menicuccis. Cardosi had a room that the couple could use.

In early May 1921, Amerigo and his bride purchased tickets for steamer passage to America. They planned to travel out of Genoa and arrive in Boston. On May 16th, they said farewells to their families, including a tearful departure between Davina and her two sisters. Davina had no experience traveling and had never left their home, except for some visits to the walled city of Lucca. They traveled in steerage class on the Princess Matuika, scheduled for arrival in Boston, Massachusetts about a week later. Amerigo could have afforded second-class passage, but he considered that an extravagance, even for a new bride. Frugality was the modis operendi with the Menicucci brothers.

Amerigo was an experienced traveler and led Davina through the immigration process. By marriage, upon arrival she became an American citizen. By the end of May, they arrived at the Cardosis, where they were greeted as returning family. They remained there until Julio arrived. The couple spent the evening discussing their new marriage and their plans. The following day Amerigo returned to Bradley where he assumed the same position as a molder. His pay was increased substantially from his previous employment. Angelina immediately began Americanizing Davina, just as she did earlier for Amerigo and Julio.[3] Davina was already an experienced cook, especially with gourmet meals. She helped Angelina.

WINE, INDEED

Julio worked hard to catch up with his brother. He had his sights on several women he had met but had nothing secured. One day Eufamia and Guilia Gragnani paid a call to Teresa. Teresa's sister, Amabele Rondina, was married to Francesco Morelli, whose son, Raffaello, married Marietta Gragnani Morelli. Giulia, Eufamia and Marietta were siblings. The women had visited for a while when Julio entered the room and was introduced to the women by Teresa. He had been gone so long that he was not fully aware of his mother's family relations. Julio took an immediate liking to Giulia. Plus, the family was well known and reasonably prosperous, certainly well above Colono.

After they left, Teresa noticed that one of the visiting women had left an umbrella at the home. Julio immediately saw the opportunity to court Giulia. The next day, he took the umbrella back to Giulia's home in Ponte a Moriano, several miles to the west of the Menicucci's home. He visited with Giulia and her family for a while. Naturally, Julio proudly listed his accomplishments in America, wowing the folks with his tales of adventures in the mines and war. Giulia was interested in the young man, but she had recently broken up with a man she had planned to marry, so she was cautious. Julio asked if he could see her again and she agreed.

Later, she discussed Julio with her father, Luigi. The Menicucci and Gragnani families were already intermarried; The Menicucci family was acceptable. The issue was whether Julio measured up to their standards. Like Amerigo, Julio's reputation preceded him. Julio was a good man, and Luigi reported that his aspirations to build a family in America were excellent. Several family members had migrated to Albuquerque, and all were doing well. He shined the green light on the marriage. Giulia was still reluctant due to her recent pre-marital difficulties and prohibition in the U.S. Wine was an essential part of her life for cooking and drinking. Without wine, she was not interested in America.

It was the middle of 1921 and there was no time to waste. Julio set his sights on Giulia and was determined to secure her in marriage. On the second meeting, Julio took her to a summer gathering in Lucca. She liked Julio and was impressed with his credentials for marriage, but she brought up the prohibition problem. She told him she needed several glasses of wine daily, and America did not allow it. Julio immediately had the answer: Americans could ferment and keep their alcoholic beverages, and he knew how to ferment wine. He pledged to supply as much wine as the family needed. That instantly eliminated a major obstacle and they parted with an agreement to meet again.

Julio let no grass grow under his feet. A day later he sent a note requesting a meeting with Giulia at her home. In a private place, which the family readily provided, he proposed marriage to her, stipulating that she would have the wine she needed every day. That was all it took and she accepted. On July 23, 1921, they were married in a small Catholic ceremony in Ponte a Moriano, Province of Lucca, in the chapel of Archbishop Volpe. Johnny Matteucci was Julio's Best Man.[4]

Wedding of Giulia Gragnani and Julio Menicucci. Courtesy author's collection.

HURRY

They planned to honeymoon in Italy and sail for America, with the destination of Kankakee where he would join his brother. Only a few weeks after the honeymoon, Giulia was confirmed pregnant. This lit a fire under Julio because he wanted the birth on American soil to ensure instant citizenship for his child. Giulia experienced morning sickness and Julio was concerned about the angry winter Atlantic seas. He believed that a southern sea route was potentially smoother. After a few weeks of preparations, they boarded the Giuseppe Verdi, sailing from Naples in November 1921 and arriving in New York Harbor on December 5, 1921. Despite all of Julio's planning, it was a horrible trip. Miserable steerage conditions coupled with sea sickness created unpleasant conditions for normal passengers. But Giulia was already nauseous when she boarded the ship. Once the ship moved out to sea, she vomited almost constantly, could hold down very little food and was completely debilitated by the cold and humidity, both of which were intense. It was a poor time to travel the Atlantic, but Julio could not delay further. The future of the Menicucci family rested on his shoulders.

As the ship maneuvered into the port at New York, Julio prepared for customs. He was a citizen, but he had an infirmed wife, a situation that always raised flags for the port authorities. Like Amerigo, Julio knew the process at Ellis Island, and he did the talking. Sea sickness is what he declared to customs for his wife's condition and her pregnancy, common afflictions that were passed over by authorities. He and Giulia were quickly paraded through. They immediately walked to the rail depot and boarded a train to Kankakee.

The two-day trip to Illinois was an improvement over the ship, but not much, as Giulia remained miserable and weak from a lack of food and sleep. Julio did all he could to comfort her, but she was beyond comfort and sometimes wondered what she had gotten herself into. As previously agreed, they planned to rendezvous at the Cardosis while they decided where they might permanently settle.

They arrived in Kankakee at Christmas time. They were greeted warmly by the Cardosi family, and especially Amerigo. Angelina quickly came to assist Giulia, who was in poor condition and showed it. Angelina sat her down and placed a blanket over her shoulders. She quickly warmed some brodo (bone broth) and Italian bread, which she brought to her as she rested. As the hours passed, Giulia's condition improved, and the nutrition, wine, and familiar Italian atmosphere breathed life back into her. She chatted with Angelina about the pregnancy and her adventures on the sea. Angelina's charm worked on Giulia like it had on her new husband. America was looking a little better to Giulia.

DREARY BEGINNING

While Giulia was recovering, Julio learned about the latest family crisis, which had Amerigo in a major state of unrest. He reported that Davina had been feeling poorly and felt feverish. The day before, he had taken her to a physician in Kankakee. She was diagnosed with tuberculosis, he said in a depressing tone. The doctor said it was a serious condition and recommended that she move to a dry climate in the western U.S. for treatment. Amerigo was conflicted and confused. He was doing well at Bradley, advancing professionally with a good future. He liked Ausutillo Giannini as his cousin, but he was cautious about his ostentatiousness. Now he learned his new wife might die.

Julio took command of the situation, addressing his brother again as mio uomo (my man), calming and assuring him that all would be fine. Then he laid out the case for Albuquerque. They had family there: Giulia's sister Marietta, the Morellis and the Gianninis. Ausutillo Giannini had offered them part ownership of this tire repair business, which was a long-time quest of the two men. It was a foothold for them in business. The Matteuccis—Johnny and his brothers and sisters—lived in Albuquerque along with many other Lucchese, all thriving. It was a dry climate, which was exactly what the doctor recommended for Davina. Further, Albuquerque was known for its tuberculosis treatment facilities, where several Lucchese were successfully treated. He declared that they were traveling to Albuquerque as soon as they could purchase passage, and Giulia had recovered. Once John Cardosi observed Julio's leadership, he backed off his proposals for the family to remain in Kankakee. Julio had spoken.[5]

As Angelina Cardosi looked after the ailing women in the ensuing days towards their departure, Julio sent telegrams to his cousin Ausutillo Giannini, accepting his offer to join his tire business and to his aunt Amabele Morelli, asking for help in locating housing for them. Amerigo bought train tickets for the following day. Amerigo and Davina packed their belongings for the trip, but Julio and Giulia never unpacked theirs from their arrival a few days earlier.

They boarded a train for Albuquerque the following day and arrived just after Christmas 1921. Giulia was pregnant, Davina had tuberculosis, and both women were ill, in poor spirits and sleepless for the entire train trip. Giulia had been nauseous to one degree or another since the day the ship departed Naples and was noticeably losing weight, not a preferable condition during pregnancy. Among the four of them, only Giulia could speak no English. The men, of course, were completely fluent. Davina and Amerigo had lived with the Cardosis while Julio was returning to America with Giulia. Angelina tutored Davina in English but not with the vigor she applied to the men. She foresaw the men, the family breadwinners, in an American business where English fluency is critical. In the Italian custom, women were destined for homemaking where the language skills were not as acute. Still, the Cardosis only spoke English in their home, so it was nearly impossible for boarders not to learn some. Davina was roughly conversant in English when she boarded the train to Albuquerque but well short of fluency. Giulia was not at the Cardosi home long enough to pick up any English. It was the first major test of Julio's leadership as he felt the weight of responsibility for five lives, one of them in a womb.

For Julio, his family responsibility now precluded all other concerns. These people lived by the rule of the Lord, as the Catholic Church defined it. While gender defined certain natural roles for men and women, all will be equal in the paradise of Heaven. Simply put, they believed that at birth, the Lord imbues each person with unique physical and mental assets for a specific role in life. Each person is responsible for developing those assets to their maximum potential in the short time they live on earth. Most importantly, they believed their greatest duty to the Lord was to grow a healthy, productive family.

CLEAR-SKY HELL

The families' arrival in Albuquerque was more of a reprieve from torment than a joyous occasion, especially for the two infirmed women. The city's desert climate provided no immediate relief. Albuquerque was a small, western city situated along the banks of the Rio Grande River. Its size and operation were analogous to the fictional town of Mayberry on the long-running Andy Griffith Show of the 1960s. Along either side of the river lay one of the greatest cottonwood forests in the world, locally called the bosque, Spanish for forest. Beyond the river, though, the landscape was barren with open land, few trees and plenty of dusty open land. Buildings were scattered about town, with only a few multi-story buildings. Few streets were paved, rendering them mud bogs during the summer rains and icy rinks in winter. It was a shock to people accustomed to Lucca's verdant lushness. Guilia later said of her first impression of the city: "When I got off that train in Albuquerque and saw no trees, I thought I'd died and gone to hell." Davina, too, was depressed and longing for the comfort of her mother and sisters as she dealt with her medical condition. The brothers had two distressed and grumpy young women to care for. For all the misery the women endured on the trip, the one bright spot was the deep blue skies that graced Albuquerque nearly year-round. Both women marveled at the clarity of the skies in the dry desert air.

The California Limited train arriving from the north at Albuququeque's Alvarado Train Depot, circa 1925. Courtesy Albuquerque Museum, a gift of John Airy, Photographer: Cobb Studio.

Immediately after arriving in Albuquerque, Julio sent Americo on a fast trot to his aunt's home to inform her that they had arrived. Meanwhile, Julio was arranging for some transportation for the women who were physically weak and needed medical care. Aunt Amabile was delighted to see Amerigo on her doorstep and welcomed him briskly into the home. She provided coffee and said that she had arranged for housing for both new families in boarding rooms that Lucchese owned and operated. A short time later, Julio arrived with the two women in a mule-pulled cart, an early 1920s version of a taxi. Gasoline-powered taxi cabs were just beginning to penetrate the American market but none had made its way to Albuquerque.

That night, they stayed with Amabele, but the next day, Amerigo and Davina settled into a small, furnished home at 505 Tijeras Street, and Julio and Giulia settled into furnished housing at 418 Second Street, just a few blocks away. This small, dry, remote, high-desert community of fifteen thousand—one entirely different from Lucca—was their home.

In early 1920, the Menicuccis traveled to Italy to acquire wives and return to America to settle. After nearly two years of travel and intensive effort, they had accomplished their objectives. It was a difficult start to their new life in America, but their adventure was only beginning.

See notes 6, 7, 8.

Notes

1. *Berry* and *Little* present summary articles about Italian wedding traditions. *Alter* discusses marriage practices in Europe in the 19th Century. Although many wedding traditions are common among Italians, each family had its traditions, most centered on Catholicism.

2. Davina's birth record can be found in the Portale Atenanti. Record #163, posted on October 10, 1897. Her date of birth was October 7, 1897. Throughout her life, she listed her birth as October 12, 1898. The records are located in the comune of Capannori, frazzione of Segromigno.

3. The words Americanize and Americanization represented the process of acclimating an immigrant with American customs, norms and societal practices. The American public supported rapid assimilation of immigrants into American society.

4. Giulia birth record can be found in the Portale Atenanti. Record #187 posted on September 17, 1897. Her date of birth was September 13, 1897. The record of her marriage to Giulio Menicucci is posted on

February 19, 1921. The records are located in the comune of Lucca, frazzione of Ponte a Moriano.

5. Albuquerque was becoming well-known nationally for tuberculosis treatment. *Lewis (Nancy)* describes it.

6. This story is well-documented in lore and is typical of how Italian men sought women for marriage. Many others in the Italian Colony, such as Johnny Matteucci, returned to Italy for wives and then returned to America to live.

7. *DeMark's* work includes many statistical and geographical details about the history of Albuquerque's New Town from the late 1800s to 1920. *Neel's* Masters Thesis describes the history of Albuquerque from it inception to around 1925.

8. The historic, real-time stories in the *Albuquerque Journal* provide valuable resources about individuals in the city. Because of its size, news articles reported on such items as when certain people were vacationing or a woman hosting a celebratory party. *Journal* news reports about a private gathering often included the participants' names and employment status, the foods or gifts each contributed, and any interesting personal information about the host. Over time, as the city grew, such details became less common, but in the 1920s, the stories were replete with personal information.

10

HELLO ALBUQUERQUE
(1922–1926)

TUBERCULIN PREGNANCY

The first order of business after unpacking was to have Davina medically examined so that she could begin a course of treatment for tuberculous. At that time, treatment was crude and mostly experimental. The Germans had developed a process in which the infected lungs were temporarily collapsed and subsequently allowed to heal free of the infection. It was a difficult and painful therapy with less-than-stellar results.[1]

They turned to Dr. John Reidy, whose office was just a couple of blocks away. John was one of two Reidys who practiced medicine downtown. tuberculosis in 1922 was serious, so Reidy rushed her in. After some examination, Reidy asked Amerigo to step into the examining room with him and Davina. Amerigo was expecting bad news as he looked at a grinning doctor. "Davina does not have tuberculosis; she is pregnant," Reidy said as he extended his hand in congratulations. Reidy explained that the symptoms of early pregnancy can sometimes mimic those of tuberculosis, excusing the misdiagnosis of his medical colleague in Illinois. Amerigo was flabbergasted and Davina was overjoyed.

Amerigo had been bracing for the worst news, that his new wife might die, and now the situation was turned on its head. Not only was she perfectly healthy, but she was also perfectly pregnant, and he would soon be a father. Naturally, he and Davina were eager to spread the good word, and they hurried back home. Amerigo sped off to inform Julio. Soon the good news was circulating among the Italians in the colony. Amabile was first to walk over to congratulate them. Matteuccis brought some appropriate maternity gifts from their stock at Champion. Others followed, including a jubilant Giulia. Now she had a sister-in-law to share the childbirth experience. It was a time to celebrate and they did.

It was a typical reaction in Albuquerque's Italian colony because many had direct roots in Lucca province, about half from Capannori. Families who lived as neighbors in Italy often became neighbors in Albuquerque. The families knew each other and acted according to their customary traditions. In Italy, mostly family members and close friends celebrated an event like this. In Albuquerque, families were young with few relatives. Thus, Albuquerque's small Italian community became its own family, substituting friends for missing family members at celebrations and assisting in stressful times.

Davina was due to deliver in May, about a month before Giulia. In the minds of these people, this turn of fate could only be ascribed to the work of the Lord. They made a special visit to the Immaculate Conception Church, lighting votive candles to thank the Lord for their good fortune and to ask the Madonna to help bring healthy babies into the world. All four immediately liked the church because of its namesake, adorning the Madonna.

Many Catholic Churches in America were named after various historic incarnations of the Virgin Mary. The Virgin plays an outsized role in Catholicism but in terms of Virgin reverence, the Immaculate Conception always believed it was the leader. The church was replete with themes of Mary, led by wall mosaics, rows of stained-glass windows and elaborate statues. It was the most ostentatious religious display of Mariology in the city. It fits the wider community because the native Hispanic community and the Irish immigrants, both fervently Catholic, comprised nearly half the population in Albuquerque and held similar reverence for the Virgin Mother. Regarding religion, the Italians slipped almost effortlessly into the local societal scene.

COUSINS UNITE

Julio concentrated on business and met with Austutillo Giannini and Amerigo. The first thing the Menicuccis learned is that Giannini had changed his given name to Johnny. He explained that it was a simpler name to pronounce and sounded American, a very important factor in business. In addition, although not stated, was the alliterative ring of Johnny coupled with Giannini. Julio and Amerigo had already Americanized their given names. Julio got his new name in the Army, and Amerigo was sometimes known as Henry. The names Amerigo and Enrico almost rhyme, and most Americans were familiar with Enrico, which is Italian for Henry. Amerigo retained his Italian name for life, except among select friends who occasionally referred to him as Henry.

Johnny set out the terms for the Menicucci brothers to buy into his Safety First Tire Company. In 1921, he acquired the company with the financial assistance of Frank Petroni and Mario Bonaguidi, both early Twentieth Century immigrants. Mario was Johnny's father-in-law and was living with his family. Frank Petroni's sister was the wife of Amedeo Matteucci, a close friend of the family. Johnny needed their investment, but they were silent partners in the business. The plan was for Frank and Mario to retain ownership in the company until they could sell their interest to the Menicucci brothers at a profit. Frank and Mario had already agreed on the price and terms. When Johnny cut this deal, the Menicuccis had not yet decided to return to Albuquerque, but he was confident that he could persuade them. Johnny was a compelling and aggressive salesman. All that the brothers needed to do was sign the paper and pay.[2]

The agreement was for Frank and Mario to sell their share of the business to the Menicuccis. Johnny retained ownership of the land. The entire transaction, handwritten on a single page, consumed about twenty minutes and money was exchanged in cash, exhausting nearly all of the brothers' savings. From a prima facia perspective, what appeared to be a chancy business endeavor was relatively safe because all the participants were direct family or close Lucchese. Amerigo and Julio were equal partners in purchasing the business as their savings had been pooled since they joined the Franklin Jr. mine. Even when Julio was awarded a fee for the foundry invention, he saw it as "their" money and lumped it into a joint fund. Though Amerigo had accumulated more savings than Julio in the Army, every penny he earned was added to the brothers' joint savings.

A FAMILY DEAL

In the Safety First deal, Johnny retained fifty-one percent, a majority ownership so that he could control business decisions. Johnny smelled opportunity and he didn't want anyone in his way. Petroni and Bonaguidi provided startup money, but they offered no day-to-day support. Johnny alone built and ran the operation. Now, with two young, healthy and powerful first cousins at his side, he had the team to thrive in a burgeoning frontier community.

At that time, and especially in the Italian colony, land and business ownership were not always synonymous. Typically, a sound business was located on land it owned or controlled through lease agreements. A typical small Italian business in 1920s Albuquerque might have been located on land it neither owned nor controlled. The risks were low as long as it stayed more or less in the family.

The trust level among Albuquerque's Italian families was extraordinarily high, even by Italian standards. The Italian colonists were deprived of one of the most dependable sources of social support: the immediate and extended family, which in Italy sprawled back over generations in families that were concentrated in small communities. In Italy, each family had many closely related relatives for direct support. Most of Albuquerque's Italian immigrants had few, if any, generational relatives in town. Moreover, communicating with Italy was difficult and time-consuming. A letter from Albuquerque took weeks to arrive in Lucca. Even an emergency telegram required days. In the absence of blood relatives, all Italians in the colony became family members to one degree or another. The Lucchese were dominant in the colony and most families knew each other in Lucca, so they were an especially close subgroup in the colony.[3] Intermarriage was common in the subgroup and so were business partnerships. Within the colony, any historical animosity between the Lucchese and Italian southerners was unapparent. Even Sicilians, who had for generations carried the stigma of the Mafia, intermingled with other Italians in town. Physical distance from their homeland mitigated prejudice. When emergencies arose among any Italian families in Albuquerque, Lucchese responded to Sicilians like family members. And vice versa. Only the Italians recognized that Safety First was a Lucchese operation. To Anglos and Hispanics, it was just an Italian business.

There were casualties with this freewheeling business approach, as Amerigo pointed out to Julio. Johnny Matteucci had repeatedly told the story of Amedeo and Alessandro Matteucci, his two brothers, who had engaged in a bitter dispute regarding a business arrangement based on a misunderstanding about ownership. The situation led to a two-decade mutual estrangement. In the 1910s, Alessandro was one of the most discussed Italian immigrants. He was boisterous and tough, and some admired him for his spunk. But his antics cost him his race for Sheriff in 1920 when the Democrats forced him to confront his record.[4, 5]

Those downbeat stories did not bother Julio. He and Johnny were steaming ahead-full on the Safety First deal. Amerigo, meanwhile, was pondering how it was going to work. Johnny's arguments made perfect sense. With the auto industry growing, vehicle owners needed three important products: fuel, lubricants and tires, the focus of Safety First Tire Company. His concern was that while he and Julio knew farming, mining, forging and masonry, none of these skills overlapped with any business needs. They needed training, which he hoped to get from Johnny, who had worked for E.E. Bliss, a tire wholesaler in Albuquerque. Johnny started work as a twelve-year-old and was a recognized expert vulcanizer.

Vulcanization is the process of curing liquid rubber into a hard, durable material appropriate for automobile tires. In the early days of the auto industry, tires were one of the most fragile parts of a vehicle and comprised the majority of auto repairs. Rubber tires had no protective steel belts or other linings on the wear surfaces; thus, they were susceptible to cuts from rocks or other sharp objects on the mostly unpaved roads. A vulcanizer cuts out the damaged section of a tire, fills the hole with liquid rubber and cures it in place, effectively patching the tire and allowing it to accept an inflatable tube. It was the primary skill needed by auto service shops of the day. Experts like Johnny Giannini commanded top dollar for his repairs.

Amerigo also knew he would run the tire shop while Johnny and Julio were out drumming up business and seeking new business deals. Johnny and Julio thrived on each other's exuberance, sometimes to the exclusion of practical matters. Amerigo knew nothing about running a business but had learned much about organizational operations while in Kankakee and the Army. Being unskilled and unprepared for a job was nothing new to the brothers, so in Amerigo's mind it was not a matter of whether, but how fast they would be up to speed.

DIRT FLOORS AND DRAFTY ROOMS

While the men were out making money for their families, Giulia and Davina were doing their jobs building homes and preparing for the births of their first children. Amerigo's quarters on West Tijeras Avenue were marginal—a shed in Pietro Dinelli family's backyard that was converted to a boarding home. It measured seven hundred square feet, including a living area, a kitchenette with cold running water, a bathroom with a toilet and large wash basin, but no tub. They used a single coal stove for space- and water heating and cooking. Several electric light bulbs hung from the ceiling.

Julio's apartment was on North Second Street and similarly rudimentary. It was an addition to a home owned by Ettore Franchini that he rented. Over half of the building had dirt floors. The houses were sparsely furnished with low-cost items. The windows were so poorly sealed that high winds swayed the curtains. These were challenging conditions for the women because these accommodations were far below the Italian standards to which they were accustomed. Further, they had no immediate family to lean on for help. In Italian culture, an expecting woman's principal advisor was her mother.

Naturally, the women turned to their family in Albuquerque for assistance, specifically from their aunts Amabele Rondina Morelli and Adelina Menicucci Giannini (Johnny Giannini's mother), Menicucci relations, and Giulia's older sister, Marietta Grangnani Morelli. They all lived within a few blocks of one another and interacted freely. Both aunts assisted the women in planning the home for the family and finding the materials they needed. Giulia needed rugs to defend against the dirt floors.

The women purchased various kitchen items, such as pots, pans and various utensils. Naturally, they procured statues of the Madonna, which adorned and protected both homes. They stayed busy through the late winter and spring preparing for the babies. The two women did little direct shopping themselves, mainly because they were not familiar with American markets and due to language differences.[6] They listed what they needed and the men did their duty to provide it

ALBUQUERQUE'S LITTLE LUCCA

In 1925, Albuquerque's Italian colony was concentrated downtown; seventy five percent were Lucchese. (See Appendix II). For many immigrants, opening a grocery store was an easy first step into business. Grocery stores sell products that the population needs to survive. Subsistence was not the only issue in the colony; immigrants wanted Italian culinary staples that typified their homeland.

Bread, olive oil and wine were hallmarks of Italian diets. Bread was available from several local bakers, one of them, Union Bakery, a family-owned enterprise run by James Giomi and Attilo Santori, a brother-in-law to James. James was born Jacopino but Americanized his name. The Domenicis sold some of the finest olive oil on the planet at their Montezuma Market. Gradi & Domenici brand olive oil was produced in Lucca from local olives. The Gradis and Domenicis were related from Marlia, a Lucca comune where the families lived. Antonio and Cherubino were sons of Luigi Domenici and Teresa Marchi. The familiar two-liter oil tins with its distractive and flowery green decorations were in almost every Italian kitchen pantry. Eventually, most of the other Italian purveyors carried it.[7]

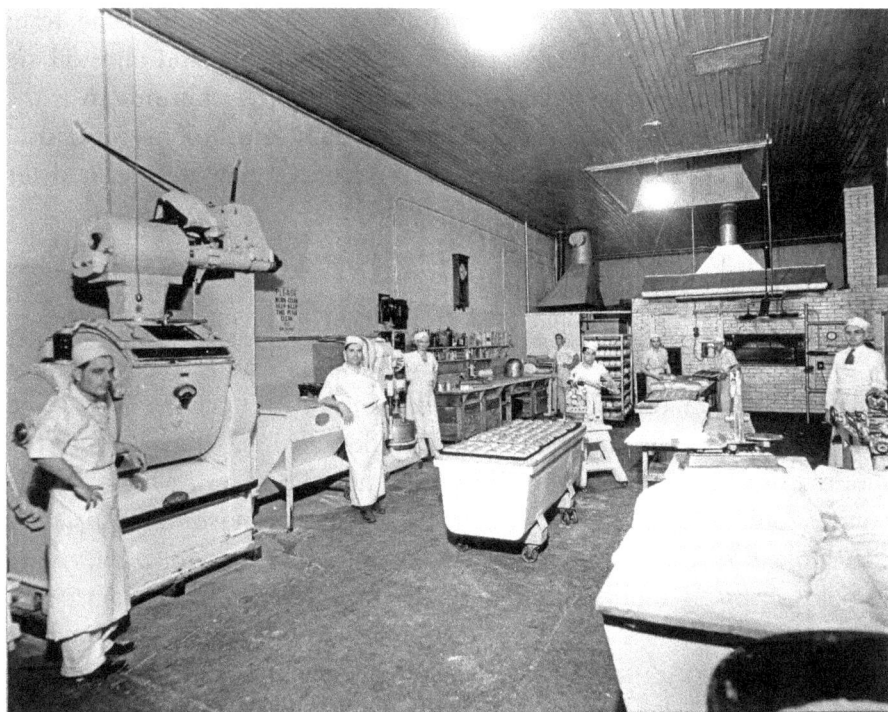

Interior of Union Bakery owned and operated by the Giomi family in the 1920s. The individuals are not identified but likely contained members of the Giomi family. Courtesy Giomi family.[8]

Wine was the biggest challenge. Neither Julio nor Amerigo had the equipment nor the room to produce wine. The problem was the law, which prohibited the transport of alcoholic beverages. Technically, it meant that giving a bottle of wine to another person for consumption in their home was illegal because the transaction required transportation. It was common for families to make large batches of wine and share it with other family members. Sharing was rarely prosecuted as long as money was not exchanged and the total volume was reasonable—as defined by the local authorities. Julio had promised Giulia that she would have wine daily, but it weighed on him. As was common in those days and until prohibition was repealed, groups of Italians worked in teams to produce large batches of wine—hundreds of gallons each—distributed to each team member. Julio was relieved to find many Italians in town and took them on as wine-making team members.

Similarly, the Menicuccis scrounged Porcini mushrooms from other Italians, particularly close friends or family. Wine and olive oil are important in an Italian kitchen, but the prized Porcini mushroom is the next priority. Many Italian dishes depend on these mushrooms for critical flavor enhancements, and in times of abundance, they are prepared for main courses.

SIMPLE DOG SENSE

Oreste Bachechi was a vigorous mushroom hunter, as were most Italians. Early in the Century, he and some other Lucchese discovered the Jemez Mountains, located about 75 miles north of Albuquerque. The mountains were similar to the Apennines near Lucca, with high-altitude conifer forests. He and several others had harvested mushrooms in Jemez that looked, smelled and felt like the Porcini growing in Italy. They were initially skeptical about the safety of the New Mexico mushrooms; they were well aware that dangerous mushrooms can sometimes mimic edible ones. To determine edibility, they cut up a Jemez Porcino (singular form of porcini) and fed it to their dogs in increasing amounts. After a day, the Porcino was gone, the dogs wanted more, and they had the green light to harvest New Mexico's version of Italian Porcini. In fact, the type of Porcini growing in Jemez was closely related to the Italian Porcini. Called the Boletus Barrowsii, this mushroom species grows exclusively in northern New Mexico and Southern Colorado. Mushrooms attracted many Italians to Jemez, where groups of families ascended into the mountains for a day of picnicking and mushroom foraging.

A closeup of a young Porcino growing in Jemez Mountain high country.
Courtesy author's collection.

Johnny Giannini, Antonio Domenici and Amedeo Matteucci, all took the brothers to Jemez on mushroom forays and fishing trips. The Menicuccis would not own vehicles for many years to come. Upon visiting the highlands of Jemez, both Menicuccis were delighted. It was relatively close to Albuquerque, about a three-hour trip one way and replete with natural resources similar to Lucca's. What is more, there were unique resources, such as the natural, steaming hot, mineral-rich spring water welling up from the ground, producing pools of water for bathers. Amergo was most interested in the baths because he believed that wet-heat was a good curative agent for whatever physical ailment might plague you. Some springs were cool but contained abundant dissolved minerals. In Italy, Italians drank water laced with various toxic chemicals. It was supposedly an elixir for various internal ailments and depression. Many Italians experimented with different kinds of natural mineral waters that sprung up around Jemez—even Arsenic-laced water. The level of Arsenic in the water must have been low because they drank it, claimed it helped and never attributed illness to it. Arsenic water is no longer sold or advertised as a health drink.

Fresh mushroom resting on screens in preparation for slicing and drying; circa 1930. Courtesy author's collection.

BACHECHI FAMILY LEADS

By 1925, the Bachechis had been in Albuquerque for two generations. Not only did Oreste encourage emigration from Lucca to Albuquerque, but he was extraordinarily helpful in the community. He provided low-cost housing for immigrants—including my maternal grandmother Pia Barsanti Dalle. The Bachechis were popular, well-known and strong advocates for Italian immigrants in the area. The family was an advocate for the Menicucci brothers. Oreste was impressed and saw them as potential rising stars in the business community. Like any good community leader, he abetted them in various endeavors. The Bachechis introduced many local Italians to the mayor and commissioners. The family also helped immigrants to understand the local politics. In his many letters back to Lucca, Oreste often touted the local immigrants' business successes as examples of the economic opportunities that lay waiting for immigrants.

He proved it in Albuquerque. The Menicuccis did not know the Bachechis in Italy, but developed lifelong business and personal relationships in Albuquerque. Oreste's and Maria's son Victor eventually became one of the closest friends of the Menicuccis.

The Bachecis had both capital to invest and advice to provide. Oreste and his wife Maria had been in Albuquerque for twenty-five years and ran two successful businesses, one operated exclusively by Maria. She was the first Italian woman to break the mold of women's domestic exclusivity by doing as many women in the Twenty-First Century do: raising a family while maintaining a professional business career. Maria was an excellent businesswoman, and she brought on Armida Bonaguidi Napoleone, spouse to Nick Napoleone, to open and operate the Bachechi Dry Goods Company. She also organized and operated the Italian Women's Study Club, which educated young Italian immigrant women in the English language, and acquainted them with American societal practices and customs. As part of their business, Armida organized the Italian Women's Sewing Club, where she trained youngsters in knitting, sewing, crocheting, needlepoint and other similar crafts. Not only did the club provide a social haven to meet and exchange information, but it also helped businesses. Teaching the women new crafts created a demand for sewing products from the Dry Goods store. Maria and Armida were the first Italian women to operate a business in Albuquerque.

Davina, being personable and outgoing, was quick to join the groups. Giulia was more reserved and preferred to remain home, letting Julio interact with the community. Oreste, a saloon keeper before prohibition, opened several new businesses, including the Pastime Theater, the New India Theater and Anchor Milling.

Giulia spent much time with her sister, who had two children, Emma and Gina, and they had lived in Albuquerque for a decade. Giulia felt comfortable with her sister at her side as she slowly adapted to Albuquerque's desert climate and the mixed cultures in the area. Julio and Amerigo were contented that the women were progressing well because it freed them to concentrate on their main job—building a firm economic future for their family by growing a profitable business. Like their husbands a decade earlier, these women were young and ignorant of the world, especially in a tiny community tucked away in the corner of the Southwest United States. Like the men, they learned rapidly how to assimilate into American society by using the Italian resources, most importantly the collective Lucchese resource in New Town Albuquerque.

During the middle 1920s, many department stores selling household merchandise were positioning themselves downtown, including JC Penny, Kistler-Colister, Meyer & Meyer, Baker Dollar Stores and Popular Dry Goods. However, new products were too expensive for the Menicuccis, so they spread the word in the Italian community about their needs and people responded, offering to sell, barter, or loan the needed articles. Some other better-established immigrants, such as the Matteuccis, Domenicis, Bachechis, Del Fartes, Petronis and Giomis, operated well-established, successful businesses and were quick to provide employment opportunities, loans and business advice.

SNUFF 'N MORE HIGHS

The brothers snuffed while wandering around Jemez. Snuff is finely ground tobacco that can be sucked into one's nasal cavity so that it releases nicotine directly into the bloodstream. They loved the quick nicotine rush from a healthy pinch of Copenhagen snuff. Julio once commented that it was like a "slap on the back of the head." He was right; I tried it several times. What they often overlooked in their praise of snuff was the sickly, brown mess it made of handkerchiefs used to blow the snuff out of their noses. It resembled a glistening, dirty diaper. After a good blow, the men walked away and shook off the kerchief, with pieces of snuff flying about in a cloud. Then they crumpled it up in their pockets for the next tobacco blast. They rinsed their handkerchief out in the stream before returning home. Washing did little but remove the bulk of the debris; the cloth was permanently dyed brown. Handkerchiefs were not always needed to snuff in the field. They held one nostril closed and blew out the other. It was important to ensure that the blow was done upwind.

Many men, including the Menicuccis, smoked Italian Stogies, a low-cost, low-value, malodorous cigar. Today, stogies are a premium brand of cigar, but in those days, it was the common Italian cigar of choice. The cigars were about five inches long, three-quarters inch wide with tapered ends, completely enclosing the cut tobacco within a single rolled leaf. The smoker bit off one end to draw smoke and lit the other. Typically, they smoked them to the point where they could no longer hold them between their lips. They reserved the tiny remainder and accumulated the bits until they had enough to fill a pipe bowl, which completed the consumption of the product. The Italians were thrifty, even to the point of miserliness, and they rarely wasted any commodity.

From almost all accounts, the stogies were repulsive with acrid, penetrating, strongly flavored smoke. That was the point. The smoke was laden with nicotine, and the first draw could quickly set a standing man in his seat. I remember marveling that they not only drew that smoke into their mouths but they inhaled it deeply, then leaned back to enjoy the nicotine rush while exhaling it through their nostrils. Coupled with wine after lunch in the forest, a nicotine-relaxing rush was just the ticket for a nap and subsequent foraging. Like snuff, I tried stogies and they indeed kicked like nicotine mules, but the taste and offending odor are a steep price to pay. For the record, Johnny Matteucci, a tobacco aficionado, disapproved of stogies: too crude, he declared. He preferred smoking fine tobacco in his signature hardwood pipes.

ALBUQUERQUE BEGINS TO ROAR

By 1922, the United States was rapidly growing out of the post-war recession as soldiers were reintegrated into civil society and employment. New technology was being invented rapidly, producing many novel products to improve the quality of life, including engine-driven farming equipment, electric lights, new medicines and telephones. It was the threshold of what came to be known as the Roaring Twenties.

The auto industry was one of the leading American industries, surpassing railroads, as mass production helped reduce the costs of constructing vehicles, enabling a wide segment of society to own them. The burgeoning auto industry produced around two million vehicles a year in 1920 and more than doubled that in nine years. This industry supported a broad swath of suppliers that produced the products and infrastructure required for a rapidly increasing fleet of vehicles, including engines, rubber tires, windows, upholstery, fuel, lubricants, road construction and repair, auto repairs, retail distributorships and insurance. Urban streets were being paved. At the national level, the mostly paved Route 66 Highway linked Chicago with Santa Monica, California and ran through Albuquerque. With increasing traffic, this new highway was destined to bring many visitors through the city, all needing goods and services. It was an ideal time to build an Albuquerque business dedicated to the automobile.

In the early 1920s, the United States was rocketing to astronomical economic growth. Albuquerque was doing even better; its economy could support just about any reasonable business venture. Johnny Matteucci, for example, returned from Italy with his new wife, Teresa Giuli, in 1922 and opened the National Cigar Store in the First National Bank. The store specialized in tobacco, cigars and paraphernalia, such as pipes. He immediately did well enough to start a family. Many Albuquerque Lucchese were grocers, and despite much competition, all were profitable as the population continued to outpace the supply of merchants. At the time, grocery stores were disbursed throughout the city, with small stores serving small localized communities. Without refrigerators, every family visited a grocer frequently, usually daily. Most people owned no vehicle, so they walked to the store. Physical convenience was important. It was not unusual for several grocery stores to be located just a few blocks from one another, each serving a handful of local customers. The only businesses that failed in Albuquerque in the 1920s were those run by wholly incompetent owners. Metaphorically, the city's business climate was so fertile that any healthy business idea that descended upon it sprouted profits.[9,10,11]

A picture of New Town Albuquerque's downtown in the early 1900s; North Second Street looking South from Copper Avenue. The streets were unpaved and the city had no storm sewer. Summer rains and winter snow created transportation problems for residents, sometimes stranding residents in their homes for days following major weather events. Courtesy Albuquerque Museum, a gift of Walter C. Haussamen, photographer: Cobb Studio.

TINGLY RIDES THE BULL

Albuquerque needed a strong leader to manage and direct the growth, which, by the middle 1920s, was accelerating. Wall Street's bullishness was descending on Albuquerque. Clyde Tingley stepped up to manage it. Tingley came to Albuquerque in 1910 from Ohio. He met and married his wife, Carrie Wooster, in Albuquerque. She was recovering from tuberculosis and required a dry climate to recover, which she eventually did. A lawyer by training, Clyde was disposed to politics and, because of his wife's condition, was a strong advocate for tuberculosis treatment facilities, especially for children. Tingley was about five feet, ten inches tall, clean-shaven and heavy-set. He sported a wide smile on a flat, square-shaped face, bushy eyebrows and dark brown hair with a receding frontal hairline. He was the consummate politician who focused on serving people and, as he put it, "to get things done." His political career began in 1922 as an alderman on the Albuquerque City Commission, representing the second ward. In this form of government, the Commission acted alone to lead the city, with the chairman assuming the de facto position of mayor, although the position did not officially exist.

Carrie Tingley's tuberculous was the reason that she and her husband took up residence in Albuquerque. This picture is dated to the late 1920s. Courtesy Albuquerque Museum, transferred from Albuquerque Public Library.

Tingley, shown standing next to his Ford Model T Roadster, frequently hunted and fished with local residents. Here he was camping in the bosque, the riparian area adjacent to the Rio Grande River. The other man is unknown. The picture dates to the early to middle 1920s. Courtesy Albuquerque Museum, gift of Mrs. Clarence Higgins.

He took his position seriously and spent most days surveying his ward for problems he could solve. By 1925, he had become chairman of the City Commission, and he treated the entire city as he did his ward—with an eye toward continual improvement in the lives of its citizens. Tingley adopted the "mayor" title immediately following the election and retained it for the ten years that he held the job. He was an unceasing advocate for Albuquerque and constantly brought in various celebrities to attract publicity and interest in the city. The way Tingley saw it, the local businessmen and women were key ingredients in the city's bubbling cauldron of growth and his job was to parade through as many potential customers as possible. Tingley's governing philosophy could be summarized as follows: The business of Albuquerque is growth, and the foundation of growth is business. He shared the common philosophy of most Albuquerqueans at the time—growth and prosperity were synonymous. They were right. At this time and in that situation, physical growth was needed to develop the city to its full potential as a haven for life in the desert. Growth expanded the tax base and business infrastructure, allowing for an extended array of services and products. In this growing environment, people could access capital needed to operate profitable businesses. A growing community lifted all ships, to paraphrase a common metaphor.

The mayor knew every businessman and woman in the city by first name. He habitually stopped in at their businesses for a purchase and a discussion about problems he could address. He advocated for laws, regulations and streamlining of bureaucracy to promote growth. He once walked into City Hall with a citizen who had been denied a business permit and demanded the reason. Frustrated with the answer, he rectified the situation on the spot by overriding the city official and signing the authorizing license himself. These kinds of actions built a favorable memory of the man that stuck with people right into the ballot box. Tingley instinctively understood that one of his most important activities was maintaining competition among the business community because that is a requisite for quality products and robust economic growth.

Tingley found the Italians to be honorable citizens with excellent business skills and philosophies of life that complimented those of most Americans. Johnny Giannini, with his sales skills and assertiveness, was naturally attracted to Tingley and vice versa. Tingley perceived Johnny as one of the movers and shakers in the community who was surfing the monumental wave of automobiles that had begun to swarm over America. It was not unusual for Johnny, the mayor and other city officials to hunt and fish together. Tingley was frequently seen at weddings, funerals and other important Italian events in the city, always sure to be photographed with the celebrants. Johnny, of course, used his connections to city hall to his business advantage and taught Julio and Amerigo those skills.

UNITE OLD AND NEW

Albuquerque's geographical bifurcation at that time was of special concern to Tingley. Albuquerque's original settlement was near the banks of the Rio Grande River, which runs north to south through the city. All of the settlements were on the east side of the river. The fate of this area was set by the railroad in the middle 1800s, as rail tracks were infiltrating the country. The Rio Grande River's flow channels were unconstrained and they often meandered east, sometimes inundating the low-lying areas and farms during the spring runoffs. These floods caused the soils in the small community to be marshy and sandy, with inadequate structural qualities to support rails. Instead, the rail and its Albuquerque depot were placed a couple of miles east, higher in elevation and well above the river's flood plain. A new city developed around the depot and became known as New

Town; the original site was dubbed Old Town. Old Town was populated mostly by Hispanics and a few immigrants. A horse-drawn trolly provided transportation from New Town to Old Town, a twenty-minute ride.

New Town, which in the early part of the Twentieth Century explosively surpassed its old sister city in population and economic growth, contained mostly Anglos and immigrants. Almost all of the Italian immigrants lived and worked in New Town. When Tingley became Mayor, one of his concerns was how to incorporate the two cities. After witnessing years of accelerating growth between the two towns, he knew that transportation between the cities was essential. And very expensive. But Tingley was clever. He figured to get the federal government to pay for it. As Route 66 was being planned in the early 1920s, Tingley lobbied heavily for the route to travel through New and Old Albuquerque. The feds were considering a number of possible routes for the first few interstate highways, and the states fiercely competed for them. Julio said, "Tingley charms off their pants," metaphorically referring to seduction. He certainly seduced the Washington crowd because the final route, which follows today's Central Avenue, passed through the middle of both towns and funneled thousands of customers to Albuquerque's business communities. It was a huge success for the mayor. Even the most conservative Republicans had difficulty criticizing Tingley.

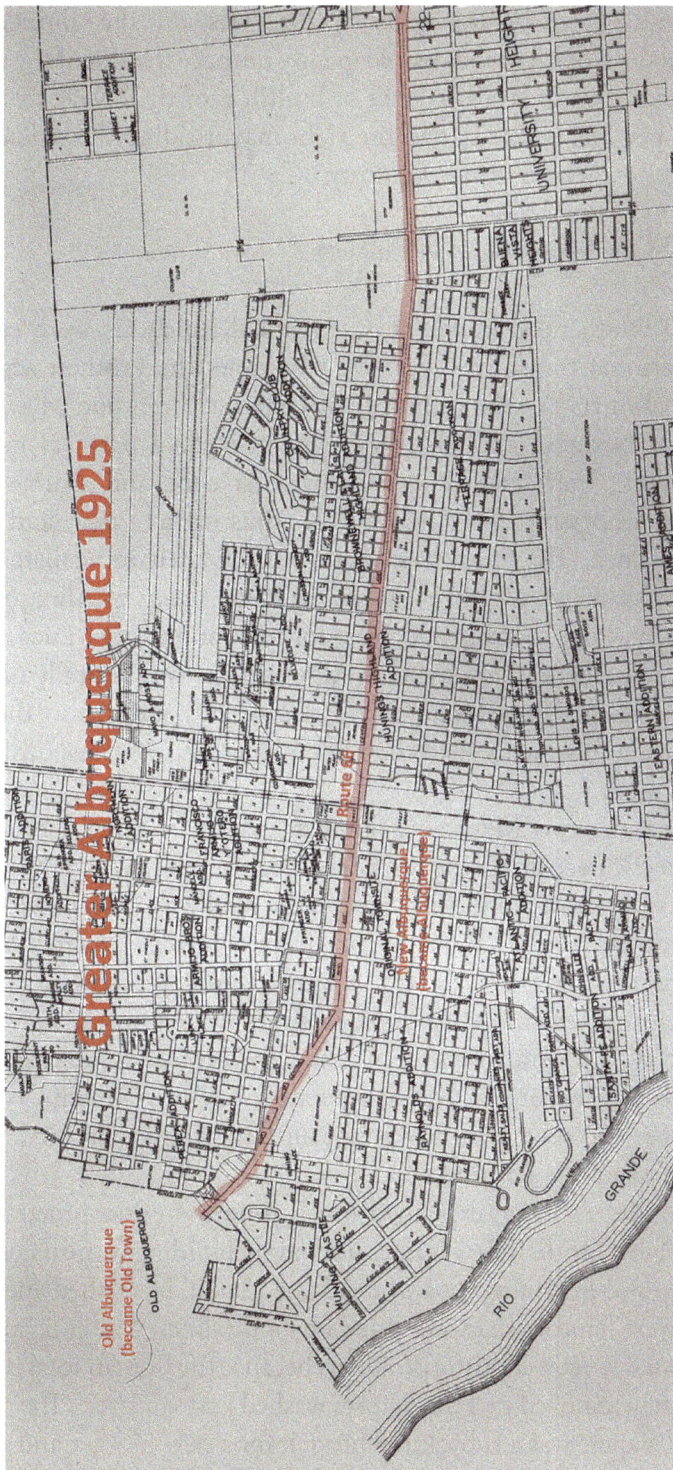

Map of the greater Albuquerque area in 1925. New Albuquerque was many times the size of Old Albuquerque and had become the flagship community in the county, assuming the moniker Albuquerque while Old Albuquerque became Old Town, a major tourist attraction. Route 66 would become the principal reason for the rapid development of both communities. Courtesy Albuquerque Public Library, Street map of Albuqueque, 1925, located in the map collection in the Genealogical Center.

Albuquerque, in the early 1920s, was on the threshold of phenomenal development that would greatly outpace the rest of the nation: the beginning of eight straight years of bullish growth of well more than ten percent per year. The city had the right mayor riding the bull and the right business owners in the community.

BABIES AND BUSINESS

As Albuquerque leaped forward, the Menicuccis were engaged in major personal transitions. For the first time, the brothers separated their personal finances, which since their birth had been pooled as a joint resource. For business, though, they remained equal partners in all of their endeavors. They both expected their first child and assumed their own families' leadership. Their wives were adjusting to a new land with a different language. The physical separation from their immediate family was the most difficult problem for the women. Many of Albuquerque's Italian women strove to supply comfort for newcomers from Lucca, but it was not the same because so much of Albuquerque was radically different from Italy. The men had spent over a decade in America, so they had fewer personal adjustments than their wives, but their new responsibilities weighed on them.

When the two Menicucci families arrived in Albuquerque, they assumed a hectic pace preparing the home for the children who were due to arrive in a few months. For the first time in the family's known history, these pregnant women received prenatal care from a medical doctor. Medical doctors were rarely or ever involved in births among the peasants in Italy. Both women were examined a couple of times prior to pregnancy by the local physician, Dr. John Reidy, to screen for obvious problems. Many births at that time occurred at home under the care of a midwife, typically an older, experienced woman. It was not until the 1930s that birthing was routinely handled in a hospital.

Julio and Amerigo expended much time and effort procuring the materials needed for their new homes, including building furniture, such as baby cradles, and providing tubs where diapers could be washed and dried. All clothes were hand washed and dried on clotheslines, winter or summer. Diapers created special cleaning problems because the human fecal material had to be safely removed and the diapers washed and sanitized. The manual recycling of diapers was a substantial burden for a new mother and created health hazards. Giulia and Davina were reasonably well-trained in home-economics but had a limited understanding of microbial activity associated with handling human waste. Many of their practices were risky and unsafe. They also had limited command of the English language, which meant that the men did all the shopping and assisted them as translators as needed. Fortunately, both Menicucci families shared properties with older Lucchese who advised and assisted the women.

In mid-May, Davina felt birthing contractions and called for help. Within an hour, word spread about the city, and people responded. Aunt Amabele was closest and likely first on the scene, followed by a midwife, who was likely an older Italian woman. Midwifery in that era required no special qualifications other than experience and reputation. Except for medical doctors, men were uninvolved with childbirths. Without fanfare, on May 27, 1922, Davina delivered a healthy baby boy, naming him Mario. Thirteen days later, on June 9th, Giulia did the same with a new son, Dante. It was right on cue in Italian patriarchal tradition. By virtue of being the first males born to the brothers, these two babies assumed heir apparency as the future leaders for each of the two new families. The local community reacted with glee. Every birth was celebrated as a gift from the Lord.

Close relatives, especially Amabele Rondina Morelli and Arduina Menicucci Giannini, assisted both women. Giulia, naturally, was helped by her sister, Marietta Gragnani Morelli. Amabele and Arduina probably spent most of their time supporting Davina because Giulia had a blood relative, her sister Marietta, by her side. All the older ladies were mothers, and their experience comforted the young mothers.

1925 photo of the Menicuccis and Morellis who were related by blood and were physically close to one another in Albuqueque. This shows the principals in the relationship. From left: Julio Menicucci, Joe Morelli, Giulia Gragnani Menicucci, Teodolindo Morelli. Courtesy David Morelli.

Baptisms were performed on the Sunday following birth. In the Catholic faith, all newborns bear the original sin committed by Adam and Eve, and baptism expunges the soul of the evil. Catholics believe a baby who dies unbaptized is eternally confined to purgatory, a place of perpetual nothingness.

Amerigo and Julio labored diligently at Safety First Tire, located on the southeast corner of Tijeras and Fourth Street, in the middle of Albuquerque New Town. They owned nearly half of the company and worked with entrepreneurs' zeal. Johnny Giannini trained both men on vulcanization, the principal service of their business. In those early days of the automobile, tires were of generally poor quality for the rough, unpaved roads throughout Albuquerque. Tires failed frequently. In the early days of autos, many carried two or three spare tires and a complete set of tire tools, especially for out-of-town excursions. Several other tire companies existed in Albuquerque, and each contracted with one wholesaler for exclusive rights to sell a certain product brand. Johnny's main tire line was Balloon Tires, one of the earliest American tire manufacturers. By then, Johnny was in his early 20s but had been in the tire business for many years.

Johnny also taught both men his particular style of salesmanship, primarily aggressive product pricing coupled with excellent service and products. He taught the Menicuccis how to use political and administrative contacts in the local government to a business advantage. He believed that politicians were the power brokers in town. Johnny loved retail salesmanship and designed advertisements for the local newspapers, notably the *Albuquerque Journal*. He ran ads titled "Come and Tell Johnny your Tire Problems." He was developing into a wheeler dealer, generating a colorful reputation in town. Julio and Amerigo were like kitchen towels, soaking it all up.

While both brothers eagerly did any needed job in the store, Amerigo was attracted to the logistical and operational jobs. Julio engaged with Johnny in strategic planning to grow the business. Julio and Johnny cooked up a plan to expand Safety First. They focused on fuel because sales were increasing, which was directly coupled with the explosion of new vehicles on the road. It would become their main product line, poised to outpace tire repair sales, which were dragging. Tire technology was improving with better quality products that required less service.

WHOLESALE GROWTH

At that time, large, vertically organized oil companies extracted, refined and distributed fuels and lubricants nationwide. Regional distributors, which covered large geographical areas such as a state, supplied products to local distributors that distributed them to specific filling stations. Those stations became the exclusive retail outlets for the specific branded products supplied by the wholesaler. Johnny and Julio believed that wholesale distribution had more profit potential than retail. A retailer is limited to the sales he can make in his filling station, but a local wholesale distributor could contract with as many filling stations as he could handle. Further, profit margins on fuel were constrained in the supply chain. In the 1920s, competition was keen, and market forces kept profit margins tight. The retail profit margin on gasoline was less than a penny per gallon from the refinery to the filling station. Filling stations were not only limited in the number of customers who walked in but also constrained in terms of profit margin. Thus, the only way to grow was to sell more products. The wholesaler is advantaged because he sells fuel in high volumes and benefits from economy of scale. He can sell more fuel with less labor. Johnny and Julio reasoned that in this situation, it is best to be in the part of the chain that sells in bulk.

With Amerigo competently running the retail business and generating profits, Julio and Johnny were free to plot their entry into wholesaling. There were few governmental regulations involved but plenty of logistical challenges, the most important of which was storage facilities. A local distributor must have ready access to tanks where bulk oil products can be stored and a fleet of distribution vehicles to dispense the products to the retail outlets. Johnny and Julio formed a wholesale subsidiary of Safety First Tire Company, calling it Safety First Oil Company. But it was a shell because it had no assets, no customers and was co-located with the tire shop.

Rio Grande Oil Company, a large, vertically integrated petroleum company in El Paso, extracted, refined, and distributed petroleum products and was Safety First's oil and gasoline supplier. Johnny and Julio wanted to become a local distributor for Rio Grande Oil. But they had no facilities. With his superb sales skills, Johnny searched for money for the new venture. His credit was excellent and he secured a business loan from one of the banks. Julio solicited filling stations to sign supply contracts for Safety First Oil's fuel products. Julio also found equipment, two tanker trucks, each around two thousand gallons, about the size of a large, modern-day recreational vehicle. They parked the two full tankers on Safety First's station property, claimed they were storage tanks and hung up a sign. Presto, Safety First Oil Company was a wholesale distributor supplying Rio Grande Oil products throughout Albuquerque. By late 1925, they began soliciting several filling stations to sign supply contracts with them.

It was a brilliant innovation, but it created an awkward situation because its storage and delivery capability depended on leased equipment, which could be easily stolen or damaged. It lacked permanency and held unique risks, but Johnny loved the excitement, and he wore it on his sleeve as he hawked his new capability in New Town Albuquerque. By early 1926, Johnny and Julio had signed up seven filling stations, including Safety First Tire, Santa Fe Grocery and Filling station, Duke City Auto, Don Wilson Garage, Franchini Brothers, RM Hall and American Grocery.

Amerigo was becoming adept at marketing and sales. In 1924,

Amerigo secured a tire contract for the Albuquerque Fire Department's large tankers. In those days, large truck tires produced the greatest profits, typically leading to more sales. Successful contractors were routinely awarded follow-on contracts; thus, they had an inside track against competitors vying to break in. Amerigo did a fine job with the deal, but Johnny's personal relationship with the fire chief, a regular fishing buddy, probably had more to do with it. Johnny whooped it up in the local papers, in which he focused on the tires' quality and his company's excellent service as the reason for the award.

GOVERNMENT FOR BUSINESS

In mid-1924, the Bachechis, Alderman Clyde Tingley and the CEO of Maxwell Auto discussed ideas for spurring growth. Tingley was keen to promote growth in the city and was open to ideas from businesses on how to do so. These three entities conjured up the idea for a contest that rewarded people for purchasing products from participating local vendors. The contest, they argued, would promote sales, providing capital for business improvements and growth. The Bachechis, who were prominent business folks and owned Anchor Milling and Grocery and the Pastime Theater, agreed to manage the event. Each participating vendor paid an initiation fee to enter the contest. For each sale, the retailer issued "votes" to each customer based on the value of the transaction. At the end of the contest, prizes were awarded to individuals based on their vote counts. Children's sales were rewarded with different votes to compete for prizes of toys and candy. Safety First was a participating vendor, and Amerigo wisely capitalized on the opportunity to place additional ads in the papers. He offered additional gifts—small trinkets or candy—to paying customers. It delighted seasoned customers and surprised new ones. Amerigo was learning the nuances of running a retail business.

The contest ran for a month, from Thanksgiving to Christmas Eve, with a grand award ceremony at the Pastime Theater. Prizes ranged from gum drops for kids to the grand prize of a Maxwell automobile, which retailed at the time for nine hundred dollars (about sixteen thousand in 2024 dollars). Tingley frequently visited and encouraged the various participating vendors in the contest. Thousands of people partook, and participating businesses earned exceptional additional income, well exceeding their participation fee. It was a major community success, with a robust holiday surge in sales.

For Tingley, it was another noteworthy city accomplishment, and it set the disposition for his upcoming administration.

The year 1924 was the busiest and most intense one the two brothers ever experienced, but it was the pace they maintained for years. They were immersed in Safety First, working seven days a week from seven in the morning to seven in the evening. At home, their respective wives were busy delivering and caring for new children. Giulia delivered her second son, Charlie, on March 22, 1924, and Davina delivered Louise just a day later on March 23, 1924. These two Menicuccis separated their finances when they married, but they carefully coordinated the timing of impregnations.

There was a problem—their low-end housing. Julio was bedraggled under the weight of the women's discomfort. He was particularly ashamed of the dirt floor in his home, the catalyst for many problems. Giulia once said she spent half of her time chasing her toddler, Dante, "trying to keep him from crawling on the dirt and the other half cleaning him up from crawling on the dirt." These were not the living conditions he promised Giulia's father when he left Italy with his daughter. There was little that either of the Menicucci men could do. They had invested most of their savings into Safety First and they were not on salary. As co-owners, their income depended on the profits from the business. It provided a mighty incentive for both men to grow their incomes to compensate for the additional economic load of a growing family.

TYPHOID GIULIA

All progressed smoothly until the summer of 1925 when Giulia woke one morning feeling ill and running a fever. Hoping the illness would pass, for several days, Julio returned home frequently to care for the family. Marietta, Giulia's sister, assisted with the children. As the days passed, her fever increased and she became increasingly weak and pale. Julio finally walked down to Dr. Reidy's office and asked him to examine her, which he did immediately. Reidy suspected Typhoid, which appeared regularly in the city. He confirmed his suspicion with a firm diagnosis. She was seriously ill with the bacteria, which was often lethal. Several days passed and her condition continued to worsen. Her fever had progressed from about 101F a week before to over 104F. Reidy's concern was that if not controlled, the fever itself would kill her, which was often the case with Typhoid victims. She was moved to St. Joseph Hospital, a first-class health facility run by the Sisters of Charity, a Catholic order of nuns.

Typhoid was a common occurrence in much of America in the 1920s. Poor sanitation and contaminated water were the principal causes of most cases, but it was also spread to foods of various kinds. Improper handling of dirty cloth diapers caused many bacterial infections. Albuquerque was in its initial phases of developing its water and sanitation systems, and operational practices that are fundamental today were unknown then. It would be many decades before the America Clean Water Act, enacted in 1972, required all drinking water in America to be safe to consume.[12]

For days Giulia languished in an open hospital ward with others struggling with Typhoid. The physicians tried various treatments with no success. Many bacterial infections were lethal at that time because antibiotics were still years from development. Typhoid treatments included opiates, turpentine, quinine, capsicum and other chemical concoctions, all of which did little or nothing for the victim. For five days, her fever ranged from 104F to 106F. She slipped in and out of consciousness as the nurses provided little more than aspirin and some cool towels for her steaming forehead. She was noticeably slipping away when Reidy asked Julio for permission to try something radical—ice immersion. Reidy said, "We have to break the fever. Sometimes ice will do it." It was dangerous, though, and Reidy warned Julio that if it failed, she might die of shock. Julio had no choice because without the ice, she was dead for sure. To be safe, Julio called Immaculate Conception Church and asked for a priest to be on site when the ice treatment was administered, just in case of a surprise death. Julio called on the Italian community for prayers, the customary beacon of impending peril of an Italian family member. He bought some votive candles and prayed as he did in the Franklin Jr. mine, calling again on the Madonna to help save his lady. He knew it was a lot to ask, but he hoped that she still had some consideration for him. The Lord always listens to his mama, Julio kept thinking.

Reidy ordered a large steel tub and dozens of ice blocks, which the nurses broke up with pics. He added water, leaving enough room for Giulia's body to be immersed completely, leaving only her nose and mouth above the water line. Stripped naked, Reidy's medical team lowered her into the ice bath. Although unconscious, her body shuddered, her eyes gyrated in their sockets, and she screamed out in horror as the frigid water sapped heat from her body. Reidy was adlibbing. He had never applied the controversial treatment but had read about it. He had no guidance about how long she should remain submerged. Too long and hypothermia could cause death. Too short, the treatment fails and the patient dies. Reidy used a thermometer in her mouth as his only medical instrument in the procedure. When her oral temperature reached a few degrees below normal, she was pulled from the bath, dried off and returned to the ward.

Once she was back in bed, Reidy, a Catholic, suggested that the last rights be administered. He believed it was a critical time when she either survived or died. Family and other Lucchese surrounded her as the priest proceeded with the last sacrament. When he was nearly done, Giulia winked open one of her eyes, dazzled by the fanfare. She asked in a whisper what they were doing. The priest answered that he was administered the last rights. She opened both eyes wider and indignantly said, "You can give me last rights all you want but I am not dying." Reidy stepped in and checked her temperature, reading it as just about normal. The fever was broken and Giulia would survive, he declared with relief. The family broke into wild festivity, with most praying, some sinking to their knees with heads bowed graciously and others thanking Dr. Reidy. Julio, once again, was humbled, knowing that the Madonna had indeed spoken to the Lord on his behalf. His already long debt of gratitude to the Virgin had lengthened considerably.

While Giulia was reprieved from death, she was far from well. She had been bed-bound for weeks, full of bed sores, had lost nearly half her weight and was fully immobile due to weakness. She needed weeks to recover fully, requiring assistance with everything from the toilet to sitting at the kitchen table. In the interim, Julio had two small children under his care and knew little about how to do it. Raffaello Morelli knew. That night, Marietta and Raffaello went to Julio's home and packed up the children and their belongings for an extended stay there. Julio, of course, pledged to provide the needed monetary support for the children. Julio could now focus on improving Giulia's health. Family, once again, was to the rescue.

Marietta and Ralph Morelli lived on Slate Avenue, just a few blocks from Julio's family. Courtesy David Morelli.

Giulia slowly recovered in her home, and Julio provided help and assistance as needed. But most direct care came from Aunts Amabele Morelli and Adelina Giannini, who took turns looking after Giulia during the day when Julio worked. Giulia resumed her full home duties in a few weeks, after which she was reunited with her children. Julio was now determined to extract the families from their marginal living quarters and into more dignified housing. It was time for him and Amerigo to make their next advancement in business.[13]

See notes 14, 15, 16.

Notes

1. *Bryder* discusses early treatments for tuberculosis. *Melzer* describes the history of sanatoriums in New Mexico.

2. *Giomi* (Ioli) presents a description of the Bonaguidi family. Published in March, 1978, Volume V, Number 2.

3. *Giomi (Ioli)*, "Punti Di Vista", presents an English language discussion about the number of northern Italians in Albuquerque.

4. Details of the dispute are incomplete, but according to Margaret Mary Matteucci Dixon, granddaughter to Amedeo Matteucci, the affair was based on a misunderstanding. Alessandro was about seven years older than his brother and immigrated to the United States in 1896. Amedeo arrived about a year later. Around 1903, Alessandro, then thirty-one years old, founded Champion Grocery at the corner of Seventh Street and Tijeras Street. Amedeo, then twenty-four years old, naturally worked in the store with his brother. Alessandro paid Amedeo like an employee but Amedeo believed he was profit-sharing in the enterprise. As the years passed and Amedeo matured, he suggested business improvements and other changes to Champion, including expanding the business inventory to include more fancy and high-end products. After all, as part owner of the store, he felt he had that right. Alessandro believed he was paying his brother as any regular employee and thought someday Amedeo might invest some of his earnings back into the business and become a bona fide co-owner. Until he was actually a co-owner, he had no such right. As the incongruencies of their respective views were fully exposed, each man hardened around his own position.

Around 1913, the situation became so acrimonious that they agreed to part ways. Of course, Amedeo felt he was owed part of Champion for all the work he had done. Alessandro felt that he had been fair with the pay and his plan for Amedeo to buy in later. Anger and emotions prevented any kind of negotiation and each was unwilling to trust their fate to the courts, which they did not fully understand. They finally decided to draw straws. Amedeo picked the short one and he did not handle defeat with grace. He went to a close Lucchese friend and long-time Albuquerque resident, Michael Palladino and asked him to join him in opening a new grocery market just a block away to compete with Champion directly. Amedeo planned to stock a line of fancy foods designed to serve higher-class citizens. The Palladino family had done well in Albuquerque and had capital to invest. He liked Amedeo's plan and readily agreed to invest and work at the store as the butcher.

Both businesses did well. Albuquerque at that time was replete with small neighborhood grocery stores. In the days before supermarkets, refrigerators and personal vehicles, foods could not be stored for long, especially in summer, so people visited the local grocery store almost daily. Albuquerque's population was growing, and all had to eat and drink so it could support new stores as they emerged. The Italians were attracted to grocery businesses because as farmers, they were knowledgeable of foods and they had sound, innate business skills.

The Italian colony responded to the spat with a yawn. From their perspective, it was a family dispute, something that happens occasionally. In this tiny desert enclave thousands of miles from their families, community members were bent on cooperating. Other than rumors and comments, the Italian community took no sides and treated Matteuccis as before. Palladino, a hardened businessman, viewed it as an investment with little personal prejudice. His goal was to earn money.

5. Alessandro was one of the most colorful and interesting Italian immigrants in the 1910s. He pushed the right to the limits of the law. In 1913, he was indicted and pled guilty to operating a saloon too close to San Felipe De Neri Church. In 1918, he was indicted for receiving stolen goods. However, he was a Republican, and so was District Attorney Craig. His case was never taken to trial. When the Republicans nominated Alessandro for Sherrif in 1920, the Democrats attacked his record and the apparent collusion between him and Craig, and he was defeated. It was one of the first true smear campaigns in the city's history, with the Democrats rolling out mothers who decried his operation of a brothel, which was not illegal but widely considered to be immoral. The Temperance Movement was at full strength at the time, and it was easy to generate animosity against a saloon and brothel operator with a criminal record. Of course, the office—sheriff—exacerbated the problem for him because candidates were expected to be model citizens.

This notice appeared in the *Albuquerque Journal* on October 27, 1920, just before the November elections. Alessandro was running for Bernalillo Country Sherriff. It accompanied a long *Albuquerque Journal* article describing a public meeting in which a group of residents at an Old Town political rally booed and hissed him off the stage. Many other similar stories were published during this brutal campaign.

6. Davina was keen on learning sufficient English to do her own shopping. Not long after arriving in Albuquerque, she befriended Maria Bachechi, who was teaching English and basic sewing skills to Italian women. Davina achieved reasonable fluency in English and performed her own home-management-related chores, including daily shopping.

7. *Giomi* (Ioli) presents a description of the early Giomi family. Published in July, 1977, Volume IV, Number 6.

8. *Giomi* (Ioli) presents a description of the early Domenici family. Published in September, 1977, Volume IV, Number 8.

9. *Lavender* and *Dyreson & Dyreson* describe the long history of development in New Mexico.

10. *Bryan (Albuquerque Remembered)*, *Cline*, *Dewitt*, *Fergusson*, *Krammer*, *Palmer*, *Twitchell*, *Stamm* and *Winkler* provide detailed descriptions of the history and development of Albuquerque. *History of Albuquerque* is a printed book with no author or publisher but presents an overview of Albuquerque for most of the period of history discussed in this book. It is available at the Genealogy Center at the Albuquerque Public Library main branch.

11. *Bohme* offers a comprehensive account of Italian immigrants in New Mexico. His was the first book about Italian immigration to the state and it contains a detailed bibliography. He also includes many statistics about the Italians in Albuquerque and their home origins, which correspond with those that are presented throughout the book. *DeMark* presents some of the most comprehensive descriptions of Italians living in Albuquerque during the first two decades of the Twentieth Century.

12. In the 1920s and 1930s, Typhoid Fever was a health menace throughout the United States. *Wolfman & Gorman* describe the situation.

13. The use of ice in treating fevers harkens from the early 1800s, well described by *Currie*. *Grodzinsky* presents a modern overview of fevers, including using ice and cold water to treat fevers.

14. This story is based largely on community lore, stories well-known in the colony. Many details are based on corroborated family lore.

15. Historic real-time news reports from the *Albuquerque Journal* provided significant information about Tingley's actions and the public's response.

16. The Albuquerque City Directory and the Censuses were major sources of information in the chapter. The directory was especially helpful because it details the businesses and their employees. The directories also include many business advertisements, which reveal much information about the products that specific businesses purveyed. Most directories are accessible online, but there are some significant gaps. A complete collection of Albuquerque directories is located at the Genealogy Center at the Albuquerque Public Library's main branch.

11

THE LAST ROAR
(1926–1929)

THE BUSINESS OF CHANGE

By the middle of the 1920s, both businesses and families were growing smartly. On Feb 12, 1926, Rena was born into Amerigo's family. Julio and Giulia had planned a birth about the same time, but that was precluded by typhoid fever. Giulia was in no condition to consider pregnancy during her recovery. But, Julio wanted to move it along. He and Amerigo had previously decided that a two-year separation in children was optimal; he did not want to fall too far behind schedule. On October 12, 1927, Giulia delivered a baby girl named Teresa. Adding a third child, six total, including Amerigo's, placed additional pressure on Julio to improve conditions. After Giulia's narrow escape with death and with rapidly growing families, Julio and Amerigo agreed to two new goals. First, new homes. Second, their own business.

They saw the opportunity in gasoline and oil, both wholesale and retail. Amerigo managed Safety First Tire well. He gained rapport with customers and developed and implemented a simple and even-handed approach to his employees. His job, as he defined it, was to ensure that all the men were productive while on the job. Like most Italians, he believed everyone should carry their while working for others. Amerigo made it simple: the men were paid to do a specific job during specific times and the boss was there to make sure they did it. He was not autocratic. "Hire good men and then let them do their jobs" was his operating principle that he recanted frequently. He also believed that men should be treated with respect, including concern for their families. His men were given time off to attend to family duties as needed. He knew from the Franklin Jr. mine how to handle employees—in many cases doing the opposite of what the mine operators did.

Amerigo's gregarious personality worked well in the retail business. He loved to interact with the customers with whom he shared interests. Trout fishing, mushrooms and upland bird hunting were the Italians' most popular outdoor sporting activities at the time. People stopped into Safety First just to talk to Amerigo about fishing or hunting and ended up buying various things. Conversations ranged freely in English, Spanish, or Italian. He and Julio knew Clyde Tingley on a first-name basis; the mayor personally traded with as many businessmen as possible. Plus, Tingley hunted and angled. Amerigo was solidifying his position in the family's business enterprise—a retail manager.

Julio concentrated on the wholesale work at Safety First Oil Company, which was co-located with Safety First Tire Company, its parent. He slowly increased the number of filling stations under supply contracts, using his language skills to woo Anglo and Hispanic customers. He corresponded frequently with Rio Grande Oil executives about different contract options for increased profitability of their products in Albuquerque. They appreciated Julio's honesty and rewarded him with various deals and opportunities. As a result, by the end of 1927, Safety First Oil Company, the local gasoline-distributing arm of Safety First Tire, was producing a healthy return on investment with good prospects for the future. Still, Julio was worried about the tenuous nature of their situation, having no permanent storage facilities and depending on rented trucks.

Both Amerigo and Julio were superb students of the world and quickly applied lessons learned to the business. Above all, both brothers believed in honesty as a business staple. Amerigo had Safety Tire humming along like one of Maxwell's Touring autos, with steadily increasing sales. Julio had Safety First Oil hitting all cylinders and producing more than half the profits.

BUSINESS FRACTURES

Johnny was growing impatient with steady growth. He liked excitement. It was in his blood. He embraced the challenge of developing and implementing a bold business venture but was bored once the venture was returning steady profits and growth, as was the case with the Safety First enterprises. In 1927, Johnny, in frustration, concluded that the local gasoline market had too much competition and some thinning was needed. He was itching for a brawl and suggested Safety First launch a gas war.

A gas war is a radical retailing tactic to reduce competition. It commences when an exceptionally sound gasoline retailer dramatically reduces prices. The public flocks to the discount gasoline, depriving competitors of business and producing cash flow problems. If other businesses match the price drop, they incur losses, which also impacts cash flow. Competitors drop out proportionally to their solvency levels, resulting in fewer businesses and less competition. In simple terms, a gas war brings a plague on all gasoline vendors and only the strongest ones survive. According to Johnny, it was a sure win because Safety First Tire and Safety First Oil Company were comfortably profitable and he thought he was well positioned financially for war.

The idea shocked Julio and Amerigo and they adamantly opposed it. They were making money with excellent growth prospects because they focused on quality and service. Julio was afraid the war could backfire and posed the possibility that there were even stronger companies that could take down Safety First. The Menicuccis were not business experts, but they were trained military men who understood the difference between bravery and foolhardiness, and it seemed innately foolish to mess with success. Together, they owned nearly half of the enterprise and did most of its day-to-day work. Johnny had to listen and backed off, but he was not convinced. The disagreement put Johnny and the Menicuccis on diverging professional paths.

FOOL'S GOLD

When Johnny was not planning gas wars, he chased gold, which marked the beginning of the end for the partnership with the Menicuccis. Placer gold deposits were discovered in the nearby Manzano Mountains and it was the type of activity that captivated him, not unlike previous Menicuccis, such as Emilio, who pursued gold in several states. Gold charged up Johnny like an electric light bulb and he frequently mined the placer sites. Whether he rendered profits from it is unknown. Julio and Amerigo, on the other hand, had no interest in mines of any kind, even placer fields at the surface. The mention of "mine" to Julio elicited a voracious negative reaction, even at the later stages of his life. With a growing reputation as a business high flyer, the precious metals added to Johnny's luster. He sometimes walked into a bar, ordered a beer and spilled out a sack of sand on the table laced with gold specs sparkling like nighttime stars. Naturally, other patrons flocked to see and hear Johnny's mining tales. Johnny was right where he was comfortable, in the spotlight. A humorous anecdote developed over time that accurately characterized this man's persona. Here is one version of it.

There were two Italian storekeepers in Albuquerque. One of their oldest and best customers, a frail, elderly Hispanic man, came in. He gathered the two men and told them how, after so many years, he knew they were honest and trusted them. The old man unfolded a dry, crackly, hand-drawn map. He explained that the map led to a small, hidden gold mine, which his family had for generations used as a family social security bank for old age. In his final years, it was his turn to tap in. He wanted the men to go to the secret location and remove enough gold for the two Italians and a tiny bit for him and his wife to finish their lives; ten percent of the booty was all the old man wanted. The man emphasized that secrecy was paramount, for if word of the mine spread, it would imperil his family's future. The two Italians were on the trail the next day. After days of arduous hiking, fighting off wild beasts, scaling one-hundred-foot sheer cliffs and being lost, they finally found the last landmark. As they carefully made their way to the mouth of the gold mine, they looked up and saw a grinning, barrel-chested man holding a shovel in one hand and an overflowing sack of gold in the other. It was Johnny Giannini.

No matter what unique business opportunity arose, Johnny always seemed to be first at it. At least, that was the perception many people had and one Johnny wanted them to have. Beyond gold, fist-fighting was fundamental to Johnny's persona. He was rambunctious by nature, a street-fighter type who never shied away from a row. In 1927, he promoted prize fights in Albuquerque. Amateur boxing was popular, involving many local residents, including some Italians, such as my maternal grandfather Modesto Dalle, an amateur lightweight fighter. Professional prizefighting, which Johnny promoted, was a brutal, bare-knuckle business full of twists and turns and plenty of sleazy characters. In one incident, Johnny was involved in sponsoring a prize fight that involved illegal gambling and match-fixing. In the event, a stranger attempted to deliver a handful of cash to one of the fight trainers in the middle of the match. The story made the front page of the *Albuquerque Journal*, and Tingly cross-examined Johnny about his role. It turned out that Johnny had nothing to do with fixing the fight but was actually a victim. Naturally, Johnny swore revenge. In another fight in which the scheduled fighters were unable to compete, Johnny and another promoter got into the ring for a faux bout, which delighted the spectators and the press. Johnny's fights were often reported in the local papers, sometimes on the front page. He gobbled up as much publicity as they could serve. The fun of promotion compensated for Johnny's meager gains in the boxing world. It was all fine because the profits from Safety First, of which he owned fifty-one percent, sustained him quite well.

Johnny extended his fighting instincts to a court of law. He cherished opportunities to argue in court when he had been cited for some violation, such as leaving one of his automobiles parked on the street overnight. A dozen other people were also cited, and all pled guilty except for Johnny, who successfully argued that the signs were improperly placed. His case was dismissed, and the story of his court maneuvers appeared in the Albuquerque papers. Johnny often appeared in court to contest citations and won all of them. One *Albuquerque Journal* story headline reported that Johnny had "outtalked the court" on his way to an acquittal.[1]

AWOL

While Johnny galivanted around town like a big shot, he spent almost no time at Safety First. It bothered the brothers, but Amerigo was particularly irked and let Julio know of his displeasure. Amerigo was keenly concerned about equity ever since he was left behind in Italy twenty years earlier. It made little sense to him that he and his brother should do all the work yet split half the profits with someone who did none. It was the kind of inequity that typically got under Amerigo's skin. Julio put their exit on the fast track.

The brothers developed their business strategy. In discussions with Rio Grande Oil executives, Julio discovered a unique automobile service station concept developed in California. Called a "super service station," it integrated all of the services needed to maintain and operate a motor vehicle under one roof. It was analogous to a supermarket, which was also developing in California and on the east coast. In those early days of the automobile, owners typically traded at a range of specialty shops for various services, such as lubrication, fuel, replacement hoses and belts, and washing and detailing. The integrated service stations provided convenience, an attractive retailing feature. In 1928, no super service stations yet existed in Albuquerque and the Menicuccis wanted to be the first. Julio correctly believed that it would give them a unique marketing position in the community and an ideal way to launch their new automobile service and supply business.

The brothers had learned much about the retail and wholesale gas and oil business and had business contacts throughout the community. They had savings, but they were growing slowly because they were spending part of their income on new children. They had insufficient funds to launch a new business. They turned to the colony. The Menicuccis knew Michael Palladino's family from Lucca. Mike, as he was known, was a partner with Amedeo Matteucci in his fine foods market. He had money to invest in the Menicucci's new business. Mike was optimistic about the future of the automobile fueling and service business. Horace, his son, who had studied auto mechanics in high school, was doing simple auto repairs at Safety First. Mike agreed to invest in Menicucci's new enterprise.

With sufficient money to launch their new station, the Menicucci bantered around several names for it but eventually decided to name it what it was: Super Service Station. The name had a double connotation. It would indeed be a super service station, an integrated, multifunctional operation like those in California, but also a super-service station focusing on service and quality products. For some time, the brothers had concluded that the best way to achieve sustainable profits was through excellent service, which builds customer loyalty and growth. Later, following the launch of Super Service Station in 1929, several other super service stations emerged, including Nevada Super Service Station and Standard Super Service Station. But the Menicuccis had coopted the three-letter name, a clever marketing ploy, giving them the appearance of pacesetters.[2]

BREAKAWAY

In early 1928, they informed Johnny of their intentions. He was unmoved because his interests were in boxing rings and placer fields. Besides, he was frustrated by Menicuccis' conservatism and reticence to market brawling. He also did not appreciate how closely Amerigo and Julio watched the books and his spending. Julio operated so autonomously, and Johnny spent so little time at work, Johnny was not even sure what he did except make a profit and resist his plans to take Safety First into a risky war. The split was mutual with no familial relations damaged.

Simultaneously, with their announcement to depart, Julio completed a deal with Rio Grande Oil to open a distributorship in Albuquerque and hire him as director. This new company, financially backed by the huge national corporation, competed directly with Safety First Oil. Rio Grande Oil invested in the property, including a warehouse building, storage tanks and other hardware.

The Menicuccis arranged to sell their Safety First shares to Frank and Johnny Dinelli, sons to Pietro, two young Lucchese brothers in Town. The men were twenty-four and twenty-one years old, respectively, with no experience in the auto industry. Amerigo and Davina were boarders at the Dinelli home at 505 Tijeras, so the Dinellis had plenty of time to discuss the Safety First business with Amerigo. Pietro was a hotel keeper and wanted to help his two sons into the business. He was impressed with what Johnny Giannini and the Menicuccis had done at Safety First. Pietro supplied the money needed to buy out Julio and Amerigo and handed the business shares to his sons. Pietro thought he was investing in a growing business in Safety First, and he was right. Except, the two men who underwrote that growth took it with them to create a competitor.

In May 1928, Julio and Amerigo signed the papers that freed them of Safety First, producing a handsome profit from their initial investment. Julio immediately bought a parcel of land at Fourth Street and Marquette Street to house their new super service station. Fred Lemke owned the property and knew the Menicuccis well. He sold it for two thousand dollars (about thirty-five thousand in 2024 dollars). It was within shouting distance of Safety First, two blocks north of it on Fourth Street. As part of the deal, Johnny agreed to relinquish his exclusive sales contract with Mohawk Tires to the Menicuccis. Johnny, in turn, contracted with Lambert Tire Company as his tire supplier, a manufacturer he thought produced superior products. Johnny's reasoning is difficult to reconcile because Mohawk was a top manufacturer at that time and has remained a profitable business through 2024.

The Fourth Street location was excellent for an auto supply business because it was on the main road through Albuquerque. At that time, Albuquerque was organized in a North-South fashion, with businesses and residences developing along the rail tracks. Fourth Street, which runs north-south, was designated U.S. Highway 85 and became the major thoroughfare through the state. After U.S. Highway 66 was completed, which ran east and west, Albuquerque's development followed it. As U.S. 66 passed through Albuquerque's downtown, it carried the name Central Avenue. Fourth Street remained a major highway for many decades, and its intersection with Central Avenue was the busiest in the state.

Building a super service station was more complex than a standard filling station, such as Safety First, because it provided multiple services requiring different workstations under the same roof. It was a new concept in a rapidly evolving auto industry. Some of these services, such as engine repairs, were foreign to the Menicuccis, and they needed to hire properly skilled people for that work. Qualified repairmen were rare in Albuquerque because automobiles contained advanced technology requiring specially trained men to repair them. Few automobile repair training facilities existed, and only one was Italian-owned—the Napoleone brothers, Nick, Tony and Joseph, on Bridge Street. They operated an auto repair shop but did little else other than sell fuel. Italians tended to frequent other Italian businesses, but Napoleones were a couple of miles from the main downtown area. The Menicuccis believed there was healthy market potential for repair services downtown, where many Italian families lived. Repair service perfectly complemented their new business and was a necessary component of a super service station.

Horace Palladino, Michael's son and Johnny's repairman, defected from Safety First to work with the Menicuccis. Horace wanted to expand his repair skills from tires and drive trains to more complex systems, such as electrical and carburation. As autos developed in complexity, auto repair work was becoming increasingly profitable. Repair service requires specialty tools, equipment and training, which were investments that Johnny was reticent to make. Slow and methodical business development failed to interest Johnny's flamboyant personality. Horace believed that the Menicucci's super service station concept allowed him the flexibility and freedom to develop the repair business he envisioned.

JOHNNY'S WAR

Johnny wasted no time in displaying his version of Napoleonic drama. On July 3, 1928, just a month after the Menicucci's departed, he launched Albuquerque's first gas war. He reduced his prices by twelve percent, from twenty-five cents/gallon to twenty-two, a huge markdown considering the tiny profit margins for service stations. Profit margins ranged from less than a half cent per gallon to as high as two, with an average around a penny. In quarter-page ads in the *Albuquerque Journal*, he taunted his competitors to match his price, specifically challenging the large companies. The tactic was front-page news in the local papers, and everyone nervously waited for the outcome. His rash act caught his own contracted filling stations by surprise and some informed Johnny that they could not operate profitably for more than a few days at the lower price. Some reduced their price in consolidation with Johnny, but most held fast and absorbed the lost business. Johnny had a banner day on July 4th, as cars lined both streets at the corner of his property at Tijeras and Fourth Streets. Unfortunately, he was selling fuel at a loss; the more he sold, the more he lost. It was part of the strategy, and Johnny held firm, hoping for capitulation from his supposedly weaker competitors. Julio and Amerigo, well acquainted with the fuel business, were stupefied at the notion that taking big losses somehow leads to big gains. In today's colloquial jargon, they considered it a non-sequitur.

From the public's perspective, it was a spectacle to behold with Johnny's newspaper ads sporting a scowling man holding out his fist in a threatening manner. His slogan: "You stick with us and we'll stick with you." Johnny envisioned leading a price rebellion with legions of Albuquerqueans "sticking" with him in this glorious battle; a David and Goliath redux. Few others, especially the Menicuccis, were interested in this kind of tussling. Johnny wanted to make a splash and he did. Ads in those days featured the quality of products and rarely openly attempted to intimidate competitors or even mention them in ads. It was a new advertising tack in the city.

An Ad With a Punch!
GILCO
GASOLINE
22c Per Gallon
Anti-Knock Ethylene Gas Reduced From 28c to 25c Per Gallon

The price of gasoline at all our stations is 22c per gallon. We've made this reduction despite a one cent a gallon increase in our cost price, and despite this increase we still maintain that money can be made selling gasoline to the public at 22c per gallon.

When we first reduced the price of gasoline we thought it would be met by other oil companies in a reduction of the tank wagon price—it wasn't. We put the price back to 25c per gallon and thought the tank wagon price would be reduced after the state attorney's investigation — it wasn't! So we've again taken the initiative in reducing the price of gasoline to 22c per gallon.

Mr. Williams, of the Ever-Ready Garage, who owns his own equipment and has had difficulty in securing gasoline to sell his customers will have no further trouble in the future—WE ARE NOW, AND HAVE BEEN FOR THE PAST WEEK, SUPPLYING MR. WILLIAMS WITH GAS-OLINE.

The public need not hesitate buying gasoline from these stations believing that these dealers are not making money at this price—every station is making a fair profit.

You Stick With Us and We'll Stick With You

Safety First Oil Company
JOHNNY GIANNINI, Manager

Safety First Tire Co.	Santa Fe Grocery	Duke City Auto Co.
Santa Fe Filling Station		American Grocery
Don T. Wilson Garage	Franchini Bros.	Ever-Ready Garage

Clipping from the *Albuquerque Journal* of an ad that Johnny Giannini ran during the gas war. At this time, the Menicuccis had left Safety First and Johnny did not know that all of his wholesale customers—those listed at the bottom of the ad—would all defect to Julio when he took over Rio Grande Oil Company. Note that Safety First Tire Company is listed as one of the retail stations that was supplied with fuel by Safety First Oil Company.

Unfortunately, the only thing that stuck to Johnny was humiliation when none of the other stations in the city budged on their prices. Some bigger operators, such as Texico and Standard Oil, got in an uppercut, publicly challenging the quality of Safety First's fuel, suggesting it might be bootlegged. It wasn't black market fuel but raised enough public doubt that it justified companies to hold their prices. The Lucchese station owners under contract for wholesale supplies from Safety First, including the Franchini brothers, stuck with him initially but finally limited sales to moderate losses. They contacted Johnny on July 5th, demanding he sue for peace. It was the beginning of the end for the stations' relationship with Safety First Oil. Rio Grande Oil was awaiting them.

Johnny stood his ground, but the next day, July 6, he took another torpedo; all of his contracted stations—including the Franchinis—refused to match the low price, returning their prices to market level. Johnny was stranded with his losses, which appeared manageable given the strong initial financial condition. In a very non-Napoleonic move, he retreated. He paid for another expensive newspaper ad explaining his situation and raised the price back to twenty-five cents per gallon. It was a humiliating loss and he stewed over it for days.

On July 8th, his ego took control and he relaunched the war. It took a while, but the result was a repeat of the first one but this time with serious financial results. Johnny was sitting on sobering, realized losses from selling all his gas below cost. All the profitless sales left him short on stock and cash. His losses wiped out the enterprise's profits from the previous few years. His customers were gone and so was his money. His reputation as a clever businessman quickly tarnished as he scrambled to dig himself out of his self-created, toilet-like whirlpool. On July 11, 1928, after his second gas war settled, the *Albuquerque Journal* printed a Limerick by U. N. Biased mocking Johnny:

> *There was a young man named Giannini*
> *Who donned the strength of a Mussolini*
> *So he said to himself,*
> *"I'll give part of the pelf*
> *To the people who buy gasolini."*
> *But—*
> *The other boys still have a punch—*

They got together and pulled off a hunch.
Said they, "We've enough
Pro bono publico stuff."
And now Johnny's back in the bunch.

In the end, Safety First was the only loser. Upon armistice, all the competitors were still standing, only now much stronger in relation to Safety First's depleted condition. Johnny had, in a matter of a couple of weeks, managed to lose substantial capital, forfeit all of his wholesale customers and ninety percent of his retail customers, and lose his repairman. Safety First, once a leading automobile service wholesaler and retailer, was metaphorically a burned shell. Johnny's dream for a Napoleonic-like victory in the gas war turned out more like a Waterloo, a total loss.[3]

BLIND FAITH

In response to the losses, Johnny convinced the Dinellis to invest in advertising to bring in more business and recover the losses from the failed war. Business growth was the path out, he argued. They agreed because they were new and unfamiliar with the business, and they trusted Johnny. Johnny invested their money in a series of ads in which a group of business owners paid for a half-page of newsprint space to complement and highlight various local businesses in Albuquerque. The ads were, at best, indirectly beneficial to Safety First and did Johnny little good. Julio and Amerigo were bewildered that a company in financial trouble, operating on borrowed money, a jaded reputation and inexperienced laborers, wasted money on ads complementing competitors. Johnny's retail business teetered with the loss of his regular gas customers. Before the end of 1928, Safety First Oil Company had become a one-man band in an empty building clinging to life.

The Dinellis walked into a bad situation at the wrong time. They had no way to assess the situation with the businesses because they had no experience in the automobile market. The Menicuccis left Johnny with two profitable and growing businesses, and they made a fair profit from their trade of equity shares to the Dinellis. Once free of Safety First, the brothers pivoted to their business. As far as they were concerned, they had done their share and Johnny was now just another business competitor.

If the Dinellis had done their due diligence, they would have recognized the risks. Johnny's clownish reputation was well known. The local papers loved him because his antics sold papers. And then there were the Menicuccis skedaddling, taking with them the cores of the Safety First businesses. All the warning flags were flying. It was bad enough that Dinellis made a bad investment initially, but then they compounded their mistake by giving Johnny more money, which he promptly wasted. It was an unfortunate situation that left them painfully realizing that Johnny's self-inflicted wounds had doomed their investment from the beginning.

Julio and Amerigo were dismayed by the events at Safety First. They knew that this was the kind of publicity that scandalized the family. Scandal was truly and deservedly raining down on Johnny. He was a blood relative who was suffering. They resolved to keep their distance as a scandal of such magnitude could spill over. Amerigo was keen on these subtleties; he wanted to eliminate any taint that could drag on business. Nevertheless, they were dispirited to see Johnny's high level of prominence suddenly plunge to embarrassing levels of shame. Moreover, they were heartbroken to see the rapid destruction of profitable companies they had so carefully crafted over the years. Being a blood relative—a first cousin—inflicted more pain. His failure embarrassed the family.

The Menicuccis were pleased to have escaped the debacle before losing money. Their timing was impeccable; it was the peak of Safety First's profitability. Julio and Amerigo believed the events validated their slow and steady approach to building a business based on outstanding service and quality products. Ironically, Johnny had once favored the same approach with early success but was lured by ego into a self-destructive and poorly conceived gas war. The brothers attributed their fortune to the Lord, who looked favorably on them due to their relationship with his mother. The brothers believed, as the family historically has, that the Lord presents special events in a lifetime that allow a person to slow down, reflect and redirect as needed. This was one of those times.

FROM GROUND UP

In May of 1928, even before they had left Safety First, Julio took out a construction permit for a new building at Fourth and Marquette Streets, a retail super service station. It was the start of an intensive period for the brothers. They labored every waking hour, seven days a week, constructing their new station. The Menicuccis were adept tradesmen; both knew carpentry and plumbing and Amerigo was a qualified mason. They constructed the buildings mostly by themselves using adobe bricks for the walls Amerigo laid. Adobe bricks are constructed of mud and straw, which provides structural strength. The bricks are formed in molds, producing a product about the size of a modern concrete block that can be handled by a mason and used to construct walls for buildings. Adobe has good thermal properties and had been a traditional building material in New Mexico for centuries. They subcontracted specialty work such as electrical and roofing. It is probable that Vicente Cimino and his son Alfred along with Angelo Bandoni, all Lucchese building contractors, assisted in the construction. Marco Donati, a young carpenter at that time, was also likely involved. Marco became one of the premier Italian home builders and would later intervene in a Menicucci family crisis. The brothers purchased gasoline pumps, lubricating equipment, repair racks, benches, tools and washing supplies. Horace personally built the benches he needed for his repair work and purchased the equipment he needed. They all worked feverishly, with the intensity of a life emergency.

An interesting decision, which came late in the construction, was to add large canopies over the pumps to provide shade for customers while their autos were being serviced. Other stations had covered pumps, but this canopy was attached to the main building. A customer could pull into one of the pumps at the station, exit the vehicle and enter the confines of the front office, all under protective cover from weather. Along with the company name, the canopy was the second innovation that distinguished Super Service Station from others in the market. It would not be long before other new stations copied the Menicuccis, a sure sign that the Menicuccis had a unique market angle. Julio and Amerigo focused on service, the namesake of their company, and a canopy over the pumps was a service enhancement. They hired pump attendants, a lubricator and a washing man, all Lucchese.

Simultaneous with the construction of the station, the Menicuccis planned for their new homes. Amerigo found a lot at 717 Marquette Street and Julio secured one at 517 Third Street. They planned to build adobe homes themselves just as they did the station.

The homes were typical middle-class construction for the early 1930s with pitched roofs, two bedrooms, a living area, a large kitchen and expansive basements, a bathroom, a coal stove for space heating and cooking and screened front and back porches. Importantly, the basement provided plenty of room to store home garden produce and to produce and store wine. A basement was an essential feature in Italian homes because it was typically cool throughout the year, making it ideal for fermenting and storing wine. The men used wooden barrels to ferment and age the wine. Winemaking is an art as much as science, and the action of yeast and bacteria in fermentation was poorly understood at the time. In wine fermentation, yeast is placed in a sugary batch of grape juice that yeast converts to alcohol, producing wine. If the vintner is not careful, bacteria could infect the wine and sour into vinegar before the yeast can produce wine. Wooden barrels minimize the risk of bacterial contamination because wood naturally resists bacteria. Various Italian grocery markets, including the Matteuccis, supplied the grapes, yeast, storage bottles and other equipment needed for the fermentation needs of the local community. These businesses brought in the grapes by the train carload, which was then divided up among various Italian families.

The last year of the 1920s was hectic for the Menicuccis as they worked seven days a week and every waking hour constructing businesses and homes. By the middle of 1929, the three buildings were complete. The families moved into their new homes and Super Service Station opened to great fanfare in town. On opening day they hosted a crowd of customers, including most of the colony, all wishing the Menicuccis well. Everyone marveled at the new building and facilities while they bought discounted gasoline and other promotional items. The brothers figured that the promotions ensured a productive start. Mayor Tingley was proud of the station and the Menicuccis because they exemplified the essence of his growth strategy. Naturally, the mayor appeared at the station to congratulate the brothers, buy some gas and mingle. From Tingley's perspective, Super Service Station was another member of the Albuquerque growth team. He was the quintessential politician and blended right in by chatting with the common laborers and customers at the new Station.[4]

Julio focused on managing Rio Grande Oil Company and Amerigo was in familiar environs running the new Super Service Station. Both men had acquired considerable professional business expertise at Safety First and expeditiously brought the innovative Super Service Station into the limelight of Albuquerque's competitive automobile industry.

The Super Service Station constructed by the Menicucci brothers in 1928. The canopy was its most innovative feature. Courtesy author's collection.

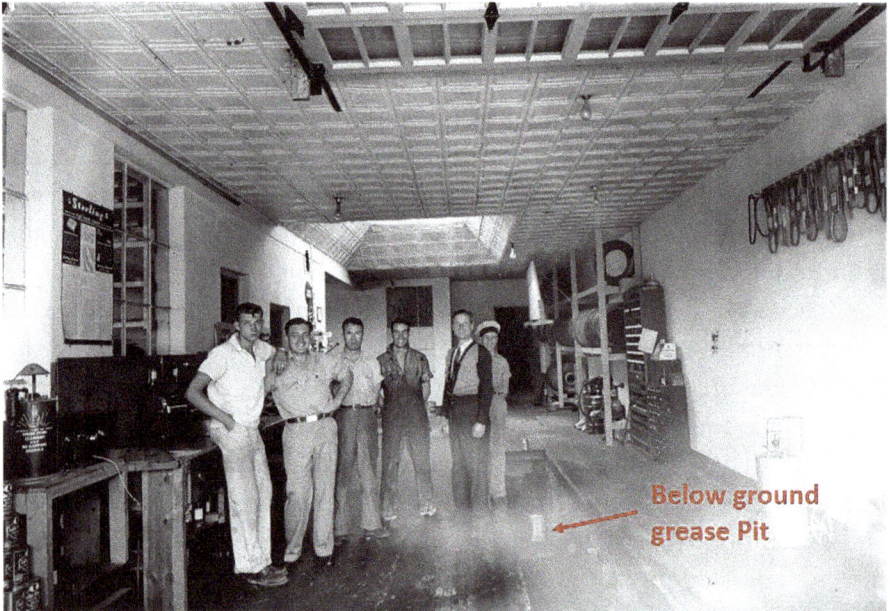

The grease pit at the original Super Service Station. Standing left to right: Herbert Bowdich, Horace Palladino, Ray Mathews, Gilbert Jojola, Julio Menicucci and Sam Jojola. Courtesy author's collection.

All of the men in the photo except Julio were part of the technical team that provided auto repairs, lubrication and detailing. The pit is a rectangular area just to the right of Sam. It was essentially a basement with a rectangular hole in the ceiling allowing men to stand while lubricating a vehicle parked overhead. Without hydraulic lifts, this setup allowed vehicles to be driven in at ground level and be easily serviced. It was, however, very dangerous and occasionally men fell into it. One of their first upgrades to the station was the installation of two lifts in the early 1930s followed by the abandonment of the pit due to safety concerns.

LUCCHESE TO ALBUQUERQUE'S DEFENSE

By the end of 1928, the stock market had been roaring for six years and Hoover's victory spurred it dizzyingly higher. To Albuquerque's Italian businessfolks, Wall Street and big business were all a distant whisper. They were focused on local market issues that affected their businesses. Most did not know the fundamentals of the stock market or economic and business theory. All they knew was that they could secure local bank loans at reasonable rates and deposit and withdraw cash as needed. Most importantly, business was so fine in a rapidly growing Albuquerque that few of the Italians had any concerns about the economy.

Two topics kept the Italians glued to the news reports: Prohibition and the Mafia. Liquor was high on the minds of Italians due to the societal and culinary importance of wine. By 1928, prohibition had obviously failed as liquor flowed freely throughout the country via the black market. In Chicago, more than twice as many saloons existed five years after prohibition than before. Along with illegal saloons came extensive, gang-related crime, especially in the large, eastern American cities.

The Italian Mafia, comprising mostly Sicilians and other southern Italians, organized into warring gangs of thugs battling regularly in American streets, often leaving bodies lying about while gun-toting murderers screeched from the scenes in black Lincoln Continentals. Much of the violence revolved around liquor, which was bootlegged into big American cities with few restrictions. Al Capone headed one of the largest and most ferocious Italian Chicago gangs with a reported 100,000 men in his militia in 1928.

Stories frequently appeared in the local newspapers about the alcohol-inspired gang warfare and its apparent migration to the western states. There were disturbing reports of the Black Hand Society operating in Colorado and Texas in the late 1920s. This society was a version of the Mafia and consisted of gangs of southern Italians who regularly extorted money from businesses and families. They brutely demanded money from businesses in letters signed with the imprint of a black hand. Failure to pay resulted in death or fire. Black Handers often preceded the Mafia into communities.

By 1928, public opinion was turning against prohibition. Congress was increasingly debating the law, and a growing number of U.S. representatives and executive officials were speaking out against it. As they did throughout the country, the Italians in Albuquerque cheered the opposition as many were eager to reopen their saloon and liquor sales businesses. There was particular concern about the Mafia infiltrating the area and taking over the liquor industry with illegal activities. Liquor, drug running and money laundering were prime Mafia business activities. The local Lucchese considered Albuquerque to be pure and free of Mafia filth, and they were—to a man—determined to keep the Mafia at bay.

In 2010, Rick Nathanson, a reporter for the *Albuquerque Journal*, published a story entitled "The Day the Mafia was Run Off...Or was it?" He reported about a 1928 picture of seven Italian men supposedly posing as a cadre of tough Albuquerque Lucchese who were purportedly prepared to defend the city against an invasion of Mafiosos from the East. The story went that these men heard that the Mafia was headed to Albuquerque to establish a foothold in the city when they were confronted at the rail station by seven rough Italian Lucchese who frightened them back to Chicago. The seven men included Cherubino Domenici, Amedeo Matteucci, Felice Barsanti, Frank Petroni, Joe Del Frate, Pete Vichi and Modesto Dalle. Nathanson told the tale but left the mystery intact regarding how and why these men came together for the picture and what transpired from it.

1928

MODESTO DALLE   PETE VICHI   JOE DELFRATE   FRANK PETRONI   BARSANTI   PAPA   CHOPPO

This original photo was published by the *Albuquerque Journal*. All of the men are hand-annotated by Lida Matteucci, daughter of Amedeo who likely took the picture. Amedeo is noted as "Papa." Courtesy Matteucci family.

INSERT Image 42. Five of the seven men in this second photo are the same as the ones in the original. A sixth was probably taking the photo and the seventh is not pictured, possibly cut-off on left. From left: Pete Vichi, Modesto Dalle, Cherubino Domenici, Joe Del Frate and Felice Barsanti. They are in front of Soda Dam, just north of Jemez Springs, New Mexico. Courtesy Matteucci family.

Considering the men's backgrounds, personal prejudices, affection for the city and aggressive natures, the mystery can be solved. All of the men were Lucchese and all were related to one another by a complex web of blood, law, marriage and philosophy. All of them were in or would be in the food business and some had sold liquor before prohibition and wished to do so again. And all of them profoundly loathed the southern Italian Mafia, and the picture was likely the brainchild of Amedeo Matteucci because his daughter Lida annotated the original photo with the names of the men. Amedeo owned and operated the Matteucci and Palladino Grocery Store and was a leader in the Italian community. Frank Petroni was Amedeo's brother-in-law; his sister was Amedeo's wife, Ancilla Petroni. Frank owned Metropolitan Market and had a boisterous personality. He was once convicted of possessing stolen chickens, but the judge deferred a prison sentence because he was only a "casual buyer." For a time in 1919, Frank worked at the Champion Grocery store owned by Amedeo's brother. Felice's wife, Eufamia Stefani, was sister to Alessandro Matteucci's wife, Maria Stefani. Joe Del Frate was the younger brother to Louie Del Frate, who was married to Amedeo's niece, Banny Matteucci. Pete Vichi's sister Alda was Cherubino's husband, making the two men brothers-in-law. Modesto Dalle Piagge, my maternal grandfather would be in business with Pete Vichi and had just engaged to marry Pia Barsanti, a distant relation to Felice. Pia had been the housemaid to Antonio Domenici for six years. The Del Frate family participated in Modesto's and Pia's marriage ceremony. The point is that it was essentially a family affair. All of these men were ambitious, hard-charging, tough and hung together. Some of them, including Frank Petroni and Modesto Dalle, were amateur boxers.

The pictures were taken while Felice Barsanti was visiting briefly in 1928. He left Albuquerque a few years earlier to work in California but had been in Chicago on business. He was passing through Albuquerque and stopped to visit. The two photos were probably shot at the same time near Soda Dam because the men are wearing the same clothes in both photos. Note the beverage containers. Visible are two wine bottles, one in the box and another half-empty on the ground. A third shorter one in the box, likely held Grappa. The teacups likely contained coffee handsomely enhanced with Grappa. Two bottles of wine and one of Grappa was a typical load of alcohol for these men on a Jemez outing. There were likely tins of snuff and stogies lying about also.

I believe all of these men gathered at Soda Dam to celebrate Felice's visit when the discussion, fueled by liquor and wine, led them to the subject of the Mafia, which Felice had experienced firsthand in Chicago. He had heard tales from his associates in the Windy City how the Mafia had extorted hundreds of dollars from some Lucchese, roughing them up and burning their business in the process. This enraged the wine-logged men, who concocted a stunt to post a picture of Albuquerque's formidable Italian men at the rail station, warning any Mafia invaders that they will face stiff Lucchese resistance in the city. They probably took the picture to Mayor Tingley and all enjoyed a good laugh. Maybe it was effective because neither the Black Hand Society nor the Italian Mafia took hold in Albuquerque. In the end, there is little mystery about how and why these men ended up in the picture.[5]

The year 1928 ended on a high note, with the stock market soaring to astronomical heights following Hoover's presidential victory. Elation was endemic in the nation's business community, including Albuquerque's. While the people blissfully slept dreaming of riches in a land of milk and honey, beyond the horizon, ominous clouds were gathering that would soon envelop the city, country and world in an economic calamity of historic proportions.

Notes

1. Johnny (Austutillo) Gianinni was one of the most colorful of the Italian immigrants, even surpassing the antics of Alessandro Matteucci a decade earlier. Johnny loved the spotlight and performed to it. He was the constant talk of the colony and was frequently mentioned by name by both Menicucci brothers. Julio once called him a mamaluccho (insane or crazy man). Mariangela Menicucci Scanlon, daughter to Julio, told the story of Julio's reaction to Johnny's antics. "Papa thought that Johnny might have been taken by the devil because he acted so crazy sometimes. Both Papa and Zio (Amerigo) thought his gas war was because he gave in to Satan. Johnny did so many crazy things that it was the only explanation."

2. *Los Angeles Water and Power Associates* describe the origins of super service stations in a short article.

3. Most of the information for this chapter was derived from lore supplied by the Menicucci brothers and corroborated by historical, real-

time newspaper reports, particularly those relating to the first gas war, which was a front-page story with great reader interest.

4. Sacks describes Tingley's mode of operation well.

5. *Mangione & Morreale* and *Laurino* discuss the Italian Mafia in the United States in the early Twentieth Century.

12

A TRANSITION FOR PEOPLE AND NATION (1928–1933)

SEEDING THE DOWNFALL

Most people believe the stock market crash in October 1929 initiated the Great Depression. It was more of a symptom of the widespread disaster. The worrisome signs of economic calamity emerged in 1928, even as the stock market wildly lurched forward in a frenzy before and following Herbert Hoover's 1928 presidential victory. The volume of trading after the election reached record highs with the stock ticker running nearly two hours behind, indicating a plethora of buyers. Six years of booming and unprecedented economic growth had created a mood of invincibility in the financial markets. Almost every reasonable business venture was profitable, stocks always seemed to rise and risky investments paid off like conservative ones but with greater reward. Risk begot risk and it encouraged more speculative investing.

Wages were adequate, employment rates were high and an increasing number of people had money to buy new devices and leisure time to enjoy them. In 1928, for the first time, average Americans, including most of the Italians in Albuquerque, could purchase many fine features of life, and they responded by procuring a plethora of discretionary items, especially appliances, autos, radios and homes. Albuquerque had been on a growth tear for six years, with the city annexing nearly five thousand acres of land with over thirty-five hundred homes. Its population increased from fifteen thousand to over twenty-six thousand in the 1920s.

Early in the decade, most consumer purchases were in cash but in later years many transactions were via installments, including personal loans from banks. Installment buying assumes the borrower can repay the loan, presumably because he or she earns a steady income. If that income stream is interrupted, the lender can lose. The banking industry increasingly hawked installment loans, which were profitable because the economy was raging along.

Loans were scarfed up by the public that needed capital for many new consumer products coming into the market after the war. With more money, citizens invested heavily in durable goods, such as homes or automobiles. It produced a spike in spending that faded over time. The problem was that durable goods lived long as opposed to many consumables, with lives measured in days. With durable goods, a purchase is made and the asset is held for years. The purchaser is removed from the market and replacement buyers are constantly needed to maintain the pace of growth. Sales of many durable goods products waned even as their companies' stocks soared, creating great disparities between the book value of the companies and their market value. Alas, the economic frenzy met the reality of an economy based largely on a diminishing supply of buyers.

By 1929, durable goods, which had been leading the economic boom, encountered market saturation. Factories laid off workers, but the overall market, in the frenzy of euphoric profit-taking, ignored the warnings. Investors' speculation drove up company valuations even as their businesses slowed. A unique form of panic buying emerged—investors from all walks of life panicked to buy stock in a soaring market. These people borrowed heavily to finance their speculative market forays. Typically, a brokerage allowed investors to trade on margin, essentially borrowing from the broker to buy stock. Later, the banks loaned to traders, including many smaller investors looking to get rich quickly but without experience in market trading. It worked well for everyone as all stocks consistently rose, producing revenue to pay back the loans and invest the profits in even larger speculations. All was fine in the first half of 1929, except for increased market volatility. The market gyrated up and down, creating losses that were quickly recouped when the market swung back up.

The banking industry, sniffing profits, offered more attractive loan terms to accommodate the panic buying. Simultaneously, banks speculated in the stock market, using it to augment their capital accounts and bolster their bottom lines. They also shrank their reserves and the money kept on hand to service day-to-day cash transactions and investments. The reasoning was that cash reserves can be reduced in a booming economy because people will likely repay their loans. Lower margins allowed the banks additional capital to speculate in stocks. Regulation was rudimentary then, and banks were allowed wide latitude regarding their reserves and investments. The Federal Reserve had only existed for a decade and was unsure how to execute its role in managing the nation's banks. What is obvious now but opaque then was that the entire U.S. banking system was operating like a Ponzi scheme, where increased risk was hedged with additional risk. The financial community felt invulnerable because almost anything they did produced profits.

As 1929 wore on into summer, economic warning signs, which a year earlier were dead cold, were flashing yellow and red. Factories laid off workers as demand for durable goods declined. Normally, an occasional business slowdown is a healthy sign for a normal market because unceasing growth is impossible. This was different because the durable goods industry was the bedrock of the economic boom and if it declined, so did the economy because there was nothing of comparable size to replace it. By August the reality was beginning to sink in as employment statistics showed a significantly slowing economy and increasing joblessness. Loan defaults were growing and traders were often caught off guard, losing money on leveraged trades and short positions.

Banks felt the pain and some smaller and undercapitalized ones failed. The banks with heavy stock market positions were especially at risk, but there was little concern because they expected the market to continue to grow. Market valuations were astronomically high following the post-election frenzy and poised for a correction. The market participants were in great peril, although few could see it at the time. Hoover could see it but he stood by the Republican philosophy of hands-off of businesses. He trusted the market to find a way to maintain growth. Lenders, too, believed that the more the government removed itself from the finance system, the better. They did not realize they were stirring a witch's brew that would lead to their demise in just a few months.

ONSLAUGHT BEGINS

It all came to a head in October of 1929. At the start of the week of October 14th, stock prices slumped, sending shivers through the market. At times, some stocks on the exchange sat for hours with no buyers, eventually purchased by market vultures scooping up distressed positions for pennies on the dollar. The rest of the week and the subsequent one followed the downward trend with increased volatility. Meanwhile, bad news of eroding overall business activity spooked the market. The general public was beginning to realize the precarious economic position of the American economy.

On Tuesday, October 29th, the market was itching for a downturn. The investment mood was sour, lenders were uncertain and millions of investors feared the worst. The beginning of the end commenced as the market opened with millions of shares of stock for sale and few buyers. Many shares closed the session at zero value, having sat for sale all day with no buyers, not even extreme bargain hunters. Technically, this meant that the associated companies were insolvent, and any loans for positions in those companies were also rendered valueless. By the end of the day, many banks were looking at balance sheets indicating that they were technically bankrupt. Banks do not operate in isolation but depend on other banks for loans and other services. Therefore, a default in New York or Boston banks could affect those in Albuquerque. Troubled banks and brokers leaned on investors to pony up cash to cover their positions, but many investors had lost so much that they forfeited their positions, leaving a growing wake of losses. Exacerbating the situation were the losses that the banks incurred from a rout of their stock positions, which they had purchased as a hedge against slowing loan applications. Throughout the day of October 29, thousands of investors scrambled for money to cover their loans and many had no money left. Many millionaires, some in Albuquerque, had the net worths of alley bums at the close of trading on that October day.

Panic of a different kind set in as word of the bank failures spread across the country. The Federal Deposit Insurance Corporation would not be in full control for several years, thus leaving bank depositors at risk of bank failures. As people sensed the danger, they flocked to the banks to withdraw their savings. It only took a few bank failures, with spectacular stories of grandpas losing their entire life savings in a day, for dread to grip the nation. For weeks, the crisis spread throughout the banking sector, leaving a trail of despair for millions as they could not withdraw their savings from banks.

The agriculture industry was hit especially hard because farmers depended on loans for operation. With many banks closing and cash reserves low, many farmers could not secure operational loans and abandoned their farms, returning to the cities, where they were relegated to bread lines to find food they once grew. Farmland rapidly lost value and farm output slowed. An extended drought in the early 1930s destroyed millions of acres of farmland in America's breadbasket, the Midwest. Farming descended into a depression that mirrored the stock market crash as massive amounts of arable land had been laid fallow. In 1929, New Mexico's farm production was nearly forty million dollars (about seven hundred million in 2024 dollars). By 1931, it had dropped to twenty million and fell to nine million dollars the following year. State livestock values plunged from nearly eighty million in 1929 to thirty-two million in 1933.

BANKING BUST

It took a couple of years for the banking problem to settle in Albuquerque. The distance from the nation's financial capital in New York and the city's geographical isolation in the desert provided a buffer. In 1933 the banking crisis arrived with a blast. The First National Trust and Savings was the first trouble spot. For years, the bank operated on the margins of ethical standards and safe loan practices. The federal government identified the bank as one likely to default. First National Bank, about six times the size, was positioned better but was also in trouble. Further, it was tainted by its affiliation with First National Trust. Albuquerque's third bank, Albuquerque National Trust and Savings, was more conservatively managed but still operated with a modicum of safety.[1] It was in poor condition but superior to the other two. All three banks were now identified as possible failures. Like those nationwide, these banks operated free of most regulation and with the irrational enthusiasm of America's Roaring Twenties. They were now in precarious financial positions. Witnessing the unfolding disaster, people attempted to cash out their savings accounts, and the national bank run was on.

Despite Hoover's laissez-faire predilection, he sensed the peril of a national banking system collapse. Such a catastrophe would impose severe losses on nearly every citizen, which could progress to anarchy or civil war.

His administration developed legislation to deal with the crisis. However, Hoover was enslaved to his philosophy, and the help he pondered was primarily for businesses, not individuals. His theory was that businesses would lead the country out of the slump. Meanwhile, the states, too, were enacting legislation to deal with the local impact of the financial crisis.

As 1933 unfolded, locals by the dozens appeared at banks demanding to cash out their savings accounts. The bank's reserves were rapidly consumed and some depositors were refused or delayed in withdrawing their holdings. It further inflamed the situation and public demonstrations, including violence, rang the government's alarm bells. On March 3rd, the New Mexico bank examiner, John Bingham, took the unusual step of imposing a bank holiday in which banks closed and each submitted to detailed state-of-New Mexico inspections. It was a kind of cooling-off period. Just as the state bank holiday ended a week later, the Federal government imposed a national bank holiday. During the two bank holidays in the spring of 1933, both lasting about a week each, Albuquerque had no operating banks, with depositors unable to access their accounts and left wondering if they ever would. During the holiday, federal examiners rated each bank for solvency. At the end of the holiday, only the financially sound banks would reopen while the others would be reorganized. Although all three city banks were reopened, Albuquerque National was the only one that even approached the lower bounds of true financial security.

First National Trust was barely operational. Deposits fell to zero while depositors cashed out and closed their accounts. It was in precarious shape and struggled to remain solvent using various operational schemes. On March 20, 1933, the state bank examiner restricted the bank, limiting withdrawals to five percent of the depositor's balance. On the day after the holiday, depositors flocked to the bank for their five percent, quickly exhausting its already limited cash reserve. The examiner also ordered that any new deposits be stored at the Federal Reserve Bank in Denver rather than at First National Trust as a safety hedge. All this was like a bullhorn warning depositors to withdraw their money as soon as possible and the holidays only delayed the day of reckoning.

A crushing blow occurred on April 8th, 1933, when bank examiners discovered a massive, ten-year-old embezzlement scheme at First Savings Bank that resulted in a loss of over one hundred seventeen thousand dollars (about two million seven hundred in 2024 dollars). What so astonished the investigators was that a single perpetrator, an employee, had embezzled singlehandedly. Among the other malefactions, the auditors also found fraudulent accounts, mortgages sold twice and personal loans to deceased people. The bank leaders had been asleep at the switch for years. The bank was closed permanently a short time later.

Friday Morning, July 14, 1933.   PRICE FIVE CENTS

Systematic Looting of First Savings Bank for Decade Shown by Audit

DEPOSITORS ASK CHAIRMAN TO CALL SPECIAL MEETING TO QUIZ BANK EXAMINER

Petition Governor to Assure Bingham's Presence; Committee Criticized, But Status Remains Unchanged; Three Members Defend Their Actions

$111,198 TAKEN FROM PATRONS, INSTITUTION BY COX, SAYS REPORT

$35,000 in 1932 and $20,000 in First Months of 1933; Trust Funds Looted of Thousands

INTRICATE BOOKKEEPING; NAMES OF DEAD USED

In Some Cases, Mortgages Sold Twice; Reported Shortage Approaches Bank's Capital

---

COOK SELECTED FOR TEMPORARY DRY DIRECTOR

Prominent Democrat of Socorro Undecided If He Will Accept Post Vacated by C. H. Stearns

BINGHAM SAYS DEPOSITORS HIS ONLY INTEREST

Bank Examiner Declares He Will Attend Meeting at any Time; "Has Nothing to Conceal"

TWO HUSBANDS GIVEN ALIMONY UNDER NEW STATUTE IN ILLINOIS

BRIDE WILL WED

RUTH SEEKS RECORD

NARCOTIC SHIPMENTS

MORE DISOBEDIENCE

NO PRI-ATE RELIEF

Clipping from the *Albuquerque Journal* in 1933 announcing the embezzlement scheme at First Saving Bank in July, 1933. It was the beginning of the end for the bank, which never reopened.

First National Trust depositors eventually lost most of their savings. The losses stung many business owners and the gloom of the national depression lurked like a specter in Albuquerque. The crisis was just getting started. On April 17, in response to a huge swarm of depositors making fearful withdrawals from their savings accounts, First National Bank's comptroller for currency closed the bank and appointed lawyer Wil Keleher to oversee its reorganization to secure one hundred percent of deposits. The Keleher family had been in Albuquerque for years and were among the most prominent families in town, specializing in law. They were respected at the highest levels of government for their expertise and ethical standards.[2]

Two of Albuquerque's three banks were now closed and the strain on the community was showing, especially among farmers. The reorganization took months and several plans were considered, including one from Albuquerque National, where they proposed buying First National. Their plan was not accepted and it took until October 25th to reopen, which they did with a half-page ad in the *Albuquerque Journal* touting its new operational condition by presenting its complete balance sheet.

THE FIRST NATIONAL BANK
in ALBUQUERQUE
Capital and Surplus $625,000.00
I; Open For Business Today

FOR MORE THAN FIFTY YEARS the First National Bank has served the business interests of Albuquerque and New Mexico, fostering development, aiding industry and forwarding the progress of the community.... So valuable has been the service performed by the bank that, when it encountered difficulties in the turbulent period of the National bank holiday, more than five hundred of the leading citizens of New Mexico and Northeastern Arizona joined with the United States Government in its complete and successful reorganization, in order that the institution might resume its place of usefulness . . . stronger and better equipped to serve than at any time in its history.

Now every detail of that reorganization has been successfully carried out. With the largest capital of any bank in New Mexico . . With cash reserves adequate for every possible requirement of its depositors . . . with every item of its assets liquid . . . with every note in its case worth 100 cents on the dollar . . . with its management amplified and strengthened and its directorate representative of all phases of the business and industry of city and state . . . THE FIRST NATIONAL BANK IN ALBUQUERQUE will resume business Tuesday morning, October 24th, at 10 o'clock.

OWNERSHIP

Strong ownership means a strong bank.

The ownership of the First National Bank is as strong as the community itself, because it is thoroughly representative of all elements in the community. Its common stock is owned by more than five hundred citizens, representative of the principal financial strength of the community. These citizens have demonstrated their faith in the institution and their realization of the essential place it occupies, by buying its entire common capital stock of $250,000.00, for which they have paid the sum of $375,000.00, thus providing as surplus of $125,000.00. These citizens may be depended upon to stand squarely behind the institution in which they have made this large investment, and to work for its welfare and growth, in order that its usefulness to them and to the community may be steadily expanded.

This group of more than 500 citizens have as their equal partners in the ownership of the First National bank, the Government of the United States. The Federal Reconstruction Finance Corporation has purchased the entire issue of $250,000.00 of preferred stock, thus completing the bank's capital of $500,000.00. In addition by acquiring a half ownership in the bank, the Reconstruction Finance Corporation has advanced $400,000.00 upon unacceptable assets of the old bank, on which the new First National has no liability of any kind.

Thus the United States Government has demonstrated its realization of the vital place of this bank in this community and its complete confidence in the soundness of its reorganization and its future.

As Hon. Jesse H. Jones, chairman of the Reconstruction Finance Corporation has said: "For the Government to be willing to buy stock in a bank and advertise to the world that it is a partner in that bank, is the greatest compliment and source of strength that could come to any bank."

MANAGEMENT

The management of this bank begins with its stockholders, who, as stated, represent all elements of the community and its principal financial strength. The United States Government, as owner of fifty per cent of the capital stock, exercised the right to pass upon the eligibility of all officers and directors and has given its unqualified approval to the bank's official organization. The Reconstruction Finance Corporation also reserved the right to name its representatives on the board of directors at any time it may deem such action advisable. The corporation, satisfied with the personnel of the initial board of directors, has not found it necessary to name any representatives on the board, thus voting its entire confidence in the character and ability of officers and directors to manage the institution successfully.

The board of directors has been chosen with a view of providing representation for all divisions of business and industry in Albuquerque and New Mexico.

Mr. C. W. Carson, President, has had a wide experience in southwestern banking and is thoroughly familiar with business and industry in this region. Moreover he has had a recent and thorough experience in Washington as deputy Land Bank Commissioner, bringing him in contact with all the Government's financial departments and loan agencies which will prove of highest value to the institution.

Mr. W. C. Thaxton, vice-president, is an experienced maker of mortgage loans and a real estate appraiser of recognized ability. He has demonstrated his capacity in handling and financial managements, his conservatism and his sound judgment.

Mr. Silvestre Mirabal, director, is a livestock owner and operator who has been successful in the conduct of his business and who knows thoroughly all phases of New Mexico's great livestock industry.

Colonel D. K. B. Sellers, director, is a successful real estate operator, who has demonstrated his judgment of real estate values and as financial management. He is one of the best informed men on the resources of the region served by the bank.

Mr. Henry G. Coors, director, is an outstanding lawyer. He is a former president of the Clovis National Bank, and rendered important service in connection with the reorganization of the bank.

Mr. B. B. Hanger, director, is a real estate operator and successful business executive whose experience in some of the state's principal industries will prove valuable to the organization.

Mr. G. L. Rogers, vice-president, is an executive of the First National, who has services invaluable to the institution, will serve as Assistant to the President, while continuing his present capacity as Manager of the New Mexico Credit Corporation.

Mr. W. J. White, Cashier, has a continuous record of more than 30 years with the bank and is expert in all departments of the technical operations of banking.

CASH and LIQUID ASSETS

A first essential of banking strength and capacity for sound public service is liquid assets and ample cash reserves.

The First National Bank resumes business with a total cash reserve of $1,373,822.10. Few banks in existence can show so large a cash reserve.

Behind this large cash reserve, stands the bank's secondary reserves, consisting of readily marketable bonds which are carried in all cases at present market prices.

With the single exception of the bank building and fixtures, which are carried at much less than their actual value, all assets of this bank are completely liquid.

The bank's note case consists entirely of prime, well-secured paper, worth one hundred cents on the dollar.

The bank has no "frozen assets," such as frozen loans, defaulted bonds, real estate mortgages. Every item of its assets is cash or can be readily converted into cash, with the single exception of the bank building.

This strong cash reserve and liquid position not only provide maximum security to depositors, but also makes it possible for the institution to resume operation with the maximum capacity for service to the business community.

And behind this strong cash position and complete liquidity of assets stands the bank's capital of $500,000.00 and its surplus fund of $125,000.00, the largest capital and surplus of any bank in New Mexico.

OFFICERS
C. W. Carson, President
G. L. Rogers, Assistant to the President
W. C. Thaxton, Vice President
W. J. White, Cashier

You, the present customers of the First National Bank, are invited to resume your normal business relations with the institution, with confidence that it is prepared to serve your every need, faithfully and efficiently. You, the business community and the public, whether you have been customers of the bank in the past, or not, are cordially invited to come in and meet its officers and to make use of its facilities whenever their services may be required.

DIRECTORS
C. W. Carson,
W. C. Thaxton,
Silvestre Mirabal,
D. K. B. Sellers,
Henry G. Coors,
B. B. Hanger,
W. J. White.

Clipping from the *Albuquerque Journal* in October, 1933 with an extraordinary announcement of the reopening of the First National Bank.

By this time, the public was so traumatized by the banking crisis that many distrusted the banks. Some, such as the First Savings account holders lost their savings. Tom Keleher suggested the ad to help regain public confidence. Keleher was a leading figure in town and was involved in many of the major bank actions of the time. The bank still operates today.

The impact of the economy on specific businesses depended on each one's financial situation and the industry in which they operated. Farmers were first to feel the pinch, followed by those who sold durable goods, such as autos and appliances. Automobile manufacturing, which had been growing at over ten percent per year for nearly all of the 1920s, by 1932 had shrunk by fifty percent. The businesses least affected included food establishments, stores, restaurants, and auto supplies. Food and mobility were essential to modern life and remained in demand regardless of the state of the economy. Housing was affected by difficulties in obtaining mortgages; people stayed put. Although auto sales had plummeted nationally, many people still owned cars that needed service and fuel. The auto and appliance repair businesses actually grew slightly during the Depression because people held their vehicles longer because they could not buy new ones.[3]

SUPER RESILIENCE

Super Service Station was in about the best possible market position, although building any business on the threshold of an economic collapse was an exceedingly risky venture. The Menicuccis had built an innovative service station that provided popular conveniences to the public. Safety First's customers followed the Menicuccis; Amerigo brought most of his many retail customers to the Super Service Station and Julio took all of his wholesale service stations to Rio Grande Oil. All of those stations were keen to jump from Johnny's ship after the gas war debacle. Like at Safety First, people stopped by Super Service Station to talk to Amerigo and buy a tank of gas. Julio, too, had his following, but at the wholesale level. He had developed working relationships with many of the big gas and oil suppliers, giving him an understanding of the wholesale market landscape.

During the depression years, Super Service Station operated year-round seven days a week, seven in the morning to seven in the evening. Their profits were not only strong but growing with a burgeoning customer base. Amerigo, whose retail management skills were advanced, continued advertising regularly, including special deals and other incentives. They advertised Mohawk tires on sale for six dollars each, including installation and a free car wash. Amerigo had customers lined up for service each morning and his entire crew was busy every day.

The new station was ideally located downtown for the convenience of the growing number of residents filling the vacant residential lots nearby. Super Service Station was new and different, and it attracted customers. Amerigo's charm was an enticing feature, and his focus on quality and service led to a cadre of devoted admirers. Julio's determined leadership and rapidly developing business acumen kept the family's oil and gas enterprise in Albuquerque's fast lane of commerce.

When the Menicucci brothers sold their interest in Safety First, they took most of Johnny Giannini's customers with them. None were more important than the Albuquerque Fire Department. When he was running Safety First Tire, Amerigo had negotiated a tire replacement contract with the department. This kind of a contract was a major profit staple because it created a steady demand for products and services at fair prices. The department followed Amerigo to Super Service Station.

An Albuquerque fire truck that was outfitted with Mohawk tires under a new contract that Amerigo negotiated. At far right is Amerigo Menicucci. A customer stands nearby. The fire truck contains the fire chief, Arthur "Art" Westerfeld, and another department employee. Courtesy Theresa Domenici Menicucci.

SAFETY FIRST SUCCUMBS

The Menicuccis, fortunately, were steeled for the depression. Johnny Giannini, on the other hand, was situated for demise. Safety First, due to the ill-conceived gas war, was deep in debt and his tire shop was becoming obsolete in the rapidly evolving world of auto service. The quality of his service and products sank as he struggled to save his sinking ship. He no longer had a wholesale business to buoy his enterprise. By 1933, he was on the cusp of bankruptcy. He made one last attempt to save it by renaming Safety First to Johnny's Super Service Station. It was too late. Menicuccis had already capitalized on the idea. He mortgaged his land but promptly defaulted on payments, triggering a lawsuit. By the end of 1933, Johnny was finished and he closed the business. The Dinellis sued Johnny to cover their lost investment and won judgments but could never recover fully. Johnny did odd jobs and spent many of his days mining gold with some success. He never reopened a business of any significance. His effect on the Menicucci family was more significant than any other individual they had encountered in America. Johnny Giannini was one of Albuquerque's most interesting Italian immigrants.

This picture was taken in 1930 after Safety First at 222 North Fourth Street was nearly destroyed by the disastrous gas war. From left: unknown, Johnny Giannini, and the two Dinelli brothers, Frank and Johnny. Courtesy Albuquerque Museum, a gift from Ray and Daniel Bandel.

BAD CHOICE

The economic crisis randomly imposed hardship on people when they made perfectly rational decisions at the wrong time. Consider the case of Modesto Dalle Piagge. He originally immigrated to Colorado in 1910 to work in the coal mines. A mining disaster, similar to the one that nearly killed the Menicucci brothers, discouraged him from the job, so he began working with Ralph Balduini. Together they moved to Albuquerque, where they worked in real estate. Modesto simplified his name to Dalle because of the Americans' difficulty pronouncing Piagge. He settled in Old Town, living on Central Avenue near the Rio Grande River. He managed apartments in New Town when he met Pia Barsanti, his future wife. Pia had immigrated to America on a blind arrangement to marry Michele Granone, brother to her sister's husband, John Granone.

The prospective groom was a successful Italian businessman who paid for Pia to travel second-class to America. She was among the few immigrant peasants to travel to America above steerage class. After Pia met Michele, she refused to marry him. She later said, "I took one look at him and said 'no.'" The decision left her isolated in Albuquerque, where she had no husband, no money, no family, and no job. As was typical at that time, Lucchese came to the rescue. Antonio Domenici hired her as a housemaid to help his wife, Emma Giomi, look after their children. She became a family member, as Emma trained Pia on the Italian way to run a home, especially cooking. The Domenici families, Antonio and his younger brother Cherubino were well established in Albuquerque and known for their Montezuma Grocery, which specialized in Italian foods and Olive Oil. Cherubino eventually adopted the nickname Chopo and went on to father Pete Domenici, who became a U.S. Senator from New Mexico. Pia repaid Granone for the travel expenses and worked for the Domenicis until she married Modesto Dalle in April 1929.

Modesto wanted a good start for his family and saw a fine ranching opportunity. After some investigation, he concluded that it was a secure business for his growing family. Old Town was mainly a farming and ranching community and many of the Hispanics had been successfully operating hog ranches for generations. From his perspective in 1930, Albuquerque's economic outlook appeared good despite the national situation. He bought a hog ranch near Rio Grande Boulevard and Central Avenue using his life savings and personal loans.[4,5]

His timing could not have been worse. Shortly after he commenced operation, land values crashed as the depression set in throughout the country. Within six months, the value of his ranch property dropped by seventy five percent. It was a particularly pernicious situation where the sale of one farm set the value for all the others in the area. In an environment of falling prices, values constantly ratcheted down.

Here is how this phenomenon works. Consider three identical hog farm properties, each adjacent to one another. Property one has a mortgage of three thousand dollars, property two's mortgage is four thousand and a third is servicing one for five thousand. Property one sells his ranch in a panic for three thousand dollars, enough to cover his debt but sacrificing any equity he had in the property. The value of all the adjacent properties is now worth three thousand, and the other two owners cannot sell their properties for enough even to cover their loans, leaving them bankrupt.

This debilitating process was playing out throughout the country and increasingly in Albuquerque.

The hog ranchers burdened with mortgages and loans—most of them—had no choice but to sell in a panic because hog prices were depressed and falling. Not only was the chance of profit gone, but they were also hard-pressed to find any buyers. Some ranchers slaughtered and buried their hogs because they were too expensive to keep, and they could not give them away. Even procuring farm products to operate the ranches became difficult. Modesto never turned a profit and in 1932 he sold his ranch for pennies on his investment. He was broken with two young children and a wife at home. He spent the next few years working various odd jobs until he had repaid his debts and had enough money to open a bar and café in 1935. In contrast to the Menicuccis, his family suffered greatly in the early 1930s.

LUCCHESE BROTHERHOOD

The Italian community stuck close together through the economic crisis. Johnny Matteucci provides an example of how the Menicuccis responded to those in the colony who were in need. In 1930, Johnny operated his National Cigar Store in the lobby of the First National Bank building on Fifth and Gold Streets. His store sold a variety of tobacco products. He had run the store for several years with sufficient success to start a family. First National was the city's largest bank and housed many professional organizations, including lawyers, real estate agents and insurance brokers. These folks patronized Johnny's store with its exclusive offering of high-quality tobaccos. Many of these people traded daily at the National Cigar Store.

As the depression evolved, many of his customers were licking their wounds over the stock market crash and its continued decline; many were wealthy local citizens, such as CEOs of large companies. Tobacco was one of the discretionary purchases many of these people eliminated to save money. Johnny first noticed that regular customers stopped in less frequently. As weeks passed, many bought less expensive products and many stopped buying tobacco altogether.

His future was bleak. As the crisis continued, with runs on the banks and hordes of angry depositors walking by, few were disposed to stop into Johnny's luxury store. Many people eschewed the bank altogether because it reminded them of the depression; Johnny's shop was guilty by association with First National. By 1932, Johnny's losses were eating through his savings, so he relinquished his lease and sold the store. He had taken a heavy loss and was looking for work, along with a growing list of others. A cigar store in a major bank building was perfect for the roaring twenties but a rotten one in a depression.

Johnny's situation concerned Julio. He felt obligated to help one of his closest family friends, a relationship that harkened back many generations in Italy. Johnny stopped into the station occasionally to visit with the Menicuccis, reporting on his failure to find employment. As the weeks rolled into months and still out of work, Johnny was running out of money. Julio interceded and told Amerigo that they would include him in Super Service as a minority owner. Johnny contributed no capital but was paid as an employee. He agreed to invest part of his remuneration in the business over a specified period, making Johnny a small co-owner. Amerigo was agreeable. A crisis was no time to quibble when it came to assisting one of the Matteuccis. Johnny, immensely grateful, came on board immediately, working with Amerigo purveying tires and fuel. He had no technical skills but possessed a business mind, and he was an excellent companion to Amerigo at the station. Best of all, the three men—Julio, Amerigo and Johnny—were friends and worked smoothly together.

It took a few years for the depression to settle into Albuquerque, but by 1933, business activity had significantly slowed. Banks in Albuquerque had been on the brink, and one had been permanently closed, leaving depositors with losses. Few businesses operated profitably and many changed their business strategy from thriving to surviving. Super Service Station was an exception and stood as one of the economic pillars of support in Albuquerque during the Depression.

The Super Service Station team during the Depression. From left: Johnny Matteucci, Pete Granucci, Julio Menicucci, Albert Nottoli, Amerigo Menicucci, Horace Palladino, Firpo Gallegos, Jim Mahon. Courtesy author's collection.

FINISHING UP THE FAMILY

The early 1930s was a frenzied time for the Menicucci families as they settled into their new homes. Davina and Giulia, maturing young mothers, were busily nurturing their young children. Each day started at about four in the morrning for both women and men. In the winter the men ensured that the coal stove was properly fueled and stoked and that the women had all they needed for a day of work. Families stored food in closed, wooden boxes outdoors during the cold season, which regularly dips below freezing. In the summer, the men recharged an ice box ice daily. The women washed and dried all their clothes by hand, including diapers, prepared all their meals, cleaned the home, cared for their children, and performed their marital duties to their husbands. They dried clothes on clotheslines and on cold winter days, moist clothes froze solidly on the line. In extreme cold conditions, Giulia placed drying clothes on cords draped across the room where the stove was. It consumed most of the open space in the home. Both women worked dutifully day in and day out.

Julio did all the shopping for Giulia. She gave him a list of items she needed each day, and he dutifully supplied them. Being friendly and outgoing, Davina developed relationships with Lena Franchini, who lived next door, and Ancilla Matteucci, Amedeo's wife. Lena and her husband Gene lived next door to Amerigo's family. The Matteuccis lived only a block to the southeast on North Sixth Street. These women shopped together for food and other products because all three could speak English and they enjoyed each other's company.

In spite of the deepening depression, the Menicuccis had some discretionary funds to enhance their home, including new furniture and clothes. Their retail and wholesale businesses were steadily advancing amongst a growing array of economic ruin that was insinuating itself in the city's business community.

TRAGEDY IN THE CRIB

In 1931, the effects of the depression were yet to be felt. Certainly, some local folks had lost fortunes, but the average resident felt little effect. Most importantly, the Wall Street turmoil did not affect the Menicucci's businesses, which were growing briskly. The risk appeared low and the timing was right for a fourth child. On January 3, 1931, Giulia delivered a healthy baby girl named Mariangela. On schedule, Davina followed on April 18th with a baby boy named Julio Henry. The given name of this fourth child was preplanned as a tribute to the family founders. Amerigo was often called Henry by close friends. Had the baby been a girl, her name likely would have been Giulia Davina.

It was all according to Julio's plan to implant the Menicucci family in Albuquerque. In his mind, one colonizes a family by bringing oneself and one's personal resources to the new land and producing good-quality descendants who can serve the community over generations. Julio Henry brought an equal number of males and females on both sides, giving an equal chance for maternal and paternal "blood traits" to be introduced into the family descendants and ultimately into the community. It ameliorated difficulties later on when businesses and properties are divided as they pass to successive generations. It was all well calculated and was unfolding as expected.

Davina was a typical Italian mother, glowing with motherly love for her new child. She gave birth at St Joseph's Hospital, which was a growing tendency countering the long-held practice of home-birthing. The Sisters of Charity managed and staffed the hospital with fully qualified medical professionals, including nuns and brothers. However, the hospital offered few other advantages beyond offering a sterile birthing environment and trained professionals on the scene. They had no electronic equipment of any kind. Thermometers were mercury-bulbed. Antibiotics did not exist and few painkillers did. Antiseptics were crude. The maternity ward provided cribs for infants but with few amenities, such as oxygen tents. Their goal at birth was to clean up the infant and get the child to the mother's breast as soon as possible. It was the best they could do and worked well for most.

Amerigo was a proud Papa but knew that this was his last child. This fulfilled his part of the plan, and he contributed to the family in the most significant way: a male who carried the Menicucci name forward. He fully endorsed Julio's colonization approach, just as he did all of Julio's business plans, and he was proud of his personal performance. He made the best of the opportunity to crow, and he purchased a couple of boxes of Johnny Matteucci's finer cigars for distribution at Super Service Station.

Davina had been through childbirth three times previously and she knew it was likely her last. She cherished this time of childbirth, when she commenced her most important activity, suckling her baby. Like any mother, she knew her son should be hungry after hours of childbirth and it was her job to provide that food, which came exclusively from her body.

Her breasts were willing but the baby was not. When the baby was delivered to her, she immediately saw a problem. He was weak, listless, pale and had no interest in eating. Bad signs, she thought, a healthy baby should be hungry. The nurses took the baby away for intense therapy, basically watching it more closely in an observation area. They reassured the parents and Davina was discharged almost immediately. She returned to the hospital for regular breastfeeding. The feedings were discontinued because the baby did not suckle, vomited frequently and rapidly deteriorated. The nurses attempted a few possible remedies but with no success. He was given last rights and within a week of birth, he lay withered and dead. The obvious cause of death was listed as a birth defect, but the underlying cause, genetic or otherwise, is unknown.

During this period, the couple spent all their spare moments praying. Amerigo, especially, called again on the Madonna. This time she did not intercede. Julio Henry's death on April 30th crushed both Menicucci families. It was the first family death that the brothers had ever experienced. What was worse, for some reason, the Madonna did not perform. Amerigo, in remorse, questioned the motives of the Lord. He knew that they had asked much of the Madonna and she had been mighty generous over the years; perhaps this was to be expected. Amerigo and Davina grieved deeply for weeks, but soon the reality of life took hold as they moved forward with renewed vigor to enjoy their surviving healthy family.

TRAVELING RIGORS

By 1932, Julio and Amerigo had Super Service Company and Rio Grande Oil marching along with escalating profits. The brothers had not taken a vacation for ten years and they believed it was time for a trip back to Italy so that their folks could meet the grandchildren. Giulia's father had recently died, and Aladino, Julio's and Amerigo's younger brother, was ill and slipping away. They planned to spend a couple of months in Italy.

Julio arranged for Johnny Matteucci and Horace Palladino to take over the management of Super Service Station and Rio Grande Oil, respectively. Both men were young but honest and the businesses were running smoothly. The men were acquainted with the operations. Horace had driven Julio's delivery truck and the customers were acquainted with him. The brothers had it all arranged for a pleasant family reunion.

Traveling with children is always rigorous for families, but this case is exceptional. Four adults planned to travel six-thousand miles across land and sea with seven children, all younger than ten, including a baby; a total travel time of two weeks. Julio contacted the Franchini Brothers, both Lucchese, who were among the first Italian immigrants and operated a travel agency out of their store.[6] They arranged the trip. They would take passenger-rail from Albuquerque through Chicago to New York, where they would board an ocean liner to take them to Genoa, Italy. From there, another rail trip ferried them directly to Lucca, where they could hire a cart to carry the two families to their paternal homes in Lucca: third class all the way.

Franchini brothers operated in the Bachechi building. Most of the Italians in the colony used Franchini's travel agency services to arrange their visits to Italy. Courtesy Lynne Franchini Peckinpaugh.

Passenger rail was in a period of rapid advancement as it was the only form of intracontinental mass transit. Third-class rail accommodations in 1930 were about on par with those in first-class in 1900, offering padded seats, a few sleeping compartments, meal cars and a medical professional on board in case of emergency.

The Menicuccis pooled all of their belongings into one huge travel container, which looked like a squarish coffin with a flat top, three feet by two feet by two feet high. Handles at each end allowed the men to carry it. A hasp and padlock secured the contents. Safeguarding the container was a top priority because it held all of the families' belongings. Containers of that size were often brought on board by passengers. On trains, luggage compartments were robust. Ships also provided large, accessible storage areas as they expected people to require access to their belongings during a long journey.

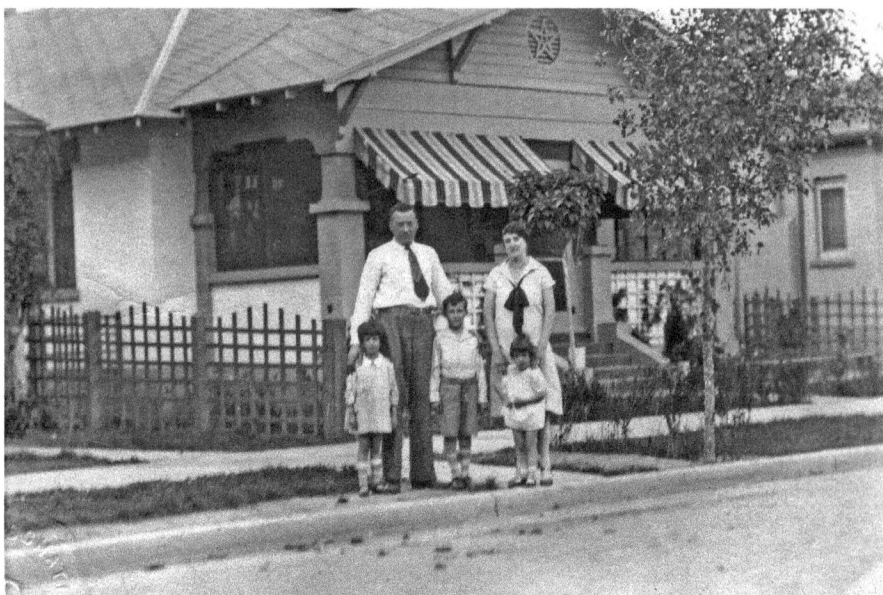

The Amerigo and Davina family in 1931, just before they left to visit Italy for the last time. From left: Louise, Amerigo, Mario, Rena and Davina. Courtesy Theresa Domenici Menicucci.

Giulia was weaning the infant Mariangela but still supplementing her meals with her breast. There were no baby carriages or special sleeping arrangements for infants, so mothers typically held infant children throughout the trip. By 1932, ocean travel had improved from the brothers' last voyage ten years previous, but it was still difficult in steerage class, especially for those with children. With a much higher density of passengers, disease in steerage was a greater concern than in second or first classes. Seasickness was a big problem, especially for those on their initial voyages. Julio had traveled the Atlantic Ocean three times—his initial immigration, World War I and the trip to wed. Amerigo had the experience of two trips. Unlike Julio, he did not leave America during the war. Giulia and Davina fared better than their initial trip when they were both pregnant, but neither was nausea-free. The children were not affected by seasickness but were often bored. And that led to shenanigans.

Giulia told the story about her son, Charlie, on the ship: Charlie was eight years old and was running around the ship. He climbed on the rail of the ship's main deck, showing off. The problem was that if he lost his balance, he would plunge into the ocean dozens of feet below the rail.

After nearly fainting when she saw him, she called Julio for help. Julio asked Charlie nicely to stand down, not wanting to frighten the boy and cause him to fall into the sea. Charlie complied and when he was safe, Julio let into him with such a verbal and physical barrage that Charlie never got near the rail again.

TERESA'S LIFESAVER

A few days later, Teresa, Julio's daughter, also had an incident. Charlie told the story: "She swallowed a lifesaver candy whole and it stuck in her windpipe. She was choking. Mama turned her upside down and pounded on her back to dislodge the candy, but it stuck. Papa got the ship's doctor, but he couldn't do anything. She was not going to die because the lifesaver candy had lodged so that she could still breathe through the hole. The doctor called for warm water, which he slowly fed to Teresa until the candy dissolved enough for her to cough it up." The whole near-death crisis consumed thirty minutes, but it was long-term anguish for the Menicuccis and for the gaggle of onlookers watching in stunned silence as a child's life teetered in the balance. Once the physician released Teresa, Giulia rushed to hug her. All of the children laughed and cheered as Teresa rose and smiled between bouts of coughing.

Julio faced Amerigo and both grinned wily—that same look they had when Giulia escaped Typhoid and Davina was cleared of TB—the Madonna was at their side again. In Julio's mind, he continued to build debt to this wonderful woman. It was a dramatic change of faith from his teenage days in Italy where his younger brother had admonished him for doubting the Virgin. The completion of these types of episodes always ended in the same way: by visiting a church—in this case, the Catholic chapel aboard the ship—to thank the Lord for their good fortune. It paid to know the Lord's mama.

They arrived in Lucca two weeks after they departed Albuquerque. They hired a car from there to bring the family to Rafaello's home. When they arrived, Teresa was first to greet them with jubilation. Raffaello and Aladino quickly followed. Raffaello had arranged for the brothers' families to board in the vacant home of a relative who had immigrated to America, as had many Lucchese. It took a couple of days for the families to unpack and settle in, but then they made the rounds to see the family. They spent the first few days with Raffaello and Teresa. Julio then took the family to Giulia's Grangnani family in Ponte Moriano where they stayed at the family's farm and silk factory. Giulia's mother, Emma Caselli, died in 1920 before Giulia married. Similarly, Amerigo and Davina visited her folks. The brothers took time to fish and hunt mushrooms, activities they had infrequently enjoyed since they had been in America. The Michigan mines, the Bradley Foundry, home building and business development, had captivated their time. Now, they were investing time to recuperate and relax.

OPPORTUNITY ARRIVES

They had been in Italy about six weeks when a cablegram from Johnny Matteucci was delivered to Julio at Rafaello's home. It read: "Sinclair Oil bought Rio Grande Oil, property and equipment." When Julio read it, he was beside himself with worry and anger. What would become of his job and the company that he was building? What about his wholesale customers? Without equipment and storage, he could not serve them. After discussing the situation with Amerigo, they decided to return to America immediately to deal with the new crisis. It was fine with Amerigo, as the family was near the end of their planned visit anyway and he was itching to get back to the station.

Julio immediately arranged the return trip, backtracking the same route to Albuquerque. Amerigo packed up the family belongings and paid the final bills. They planned to leave the following day as Julio was like a hungry lion, itching to get to Albuquerque where he could defend his business and family. The dearth of information was a particular irritation. All Julio and Amerigo had for details was contained in nine words in the cablegram. International phone calls were virtually impossible in Lucca due to a lack of equipment. Letters took weeks to deliver. Cablegrams were expensive. Julio was climbing a wall of worry, imagining every sinister scenario that might be playing out in Albuquerque.

The return trip was replete with tension, and Julio's and Amerigo's foul moods dragged on everyone. The families arrived back in Albuquerque in the middle of September 1932. Julio and Amerigo immediately went to the station for a debrief directly from Johnny Matteucci and Horace Palladino. They confirmed that Sinclair Oil, a large, national, vertically integrated oil extractor and refiner, had taken over. Sinclair had cleverly been preparing to deal with an economic downturn by hoarding cash and buying distressed companies at fire-sale prices. Like many national oil and gas distributors of the day, Rio Grande Oil found itself in financial trouble and Sinclair was there to scoop them up. Julio was dumbfounded that Rio Grande was financially teetering; it looked good when he left. Now, his attention was on Sinclair, the new owner.

Julio and Amerigo arranged a meeting with the Sinclair representative who was coming to town. The Sinclair-Rio Grande deal was still not closed, so Rio Grande Oil operated normally, delivering gasoline and kerosene throughout the city. Sinclair had intended to hire a manager for its new Albuquerque wholesale operation, and had its eye on Julio for the job. His reputation as an astute businessman was spreading in the wholesale community. He was hired immediately and resumed his management job. It was a huge relief; but there was a catch. The Menicuccis could not fly the Sinclair flag. In other words, Julio had fuel to sell and tanker trucks to deliver it but could not display the Sinclair brand on either his business or his trucks. A few other stations in Albuquerque were exclusively selling Sinclair products and the Sinclair executives wanted to avoid the appearance of adding competitors. Since Julio couldn't sell Sinclair fuel under its regular brand, he needed a new name for the distributorship.

The Menicuccis had succeeded with the name Super Service Station, which was becoming synonymous with super service and superior auto products. They decided on the name Super Oil Company, implying that it provided super-service and superior oil. By 1933, Julio steadily grew Super Oil Company, regularly adding to his expanding list of stations and individuals under supply contracts. Super Oil had only one delivery tanker, and Julio operated it himself. Super Oil's headquarters was at Super Service Station, where there were two desks in the front office—one for Julio and another for Amerigo. The tanker was typically parked in the street in front of Super Service Station.

In those days, kerosene was the most demanded fossil fuel because many families used it to illuminate their homes and barns. Some used it for heating and cooking, especially mobile homes, a growing group of homeowners. Kerosene was not discretionary. People needed it to live, regardless of the economy. Super Oil delivered the fuel throughout Bernalillo County, but mostly in Albuquerque. The discovery of the domestic kerosene market delighted Julio because it diversified their product line. Johnny Giannini never had an interest in kerosene. Julio not only delivered gas and oil to the service stations under delivery contracts, but he also had a steadily growing demand for kerosene. Super Oil kerosene and gasoline were delivered directly to end-use customers, many of whom were residential, by filling their small home storage tanks weekly and billing them monthly. Some small organizations, such as trailer parks, had their own overhead storage tanks, typically a couple hundred gallons each.

The 1930s were years of transition for both the Menicuccis and America. The family businesses were up and running, their homes were built and their children were fine. The tumult was behind them and they could concentrate on business and family life. America, meanwhile, was transitioning from a rural, agrarian society to a capitalist goliath. During the depression years, the nation concentrated on developing new banking and stock trading rules to help avoid economic panics and new labor laws to reduce worker exploitation. This challenge was accomplishing both objectives without stifling creative innovation synonymous with American capitalism. Both Menicucci brothers had no problem adapting to a burgeoning market for their purveyed products. However, they were yet to be fully tested.

See notes.7, 8, 9, 10.

Notes

1. Albuquerque National Trust and Savings eventually became Albuquerque National Bank.

2. The Keleher family has been in Albuquerque since about the time of its founding. It still produces some of the finest lawyers in the state of New Mexico.

3. *Grant* provides an overview of the Great Depression.

4. *Giomi* (Ioli) presents an account of the history of Modesto and his family. Published in September, 1977, Volume IV, Number 8.

5. *Pedroncelli* discusses farming along the Rio Grande Valley in the Albuquerque area. Pedroncelli was an Italian immigrant.

6. *Giomi* (Ioli) presents an account of the history of the Franchini family. Published in October, 1977, Volume IV, Number 9.

7. Much of the details for these stories are based on well-corroborated lore.

8. Much of the information for this chapter was gathered from newspaper reports in Albuquerque.

9. *Melosi* describes how the automobile shaped Western American cities, such as Albuquerque.

10. The census provided many details for the chapter.

13

A DEAL FOR
ALBUQUERQUE (1929–1939)

AILING NATION

The Southern Italian Mafia never infiltrated Albuquerque but the same cannot be said of the federal government, which was about to implement some of the greatest social programs in national history. Many programs reached deep into Albuquerque, which took advantage of all of the largesse that Washington DC could generate.

Herbert Hoover's reaction to the market crash, the growing number of bank failures and skyrocketing unemployment was less than inspiring. He and Andrew Melon, his Secretary of the Treasury, both reportedly expressed glee when the market crashed, thinking that it was merely a needed correction to overheated trading conditions. There was little panic in the White House in late October of 1929, even as billions of dollars of business value was tossed to the wind. They had complete confidence in the free market system to self-correct. Unfortunately, the system was in freefall and needed intervention to stem further damage and possible collapse. The Federal Reserve, in modern times, is one of the first government entities to intervene in an economic crisis by adjusting interest rates, buying bonds to increase national liquidity and managing the money supply. In 1929, the Fed was new and relatively impotent. It was unsure of its authority, so it dawdled while the country's economy lurched down.

Melon was one of the most prominent economists of the era and had served as Treasury Secretary since Warren Harding appointed him after he defeated Woodrow Wilson in 1920. He served until 1932, when Franklin Roosevelt defeated Herbert Hoover. Melon had been Hoover's principal advisor and had engineered the massive growth in the 1920s. He was a principal campaign advisor to Hoover because economics was the heart of the presidential race. In response to the growing economic crisis, Hoover established the Reconstruction Finance Corporation to make emergency loans to large businesses. He also signed the Emergency Relief Construction Act that provided one and a half billion dollars for public works in states. (Around thirty-two billion in 2024 dollars.)

By 1932, the economic situation weighed heavily on the voters' minds in the presidential campaign. From 1928 to 1932, unemployment rocketed from three percent to nineteen percent. Hoover tried to convince the voters that regardless of what they were seeing with their eyes, the economy was improving. It failed. Unemployment was nearly twenty percent by voting day and increasing steadily. The reality of the sinking economy obviated Hoover's rose-colored fantasy claims. The national crisis needed valiant action and his laissez-faire philosophy constrained him from proposing the required solution. Hoover's dogged adherence to a political ideology dragged on his campaign because his policies were out of sync with the nation's needs, and he refused to consider new ideas.

Roosevelt, a Democrat, lived the party's philosophy of supporting small businesses and defending individual and employee rights. In his presidential campaign, he proposed to take the country on a huge and costly experiment to reverse the nation's economic decline by injecting huge amounts of public money directly into the economy. He made the case directly to the public that the federal government would provide the necessary relief to the common man, allowing the economy to regain its footing. His greatest campaign speech was dubbed "The Forgotten Man" because in it he declared that if he were elected, he would focus his attention on "the forgotten man at the bottom of the economic pyramid." It hit home with the vast majority of Americans, from those at the lowest societal levels to previously wealthy citizens devastated by the crash, all of whom felt betrayed by Wall Street and longed for government assistance. The Menicucci families were pleased with what they heard. Most Italians had been attracted to the Democrat party because of their ideological support for common men and small businesses. This speech, though, solidified their affiliation with the party, as many average Americans at that time viewed themselves as forgotten people.

The country rejected Hoover in a landslide. Roosevelt carried forty of forty-eight states and secured nearly sixty percent of the raw vote totals, along with a veto-proof Democratic majority of three hundred thirteen to one hundred and seventeen in the House and a substantial fifty-nine to thirty-six in the Senate. Although the Senate was technically not veto-proof—requiring sixty-four for an override—it was essentially so because it was unlikely for Roosevelt to veto any bill that had passed through the Democratic Congress.

Harding, Coolidge and Hoover, all Republican presidents during the 1920s, governed with the philosophy of minimal business regulation, low taxes and hand-off administrative practices. It was a classically conservative approach and perfectly suited for the 1920s following a war when the country was primed for explosive development and prosperity. It flourished until it flamed out in 1929. In 1932, the Democrats garnered a smashing victory that rendered the Republicans politically helpless for the remainder of the third decade and well into the next.

Roosevelt and his team correctly diagnosed the situation: Too many Americans were not working, which meant that they had little money to spend on products, which negatively impacted businesses, all leading to reduced business and layoffs. It was a vicious, deteriorating economic Catch-22 that beaconed for administrative action to thwart it. Roosevelt adopted the Keynesian principles of massive government investment in the populace rather than in businesses. Keynes's new theory, in simple terms, was to give people money, whether from direct subsidies or through government work programs, so they had money to spend. Before he took office in 1933, he and his team had lined up a series of measures and bills that constituted a New Deal for America that directly affected every American. He knew that the spending would exceed the budget, a condition that neither party found acceptable, so Roosevelt also campaigned on a pledge to balance the budget once the crisis passed.[1]

On March 4th, 1933, Roosevelt delivered his inaugural address, broadcast by several radio networks, reaching over ten million listeners. The speech has long been noted by his remarks about fear, but it was his overall confident and calm demeanor that resonated with the populace. With solid majorities in both the House and Senate, Roosevelt pushed through every bill he proposed within the first ten months of his administration. In rapid-fire succession, the following actions were approved into law:

Emergency Banking Relief Act; which broadened presidential powers over banks and restricted gold hoarding;

Federal Emergency Relief Administration, designed to provide grants to states;

Economy Act, which would balance the federal budget;

Public Works Administration, intended to fund infrastructure projects throughout the country;

Beer-Wine Revenue Act, proposed legalization of low-alcohol beer and wine;

Civilian Conservation Corps Reforestation Relief Act, which authorized money for jobs in reforestation and construction;

Abandonment of the Gold Standard;

Agricultural Adjustment Act, which helped to reduce agricultural commodity surpluses by subsidizing farmers from producing certain crops;

Federal Emergency Relief Act, which established a system of direct grants of public money to the states;

Tennessee Value Authority, which authorized the construction of 49 dams along the Tennessee River in Tennessee designed to prevent flooding and produce electricity;

Federal Securities Act, designed to ensure full disclosure about stocks;

Homeowners Refinance Act, which provided money to refinance mortgages;

Glass-Steagall Act, creating the Federal Bank Deposit Insurance Corporation;

Farm Credit Act, which provided low-interest farm loans;

Emergency Railroad Transportation Act, designed to improve the rail industry;

National Industrial Recovery Act, which focused on reviving industrial production;

Public Works Administration, which sets aside money for public projects;

Commodity Credit Corporation, which extended farm loans;

Civil Works Administration, authorizing four million jobs on federal construction projects throughout the country;

Repeal of the 18th Amendment.

These actions, most of which were passed by huge Congressional majorities, pumped bountiful amounts of cash directly into the economy while creating government fiscal deficits comparable to those of the war years. The U.S. sported a surplus of around eight hundred million dollars in 1929 (around seventeen billion in 2024 dollars). By 1933, after Roosevelt's spending extravaganza, the deficit grew to nearly four billion. Roosevelt's approach was radically different from that of the Republicans and was unprecedented. No peacetime president had spent as much public money in such a short period. But no peacetime president had ever faced an economic crisis of the severity that faced the nation in 1932, and he felt bold action was needed to prevent a national economic collapse. Besides, the Republicans had three years after the crash to correct the situation and failed. Roosevelt believed the odds were with him if he followed the opposite path. Roosevelt sensed that he needed to build the people's confidence by demonstrating the government's concern about the plight of its citizens and that he was responding audaciously. Roosevelt understood the old saying, "Money talks and bull shit walks."

ALBUQUERQUE TAPS IN

Clyde Tingley, a solid Democrat, was congruent with the Roosevelt administration and lobbied for the government munificence that was soon to follow. With his emphasis on growth, he saw the opportunity to fund many public work projects in Albuquerque that engendered tourism, fostered development and beautified the city. Tingley worked feverishly following the presidential election and funneled thousands of federal dollars into the city. By the end of 1933, Tingley had secured nearly one hundred thousand dollars (around two million in 2024 dollars) for his favorite project, the creation of Terrace Park, which would later be renamed Roosevelt Park and remains one of the largest city parks. He also negotiated for funds to build Lew Wallace School and upgrade the University of New Mexico's football stadium. It was quite a display of handiwork by the nimble mayor, who was planning his campaign for New Mexico Governor the following year. Tingley was like a child in a candy store and he kept the money flowing into the city in 1934, initiating city waterworks upgrades and construction of Scholes Hall at the university.

In 1935, Tingley's gubernatorial campaign highlighted his support for Roosevelt's New Deal and his record in Albuquerque, seen by most as impressive. Interestingly, the *Albuquerque Journal*, Republican-leaning at the time, editorialized against Tingley. It did little good. Nobody was listening as bundles of money were flowing into the area and most believed that the best man for the job was one who could snatch even more of it. Tingley's successor in Albuquerque, Charles Lembke, also a Democrat, took up where Tingley let off and continued to bring public works projects to the city, ranging from sidewalks to land surveying. Thanks to Roosevelt's programs, despite the depression the city continued to grow modestly in the 1930s, producing a steady decline in unemployment. Over the decade, Albuquerque captured and spent over twenty-two million federal dollars (about four hundred sixty million in 2024 dollars). For comparison, Albuquerque's annual budget at the time was less than one million dollars (about twenty-one million in 2024 dollars).[2]

Well-positioned Albuquerque businesses, such as Super Service Station, not only survived but prospered during the depression years. However, the overall sluggish economy dragged on its bottom line. Still, the brothers provided work for more men than they needed because they supported the community, especially the Lucchese. Johnny Matteucci would not likely have joined Super Service Station had he not lost his cigar business. Similarly, Julio hired laborers for Super Oil who were superfluous because the men needed work. The Menicuccis tended to dip into their profits to support their fellow Albuquerqueans. They knew the men would do the same for them if the situation were reversed.

PROHIBITION'S MERCIFUL END

Roosevelt's proposal to repeal prohibition was especially well received among Albuquerque's Italian community. Wine was an important culinary and gastronomical necessity. To those who had been in the liquor business before prohibition, including the Matteuccis and Bachechis, they were itching to get back into the fray. The nation's great experiment to improve social order—one of the cornerstones of the progressive era policies—had miserably failed. It was obvious from its inception that the prohibition laws could not deny people a product they desired. One way or another, diligent and persistent people in a free land find what they want on the black market.

A major flaw with the law was that it proposed to enforce prohibition by limiting the transport of alcohol. People could still possess and consume it and plenty did, especially Albuquerque's Italians. Demand for alcoholic beverages during the Depression remained relatively constant, even growing in some areas. The federal government had little chance to curb the demand with a law that controlled its transport instead of inducing demand reductions. Some viewed the experiment as an embarrassing episode in the country's legislative history. Many said it was a slipshod piece of legislation that was bamboozled through Congress when people were preoccupied with World War I and its aftermath. It generated continual criticism of the government.

In Washington, DC, the discussions were almost comical relative to the situation and out of touch with reality. The Wickersham Commission provides a good example.[3] On May 20, 1929, Hoover commissioned eleven prominent people—mostly lawyers—to examine prohibition and recommend improvements or reversals. Their primary objective was to investigate the crimes associated with illicit liquor and recommend corrections. Former Attorney General George W. Wickersham led the team. After twenty-one months, including numerous hearings, expert witness testimonies and long and contentious meetings, the commission issued a two hundred eighty-six-page report on January 7, 1931, recommending retaining prohibition but enhancing state enforcement with considerable additional federal law enforcement resources. The committee also recommended that beer and wine with low alcohol be allowed for sale.[4]

Cynicism and ridicule erupted in communities nationwide, especially those familiar with the depth of the crime problem. Local police, who were on the front lines of enforcement, were the clearest-eyed of all, and most officers regarded the law as unenforceable. It was obvious that the only way that prohibition could work was through a federal police state, a concept anathema to every American. Nonetheless, the Hoover administration continued to doggedly support it. A poem by Franklin Adams, a journalist for the *New York World*, published in November 1931, brilliantly encapsulated the situation:

> *Prohibition is an awful flop.*
> *We like it.*
> *It can't stop what it's meant to stop.*
> *We like it.*
> *It's left a trail of death and slime.*
> *It don't prohibit worth a dime.*

It's filled our land with graft and crime.
Nevertheless, we're for it.

The poem was the galvanizing moment for the country in the movement to repeal the 18th Amendment. Tingley, of course, strongly opposed prohibition for many of the typical reasons: It tied up city police resources vainly enforcing a law that was widely violated and had failed to achieve the objective of eliminating alcohol use. People in the city either brewed or fermented their own—as the Germans and Italians did—or bought it off the black market, which flourished across the county. Alcohol was as easy to obtain as carrots or milk. The only issue was which unlucky individuals among the many violators were selected by the police for punishment.

There were other reasons why the mayor favored repeal. It would generate business, put people to work and broaden the tax base. Tingley lobbied both New Mexico's senators, Sam Bratton, a Democrat and Bronson Cutting, a Republican. He received a positive reception from both as they had sensed widespread voter discontent with prohibition. In February 1933, the Twenty-First Amendment to the Constitution repealing prohibition was approved by Congress and sent to the states. It took only eleven months for thirty-six states, a three-quarters supermajority, to approve it. South and North Carolina voted not to approve it. Georgia, Kansas, Louisiana, Mississippi, Nebraska, North Dakota, Oklahoma and South Dakota took no action. On December 4, 1933, Congress declared that the amendment was ratified. With repeal, the issue of managing liquor fell to each state. Liquor trades between states would be managed under existing interstate commerce laws.

The rousing cheers in the community overwhelmed the few remaining prohibitionists. Many people, especially the Italians, Germans and Irish, whose cultures incorporated alcohol, were full of glee. Many previous liquor businessmen were primed and ready to restart their businesses. The Francini brothers, the Domenicis, the Bachechis and the Matteuccis were among the first liquor dispensers in Albuquerque and were first in line for new ones. Others without prior experience were also keen to compete in the liquor industry. Many of these Italian men made repeated trips to Santa Fe to lobby for specific provisions in the developing liquor laws that would benefit them. They were like kids at a pinata party flailing away for the big prize—a chance to sell liquor to a very thirsty populace.

The Temperance movement was badly beaten, but the Anti-Saloon League, reorganized and turned their attention to the states. They lobbied hard. Given the public's widespread contempt for prohibition, they were doomed from the start; the legislature was primed to act and nothing could stop it. Dollar signs were dancing in the heads of New Mexico politicians as they envisioned tax revenues surging from liquor sales. Within a year following the repeal of the 18th Amendment, liquor establishments appeared throughout the state.

INNOVATING A RESTAURANT

Modesto Dalle, driven off his hog ranch a few years earlier, leaped at the opportunity in the new liquor industry. He was a proud and fiercely independent man struggling to recover from his losses. He was determined to reboot himself and believed a liquor business would suit him. Modesto had some ideas but no money.[5]

He and Pete Vichi developed plans for a new kind of saloon, one that provided both full liquor and restaurant service. At that time, full-service restaurants sold food and saloons sold alcohol, but the two were not combined. Pete owned a building at 212 Third Street. He was so convinced of the viability of Modesto's project that he remodeled the building in exchange for a share of Modesto's profits. Pete added neon lighting to the building, a unique feature that made it the brightest spot for Albuquerque's nightlife community. Modesto named his establishment the Mint Café and Bar after the famous Café Mint Bar in Juarez, Mexico, which catered to Americans wishing to escape the confines of American prohibition. His place, he envisioned, would be Albuquerque's post-prohibition escape venue—Modesto style.

Modesto had been working with the Vichi family since he married Pia Barsanti. Pia worked for the Tony Domenici family, which owned and operated Montezuma Grocery and became the exclusive distributor of Falstaff beer to Modesto's new café. Pete's sister, Alda, was the wife of Chopo Domenici, one of the two Domenicis who owned Montezuma Grocery. Pete vouched for Modesto's bank loan. At the new establishment, Vince Vichi, Pete's twenty-four-year-old son, worked for Modesto.

The Mint installed all new, modern equipment. Modesto believed quality products and services required professional tools, which were evolving rapidly. After over a decade of prohibition, any used liquor equipment was old and obsolete; new equipment was all that was available. He invested in an electric refrigerator, a recent innovation that greatly extended the time that fresh vegetables, meat and cheese could be stored for an extended time. More importantly, he could serve cold beer, about 38F, which enhances the flavor and appeal of lagers such as Falstaff, one of the Mint's most popular beer brands. Chilled beer was not standard fare at bars at that time.

Pete Vichi was delighted to see Modesto take full, professional command of the business. A profitable Mint was money in the Vichi pockets in two ways: as the lessor of the property and as an investor in the business. Modesto was fine with the arrangement because Vichi's money provided him the opportunity to rebound from his hog ranch disaster.

The new business was so unusual for Albuquerque that it warranted a story in the *Albuquerque Journal* on Friday, July 20, 1934, the day before the grand opening. The story ran adjacent to ads that consumed nearly half a newspaper page celebrating the Mint's opening. The Mint had two distinguishing features. 1) Alcohol and food were served and consumed in a single establishment, and 2) It offered a variety of cuisines. The Mint opened the next day at ten to a full house of guests.

The Mint was a saloon-restaurant. The modern equivalent is a Bar & Grill. Typical saloons were operated by bartenders who sold liquor over the bar--period. Patrons purchased beer at the bar and either sat there or carried it to a table. Restaurants typically served food but no alcoholic beverages. The Mint did both. Modesto delivered beer to the tables for consumption with a meal. It was an innovation that made for a captivating marketing angle.

Modesto built his business on fundamentals. Service was at the top of the list. It was a top priority for most food businesses because of the competition. At the time, plenty of other restaurants existed, so service was often the only differentiating feature among them. Excellent service was a requisite for any competitive food or drink business. His large ads, which ran a few times a week, proudly stated that Falstaff Beer was "Served by Modesto," implying that when you came to the Mint, Modesto personally cared for you. The man was consumed with serving his customers like royalty because he knew they would reward him with patronage.

His major innovation was the food. Most restaurants specialized in a specific cultural cuisine. The Mint offered a multicultural menu designed to appeal to the major local ethnicities: Anglo, Hispanic and Italian. But it had no full-time chef. Instead, several part-time chefs cooked their specialties on the days dedicated to their specific cuisine. Certain weekdays were dedicated to particular ethnicities. A middle-aged Hispanic woman from Old Town prepared New Mexican plates for the Mint's weekly "Spanish Food" days, as Modesto dubbed them. Modesto had lived in Old Town, which was dominated by Hispanics, where he learned the language, customs, and cuisines. His new cook prepared the typical New Mexico fare: enchiladas, rellenos, green and red chiles stews and tortillas. An Anglo man prepared typical American dishes of meat, potatoes and vegetables. A part-time Italian chef did the same for Italian cuisine but was augmented by Pia's specialty Italian dishes that she prepared for holidays and special occasions. Pia cooked spaghetti sauce and made ravioli, using recipes she learned while working for Emma Giomi, Tony Domenici's wife. While American palates rarely notice the subtle differences among the Italian cooking, Lucchese were attuned to the differences. Pia's recipes and cooking style mirrored the Giomi family's style, which some in the colony recognized.

Every Wednesday Pia cooked a ten-gallon pot of barbequed shredded pork and homemade sauce using a distinctly Southwest American recipe augmented with her adjustments for Modesto's customers. She slow-cooked the meat in an enameled, steel pot that simmered at the Mint kitchen all day. It provided sandwiches consisting of a bun, a leaf of lettuce, a slice of pickle and a scoop of steamy barbequed meat. A very fine deal for just the regular price of a beer. It was a huge hit. Local businessmen stopped in for their Wednesday lunches. Despite the giveaways, Modesto profited handsomely due to big markups on liquor.

Modesto did his own culinary development with his famous cocktail drink, one that perfectly complemented Pia's Cenci, strips of deep-fat fried sweet bread dusted with confectioner's sugar. His hot Tom & Jerry was an amalgam of various liquors, spices, cream and butter. When the heated mixture is whisked together, it produced a thick, silky smooth, sweet drink with a dense, foamy head. Topped with Nutmeg, it was a delicious beverage for celebrating on a cold night. The drink became a holiday legend in both New- and Old-town Albuquerque. These offerings alone brought in hordes of guests. It became so popular that patrons needed reservations to experience his famous drink.

The Mint operated every day except Sunday, Christmas and Easter. Normal hours were ten in the morning to ten in the evening. On New Year's

Eve, instead of closing out his patrons before midnight, he invited them to his home where Tom & Jerrys and Cenci were free. The local code forced the closure of liquor establishments at ten in the evening. Otherwise, he would have remained open well past midnight to accommodate the local revelers. Given that Albuquerque by 1934 was still reeling from the banking crisis and many residents were unemployed, his business was impressive.

Modesto was an extraordinary marketeer, repeatedly advertising new dinner or drink specials, all appearing to be good deals for his patrons. His clientele was enamored with the free snacks he regularly offered with a first beer. Modesto knew that salt-induced thirst was advantageous because his most profitable products were beverages, especially alcoholic ones. Salted nuts, chips of various types and pretzels were placed on every table and along the bar. It was more or less standard fare in every bar in the city. Modesto extended the concept of snacks to mean real food in tiny amounts, such as miniature tamales, tiny biscotti and some exquisite Italian specialties, such as fried slices of Porcini mushrooms picked fresh in the Jemez Mountains. It was not unusual for patrons to pack the Mint trying to sample some specialty hand food he had advertised. Pia's Cenci and the Tom & Jerrys always drew overflow crowds, but he always had one deal or another going. Sadly, both Modesto and Pia died with most of their specialty recipes locked in their brains. Cenci lives on, though, still prepared for New Year's Day by Modesto's descendants.[6,7]

In those days of depression, even big shots in Albuquerque counted their dollars carefully, and Mint deals looked like genuine bargains. It was an enclave of cheer in a city struggling with the doldrums. People from all walks of life craved the confines of the Mint following a day of work. Modesto set the scene at the door with warm greetings. Inside were tasty snacks, icy cold beer, spirited talk among friends and excellent food. All housed in a bright building—the signature physical features of the Mint. Despite the hard economic times, Modesto recorded respectable profits over the middle and later 1930s. His weekly and holiday specials usually sold out before the close of business, enhancing customer interest. Each daily special drew people clamoring to get in early and sometimes there were lines outside. Modesto treated each one like a family member, often giving out free snacks to those waiting outside.

Modesto's dream of a modern, bright, and vibrant food and drink establishment was bolstered by its location in Vichi's building, which, with its new neon lights, bellowed loudly with its presence. Vichi liberally used neon lighting to draw attention to the building, a multistory structure that could be seen throughout most of the city at night. It perfectly matched the Mint business.

The Mint was one of Albuquerque's most unique and fully modern restaurant and bar facilities of that era. It attracted a range of customers, from Hispanic farm laborers in Old Town to the CEO of First National Bank. Culinary diversification kept the Mint competitive throughout the Depression years and beyond. Modesto's welcoming personality and his excellent service were its defining features. Like so many other Italian immigrants in Albuquerque, Modesto arrived in America with little education and no experience. He flourished due to a confluence of events and situations. He was honest, diligent and hardworking, a perfect match for American capitalism, which allowed him to develop his innate business skills into a noteworthy contribution to Albuquerque. Like so many others, he availed himself of help from fellow Lucchese. In contrast to his hog farm, this time his business timing was impeccable. The liquor business was rising from the ashes of prohibition. Lastly, he was entrepreneurial in spirit. The hog farm failure did not deter him from trying anew. He said, "America gave me another chance to live a good life."

PROSPERITY CREEPS BACK

As Roosevelt's programs pumped money into Albuquerque's economy, it was not just Modesto innovating. It was endemic throughout the city. New technologies appeared, such as autos, kitchen appliances, telephones and other conveniences. The Italians, most smart and enthusiastic, never let an advantage like this slip by. The Franchinis, Matteuccis, Giomis, Domenicis, Bachechis, Palladinos, Dalle and other business owners used new technologies to grow their businesses. Home deliveries of food became common, with orders taken by the newly invented telephone and delivered in a new auto. Matteucci and Palladino Grocery store was one of the first to implement a full call-in and delivery service, which was quickly duplicated by others.

New, reasonably priced commercial refrigerators allowed small grocers to expand their offerings to include products with normally short shelf lives, such as meat and cheese. Cheeses, for example, were difficult to purvey due to their propensity to mold quickly. Cheeses were typically stored in small amounts and promptly sold. But with a refrigerator, mold is inhibited and a grocer might be able to stock full wheels of cheeses and hack off pieces to sell over time. It greatly improved not only the grocer's profit margins but also the value and convenience to the customer. For the first time, a customer could visit a grocer, purchase three pounds of parmesan, store it in his own home ice box, and eat on it for a week. Phones and autos became necessary business accouterments, spurring the auto service industry and ancillary ones, such as taxis.

The Menicuccis, as usual, were in the thick of business innovation. In the middle 1930s, Amerigo got a phone call from a customer who had run out of gas. His car was parked about a block from his home. Super Service was a walk-in business; it did not deliver products or services. Amerigo packed a one-gallon can of gasoline in the company pickup truck and headed over to the customer's auto, where he poured the fuel into the tank. The customer then drove to the station for a fill-up and full service. Amerigo charged a fee for the delivery, which was happily paid. The customer gushed over the fine service, praising Amerigo and thanking him. Julio watched the whole thing unfold. As soon as Amerigo returned, he proposed developing a fuel delivery service, a microcosm of how he operated Super Oil. Amerigo went a step further. Why not offer to tow a customer's broken vehicle into the shop for repairs? Until then, only auto repair shops, like the Napoleone's, provided towing. His idea was to buy a chain that they could connect to the broken auto and hook it to the bumper of their pickup truck. Then, they dragged the vehicle to the station, where it would be repaired and fully serviced. They advertised the service, sporting the Super Service phone number for emergency help with a vehicle—gas or towing. They profited immediately.

By the later 1930s, modern taxis were being equipped with new two-way radios that allowed the vehicles to communicate wirelessly with dispatchers at a central location, usually located near the. For the first time, customers could use phones to call the taxi company for a ride, giving them the passenger's location. The company used a radio to dispatch a driver to the customer's location. Once the ride was complete, the taxi driver used the radio to inform the dispatcher that he was free for more rides.

New technologies spurred businesses and improved lives. Saloons and restaurants sprang up in brightly lit establishments due to the growing application of incandescent light bulbs for lighting and neon tubes for decoration. The wholesale suppliers upgraded their warehouses with new technologies, such as mechanical forklifts, that allowed them to move crates and equipment more efficiently. Building codes required electrical wiring to be installed in all occupied buildings. In general, new technology raised industrial productivity, making America the emerging envy of the world. Even the Europeans, who had long harbored feelings of superiority, now marveled at the American economy flourishing under free-market capitalism.

The Menicuccis continued to lead. In 1935, they installed a new set of men's and women's restrooms exclusively for customers. Employees had their own single, unisex restroom. They also provided customers with free coffee and cookies while waiting for their vehicles to be serviced. Some services, such as an oil change, came with a free car wash. So, a customer might be waylaid at the station for a while. Julio and Amerigo wanted customers to be as comfortable at the station as in their homes. It was the Menicucci's version of a modern customer loyalty program. To them it was simple common sense. A customer who enjoys being in your establishment will become a regular customer. No gimmicks, cards or point programs were needed. A man could roll into Super Service Station fuel bays during a heavy rain storm for a fill-up, walk inside, grab a cookie, use the restroom, chat with Amerigo, pay his bill and happily drive away without a drop of rain ever hitting him. In those days, this type of pampering was unique and customers rewarded the brothers with steady patronage.

Super Service Station in the mid-1930s that shows the considerable expansion. Two new work bays were added, as can be seen on the left side of the photo. The brothers performed the addition during the depression years, indicating that the station grew during the worst of economic times. Courtesy Theresa Domenici Menicucci.

Even Johnny Giannini became a regular customer, stopping in with his usual bravado about the gold he was reaping in his placer mines in the Manzano Mountains. He admired the Menicuccis' work, pridefully knowing he was the springboard for their success.

JURY RIG FAILS

Julio alone operated Super Oil Company and was always bubbling over with ideas for improving business and maximizing profits. While the company headquarters was co-located with Super Service, the company's storage tanks were found at its warehouse on the east side of Summer Street and First Street. First Street was named such because it was the first street paralleling the railroad tracks on the west side. Thus, the rear of Super Oil's property lay adjacent to the railroad, and for good reason. Gasoline and kerosene were delivered to wholesalers by tanker railcar. Super Oil had two large overhead storage tanks on site, about ten feet above ground. One with a sixteen-thousand-gallon capacity for kerosene and another twelve-thousand-gallon tank for gasoline.

In 1933, when Super Oil took ownership of the Rio Grande wholesale business, the purchase included only the real property, including the tanks. Various claimants took all tools and equipment not affixed to the property during the sale. Julio needed a delivery truck, so his first equipment purchase was a twenty-five-hundred-gallon tanker. It was about the size of today's two-ton Ford pickup truck with a tank lying in the bed. It had two purposes: deliveries and pumping. Julio parked the truck at Super Service Station, which occupied one of the station's service bays.

Having only one delivery truck complicated delivery schedules because Julio wasted time repeatedly draining and refilling it to meet customer orders for one fuel or another. Logistics were complicated because Julio tried to batch up orders of the same fuel type to minimize switching, but he risked angering customers with delays. And there were always emergencies, e.g., one of his stations holding a sale over a weekend and running out of gas, requiring Julio to deliver replacement fuel immediately regardless of the type of liquid in Super Oil's delivery truck.

Rail tankers typically dispensed liquid products by gravity fill. A valve at the bottom of the tanker car allowed fluid to flow through a hose to a customer's underground tanks. For those with overhead tanks, electric pumps were used to fill them directly from the rail tanker. Julio inherited Super Oil's overhead tanks when Rio Grande Oil sold out early in the decade. Overhead tanks are advantageous because leaks are easy to spot, and gravity can drain them. But they were a liability to fill without the right tools. Rio Grande had large commercial pumps to charge the overhead tanks at the First Street location, but they took them when they sold out.

Super Oil could not afford such luxuries. Julio used his twenty-five-hundred-gallon delivery truck to fill his overhead tanks. It had a small on-board pump used to pump liquid from the delivery truck into their customers' overhead tanks. When a rail tanker arrived with his order, Julio gravity filled his delivery truck from the larger rail car and drove it seventy-five feet to his overhead tanks where he used the onboard pump to transfer the liquid into the storage tank. For gravity feed to work, his truck had to be below the level of the bottom of the rail tank. His truck was too tall, so he dug out a trench alongside the dock that allowed the delivery truck to back into position below the rail tank, allowing gravity to fill the tank.

Depending on how much fuel he needed for his storage tanks, he often made a half dozen trips between the rail tanker and his storage area. It was a jury-rigged system laden with risk but it worked.

1930 Rio Grande Oil Company. Rio Grande Oil, managed by Julio Menicucci, had two overhead tanks, one for gasoline and the other for kerosene. They were located on the southeast corner of First Street and Summer Ave. One of the overhead tanks can be seen in the background. The truck was used for fuel deliveries and as a service vehicle for Super Service Station. This is the truck that Julio used to transfer fuel from the rail tankers into his overhead tanks. Courtesy Author's collection.

In 1935, Julio discovered the risk in the flesh. One afternoon, he and Albert Nottoli were engaged in the typical game of transferring fuel from the rail tanker to their storage tanks. Albert, twenty-eight years old, was the son of Tista Nottoli, an immigrant from Lucca. When the train pulled up for a delivery, the rail tanker was placed in the approximate position to release the fuel. Julio hooked up a three-inch hose to the rail car and Albert dropped the other end into Super Oil's truck's tank. Julio opened the rail car valve and gas spilled into the tank, which took about twenty minutes to fill. Both men walked away to attend some other work. Just after they left, the hose burst halfway between the rail tanker and Super Oil's truck, leaving the end connected to the rail whipping to and fro on the ground like a crazed rattlesnake. It took a few minutes for the men to notice the problem, and Julio tried to shut the valve, but it jammed. Albert ran for a wrench as Julio struggled to capture the wriggling hose spewing out gas, which looked like gushing dollar bills to Julio. He tried to get the broken hose ends together, but it failed and drenched him in gasoline. Albert brought a wrench and Julio closed the valve, but he was dripping with gasoline from the top of his head to his shoes, which were full of fuel. Over seven-hundred gallons of raw gasoline were dumped directly on Julio and the ground.

The panic was on to clean him up before the gasoline killed him. Tears followed later when Julio calculated his losses from the episode. At that moment, Julio's health was the primary concern because the life expectancy for men immersed in gasoline was short. Gasoline is not readily absorbed in the skin, but covering the entire body provides enough skin surface area for toxic levels to build up in the body. The biggest problem is inhalation. The lungs easily absorb gasoline, and the vapors can cause serious and permanent injuries to the cardiovascular system and brain. Julio breathed many fumes in his battle with the hose. Gasoline also causes skin irritation and sometimes fatal allergic reactions.

Julio stepped aside his tanker truck and disrobed completely. It was a cold March day. Albert ran for towels to dry Julio off and cover his privates while he drove Julio to his home, just a few blocks away. Julio was already feeling dizzy and shivering with cold, so Albert drove the tanker like an ambulance, thundering it into the driveway at his home on Third Street, honking several times as he pulled to a stop with fuel sloshing around in the partially filled tanker.

Giulia was alone because the children were in school. She came running to the commotion. Shock is an understatement to describe her after she saw her husband sitting naked in the truck, hair dripping with gasoline and wreaking like a mechanic's rag. She took command immediately. She managed the family's health and directed Albert to hook up the garden hose and bring some soap. In those days, soaps were made into bars for hand and body washing, and much stronger granules were used for dish and clothes washing. She specifically requested the granulated soap because she wanted all the cleaning power possible. This granular product is nearly identical to today's Tide detergent and is a powerful degreaser. She stood a naked Julio up in the driveway and drenched him with cold water as he stood shivering in the 50F degree temperature, his face color tending toward a shade of blue.

Here is a summary of Albert's story: As Giulia scrubbed her man, she declared that Julio had not been careful. She yelled at him: "This is what the Lord says to you. You work too hard. You take too many chances." She applied a lather of soap over his body as she lectured and rinsed him with the hose, ignoring his shivers, figuring he deserved to suffer a bit after exhibiting such negligence and causing her worry and trouble. By the time she was finished, the hot water in the house was ready. They had a gas-fired water heater but only lit it when needed for washing or bathing. She gave Julio some towels to dry off while she went inside to draw water into the tub, which she loaded with detergent. She would get her man clean and healthy so he could do his job for the family. He scrubbed himself thoroughly in the soapy bath water and rinsed off a couple of times. He felt better after the bath but still stank of gasoline. It took days for the odor to disappear and he wore it like a red badge of courage at the station, regaling the staff and customers with his various versions of the event. For a week, Julio was the heroic survivor of a gas bath.

The event engendered a major discussion at Super Oil headquarters at Super Service Station. It required the three owners, the Menicuccis and Johnny Matteucci, to confer in private. They stored various stock items in the basement under the main station building, mostly tires, fan belts and batteries. A smaller room in the corner was used for storing tools and smaller items. The three men fit tightly in the area and it provided privacy for the forthcoming discussion, fully in Italian. Amerigo and Julio allowed only two languages to be spoken in the businesses: Spanish and English. Italian was reserved for private conversations, and it was well away from the customers and employees.

Amerigo did not like the sound of possibly losing his brother. The Franklin Jr. mine accident still weighed on his mind and this event was in the same vein. That mine accident was caused by negligence by the owners. Our negligence could injure an employee, Amerigo declared, envisioning the liability they would incur to help an employee recover. The employee might even sue, he fretted. Unemployment and worker compensation insurance did not exist. Typically, employees unable to work due to injury were uncompensated. Since men were typically the only breadwinners in the family, an injury imperiled the family. The Menicuccis cared for their employees, paying them when ill or injured. Amerigo was ever concerned about risk, and this situation caused an outsized amount of worry for both men. The Menicuccis were applying the lessons they learned in Hancock,

Michigan. Everyone concluded that the current process was impractical because of the potential for loss, just as seven hundred gallons were lost on the ground. Without any insurance, those losses fell directly on the bottom line, very bad for a new business in the Depression.

The second risk was fire, the foremost concern in handling gasoline and was high on the owners' priority list. A spark could have ignited an inferno under Super Oil's storage tanks, possibly igniting an explosion of the rail car, the losses would have been exorbitant. There was no environmental concern by either Julio or the city regarding the spill, even though the shallow aquafer was only ten feet below the surface in that area and some people were pumping out of it for irrigation and drinking.[8] Today, a spill of that magnitude warrants a major remediation effort, including excavating the contaminated soil and monitoring the area for years to detect lingering contamination. The Menicuccis' only solution was to invest in new equipment for the warehouse, including the improved, high-voltage, high-efficiency electric fuel pumps that were available and affordable.

Amerigo and Julio dominated the conversation. Johnny puffed his pipe, producing clouds of flavorful smoke that masked the nauseating smell of tires. Johnny never had much to say; his forte was sales, not strategic business development. Julio and Amerigo agreed they needed money to upgrade Super Oil's facilities, but Amerigo was none too happy about it coming from Super Service. He used hard-earned savings to help employ Lucchese who needed assistance. Amerigo's cautious nature emerged and Julio knew how to respond. Julio looked at Amerigo and set the situation straight. "Mio uomo, we need to invest the money to grow," invoking that special Italian brother-to-brother invocation. The answer would have been no if it had been any other human than Julio asking. Amerigo trusted nobody more than Julio. It was a difficult time for such an investment, but Julio needed to improve his fuel-handling capability to grow. The current system was hampering growth and creating risk, an intolerable condition for the Menicuccis. Ultimately, they agreed to invest about seventy five percent of their savings. This was typical of how the Menicucci's handled these types of situations.

Julio, in his mid-forties, was strappingly young and vigorous. He approached any challenge as a call to arms, attacking whatever problem he faced with his full might. Within a minute after the meeting ended, he worked the telephone, seeking materials he needed for the upgrades. He located a used water tanker with a fifteen-hundred-gallon capacity that he upgraded to handle gasoline, an easy process because virtually no regulations existed for fuel wholesalers. This tank truck gave him one truck for each of the fuel types. Today, tankers that handle products as different as gasoline and water are not easily interchangeable due to environmental laws. He also purchased a new, professional pumping system for the warehouse that properly and safely transported fuels directly from the rail tanker to his storage tanks. The new enhanced-efficiency pumps worked on high voltage electricity, 440 Volts, necessitating an electrical upgrade to the warehouse. Menicuccis knew little about the electrical trades, so the work was contracted out to one of the Anglo electricians in the area, the only ethnic group that contained properly trained men. His professional pumping system had many safety features, such as double clasps to secure hose connections. The new hoses were steel-sheathed to prevent blowouts of the type that happened to Julio. Safety controls could sense a pressure loss from a ruptured hose line and shut off the flow before significant fuel can be spilled. It was expensive, so Julio redoubled his efforts to seek new customers to help pay for the investment and the losses from the gas spill. He picked up many new ones, including many Hispanic families and businesses.

SPURIOUS INNOVATION

Julio innovated in real time as he talked to prospective customers. Once, he was talking to the owner of a mobile home park, one of the many new ones being built to provide housing to a growing community. Mobile home parks could not access the city's utility services. All mobile homeowner provided for their own sanitation and heating. The mobile park provided a metered electric outlet to connect each mobile home to electrical power. Each mobile home accessed city water by connecting to a hose bib located on every home site. Each home needed kerosene for heating and cooking during the winter. That meant every mobile home park could potentially burn much of Super Oil's fuel. As Julio talked to the owner about a contract to supply kerosene, the man demurred, saying he had an insufficient number of tanks for each trailer and he was short of money to install more of them. Julio did not hesitate to tell him that Super Oil would buy and install the tanks for free but would charge rent for them. Julio would add the rental fee to each customer's fuel bill. Julio agreed that the rental contract applied as long as it was used to store the kerosene he delivered. It was a deal too good to refuse, so he reached out to shake Julio's hand and signed the contract. Julio was now in the storage tank installation business. He was one of the first wholesale distributors in the city to install and rent fuel storage tanks and dispense fuel to them.

Julio never contemplated a tank installation and rental program. He had no idea how much to charge for rent nor had he any rental contract forms. He had not discussed it with his brother. He had no expertise in tank installation or tanks themselves. He had no tools or experience. These shortcomings never fazed the Menicuccis. They did what was necessary to maintain a successful business and support their family. He promised to contact the park owner shortly with a rental and fuel supply contract to sign.

Before Julio returned to the Super Oil warehouse, he drove around town looking for overhead storage tanks. He was discovering how they were constructed. Once he saw a few, he designed a simple overhead support structure for a fifty-five-gallon drum that could be built using a 2X4 wooden frame that was nailed together. He stopped by Baldridge Lumber and bought some lumber and nails. When he returned to the warehouse with the materials, he and Albert Nottoli quickly assembled a prototype where the tank would lie on its side on the overhead frame. They tried it out with a full barrel of kerosene and it worked. It was the first of many. Julio computed the total costs and time needed to build the frame and buy a tank. He then selected a timeframe for recovery for his investment, which he put at five years. Dividing the total cost of the tank by five and adding his markup gave him the annual rental fee to charge. It was crude calculating by today's standards but sophisticated for a man with only three years of grade school education. It seemed that the Menicuccis were always a half step in front of the competition.

THE LANGUAGE OF THE PEOPLE

Julio often told an interesting story of how his language skills aided his business. Dante, his oldest son, worked part-time at Super Oil while attending school. He was in his teens and was being primed to eventually take over the business, as was typical among Italian business owners. Like all the Menicucci men, they were fluent in accented Spanish and English, but the youngsters spoke all three languages with no accent.

Julio told the story: One summer day in the later years of the

1930s, he and his young protégé Dante were out cold-calling prospective customers. They stopped at a filling station under construction. It was owned and operated by a Hispanic family, a father and his two sons who were on site. He introduced himself and Dante in English and gave them his sales pitch: He would supply quality gasoline at guaranteed lowest prices and deliver it on demand; he emphasized service and quality, which were the hallmarks of the Menicucci's businesses. The owner and his sons politely excused themselves, stepped to the side and discussed the situation in Spanish, assuming that the Menicuccis spoke only English, as did most Anglos, the racial group the Menicuccis were often lumped into. Typical Anglos could not understand any Spanish, yet he and Dante could understand every word.

Julio interrupted in Spanish, "Perdoname Senores, pero entendemos todo que dicen," (Pardon me, gentlemen, but we understand what you are saying.) It startled the family but they quickly broached smiles and responded in Spanish, immediately discussing the terms of the contract. The remainder of the conversation and all future ones between the five men were in Spanish. They remained regular gasoline and oil customers for Super Oil for the life of their business and were personal friends with Julio, Dante and Albert Nottoli, Julio's twenty-five-year-old driver.

A Sinclair Service Station under construction in Albuquerque following the depression. Julio sought out stations like this one because they were potential wholesale customers. Courtesy Albuquerque Museum, a gift of Albuquerque National Bank.

All of Julio's drivers were either Italian or Hispanic, thus they were multilingual in Spanish and English. Like Modesto, Julio saw the Hispanic community as a potential customer base and knew that they preferred to use their own language, just like Italians. Additionally, the Hispanics and the Italians shared a religious heritage, both tending heavily toward Catholicism and many were members of Immaculate Conception Parish, where the Menicuccis worshiped. He recognized that the Hispanics had longevity in the community, with families here for centuries. Spanish was the native tongue of many Albuquerqueans, and the Menicuccis believed one should learn the people's language. In Albuquerque, that meant English and Spanish. Some of the Menicuccis' customers spoke only Spanish.

Amerigo's employees were mostly bilingual because most were Italians—and nearly every Italian—was at least conversant in Spanish. He had a few specialty employees who did not speak Spanish, such as Anglo mechanics, the only group of men with mechanical skills. Italians, such as Horace Palladino, were on the track to learn the technical skills to repair automobiles, but he was not on pace with the Anglos, who had a head start in education and training over the immigrants. Technical tasks are difficult to learn without a primary education that includes the reading and math skills needed to comprehend complex trade manuals. Public schools offered training in the trades.

The underlying racial tension between the Anglos and Hispanics, of which the Italians were often grouped, had existed for years and stemmed from the perception among many that the Anglos had stolen land that had been granted to the Hispanic community by the Spanish crown. These racial differences were immaterial to the Menicuccis because they saw all Albuquerqueans as potential customers. As Julio often said, "Their money is as green as the Gringos," the slang term for Anglos. All customers, regardless of race, color or creed, were pampered and valued, an attitude that enhanced the popularity of the businesses.

Julio and Amerigo were solid capitalists but were driven in business more by need than greed. To these men, the business provided not only sustenance for the families but also an opportunity to help the next family progress socially and economically. They never wanted the Menicuccis to live as peasants again.

In the closing years of the 1930s with the depression winding down, the outlook was rosy. The country had emerged from the depression, and the refurbished banking system was sound. However, a recession interrupted the steady economic improvement in the late 1930s due to congressional spending cuts to some programs. The theory among the national politicians was that the spending had done its job, the economy was humming along and it was time to balance the budget, which was in deficit due to Roosevelt's eight-year New Deal spending spree. At that time the debt measured forty-three percent of the United States budget, the highest in history. It was nothing like the deficit spending to come. At that time, most of the populace believed that a balanced budget was fundamental for any organization, from a Kool-Aid stand to the United States Government. Citizens expected the government to keep the books balanced.

Roosevelt had correctly diagnosed the nation's economic problem, and the New Deal was an appropriate remedy. His many government spending programs were widely credited with bootstrapping the national economy back into the fast lane. Albuquerque's leaders adeptly shepherded more than New Mexico's share of the New Deal bounty into the community. People found jobs building Albuquerque's new public infrastructure, much of which directly benefitted common folks. Folks returned their savings to the two remaining banks because the federal government insured their accounts. Families bought homes and autos and vacations, traveling to new places made accessible by the rapidly expanding rail lines. Farming improved, with food prices stabilizing. Local businesses sprang up as people had jobs and money to spend on discretionary items.

By the end of 1930, the populace was content that the worst was past. A new threat was brewing, though one purposely ignored by most Americans, but it had a familiar ring to the Menicuccis. The Germans were back at their mischief in Europe, just two decades after the Menicuccis had fought to drive them from France. This time, it appeared that they were fielding a better team. The brothers were U.S. Army Veterans and they knew the situation was growing serious but it was not long before it engulfed the Menicucci family in a multi-year drama.

See notes.9, 10.

Notes

1. Keynesian theories are presented in *Keynes'* original work.

2. *Sacks* presents a detailed summary of Tingley's actions during the depression years.

3. Officially, the committee was the National Commission on Law Observance and Enforcement.

4. The *Wickersham* report is presented in full.

5. Modesto believed in self-responsibility and self-reliance, as did nearly every other Italian immigrant. He abhorred the concept of government aid of any kind. In the early 1930s his brother-in-law, John Granone, died in an accident. John's wife, Teresa Barsanti Granone, was left at home with young children. John had no insurance and Social Security was starting up, so the family was essentially broke. At the time, some social programs existed. But Modesto said, "This is family. We take care of our family." For years following, Modesto adopted the role of caretaker. He paid for their health care, school tuition, clothing and food. Mary Dalle Menicucci told the story. "Papa bought food for Zia (aunt) so that she did not have to get it from the government. He said, 'When you take money from them, they own you.' Every week we went over there with the trunk full of groceries. I helped unload the car. There was everything in there like toothpaste and celery, things for the home. Then he worked around the house fixing things. He did that for years."

6. Pia developed this simple recipe for the Mint's New Year's Eve celebration. Kathy Menicucci Meadows, daughter to Charlie, still regularly prepares Cenci for the greater family on New Year's Day. Cenci is ideal for coffee and other hot drinks.

Ingredients: 3 eggs, ½ cup sugar, 1 cube softened butter, ½ teaspoon salt, 2 tablespoons of Rum, ¼ cup milk and 3-4 cups of flour or enough for the consistency of a pie dough.

Procedure: Cream butter and sugar. Add beaten eggs, milk and Rum. Mix well and add flour. Knead well, roll out to about ½" thick. Slice into hand-sized pieces and fry in deep fat until golden brown. Drain, cool and dust with ample amounts of confectioner's sugar.

Tips from Kathy: "I use about 1/4 cup of whiskey or brandy. After kneading, let the dough rest on the counter, covering it for about 10 minutes. Cut the dough in half. Roll out on a lightly flour-dusted surface till about 1/4 inch thick. Cut into strips 6"x 1" thick. Carefully stretch the strips to tie them in a loose knot. Set aside until all strips are tied. Fry in canola oil at 350 degrees. Working quickly, add half of the strips to the oil and fry for 1-2 minutes until lightly golden brown, then flip and fry on the other side. Remove from oil to paper towel to drain. Fry remaining strips. Roll out the second half of the dough, cut into strips and fry. When cool, dust with sifted confectioners' sugar. They take two dustings depending on how much sugar you like."

7. *Artusi* wrote the first Italian cookbook in the late 1800s. Many recipes used in the Italian colony were based on the fundamentals he described. However, he did not develop many of the recipes he presented. His original book was a compendium of typical Italian cooking that reflected how people in Italy prepared food. *Dickie* describes the history of Italian food.

8. Albuquerque has two underground aquifers. One is shallow, and in the valley, it can be found at only five feet below the surface. Today, it is used for irrigation. The deep aquifer, hundreds of feet below the surface, supplies drinking water for the city.

9. Much of the information for this chapter was gathered from newspaper reports in Albuquerque and corroborated lore.

10. The census provided many details for the chapter.

14

ALBUQUERQUE LIVING, ITALIAN STYLE (1932-1940)

ENTRENCHING FAMILY LIFE

After the families' 1932 visit to Italy, they knew two realities of life. First, the families' move to America was done, at least the physical relocation. Whether it was fertile ground for the generational growth of the family was yet to be discovered, but for now, Albuquerque was their home, not Italy. Even the women on the voyage back to America longed for Albuquerque where they had their own homes, kitchens, friends and gardens. They were by now accustomed to growing their families in Albuquerque. The men, of course, had been sold on America for years and their livelihoods were in the desert. And the children knew no other home but Albuquerque, where they had friends and relatives to play with.

Second, the Menicuccis sensed that the political situation in Europe was worse than they had imagined. They had seen the effect of Benito Mussolini in Italy. He was a bombastic prime minister who was fundamentally altering the character of Italy with a new form of government called fascism. As they understood it, a fascist government is run by a single powerful dictator who uses race as the basis for a ruling philosophy and controls the press and schools. By 1932, Mussolini's influence on Italy was growing, and he contemplated military campaigns in Albania and Greece, both militarily easy conquests, even for the Italians. The family knew that fascism was neither good for Italy nor America.

Mussolini became concerning to the Italian colony in the late 1920s, and Julio and Giulia were among the first to notice because Giulia subscribed to two Lucca newspapers. The Italian press glorified the Mussolini regime and all its acts. America's free press presented the situation as it was—Italy was a lagging European economy with marginal military capability and a dictating fascist at the helm. The families also experienced Italian government meddling in their personal affairs. In the early 1930s, personal letters from Italy showed evidence of tampering: some envelopes had been opened and some pages of letters had words scratched out. By 1932, entire pages of multi-page letters were missing, and others had missing paragraphs. Italian government censors were at work. Italy was on a sinister path and the Menicuccis, and nearly every Italian in the colony, wanted nothing to do with it.[1]

Their concern about Italy did not last long as both families had a cadre of pre-teen children to nurture. Dante and Mario, the oldest males in each of the two families, were automatically slated as heirs to the family businesses, and both families were convinced of the value of education. The brothers had seen how their educational shortcomings had impeded them and saw an American society increasingly dependent on technology. They knew that to remain competitive, all citizens had to be educated. Even in their own businesses, the mechanics were their highest-paid employees and the most difficult to replace. They also observed that highly paid professional employees, such as bank officers or lawyers, were all well-educated and well-compensated. They knew that education was one of America's greatest gifts, one that Italy could not provide.

Over the years in the 1930s, the Menicuccis experienced trials and misfortunes similar to those of normal residents, including fire. In 1935, Teresa and Mari Menicucci, in a tribute to the Madonna, lit two candles in front of her likeness on a table near an open window. A gust of wind blew a wispy window covering over the candles, alighting them. Before anyone noticed, a fire was raging in the living room. Julio was at work, and Giulia scattered everyone from the home. They ran next door to the Puccis to call the fire department. The fire was extinguished, but the damage was considerable, mostly due to water and smoke. The girls, of course, were disciplined for lack of forethought, which both Julio considered to be a requirement of all children older than seven, which all of his were.

CATHOLIC SCHOOL PRESENCE

Immaculate Conception's main facilities consumed nearly the entire city block bounded by Sixth and Seventh Streets; Tijeras and Copper Streets. Two-thirds of the property was dedicated to St. Mary's School. The school's outsized physical presence reflected its value to the parishioners. St. Mary's School opened in 1921. It was part of a national trend that set up Catholic schools to become the largest non-public Christian school system in America, one that was and still is widely admired.[2]

Immaculate Conception church in the early 1940s It replaced the original church.
Courtesy Albuquerque Museum, a gift from Albuquerque National Bank.

St. Mary's School in the 1930s. The top of Immaculate Conception's bell tower can be seen in the background off the left side of the building. Courtesy Albuquerque Museum, gift from Margaret R. Herter, Photographer: Alabama Milner.

Nuns ran the Catholic schools, most connected to a parish. Each parish had a pastor and attending priests, some of whom taught religion, especially to high schoolers. The Catholic Church was hierarchical with strong paternal overtones, much more so than today. Men held the most powerful positions and women were assistants. Using a military analogy, men were the officers and the women were the enlisted. Like an army, members agreed to the system and they worked as a team for the shared goal of bettering humankind, which is equivalent to serving the Lord and community. Throughout the first half of the Twentieth Century, the Catholic church operated one of the most efficient educational systems in the country.

A top-notch private education at St. Mary's was almost free—around two dollars a month per student (about forty-two in 2024 dollars), not including family discounts. On the surface, the Catholic machine seemed to violate all of Adam Smith's economic rules. Critics missed several subtle but critical aspects of the church's underlying business situation. Catholics had a huge force of high-quality, extremely low-cost professional labor.[3]

American society was largely religiously oriented and ministers of any faith were respected. Not a single sane American at that time fancied any religious minister engaged in criminal activity. Catholics capitalized on the situation like no other religious group. They developed extraordinary marketing acumen, attracting thousands to forswear a family to labor for life with little remuneration. These recruits believed they were providing the ultimate service to the Lord. Italians often bragged about their family members serving in religious orders.[4]

The Catholics cleverly marketed into this environment by offering a superior career to the traditional one, starting with professional training and guaranteed employment. The basic concept was that since nuns, brothers and priests were free of the rigors and distractions of family life, they could apply all of their time, talent and energy to their professions. Many nuns and priests were first-class teachers. Religious life was hard work but with guaranteed shelter, meals and health care until death. The Catholic hierarchy applied the same recruiting technique to lay people, especially professionals, beaconing them to assist in parishes and schools. They offered the same package to lay folks: if they volunteered their time, it improved their standing in the eyes of the Lord. Besides, it was a socially noble activity, along with regular contributions to the church, of course. Like the U.S. Marine Corps, the Catholics advertised for the brightest and best to fill their quotas. And like the Marines, they filled them with fresh, vigorous, intelligent people stepping up to a life of Catholic service.

Low-cost labor is a major advantage to any business and the Catholic Church was a huge, global business endeavor. The American Catholic School system had operated in the United States since 1783 based on the concept that it would produce a continual supply of well-educated Catholics to support the church. It was a good plan and they had the labor force to implement it. The Catholic Sisters of Charity was one of the largest and most powerful of all women's religious orders; it concentrated on education. All nuns were college-educated, usually in a career area that served the needs of the church. Many young women became nuns because it was an easy path to an educational career. More than religious zeal brought people to the church; many believed it was an attractive deal for life.

The Catholic school system grew steadily, but a vigorous boom did not occur until after World War I. Immaculate Conception parish, founded in 1883, comprised most of downtown Albuquerque and nearly all of the Italian families. At that time, the Catholic parishes were structured much like political wards, with clearly demarked boundaries. If one lived within the boundary of a parish, that was the church residents attended. While the church was open to all, only Catholics within the boundary could formally join the parish. St Mary's school admitted all parishioner children and only accepted students from Catholic parishes without a school. Non-Catholic children could apply if their parents were actively converting to Catholicism.

The Menicucci brothers were fervent Catholics with the kind of deep devotion that comes from near-death experiences in a deep hole. Their first priority was religious training, a goal in which the women had special responsibility. While the church and school provided the theory of religion and guidance in applying it, the parents—particularly the mothers—were responsible for implementing it in real life. It was a serious family occupation, one in which quality was never compromised. The women also led in discipline. In the homes, Giulia and Davina were first to issue punishments for their children's transgressions, but if the violation were serious, kids could expect even harsher repercussions from the men. A child disciplined by the school principal, considered as infallible as the Pope in terms of student accusations, created a major problem at home. If the principal said a child was guilty, it was true and the parents always agreed. The families generally put their full trust in the Sisters of Charity who ran the school.

The men were generally so encompassed by work that they did not attend Sunday Mass. In the early days of the family business, Super Service Station and Super Oil Company were open seven days a week, 365 days a year, from seven in the morning to seven in the evening. Few Italian men attended Sunday services. The Church did not officially dispense them from the weekly service, but they understood they were earning money for their families and the Church. The Church looked the other way. Ergo, the task of family church attendance fell to the women.[5]

Children walked to and from school, regardless of the weather. Schools were rarely closed or delayed for snow.[6] School was scheduled for a certain time and students were required to be there. For lunch, many students ate at home. Most students lived only a few blocks from school and most women were full-time homemakers. In those days, there was little fear of violent threats against children walking alone between school and home as few lawless persons roamed the streets. Attacks of any kind, such as child kidnappings, were extremely rare. The biggest threats to St. Mary's' young students were stray dogs and mischievous older students.

ST. MARY'S SEX TRAINING

The nuns provided religious sex education through ninth grade. In high school, the priests assumed the teaching duties. The parish housed a dozen permanent religious staff, mostly priests and occasionally brothers. Sex education began in the ninth grade. The priests handled the boys and the nuns worked with the girls. Children were taught that sexual activity was part of the Lord's plan to reproduce, a vitally important life function. It was to be practiced as much as necessary to produce a family but not too much that it became a recreational activity. Too much recreation can be corrupting, as was the teaching. The fundamental message was that the deeply pleasurable feeling that results from sex was the gift that God gave humans to reward them for reproducing, not having fun. The church's policies made sense when population growth was desired—as it had been for most of its existence. When so many people died early and the government provided no backdrop, large families were advantageous. Italians and almost everyone else agreed that the focus of sexual education was to help youngsters do what is natural but with the purpose of family. The church wanted the sexual activity to keep growth fueled, but they did not want it to run amuck.

YES, SISTER

Catholic school nuns of that era are often characterized as military drill sergeants, and the term is not inaptly applied. Their job was to provide the basic training for a life of service to God and the community. Nuns' uniforms, including some with elaborate habits covering their heads, commanded students' attention from the moment they walked into the first-grade door to the day they walked out with a diploma. Students were told how to stand and walk, when to speak and be quiet, when to work and when to pray. Religious studies were based on Catholic texts, which interpreted the Bible's New Testament for easy comprehension by the children. The Bible was not used directly in the instructions, except for readings, which were often interpreted for the audience lest the parishioners draw their own erroneous conclusions. All the religious instruction in the school, along with the Missal used in the Masses, were Catholic publications that contained what a lay person needed to know about how to live a Catholic life.[7]

Catholic Carmelite nun and novice. The Sisters of Charity at St. Mary's school were similarly attired. They lived in a convent on Seventh Street and Copper. Nuns ranged in age from around twenty-five to about seventy-five. Sister Bernadette, who was the second-grade teacher for over half a century, taught both my father and me. She had a reputation of having eyes in the back of her head because she could recognize any student speaking out of turn by voice. Courtesy Eugenio Hansen, OFS; in the public domain via Wikimedia Commons, www.commons.wikimedia.org, 2024.

Nuns were supreme rulers of their classrooms and they demanded discipline. Offenses, such as being improperly prepared for a spelling bee, could result in a stint after school to study spelling words. Nuns had no family to return to in the afternoon, so they spent as much time as needed to ensure students succeeded. Students prized the post-school camaraderie in the playgrounds. Staying after school with a nun pounding away with learning exercises was a significant incentive for students to behave and learn. Particularly difficult cases were sent to the principal for additional discipline, including paddling, an acceptable child-rearing practice of the day. It might also include suspension from classes, which was serious because the student could fall behind and have to repeat the grade. A trip to the principal's office often led to a call to the parents, which escalated the disciplining experience from school to home. St. Mary's School was completely meritorious and students were often issued failing grades. Each grade had a student or two who did not make the cut and were forced to repeat the grade. Parents were nearly one hundred percent supportive of the teachers, often giving the nuns blanket authority to hold back or strike their child if he or she deserved it.

First communion was a major event for students and the Menicucci families robustly celebrated it. In a Catholic Mass, the faithful believe that the bread that the priest holds over the chalice of wine is converted into the body of Jesus Christ, which the people then consume. It is a solemn and holy event that incorporates the recipient into the true body of Christ, the third sacrament to augment life's journey to Heaven (Baptism is the initial one, and confession is the second).

First communion was typically scheduled for the end of first grade, meaning the entire year was spent carefully preparing the children. The training was arduous; it included not only classroom instruction but physical preparation—what to wear on the day of the event, what not to eat or drink—at that time, no food or drink was allowed after midnight on the day of the communion—how to file into in church, how to behave at the altar rail when receiving the bread and what was allowable for celebration at the church following the event. Each family had its own traditions. The nuns often celebrated with the first communicants at orphanages because they had no family and neither did the nuns. On the Friday before First Communion Sunday, all of the communicants performed their first confession. Typical offenses included talking back to parents or fibbing about the results of a school test. Absolutions included a certain number of

Hail Marys, but more serious offenses could result in heavier fines, such as a series of Hail Marys and Our Fathers.[8,9]

On the Sunday of the first communion, the nuns queried each prospective communicant on whether they had complied with the rules leading up to the event. No food or drink could be taken after midnight on first communion day. Occasionally, a student might slip up and sip some water. If so, he had to wait until the next year to try again or attend a special summer event for the scofflaws. The seriousness of the situation and the plethora of threats of dire consequences typically produced no infractions. To fight temptation, the nuns tied bedsheets around all of the water fountains and valves in the lavatories. Naturally, the top-rung nuns stood guard over the event to ensure appropriate solemn behavior as everyone gathered for the First Communion Mass.

The church and school often provided a sizable reception for the new communicants, including food, drinks and sometimes music and dancing. The Menicuccis celebrated first communions lavishly, including large family parties with plenty of wine and Italian foods, which were readily available in Albuquerque. Since most Italians had settled in New Town Albuquerque, there were sufficient Italian first communicants to spontaneously produce block parties of reveling family members, exchanging gifts similar to a wedding. Although The Menicuccis were two separate families, they celebrated their first communions together. It was easy because most of the birth dates of children on one side matched those on the other, which meant they had first communicants every couple of years for nearly a decade.

Familial participation in the Church was required. Women attended the altar, doing things typical in a home, such as stitching and repairing the holy clothes and vestments, and washing and dusting the statues. The clothes were most important because they were integral to the Masses and ceremonies. Both women and men served in the choir. The school had its own choirs—one each for the grade school and high school. School choirs performed at all the weekly student Masses and special events, such as the Christmas Pageant or recitals. Young men served as altar boys, an institution in its own right that had grown into a large and essential component of the Masses. Large events, such as solemn-high Easter Vigil mass, required a squad of properly trained boys to assist the priests.

At Immaculate Conception, most altar boys were St. Mary's students. They were exempt from classroom attendance to serve special church events, such as noon Masses, funerals and weddings. They were not exempt from learning the material they missed while at church. While Masters of Acolytes commanded the highest respect and the most prestigious altar-boy rank, the opposite was true about young, six- or seven-year-old postulant servers assigned to the least desirable jobs, such as serving the six o'clock mass for a full week in January. About a tenth of St. Mary's' boys served as altar boys. Typically, boys progressed in rank via experience, but as they grew older, they garnered the more coveted positions. Senior boys lobbied early in the year for the position of Master of Acolytes, a critical ceremonial position during major holy events, especially Christmas and Easter. Candidates ran campaigns for the position just like politicians, but the priests made the final selection. Masters of Acolytes were students who had already exhibited leadership skills in both the church and school and who were physically capable of holding the missal, a ten-pound book, for the priest during special parts of the service. Young men chosen for the position donned special garments and had distinct duties at the altar, serving the celebrant directly. It was equivalent to a military sergeant major, the top-ranked enlisted position. Dante Menicucci was chosen as Master of Acolytes for his senior year and he spoke of it with pride years later. The entire family celebrated his achievement.

Men served as ushers, which was important to maintain order in seating congregants during large events. Midnight Mass, for example, usually attracted so many attendees that the church could not comfortably seat all, and ushers were responsible for accommodating as many as possible, with some standing through the two-hour ceremony. Ushering was considered a security job, thus one for men only and typically assertive ones who commanded authority. Men, especially those with professional business skills, were tapped to serve on professional church committees, such as the finance council, a group of financial advisors to the pastor.

Both the ushers and altar boys were organized as clubs. The clubs continuously sponsored one family-oriented event after another, ranging from enchilada dinner fundraisers to overnight camping trips. For a typical family such as the Menicuccis, these activities captivated their lives and built special friendships and bondages among its members.

The church sought out Julio and Amerigo to apply their skills to parish problems. Julio enthusiastically responded as he was a bright, aggressive and clever businessman with technical attributes and a penchant for leading work activities. He served on the building and maintenance committee. Amerigo, on the other hand, was uncomfortable working in groups. His preferred face-to-face interactions as are typical in retail sales work. His and Davina's contributions lay more in the monetary arena, along with their lifetime dedication to the church. The couple often purchased votive candles in homages to the Madonna; her caricature emblazoned in mosaic glory on the west wall of Immaculate Conception Church.

By Twenty-First Century standards, the description of the Catholic community at Immaculate Conception and St. Mary's School may appear harsh, inflexible, and violating students' rights. It was indeed strict and highly disciplined, but many benefits spread to the greater community. For one, the nuns and priests taught from the Bible, with the Ten Commandments as the basis for instruction. The basic theme was that a good person is one who follows commandments, except for the sixth regarding murder, which can be ignored if your enemy is recognized as evil. Importantly, they explained how to differentiate between good and evil. They presented simple, vibrant and memorable Bible stories as examples of moral living. The characters in the stories were of common people struggling to live according to the will of God and it brought religion to the average person. In total, the Catholic faith fixed the mystery of the greater force of God in an anthropomorphic context, including communication with humans who could plead for divine intervention for special problems.

In Catholicism at the time, God was the invisible but every present almighty power driving the universe. The church emphasized personal restraint in thought and actions, especially discouraging rouge acts that injure others. Honesty was rewarded as a virtue, as was personal exertion. Each student was expected to put forth the maximum effort to learn, and laggards were punished with low grades not only for the subject areas but also for effort. The church heavily emphasized charity according to the Gospels of the Lord. Children were taught at an early age to share with those in need. Altruism was a pillar of Catholic faith, and its philosophical principles were integrated into school lessons and church homilies alike. Students—all of them—were expected to contribute their time to the church and school because they continuously sponsored one charity event after another. There were ample opportunities for continual service, such as the altar boys and the Altar Society, a group of women who cared for the linens and other articles for religious services.

In the end, students graduating from St. Mary's High School knew and understood the basic principles of Christianity, including how to differentiate between good and evil. They were academically competent, as well. There were, of course, students who did not possess the intellectual capability to excel, but they knew the fundamentals. In those days and for decades following, St. Mary's goal was that one hundred percent of students—regardless of background, ethnicity or family situation—had to prove knowledge commensurate with the grade level to progress to the next grade. There were no idle threats. The nuns routinely held back students for poor academic performance, including all of Amerigo's and Julio's children, who repeated first grade because they could not speak English. Fear and embarrassment of being stranded behind their peers powerfully motivated students.

St. Mary's taught civics, with special emphasis on freedom of religion, a pillar of the U.S. Constitution, and the implications for Catholics to go forth into the community to perform charitable works for the underprivileged. In short, the school produced appropriately educated young Catholics who understood how their religion worked within America's unique governing system. They were imbued with a duty to obey civil laws while serving the community through charitable organizations. Students who graduated from St. Mary's High School were prepared to work in society or to enter higher education. Catholic training served the community well.[10]

Interior of Immaculate Conception Church in late 1930s. This worn photograph shows a St. Mary's High School graduation class. The backdrop of physical articles around the alter were solid gold. Courtesy Dante Menicucci family.

Three first generation Italian immigrants enjoyed showing off their Easter outfits in the mid-1930s. Traditionally, women bought new attire for Easter, with an emphasis on bonnets. From left: Jeannette Franchini, Mariangela Menicucci and Teresa Menicucci. Jeannette's identity was deduced based on her known friendship with Teresa and an annotation on the photo. However, her grandchildren cannot confirm the deduction. Courtesy Guili Scanlon Doyle.

WEEKEND HOMEWORK

Weekends at the Menicucci homes were devoted to domestic work—inside the home for the women and outside for the men. Giulia and Davina were typical Italian wives striving for perfectly clean homes and occupants. Each weekend, the women gathered the girls together as a cleaning team. Even children as young as three were expected to help in some fashion—really as training for the real thing later on. There were floors to wash; dust to remove; clothes and bed sheets to strip; linins to wash, dry and iron; toilets, basins and tubs to scrub; and various articles of clothing to mend or stitch. Any large meals, such as a three-gallon pot of minestrone, which could provide several meals, were cooked on the weekends and the leftovers were stored in an ice box for subsequent meals. Regarding cleaning, Davina and Giulia were serious and demanded perfection from their young protégés. Typically, Saturday indoor chores consumed a full day of hard labor.

The men concentrated on outdoor chores, such as home repairs and gardening. Both Menicucci families raised animals, including pigeons and rabbits, providing fresh protein for meals. Julio was constantly innovating, building one device or another to enhance yield from the garden or the animals. He built automatic feeding and watering systems that reduced labor. Amerigo built special hutches for his animals to protect them from winter cold. Both families had robust gardens that produced a wide range of fresh vegetables and fruit. The Menicuccis were farmers, so their gardens were immense, filling their backyards with vegetables ranging from zucchini to radishes to corn. They also grew fig trees, as it was one of the favorite fruits in their youths and a living connection to their homeland. Figs, unfortunately, are not well acclimated to Albuquerque's winter weather, so without protection they froze to the ground every winter, killing off the growth from the previous summer. Julio and Amerigo, with their boys helping, built special enclosures for their figs, which they grew from seeds smuggled from Italy. The enclosures were ten feet high by about four feet wide and could be completely sealed up with wooden sides, sheltering against deep freezes. In the summer, screened planks replace the wooden sides to keep birds out. Finches, which did and still have a large population in Albuquerque, have strong penchants for figs.

The brothers knew organic farming. They mixed animal manure, garden compost and water in a barrel with a closed lid. They let it sit, allowing the bacterial decay to continue. From time to time, they drained some of the water out of the bucket and applied it to the plants. This liquid was rich in plant nutrients. It was also rich in odor and had to be stored in a sealed container. Their composting systems consisted of a fifty-five-gallon drum with the top cut open and a metal lid to seal it. I once asked Julio how his tea worked. He said, "It kicks them in the ass." Indeed. The mixture was so powerful that it could easily damage the plant with chemical burns. Used judiciously, it produced abundant harvests. The brothers rarely hired others to do any domestic work, so they were plenty busy. It was an opportunity for the boys to learn a wide range of technical skills.

ITALIAN CLUBS

The Albuquerque Italian community was tight-knit, determined to assimilate into American culture but to preserve as much of their heritage as was fitting. They needed support in doing so. Oreste Bachechi, one of the earliest immigrants, saw the need for a civic organization where Italians could meet and share resources with other immigrants. He founded the Colombo in 1892. Located in the middle of downtown Albuquerque at 401 Second Street, its primary purpose was to support the Italian community. For example, they had formed an insurance fund from the members' dues to help families facing the tragedies of death or disease. They also assisted immigrants with legal problems, housing assistance and job placement. They ensured that the colony preserved the Italian wine tradition by loaning out fermentation and distillation equipment and advising youngsters. Although the Colombo hosted family events, such as parties and dances, the main recreational activities of the organization focused on male-oriented activities, such as Bocce Ball and card games. The Colombo's name is a testament to the Italians' pride in Columbus and other Italian explorers.

The Columbus Hall was built by the Colombo society in the early 1900s. The Colombo rented the hall to others, giving preference to Catholic or Italian organizations, such as the Knights of Columbus and the Italian Women's Charity Club. The identities of the people are unknown. Courtesy Albuquerque Museum, gift from Yolanda Matteucci Marianetti.

The Colombo grew quickly with dozens of members, all men. It became a clearinghouse to meet, greet and confer. Card games were often held, mostly informal matches, but tournaments with high betting stakes brought out the top competition. They played many different games, including Scoapre, Tressette and Scala Quarenta. But the most popular was Briscola, a cerebral game similar to bridge, played by four. Unlike Bridge where trump is determined by a complex set of bids, in Briscola it is determined by a random card draw. The Colombo Hall's main asset was a large room used as the main recreational area for dinner parties and other recreational activities, such as dances. It was the largest in town and in constant demand for all. For years, hall rental was the organization's main source of income. Dances were popular and often a source of concern for Italian wives who were always on the lookout for their husbands' wandering eyes among the plethora of Italian women. More than a few married men were taken to task for dancing with other wives.

PLAY BALL

The Colombo maintained a multi-court Bocce Ball arena in its basement. Bocce is often compared to American Bowling, but it is different. The only similarity is that both involve rolling balls on the earth's surface. Bocce is played on dirt lanes about four feet wide. One's objective is to get a player's ball closest to a target ball, called a Pallino, placed randomly near the end of a dirt lane. At the other end of the lane, about fifteen feet away, were the competitors who each took turns rolling one of their balls (usually four) toward the Pallino. An important tactic in the game was for one team to use their balls to bump another team's ball out of position. Thus, strong-armed players could produce some dramatic results by violently jolting an opponent's ball completely off the court. Peals of cheer and groans sprang from the windows of the Bocce Ball arena along with rolling clouds of tobacco smoke. Special occasions, such as Easter, brought Bocce Ball tournaments involving a dozen men who competed over two or three days. Naturally, some men were more skilled than others, producing what today are local sports dignitaries. Choppo Domenici's family was particularly athletic. Pete, their son who became a U.S. Senator, was a notable high school athlete and was such an accomplished Bocce Ball player that he was affectionately called "Bocce," a moniker that stuck with him in the Italian community for his life. Gino Matteucci, son of Amedeo, and Charlie Menicucci, son of Julio, were also known for their aggressive play. According to some, the team of Nello Matteucci, son of Amedeo and Angelo Bandoni was legendary, never losing a match. But they never went up against Bocce.

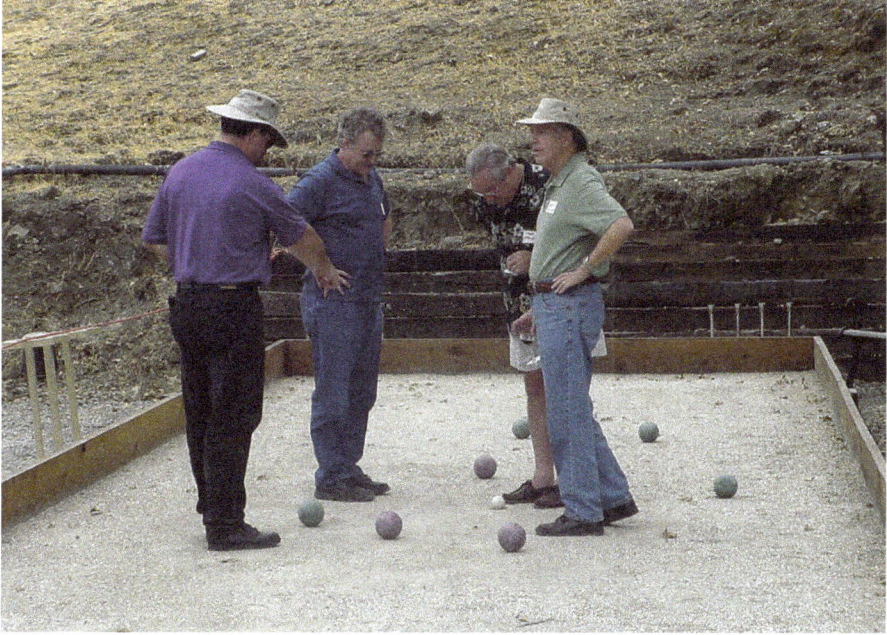

Four men playing bocce ball. The pallino is the small ball in the center. The men are arguing about the score. One of the constantly contentious issues is the distance between a ball and the pallino. Only the closest two balls provide points to a team. Courtesy Xaven; in the public domain via https://commons.wikimedia.org/wiki/Category:Images, 2024.

The Colombo was just fine for men but left women without a social gathering place. In 1923, Maria Bachechi, wife of Oreste and a leading businesswoman, started the Italian Women's Charity Club. Originally the club was limited to women, but men were the officers. It took about fifteen years before women took total control of the club, holding all of the leadership offices. Their primary purpose was charity, not only to Italians but to the community. They also offered classes in domestic work, sewing, cooking and child-rearing. Many of the young Italian women who would normally learn from their mothers lacked that guidance in America. Maria's club supplied a vital service to the community. Davina Allesandri Menicucci and my maternal grandmother, Pia Barsanti Dalle, were active members. Giulia was content to learn on her own in her home, although she did call on neighbors for help, especially Ida Toti Pucci, wife of Luigi, who was a long-time neighbor to Julio going back to Italy.[11,12]

By 1931, the women's club had closed out its training mission and it was reorganized into a social and charity club, sponsoring regular spaghetti dinners, dances and picnics. Proceeds supported local charities, especially religious ones. They reasoned that they could support charities better by providing money rather than direct labor. During wars, they comforted women who had lost husbands and sons in the war by supplying flowers and other decorations at the funerals and providing financial support until the stricken families could recover. After the war, the club disbanded. It was reorganized again in 1956 to help the Italians understand American civic patriotism and civic responsibilities. The club believed that too many immigrants were failing to assimilate and eschewed some American societal practices.[13]

Over time, many of the first-generation offspring of the immigrants became impatient with the Colombo, which was dominated by older men with little interest in youthful activities. In 1939, a group of young Italian men founded the Italamer Club. Its name was a concatenation of the words Italy and America. It was mainly social, hosting dances, birthday gatherings, holiday feasts and special outings. The annual Italamer picnic in the nearby Manzano Mountains comprised nearly the entire population of the colony.

WINE AND MORE

Prohibition ended in December of 1933, but it had little effect on the Menicuccis because they had been fermenting their own vintages since arriving in Albuquerque. Wine was a staple in Italian recreational and culinary culture. In the early years, they fermented small batches but never enough to satisfy their entire annual consumption, so they bartered to cover any shortfall. Almost all Italians fermented their own vin de table (table wine), so bartering was common among Italians, although it was illegal to do so. As they established their own families, they fermented their own small batches. With the depression settling in, home fermenting became all the more important as an economic measure.

As the Italian community grew, the families competed with others for the materials needed to ferment, especially grapes and yeasts. It was one of the first major issues taken up at the Colombo Hall, a meeting place for Italian immigrant men to recreate and discuss business. Wine was an important element, one that commanded the attention of the Colombo leadership: the Italian community was growing so rapidly that the onslaught of fermenting every fall created a rush for materials and ingredients that sometimes led to anger and resentment among friends as shortages occurred. After consuming much wine and considering many suggestions: a solution emerged—a grape co-op. One just like the modern ones where a clearinghouse takes individual orders for grapes and when a sufficient number of orders could be batched into a bulk order, then they ordered a rail boxcar of grapes. Bulk buying produced considerable savings, an important consideration when so much wine was consumed in the colony.

Arthur Bachechi took the lead. He was influential at the Colombo, owned Anchor Liquors and had been in the liquor business before prohibition. He had a large warehouse with a rail dock and a commercial address so he could receive and unload rail shipments of grapes to disburse. Arthur worked the order through Hutchison Fruit Company in Albuquerque for a couple of boxcar loads of Mission Grapes from California. Mission grapes, dark blue and very juicy, were introduced to California by the Spanish missionaries in the early 1800s to produce wine for Catholic Masses. The grape was perfectly matched for the climate and quickly became a cash crop for many farmers after prohibition. It was recognized as the grape that produced top-quality California wines and put the state on the global vintner map. If properly fermented, it produced a fine table wine roughly comparable in flavor to Chianti.

The first boxcars arrived at Anchor Liquors in the fall of 1932, each loaded with deeply purple grapes. Hutchison purchased grapes at farm prices and had them delivered to Albuquerque with a markup. Arthur added a handling fee for his dock and storage and then divided the costs proportionately to all the participating families, each of which had prepaid for their order. It worked well. The families realized a fifty percent savings on the cost of the most expensive ingredient in winemaking. Hutchison and Arthur made their profits and all were delighted. Montezuma Grocery, a wholesale food and equipment distributor, cheerily provided retailers with all of the tools needed to ferment, including presses, barrels, yeast and storage bottles. The coop remained in existence throughout the World War II years and Albuquerque Italians had all the wine they needed.

At this point in time, the two Menicucci families required about one hundred and fifty gallons of wine per year, which was typical for an Italian family of six—it averages to about a fifth of a gallon a day. All family members drank wine during meals. Even toddlers were often given sips of water tainted with wine. Children drank diluted wine, with the dilution inversely proportional to age. By the time the children were eighteen, they were allowed to consume pure wine and many did. The two families consolidated their wine-making operation into one, purchasing larger-scale equipment and processing larger batches of wine as a two-family operation. The economy of scale they achieved in the joint operation saved considerable money.

They purchased a large grape press that could handle a half lug of grapes in one pressing. About a lug of grapes, weighing thirty pounds, produced a finished gallon of wine. The press consisted of an oak barrel, about three feet in diameter and several feet high. It had a sealed bottom and open top. Along two sides and over the top was a heavy metal rail. In the middle of the rail was a large screw fitted through the rail connected to a flat saucer that fit snuggly into the top of the barrel. Turning the large handle at the top of the screw slowly pushed the flat saucer down, squeezing the grapes between the saucer and the vessel bottom. A valve at the bottom of the press allowed the grape juice to be drained into containers. It was much superior to laboriously mashing by hand.

It was a family operation with the women washing the grapes in preparation for the press, cleaning storage equipment and removing waste. The men concentrated on the heavy work, including hauling the grapes and juice and operating the press. As they pressed, they collected the juice and placed it in large oak barrels for fermentation. In most cases, they added sugar to the juice in order to produce an appropriate alcohol level for the type of wine they were fermenting. Most Italians, including the Menicuccis, made the driest wine possible, about thirteen percent alcohol by volume. Some families fermented with commercial wine yeast. Others depended on wild yeasts, those that naturally float around in the air. Julio was particular, using only specific strains of prepared yeast. Various yeast strains were available at some local grocery stores and, of course, at bakeries. Fermentation typically required about two weeks and if successful, the barrel contained a bifurcated volume of liquid with clear wine at the top and a small amount of waste material that settled at the bottom. They siphoned the wine into one-gallon jugs. They stored the jugs in the basement to be retrieved as needed throughout the year.

Wine was not the only objective; Grappa was integrated into the process. Grappa, which is similar to brandy, is a name derived from Latin meaning a bunch of grapes. The grape-press produced juice along with ample waste of skins and stems. They collected waste into separate barrels after which they added sugar, water and yeast (if using prepared yeast).[14] Fermentation required a couple of weeks. Then they transferred the alcoholic liquid into a still. The distilled product was Grappa, which was similar to Brandy. The families borrowed a still from the Colombo, which had purchased several for use in the Italian community. They distilled in Julio's backyard, where he fired the still with wood. Their homemade Grappa was typically about 80 proof, but sometimes as high as 100. It was not as refined as commercially produced Brandy, but certainly adequate for home use, which focused on its inebriating qualities not for aromatics or sipping. They produced about five gallons of Grappa a year, plenty for both families. Typically, only the men imbibed the Grappa but the women used it for cooking. Plenty of Grappa was consumed at the Colombo Hall, especially during Bocce Ball tournaments.

See notes.15, 16.

Notes

1. *Smith* (Denis) presents an excellent description of the history of Muzzolini. *Churchill* (*The Gathering Storm*) comments on Muzzolini.

2. The Catholic Jesuit order of priests founded Immaculate Conception Church in 1863. These priests were refugees from Italy; they were on the wrong side of the Italian unification and were all exiled, many to America. The history of the church is documented in *Immaculate Conception Parishioners*.

3. *Smith* (Adam) is considered the father of modern free market capitalist theory. He presents in full detail how such theory works, why it works and how it is applied. His original work profoundly influenced the creation of the U.S. economic system.

4. Giulia's brother Angelo was one who sacrificed a family to join the priesthood. He was a Monsignor in the Vatican and served as the head of recruitment. Generally, families that were financially secure with many members welcomed the sacrifice of a family member to the church. It was like a huge, visible gift to the community, and widely acknowledged. This was the case with the Gragnani family, which owned property and operated

a silk farm and fabric business. It was not true for most of the Mezzadria, who struggled hand-to-mouth and needed every family member to work productively to survive.

5. Over time, the practice of closing on Sundays and holidays spread in the business community and by the early 1930s Super Service Station closed on Sundays, Christmas, New Year's Day and the Fourth of July. It was not until the 1950s before Saturdays came to be seen as part of the weekend and shops closed. The Menicuccis kept the businesses open on Saturday mornings for years, not wanting to let the competition creep up on them. It was not until the 1960s that Saturday closings became the norm for the station. During this transition period, the men returned to regular Sunday church attendance and increasingly participated in the affairs of the church, such as serving on the parish council and ushering.

6. Albuquerque in the 1920s and 1930s was cooler than it is today. Winter often produced heavy snowstorms that dumped up to a foot of snow. The city had no snow plows or snow removal equipment and most streets were dirt. These snow events and heavy summer rains created much difficulty for residents, especially businesses because it prevented customers from visiting.

7. *Kuhns* describes in detail the history of clothing for Catholic nuns.

8. My own experience in the 6th grade at St. Mary's School is a good example of how this worked. I was disciplined for talking during class. I stood in the corner several times, but Sister Lila had no patience with continuing offenses because it disrupted the class. She sent me to the principal. I had a reputation; it was not my first trip and Sister Loyola pulled the plug. She declared that she would call my father Charlie. She kept me in the office for the remainder of the day. I figured it was a bluff, but in case, I put my previously conceived plan into action. When the phone call came in the evening, I answered it and then ducked into a nearby room to cover my voice. When Sister Loyola asked to speak to Charlie, I changed my voice and pretended to be a babysitter. I told her that he and Emma had gone on a long vacation. She politely told me to report that she had called. I was riding high when I got to school and settled into my desk with no repercussions. I wasted no time telling my buddies of my ruse. They were impressed. The jubilation was short-lived as Sister Lila pointed at me and told me to go immediately to the principal. When I arrived, my father, Charlie, was standing right next to Sister Loyola and she

informed me that I would after school every day for a week doing menial tasks instead of playing ball with my buddies. A bitter blow it was, but only the beginning. He then escorted me to the rectory where he explained the situation to one of the priests. Immediate confession was the remedy, which resulted in a full rosary for reconciliation—very severe. I shuttled my broken ego back to class but the trouble was not over for the day; I still had to go home after visiting with the principal after hours. The effects of that episode taught me not to speak out of turn in class. I was a model of behavior in that regard, but I found other ways to engage in mischief, such as spitballs hurled toward the girls.

Surprisingly, few words were uttered by any of the adults during the entire affair. They knew that I knew that I had violated commandments and no further explanations were needed. Their actions conveyed the appropriate message with clarity.

9. The Hail Mary and Our Father are fundamental prayers in the Catholic faith, ones which are memorized by children in the first grade.

10. *Sanders* presents an article reporting on a study of the educational value of Catholic schools in Chicago.

11. *Giomi* (Ioli) presents picture of Colombo members managing a float for the Albuquerque City Christmas parade around 1920. It includes, Alberto Lencioni, Louie Del Frate, Tartaglia, Mario Bonaguidi, Ovidio Franchini, Victor Bachechi, Frank Petroni, John Bonaguidi, Battista Nottoli, Vicenzo Cimino, Tony Rossi, John Tabacchi, Guido Del Frate, Joe Del Frate, Mattia, Aldo and Dante Vaio, Felice Barsanti, Aladino Viviani, Teodolindo Morelli, Lena and Edwardo Vaio, Alessandro Matteucci, Vincenzo Shifani, Joe Morelli, Pete Giacomelli, Ettore Franchini, Oreste Bachechi, Pete Dinelli and Leo Bonaguidi. Published in April-May, 1978, Volume IV, Number 8.

12. *Giomi* (Ioli) describes the early Bachechi family. Published in June, 1977, Volume IV, Number 5.

13. The Women's Club disbanded in 1974 and was replaced by the Club Culturale Italiano, organized by Italians who had immigrated from the East Coast cities to Rio Rancho, a burgeoning new community just west of Albuquerque. Its purpose was to promote Italian heritage and customs. Many of the club's Italians were from Southern Italy. But most of Albuquerque's Italians had fully assimilated into American life, with many of them educated and successful.

14. Wine can be fermented with natural yeasts that are a normal

part of the environment. Prepared yeasts provide the vintner some control over the quality. The type of yeast to a great extent determines the quality and characteristics of the wine. Winemaking is fundamentally simple but complex in detail. The Italians have been fermenting wine for a long as the Germans have been brewing beer—centuries.

15. *Goldberg* describes American life in the 1920s.

16. Much of the information for this chapter was gathered from newspaper reports in Albuquerque.

15

EXCURSIONS (1930–1940)

MOUNTAINS CALLING

The Menicuccis, like many other Lucchese in the colony, were drawn to mountains. Their Italian home in Lucca was located on the alluvial fan of the Apennines. The Sandia Mountains, oriented north-south, lie directly east of Albuquerque, with its signature ten thousand six-hundred-foot Sandia peak. Sandia in Spanish means watermelon, which is how these mountains were named. To the early Spanish inhabitants, the red and yellow hues of the setting sun created a greenish color on the Sandia, creating the resemblance of a watermelon in the field. The Manzano Mountains are situated just south of the Sandias. Both of these mountains were easily accessible from Albuquerque.

However, it was the Jemez Mountains that captivated Albuquerque's Italians. It was farther than the Sandias and Manzanos, but richer in resources. Fishing and hunting were its principal attractions. Jemez offered many fishing streams teaming with trout and a wide range of big-game animals. There was nothing comparable in the Sandias or Manzanos. Jemez offered much more recreational area than the other two mountains. Another factor was development. Jemez Spring was growing steadily and many resorts and lodges were available in the village. The west side of both the Sandias and Manzanos are rugged and dry. The east side of those mountains, where some development was occurring, was wetter but less so than Jemez.

The Valles Caldera in the Jemez Mountains and the many hot springs added to its allure. Sulphur Springs was the first feature that attracted people to the area from 1890. The Springs are located on the Caldera's west rim and are surrounded by towering conifers, including many varieties of Fir and Ponderosa Pine. Aspens grow in abundance along the Sulphur Creek, which runs from the springs down to the La Cueva cave area where it spills into the San Antonio Creek.[1] In the fall, large groves of aspen become a natural bloom of golden splendor. Many people still travel to Jemez to view the autumn colors.

Elevation dominates the Jemez Mountain climate. In elevations above eight thousand feet, the summers are warm but rarely reach 90F. Summer monsoon rains from July through September produce roughly half of the annual rainfall. Mid-summer low temperatures can dip to the mid forty degrees after widespread hail storms. Midday temperatures are pleasant. Winters are cold, with lows of -twenty F degrees regularly observed at high locations. Fifteen feet of accumulated snow over a winter is not uncommon. Droughts can produce years with little rainfall; a dry year with twenty percent of normal precipitation is occasionally recorded. Lower elevation locations project similar trends but with less severe winters and longer growing seasons. The climates in the Jemez Mountains are similar to those in the Apennines.

MUSHROOMS

Besides wine, one of the most important culinary items for Italians was mushrooms, particularly wild ones that they gathered themselves. The favored mushroom species was the New Mexico Porcini, a variety of Boletus Edulis that grows throughout the northern hemisphere mountains. Porcini grew plentifully in Italy and the Menicuccis had for generations foraged for them in the Apennines near their ancestral home outside of Lucca. The only difference between the New Mexico Porcini and their Italian cousins is a slight DNA mismatch. There is no difference between flavor, size and usefulness between the two types of Porcini. These mushrooms can grow large, up to a few pounds each and are nutritious. But, their most valued property is the robust flavor they impart to dishes. It is one of the principal ingredients of Italian food and was a significant part of the Menicucci's regular diet.

The Menicuccis used Porcini liberally in their main meals. A majority of Giulia's recipes either called for Porcini or had an option for them. Sometimes, Porcini were stewed and served as a main dish.[2] The women used Porcini mushrooms throughout the year, even though the harvesting period was restricted to the summer rainy season. Freshly harvested mushrooms can be introduced to various dishes, but most are dried and stored for use throughout the year. Fresh mushrooms were sliced and placed on screens to dry in the sun. Once dry, they stored them in onion or gunny sacks and hung them in a dry place, such as a basement. Whenever mushrooms were needed, the Menicuccis plucked a handful of dried slices from the bag and hydrated them in warm water to about the same consistency as fresh ones. Once softened in the water, they were sliced or chopped for inclusion in a meal. Dry mushrooms can remain in a storage bag for several years before becoming stale. Often, the two Menicucci families we forced to dip into their historic mushroom stash if a particular summer's harvest was lean. In New Mexico, it is common for some wet seasons to be dry, with almost no moisture. Those years they produced no mushrooms of any kind. Thus, Italian families always scurried to collect as many mushrooms as possible when they were available, squirreling away extras.

One of the Menicucci brothers' initial concerns about Albuquerque was the desert environment, which they concluded was not conducive to mushroom growth. Early on various immigrants dispelled that notion—there were Porcini mushrooms aplenty in the Jemez Mountains and occasionally some in the Sandia Mountains. The Bachechis, Domenicis and the Matteuccis discovered Porcini in Jemez in the early 1920s as they were one of the first families with a vehicle. Later, several Italians discovered Porcini mushrooms growing north of Santa Fe in the Sangre de Christo Mountains. As word about the Porcini spread about the colony, each summer became a scramble to forage for mushrooms. As people bought new automobiles, more foragers appeared in the mountains.

When the Menicuccis arrived in Albuquerque in the early 1920s with their wives, they had no vehicle. It would be several years before they owned one. Johnny Giannini had an automobile and a pickup truck as part of his business at Safety First Tire Company. The Menicuccis borrowed it for mushroom foraging, hunting and fishing. Of course, the brothers also scrounged dried mushrooms from neighbors, bartering as needed to maintain a supply of mushrooms for their families.

SULPHUR BATHING

What captivated the brothers' imagination even more about Jemez was Sulphur. Local Italians were familiar with it because it was widely used in Italian homes and farms for everything from diaper rash to insecticides to gunpowder. Sulphur is a natural element and relatively benign to humans, but it is thought to possess special therapeutic and medicinal properties. Many of the hot springs in the Jemez Mountains were laden with Sulphur and other minerals due to the geologically recent volcanic activity that created the Valles Caldera, one of the largest in the country. Sulphur is present in many of the hot springs in the area, all churned up from lingering volcanic heat under the surface. Sulphur Springs comprised a robust family of hot mineral water pools that naturally welled to the surface. Located about ten miles north of Jemez Springs, it had been used for therapeutic bathing for centuries, dating to the time of the earliest native Indians.

The Italians, particularly the Menicucci brothers, carefully noted Sulphur Springs as a possible vacation spot. The Sulphur baths helped generate interest in the Jemez Mountains, as opposed to the nearer Sandia Mountains to the east of Albuquerque, which also contained mineral waters, but not in the abundance or quality of those in Jemez. The major difference between the waters of Sulphur Springs and those of Jemez Springs is the mineral content of the water. Sulphur Springs offered baths that contained Sulphur, while the waters at Jemez contained only sulfates, the fully oxidized form of Sulphur. The Jemez waters lacked the Sulphur odor and some people favored them over the Sulphur Spring baths, which produced the distinctive rotten egg smell. The Menicucci brothers and many other Italians believed Sulphur did the curative heavy lifting in Balneotherapy and the odor is proof positive that the water contains the element. Like many folks, Italians liberally used Epsom salts to treat skin lesions and irritations of various kinds; Sulphur is a major constituent of Epsom salt. The Menicucci brothers also smoked cigars and snuffed Tobacco, both of which they agreed added toxins to their bodies but produced desirable pleasure. Hot Sulphur water was reputed to extract those toxins. Many physicians prescribed hot Sulphur baths to eliminate skin fungus. The Menicuccis also believed Sulphur treated neurological problems, such as lower back pain or joint problems. They were destined to be regular bathers.[3]

CABINS FOR THE MASSES

Art Routledge's family operated a ranch a little over a mile directly south of Sulphur Springs where they grazed both beef- and milk-cattle and raised chickens and goats. They also farmed parts of the ranch and in summer produced a variety of vegetables, including potatoes, carrots, corn and various grains. Routledge capitalized on his location. Routledge's rentable, low-cost cabins along the Sulphur Creek allowed average folks to enjoy Sulphur Springs bathing. The cabins were sparse and rugged but much less expensive than the resort hotel at Sulphur Springs.

The family sold milk, eggs, vegetables, beef and goat meat to guests during their stay. Routledge's ads in the Albuquerque papers caught the eye of many Albuquerqueans, including the Menicuccis. To Julio and Amerigo, vacationing in rustic cabins among the cool pines was ideal. From the Routledge ranch, a fifteen-minute walk up the road puts a person in an odiferous Sulphur bath. Routledge's cabins were popular in Albuquerque's Italian colony and they occupied many of the cabins in summers. It was a favorite spot for the Menicuccis for more than a decade. See Appendix II for more on the history of Italians with the lodges in the Jemez area.

Typical Routledge cabins along Sulphur Creek, just below Sulphur Springs. The bridge crosses the Sulphur Creek, which is dry in the photo. It flows only during the spring runoff and the summer rainy season. Courtesy Cindy Tartaglia Spurlock.

The Routledge barn and shed. Leonard Tartaglia later remodeled the barn when he took over the property. Courtesy Cindy Tartaglia Spurlock.

THE ROAD

The Jemez Mountains attracted Albuquerqueans from as early as 1900 but traveling to them was challenging. Until about 1915, only stagecoaches could navigate Jemez roads. Most of them provided service from Santa Fe to Sulphur Springs, the top Jemez attraction until about 1925, when Jemez Springs developed into a competitor for tourists and vacationers. Stages ran from the ATSF rail stop at Thronton to the Springs and back. By around 1915, stage service from Albuquerque to Jemez Springs began to flourish. Motorized vehicles were increasingly employed as coaches and they used the same road as the stage lines. In the 1910s and into the mid-1920s, the all-dirt road from Bernalillo to San Ysidro was sandy in places, sometimes bogging down and stranding the thin-tired tin lizzies of the day.[4] Summer thunderstorms filled a few arroyos that crossed the road, requiring coaches to ford them. In bigger storms, the road washed out in several areas, stranding travelers between the breeches. In the middle years of 1920, when the road was shared with stagecoaches, rutting was a problem for autos. Stagecoach tires have large diameters and narrow widths, which allows them to sink deep in the ground before high-centering.[5] The ruts were sometimes eighteen inches deep, fine for a horse-drawn stagecoach but well too deep for the automobiles of the day, with ground clearances of around ten inches. Motor vehicles had to straddle the ruts, but when it slid into them—which often happened in icy or muddy conditions—the vehicle bogged to a stop. The problem was the same as modern rear-driven automobiles with differentials that put all of the engine power to the wheel that is slipping the most. Thus, in low traction conditions the vehicle is essentially driven by a single wheel.

At San Ysidro a driver turned north on Road 4, a seventeen-mile stretch that followed a meandering Jemez River up to Jemez Springs. It was reasonably smooth. A number of areas were prone to washouts by seasonal arroyos that traversed the road as water rushed from the hills on the east side of San Diego Canyon and thundered its way to the Jemez River below. In the summer, when flash flooding was a regular weekly event, storms developed rapidly, sometimes growing from puffy clouds to pouring rain in less than twenty minutes. In the 1920s and 1930s, it was not unusual for drivers to be stranded between two washouts on Road 4 south of Jemez Springs, waiting for hours for the runoff to recede to fordable status. In the spring, the same areas of the road were frequently inundated by snow-melt runoff that breached the banks of the Jemez River, flooding the entire canyon.

Once a driver arrived at Jemez Springs, Soda Dam was just a mile north and until the late 1920s, it was the end of the line for most people. The dam is composed of travertine that had accumulated from mineral-laden hot springs in the narrow area of the canyon. Over eons, a small mountain of travertine had amassed over the eons, sprawling across the river valley. For many years, the Jemez River had flowed over the rock-hard dam, but by the 1900s, it had found a way under the dam on the east side, exactly as it is today. The only way up the canyon was over the travertine mound. It was a steep climb on either side, about a twenty-five percent grade. The Model T Ford, owned in abundance by average folks, could not traverse the dam in the forward gear because the vehicle's tilt starved the engine of fuel. The fuel tank was under the seat in the cabin, only a foot or so above the carburetor. It was a gravity-fed system, so when the front of the vehicle angled up, fuel stopped flowing because the fuel tank rose above the carburetor.

Backing over the dam was the solution. Fortunately, the reverse gear produced forty percent more power than the lowest forward one. Backing the vehicle creates a front-wheel drive machine with better traction than rear-driven ones. Traction was a principal concern with the tires on the

Ford vehicles. All were thin, about three to four inches in width, and were pressurized rock-hard to prevent the tube from being pinched if the tire was violently compressed by running over a rock or plunging into a pothole. The thin, hard tires allowed less rubber to contact the road, yielding less traction. Lower tire pressure, as is typical in modern tires, allows more tire flexibility, a softer ride and a wider footprint with more traction. Ford's new Model A, produced in the late 1920s and early 1930s, mounted the fuel tank higher on the vehicle and had lower forward gear that allowed drivers to traverse the travertine bar in a forward direction. Soda Dam at that time, would have challenged modern two-wheel-drive pickups.

Soda Dam around 1920. The area just beyond the horse and wagon is the steep dam wall that had to be traversed to proceed up to the Jemez Mountain high country. Many early day-visitors picnicked in this area. The state of New Mexico blasted the walls of the dam to make an opening for New Mexico Highway 4. Courtesy Jemez Springs Public Library.

For many of the Italians in Albuquerque, the Dam was a coveted destination for weekend picnics and family outings. In the 1920s, Tony Domenici and his family regularly traveled to Soda Dam in a convoy of two or three vehicles. The Italians, in particular, traveled in packs of family members, mainly because they were close-knit but more importantly for safety and security. Multiple vehicles provided additional resources for problems, such as engine failure or flat tires. He and other family members appear in numerous family photos picnicking at Soda Dam in the 1920s. The Domenicis, Gradis, Palladinos and Giomis were some of the first Albuquerque Italian families to own vehicles and some of the first to take their families to Jemez. Many of Albuquerque's Italian descendants have pictures of relatives posing at Soda Dam because it was as far into the Jemez mountains as they could go. Only later into the mid-1930s were vehicles regularly traversing Road 4 over Soda Dam and deep into the Jemez Mountains.

Tony Domenici was one of the earliest Italian immigrant visitors to Jemez. This 1924 photo shows his family in front of Soda Dam. From left the adults were: Pia Barsanti Dalle (my maternal grandmother), Tony Domenici, Emma Giomi Domenici. The others were his children. The young man was likely a Giomi. Courtesy Theresa Domenici Menicucci.

DREADED HAIRPINS

Beyond Soda Dam, the road was replete with hazards. Especially feared was the stretch of Road 4 between what is today Battleship Rock and the La Cueva caves. The road in that area was steep, with an average grade of about six percent, but with some short stretches reaching fifteen percent. Cut into the sides of the San Diego Canyon walls, the road followed every curve and turn of the valley, with the San Antonio Creek flowing at the bottom. For most of that stretch, a rock face loomed on the west side of the road while sheer cliffs menaced on the east. Only about ten feet wide, the road snaked around hills on tight turns that limited sight distance for drivers. In that stretch of road there were about ten hairpin turns, those effecting as much as one-hundred and-fifty-degree directional change.[6] Most of them were of short lengths and all provided pullover spots before and after each hairpin where vehicles could pass one another.

The infamous hairpins near Spence Hot Springs lay about a mile and a half north of Battleship Rock. Known colloquially as "The Hairpins," the road in the area was steep, rocky and narrow, accommodating a single vehicle only. There were several long hairpins in the stretch, a few measuring over a hundred yards. The pullout areas for The Hairpins were barely sufficiently wide for two vehicles to pass each other. The steadily increasing width of newer vehicles exacerbated the problem. There were a couple of passing areas where opposing drivers could become acquainted face to face; one driver could easily reach out the window and grab the other steering wheel. As the vehicles crept by each other at about toddler-walking speed, the wheels of the outside vehicle rolled within eighteen feet of a sheer eighty-foot cliff plunging down to the San Antonio Stream. Vehicle passengers in the hairpins looked at a rock wall on one side and peered out at a sheer cliff on the other. Rocks and debris jarred loose by the tires careened down the cliff, bouncing and bobbing for four or five seconds before splashing into the stream. In the 1930s and well into the 1940s, the three-mile stretch from Battleship Rock to La Cueva often consumed twenty minutes in good conditions, an average of around nine miles per hour, but travel time could be double or triple that in inclement weather. The Hairpins was the site of many accidents, some fatal. On November 2, 1938, Leonard Lewis, a U.S. Forest Service Ranger, lost control of his truck-trailer rig and tumbled off the snow-packed road. His truck and trailer plummeted down the slope, with Leonard bowled over and killed on the way down. It took several days to remove his body and weeks to recover the vehicles.

Leonard Lewis, Jemez pioneer, who was killed on the Spence hairpins north of Jemez Springs, New Mexico. Courtesy Katie Lewis Riley.

Hairpin turns on mountain roads were common in the western states. Engineers at the time followed the landscape for a road because they could not move enough earth to provide a straight road, especially in the mountains. Hairpin safety rules evolved over time by road users. It was based on a simple system of loud blasts, as from a horn, to communicate. Many American Indian tribes use smoke instead of sound for the same purpose. That warning system was used on the Hairpins. As a driver approached the entry to a hairpin, he stopped and listened. Every seven or eight seconds, oncoming vehicles already into the turn regularly gave two honks of the horn to indicate their presence in the hairpin and their approximate location. If the driver heard nothing, he honked once and waited for a two-blast response. A return honk indicated another driver enroute, so he waited for the oncoming traveler to exit. Hearing nothing, he proceeded into the hairpin and began double toots. Three blasts of the horn always indicated distress of some kind, usually a broken-down vehicle or an injury. In those situations, those waiting out of sight around the bends would either creep forward in a vehicle or walk to help the distressed driver. The system was impeccable as long as people followed protocol. Occasionally, a neophyte traveler, ignorant of the rules, found himself in a head-to-head confrontation in the middle of a hairpin. The vehicle closest to an entry point backed out to the passing area while the other followed in forward gear. The Hairpins were the heart of many discussions among the Italians in Albuquerque because the best mushroom hunting is beyond Jemez Springs, in the area of Sulphur Springs.

Applying the current US Forest Service designations for mountain roads, the Hairpins would likely today to be designated Class 2, the second most difficult of five classes of roads for modern 4X4 pickup trucks. This road would challenge a 2023 Dodge Ram 4X4, operating with the most advanced traction features available and riding on 8ply, steel belted, all-terrain tires.

Tires were the weak links in automobiles of that era and caused a majority of automobile failures in the Jemez Mountains. Much of the Jemez was formed by volcanic activity that creates a volcanic glass called Obsidian. When shattered, it produces extremely sharp edges· and these razor-sharp shards are found on many Jemez Mountain roads. Obsidian has been used for centuries by indigenous people as spear points and arrowheads. It has also been used in recent times for the cutting edges in precision knives, such as surgical scalpels. Automotive tires at the time were designed for travel on relatively well-maintained roads, such as city streets. The unbelted rubber tires of the day were no match for Jemez. Visitors from Albuquerque carried one or two spare tires and frequently used both in a round trip to Sulphur Springs. They brought along extra tubes, tires, and rims to make repairs in case the spares had already been used. In a field repair, the wheel was removed from the axle, the tube was deflated and the tire and tube were busted from the rim. The inflatable rubber tube was either repaired or replaced. Some of the replacement tubes had been repaired many times. A split rim, a unique Ford invention, can collapse inward, reducing its diameter sufficiently to expedite the repairs of Model T and Model A tires. Yet, removing, repairing, and reinstalling a tire on the road might consume an hour of effort, even for an experienced man with proper tools. Talcum powder was used in great quantities in tires as a dry lubricant, allowing the inflated tube to slip as needed inside the tire and preventing pinching, which was one of the major causes of tire failures in the mountains. Talcum aroma interacted with the odiferous rubber tires, producing a unique aromatic signature of a mountain tire change. The powder was liberally applied to the final tire assembly process in a messy process of massaging the tube into the tire and properly seating both on the rim. By the time the tire was mounted, powder coated the tire, the ground where it was repaired and the men who did the work produced a plume of fragrance. Julio said, "It is like changing a diaper; it smells sweet when you're done." Small white areas could be seen sporadically along Road 4, telltale signs of previous tire repairs. It was not uncommon for other travelers to stop to aid a fellow trekker who was struggling with an automobile problem along the road.

The summer rains regularly deposited slides of rock, mud and boulders on the road, often necessitating a team of vehicles to clear the debris by pushing it over the edge down into the canyon. Mud was frequently an issue when repeated summer rains flooded sections of the road, leaving deep bogs that could swallow the thin-wheeled vehicles up to their axles. Most visitors carried well-stocked toolboxes, including shovels, picks, chains, ropes, pinch bars, mechanical winches and other equipment to nudge boulders out of the road and to pull the vehicles through mud holes.[7] In some cases, drivers teamed up with their joint tools to move large or stalled vehicles. For about five winter months, the road was impassable due to snow and ice. Some of the Road 4 road was privately owned, with the road running through easements, while the other areas were state and federal government-owned. Local folks and visitors provided much of the maintenance. Stopping and filling potholes, for example, was as common as tire repairs.

LURE OF THE TALL PINES

By the end of the 1920s and into the early 1930s, the Menicuccis had completed their final visit to Italy and they were settling into their businesses. After Super Service Station opened, the Menicuccis purchased a pickup truck for the business. In the late 1920s, they used the company truck for their own excursions to Jemez to fish and hunt mushrooms, typically day trips for the two men. During the depression the families sat tight in Albuquerque, counting their pennies and nickels and managing the businesses.

By 1934, they discussed locations for summer vacations. The brothers were doing what they could never have done in Italy: enjoying a genuine vacation, American style. Besides, the kids were aging and would soon be too old to vacation as a family. At about fifteen years of age, Italian males (and nearly all American males) were slated to work during summer school break. In the mind of the Menicuccis, young men should work when not studying. Two destinations beaconed the families for summer vacations: the Routledge Ranch in the Jemez mountains and California.

Mushroom trips often included family members convoying up to Jemez for a day of mushroom picking and picnicking. By the middle of the 1930s, a Jemez trip was an easy one-day outing from Albuquerque, about two and a half hours of travel one-way. Long summer daylight hours allowed for twelve-hour outings for the families and often resulted in plenty of mushrooms for the family.

Beginning in the mid-1930s, the Menicuccis regularly visited Routledge's ranch, renting a couple of cabins for several weeks at a time. The family carried everything they needed, including food, cooking utensils, clothing, bedsheets, blankets and any other tools or equipment needed for the stay. Planning for the annual trips was extensive, consuming hours of shopping and packing of vehicles. Routledge sold milk, butter and some vegetables from his garden. Other staples were available in Jemez Springs General Store, but they were limited to essentials. Typically, the Menicucci family's trips to Sulphur required three vehicles—two to carry people and a third, a truck, ferrying supplies. A business employee drove the supply truck, unloaded it and immediately returned to Albuquerque. The families usually carried tire repair gear. It was not unusual for at least one tire failure on the trip to or from Albuquerque. The brothers accompanied the family to Routledge's and helped them settle in, but one brother returned to Albuquerque to oversee the businesses. During the stay, the remaining brother fished and took baths, walking from the Routledge's farm to Sulphur Springs where he paid a fee for a soak and massage. The next week the brothers traded places.

Americo was the family's proponent of mineral baths. I cannot recall a trip to Jemez with Amerigo where he did not regale me with this same story. Here is a summary: He and Julio smoked cigars and snuffed tobacco. Davina, Amerigo's wife, worried about his habits, surmising that breathing smoke is unhealthy. He claimed that after a Sulphur bath he had lain on a table with towels below him and blankets above and when he arose, he could see a tan outline of his lungs on both towels. He concluded that these were the tobacco poisons that were driven from his lungs by the mineral water. He proudly stated how he took one of the towels home to show his wife Davina, who was dazzled. He said, "She never bothered me about smoking again." He always added a wink and a pinch of my arm to accentuate the subterfuge.

Julio and Amerigo also upgraded cabins. Several cabins were subject to flooding from Sulphur Creek during heavy summer storms. Those at-risk cabins were usually not rented for anything more than a day or two due to the risk. The brothers loved those particular cabin locations—somewhat remote and sufficiently large for their two families. They wanted to rent them for weeks. The solution was easy. Julio and Amerigo built a divertor on the stream to prevent it from flooding and they constructed a higher and stronger bridge over the stream to allow easy vehicle access. The bridge was so well constructed from large timbers and masonry that it was in use until the area was sold for residential development in the late 1900s. The diversion still operates today.

The families often coordinated their trips with other Italian families and then enjoyed the camaraderie of the group. Giulia told the story of one trip: It was in the mid-1930s that the Menicuccis and two other families, likely the Domenicis and the Morellis, rented a group of cabins next to one another. One day the men decided to fish and hunt mushrooms for the families' dinner. They set out in the morning and by midafternoon had returned with ninety-nine trout, all about ten inches long. They had also harvested a couple of bushels of New Mexico Porcini mushrooms. There was certainly plenty of food for dinner but a lot of work to prepare it.

The women sprang into action. The men had spent hours gathering food for the families and now they would demonstrate their talents to prepare it for eating. They spent hours cleaning trout and mushrooms. They grilled the fish on an open flame bonfire that the men built. The women added soup, fried and stewed Porcini mushrooms, boiled and grilled vegetables, which they had purchased from Routledge's farm and dessert of Grappa drizzled over slices of Routledge's Apples. All was prepared Lucchese style and overseen by Davina, the most experienced and accomplished cook in the family. The families feasted for hours around the bonfire, swilling wine and grappa to ensure proper digestion, as they claimed. The women basked in the contentment of witnessing the delight among the family members who enjoyed the fruits of their efforts. The story has become part of family lore and is an excellent example of how Italian families of that era divided the tasks for raising a family either at home or in the forest. The families' interest in mushroom foraging and wine fermenting headlined the cherished Italian customs they firmly wished to retain.

Competition from the Jemez Hot Springs added to the economic woes of Sulphur Springs. The Jemez bathhouse was of comparable size to Sulphur's; the waters contained similar minerals and temperatures, the massages were of equal quality and nearby cottages and lodges provided high-quality living accommodations, but access from Albuquerque was much easier and year-round. The crowning blow was its lower prices. Their operational costs in Jemez Springs were lower than those at Sulphur Springs due to its location. Into the 1940s, the road from Albuquerque to Jemez was steadily improved as more people realized the recreational potential of the Jemez Mountains. Unless one was picky about the Sulphur content of the water, Jemez Springs was fine.

Many Albuquerqueans, including Italians such as the Menicuccis, who initially were attracted to the Sulphur Springs resort for mineral baths, instead pivoted to the Jemez Springs as the Sulphur Springs economically sputtered. Still, all through the 1930s and into the 40s, Sulphur Springs remained the bathing site of choice for those vacationing at the Routledge's cabins. Julio and Amerigo were frequent Sulphur Springs bathers during the multi-week family vacations but favored the Jemez Springs facilities for one-day or weekend visits from Albuquerque.[8]

LADY IN STONE

Giulia instigated an interesting bit of lore concerning the western rock faces west of Road 4, a couple of miles south of Jemez Springs. The cliff faces on the west side of the river valley are craggy and undulated. She was the first to claim to see an image of the Madonna embossed on the cliff face. Once she saw it, others also saw it. A trip to Jemez frequently included a brief stop at the site of the image to marvel, at least for those who could behold the lady in the stone.

Initially, people scoffed, including me. As word spread in Albuquerque's Italian community of the Madonna sightings, speculations were regularly proffered as to its religious significance. The Jesuit priests at Immaculate Conception Church caught wind of the controversy and put the issue to rest, declaring that if a person spotted the image on the cliff faces, then he or she was on the path of salvation. This put a serious spin on the whole controversy, and many lied about seeing her to avoid humiliation and possible damnation.

Julio uncovered my mendacity when we stopped at the holy site for nature's call. I wanted to impress Julio with my brilliance. I was young, and I played a hunch that the whole Madonna rumpus was foolish imagination. I pointed to an area at random and declared that I could see the Lady. Bad bet indeed as Julio pointed to a spot about thirty degrees north of where I was looking. He said, "There is the Madonna." I was embarrassed that he called my bluff and I looked like a fool. It was quickly replaced with shock. It implied that those who had seen the image had, in fact, seen something real. There were too many credible people who claimed to have seen her in the same location to dismiss the sightings out of hand. Maybe it was the Madonna or maybe it was something else; a craggy, rocky surface makes a poor canvas. In any case, it dogged me for years and I still cannot see her.

Cliff face on the hills south of Jemez Springs where the image of the Madonna is supposedly embossed. Courtesy author's collection.

ITALIAN CALIFORNIA

Between 1928 and 1940, the brothers and their families vacationed together. They confined their annual retreat to Jemez for the initial six or seven years because it was relatively close and reasonably priced. As the quality of their vehicles improved over the years and the business profits steadily grew, California became the vacation destination of choice in later years. California was interesting to many of Albuquerque's Italians, especially the Lucchese. Many had migrated directly to California. Others, such as Marietta Gragnani Morelli, Giulia's sister, moved from Albuquerque to California for the climate, which was similar to Lucca's. Small Italian colonies dotted the coastline of California. Many Albuquerque Italians viewed California as a premier vacation destination.

Teresa Clark Menicucci told the story of the families' calamitous initial California visit: Around 1933, in late winter, Julio wrote to one of Giulia's relatives, likely Dominico Caselli, who at that time lived in downtown Los Angeles with his wife, Josephine. She managed apartments. Dominico, one of Giulia's maternal forefathers, emigrated from Lucca directly to California. Other distant relatives and friends in the southern California area, such as Felice Barsanti, who had labored at the Champion Grocery and was a popular figure in Albuquerque's colony. There were plenty of reasons for Italian immigrants, even distant relatives, to crave reunions and Dominico agreed to help find accommodations for the Menicuccis.

By July, Julio had housing reservations in Santa Monica, near Los Angeles, and he decided to drive to save money. Besides, the family was in the automobile business and it was a logical conclusion. In Julio's absence, Albert Nottali was tasked to manage Super Oil. At Super Service, Amerigo asked Johnny Matteucci to oversee the station's operations. The families spent days shopping and packing, which was more difficult than the Jemez trips. There were plenty of food and merchandise vendors in Santa Monica, so they packed little food, but it was a much longer trip than to Jemez. Additionally, they had never traveled out of state and certainly had no experience with the unique challenges of navigating within a large American city. Julio, a planning devotee, thought out every detail, along with contingencies. Amerigo, as usual, worked right along with Julio, just as he had since the family days in Lucca. As departure day approached, Julio asked Horace Palladino, Super Service's chief mechanic, to give both vehicles a thorough inspection, replacing any part that showed signs of wear or potential failure en route. The Menicucci's California trip was analogous to a modern spacecraft mission with multiple interacting systems, all of which must perform to specifications to ensure mission success: arriving safely at the rental home.

On the day of departure, the families rendezvoused at Julio's home around two-thirty in the morning where they did their final inspections and shoved off. In July, sunrise in Albuquerque is around five-fifteen Mountain Standard Time. (Daylight Savings Time was not used.) Julio's pointillistic plan was complete with a detailed checklist, of course and he used it. Finally, with everything set and all passengers on board, he stuffed the rental contract in his shirt pocket, locked the front door to the house and they were off. Julio led the two-vehicle caravan south on Third Street to Central Avenue, the Route 66 highway that led to Santa Monica.

Julio expected the trip to consume fifteen hours of travel, and he planned to drive it in one day to avoid a costly overnight hiatus. They departed Albuquerque at three, with Julio leading and Amerigo closely following behind with strict directions to remain in visual contact with his lead vehicle. Julio's auto contained his family, Giulia was the right-front passenger on the bench seat with pre-teen Mariangela in between her and Julio. Dante and Charlie jumped in the window seats in the back, leaving Teresa in the middle. Amerigo's three children sat in the back, with Mario at a window seat of his choice. The oldest Italian males retained overt privileges.

When they left Albuquerque, the temperature was a mild sixty-seven degrees. In the afternoon they were sloughing through the fiery hot Arizona desert, where ambient temperatures exceeded one-hundred and fifteen along the scorching hot pavement of Route 66. Car windows provided "air conditioning," as long as the car was moving. Open windows forced in a wash of oven-hot air over the passengers, who hopefully were perspiring enough to gain some cooling. It was an agonizing journey for certain, but as the sun was nearing the western horizon and as the Los Angeles Basin came into sight, Julio sensed victory. They were into the final couple of dozen miles and they would soon arrive at the rental home where they could enjoy a nice glass of wine before a late dinner.

He fallaciously concluded that they could continue at highway speed directly to their destination, in downtown Los Angeles, one of the most auto-congested areas in America. They were not prepared. Driving in Albuquerque was simple because there were relatively few streets and drivers. The Los Angeles Road map resembled a spider web and the roads were crowded with autos and littered with strange markers and warning signs, all normal for California's auto scene but flummoxing to the brothers.

As Julio groped his way through the evening traffic, Amerigo's meager big-city driving skills came to the fore and he fell behind. Amerigo was too diffident for big-city driving, courteously allowing drivers to cut in front of him. Timidity was not a virtue in Los Angeles rush-hour traffic but neither was Julio's temerity. The complexity of big-city driving shattered his confidence. He was so consumed with obeying rules, avoiding crashes and following poor directions to the rental home that he had not noticed Amerigo's lagging position in traffic. When Julio finally could no longer see Amerigo, he shuddered--they were separated. Panic welled in both vehicles because Julio had the rental agreement and directions.

Julio tried to slow down, but was forced to a side street by various city-street impediments. He took up a position where he thought his brother might pass by, but it was too late. As Amerigo hustled down a busy boulevard, he knew two truths. He was hopelessly lost and their plan, which was supposedly well thought out, had a major flaw: there was no contingency for being lost. What was worse, the plan depended entirely on Amerigo remaining directly behind Julio for the entire distance because only Julio knew the destination. It jolted Amerigo into a high gear and he sped up to catch Julio. He was panic-driven and did not know where his brother was.

Meanwhile, in desperation, Julio spotted an Italian restaurant along the road and pulled into a parking spot near the front door. The families piled out and opened the diner's door. Just as in Modesto Dalle's Mint Café in Albuquerque, the proprietors, a man named Pietro and his wife, Maria, greeted them at the door. Julio, out of breath and panting, immediately engaged Pietro in the problem. The two men recognized their Tuscany Region dialects as they spoke, establishing an immediate bond. In Italian, he lamented that he had lost his brother and had no clue how to reunite with him. While the two men talked, Maria attended to Giulia and the children, seating them, showing them the restrooms and providing drinks and snacks. As an Italian woman, the comfort and health of guests were her responsibility and priority. As Julio talked, Pietro assimilated the information in the hopes of recommending a solution. Pietro knew the area well.

Suddenly, Giulia, who was seated near a picture window, shouted that she saw Amerigo drive by. Both men lunged forward to see, but the vehicle had passed. Pietro exhorted Julio to get into his car, which was parked in front of the restaurant, declaring that he could catch up to them. They scrambled into Pietro's vintage Model A Ford and Pietro revved it up, laying tracks of rubber in his parking lot as it rocketed into action like Batman's famous Batmobile. Pietro raced down alleys, cut through private land, ran stop signs, exceeded speed limits and finally ended up at an intersection on the same highway on which Amerigo was driving when he passed the restaurant. Pietro believed that he had beaten Amerigo to that spot and that they would soon see his car emerge in the traffic. He was right. Just moments later, Amerigo, staring straight ahead on the road with white-knuckled hands gripping the steering wheel, drove right by Pietro's car with the two hollering Italian men standing alongside it pleading for him to stop. Amerigo pushed forward unabated, determined to catch Julio.

Pietro and Julio screeched back into action, rocks and debris scattering in a cloud from the rear of the Model A as they sprinted off to catch Julio. Finally, Pietro nuzzled his car in the back of Amerigo's, honking and blinking his headlights. Amerigo, confused and scared that he was under attack, stomped on the accelerator to escape. Pietro followed, still honking. Julio hung out of Pietro's vehicle, hair whipping wildly, shouting and waving his arm out the window. It was a wild scene akin to a Three Stooges skit. Finally, Mario, son of Amerigo, looked back and screamed out, "It's Zio (uncle) in the car."

When the two vehicles finally parked and the passengers exited, Julio explained the situation. Amerigo, completely out of breath and bedraggled, was relieved that the families were safe but was heartbroken when Julio reported that he was confused and essentially lost in the complexity of California driving. In all his planning, he did not consider road construction, map errors and a host of other big-city impediments that threw him off course. Pietro reassured them as he led them back to the restaurant.

The reunion scene in the restaurant was one of wild, festive glee, complete with ebullient dancing to Italian music wafting from Pietros' music box. The two brothers looked as if they had been in battle, hair wildly strewn about and sweat embedded in their eyebrows, but they delighted in the revelry. They were a little embarrassed that they performed so poorly in the traffic but tall glasses of water and wine quickly whisked away those concerns, compliments of the house.

Naturally, Pietro and Maria insisted on hosting dinner for the families. Pietro had the chef, his younger brother, come out to meet the Menicuccis so he could plan the dinner. Pietro reported to all that he had inspected the rental agreement and knew the exact destination of the rental house because his cousin worked there. He said he would lead them to their temporary rental home after dinner.

Pietro's multi-course meal was one to remember. Being a Tuscan, he served a number of northern Italian delights, including ravioli and manicotti, along with various cold cuts, fried cheeses, polenta, grilled Porcini mushrooms, seafood salad and an Italian dessert. Wine flowed plentifully and, in the end, Pietro charged them "family prices," which were substantially lower than his retail prices. The brothers knew about "family prices," which they applied in their businesses; it was selling at cost. They both resolved to return to the restaurant and pay full price for meals to give Pietro a profit. After the two-hour dinner, Pietro proudly led a three-vehicle convoy to their rental home. The family visited Pietro's restaurant several times during that initial two-week stay in Los Angeles. All of the families' future trips to California included a stop at Pietro's restaurant for fine Italian food and hospitality. The families remained in contact with Pietro and Maria for years following that momentous day.

Teresa said: "It was ridiculous. Here were two families celebrating for hours as if they had been separated for decades but they were apart for less than forty-five minutes." She recanted the story numerous times, every time interrupting it with bursts of her own laughter. Both Teresa and Mariangela said that of all the family vacations, that initial California trip was the most memorable.

A STRUCTURE OF TRUST

This story is a good example of the echelons of personal trust in Italian culture. When Julio found himself in trouble, he looked for help at an Italian restaurant because the owner was likely to be Italian. Being Italian is an echelon of trust, certainly above California Anglos. But when Julio and Pietro recognized by the dialect that they were both Tuscans, they both immediately extended trust to the next higher echelon. Being Italian was good, but being from the same region of Italy enhances the trust level.

Pietro reacted like most Italians in his position. He would have helped anyone in Julio's predicament, but a fellow Tuscan warranted actions well beyond normal. It is unlikely that Pietro would drive crazily for an Anglo-American in similar trouble. People of Tuscany share similar value systems, appearances, religious beliefs, customs, dialects and practices. Within just seconds, Pietro and Julio instantaneously meshed into an effective chase team.[9]

The subsequent celebration was a customary Italian method to celebrate great achievements: feasting on multi-course meals with plenty of music and wine. For all parties, the achievement was as much for the actual reunion of the two families as it was for engendering a new friendship with fellow Tuscans. Most people employ some value system as they interact with others, but likely not as deeply ingrained in the culture as it is with the Italians.

Throughout the 1930s, the two families vacationed together because the children were young enough to travel with the family. By the time boys were in high school, as they were in the later 1930s, they worked full-time in summer and part-time after school. There was plenty of trouble brewing across the Atlantic, but the family and most others in the colony were secure in the belief that the distance plus the vastness of the Atlantic Ocean insulated them from the political tumult engulfing the European continent. While people continued to look east with interest, a witch's cauldron of trouble was brewing in the western Pacific.

See notes 10, 11.

Notes

1. The headwaters of the East Fork of the Jemez River and the Rio San Antonio are on the Valles Caldera National Preserve. They flow east to

west and join at Battleship Rock, where their confluence creates the Jemez River that flows south to the Rio Grande, joining it just north of Bernalillo.

2. Giulia Gragnani Menicucci developed this recipe specifically for the New Mexico Porcini. The recipe was often doubled or tripled when it served as the main dish.

Stewed Wild Porcini*
Giulia Gragnani Menicucci

Ingredients:
1 to 1.5 pounds fresh porcini, washed and cut into 1" cubes
4 T butter
1 T olive oil
Half yellow onion, chopped
4 cloves of garlic, chopped
3 T chopped parsley
2 T tomato sauce mixed in ½ cup warm water,
1 teaspoon beef bouillon powder or cube.
Red pepper flakes.
Salt, black pepper, allspice
For the roux: 1 T butter in 1 T all-purpose flour.

Procedure: Put butter and oil in a pan. When hot, add onions and parsley. Sauté for a couple of minutes. Add the garlic and cook for another minute. Add mushrooms and the warm water with tomato sauce. Add bouillon and a pinch of red pepper flakes. Cook for about 30 minutes.

Make roux to golden brown and add to the stew. Cook to a thick consistency. Add salt and pepper to taste. Add a pinch of allspice. Top with grated parmesan cheese and serve with garlic bread.

*Any fresh mushroom can be substituted for Porcini.

3. *Falagas* discusses the science behind balneotherapy.
4. Tin Lizzy is the colloquial name of Ford's Model T vehicles.
5. High centering occurs when a vehicle encounters an obstacle in between the right-side wheels and those on the left, resulting in the entire vehicle being raised so that neither drive wheel contacts the ground, stranding the vehicle.

6. A hairpin curve is similar to a switchback on a hiking trail where the trail makes a sweeping turn of up to a hundred and fifty degrees with a small inside radius that produces a track that resembles a hairpin.

7. A pinch bar is a long, solid steel rod, usually one-inch in diameter, with a chisel end. It is used to finely adjust the position of rail cars on a delivery platform. By levering a long pinch bar between the track and a rail tire, a man could nudge a full rail car a few inches forward or backward. Pinch bars were similarly used to roll oversize boulders off the road.

8. *Routledge* describes the Jemez mountains and his ranch and cabins.

9. In the story, Pietro was a Tuscan; he and Julio originated from the same region of Italy. The connection provided the impetus for an immediate acceptance and trust. An additional example provides more clarity on Italian trust levels. Had Pietro been a southern Italian with all of the customary body and language features, the attachment between the two men would have been more guarded, as both hesitated for a moment due to the differences between northern and southern Italians. Given the urgency of the situation, those differences would be obviated by country-level trust. Being from the same country is an attraction and worthy of trust at an echelon below a Tuscan but above that of a non-countryman.

10. Much of this story is founded in well-corroborated lore.

11. Stories in the *Albuquerque Journal* were important sources of information for this chapter.

16

WESTERN WINDS OF WAR (1938–1945)

JOURNALISTIC MERGER OF FATE

As Albuquerque was seeing a light at the end of the dark tunnel of economic depression, a fateful event occurred, greatly alleviating a problem of chronic irritation among smaller businesses, including most Italian immigrants: biased news. From its founding in 1882 to 1933, the *Albuquerque Journal* was owned and operated by the Republican Party. The Republican party comprised many affluent citizens with a wide range of skills, including journalism. They published a well-edited paper, presenting a variety of stories ranging from Mussolini Fascism to the luncheon menu for the Italian Women's Charity Society. From its earliest years, the *Journal* highlighted its membership in the Associated Press, a national news agency with access to wire stories. Most of the Associated Press newspapers assumed the same political lean towards the Republicans. In its initial forty years of existence, the *Journal* was unabashedly a conservative voice for the community. The paper stated so in its publishing information box, which clearly stated ownership and political lean. The *Albuquerque Journal*'s major logo was born in the 1800s: its widely recognized American eagle, with its elongated wings spanning from one side of the masthead to the other. Over it is inscribed "The Albuquerque Journal."

Into the 1920s, the *Journal* increasingly referred to itself as "independent," downplaying the political connection. Many in the Italian community, including Julio, were pleased. Most wanted balanced news to assess the business climate. In Michigan, Julio and Amerigo had seen how newspaper bias affected a community. The Michigan newspapers favored the owners in the mining strike, which resulted in heavy losses for the mine workers. New Mexico's Democratic party, which at that time claimed to support small businesses, was particularly irked by the potential bias. During Clyde Tingley's time in office—as city manager (i.e., Mayor) and Governor—he and the *Journal* frequently dueled in the public arena. The Italians believed the Democrats did most to ensure the needs of the small business community. Julio, a strong Democrat from the late 1920s, especially bristled at the Republican party's control over the *Journal*. He saw what the Italians were doing with their papers and he wanted none of that in Albuquerque.

A few other newspapers attempted to compete with the *Journal* during its dominant period in the first third of the century. For example, early in the century, the Daily Citizen published an evening paper. It was outmanned and outgunned. The *Journal* had a lock on resources, equipment, labor and suppliers, and it paid higher wages with more benefits. At six months, the paper became the Weekly Citizen, on its way to becoming the "never" Citizen before the year was out. It was never heard from again. Through the years, others met similar fates.

Later, in the early 1930s, United Press International, a rival news agency to AP, offered access to its news stories to any newspaper, associated or not. Although these journalistic intricacies were of no interest to Albuquerqueans at that time, citizens suddenly became interested when the *Albuquerque Tribune* came onto the journalistic scene around 1932. It broke in as an evening paper using the independent United Press International as its primary source. Unlike previous upstarts that tried to slay the goliath, the *Tribune* brought a better quiver of weapons to the match. Not only was it an afternoon paper, but had access to a different and independent news source. The *Tribune* advertised that it would publish reports of morning events in its afternoon edition, twelve hours ahead of the *Journal*.

The *Tribune* had a winner and the *Journal* knew it. Even in the depths of the depression a young bull came in and gave the champ a black eye. In 1932 the *Journal* had no stomach—or money—to carry on a competitive battle. The *Journal* could not handle two editions a day and they knew the public was hungry for news that was breaking at an increasingly rapid rate. The *Tribune* was in a strong position. The *Journal* ceded the afternoon publishing space to the *Tribune* and agreed to a production merger where each company retained its status as an independent corporate entity. They agreed to jointly own and operate the same publishing equipment and share a unified labor pool working under standardized pay scales. A wonderful solution it was, as it increased the production efficiency for both companies, reducing costs to the subscribers.

It was not only a good business decision for both papers, it had its altruistic bent. The publishers of both periodicals were firm believers in the old-fashioned concept that readers deserve accurate information delivered as quickly as possible. Now the two papers operated like a boxer delivering the old 1-2, a pop of news in the morning and an update of new information in the afternoon, with one- and two-page extras as needed to fill in the news delivery gaps. By the end of 1930, the papers grew rapidly, serving a public hungry for truthful reporting. When the decade ended, the conglomerate became a local news giant. They had no idea their news reporting system would soon be tested like never before.[1]

ISOLATED FROM CHAOS

On September 3, 1939, at seven in the evening, Julio listened to the radio in his living room. President Roosevelt, in his fourteenth fireside chat, suavely and confidently stated: "I hope the United States will keep out of this war. I believe that it will. And I give you assurance(s) and reassurance that every effort of your government will be directed toward that end." It resounded well and placated his critics, who had been clamoring to prevent America from entering the European war, but it was deceitful. Roosevelt had for years seen the inevitability of American injection into the war but knew that public opinion was firmly affixed to isolationism. Isolationism is a political approach where a sovereign nation seeks to remain apart and distinct from the governmental affairs of other countries. He was placating the public until a specific act or event could sway the public to his position. Like thousands in Albuquerque and millions throughout the country, Julio wanted America to avoid the conflict. Many Albuquerqueans were World War I veterans who experienced the perils of conflict and lobbied Democrats strongly for political isolation.[2]

Isolation had been alive and well in the United States since the end of World War I. Isolationists, headed by a mixture of Democratic Progressives and conservative Republicans were hellbent on America avoiding another European conflict. They argued that the costs to defend

Europe exceeded the value of doing so. From their perspective, America need not have entered World War I at all and should never again. The position was extreme and of questionable accuracy, but it resonated. From the colony's perspective, it was a European problem and they were content to leave it there. During the 1930s, three Neutrality resolutions were signed into law in 1935, 1937 and 1939. They mostly prohibited the United States from selling or bartering weapons with foreign countries. Roosevelt had opposed the resolutions, but each time acquiesced to public opinion and overwhelming support in the House and Senate. He knew that neutrality was a long shot but as long as America had not suffered substantial losses, he realized that Americans would not support involvement in another foreign war. It was his only viable option.

The specific triggering act that Roosevelt needed was drawing near. Just two days before his speech, the Germans squashed Polish defenses and occupied the country; they were hinting that France was next. That was enough for the Menicucci families. They had been discussing the prospect of war for many months, and it was a hot topic at both the Super Service and the Super Oil companies. Many of the senior employees were World War I veterans. They concluded an attack on America was inevitable, many expecting a German attack on an American asset, such as a Navy ship off the American coast, killing many. These men had seen Germans menacing Europe before and it appeared no different now. Many veterans had also learned the lesson of enlistment: If you bring skills to the Army, you have a better chance to land a less hazardous job.

Both the Menicucci and Matteucci families had sons nearing the minimum age for conscription. Congress was targeting men from twenty-one through thirty-five years of age. Amerigo's son, Mario, and Julio's oldest son, Dante, were born just a few weeks apart in 1922. They and Larry Matteucci, Johnny Matteucci's nephew, were all seventeen years old and graduating seniors at St. Mary's. Like Johnny Matteucci and the Menicucci brothers, the three men were close personal friends.

Italy's political stance also concerned many Italian veterans. In World War I, Italy was part of the Allied Powers. This time, Italy was a belligerent, standing shoulder to shoulder with Hitler while making war on its less defensible neighbors. What would happen, they surmised, if the Italians were first to strike the Americans? Would Italian Americans be targeted for internal harassment as were some German Americans in 1917? And would Italian Americans on the front lines be faced with shooting their Italian countrymen? These were constant topics of discussion.

JEWS

Jews had been on Hitler's radar screen since his early days in his military service. In 1919 he penned a report to his commanding officer outlining the evils and threats that the Jewish race posed to German heritage and security. His thesis was that Jews must be removed from Germany. The process of elimination commenced immediately after he took power in 1933. By 1938, Hitler had insinuated his Fascist dictatorship throughout the country and was about to initiate one of the bloodiest genocide campaigns in human history. The target was the Jewish population, which Hitler blamed for many of the ills of German society as well as bringing defective bloodlines into Germany's Arian society. But he was not satisfied with Germany. He knew that as he took control of countries, he had command of the civil systems and the opportunity to eliminate all Jews from Europe.

The German genocidal assault commenced in the latter half of the 1930s with a series of restrictions on German Jews that effectively stripped them of their civil rights and personal wealth. Life for German Jews steadily degraded as new restrictions appeared daily, many of which were not advertised beforehand and which led to accidental violations that justified arresting and incarcerating Jews. Many were jailed on frivolous charges that led to torture and often death. In November of 1938, a Jewish man assassinated a German diplomat in Paris. Hitler and his acolytes exploded with rage and imposed a fine of one billion marks on the German Jewish population, which essentially meant that the government could take all of the Jewish wealth in the world and still be well short of collecting the full fine. It was impossible to pay and was an excuse to pillage the Jews.

This ugly theater of persecution was noted in the local Albuquerque press, but many of the reports were buried on the back pages. Towards the end of the 1930s, as attacks on the Jews escalated in intensity, a few editorialists declared moralistic outrage but the message fell largely on untuned ears. The European political situation was a principal distraction and the plight of German Jews was of secondary interest. Besides, many Albuquerqueans, especially most Italians, held dim views of the Jews, which muted their reactions. The outrage came sporadically from the Catholic Church, as they saw the evil in Hitler's acts, regardless of racial intent, but even within the church, the reaction was carefully modulated because many clergy members quietly disparaged Jews and their religion. Many

Catholics had been taught that the Jews were the antithesis of Christianity because, as Julio said a few times, they had "killed Jesus." Some Protestant religions also held the same belief, but not with the fervor of the Catholics. This strongly held belief was as illogical as it was inveterate. First, Catholic Christianity is based on the belief that Christ rose from the dead, which required him to die. His death was superfluous to his defining event, resurrection, the foundation of Christianity. Second, the Romans had plenty to do with Jesus' death. They treated Jews as lowly, expendable subjects. They coldly viewed rampaging mobs of Jews salivating over a new religious prophet as an existential threat to the Roman rule, one easily eviscerated with a simple execution, which they regularly imposed on quiet mobs. In the minds of many Catholics, including the Menicuccis, additional bias lay directly in the Bible with all four Gospels describing Jesus' rout of the Jewish temple, casting out the money changers that he labeled "robbers." These robbers were wealthy and influential Jewish families that specialized in finance, which the Menicuccis and other Italians equated with bankers.

Another issue was fear or perhaps envy. The Menicuccis and many other Italians believed the Jews had special business skills in their blood; traits passed down through the generations. Jews had a reputation as shrewd negotiators and clever business operators. Charlie Menicucci said it plainly, referring to Albuquerque's Jews. "They are damned smart. You gotta watch your butt when you deal with them." Alas, there was no love lost between many Christians and the Jews.

The Menicuccis were U.S. Army veterans of a World War. They understood the military mindset and were experienced in the type of political dialogue that leads to conflict. They had heard the neutrality exaltations before and knew they were hollow. They had seen the Unni (Huns) twenty years previous and it appeared to them that the corpse that they thought they had slayed in 1918 was rising from the grave like a zombie.[3] They watched with disgust as Mussolini continued his Fascist ways in Europe. In spite of long-held feelings, they knew that the Jewish situation with the Jews heralded a new horror in warfare. The family disdained the Italian dictator, especially fearing for their extended families in Lucca. They followed the news carefully because their own boys were close to draft age. These boys were slated to run the family business, and their absence during the war would impact their business operations. Their deaths could spell economic disaster for the families. In spite of all the money spent by Roosevelt for his new social programs, families still had little protection against the losses of men, usually the family breadwinners. At that time in America, people were expected to support themselves and except in rare instances, the government would not rescue them.

EUROPE SHUDDERS

Any isolationist dreams were dashed in September of 1939 when the Soviets and German Wehrmacht invaded Poland simultaneously. Stalin attempted to reclaim Polish land granted him under the Molotov-Ribbentrop Pact, the 1939 agreement between Russia and Germany not to attack each other and to divide the Polish land that lay between them. It was a land grab by both countries, but Hitler had the entire Polish nation in his crosshairs. The Nazi war machine bowled over Polish forces like rats under a steam roller. Nevil Chamberlain, British Prime Minister, was shocked. He had spent significant political capital in 1938 attempting to appease Hitler and stop the aggression. He brokered a Munich Accord on September 29, 1938, in which the Sudetenland and all Czechoslovakian fortifications were ceded to Germany with virtually no concessions. Chamberlain happily announced to a large gathering in London that he had achieved "Peace for our time" and reported that "Hitler said he had 'no more territorial demands to make in Europe.'" Hitler got exactly what he wanted with no losses.

Ignoring the Munich accord, the Wehrmacht cleverly marched around the north end of the French Maginot line and through a dense forest area that the French considered to be non-traversable. The Germans sliced through it like a two-thousand-pound bull barging through a backyard garden. It was the innovation of Blitzkrieg. It is a tactical concept of ground warfare that applies a full range of military assets in a single, integrated, rapidly moving force. The German assault was on breadth and timescale never before seen in ground warfare and nothing resembling the stalemating tactics employed in World War I. Europeans had never observed such a devastating military force on the continent since Napolean and it was rapidly becoming clear that even that comparison grossly understated the military supremacy of the Nazis. On June 13th, 1940, German tanks triumphantly parked under the Eiffel Tower and by July, the French parliament produced a new, completely totalitarian Fascist government under German control.

On May 25th, the Germans surprised the British Expeditionary

Force and the French and Belgian armies in northern France, forcing all three to run for their lives. By June 4th, history records a historic evacuation at Dunkirk of more than three hundred thousand Allied soldiers, a successful retreat but a tremendous setback for the Allies. They were defending the last allied-held operational territory on the European continent. It left the entire western continent in Axis hands. The only sheen on the debacle was a demonstration of the efficiency and skills of the Royal Navy during the evacuation. Chamberlain, weak and frail, completely discredited, and vilified domestically and internationally, resigned as premier. He died within a year, replaced by the venerable Winston Churchill. Churchill praised the effort but with the perspective that well-executed retreats do not win wars.

In late 1939 Britain faced its greatest threat since William the Conqueror in 1066. After Churchill gained command of the government in 1940, he quickly consolidated power around a new philosophy: to fight the Germans with all the might the nation could muster. Churchill, in a stirring speech to the public, declared that Britain would never surrender to Germany, a pledge that he repeated frequently throughout the war and which became a rallying cry for the British forces. The speech was reported in Albuquerque and many hoped the Brits could rally militarily without the Americans. Isolationism was the policy-speak of the nation.

By early 1941, the Royal Air Force had won the Battle of Britain, a defensive British victory that was as bittersweet as it was admirable. They had rebuffed the Germans from invasion but their capital city lay in tatters due to the indiscriminate bombardments. They had retained their land, but at a huge cost, one that imperiled their ability to proceed without allied help. The United States, still claiming neutrality, responded with several acts of Congress, including the Smith Act governing the legal status of aliens in the country, the Act of Havana, in which all of the Latin American countries in the western hemisphere agreed to a pact of common defense, the creation of a Joint Board of Defense and the creation of the Selective Service Act, which provided for the training of nearly one million American soldiers. Of course, the America officially remained neutral.[4]

JOHNNY PLOTS AGAIN

The Menicuccis and Johnny Matteucci concocted a plan to protect the boys: quickly train them with a skill before the draft. Johnny jumped on the task of getting the boys set up with technical work. He had learned his lesson from World War I, and he pushed hard for the same approach in 1917 when he convinced Armerigo and Julio to enlist with him. Of course, both Menicucci boys worked in the family businesses, Dante at Super Oil and Mario at Super Service. They learned the oil business, especially accounting and bookkeeping, both marketable skills. Larry Matteucci also labored at Super Service but in a non-technical sales position. This situation was fine until they graduated, but then they needed to move quickly because many young men were being notified to prepare for orders. Young men in this position had two realistic options: enlist in the National Guard or work in an industry critical to a war effort. In spite of what was publicly professed by politicians about neutrality, the country was steadily building factories that were pumping out munitions for the U.S. stockpile.

They reasoned that the National Guard could allow the boys to gain a skill within the military complex, but they also knew that Guard troops are the first ones called to battle. Nonetheless, many Italians pursued the National Guard gambling that isolationism would prevail during their service time.

Julio and Amerigo had worked in the railroad factories in Albuquerque prior to the war and the results were good for them. The key was to find an industry that provided critical components for national security and learn the associated trades. The reasoning was that men with essential skills would be exempted from military service. More importantly, even if they were inducted, they would possess a skill that could lead to a safer military assignment. They figured that there was nothing more important to an Army than weapons. So, they sought employment opportunities for their sons in weapons factories.

The brothers used their business connections in Albuquerque to gain inside information on the boys' job prospects. They knew just about every businessman in the city and they implored many of them for tips and ideas. The Colombo was also an excellent hub for information as many Italians were members and some, such as the Bachechis, were prominent with political and high-level business associates. If anyone needed advice on any subject, the Colombo was the venue to find it. In this case, they found several Italian families whose sons had landed jobs in a newly built warplane factory in Kansas. The factory sought employees. It was ideal and they quickly obtained the contact information and sent off a letter offering their three boys as potential employees. They used the Albuquerque

Italians who were already employed as references. Within a week, they were notified that all three were hired and would begin work upon arrival. It was all going according to plan.

Like Julio, Amerigo and Johnny Matteucci twenty-three years earlier, two Menicuccis and a Matteucci marched off to a world event together. Johnny cooked up the plan in 1917 and he rewarmed it and served it up again in 1941. By mid-1942, Mario, Dante and Larry were hand-fabricating airplane cowlings, skilled factory positions. Julio's younger son, Charlie, was still two years from graduation and the draft, so Julio sent him to work part-time with Horace Palladino at Super Service, learning electrical and mechanical skills. Julio insisted that Charlie spend as many hours working and training as possible. Everyone—fathers and sons alike—was ready for whatever ensued.

Europe remained the global focus in the closing years of the 1930s. Europe had an historic reputation for conflict and war was not surprising to many. The Menicuccis, of course, exclusively focused on European news because it involved their homeland; many family relatives and friends remained there. They, like most all Italians in town, despised Mussolini, whom they considered an enemy of freedom. They had tasted real freedom in America, and Mussolini was at the extreme opposite. Their loyalties lay entirely with America.

What the families missed by focusing on Europe—what almost everyone missed—was a new menace in the West. Japan had aligned with Germany and was building its military forces with an eye to conquer the Pacific Ocean and its nations. There had been reports of the Japanese invasion of Indochina in 1941 and that they were eyeing more territory, with the Philippines next on its list. But the stories paled next to the war atrocities reported in the European war. In July 1941, Douglas MacArthur was named commander of the United States forces in the Far East. He and the president issued a series of threats to the Japanese and the situation was clearly devolving into a major fray. Still, the public's eyes remained squarely on Europe.[5]

IGNOMINIOUS SUNDAY

It was a bright Sunday morning on December 7th of 1941 when the Menicucci families were preparing for the midday meal, the largest of the day on Sundays. A knock came on Julio's door. Then, it was followed by a more forceful pounding and a call to Julio. It was the neighbor, Luigi Pucci, who told him that the Japanese were invading the West Coast. It was early in the reporting, so the facts were wrong, but the details were unimportant because America was now under military attack. Giulia caught wind of the conversation and rushed to the door. As usual for her, she showed little emotion hearing the news but knew that life would soon change for her family, in a way that was none too good in the short term. She did what she knew best and quietly called upon the Madonna to intervene with the Lord to protect them.[6]

Julio ordered the radio on and told the family to gather around to hear the news. Everyone listened to the nonstop reports of the destruction of America's Pacific fleet and its sailors, the ones supposedly there to protect the Western United States. The fact that this attack came from Japan added to the shock because most people expected Germany to throw the first blow. The situation at Amerigo's home was a little different. He and his family listened to radio reports with trepidation. Naturally, all attention was on Mario because he was on the line to be called up after his upcoming graduation. Mario attended Albuquerque High School because several years earlier he got crosswise with the nuns and divorced himself from St. Mary's. He retained his friendship with his contemporaries at St. Mary's, especially the Italians. At that time Amerigo held more anxiety than Mario because he had the experience of war and he prayed that his son survived to assume the family business.

The *Albuquerque Journal* and the *Tribune* cranked out Extras for several days following the attack. An Extra was usually a single newspaper page printed on one side only so it could be pinned to bulletin boards. Albuquerque's radio stations produced news continuously—typically full reports on the hour and updates on the half hours, with interruptions as needed for breaking news—but newspapers were what most people considered the most accurate source of information.

It took hours of listening and ruminating to fully understand the situation, and by that time, the Colombo Hall was full of men, all discussing the impending war. Amerigo was nervous, his personality's first induced impulse. Julio was confident in their plan. He heard numerous rumors that the government did not conscript men engaged in critical industries, such as weapon production. It was comforting, but anything could go wrong, as it did when he and Julio assumed that if they enlisted with Johnny Matteucci, they would be assigned together. Still, he believed they had the best plan available. But so did everyone else. Each family with sons or husbands of draft age had their own schemes, including some who deliberately did no preparation.

The brothers' second concern was business. The war presented a challenge because the administration was discussing gasoline rationing. Not only would they likely lose employees to the draft, but gasoline sales would also be restricted. Both businesses were focused on personal service, which by necessity is rendered by humans. If materials, such as motor fuel, became scarce, both businesses would suffer. It was looking like the brunt of this conflict was falling upon the Menicuccis.

ARMY TYPISTS

Mario, Dante and Larry graduated in May 1941. Mario and Dante attended the University of New Mexico in the fall to study business and administrative skills, but by the end of the summer the three men were laboring at Aero Parts, an airplane component factory in Wichita, Kansas. The men worked on the assembly line riveting cowling parts and fittings on military bombers. As planned, they rapidly learned the assembly trades, hoping to remain in place for the duration of the war.

It did not go as planned. Shortly after arrival, Mario contracted a serious fungal lung infection, one that resisted the treatments he received in the local clinics. He returned to Albuquerque where he was hospitalized for a couple of weeks before he was released. He remained in Albuquerque for a year, attending the University of New Mexico while convalescing under Davina's care. He studied business and typing. He also worked part-time at Super Service Station. Dante and Larry Matteucci remained in Kansas. In late 1942, Mario returned to Kansas and resumed his job.

A short time later, in early 1942, all three men were inducted into the Army and sent to basic training where they were tested for aptitude and assigned a rank and duty. For all their preparation in the factory, it was typing skills that the Army noticed about Mario and Dante. Typing was an important skill for the Army. The typewriter was new and usually was found only in professional or commercial offices. Firm wrist action was needed to operate the mechanical keyboard with sufficient force to complete military forms, which were often layered with carbon copies. Mario and Dante were designated enlisted clerk typists.

Larry Matteucci capitalized on his factory skills. He was assigned to the 353th Fighter Squadron of the 354th Fighter Group in France as an airplane armorer, a man who loads munitions on fighter aircraft. The Army understood the ethnic differences among the Americans and the fear of fighting their countrymen. Thus, many Italians were assigned to the Pacific Theater where no Italian nationals fought. For others, such as Larry, his assignment as an armorer in England greatly reduced the possibility of him facing another Italian on the battlefield.

Dante passed through basic training and served stateside for about nine months. His exact assignment was unknown. He injured his back in a military exercise and spent several weeks in a military hospital recovering, but his injuries were sufficiently severe that he was medically discharged. His injury reportedly involved a ladder that slipped out from under him, throwing him backward. He was honorably discharged after a year, just before he was to be deployed. Unfortunately, these kinds of discharges were often viewed by some suspecting malingering, which in the patriotic fervor of the country was considered a severe infraction by the populace, one punishable by court marshal and incarceration. There is no evidence that Dante's injury was not genuine, but it was a stigma that he nonetheless wore for years and one that had personal repercussions later in life, as we shall see.

To Julio, Amerigo and Johnny Matteucci, their plan worked, just as it did in World War I. The boys were relatively safe. At least none of them was carrying a rifle through a forest with enemies firing at them from behind trees. And Dante was relieved from any service at all; he was heartily welcomed back to the family less than a year after he left. Giulia was especially delighted because her oldest son, the one destined to lead the family, was safely in the saddle. Julio, too, was energized because he needed all the laborers he could find to operate Super Oil because many of his employees, notably Albert Nottoli, marched off to war.

As their boys entered the Army, the Menicucci brothers wondered how they might communicate their locations to their families. The Menicuccis knew that the Army censors scrutinized outgoing letters from servicemen to ensure that they did not reveal American strategic secrets, especially the location of forces. Charlie, just a sophomore at St. Mary's at the time, devised a code system for their overseas letters going back home. The first character of the third word of each paragraph spelled the name of their location. Although the most modern Twenty-First Century Artificial Intelligence algorithm might be able to break the code today, it was impossible for the censors to detect, and not a single letter from the Menicucci boys back home was ever altered. The family knew the boys' whereabouts continuously. The sensors knew that coding was ongoing and the best they could do was to remove the obvious ones. The Matteuccis also had codes. Nello Matteucci, Larry's brother, was stationed in Puerto Rico. He wrote back to his folks asking if his uncle had sold the Porto Rico, a bar they had owned. The family knew it was a code because the bar had long been closed. Then they realized that he was in Puerto Rico. (Porto Rico is the Italian equivalent to the Spanish Puerto Rico, both meaning rich port.)

DISPIRITING LOSSES

The Japanese surprised the Americans with their attack on Pearl Harbor and used the momentum to immediately assert their advantage. The Battle of Bataan in the Philippines was the first and largest American defeat in the Pacific Theater after Pearl Harbor. New Mexico's 200th Coast Artillery was called into action on December 8th, 1941. The mission of the eighteen hundred New Mexicans was to defend the Philippines. The Japanese had originally intended to attack the Philippines simultaneously with Pearl Harbor, but logistical problems prevented all but a handful of Japanese bombers from getting through. In January of 1942, though, Japan launched a massive invasion of Luzon, on the north end of the Philippines. They strove to drive the Americans out, giving the Japanese a launching point to prosecute the war south toward Australia. The intent of the U.S. commanders at the time was to constrain the Japanese expansion to the northern half of the American commonwealth. U.S. forces were badly outnumbered in terms of equipment and personnel and in spite of a spirited defensive effort, the Americans were pushed south.

In July 1941, Douglas MacArthur took command of the Allied Forces in the Far East and organized his headquarters on the Island of Corregidor, located just to the west of the Philippines. His strategy was to have his army hold its ground until he could secure additional resources to move offensively. It failed. The Japanese overpowered the Americans, chasing them south on the island. As they gained momentum it became clear that the Philippines could fall. Roosevelt, fearing the loss of one of the top American commanders, ordered MacArthur to move his headquarters to Australia. On March 11, 1942, he and his family snuck out of Corregidor at midnight and landed safely in Australia a few days later.[7]

General John Wainwright took command of the army that was being driven south into the Bataan peninsula. MacArthur's exit both terrified and outraged the troops. MacArthur had been heavily criticized by soldiers for the location of his headquarters, far from the battlefield. Many of them believed that the situation they faced was a result of command mistakes. MacArthur gained the nickname "Dugout Doug," a metaphorical reference to their belief that while troops were under constant fire, MacArthur was living well in his headquarters.

ITALIAN BATTLING BASTARDS

Giuseppe Bandoni was a member of the 200th serving as a building technician. He was the son of Antonio who immigrated with his brother Angelo to Albuquerque in the first decade of the new century. Antonio worked as a carpenter for the Santa Fe Rail Road and did odd construction jobs around town. Giuseppe often helped Antonio and picked up construction skills. Giuseppe, who had acquired the nickname Beppe, graduated from St. Mary's in May of 1939.[8] Like most of the Italian immigrants, he repeated first grade because he could not speak fluent English. He joined the New Mexico National Guard out of a combination of patriotism and the belief that he could provide military service while remaining in Albuquerque.[9] He had an aptitude for construction and had worked as a carpenter with Marco Donati, another Lucchese in town. His skills led to his promotion to E4, a non-commissioned officer with the rank of Sergeant.

By early 1941, the defense of the Philippines became concerning to the American Joint Chiefs, who managed the Army and Navy operations. Beppe was called to service in the regular Army and transferred to the Philippines, serving in Luzon, which was under U.S. control at that time. He was assigned to an engineering group. The Japanese pushed the offensive against the under-equipped and marginally experienced Americans, such as Beppe.

He and his fellow soldiers battled the Japanese as they pounded the island from the north, forcing the action with overwhelming soldiers and firepower. The Americans steadily retreated and Wainwright and his commanders steadily requested support and were steadily ignored. As losses mounted and the Americans retreated, morale sank. A famous poem by Frank Hewlett vividly describes the aura of gloom that had descended upon the retreating troops:

We're the battling bastards of Bataan;
No mama, no papa, no Uncle Sam;
No aunts, no uncles, no cousins, no nieces'
No pills, no planes, no artillery pieces
And nobody gives a damn.
Nobody gives a damn.

The United States was fighting two wars, and domestic war production had not yet been geared up for either one. The flagging American forces received little additional materiel and no additional troops. By April, the situation was desperate and hopeless. The troops had been battered, with high casualty losses, dwindling supplies and exhausted and sick men. In the first major blow to American efforts, General John Wainwright surrendered to the Japanese on May 6, 1942. What followed was one of the most brutal campaigns of anguish and torture of prisoners in the history of war.

JUNGLE HORROR

After Wainwright capitulated, the Japanese rounded up the American soldiers for transport to internment camps. They placed them on train cars suited for cattle. The Japanese forced as many standing men into the cars as possible and locked the door on the windowless carriage. No man could sit as they were so cramped they could not move. Many had dysentery with no sanitation. Their boots were their toilets. Besides the horrendous odor, the heat was sweltering, as always in the Philippines. With temperatures in the box cars exceeding 120F, many men died en route to what they thought was a prisoner of war (POW) camp. When they opened the doors to disembark, the dead men collapsed as the others trampled them as their captors rushed them out with bayonets at their backs. The dead were swept out of the cars and gathered up by tractors with large front-loading buckets. It turned out to be a staging area for one of the most brutal campaigns against POWs in history.

Beppe and the other American prisoners were forced to walk sixty-five miles in the blazing heat to their POW camps that would be their homes for the remainder of the war. The "Death March," as it was later dubbed, caused about one hundred deaths a day as many men were killed for incidental actions, such as stepping out of line to urinate. Most of the men were ill. The Japanese shot men on the spot if they fell while marching. Typically, those rushing to their aid were beaten and killed if they persisted. The corpses were left on the road to be gathered up by bulldozes that pushed them into mass graves the Japanese had dug along the walking routes in anticipation of burying Americans. The only limit to the Japanese massacre was the physical burden of burying corpses. They were not allowed to leave rotting bodies on their land and it was laborious to bury them. Once at the camp, the torture continued daily and although the death rate slowed from the march, dozens a day expired.

Surviving the forty-month ordeal in the Japanese POW camps depended on a mixture of good fortune and cunning. Beppe had construction skills, which he openly demonstrated to his captors. He cooperated fully and feigned respect and admiration for the Japanese, holding his derision in check to preserve his existence. He was rewarded with various construction jobs. Typically, these jobs involved manual labor but sometimes he was asked to construct various objects for the commanders. He was nonetheless beaten on a routine basis and sustained life-long injuries to his back due to crushed vertebrae from a blow from a rifle stock. Worst of all, he could not communicate with his family. His only consolation in captivity was his belief in God and faith in the Lord.

At home in Albuquerque, the Bandonis knew nothing except that Beppe was part of the American unit that had surrendered to the Japanese. After that, letters from Beppe ceased. By 1943, his name appeared on a list of Japanese POWs being held in the Philippines. It was not until 1944 that the details of the Bataan Death March were revealed to the public. When they were publicized, it drew the ire of the public like no other event since the Pearl Harbor attack. The homicidal brutality outraged the American spirit and hardened its hatred of the Japanese people, further galvanizing the national determination to defeat them. During the forty months of his captivity, the family assumed that Beppe was dead, but they prayed daily that he remained a prisoner. If dead, they had little hope for his body to be returned, even if it could be recovered.

I clearly remember Beppe telling the story of Bataan in about 1961 while he, my father, Charlie and I traveled east of Albuquerque to hunt doves. Charlie was driving and Beppe sat in the front passenger seat talking about the war. It was one of their favorite topics. From the middle of the back bench seat, I leaned forward with my elbows on the front seat-back, fascinated by the banter. Although only ten years old at the time, his tale was so engrossing and graphic that the details remain clear and are among some of my sharpest memories.

As we drove along old US 66 west of Albuquerque, Beppe and Charlie told the horrid actions of the Japanese toward American troops. These two men still viewed the Japanese as enemies. Beppe talked about how he had collaborated with the Japanese in the POW camp. It startled me because he had just said he hated the Japanese and wanted to kill them, but now admitted to helping them, an obvious contradiction. I asked him why. It opened the floodgates. He turned to me, put his hand on my arm and said, "David, you have to understand that the devil was working in these people. They were beyond vile. But when you are a prisoner, you try to stay alive." He repeated it several times to ensure I understood and used words I could understand. The devil was the opposite of good, it was part of the moral education provided at St. Mary's, which I attended. Charlie sat silent, but he clearly agreed, only interjecting at one point, "The Japs had to be killed or they would have come over here and killed us. We couldn't let this happen to our families."

Beppe had collaborated with the Japanese in order to gain favors and live. He had construction skills and he showed them off frequently to his captors, who in exchange offered him opportunities to work on camp construction projects. He picked up a little Japanese, which also added to his acceptance by his captors. He despised the Japanese but he knew that any display of antagonism would result in instant punishment, with torture and death appropriated to more severe infractions. "I did what I needed to survive," he said, "And if that meant I had to work with those bastards, it was because I wanted to live long enough to see Americans kill them." Besides, he added, "It wouldn't do anybody any good if I died. I was a sergeant and I had a duty to stay alive to help my men." These words were likely the harshest that I ever heard from Beppe's mouth and entirely out of character. He was a gentleman, standing about 5'8" tall, medium build, reserved, polite, and congenial. Then he qualified, somewhat apologetically, "David, when you have seen the devil, like your dad and I have, it is hard to forgive them. But I hope I can before I die."

Beppe went on with a long list of atrocities that he had witnessed. He described how men were beaten to death every day, some with sticks, others with whips and others with rifle butts, many for slight infractions. Men were tortured by stripping them naked, tying them to a table in the broad sun and leaving them to die slowly. Others were forced to go without water for days and then given deliberately contaminated water, ensuring that they died in the most painful way possible. Others, he said, were locked into nearly completely sealed prison cells with no facilities, not even a bucket for human waste. The temperature inside the nearly totally dark cells was well over 140F with high humidity. Men who were already emaciated from abuse succumbed after a day or two of this treatment. "The Japs baked them to death," Beppe said with scorn. "The next time you see a turkey cooking in the oven, think about a man inside instead of a bird." Even today, a Thanksgiving bird glistening in a hot oven brings Beppe's words to my mind's eye.

As punishments for severe infractions, such as escape attempts, some men were buried up to the chests near hills of flesh-eating ants and the men in his group were forced to watch the victim slowly eaten alive by hordes of insects that left nothing but his skull. Of course, he added, some men were shot or stabbed to death based on the whim of a captor satisfying his zeal for putting American blood on the ground. They dumped American bodies in a hole like trash. "David," Beppe added, "Some of those men were friends from Albuquerque. I saw their bodies thrown in a hole like banana peels." He continued, "It was a game for them. They often gambled on when a prisoner might die or which one of a group might succumb first. "They even used American dollars that they stole from us to do the betting."

He said they he had been given so little to eat that he had one bowel movement a week. "There was nothing going in, so nothing came out," he said. He limped badly due to his back injury, which plagued him for the remainder of his life. Prisoners were given no medical care and when the infirm died, they were carted off and dumped in a hole. The Japanese were much more proficient at killing Americans than housing them. Bulldozers buried bodies in nearby landfills. American physicians were imprisoned along with the soldiers, but they had no supplies and were often tortured if they attempted to treat Americans. Nurses were herded into a separate camp. Surviving men typically watched helplessly as their comrades died of diseases and torture wounds that could ordinarily be successfully treated. The families in Albuquerque, knowing nothing and imagining the worst, suffered almost as much mental anguish as the prisoners suffered physically.

Beppe followed his commander's orders—do what is needed to survive without divulging any intelligence information. Of course, Beppe, an Army sergeant, had little intelligence to share with his captors and they knew it. His rank was an excuse for his captors to beat him. The daily regimen of Japanese atrocities he had witnessed for four years permanently changed him and like Charlie, he never shook his distaste for the Japanese people. Charlie refused to eat rice after the war because it reminded him of Japan.

By the time Beppe was liberated after forty months in captivity, he had lost nearly half his body weight. He was malnourished and feeble with various ailments, including malaria and dysentery. His extremities shook and his body had shrunken to a skeleton with a paper-thin skin hanging on it. "I was so skinny I could almost get my hands around my stomach," while putting his two hands together, his thumb touching the other thumb and the middle fingers touching. But he added, "After the Americans arrived at the camp and liberated us, any of the Japs that were left all turned their backs to us when we walked by because they were ashamed of the way they had acted." There are records of the Japanese turning their backs on conquering troops as a measure of respect to the victors.

Beppe invoked Catholic thinking in his tales because it provided the context in which to discuss the heinous acts of the Japanese. A critical feature of Catholic Christianity is the creation of mythical, earth-like creatures to exemplify the obvious facts of life: Evil exists along with good. Evil is the invisible force influencing every human to break with norms and act in ways that are destructive to civil society. In Catholicism, the devil, a sinister creature of pure malice headquartered in hell, roams the populations of the earth seeking opportunities to tempt dastardly acts. On the side of good is God the Father, who commissioned his son, Jesus, to counter the great sinister beast. It is through Jesus, according to Catholics, who leads people through the jungle of evil to Heaven with the Father.

The Ten Commandments, a Judean concept, is fundamentally a set of rules for proper, civilized life leading to a place in paradise upon death. Stripping away the Commandments' religious inferences, they are common sense rules for civilized behavior. A society where all people followed the commandments would be perfectly peaceful and productive. Not without conflict, which is a condition of all life that competes with other living creatures, but one where conflict is resolved peacefully. Catholicism is the suggested method of applying the Commandments in life.

Catholic schools taught children the fundamental difference between good and evil. Those who grossly flaunt the Ten Commandments are evil. The Japanese running the Filipino POW camps violated most of them continually. Thus, the Japanese were clearly acolytes of the devil. Conversely, the Americans were on the side of good, destroying the evil oppressors and liberating those who they oppressed. Even by fourth grade, as I was when Beppe told his story, the message was clear.

Below is a list of all of the Albuquerque Italians servicemen who were captured during the early battles of WWII in the Philippines.[10,11]

Last Name	First Name	Rank	Outfit	Prison	Disposition
Bandoni	Joseph	Sergeant	200th	Bilibid	Liberated
DeVenzio	Orlando	Sergeant	200th	Oyeama	Liberated
Del Frate	Armando	Private 1st	200th	Unknown	Liberated
Domenicali, Jr	Peter	Private 1st	200th	Cabanatuan	Liberated
Donati	Peter	Private 1st	200th	Cabanatuan	Liberated
Franchini	Frank	Private 1st	200th	Cabanatuan	Liberated
Giannini	Louis	Private 1st	200th	Unknown	Liberated
Malnati	Lloyd	Private 1st	200th	Bilibid	Liberated
Micheli	Arthur	Sergeant	200th	Nagoya	Killed in action
Simoni	Tony	Private 1st	200th	Cabanatuan	Died in Camp
Maurino	Tony	Corporal	31Inf.	Clark Field	Liberated
Panici	Michael	Private 1st	19BG-Hq	Davao	Died in Camp

List of Servicemen Captured

MENICUCCIS IN THEATER

In late 1942, Mario was credited with one and a half years of college at his military induction, a huge advantage in obtaining a favorable job assignment. Mario and Dante both attended local schools where they studied accounting and typing part-time. An army is composed of a great variety of duties, from typing memos in a headquarters building to repairing damaged equipment to manning a machine gun in a bomber gun turret. Obviously, the safest job was behind the typewriter or organizing shipments of materiel and both boys knew it. Although they were resigned to do as ordered, they hoped that the Lord would help them to serve in a job with a high probability of survival. Like General Pershing in World War I, MacArthur insisted that all soldiers, regardless of rank or job, be fully trained as fighting men, including proficiency with rifles and other personal weapons of war. Mario qualified as a rifle marksman. Prowess with firearms was part of the Menicucci family's DNA as they had been using them for hunting for as long as guns had existed.

In 1943 Mario completed his basic training and was permanently assigned to a base in the continental U.S., where he performed clerical duties in support of the Lend-Lease program. He served for a year in the relative peace of the continental U.S. In late 1944, the Joint Chiefs authorized MacArthur to initiate the final phase of his plan to return to the Philippines on his way to conquer Japan. MacArthur consolidated the most capable men from across the Army for the effort. Mario, who had performed well and had some college education, was the kind of man the general was seeking and he was assigned to MacArthur's headquarters in downtown Brisbane, Australia. There he clerked for various commanders as they prepared to move out. Until now, Mario's typing and administrative skills resulted in favorable and relatively safe assignments. For the first time he was in a combat theater. It was far from safe.

Just as Mario settled into his job in Brisbane, MacArthur was setting foot in the Philippines, subsequently building his headquarters at Dagupan City. Within weeks, Mario was reassigned to MacArthur's new command headquarters. The entire command had moved in just a couple of weeks, a remarkable logistical achievement by the Army. As Mario arrived at the headquarters, the quest to recapture Luzon was just underway, which put him in the battle zone for the first and only time. There he retained his job code and clerked, but it was a treacherous time with constant air raids and Japanese commando raids on sites all around him. Security was tight and all the men regularly honed their rifle skills in case of an attack.

Mario typed the command instructions that were sent to field commanders. It was a demanding job, requiring perfection because errors resulted in accidental American deaths. Like all soldiers, he was ready to take up arms and he knew how to use them. It was the only time during the war that Mario was unable to write regularly to his family in Albuquerque, which was distressing for both. Mario served at the headquarters for the remainder of the war, which was brief following the Luzon conflict. He had been slated to serve in MacArthur's occupation force in Japan, but the war's conclusion preempted it.

Mario Menicucci in his gas mask just before he was deployed to the combat theater as part of General MacArthur's command in the Philippians.

Mario's contribution to the war was considerable, yet in his humility he rarely spoke of his accomplishments. His story, largely untold until now, adds to the body of testimony as to the dedication and talents that Albuquerque's Italian community contributed to the American war effort.

AMERICAN TECHNOLOGY

In 1943, Charlie, Julio's second son, was preparing to graduate from St. Mary's High School. It was March and the school year was not complete, but he received orders to report for induction. As customary, the school issued a diploma on the spot and graduated him. There was no traditional graduation ceremony in the aura of dejection that prevailed in the country. Young men in schools throughout the United States experienced the same.

Charlie brought a range of technical talents to the Army, not the least of which was his prowess with electrical systems. He listed his civilian job as an automotive electrician and had a strong aptitude for mechanical work, both of which had been honed by his tutelage under Horace Palladino at Super Service Station. He performed well on technical aptitude tests and the Army Air Force assigned him to electronics training where he learned to operate and repair aircraft radar and radio systems on American bombers, essential tools for aircraft in the US inventory. Radar was an advanced technology that required highly trained men to operate and maintain. In fact, radar was considered one of the mission-critical systems aboard the plane. The Army Air Force sought men who already had skills working with electrical equipment and could pick up advanced concepts quickly. They created a series of six-month-long schools, each successive one involving more complex concepts and applications. The Army Air Force Training Command (AAFTC) included schools at Boca Raton, FL, Sioux Falls, SD and Chanute Field in Champaign, Illinois, the largest and most intensive training center for airmen. By the time he had completed his fourth school, about a third of the men who started with him had been dropped and sent back to regular Army jobs, such as carrying rifles in the jungles.

Charlies aced the schools. Interestingly, he was not an exceptional school student—B range, at best—but when it came to electrical technology, he was in his element. It was almost like he knew much of the material before it was presented and he became a top performer. At completion, he was promoted to E3, a Corporal. He was assigned to the 940th Air Engineering Squadron with the job code of Radar Mechanic (852). A radar mechanic officially performs first and second echelon maintenance, repairs and operation of radio and radar equipment on air bases and fields.

Radar technology, which at the time was highly classified, was advancing quickly as the military sensed the value of spotting aircraft before they could be visually seen. For bombers, radar had become a priority system to identify approaching enemy craft and to convey their location to the pilot. The radar man ensured that the equipment remained operational, which was no easy feat. At the time, well before transistors, all electronic communication and surveillance devices were composed of vacuum tubes that were bulky and finicky. Tubes, which resembled incandescent light bulbs with internal elements burning at red-hot temperatures, had limited lifetimes. The delicate glass bonnets on the tubes easily fractured when dropped or bumped. The tumultuous ride of the World War II bombers, especially when under attack, frequently jolting and rocking from concussions of aerial explosives, was a rough environment for these complicated and delicate systems. A plane typically had redundant radar and radio systems, as failures were expected.

In addition to on-ground repair of equipment, Charlie flew bomber missions; seventeen, in fact. He explained that his job was supposed to be ground-based. Each plane had regular crews, but if one was ill or missing, ground-based radar men filled in. Dysentery was an ongoing problem for the crews and was the cause of many of Charlie's mission substitutions. Caused by contaminated water—which was replete on Pacific islands— the disease produced vomiting, abdominal cramps and severe diarrhea. For bomber crews, any crew member with the disease was not only ineffective on the plane but was extremely contagious. Dysentery came on suddenly and often incapacitated men just prior to a mission, which opened the door for replacements. Bombing missions were risky endeavors requiring top-performing crews to succeed.

CHARLIE'S BATTLES

Charlie served in combat at a rank of E4, a sergeant, the same rank that his uncle Amerigo achieved in World War I. As a non-commissioned officer he was part of the enlisted men whom the Army designated as the backbone of the American military forces. Officers were considered management. He was the first Menicucci who actually saw combat in the Army. He served as a radio and radar man for various bombers, including the Boeing B-17 Flying Fortress, the Consolidated B-24 Liberator and the North American Aviation B-25 Mitchell. In 1944, he received field training on the advanced radar systems in the new Boeing B-29 Superfortress, the first pressurized bomber in the American air arsenal and the kind that delivered the atomic bombs to Japan to end the war. About half of the missions that Charlie flew in the war were in the B29, including a number of bombing raids over Japan.

Charlie enjoyed the comfort of the B-29s as compared to the older bombers. They were pressurized and heated, meaning that crews at high altitudes could perform their work in warm temperatures instead of the subzero ones on other aircraft. He reported that men often returned from B-17 missions with frostbitten toes and fingers. Temperature changes in the older planes also altered the performance of radios and radar systems, requiring the operator to constantly retune their units. Sometimes mechanical controls on the radios froze due to moisture condensing on them. Charlie reported using his bare hand on the radio knobs to melt them free to operate. Most of all, he was impressed with the B-29's technology: the advanced radar and navigation, computerized gun turrets and heavy weapon brigade. "It was the best bomber in the skies. We could take it easy on bombing runs because we were so high the Japs couldn't reach us. Sometimes, we made our runs without any resistance," he said.

These breaks were times when many of the men lit up cigarettes. Charlie was typical and puffed along with the others. He said that almost every airman lit up before boarding the plane as that was when tensions were high. He said, "A good couple of drags took the edge off the prospect of dying." Charlie smoked the Italian Stogies before the war, but he favored cigarettes for their filter, which he believed provided a better-tasting product.

He fought in four Pacific Theater campaigns, including the Air Offensive, Eastern Mandates, Western Pacific and Rvukyus.[12] He was designated a Carbine Marksman.[13] The Air Offensive was the moniker describing the U.S. ariel strategy in both the European and Pacific Theaters. The plan was to use heavy strategic bombing to degrade the enemy positions before land assaults. In the Pacific, the additional goal was to destroy Japan's floating assets on the open sea before they could attack land bases. The strategy involved three classes of aircraft: fighters, bombers and reconnaissance. Fighters were small, fast, and agile and suited to dogfights with other fighters and to attack ships and land bases. Fighters in the Pacific were typically based on aircraft carriers, although many were also deployed on land bases. Carriers carried small dive bombers or torpedo bombers, both designed specifically to attack targets on or near the water. Reconnaissance and bomber aircraft, especially the heavy bombers such as the B17, were land-based because of their size and their large bomb loads, which required runways longer than a carrier's. Some smaller bombers, such as B-25B Mitchell that Jimmy Doolittle flew in his famous raid of Tokyo in April 1942, were carrier-based.

B17 Flying Fortress. Courtesy Airwolfhound; in the public domain via https://commons. wikimedia.org/wiki/Category:Images, 2024.

Eastern Mandates was part of the U.S. Joint Chiefs of Staff (JCS) "Strategic Plan for the Defeat of Japan" developed by the British and American Conference in Washington DC in May 1943. Admiral Nimitz, commander of Pacific naval operation, was ordered to attack Japanese positions from the west while MacArthur attacked from the south, keeping the heat on the Japanese on two fronts. The Mandates was the first major campaign involving island groups that Nimitz targeted for invasion. These islands are known today as the Marshall Islands, ones that Germany had occupied but had been mandated to the Japanese by Article 22 under the League of Nations charter. Charlie was assigned to a heavy bomber unit in the campaign, which lasted five months, ending in June 1944. Charlie did not fly in this campaign because he was new, but he was in a combat zone and serviced those fortunate bombers that although battered and bruised, wobbled back to the base. Speed was of the essence in the repair work. Charlie said that they worked double and sometimes triple shifts during the heat of a campaign. "Our job as radar men was to get the plane flying with operational radar as fast as possible," he explained. "We'd rip out the old units and replace them in two hours, about half the time recommended by the Army manuals. He added, "Our job was to help our men kill Japs and they can't kill anything when they're stuck on the ground."

At the end of each campaign, the men rested for several weeks and some furloughed. Typical furloughs involved time in Australia or Hawaii. A few furloughed to the mainland during the years of heavy conflict from 1942 through 1945, but they had to pay for their transportation. The vast majority spent time away from the front for rest and relaxation. Bomber crews were often given liberty on a newly captured island for rest and relaxation before they were called to attack the next one. The rest times typically lasted a week or more as crews usually flew several missions in relatively rapid succession over three- or four-day periods, thoroughly exhausting the crew. Each bombing mission demanded heightened attention to detailed tasks for long periods, which required a fully attentive crew. As Charlie put it, "It was exhausting but they gave us plenty of R&R time where we could pick up some fungus for the next mission." He suffered from Jungle Rot, a type of stubborn foot and ankle fungus that lasted his entire life, including some bouts of severe flareups that caused numbness and itching in his feet.[14]

The Western Pacific Campaign took up where the Eastern Mandates ended. The objective was to control the Marianas archipelago, a string of volcanic islands including Kwajalein, Eniwetok, Saipan, Tinian, Guam and the Palaus. Again, heavy bombers led the way, followed by naval bombardment and amphibious assaults by the Marines. Once the Marines had established a firm beachhead and the Navy Construction Battalion (CBs) had built airfields, the Army moved in to take control of the island. MacArthur was hopping up the chain of islands to the Philippines. Typically, at the outset of a campaign the Japanese resistance was fierce, but as the bombing rolled on and destroyed the enemy antiaircraft positions, resistance dropped as the Japanese hunkered into caves where they expected to fight the Marines to their deaths. The Marines obliged and killed them. The Navy CBs drew widespread praise for both their valor and construction expertise. Charlie spoke of them often with admiration. "They followed the Marines onto every island and built runways with one hand and shot damn Japs with the other," he said with a distinct air of admiration.

By the opening of 1945, Nimitz's navy attacked from the east, and MacArthur's army hopscotched islands northward. The Americans were tightening a ring of fire around Japan. In March of 1945, Charlie was in a B29 Superfortress, flying both reconnaissance and bombing missions over Okinawa, the largest island in the Ryukyus, a chain of islands south of Japan. The island was of sufficient size to house base military facilities and was strategically well-located near the Japanese mainland. It was viewed as the staging site for the final assault and invasion of the Japanese island. The initial air campaign against the island was some of the most intense of the war with men flying difficult, long missions with only short rests in between.

The bombardment persisted nonstop for several weeks before the Marines commenced their invasion. Okinawa was projected to be a relatively easy duck to down, but the Japanese proved differently. They saw Okinawa as the last defensive land between Japan and the Americans; only nine-hundred miles of water lay between the island and Tokyo, well within the operational capability of the American bombers. The island's harbors were also well suited to defensive military vessels. The Japanese defended the island with the vigor of a trapped, wounded animal, often fighting to the last man in impossible circumstances in lieu of surrendering. The Japanese were bunkered well into the opposite sides of the mountains from their American attackers. Thus, they could survive the Naval artillery bombardment and then step out of the bunkers to shoot down on the troops as they ascended the hill from the opposite side. Once the Americans scaled the hill and took it, the Japanese quickly retreated to the next hill where they bunkered in to wait for the next assault. It was cleverly designed to force the Americans to constantly fight uphill. By July 1945, the Americans had control of the island, but at a steep cost. America had lost over twelve thousand five hundred soldiers, sailors and marines, thirty-six ships and over seven hundred airplanes. Japan lost an astonishing hundred and ten thousand troops and another seven thousand captured. It was the bloodiest battle in the Pacific theater in World War II.

As the Americans pushed north, Japanese defenses waned as the Americans were literally bleeding them to death with ferocious firepower. The B29 was designed for high-altitude flight, up to thirty thousand feet, beyond the range of the Japanese fighters and the ground-based antiaircraft guns. The plane, with its computerized targeting system, was brutally effective from high altitudes and even more so at lower ones, at which they flew with impunity as enemy resistance petered out.

ChARLie's ENSIGNA
Nov 8, 1943

Enlisted airman's embroidered wings issued to Army Air Force combat aviators. Officers were issued metal insignia. Courtesy author's collection.

A WARRIOR'S VIEW

Charlie talked frequently of his missions over the Japanese-held islands: "We never knew what was worse, the flak from Japanese cannons or the anti-aircraft guns." The flak cannons produced nearly continuous aerial explosions that spread shards of hot metal scattering in all directions, penetrating aircraft skin and damaging crew and equipment. In some instances, the flak could cut down a plane. The concussions from explosions rocked the plane, affecting the accuracy of the bombing runs. He said, "The rocking and bucking of the plane played havoc with the radios and we always took a box of spare (vacuum) tubes to repair broken devices during a mission." He likened the flak to a shotgun and the antiaircraft guns to rifles. "A single bomb could splatter you with flak coming from any direction." Bullets did more damage when they hit the plane, but they usually missed."

A similar B29 Super Fortress carried the atomic bombs over Japan to end WWII. Courtesy Michael Barera; in the public domain via ttps://commons.wikimedia.org/wiki/Category:Images.

It was during the Japanese mainland missions that Charlie saw the havoc the bombardment did on the ground. By the summer of 1945, Americans had nearly total air superiority, so the bombers approached targets at low levels where the plane's bombs were extremely accurate. He twinged when he saw for the first time people scrambling in desperation as the plane's bombs killed them in mass. It was the incendiary munitions that were the most impressive man-killers. "It looked like ants under a blow torch. As they came out of buildings running for the hills, they fried." It shook him, but then he remembered Pearl Harbor and "The feeling went away fast," he added. There was not a single man on any mission that had any other intention for the Japanese other than death and Pearl Harbor was never far from the lips of men during battles. He recalls many crewmen cheering when they hit a target: "That's for Pearl Harbor, you Jap bastards." Similar cries came from other quarters on the plane, with the crewmate cheering the team on. Charlie said, "It was a lot like in a ball game, where the dugout gets all excited after a big hit. Our goal was to win and go home. Killing Japs was the way to win and we were damned good at it." The B29, a true aerial fortress, had considerable armor and aerial offensive capability with numerous turrets, each equipped with multiple guns operated with analog computers, most of them firing 50 caliber Brownings. Many Japanese fighters that tangled with a B29 had short lives.

Occasionally, a bullet got through. He told the harrowing story of a B29 mission where his life was narrowly spared by the "grace of the good Lord:" "We were at a few thousand feet, hiding in clouds for a low-level run. We had light resistance, so I took a break. We ran out of clouds and a Jap bullet ripped through my number one radio and my vacant chair. It was the best piss break of my life. When I saw the mess, I would've pissed for sure, but I was empty." He said, "There is nothing like the loneliness you feel when somebody it trying to kill you. Your only friend is the good Lord." Charlie's Catholicism was the philosophical pillar that saw him through the war.

FINAL MISSION

On January 13, 1945, MacArthur established his headquarters at Dagupan City on the West Coast of the Philippines. After Luzon was liberated and the air and naval bases in the Philippines were secured, the final staging for the invasion of Japan was complete. Heavy Bombers were consolidated on the island, with the B29s expected to do the heavy lifting in the raids over Japan. By early summer, Charlie was with his engineering unit in the Philippines ready for action.

In late July 1945, Charlie and several other radio and radar men were ordered to stand by as backup crew members for a special mission. He did not know it, but he was a candidate to serve on the backup crew for the "Bockscar," the B-29 set to carry the Fat Man atomic bomb to Nagasaki. The pilot, U.S. Army Air Force Major Charles Sweeney, had selected the primary and backup crews from among those men who were available, qualified and had reputations for excellent service. Charlie was one of those men. He was experienced with B29 radio and radar and had flown bomber missions over the Japanese island. He also had a reputation for innovating repairs, specifically his ability to get damaged equipment running in minimal time. His eyesight was also exceptional, somewhere around 20/10.[15] The commanders were uncertain how much the atomic bomb could affect the delivering plane, but he wanted men with the best possible eyesight in case of difficult seeing conditions.[16] Charlie was also an E4, a non-commissioned officer (NCO) of sufficient rank for B29 crews, which typically included four officers in the cockpit and eleven NCOs manning the communications and guns. Plus, he was a small man, at five feet, nine inches and one hundred and fifty-five pounds, ideal for the B29, carrying a maximum load of the nuclear bomb and associated equipment. While being briefed he realized that the mission was to bomb Japan. He did not know the exact location nor the kind of bomb, but he surmised it was the opening of the final invasion and defeat of the island nation. It was indeed, but the invasion was conducted by just two airplanes, one delivering an atomic bomb over Hiroshima and another a few days later over Nagasaki.[17]

VICTORY

By 15 August, it was all over as Emperor Hirohito announced Japan's unconditional surrender. Charlie later said, "It was the best ending because we would've lost a lot of men invading." Charlie was unequivocal in his belief that the atomic bomb saved countless lives. His point was that the U.S. had total superiority over Japanese skies, giving them unlimited ability to fly low and lay waste to the entire country with bombs and incendiaries. "We could've killed more than half the population by air," he said. But the Marine casualties would have still been high because the Japanese were desperately fighting to the last man—never surrendering. Charlie said, "They'd put second graders out on the beaches with rifles." The Americans were still reeling from Okinawa where the Japanese resistance was fanatical. Charlie said frequently, "We killed a lot of Japs with the A-bombs, but we did it all at one time instead of killing three times as many and losing a lot of Marines." It was true. In 1945, the Americans were pummeling the Japanese Island with wide latitude. The bombs they had already dropped had laid waste to millions of acres of Japanese civil society. A sustained, full-throated American air assault over months would collectively have the same effect as an atomic bomb but on many cities. Many American veterans of the World War II Pacific Theater agree.

The Menicuccis and most Italians were delighted with the outcome, especially with the outrageous details about Bataan leaking out. Julio put it bluntly: "American lives were more important than those damn Japs." The realities of war modulate humanistic tendencies toward other people.

Julio and millions of Americans cheered American might. At home, the Menicuccis were exuberant. Their son was returning home alive and the Japanese, like the Germans, had been taught a lesson. "Only damn fools bet against America," Julio told me many times. On September 2, 1945, Charlie stood on the deck of a humid and crowded American destroyer in Tokyo Bay when General MacArthur signed the instrument of surrender. It was a monumental time for a young warrior: the conflict was over, he was an NCO going home alive and healthy, and he stood in awe and respect for one of the greatest U.S. generals in history. Charlie expressed unbounded respect and admiration for MacArthur, as did nearly all of the men. "He said he'd come back and by damn, he did," Charlie frequently exclaimed. Charlie was the only combat warrior in the living memory of the Menicucci family.

America had no professional army. Citizens did the fighting and their tales of the horror were conveyed directly to the populace. The widespread dissemination of factual information helped common folks to fully appreciate the horrors of war. In contrast, Twenty-First Century America maintains a professional army that can conduct battles while the populace remains at home with little personal impact. A citizen army brings a country together like no other factor because all citizens have a stake in the outcome. Mario's and Charlie's service in the war was a testament to the value that the family had brought to the United States. The family had progressed mightily, but setbacks were lurking.

See notes 18, 19.

Notes

1. *Goff* outlines the history of newspapers in Albuquerque. The *Broadcasting Yearbook* discusses the state of commercial broadcasting in 1940

2. *Collier* describes the conditions in the West that led to the bombing of Pearl Harbor. *Churchill* (Gathering Storm) describes the conditions in Europe that led to war.

3. Italians frequently referred derisively to the Germans as Uni, or Huns, a nomadic and uncivilized group of Eastern European troublemakers who lived in the area of Germany around 500 AD.

4. *Churchill (Their Finest Hour and Triumph and Tragedy)* presents a detailed discussion of the war in Europe.

5. *Bertoletti* describes the impact of WWII on the Italian populace.

6. Emma Del Frate lived on the west side of Albuquerque on 14th street. The chief of the Albuquerque Fire Department lived next door and kept his police radio in his car on during the day so that he could respond quickly to calls. She told the story: "We could sometimes hear his radio. That Sunday we could tell that something was wrong because he had it on loud. It was very scary hearing the men shouting about the war. We knew it was bad." She heard the report about forty-five minutes before it was broadcast to the city.

7. Douglas MacArthur was one of the greatest American generals. *Manchester* and *Perret* write extensive biographies of the general and full descriptions of the United States' war against Japan.

8. Beppe is derived from the Italian name Guiseppe.

9. Service in the National Guard involved only brief monthly training exercises and a two-week annual training, which allowed the member to remain at his or her home.

10. The list of men was developed based on newspaper reports and the work of *Matson*.

11. *Chisum, et. al.* describes the death march. *Matson* discusses the role of New Mexicans as POWs in WWII.

12. *Wright* describes the Mandates from the League of Nations.

13. A carbine is a short-barreled, lightweight, rifle favored by aviators. The standard issue rifle for the Army was the Winchester's M1 Carbine 30 caliber rifle, developed in 1938.

14. *Historical Studies Branch* discusses how combat crews were rotated during the war.

15. 20/10 is a measure of visual acuity where the 20 is the distance that an average person can see clearly and the 10 designates what distance the measured person can see the same thing with identical clarity.

16. "Seeing" is a technical term indicating the level of clarity of the atmosphere relative to seeing a target.

17. *Simpson* presents a detailed discussion about the American combat squadrons in WWII.

18. *Beever* presents a comprehensive summary of WWII. *Morris (Barry)* and *Langer* present in an encyclopedic format the history of events relative to WWII.

19. Much of the information for this chapter was gathered from newspaper reports in Albuquerque and New York.

17

WORLD WAR II AT HOME
(1941–1946)

SPECTER OF RATIONING

Immediately after Pearl Harbor, the Menicuccis realized that while knew about war from the military side, they had no experience from the civilian side. A ton of problems hit them—How would this affect the businesses, the families' source of support? How would the temporary loss of their sons affect the family; they had provided a great deal of support around the home and business? What would happen if they were killed or disabled? It was all a swirl of unknowns that affected each man differently. In meetings, Johnny was stoic, puffing madly on his pipe. Amerigo was agitated. Julio expressed steely determination, just as expected for the family and business leader. The overriding fear was that a Japanese invasion or, worse, a loss to the Axis powers, would place America under Fascism, a thought that horrified every American, from youngsters to the elderly.

Super Oil Company in 1940. By this time, the company had four tanks for storing fuel, which included kerosene, gasoline and diesel. Diesel was only beginning to be demanded, but the market was growing quickly. Kerosene was the most demanded product from Super Oil Company. The facility was an unmanned warehouse. Courtesy Dante Menicucci family.

While the Menicucci's first concern was labor, their second was supplies. They knew that wars create shortages of materials, especially fuel and materials such as steel and copper, the materials that power armies. Gasoline rationing had been discussed publicly for months but it became a reality in late 1942 with a nationwide mandate. Rationing had several purposes. Roosevelt knew that the U.S. military would overwhelm domestic resources with mushrooming demands for merchandise and materials, especially gasoline, needed for thousands of new military vehicles soon to operate in Europe and the Pacific. When supplies are restricted in a capitalist society, prices naturally rise to compensate. Rationing was meant to control inflation, which normally occurs when sudden government demands induce supply shortages in the domestic market. Inflation leads to hardships as rising prices sap buying power, leading to a recession or worse. It was also intended to prevent hoarding, especially by those who could buy in bulk, leaving the shelves bare for others.

Julio and Amerigo complained bitterly to the mayor and anyone else who listened. Gas rationing would harm their businesses, both of which purveyed fuel products. They had plenty of supporters, including all the gasoline business owners, most other business owners, the mayor, the city commission and John Miles, New Mexico's governor. Miles traveled to Washington DC to argue that New Mexico's large, open spaces required more traveling to live than those in the East. Thus, he claimed, western states should be given special rationing targets. It had no effect because the needs of the war superseded any local inconveniences or subtle inequities.

Under the system, gas station owners sold a prescriptive amount to each customer. The federal government issued gas rationing cards to every licensed driver in the country. Every card had removable tabs at the bottom with a number printed. When a customer drove up to the pump, he surrendered a tab to the gas station owner, and the attendant pumped the number of gallons indicated on the tab into the vehicle. At the end of the month, the station owners were required to report and prove, using the tabs and station records as evidence, that they had sold products in accordance with the rationing limits. Stations were periodically audited to determine compliance. An average person could purchase four gallons a week, but others, such as traveling salesmen, could purchase more. Super Service Station and Super Oil moved from a posture of profit and growth to defense and belt-tightening. They knew that as long as there were automobiles, they needed gasoline. Squeezing a profit from this situation was a challenge.[1]

A severe global rubber shortage developed on December 8, 1941, after the Japanese overran Malaysia, taking control of the rubber plantations that produced a majority of the world's natural rubber. Synthetic rubber was well-known but had not gained any market traction due to its high cost relative to natural rubber. The Army needed much rubber for its war machine. The situation changed with the Malaysian conquest, but it would take a couple of years before U.S. synthetic rubber production could gear up to meet military demands. In the interim, rubber tire rationing was implemented in January of 1942. The government simultaneously instituted a national speed limit of thirty-five miles per hour to reduce gasoline consumption and tire wear. It was a double whammy to Super Service. Sales of tires and gasoline and associated services produced most of the station's income.

Sales of new rubber tires were all but prohibited. The restrictions generated interest in repairs, a principal service at Super Service. Rationing encouraged the retreading industry. Retreaded tires are used ones in which the tread had been removed and replaced. The Menicuccis learned about tires at Safety First Tire Company, which specialized in vulcanized repairs and retreads. Super Service had never invested in retread equipment because new tires were available and much more saleable and profitable. Super Service pulled money from savings to purchase retreading machinery for passenger- and small-truck tires.

Julio found several sources for non-rubber tires, including wood and textiles. All of the replacement tires worked to some degree, but they produced rough rides because they did not have the air cushion of pneumatics, which absorb irregularities in the road surface. Wood tires, which had a welded metal band around the tread surface, created a rugged, hard tire that produced a jaw-breaking ride of jolts and jerks sufficient to bounce drivers off of their car's ceilings. Plus, the substitute tires had limited lives. New pneumatic tires lasted fifteen thousand miles. Retreads were done in half the distance. Wood or textile tires wore even faster, a couple of thousand miles at best. These were not good solutions, but rationing was the only way for the country to support the war and continue to operate their civilian lives normally. Super Service Station was one of the first in town to offer these innovative products. The brothers worked to stay ahead of the competition.

As time passed America's efforts raged on two global fronts and more shortages developed. This time with food. Rationing was mandated on sugar, coffee and meat. Restaurants felt the blow as supplies for their most profitable dishes dwindled. Many recipes were altered for less sugar and butter. Coffee was brewed with fewer grinds, leading to cups full of tan-colored water that only hinted at coffee. At the Mint, Modesto Dalle and his wife, Pia, continually battled shortages while trying to maintain profitability.

Modesto was peeved at the price gouging among some of his competitors. When military men came through Albuquerque on liberty, they often flocked downtown to swill beer and wine. Some vendors deliberately doubled beer prices to grab a quick profit. Modesto, a man of principle, was livid and advertised special prices for military men. He sold his beer at his regular price, but it seemed cheap relative to the others. He reckoned that military men were fighting for our freedom, and it was a crime against America to treat them with anything but respect. During the war he offered dinner and lunch specials to military men, including a free glass of beer with a full meal. The Mint remained profitable throughout the war. Modesto did not serve in World War I because he had not yet immigrated and was deferred for World War II due to age and family.

VICTORY WITH LETTUCE

From early in the war, the government was concerned about food shortages. They encouraged citizens to grow as much food as possible in their yards. "Victory Garden" was the catchphrase and many people obliged. Roosevelt believed that home gardening would somewhat compensate for the shortages created by the war. Victory gardening had a dual purpose: Produce additional food to offset shortages and boost morale. It gave every American a sense of contributing to the war effort, whether or not they were involved in the military. At that time, a deep sense of patriotism had enveloped the country and most people, even some pacifists and conscientious objectors, participated.

The Menicuccis, experienced farmers, grew gardens in just about all the available space in their yards, front and back. Amerigo grew lettuce between the tire paths along his dirt driveway, allowing cars to pass over them. Their gardens were much larger than in pre-war days. Both families had always raised rabbits and chickens but these animals took on greater importance as meat rationing took hold. The families increased the number of animals and trained the girls to provide care for them while the men were off to war. Still, the families' diets became increasingly vegetarian as the war progressed and meat became scarce. Similarly, women replaced men in factories and manufacturing plants, doing traditional men's work. Giulia was mostly unmoved by all the events, expressing little emotion except to repeat one of her favorite phrases in life, one she often repeated to characterize events that were out of her control: "Cosa sai fare," meaning in the slang vernacular, "Whatta you gonna do." Her approach was to leave the situation to those in charge and hope that the Lord guides them to proper decisions.

America had no professional army; the citizens became the Army through the draft. In contrast to America's modern military, where professional soldiers can fight wars with virtually no disruption to the civilian populace, World War II involved everyone. There was hardly a single person in the nation who was not affected in some way by the war. It bound the country toward a common goal to preserve American freedom and its way of life. Most people saw a global threat so potent that only a concerted national effort could defeat it. By the end of the war, America was united philosophically and purposefully like no other time since the revolution.

ITALIAN ENEMY ALIENS

The attack on Pearl Harbor led to an immediate declaration of war with Japan. Germany and Italy, at that time Axis members, declared war on the U.S. These declarations automatically enacted the 1798 Alien Enemies Act that declared any person in the United States who was a native of an enemy state automatically became an enemy alien and was subject to internment or deportation. The law was part of a series of alien and sedition acts that were enforced when U.S. was grappling with France in the 18th Century. The country feared that if war ensued, French nationals would turn against America and create an internal threat. All acts had been repealed except the Alien Enemies Act, which prevailed in 1941. The law technically applied to Italian World War I veterans, such as the Menicucci brothers and Johnny Matteucci. Under the self-enacting law, Italians or Germans were not allowed to own guns, and the Albuquerque police raided some Italian homes. My maternal grandfather, Modesto Dalle, was one of them. Pia Barsanti Dalle, told the story of the police raid on their home: "A bunch of police showed up at home in January of 1942 and searched our home. Nonno (her husband Modesto) was working. They didn't find anything except they took our radio. Nonno was mad because he was an American citizen. And so was I. Later they gave the radio back."

The federal law was quickly amended but even before the formal changes, local officials directed police to stop inspecting U.S. Army veteran homes. Few other Albuquerque Italians experienced any similar injustice, although a number of unnaturalized aliens were deported, especially ones with criminal records. The German Americans, too, were spared the harassment, but Japanese Americans did not fare as well. Anger towards the Japanese—which spanned from the youngest of children to President Roosevelt--eviscerated any considerations of leniency and many naturalized Japanese Americans were illegally tossed in intern camps.[2]

FIRST ONE BACK

Dante's return in 1942 brought joy to the family. He took a position at Super Oil Company but helped out at Super Service Station when needed. His presence did not obviate the labor problems. Both businesses had lost men to the war and sales were off. They were rationing gas and rubber, their main products and the rules were in constant flux, with new diktats coming from Washington almost on a weekly basis. Fortunately, kerosene was not rationed and it was one of Super Oil's major products. In Albuquerque and surrounding areas, many people used it for heating, lighting and cooking. As gas sales flagged, kerosene sales continued to grow and quickly became the major profit generator. Julio put Dante, a young twenty-year-old, in charge of kerosene sales and built for him a one-hundred-square-foot office located under the large overhead gas and kerosene tanks in the middle of Super Oil's property on First Street. It was an unheated shack with a door and window and no phone. But it was Dante's office and he had his task, which he attacked with vigor.

Dante immediately began a sales campaign, traveling to outlying areas of the city to solicit more customers, mostly for kerosene. As new customers came on board, the profits buoyed the finances of both companies. Julio split his time between Super Oil and Super Service, directing activities for both from his position as CEO of the family enterprises. Most of his efforts targeted his wholesale service station customers, whom he had contracted to supply fuel. Julio's main concern was finding gasoline. A black market for gasoline developed organically and was constantly a temptation, but Julio demurred because of the family's commitment to quality products. However, he prioritized his customers—Super Service Station first, then his Italian retailers, such as the Franchinis and then others. He ensured that Super Service always had sufficient gas to sell. In the meme of blood being thicker than water, he and Amerigo held a little fuel in reserve to sneak into the tanks of family members for emergencies. Of course, those transfers were done on the sly, usually at Super Oil, out of sight of other customers. It was not an uncommon practice in Albuquerque.

Amerigo struggled with Super Service. Gasoline profits were anemic. New tire sales dropped to nearly zero as only institutional customers could buy them. But even those sales dimmed as the war raged. They stocked new and different tire products, of which they had no experience. Johnny Matteucci managed the tire sales while Amerigo sought suppliers and dealt with customer needs. Labor was a continual problem. They were reluctant to hire men of draft age because they could disappear anytime. They sought out young men who had returned from the war or had been rejected for service, such as Dante. They were in short supply.

Julio and Amerigo decided to concentrate on service, assuming that people would repair their vehicles rather than purchase new ones. They ramped up tire repair work. Over time, the tire repair business led the way as people sought to extend the life of their tires. Johnny stayed busy full-time managing tire repairs, including retreads. Within a year, the Menicuccis had absorbed the blows to their business, stabilized their product lines and enhanced service to meet the current war climate. While many other businesses failed, the Menicuccis continued to march forward. Perhaps not with the vigor of a few years earlier, of course, but certainly a fine outcome in the stifling business environment of World War II.

A SOAPBOX ON CENTRAL

Julio and Amerigo were both patriotic and loyal Americans and they supported the war effort, but Julio was the most aggressive in bringing his patriotism to the fore. He led an effort at the Colombo to solicit men to sell war bonds. For several years, he headed the Colombo's War Bond Committee, which consisted of about a dozen men, all business owners. They each solicited bonds in their own ways.

Julio's way was in the middle of the busiest intersection in the state. Julio stood on a wooden box in the middle of the Fourth Street and Central Avenue intersection every workday at noon with an American flag in his hat. He clutched the paperwork needed to buy war bonds. Akin to an auctioneer, when he spied someone he knew, particularly if they were wealthy, he shouted out a public challenge to buy the bonds, e.g., "Hey Bachechi, get over here and buy some bonds to support our boys." He similarly yelled and pointed at drivers as they passed by. Many stopped, turned around and bought bonds. The Albuquerque police ignored the several ordinances Julio violated that prohibited people from interfering with traffic and peddling on a public street. From the mayor down to the cop on the street, Julio was free to sell at will. He did. As the war wound raged on, the Colombo recognized him twice as a top salesman; his bond sales equaled that total collected by the remainder of his team. As the war drew down, the governor recognized Julio's efforts with a letter of commendation.

Albuquerque's downtown at noon in 1940s. This view is looking north on Second Street from its intersection with Central Avenue. Forth and Center was even more congested. Courtesy Albuquerque Museum, a gift of Albuquerque National Bank.

FEAR SETS IN

The threat of a Japanese attack on the mainland terrified every citizen west of the Mississippi. Everyone had all been looking east, especially the Italians. The attack came from the west. And from a country that many thought was controllable. In the space of a day, those visions were ejected from the minds of sane people. Proximity mattered. The Italians knew better than most that the East Coast was a lot farther from them than the West Coast. There is a lot of distance between Albuquerque and the Germans in France. But the Japanese had been as close as Hawaii and California could be next. Many feared that the US Naval fleet had been so damaged at Pearl Harbor that it could not defend the West Coast. Now, suddenly, a formidable enemy appeared to be close. Many Italians, including the Menicuccis, had relatives in California, so the enemy was even closer for those families.

Ignorance added to the terror level. Most Albuquerqueans knew nothing of the Orient. The names were foreign and difficult to pronounce. The people looked different from Europeans. And their military power, which most Americans had dismissed as second rate, had just decimated what most thought was a mighty American Pacific Naval fleet. For the first time since they had arrived in America, a deep-seated dread fell upon the Italians, similar to what their families had frequently experienced in Italy. It quashed their belief that America's physical isolation from both Europe and the Orient was protection.

The Menicucci brothers were the first to grasp the severity of the situation. They were military veterans. They could see a weakness on the West Coast, especially with the U.S. Pacific fleet in tatters. Their jobs were to protect their families and this was a call to action. To the women, there was fear but deep faith. There was the Madonna, of course. But going directly and politely to the Lord was also in favor. Their first thoughts were how to protect their children, especially in a physical attack. Interpreting all of this for the children was challenging. There is a fine line between informing and alarming. They knew only one thing: the Lord guided them and prayer induced courage.

The children were initially shocked and felt nothing. They could not understand the situation. Over days, depending on age, they grasped the palpable trepidation in Albuquerque. Emma Dalle Menicucci (my mother) told the story: "I was only ten, but I understood how serious it was. All of us worried every hour of every day about invasion."

In the last years of the 1930s, the local Albuquerque papers concentrated their reports on the European war, but Pearl Harbor changed that. Suddenly, both Western and Eastern theaters of war were equally represented in the news. The Albuquerque papers and radio stations provided ringside seats to the action. But the action was not pretty. The Hawaii disaster was followed by one setback after another. The local newscasters, of course, sensing public angst, accentuated any US gains and placed the best spin on the losses. But no amount of journalistic equivocation could disguise the licking Japanese were putting on the Allied forces in the Pacific. Double-line, two-inch letter headlines regularly belched out news of American setbacks. There were many and they were grim. On

December 8, 1941, Guam was taken by the Japanese. Simultaneously, Wake Island fell. In January, Japan captured Tarakan, which gave them a source of oil that was critical for their armed forces. In January 1942, Malaya capitulated, with British and American forces routed. Now in wait for the Japanese was the Philippines, an American territory. Confidence was high that the U.S. military, composed of many New Mexicans, would rebut the Japanese invasion from the north. Emma Dalle Menicucci said, "Every day there was bad news. Everyone was sad and worried all the time."

LOS ANGELES UNDER ATTACK

On the morning of February 25, 1942, the locals were traumatized again as the *Albuquerque Journal* screeched headlines that guns in Los Angeles had fired on "unidentified aircraft" off the West Coast. The story implied that it could have been Japanese planes. It was more or less true because there were objects in the air. Not Japanese planes, though. It was likely the American weather balloons launched from a nearby weather station. An Army Airfield apparently fired on the invaders, but the only thing that survived the incident was the story itself, no evidence. Nonetheless, the media frenzy was monumental for its day. People were on edge. Information was chaotic and confounding. In Twenty-First Century vernacular, it went viral with a vengeance. News of the false attack reached the New York papers before officials refuted it. It imbued a kind of terror upon the people that does not easily fade. This was especially true with children with limited perspectives.

The Albuquerque Tribune

HOME EDITION

PRICE THREE CENTS

MYSTERY PLANES ON WEST COAST

Three U-Boats Sunk, Knox Reports

ANTI-AIRCRAFT BATTERIES FIRE; ORDER BLACKOUT

FOUR DAMAGED BY NAVY SHIPS IN 56 ATTACKS

Found Guilty By U. S. Jury

30 JAP PLANES ARE BAGGED BY ALLIED FLIERS

FIRST PICTURE OF U. S. FORCES IN TRINIDAD

Police Report Seeing Unidentified Fliers as Far Inland as Los Angeles Suburb

REDS CELEBRATE WIN IN STARAYA

Bataan Battle Appears Stalemated As Japs Delay Move to Crack Lines

U.S. Closes Viereck Case

FIND NAZI CLUE IN PAPEN CASE

President Asks Defeat Of Farm Price Measure

DEFENSE MEET TO BE CALLED

Sold Books To Germans

NOTED FLIER HERE

Albuquerque Air Base Pilots Heroes In Great Air-Sea Battle Near Java

Snow Predicted For Albuquerque

PVT. BECK IS SAFE

Theater Aids Milk Fund Here

ZOO GET CERTIFICATES

Wake Up Americans!

CONGRATULATIONS

Clipping from the *Albuquerque Journal*, **February 25, 1942**

Shocking morning news became a staple, like Albuquerque's dusty afternoon spring winds. On March 11, 1942, MacArthur was reported slinking out of the Philippines in the dead of night to avoid capture. He left Wainwright in charge of the flagging American forces. As the Americans and Filipino allies retreated south from Luzon into Bataan, the city residents were shocked again on April 9, 1942, with the *Albuquerque Journal*'s massive headline: "Enemy Overwhelms Bataan." For days, the stories and sidebars poured out a plethora of horrific news of thousands of Americans taken prisoner by the Japanese Army. The information was sketchy, but dozens of Albuquerque men were directly involved via the National Guard and were deployed in the Philippines.

The fear of a West Coast invasion was so visceral that the government instituted civil defense drills, including blackouts. Night bombing raids required bomber pilots with relatively primitive navigation equipment to visually identify terrestrial features for targeting the bombs. In the dark of night, a city is a large, illuminated area that makes a good marker and an excellent target. Blackouts were an effective defense against nighttime marauders. The periodic blackouts in Albuquerque unnerved the public, but all knew it was necessary, which the Los Angeles scare punctuated. Officials measured the effectiveness of blackouts with overflights that recorded the degree of "blackness" the community had achieved. Wailing air raid sirens accompanied the blackouts, providing a wartime feeling. The federal government randomly scheduled tests for various communities, each lasting a few hours.

The Menicuccis ordered everyone to bed on the blackout dates. They thought it was best to sleep through them, especially for the children, who had already been sufficiently agitated and were constantly fearful. Besides, they got sufficient practice at schools when the city's air raid sirens wailed periodically, sending students scurrying to basements and safe houses. These drills created high anxiety levels in people as they sat in silence in their shelters imagining the sound of enemy aircraft approaching.

It was not until May of 1942, at the battle of Coral Sea, that the appalling litany of American military failures finally ended. The U.S. Navy repulsed a Japanese attempt to claim a base of operations from which they could attack Australia. The battle was essentially a draw, with both sides claiming victory, although losses were substantial to both. However, it was the first battle of the war where the Navy prevented the enemy from achieving a strategic objective. Given the string of losses over the previous month, a draw was a welcomed outcome.

At the outset of the war as the Americans mobilized men, national industrial production dipped due to the loss of laborers who were being drafted. Later, as the country adjusted, including the addition of women to the national factories, output soared, producing materiel and munitions for the allies. Much of the manufacturing success was due to the women who stepped up to do heavy manufacturing. Rosie the Riveter became a well-worn symbol that appeared on billboards throughout the country. By the spring of 1943, the Americans were outproducing the Japanese by a factor of three to one. At the same time, it was producing a major share of the war materiel for the Allies in the European theater. The Americans could produce more and better products than the enemies and do it faster than any other country. America's unique government, one based on freedom, capitalism and meritocracy, governed businesses throughout the country and spurred efficiency and technological innovation. This philosophical precept was a societal staple.

AMERICAN MAGIC

Magic was a critical facet of American success in the Pacific. Military code cryptanalysts had successfully broken many of the Japanese communication codes, providing the American commanders with inside information about Japanese plans. Called Magic, it produced a continual stream of intelligence that proved pivotal in many battles. Magic Reports supplied intelligence about Japanese plans in the Coral Sea, which led to the American's successful stalemate in that battle. But the best was yet to come.

Magic's influence proved its real worth as the Americans picked up reports about Midway Island. Located about halfway between California and Asia, the island would provide the Japanese with a strategic base of operations for attacking Hawaii and the mainland U.S. Magic operators learned that Japan planned to attack the island. Midway was a good strategic goal for the Japanese and a way for Admiral Isoroku Yamamoto, the Japanese fleet commander, to repay the Americans for the Doolittle raid, an embarrassment to the military establishment.

Nimitz positioned his carriers away from the island, giving the appearance that they were unaware of the planned operation. On June 7, 1942, the Japanese carriers began their attack on Midway's military base and its airfield. Over an hour, the Japanese fleet launched all of its planes, hoping for success similar to Pearl Harbor. They did so with confidence that the Americans were no-shows to the battle because of the damage they had sustained at Pearl Harbor. It was Yamamoto's biggest judgmental error. After the attack on Midway was underway, the U.S. carriers moved in and attacked the Japanese carriers and destroyers that floated naked on the seas with no air cover. It was like shooting fish in a rain barrel, with the

Americans raining bombs and torpedoes on the Japanese. The American Navy sank four aircraft carriers, and since the carriers' planes were in the air when the attack started, those planes had nowhere to land. Many ran out of fuel and crashed. American Navy fighters engaged others as they attempted to return to their ships without ammunition. All they could do was fly wildly and die as the Americans thumped the helpless Japanese pilots into the sea. It was the largest Japanese debacle of the war. Magic, which was never known to the Japanese, was one of the most significant and underappreciated factors that led to the ultimate American victory.

The Americans, meanwhile, had their own secret code—the Navajo language, which consisted of American Indians speaking in their native tongue. It baffled the Japanese code breakers because the Navajo language was spoken but not written, so the Japanese had no documents from which to work. The language's construct was unique in the linguistic world. Called the Code Talkers, these Americans—all US Marines—provided secure communications for every significant campaign in the Pacific throughout the rest of the war. The Japanese never broke the Navajo code. It and the American Magic provided secure communications and intelligence throughout the war. The prowess of America's racial diversity was proven.[3]

News of Midway thundered off the Albuquerque presses. "The US Smashes Jap Invasion Fleet in Great Naval Victory" blasted the *Journal* headlines the next morning. People were gleeful, neighbors called each other to discuss the news, the Italian men talked of victory at the Colombo, and the mood brightened as the citizenry sensed that the tide might be turning on a bleak first half of the year. One battle won does not make a war victory. On June 13, 1942, the Japanese attacked Dutch Harbor, Alaska, as part of their campaign to divert American attention from the South Pacific to the North. They took Attu and Kiska Islands and established bases of operation. The attack jolted the citizenry back into the reality of a war that had a long way to go. The Japanese were not defeated and the threat to the U.S. Mainland remained intact. It was not until March 1943, in the battle of the Komandorski Islands, that the Yankees finally ran off the Japanese invaders and reclaimed full control of the islands. The Japanese never again threatened American territories but they were not through menacing the eastern Pacific.[4]

ALBUQUERQUE JOURNAL

62nd Year   Published Every Morning   Monday Morning, June 8, 1942   Price Five Cents

Bulk of Japanese Seapower' Foiled at Midway, Says U.S. Fleet Chief; May Decide War's Course

Fight in North Pacific, Off Alaska, Continues, With Reports 'Obscure'

Clipping from the *Albuquerque Journal*, June 8, 1942.

The women's main job on the home front was to manage mental and physical health. Giulia and Davina, both intensely religious, insisted on nearly constant prayer, with Sundays highlighting their efforts. Sunday Mass was essential and all were expected to attend. Prayers at the kitchen table were typical, with long pronouncements and pleas to the Lord to ensure their boys' safety and the country's success. They dealt with the rationing of sugar, meat, butter and other staples, challenging them to adjust their recipes. Davina, an excellent cook who was trained by professional chefs in Italy, had little trouble making the changes. Giulia struggled but eventually adjusted to the war economy. Grapes were not rationed, so families continued to ferment wine. Unfortunately, fuel shortages curtailed mushroom foraging, so stocks of dried Porcini mushrooms hanging in the Italians' basements dwindled as they imposed their own rationing to extend their supplies. The men, who were used to supplying at least some of the families' food from bird hunting, were restricted and their production fell dramatically, straining the women to adjust. The women performed their jobs to maintain the health and vigor of a family, a strictly local issue. They expected the men to do their jobs to maintain security and adequate resources. But the women were every bit as eager to help the war effort as the men. They had their chance in 1943.

CAMP ALBUQUERQUE

On October 15, 1943, 165 Italian POWs were transferred to the old Civilian Conservation Corps (CCC) barracks at Iron and Fourteenth Streets, SW, near Rio Grande Park. Shortly after that, small groups of men in prison garb reportedly worked on farms around the city. Others were seen working on the irrigation ditches and laterals that are the backbone of the ancient Acequias Rio Grande water distribution system for farmers. Italian prisoners were deployed in small groups of men, all in bright prison garb and heavily guarded by armed soldiers. Albuquerque was one of dozens of cities housing POWs who worked in local farms. The city participated in one of Roosevelt's programs to alleviate overcrowding in Britain's POW camps. The POW problem originated when the American Armies joined the fight in Europe. The Americans quickly turned the direction of the war and, along with the British, took prisoners in increasing numbers. By default, POWs were housed in Britain. Churchill asked Roosevelt to share the responsibility of housing enemy POWs in America.

While the POW problem mushroomed in Britain, a labor crisis was developing in America's agricultural sector. As the draft drained young men from communities, farmers were affected disproportionally more than other industrial groups. Farmers ran high-risk, low-margin, labor-intensive operations. Draft boards minimized the impact on the agricultural sector by deferring farmers and farm workers but inevitably, many were called. For months in 1942, elected officials in Washington heard dire forecasts of gloom from farmers throughout the nation. Food would be left in the fields to rot, op-ed columnists and local politicians cried. The clammer increased steadily as more men were drafted and labor pools shrank. What especially flustered the administration was the U.S. Department of Agriculture's own assessments that labor shortages actually were affecting harvests. With food rationing riling plenty of voters, the vision of food rotting fields was a political nightmare for the administration.

The solution was obvious. History exudes examples of waring nations using each other's POWs to supplement domestic labor, so why not America? Roosevelt issued an executive order to develop POW camps throughout the country and distribute German and Italian POWs throughout. It was a two-run homer. First, he could show Churchill that he was addressing the POW problem. Second, he could address the domestic labor shortage, especially for farmers.

Security is a serious problem when using enemy war combatants in the civilian population of the opposing nation. Escapees could be dangerous, seeking revenge against Americans. Or, they might act as spies for their home countries. These are all valid concerns, but the crops needed harvesting. Over the winter and into the spring the men worked farms around Albuquerque, serving one farmer after another to complete specific tasks. Later, German POWs were reported working in Bernalillo.

Throughout the winter of 1943 and into the spring of 1944, the Italian POWs labored in the local farming communities for eighty cents per day (about fourteen dollars in 2024 dollars). The local Italians in the colony knew of the POWs, but since Italy remained an enemy warring nation, the Italian POWs were barred from interacting with any of the local populace. Outside some spontaneous interactions among a few locals with the working men, the POWs were isolated from the city.

INSTANT ALLIES

In 1944, an event in Italy perpetrated a change in the status and size of Albuquerque's POWs. A group of citizens ambushed and killed Mussolini, hanging his dead body upside down in a public square. Then

Italy declared war on Germany. While Albuquerque's German POWs remained combatants, the Italians were now instant allies.

Initially, the Army maintained restrictions at the camp, but over weeks new rules evolved that allowed small groups of Italian POWs who met certain standards for behavior to work in the community unsupervised. As word leaked about the new freedoms, more of the local Italians interacted with the men as they walked to and from their job assignments. Many of the local Italian women baked Italian desserts and other ethnic favorites; their husbands delivered the food to the men in the fields.

As the POW population grew nationally, Albuquerque's German POW population was slated to grow commensurately. Apparently, local farmers had requested the Germans because of their supposed farming expertise. Thus, around April of 1944, the Army ordered seventy-five German POWs to Albuquerque to assist in farming operations. When some of the local Italians heard of the decision, they exploded with outrage. Bachechis, Gradis, Giomis, Franchinis, Matteuccis and other politically influential people contacted political representatives to set them straight. Italians are natural farmers, they explained. They were farmers. Their fathers and grandfathers were farmers. They knew about farming. It was the *Italians* who were expert farmers, they said. Besides, they argued that the Italian POWs would have plenty of support from the local Italian American community, especially women. The decision was rescinded, and seventy-five Italian POWs were consolidated with the existing one hundred and sixty-five and transferred to a new facility dubbed Camp Albuquerque. It was located in an open tract in the south valley about three miles south of the CCC barracks between Second Street and the Rio Grande River.

The news was cheered by local Italian men and women alike. For women, these POWs were the closest connection to the old country they had had in years. They thought the men might supply news about Italy. During the war, communications between the Italians and Allied nations essentially collapsed, isolating Albuquerque's Italian colony from their families in Italy. Moreover, it was an opportunity to welcome young men in an Italian style, comfort them, and even introduce some to their available daughters. Most of all, they wanted the POWs to have proper Italian meals. They presumed the men were not properly fed because Italians were not doing their cooking.

Businessmen, especially farmers, fully appreciated the benefits of additional labor in the community. Super Service and Super Oil had serious labor issues. While the Italian POWs targeted the farming community, Menicuccis knew that any labor improvement in one area helped others. Throughout 1944 and until the war concluded in the summer of 1945, local Italian women baked regularly for the POWs, especially mindful of special events favored by the Italians, such as holy days venerating the Virgin Mary. Local men often brought gifts, tobacco, and even wine and grappa, which had to be smuggled to the POWs. At least one local couple met and married due to their altruistic efforts at Camp Albuquerque. Fannie Sai and her future husband, Beppe Corradini, were frequent visitors to the Camp. Both were in their twenties and they often coordinated their visits to the camp. Over time their friendship became a courtship. Beppe was a naturalized citizen and they married just before he was conscripted into American military service. The couple settled in Albuquerque after the war.[5]

FINISHING THEM OFF

Interest in Europe waned after the United States joined the fight and the war turned in the Allies' favor. Once the Allies, led by American forces, established a beachhead on the European continent in the summer of 1944 and with General George Patton running roughshod over the Axis forces in Italy, the Germans had finally begun to choke on their own excesses and stumbled in retreat to Berlin. The Soviets, officially an ally but harboring disdain for the Western leaders, were marching east to Germany, creating a pincer that spelled the death knell to the German high command. On April 30th, 1945, as the Soviets and Americans closed in on his bunker, Hitler put his Walther PPK 7.35 mm pistol to his temple and pulled the trigger.[6] On May 8th, German General Alfred Jodi signed the country's unconditional surrender to the Allies in Reims, France. The war in Europe was over and American boys returned as American war veterans.

Albuquerque's populace then turned its attention squarely to Japan as America's Allies called for its defeat. Many in Albuquerque's Italian colony were always more focused on the Pacific theater because that was where many of its sons were deployed.[7] The British were first in action, sending a carrier and its fleet of warships to the Pacific to support the Americans. The Soviets rescinded its neutrality agreement with Japan and declared war on it. They moved their troops to the east to engage the Japanese. It was nothing but political symbolism as MacArthur and Nimitz were thrashing the Japanese and needed no additional help. By the time the Brits and Soviets had a chance to assemble and integrate their forces in the area, the Americans had terminated the war with overwhelming military might, including the most potent bomb in human history. The Soviets and British contributed little to the Pacific war effort.

As Americans were liberating islands, they often collected many of the local citizens to fight alongside U.S. troops. The Filipinos' efforts were frequently noted. In general, the Pacific theater was America's war, much more so than Europe where "allies" meant that other nations were meaningfully involved. In fact, it was the Americans who turned the tide in Europe, but the British, French and Poles all contributed mightily to the war effort. Among the allies, Britain was the most courageous, stalemating the mighty German war machine for over a year until the United States came to the rescue.

As 1945 mercifully ended, both Mario and Larry Matteucci returned to their families. They arrived in Albuquerque about the same time, in February 1946. Mario was greeted gleefully by both his family and Julio's. Larry Matteucci returned safely and was similarly greeted. He went to work with his brother Nello, who was stationed in Puerto Rico and had returned. Charlie's reunion, a few months later, was more eventful. He walked up to the home on Third Street and surprised Julio, who was repairing the roof of the family home. Julio was so startled to see Charlie that his circular saw cut off about a half inch of his middle finger on his left hand. The severed finger piece fell to the ground as Charlie rushed to help. Bleeding, Julio scrambled to the ground and directed Charlie to find his finger. They found it and instead of heading to the hospital, Julio put the fingertip back in its place and taped it there. No stitches and no anesthetics; the joy of seeing his son alive masked any pain. Later, both the families celebrated with a huge dinner of traditional Italian favorites, including ample supplies of wine and grappa. The finger was "glued back," as Julio later characterized it, but he added that he was left with a numb, dark-colored, nail-less fingertip on a middle finger that was shorter than the index one.

Julio and Amerigo wore their pride in their boys on their shoulders. The public admired men who had served in a combat theater, especially ones who had actually seen combat. Numerous celebrations occurred around town, including many organized by the Colombo. Their two young sons often wore their Army Air Force uniforms at parties and other events.

The Italian Women's Charity Club hosted talks by returning veterans. Joy and thanksgiving swept through the city like a tsunami.

Unfortunately for Dante, it was a mixture of happiness, despair and embarrassment. He was delighted to rejoin his brother and cousin. But he saw adulations heaped upon them while he had missed the whole thing. As the oldest male, the sight of his younger brother in the spotlight distressed him. The stigma from not participating in the war was a deep-seated, depression-causing angst that plagued him for years. Even though he had been honorably discharged, he was largely ignored during the celebrations with the populace clearly focused on returning warriors. Many still looked askance at those who were medically discharged before seeing action. Nothing had changed relative to his position in the family business; he was destined to become CEO of Super Oil Company, but his military record weighed heavily on him.

OPTIMISM, JULIO STYLE

As the 1940s faded into history, the Menicucci brothers collectively sighed with relief. It was a nasty five years of war that displayed an astonishing waste of sixty million lives, destruction of hundreds of large, vibrant cities and exposed the most grotesque human atrocities in history. The global population had never witnessed such a man-made cataclysm and the application of weapons of unimaginable destructive power. The Americans were left standing as the preeminent power on the globe and it set forth a determined effort to reorganize and stabilize the world order, finally making the world safe for Democracy. At last, people thought Woodrow Wilson's wispy World War I dream was at hand.

The war's end was not a simple defeat for the Axis powers; it was unconditional surrender. Hitler and Mussolini were dead, along with most of Germany's military commanders. Those commanders who escaped death in battle were duly executed after showy trials at Nuremberg. One by one, German Nazis were systematically ejected from the human population. The German nation was poised for reconstruction under George Marshal's master plan to rebuild the newly liberated nations in Western Europe in the model of American democracy and free market economy. In 1948, congress appropriated thirteen billion dollars for the Marshal Plan (about one hundred seventy billion in 2023 dollars.)

In Japan, MacArthur was essentially a dictator, reconfiguring the battered nation into a Western-style economy and a democratic political structure. Immediately following Japan's capitulation, the United States initiated a two-billion-dollar (about twenty-eight billion in 2024 dollars) campaign to provide essential commodities to the Japanese people. MacArthur believed that the first step to recovery was to engender healthy people to work on rebuilding their own country. Simultaneously, he conducted a series of trials to rid the country of the military leaders who had prosecuted the war. The government was reconstructed in the American model with a new constitution that improved women's status, expanded civil rights, fostered capitalism and encouraged individual productivity. It radically reconfigured or replaced long-held economic and business practices incompatible with the American economic model. The master plan to rebuild Japan incorporated many of the principles advocated by Niccolo Machiavelli in his guidance to his prince in 1512 about how to seize and hold power in a conquered nation. It worked. By the end of the decade, Japan had risen from the ashes of its self-made immolation and was operating, more or less, like a free-market, capitalistic society, which historically is the most effective means to achieve organic economic growth.[8]

In San Francisco in April 1945, the Americans sponsored a meeting of the world's countries to discuss the creation of a United Nations, an international body tasked with maintaining peace and order worldwide. By June, the group adopted an operational charter and by October, it held its first meeting at its world headquarters in New York City. Just as in World War I, the U.S. had intervened to preserve world order and to eclipse the specter of totalitarianism. This time, it seemed different. There was widespread optimism that American leadership had finally forged a lasting world peace.[9]

These events were faithfully reported to Albuquerqueans by its two papers. Citizens were ecstatic with the results. They had every right to be gratified as the victory was a true national accomplishment shared by all citizens. Importantly to the Menicuccis, their sons served proudly in the defense of the country they passionately cherished. Their businesses had not only survived but had grown during the war years. Their families were healthy, and the oldest son of each family was positioned to begin their apprenticeship and assume the reins of the two businesses. It fits perfectly into the Italian social model where birth date automatically infers privileges to the oldest male, who has implied the first right to refuse family business leadership. It was how it was in Italy for centuries. It was just as Julio had master-planned twenty-five years earlier when the two families arrived in the city. Amerigo was equally confident in the economic outlook but with less ethereal aspirations. He desired steady retail growth unencumbered with governmental intrusion or constraints.

DREAMING A FUTURE

Julio, emboldened with optimism and vigor, envisioned unlimited monetary and social growth for the families. As in Italy, societal growth usually occurs when young men of lower status marry women from more prominent families. He and Amerigo had both stepped up societally when their newfound wealth from American jobs allowed them to court and marry women of higher status. Both he and Amerigo were on the lookout for potential brides for their two oldest boys.

He also envisioned major expansions for the two businesses, including adding new fuel choices from Super Oil and expanding service at Super Service Station. Charlie, Julio's second son, was not slated for upper management but was tasked to expand the repair service at Super Service. He was an Army veteran with combat experience and expertly trained in electronics, perfect preparation to build a repair business for new vehicles with ever more complex electronic and mechanical functions. To foster the idea of family-owned and operated businesses, women performed clerical work, as they were considered too physically weak to perform heavy work, such as that at Super Oil Company.

Gloom was vanquished, and Julio was like a racehorse champing at the bit to bolt from the starting gate. In his mind's eye he saw fame, money and glory for the family and he believed he had the team to do it. He could not see the storm clouds hovering just out of sight over the horizon, which would test the man like never before.

See note 10.

Notes

1. During WWII, the *Office of Price Administration* regularly published specific updates on the rationing program.
2. *Robinson* discusses the internment of immigrants during the war.

Although the focus of his work is on Japanese Americans, he also discusses the internment of German and Italian Americans.

3. *Lewis (Ronald)* tells the story of the Magic reports. *McClain* discusses the Navajo code talkers.

4. The Battle of Midway is fully described by *Prange*. The victory was so extensive that it essentially decided the war's eventual outcome by destroying so much of the Japanese Pacific fleet. The victory is often referred to as a miracle due to its improbability, which led to the belief that Americans were in some way divinely endowed during the war. Americans, of course, were the keys to victory in both world wars but whether a deity guided their actions continues to be debated today.

5. This story is based on accounts from Theresa Domenici Menicucci, newspaper reports and the work of *Doyle*.

6. There remains debate about the exact disposition of Hitler, with some arguing that he fled to South America. The official reports are that he shot himself to death.

7. The United States Army had learned from WWI how to deal with an ethnically diverse populace during war. The main concern was to prevent an American from combatting an enemy with the same ethnicity. Thus, Italian and German Americans were often deployed in the Pacific theater.

8. *Machiavelli's* descriptions of the techniques to hold and rule seized territories have been debated for centuries because of their callousness and crudity, but they are effective. He has become both infamous and famous for his work.

9. *Jeansonne* discusses the changes in America between the two world wars. *Chavez* presents her account of living through WWII in Albuquerque.

10. Stories in the *Albuquerque Journal* were important sources of information for this chapter.

18

TRANSITIONAL YEARS
(1945–1951)

FIRST GENERATION TAKES HOLD

At the dawn of the Twentieth Century, as their children became adults, Julio and Amerigo agreed it was time to promote their two company CEOs in waiting. Mario, the oldest son of Amerigo, and Dante, the oldest son of Julio, were both in line with Italian customs. Both worked at Super Service and Super Oil for several years after the war.

Julio was fifty-seven and Amerigo fifty-five and they looked to the future and took stock. Julio correctly read the industry trends and believed that the automobile market would grow rapidly and both family businesses could grow right along. Both brothers agreed that their principal product was service. It was in their business names and in their blood. As it was among many of the Italians, service was a key differentiating feature from the competition. They also decided to continue to honor their business name and provide a full range of automobile services and fuels. As a result of the war, new technology was appearing in every new automobile model parked in dealer lots. Super Service provided repairs, meaning that their mechanics and service staff needed to be competent. They needed a good serviceman to remain abreast of the technical trends commensurate with super service.

Wholesaling was different. At a retail outlet such as Super Service, the customers come to purchase products. In wholesale, such as Super Oil, the product is delivered to the customer. A wholesaler operates in a different environment based on fewer but much larger business-to-business level transactions. In the case of Super Oil, their customers were service stations, which provided the fuel for retail sales. Costs and prices are critical issues in the business, which is driven by bulk fuel purchases. Suppliers, the large oil refiners, delivered bulks of many thousands of gallons of fuel to each wholesaler, such as Super Oil. The wholesaler stores the products on-site, assuming responsibility for safety, logistics and security. Heavy machinery was needed to manage the storage facility and safely deliver large loads of various fuel to customers as far as seventy miles away. Purchasing bulk loads of gasoline from rail cars had its own hazards, including fire. More importantly, a bulk sale carries a bulk financial risk. Since so much fuel is traded in every transaction, a small error up front propagates to the bottom lines. Wholesaling had a greater profit potential than retailing.

An important part of the Super Oil CEO's job was managing the physical facilities, which involved considerable plumbing, large concrete structures, steel tanks, two-inch hoses, three-axil trucks, tractors and other equipment. There were storage tanks that Julio had put in the field a decade earlier that needed constant maintenance. The job demanded mechanical and construction expertise as much as bookkeeping and marketing acumen. Dante had the perfect temperament and skills for the job. He had studied business with Mario before the war and studied more after he was medically discharged. Dante gathered mechanical experience in his first job assignment with the Army Engineers. By the end of the 1940s, he had been working at Super Oil for five years and had learned much of the physical aspects of the business. He was a large, muscular man, standing about six feet two inches tall and around two hundred twenty pounds, similar in build to Amerigo. He had apparently inherited Julio's technical and business aptitude as he was equally at ease with punching an adding machine in his tiny office as he was manhandling a couple of thirty-six-inch pipe wrenches wrapped around a two-inch pipe.

Similarly, Mario had been working at the station for several years and like Amerigo, was blossoming into a notable salesman. He delivered state-of-the-art organizational skills that he had learned in the Army. What is more, his natural demeanor was friendly and welcoming, perfect for retail service. But there was more to the business than shaking hands and counting money. There was inventory, customer relations, costs, labor, regulations, safety, taxes, competition, business planning and many other facets of the job that could not be learned in college or the Army. Amerigo became a tutor.

Julio and Amerigo, of course, were old veterans of the gas and oil trades. They knew their respective businesses and exactly what their boys should know and in what sequence. The brothers understood that book learning and aptitudes do not ensure competence. They placed Dante and Mario, both twenty-eight, into executive on-the-job training programs. The boys had been groomed from birth for their jobs and now was delivery day.

Julio was insistent that both boys learn all facets of the businesses before they manage them. That is why both Mario and Dante started at the lowest levels when they returned from military service. For Mario, it meant serving customers by pumping gas and cleaning windshields. He quickly advanced to the wash rack, detailing vehicles and then to grease and oil vehicles. Once he had mastered the physical trades, Amerigo moved Mario to the front office to learn the business, starting by keeping the books. Many years later, Amerigo once told me his prideful story of when he first noticed that Mario had developed significant prowess as a tire salesman. Pointing to a rack of tires at Super Service, he said, "Every time I looked up there, more tires were gone…," then pointing to the tire lane said, "They were going on a car." Moving the product generates profits that directly benefit the family. Mario's personable and professional manner, traits he was learning from his father, precisely fit the Super Service bill.

The repair work was considered a separate and special area, one conducted by technical experts. Therefore, Amerigo absolved Mario from having to learn that particular specialty. Amerigo completely trusted his nephew, Carlino, as Charlie was affectionately called, to handle repairs. Like him, they were both Army veterans, and he was confident that Charlie knew about his technical business.

Dante traveled a similar path, initiating his apprenticeship as an axle-grease delivery boy after the war, but he progressed to larger trucks and managed rail deliveries by the end of the decade. Super Oil was growing rapidly, producing one physical challenge after another to accommodate on-site product storage. He managed various construction projects on the premises, performing many technical tasks himself. Both Dante and Mario spent time keeping books for the businesses. Julio believed proper financial management was critical to business profits.

Charlie, two years junior to Dante and Mario, was ideally qualified to manage the auto repair service, which was becoming a critical attribute of Super Service Station's service in a technologically advancing auto industry. American manufacturers had developed a plethora of advanced mechanical and electrical technology for war vehicles. Now much of that technology was integrated into new domestic vehicles. What used to be rather simple vehicles in 1938, modern ones of 1950 were loaded with electrical features such as power brakes and power steering, safety and space lights, radios, cigarette lighters and forced air heating and ventilating systems. Every year, new and different models rolled into the auto dealers' showrooms, each sporting some unique luxury or safety device, all of which increased technical complexity. Auto repair shops struggled to maintain competent repair teams that could stay abreast of technological advances. They could only repair what they understood and manufacturers of various products regularly presented evening seminars, demonstrating and explaining the operations of new systems and their maintenance methods.

To the Super Service management team—Mario and Amerigo—their goal remained as it did when it was founded: to provide a complete line of products and services to maintain the community's motor vehicles. Horace Palladino had headed the repair work from before the war and trained Charlie before he was inducted. He was partially responsible for Charlie's war assignments and rank. Horace did not serve in the war and instead ran Super Service's repair department. Normally, he might have had the inside track on retaining the job after the war. But there was Charlie, Julio's second son. It was more than familial preference.

OVERWHELMING TECHNOLOGY

In 1946, Charlie stunned Horace. The young war veteran, sprouting his uniform festooned with the insignia of advanced technological warfare, was far different from the skinny, silly high-school kid who had departed a few years earlier. Charlie's technical expertise, especially with vehicular electrical systems, coupled with his intensive hands-on field experience, dwarfed Horace's capabilities. Horace spent the war in Albuquerque, where the business goal was survival and few new technological products appeared for repairs in Horace's shop. While Charlie was operating and repairing advanced electronic systems, Horace was stuck in the 1930s. Plus, Charlie was a non-commissioned officer in the war, which meant that he could lead people in performing technical work. Most important—and Horace knew it—Charlie was Julio's son and he had first right of refusal for the job if he were considered worthy. Charlie was more than worthy.

Horace could read the writing on Super Service's walls and in early 1947 he notified Julio and Amerigo that he planned to leave Super Service to build his own business. Julio was relieved when Horace would not compete head-to-head with Super Service Station on mechanical repair work. Horace admitted that Charlie was a powerful young technical buck but he believed his advantage was his knowledge of the local automobile business community. He planned to sell auto parts. He reasoned that he could sell advanced technology products without knowing all the technical details required to repair and maintain them. All he needed was a bookkeeper with some logistical expertise. He stayed on at Super Service working under Charlie while looking for an opportunity to exit. Carburation was the only area of auto repair where Horace's expertise still exceeded Charlie's. A carburetor was a complex mechanical device used in automobiles and airplanes, but Charlie's expertise was in electronics. Charlie learned as much as he could before Horace departed and even afterwards, Horace consulted for Charlie.

Amerigo and Julio saw the value in the split. The Palladino family had long held an equity position in Super Service. Michael Palladino had provided seed capital to help found Super Service Station. Over the years, the Palladino position had dwindled to a few percent. Julio wanted to clear the books.

REORGANIZING

Similarly, the Menicuccis wished to reformulate the partnership relationship with Johnny Matteucci, who was aging, well-worn and retiring in place. He had only one son who was interested in the business. Pete tried working as an apprentice for Charlie, but he had no mechanical or electrical foundations and was disinclined to use tools and instruments. Charlie tried for about a year, but it was a poor fit. Pete moved up front to repair and sell tires but was often found sleeping in the back room. When Amerigo found him slumbering in the corner, he snuck up and pinched his pectoral muscles. Amerigo was a large man with extraordinarily large and strong hands, typical of masons. When Pete bobbed his head awake, there was Amerigo face-to-face. "Vai a lavorare." (Get to work.) Then, Amerigo would report the incident to Johnny. Julio frequently said, "Non ha la voglia" ("He doesn't have the desire"), chalking up the experience as another confirmation that aptitude is important in employee development. Pete fit in better at Southern Union Gas, the local natural gas supplier. That left Johnny alone at Super Service, and he knew that Julio wanted an adjustment in his equity share.

After Pete left, only Johnny remained and did very little work. In fact, Amerigo and Julio both heard complaints about Johnny "being in the way" and "hogging the stove." At that time, Super Service was heated with coal stoves, two of them for a sprawling five thousand square foot building. They left plenty of cold spots. During extremely cold weather, the stoves were coveted spots for men to warm their hands after servicing vehicles outside. Super Service had two indoor bays for Charlie's auto repair work. He had two car hoists, one inside and the other out, capable of raising a car overhead for work on the undercarriage. Much of Charlie's work involved mechanical repairs on the undercarriage, which meant he and his men worked outdoors in all conditions year-round, rain or shine. In winter, he and his men spent long periods in the cold and snow. Thus, Charlie believed that due to their hardships, his team should have priority positions for warming themselves at the stove.

Johnny's view differed. On very cold days, Johnny was a co-owner, so he stood in the ideal spot in front of the best stove in the station. Charlie told the story: "That Johnny. All he does is stand in front of the Franklin (stove) puffing on that damn pipe. We're out there freezing our butts in twenty-five degrees and he makes us go down and get coal. Then he tells us that "it's not that cold." Johnny was unfazed; it was nothing that a few puffs of premium, imported tobacco could not remedy. Julio knew Charlie was right, although he did admonish him for how he complained about one of the family's dearest friends. Johnny placated the situation by agreeing to supply coal to the stove while standing in front of it. Charlie was still irked about it forty years later.

Julio saw the opportunity to clean up the partnership equity split by liquidating the non-productive positions. He bought out Johnny's small position but gave him a sinecure, a kind of honorary employee with some compensation but no duties, save for his agreement to supply coal for the stove. He had not accumulated much money and still had children at home. Most of all, Julio and Amerigo wanted to officially turn all the business shares over to their sons. Ultimately, their goal was for Julio's half of the business to be split among his two boys, Dante and Charlie. Amerigo's half went to Mario. By 1952, the goal was accomplished. Super Oil and Super Service Station were owned free and clear by the Menicucci family.

Albert Nottoli returned from World War II about the same time as the Menicuccis boys. Since he had worked at both Super Oil and Super Service, they were the first places he visited. When Horace heard of Albert's qualifications, he thought he might have the right partner for his business—an auto parts supply house. Albert served as a US Marine Corps Supply Sergeant. A man in that position is not only a fighting Marine but is also responsible for organizing and managing supplies, one of the most important functions in any military force. He is specially trained for the job, which emphasizes organizational efficiency. When Horace fully realized the extent of Albert's new skills, he knew Albert was the perfect partner. Albert had studied accounting and worked as the bookkeeper for both Super Service and Super Oil Company through much of the 1930s and early 1940s. He also served as Julio's helper at Super Oil during those same years. Albert is best characterized as a multi-talented handyman who can keep books. In April 1947, Horace and Albert announced the opening of the Automotive Electric Service at 800 Third Street, NW. Although the company initially offered minor repair services, it quickly evolved into one of the leading auto parts suppliers in the city. Super Service headed their list of preferred customers.

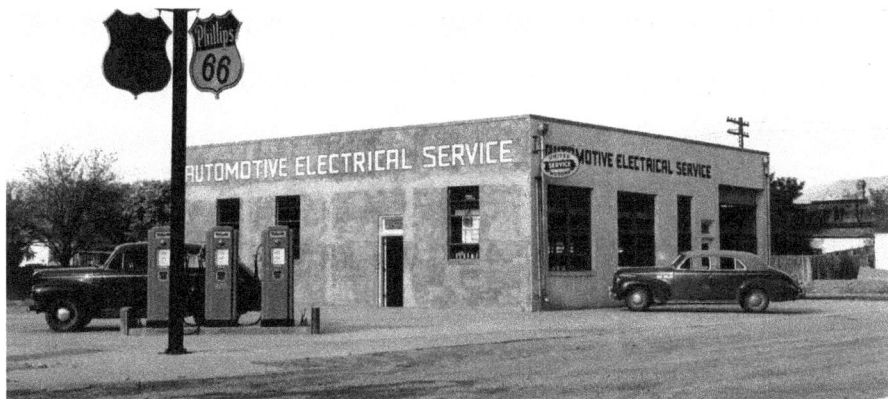

Automotive Electric Service after it opened in 1948 at 800 North Second Street. Super Service Station was its biggest customer. Courtesy Albuquerque Museum, a gift from Albuquerque National Bank.

NEW USED TRUCK

One of the first actions of the new CEO team was regarding its service truck. The station's existing vehicle was a relic of the 1920s, probably a half-ton Ford Runabout. It was constantly under repair. Charlie reported that he spent more time repairing it than he used it to service vehicles. It was so old that he could not find replacement parts. Mario had trouble finding tires to fit it. It was wasting time and degrading efficiency. Efficiency loss affected the bottom line and captivated everyone's attention. Something this big involved Amerigo, Julio and Dante. They all headed to the tire basement for a meeting.

Charlie wanted to outfit a new one with a service kit, including tools and materials to allow him to provide emergency service. At the time, a substantial portion of their profits was from field service. Other than tires, the other major Achilles Heel for automobiles was the battery. Their lives were short and they were fussy about temperature. Batteries supplied less power in cold temperatures. As they aged, their electrical capacities steadily decreased. High summer temperatures enhanced aging. Older batteries successfully cranking an engine in fifty-five-degree weather fell short at twenty-five. Cold weather events produced so much work in the fall that Charlie hired part-time helpers, lower-paid people who could do simple things, such as fetching parts, which freed up his mechanics to focus on valuable mechanical work. By the late 1940s, Super Service was reaping increasing profits starting cold vehicles for people and selling them new batteries.

It did not take long to decide on a "new" truck. Of course, "new" to the Menicuccis meant newer than the old one, but certainly not off a dealer's lot. Charlie and Mario were biased toward Dodge. During the war, they witnessed the exemplary performance of the Dodge T214 series of half-ton pickup trucks. They were rugged, reliable and serviceable vehicles that were used in a wide variety of military applications and in extreme environments. Almost immediately after Japan surrendered, Dodge produced a consumer version of the T214. Called the Power Wagon, it had a single bench seat in the two-person cabin, a ninety-five horsepower, four-cylinder engine under the hood and a four-speed transmission with a granny gear. A granny gear is an ultra-low gear to provide extra power for a heavily encumbered vehicle. The granny is so low that even at four thousand rpm, the vehicle moved only about walking speed, yet with enormous power. When lightly loaded, only three gears were used, second through fourth. The instrument panel had four instruments: In the middle was a round dial speedometer, about five inches in diameter. Four smaller gauges, two on each side, reported engine temperature, oil pressure, fuel level and electric current.

A 1946 Dodge Power Wagon, identical to the one purchased by Super Service Station. This one is rigged for drilling. Dodge continues to manufacture the Power Wagon. Courtesy Albuquerque Museum, a gift from Judy Korber Elstner.

Charlie quickly found one for sale; a used 1946 Power Wagon with only one hundred thousand miles on the odometer. They quickly negotiated a sale and took ownership. Mario had the truck painted bright yellow with a large, colorful Standard Oil chevron on both doors. To save money, Charlie did the sign lettering himself with professional looking results. "Super Service Station" was painted over Standard's chevron in large black letters. Charlie was no artist, but his philosophy on various tasks was that if someone else could do it, he could do and he worked for free. He took that attitude from Julio, who often said, "Don't worry if you don't know how to do it. When you're done doing it, you'll know."

Charlie designed and outfitted the modern truck with a heavy-duty automotive cold-starting kit, including an auxiliary bank of two large batteries wired in parallel, providing plenty of power to crank even the largest engines on the coldest days. Charlie had installed an industrial-duty alternator capable of recharging both the truck's starter battery and the auxiliary ones too, so they remained fully charged at all times. He built a lockable steel toolbox and bolted it to the bed. It housed the typical tools and instruments needed for road repairs. As an expert welder, Charlie also designed and installed a tow bar, which is the safest way to tow vehicles because it solidly connects both vehicles together with a steel bar, preventing the towed vehicle from accidentally rear-ending the lead one, as is prone to occur with chain towing. The station had previously experienced some rear-end incidents when towing vehicles with chains. Further, a tow bar requires nobody in the towed vehicle to steer and apply brakes, as is the case with chain towing.

Towing was an important service because sometimes a stalled vehicle could not be started in the field and had to be towed to the station for service. Once an auto was in for service, Charlie typically found other vehicular needs. Mario too, might sell the customer some additional gear, such as tires, belts or wipers. One of the ubiquitous sites in the 1950s and 1960s Albuquerque was the little yellow 1946 Super Service pickup crawling through the downtown streets with a hulking, late-model Cadillac in tow. The truck was an integral part of the Super Services business and was in constant use performing all manner of tasks, including hauling trash, picking up parts and shuttling customers to and from the station. Dodge manufactured a series of trucks using a similar design, most of which were acclaimed as some of the most durable ever produced. This vehicle fixed Dodge's reputation for tough, hard-working trucks, a repute that prevails a century later.

Mario capitalized on changing seasons. He cultivated a group of customers who every fall regularly swapped out their rear street tires for snow-treaded and studded ones. Super Service stored the unused pair for an exchange at the end of each season. Many customers owned six tires per vehicle, of which two were always stored at the Super Service Station. Mario's philosophy was that once a customer was at the station, he intended to buy something, so his goal was to keep him coming back. He was trained by Amerigo, a master. Charlie had a steady stream of winter customers with battery and starter problems. He ran regular ads with special notices, such as the fall season service, where they offered package deals to winterize the vehicles with new antifreeze, wipers and fan blades.

MARRIAGE SPIRIT

By 1950, Julio and Amerigo had reconfigured the company and properties. Like Johnny Matteucci, they were emeritus employees but with better benefits and duties to consult as needed. It was time for the next step in the family's development, one similar to the ones the immigrant brothers trod thirty years previously. The boys needed wives to grow their families. The Menicuccis believed that a person's prime duty in life is to create new life. To these men, the obvious physical differences between men and women clearly indicated God's intention for them to procreate. Julio was often blunt: "Look how you're made. It tells you why God put you here." In Julio's mind it was clear. One cannot instill a family in a new land by producing just one generation. A quality family produces successive generations of virtuous, successful and productive people. Only that kind of propagation could ensure Menicucci's blood takes hold in America.

Both brothers looked over their customers for those with eligible females of marrying age. Italian women were certainly preferred, but Anglo gals might also work. Tony and Choppo Domenici, owners and operators of Montezuma Grocery, were long-time Super Service Station customers, contracting for service for their personal and professional vehicles. Importantly, both had girls who were of marrying age. Amerigo made a point to talk to either Domenici brother each time he drove into the station. The topic always involved family and that led to the prospect of marriage. Marriage was endemic in the community as servicemen, returning in droves, sought wives for their families. It was the Sujet du Jour, the hot talk of the day.

Mario was active in the local social scene, including the Italamer Club and church groups. He had his eye on Theresa Domenici, Tony's daughter. Tony and his brother had dealt with Amerigo for years and respected his integrity. He was impressed with the Menicuccis' businesses. Amerigo suggested to Mario that Tony had an eligible daughter in a not-so-subtle hint to act with an all-clear signal. He acted. Mario found the opportunity to introduce himself to the young lady in question. He and

Theresa hit it off and after a series of dates, they discussed marriage. In May 1948, the Albuquerque reported that Theresa Domenici and Mario Menicucci planned to wed in June.

Her father, Tony Domenici, was legally related to the Giomis; he married Girolomo's daughter, Emma. Girolomo Giomi was one of Albuqeurque's early Italian pioneers, landing in Albuquerque about the same time as the Bachechis in the late 1800s. The Giomis had accumulated sizable professional positions in real estate and business and were considered among the most respected professionals in town. Montezuma, Domenici's sizable flagship business, was solidly established in Albuquerque. Davina and Amerigo were delighted because in their minds it was a perfect match. They believed that the Domenici-Menicucci match had the potential to yield much fruit. It was working out just as Amerigo had hoped. The Domenicis were investing in the Menicuccis and both families brought high value to the new relationship. It met Menicucci's goal of advancing the family by improving the quality of each successive generation.

The Domenici name was well known in Albuquerque outside the Montezuma Grocery. Chopo's son, Pete, was making himself famous in the sports arena, where he excelled in several athletic endeavors, notably baseball. He went on to serve as the Chairman of the Albuquerque City Commission and a U.S. Senator from New Mexico. He was once suggested as a candidate for Vice President of the United States. The Domenici families were among the most respected in the city and the name today adorns various buildings around the city. Mario and Theresa married in June 1947.

Next to bite was Charlie. He had considered college but opted to devote his life to automotive work, where he excelled. He was doing well and had little pressure from his folks to marry because they were focused on Dante. Charlie married Emma Dalle, daughter of Modesto and Pia Barsanti. Modesto owned the Mint Café and Bar, a popular and profitable eating and drinking establishment. Modesto was an Italian immigrant who arrived in Albuquerque in the early 1920s. Pia was an immigrant who had worked as a housemaid for Tony Domenici's family for eight years before she married Modesto. Tony and Emma Domenici counseled Pia about Modesto as she considered his marriage proposal. Pia said that Tony said, "Modesto is a good man and you should marry him." They married in 1929. Julio and Giulia fully approved the arrangement with the Dalles and they announced the wedding in the *Albuquerque Journal* in May of 1950. Charlie and Emma Dalle married on June 27.

The Menicucci girls were all younger than the boys, so most married later. Rena, Amerigo's first daughter, was the first to marry. She chose an Italian man from the Chicago area, Albert Arigoni, a businessman and real estate professional. They wed in May 1951. Louise, Rena's younger sister, married William Stein, a banker. Mariangela, the youngest of all the girls, married Jerry Scanlon, an accountant. This was all good family news for Julio, but his real interest was in the men. They carry the family blood and name, he often said. Dante was lagging. Teresa remained single.

See notes 1, 2, 3, 4.

Notes

1. The chapter is based largely on corroborated lore.
2. Albuquerque Progress is a set of periodicals reporting on business activity in the city between 1934 and 1956.
3. Stories in the *Albuquerque Journal* were important sources of information for this chapter.
4. The Albuquerque City Directory and the Census provided much personal family information.

19

DARK TIMES (1950–1956)

PRESSURE BUILDS

After Mario's and Charlie's marriages, Dante felt heat and knew he had to move. It was 1951 and Julio was increasingly itching for him to marry. Like Amerigo a couple of years earlier, he kept his eyes out for possible mates. Dante was unsure. He still wore the stigma of the military service, although it had faded from the minds of almost everyone. It was, nonetheless, a depressive force that weighed on him. As he dwelled on the situation, he lapsed into depression. He doubted his ability to step into Julio's shoes. Julio was such a great man that it was increasingly difficult to see how he could meet that standard. Dante's frustration grew as his depression inhibited him from impressing young ladies with confidence and strength. Instead, he grew to loathe the idea of dating, fearing rejection, which engendered more depression. Other family members, including Charlie and Mario, observed Dante struggling, but Julio worked diligently to obfuscate the situation. Julio watched in desperation as his son sank. He turned to the church for help and advice. Father Veale, one of the church ministers closest to the family, counseled Dante and Julio. Whatever the priest did, it helped Dante pull out of his funk and into his stride to secure a bride. Frequent prayer, it turns out, was the prescription, and it worked.

STEPPING UP

Charlie Brunacini, a Sicilian, had been living on the East Coast since his family emigrated from Sicily in 1904. Charlie, born in 1901, was a college-educated and seasoned professional. He arrived in

Albuquerque with his family in 1921. He landed high-level jobs, including county manager and director of the local Indian hospital. In short order, Charlie accumulated wealth and universal respect. In 1940, he opened a campground and filling station on north Fourth Street, just south of the Sandia Indian Pueblo, well beyond the northern boundary of Albuquerque and about halfway to Bernalillo. Trailer homes renting space at his camp burned kerosene for heat and cooking. Julio knew the Brunacinis and was the first to solicit Charlie's business. Julio completely dismissed any past prejudice regarding southern Italians, instead viewing Charlie as an example of the societal value of Italian Americans.

Dante, still apprenticing at Super Oil in 1951, delivered fuel to Charlie's mobile home tenants on North Fourth Street. It was there that he met Charlie's daughter, Lola. She was a beautiful, sophisticated woman with smooth Italian facial features and a broad smile. In addition to beauty, she was intelligent, graduating from St. Vincent Academy in 1942 with honors and earning a scholarship to Loretto Heights College, where she earned a bachelor's degree. She returned to Albuquerque and completed training as a registered nurse at Albuquerque's Regina School of Nursing. Upon graduation, she found immediate employment at St. Joseph Hospital as the chief nurse for the maternity ward. The couple dated for a few weeks and were progressing normally towards marriage.

Giulia was pleased, but Julio was ecstatic. The Brunacinis were well above the status of the Menicuccis and would pull them up socially. And Charlie was already connected to the family via a business relationship that he was developing between Charlie Balduini and Al Arrigoni, who was married to Amerigo's daughter, Rena. The two Charlies (Brunacini and Balduini) started Pueblo Agency, a real estate brokerage. Charlie Bruncini's connection to the business community was excellent, Julio thought, because it expanded the family name in a professional context. What is more, Charlie was wealthy, with ample resources for investments. Julio metaphorically licked his chops as he saw access to capital that could be injected into the family businesses. Borrowing from in-laws was common for many Italians who wanted to grow family fortunes. He believed the marital union could be the greatest accomplishment that any Menicucci ever pulled off in a marriage.

Julio was well on his way to complete his long-standing family mission. The first-generation Menicucci men would marry into respected families and they would assume control of the family businesses. Julio was not shy in his pride and basked in the light of success. His family, which only fifty years earlier were dirt-framing paupers in Italy, had advanced so significantly that a high-level individual like Charlie Brunacini embraced them as family partners. It was impressive.

On July 10, 1951, the *Albuquerque Tribune* published a three-column, twenty-column-inch lead story on the Women's page announcing Lola's engagement to Dante, with the wedding set for September 12. The upbeat story highlighted the success of both Italian immigrant families. Brunacinis and Menicuccis alike celebrated the engagement with a lavish, multi-course Italian meal hosted by the Brunacinis at their home. Lola and Dante, of course, sat at the head table with their proud parents on each side. In the following weeks, the Menicucci girls sprang into action like a military strike force, hosting parties to shower Lola with gifts and goodwill, all in accordance with long-held Italian tradition to celebrate the marriage of the oldest male in the family. Lola shopped with her mother for a wedding dress. The *Tribune* highlighted the engagement on the society page again on August 23rd, the same night that Dante attended a Knights of Columbus meeting, where he had professional duties. There he and other soon-to-be grooms were honored.

Proudly preparing for her upcoming life as an Italian wife, Lola resigned from her professional nursing position at the hospital. At that time, working Italian wives were a rarity and she was ready to raise a family. Lola's goodbye party at the hospital was another excuse to honor the young bride-to-be. The Brunacini family was as pleased as the Menicuccis. It was all perfect.

NOT SO FAST

There was a problem. During the summer Dante's depression had returned, aggravated by the engagement. He worried that he was now dedicated to a life-long commitment with huge implications. What's more, Lola was college-educated, a goal Dante long held for himself but fell short due to circumstances. He worried how it would appear if he, the man of the family, were less educated than his wife. That image was socially important at the time. Charlie Brunacini, too, was a man of stature and Dante questioned his ability to measure up to a commensurate professional level. Basically, he was conflicted and unsure, which stood in stark contrast to Julio's ebullience. He grew progressively more agitated as he mulled the situation in his head. He tried to carry on, masking his ever-increasing gloom, but the weight was too much to bear. He rotely attended the August 23rd Knights of Columbus meeting, but the charade was over. When he got home, the weight of his depression-induced woes was beyond bearing and he collapsed.

It was clearly a mental condition, and it perpetrated a massive family crisis because mental illness was universally misunderstood and feared. To Italians, it was the basis of scandal, a black mark on the family that might pass on to future generations, spoiling opportunities along the way. Legends of devastating, generation-long scandals revolving around mental disorders universally haunted Italian families. Julio and Giulia sprang into action, best described as panic. It had to be concealed from everyone, including close family members. Julio had to preserve the family name and hastily concocted the cover plan: He assumed that Giulia could quickly nurse Dante to health before anyone was the wiser. Meanwhile, Julio protected the home from visitors so nobody could see Dante's actual state. Julio cooly reported to the family that Dante had a sudden hankering to participate in a faraway religious retreat to prepare for the wedding. The message spread among the family but few believed it. The sense of something amiss hung heavily in the air. Emma Dalle Menicucci, said that "We all knew it was phony but could do nothing but wait."

In the following days, and in spite of Giulia's constant care, Dante's condition steadily worsened, producing a desperate crisis. Julio knew his pretentious cover story was weak and that time was running out. He remained steadfast to contain and sequester the scandal that was brewing. Julio called again on Father Veal, who rushed to the Menicucci home to provide his counsel. After he saw Dante's condition, he realized the case was beyond his capabilities. He insisted that Dante be admitted to Nazareth Sanitarium, a Catholic facility operated by the Dominican Nuns. The facility specialized in mental health disorders. Julio was hesitant; visions of his own father's depression-induced abandonment of the family danced in his head. Now, just a month away, the fabulous wedding hung in the balance. Veale knocked Julio back to his senses. His son's health was at stake. Julio acquiesced and asked for the priest's assistance in the admittance, a process for which he was well qualified because several parishioners, including some other Italians, had been directed to Nazareth by the Jesuit Fathers at Immaculate Conception.

Teresa Menicucci Clark and her sister Mariangela, who lived at the family home on Third Street, told the story of the crisis. Teresa said:

"Dante came home when we were already in bed. The next day they told us nothing except that Dante was sick and needed to be left alone. Papa kept us away from Dante's room while Mama attended to him. Dante's room was at the far end of the house with only one hallway leading to it, so papa could easily guard the hallway to keep us away. We knew something was terribly wrong. We finally snuck some peeks by crawling outside, looking through his window and eavesdropping." Mariangela said Dante was "so mentally confused that he was incapable of ordinary tasks, such as eating or even carrying on a conversation." In the vernacular of the day, he had a nervous breakdown and he needed immediate professional medical help. In Twenty-First Century vernacular, the term is a Mental Health Crisis.

Giulia was horrified and humiliated as her oldest son was carted off to a mental hospital. For Julio, it was a double-edged sword. On one edge he lost a quality daughter-in-law from a prominent family. On the other, he had to admit to Chalie Brunacini, the family and the community that Dante was under treatment at Nazareth. Mental disorders, especially among the Italians, were baffling maladies that had the hallmarks of demonic intervention, causing victims to act irrationally. Worse, it was scandalous because it reflected negatively on the parents, Julio and Giulia. It implied that their son was imperfect. In the minds of many Italians, the appearance of familial stability and perfection was necessary to maintain the family's image. Any deviation implied that the parents had somehow failed. Money, of course, was also a factor because Nazareth was not inexpensive, charging several hundred dollars a month or more, depending on the treatment (about thirty-six hundred in 2024 dollars). The Menicuccis had the resources, but that was beside the point of the scandal. However, Dante's health was rightly becoming Julio's principal concern.

Veale drove the parish auto to Julio's home to ferry Dante to Nazareth. He had already completed the preliminary forms, and Julio signed them, which was one of the most difficult acts in his life. Veale loaded Dante and Julio into his auto for the forty-minute journey to Nazareth near Alameda in Albuquerque's north valley area. On the way, they stopped by the bank and Julio withdrew cash. At Nazareth, as Veale prepared Dante for admittance, Julio paid the fees and prayed for a quick recovery that would allow Dante to jump back into the saddle in time to wed without anyone knowing any better. It was an ephemeral pipe dream. The attending physicians informed Julio that Dante's condition was serious and that treatment could last months, perhaps a year.

Nazareth Sanatorium, copied from a postcard located in the Vertical file: "Nazareth Sanatorium," stored at the Albuquerque Public Library Special Collections.

Julio was heartbroken as he faced the facts, one of the most difficult of which would be facing Charlie Burncini. Later, to add insult to his injury, he would face the public and the scorn that surely would follow. It was an exaggeration born from a combination of remorse, fear, ignorance and embarrassment harkening from an Italian bygone age and overactive imaginations. In Julio and Giulia's minds, it was a scandalous tragedy that was way out of proportion with reality. In reality, many people suffered with mental problems. Plus, broken engagements were not unprecedented in the colony. A decade earlier, Pia Dalle was treated at Nazareth and had broken an engagement to Michael Granone, with no long-term scandalous consequences.

Within a few days of Dante's admission, Lola noticed that he was missing and her angst passed up to her dad. Charlie called Julio to inquire. The jig was up and Julio privately met with him and laid out the story. Julio spun it the best he could, but it was beyond spin control. The bottom line was the wedding was off, Dante was in Nazareth and he did not want to marry Lola. Julio offered to repay Charlie for the dinner, but money was not the problem. His distressed daughter concerned him, and he looked squarely at Julio to blame. Julio was powerless, the most ashamed he had been in his life. It was so perfect, he kept thinking, how did it so quickly come to this?

Lola was devastated and full of grief. Jilted, laid low by the events and uncomfortable among her peers, she believed it might stigmatize her as possibly a flawed mate, imperiling her future. It was the stuff of soap opera drama.

Julio's shame finally caught up with him, and he opened up to the family. There was no surprise, for everyone long knew something was askew. Still, shock and dismay swept through all as each considered a seriously ailing key family member and grasped the depth of the multi-faceted social adversity. The entire family overreacted based on old-world myths and outdated traditions. In fact, many others in the community had been treated at Nazareth. Their cases were well known, but to Julio and Giulia, the Menicucci situation was unique because it involved a promising marriage.

TREATMENTS

Each Nazareth patient was assigned to one of the psychiatric physicians on staff. The staff physicians developed customized treatment programs for each patient that the clinicians carefully implemented. Typical treatments for mental problems at that time included electroconvulsive therapy, Lithium and psychiatric counseling.

The electroconvulsive treatment was the most violent and painful, but they seemed to have some positive effects. The treatment applied electrical shocks to the head. The patient was tied to a table and electrodes were applied to both sides of the head, near the ears. Then electricity was passed between the two and through the brain. The patient recoiled from the shock and writhed in pain and involuntary convulsions. Sometimes, hearing, speech and sight were temporarily lost. Most patients recovered and experienced some relief from the effects of depression. Some were unresponsive to the treatment and a few died, often due to stroke or heart attack from the treatment itself. Electroconvulsive therapy is still used in the Twenty-First Century to treat mental disorders, but the patients are treated under general anesthesia.

Lithium too, was clinically proven efficacious in treating depression but produced uncomfortable side effects, such as uncontrolled shaking, shivering, nausea and fatigue. Nazareth's' Lithium treatments often extended beyond the hospitalization period on an outpatient basis. The staff psychiatrists counseled patients on coping with the treatments and dealing with the depression itself. In Dante's case, they worked to help him ease his feelings of inadequacy and deal with periodic anxiety that led to depression.

Dante was treated in the advanced care ward for the first six weeks, which handled serious cases. No visitors, including family members, were allowed. It was terribly difficult for the close-knit family as they had no realistic idea of what treatments Dante was undergoing and feared that loneliness could worsen his condition. They trusted the nuns at the hospital but wanted to be at his side to assist him in his recovery, just as they might do at the regular hospital. Unfortunately, Dante was in no condition to see anyone but his caretakers.

RELIEF

As the weight of the wedding was lifted from Dante's shoulders and the treatments took effect, he steadily improved. By the year's end, Julio and Giulia were his first visitors, and they were delighted to see their son nearly as sunny and bright as a year earlier. My father, Charlie, and mother, Emma Dalle Menicucci, carrying me as an eight-month-old baby, visited him in early 1952. Emma reported that his condition was good, as he bantered with his brother and played with his new nephew. By the early summer of 1952, his physicians declared that he was sufficiently recovered and released him to the care of his family. But his full recovery required home care for the remainder of the year, including rest, plenty of exercise and avoiding stressful events. Certainly, reasonable suggestions given that mental illness was not well understood.

In various promotional publications, Nazareth claimed high curative rates, implying that one walks out with a clean slate and a new lease on life, similar to a cured Strep infection. Many patients, probably most, were not cured and, like Dante, were treated for years following their admissions. Many also returned. People such as Lida Matteucci, Ancilla Petroni Matteucci and my maternal grandmother Pia Barsanti Dalle were treated at Nazareth multiple times, but all three struggled with depression throughout their lives. In the modern Twenty-First Century, most of the people treated in 1950s mental institutions would today be treated by their primary physician using common antidepressant medications.

Giulia and Julio understood the doctor's order about rest and exercise, but the one edict caught their ears: remove stress from Dante's life. The physicians logically reasoned that convalescence is a quiet time. Giulia and Julio interpreted it as implying that stress caused the disease and could rekindle it. This line of thinking has some scientific truth, but at that time, even the experts knew little. However, the watchword in the future was "Don't upset Dante." Giulia counseled family members with this warning well into the 1970s, decades after the episode and with Dante fully normalized.

In their minds, thinking in the old culture, they greatly exaggerated the ramifications of mental problems on family reputation. To this couple and to many of the original Italian immigrants, mental disorders were bewildering and difficult to comprehend. From experience over generations, they had observed some repeatable characteristics: It came on suddenly and randomly and often with the potency to incapacitate even the heartiest individual. It equally infected both sexes. It had no apparent cause or cure, but it was sometimes gone for long periods before returning with a vengeance. Irrational or unusual behavior was always a symptom. It seemed to follow the blood in a family. "Follow the blood" is a figurative translation from Italian, which means it could be hereditary.

By the summer of 1952, Dante was interacting with friends and relatives. He reappeared at meetings of various clubs to which he was previously a member. By January 1953, Dante returned to work at Super Oil, where, in good spirits, he reassumed his CEO position. Julio was pleased to vacate the chair. It was a sign that he and the family were back on track, just like before Dante's medical mishap. In reality, it was not the same as before. Dante remained under the care of Nazareth as an out-patient and he was still on drug therapy. He still saw a psychiatrist at the hospital regularly to deal with twinges of depression. The treatments at this point focused more on teaching him to manage symptoms over his lifetime rather than restoring him to normalcy. The medical staff had provided the best remedies possible but they were far from efficacious and most patients wrangled with life-long symptoms.

Giulia, the most superstitious of the four immigrants, was especially agitated and shaken by the events. She had a propensity for the oldest males, especially the family's firstborn, who became heir to the family leadership position by virtue of timing. In Giulia's old-world Italian vision, Dante was the rock of the family, one to step into Julio's shoes seamlessly, one to lead as Julio did. A mysterious mental monster crushed that rock. Now, he is glued back together, but the nag of fear prevailed: What if it struck again? In her head, all was fine for now and the goal was to keep it so.

There was a silver lining. Julio so fearful of inducing stress, purposely reduced his oversight of Dante at Super Oil, leaving him to find his way in the job. He moved Dante's office from his shack under the fuel storage tanks to the main warehouse building. Julio withdrew from the day-to-day management; he became a delivery truck driver, leaving the office for long periods for Dante to manage alone. It was the freedom that Dante needed and he blossomed in the job.

BACK ON TRACK

At an Italamer Club charity event in the spring of 1953, Dante met Mary Nicola, a lovely young daughter of Maggiorino. The Nicolas, like many Italian immigrants, were grocers. They owned and operated Paramount Grocery and Meat on 1605 Fifth Street NW, close to his home at 1321 Sixth Street. Julio and Giulia were delighted at the choice but nervous. The Nicola family was related to the Vaios, a prominent and reasonably wealthy family in town. In quick order, they announced their engagement to wed. On August 16, 1953, the *Tribune* published the announcement of the September 7, 1953 wedding in a modest, eight-column inch story in the bottom center of the Women's page, just as Julio and Giulia desired. Even that meager announcement embarrassed Giulia as she feared it might stir talk about the previous broken engagement, the stuff of scandal. But it was unimportant at this point, and Julio's concern about social status disappeared. The goal was for Dante to marry and complete his transition to his leadership destiny as CEO for both family companies.

The Immaculate Conception nuptials came off with typical fanfare in September of 1953. Anita Palladino, Horace's sister, served as Mary's bride's maid and Dante's younger brother, Charlie, was best man. The ceremony also included Mario Menicucci, Dante's cousin. A spectacular reception followed at the prominent Alvarado Hotel with food, wine, music, dancing and the customary Italian toasts and well-wishes. For a while, at least, Giulia was content. Her oldest son married a good Catholic Italian woman. Not as prominent as Lola Brunacini, Mary was intelligent and harkened from a fine, honest family and, importantly, her son loved her. Julio was pleased that Dante was finally on the proper Italian path and that the ugly affair could finally be put behind them, notwithstanding, of course, the specter of scandal that would haunt the family.

A fully recovered Dante marries in 1953. From left: Mario Menicucci, Charlie Menicucci, Dante Menicucci, Mary Nicola, Anita Palladino, unknown. Courtesy Dante Menicucci family.

Lola eventually married Irvin Lenz, an Albuquerque professional, on April 28, 1954. Lenz was a research engineer at Sandia Corp. He and Lola grew a family in Albuquerque, and both retired in Santa Fe. They had three children. Lola worked on parent-teacher organizations and part-time as a fashion model in Albuquerque. Lola and Irvin died around 2017.

COLLATERAL DAMAGE

Even as Dante regained his professional footing, Julio and Giulia were shaken badly. It was Julio, though, who took the cross on his shoulders. To him, the entire affair was a negative reflection on him personally, as though he could control the details of his children's lives. He feared that the scandal had negatively affected the family's future. He was still taking it hard.

Dante assumed his position at Super Oil Company and was in good spirits. Freed of the yoke of a planned marriage, he could relax and enjoy his work for the first time in years. But Julio continued to languish over what could have been as he slipped into depression. He spent less time at Super Oil and more time at home sulking. Mariangela Menicucci Scanlon told the story of Julio sitting in a rocking chair on their front porch for hours, staring into the street. "He was there when we left for school and was still there at lunch. When we got home after school he was still in the same place. For weeks he hardly ate anything." Finally, his condition worsened; he became visibly disheveled, and Father Veale was consulted. His prescription was identical to Dante's—admission to Nazareth.

Depression is a sinister malady because it robs the victim of the ability to think rationally. The suggestion jolted Julio from his moribund state like a snort of smelling salts. He sat at attention with a growling face. It was bad enough that his son was treated for mental illness; he would not add to the family's shame. Teresa Menicucci Clark quoted him repeatedly shouting one invective after another toward the priest: "I'll die before I go to that damned place." His word was final.

CARPENTER CURE

Fretting, members of the family ferreted suggestions from friends and family members. Marco Donati, who had emigrated from Lucca in 1915, operated a growing home construction company in Albuquerque. He built speculation homes in Albuquerque, borrowing money to purchase land and materials, building a home on it and then selling for a profit. He also constructed custom homes. He lived in downtown Albuquerque, was a Super Service Station customer and was a close family friend.

In early 1953, Charlie contracted Marco to construct a home for his family in the new Huning Castle Addition, colloquially known as the Country Club Area, located in the southwest corner of the city near the river and Central Avenue. Charlie knew that some of the Donati family had had mental problems and survived. He confided in Marco about Julio's condition, which had been dragging on for weeks amid his refusal to be treated at Nazareth. Marco knew Julio and had an idea to snap him out of his dilapidated state. He hired Julio to work with him on Charlie's home. He surmised that he would bounce back if he could distract Julio from his woes with physical labor. Charlie encouraged him because no other option existed. Marco stopped by Julio's home, greeted him and concocted a tale about Charlie's home. It piqued Julio's attention because it involved his son. Marco claimed he needed help because some of his carpenters were sick, possibly delaying construction on his son's home and impacting the construction loan. He knew Julio had excellent construction skills and asked if he could come and help for a couple of weeks.

It was the elixir of the hour. Julio agreed, grabbed his bag of tools and commenced working immediately. At sixty years old, Julio could still out-work thirty-five-year-olds. Within an hour of Marco's visit, Julio was mortaring concrete blocks and fitting 2X4s at Charlie's new home. He worked with Marco until the project was complete, a few months later. Marco passed the savings from Julio's free labor to Charlie in terms of a discounted price for the home, charging five thousand dollars (about fifty-seven thousand in 2024 dollars).

The main benefit of Julio's stint with Marco was distraction. Once he focused on something other than family, he realized no crisis existed. Dante was sick and has now recovered. He also learned the value of work as an antidepressant. Julio had seized on physical labor to clear his mind so he could employ his own logic to work himself out of his depression. Fortunately, he succeeded. Mariangela Menicucci Scanlon told the story of Julio's transformation. "When we went to school that morning Papa was on the porch staring just like every day. When we got home mama said he was working with Marco Donati. When Papa got home, he acted completely normal, asking for wine and dinner. Dante took a year to recover and a carpenter cured Papa in one day."

Julio never discussed this incident with me or anyone else. Giulia is on record denying that it ever happened. Her approach to any crisis was to attend Mass weekly and purchase candles to venerate the Virgin. Teresa and Mariangela confirmed that Julio believed, to his death, that one of his finest moments in life was his escape from mental illness without treatment at Nazareth. Italian old-world societal norms die hard.

In the 1950s, mental health issues in the community as a whole remained a touchy subject. Many families continued to protect the identities of family members treated in local sanitariums. In contrast to folks who were treated for physical injuries or disease, which were often reported in the press, mental health care cases were often veiled until a tragic ending. On November 20, 1950, James Forrestal, former U.S. secretary of defense, was reported dead by suicide while under treatment for a nervous breakdown. Roosevelt's son-in-law, John Boettiger, died under similar circumstances. Many press reports hyped the negative aspects of mental care, which exacerbated the public's anxiety regarding mental health issues.

Details about Dante's exact treatment, including his caretakers, will never be known because his records and those of all the other Nazareth patients during the period 1938 to its closure in 1978 were deliberately destroyed in July 1988. Details about the institution's treatment methods, physicians, caretakers, operational staff, budgets and other historical details are gone. Also destroyed were records from Vista Sandia, a private alcoholism treatment center. Fearing future stigmatization, relatives of patients likely requested the destruction. The Italians were not the only ethnic group concerned with scandal and the potential agony of mental treatment, but they certainly led the pack.[1]

Appendix VI explains the concept of scandal in Italian culture.

TURNING POINT

By the middle of the 1950s, the outlook for both families brightened. Dante and Mario were performing beautifully. Julio and Amerigo were growing confident enough to increase their recreational time. Both men had well-worm sexagenarian bodies. The brothers engaged in spontaneous fishing trips to Jemez, complete with baths. They justified the trips by claiming that they were not recreating but improving business relations among Super Oil customers in the area. Super Oil and Super Service provided fuel and mechanical repair services to many businesses in Jemez. The men were progressing into their retirements, something that their relatives in Italy could only dream about.

What was more, Julio had found the ideal remedy for depression—physical work. Indeed, modern medical therapies for depression include physical exercise. Subsequently, he became the family contractor for hire at an attractive price: free. Julio relished his dual-fold purpose of directly aiding his family and consistently defraying the depression demon that forever lurked. In 1952 he and Amerigo did a masonry project in Mario's new home, a spec home that Mario grabbed just following his wedding. In 1954, he completed an addition to Mario's home, acting as general contractor and carpenter. Later, Julio constructed an addition to Charlie's home. He and Beppe Bandoni jointly did construction projects for Immaculate Conception Church and St. Mary's School.

By the early 1950s, Albuquerque was expanding the central business district and its environs. Some residential sections were to be vacated for a new Albuquerque National Bank building. The city bought Julio's property on Third Street at a favorable price, providing him with a large profit over his initial investment. But his home was not destroyed by the new development. He sold the home itself and subsequently hired a company to elevate it onto a mobile platform and move it to the new owner's lot on Girard Boulevard, south of Lomas Boulevard. Today, most homes are constructed on a slab on grade, where the floor is solid concrete, rendering the home impossible to move in one piece.

A home being moved by Springer Transfer Company in the middle 1920s, which is similar to the method that Julio employed when he sold his property on Third Street. Courtesy Albuquerque Museum, a gift of David Schifani.

Julio needed a new home and Marco had located two adjoining residential lots for sale in the Huning Castle Addition. Both were located on San Carlos Road, just a half block away from Charlie's new home and two blocks from the Albuquerque Country Club. As one of the most elite subdivisions in town, it attracted many wealthy people, including successful Italian immigrants. Julio immediately bought the Huning Castle property and contracted Marco to construct his new home. Under the same situation with his property next to Julio's on Third Street neighbor, Luigi Pucci bought the second property adjacent to Julio's on San Carlos Road. Luigi's family lived next to the Menicuccis in Lucca and lived next to one another in Albuquerque's downtown area. Now, they continued that neighborly arrangement. Both men died in those homes, and in the end, they had been next-door neighbors for nearly a century.

Julio contracted Marco to construct his home under the same arrangement as with Charlie: Julio worked for free and Marco provided a discounted price. Although Julio planned to do much of the work himself, he needed Marco to pull permits and provide subcontractors, such as the Granone brothers, for specialty trade work. Frankie and Charlie Granone, in-laws to Charlie, operated an electrical contracting business.

FIRST, THE MADONNA

When constructing his home, Julio had only one stipulation: he would first build and dedicate a stone grotto to the Madonna in the backyard. It was the most important landmark on the property. He carefully chipped and carved lava rocks to fit in the stone wall for the backdrop to the statue of the virgin. He selected a fine marble rendition of the Madonna holding the Baby Jesus, which he placed in the central spot in the grotto. He lined the front with a row of bricks, all carefully mortared in place. It took him a couple of weeks of time-consuming, exacting work, but he was finally ready for the dedication. It was a private religious affair involving him and his brother and their spouses. But it was really about the two Menicucci brothers who had developed a personal relationship with the Great Lady and credited her with providing them the most important gift when they were in peril: hope. Father Veal presided over the impromptu Catholic ceremony by reading a few appropriate passages from the gospels. Naturally, the ceremony included holy water and multiple blessings.

In total, by the middle 1950s, four Lucchese lived on San Carlos: Charlie and Julio Menicucci, Luigi Pucci and Johnny Matteucci. Later, in the late 1970s, my wife and I added our family as the fifth Lucchese descendant to live on San Carlos. All of these Lucchese lived on the same side of the street within two city blocks of one another. Other Italians lived nearby, including the Domenicis, Ciminos, Seis, Del Frates and other Matteuccis.

The author at age eight in front the grotto Julio constructed in his yard for the Madonna.
Courtesy author's collection.

By 1956, the outlook for the family was excellent. Children were appearing with regularity throughout the family. Julio and Amerigo believed that it was the second generation of Menicuccis who would firmly establish the family in the city. The family was hitting on all cylinders, a metaphor in concert with the family automobile business. Amerigo was pleased that his brother was apparently cured and his family had escaped the kind of calamity that had befallen Julio's clan over the recent years. Amerigo and Davian lost Julio-Henry, and perhaps that was the last of the family tragedies on his side, so he prayed. It did not take long for him to discover he was wrong.

See notes 2, 3, 4.

Notes

1. Events before 1950 are considered public information because the census for that year has been released to the public, divulging complete personal information for the populace at that time, including Social Security numbers, birth dates, spouses and other personal data. Even for events after 1950, if the individuals in question are dead, they cannot be harmed by publications and, therefore, cannot create a scandal. Logic rarely matters to families haunted by the specter of scandal. It is an inveterate fear that to this day menaces the lives of many of Albuquerque's Italian descendants and confounds researchers seeking to document Italian history. See Appendix VI for more information.

2. The chapter is based largely on corroborated lore. Charlie Menicucci, Teresa Menicucci Clark, Mariangela Menicucci Scanlon, Emma Dalle Menicucci and Adele Morelli Davis supplied the bulk of the information about Dante's condition. Teresa and Mariangela supplied the information in private settings, with no recordings, fearing recriminations while they were alive. It took me three visits to Louisiana over seven years to squeeze the entire story from Teresa. Adele was not directly involved, but provided some counsel to the family at that time and reported her observations for this book, again with the stipulation that they not be reveled during her lifetime. Margaret Mary Matteucci reported on numerous Matteucci members who struggled with depression, but with the caveat that the information be concealed until she had passed. Stories of other Italians who were similarly treated at Nazareth came from the Del Frate and Domenici families. Many others were treated at Nazareth, but their stories have been systematically suppressed by the families. No other issue confounded the immigrant community like mental health. Thus, no chapter in the book was more difficult to research due to the continued dearth of folks willing to discuss it, even though the people who were involved have been dead for decades. All records from Nazareth have been deliberately destroyed, compounding the difficulty of extracting quality historical information about the situation.

3. News reports from the two Albuquerque newspapers provided

considerable information for this chapter. For example, newspapers regularly reported the activities of Dante leading up to his collapse, including his progression up the ranks of the Italamer Club and the Knights of Columbus. His name was mentioned every couple of weeks in a story. Suddenly, after August of 1951, the reports about him ceased for over a year while he recovered. About sixteen months later, his recovery was noted by news reports about him operating in his usual forums, such as the Knights of Columbus. From there, he was on an upward trajectory that never abated as he solidified his role as the family and civic leader. Like many stricken with an ailment, he recovered and flourished.

4. The Albuquerque City Directory was a major source of information for the chapter. The directory was more helpful than the census because 1950 was the last one that had been released to the public. The directories are available for this period and well beyond. Most of the directories are accessible online, but there are some significant gaps. A complete record of Albuquerque directories is available at the Genealogy Center at the Albuquerque Public Library's main branch.

20

ANGELIC TRAGEDY
(1957–1968)

THE BABY SHOULD DIE

In 1957, Amerigo and Davina were thankfully welcoming their new grandchildren. It was early in the morning on October tenth that Amerigo took a call from his son-in-law, Al Arrigoni, reporting that their daughter, Rena, had begun labor and he was fixing to bring her to St. Joseph Hospital, which at the time had the most modern maternity ward. This was Rena's second child. Regina, her first, was just a little older than one year and growing rapidly.

The couple quickly dressed and Amerigo brought Davina to the Arrigoni home where she took over Rena's home duties looking after her granddaughter, cooking and preparing the crib and other facilities for the new arrival. Amerigo set out for supplies, as dictated by Davina. By the afternoon, Davina and Regina sang songs and played happily as they awaited with great anticipation for Regina's new sibling. Amerigo, confident but wary, wandered around Super Service Station waiting for news.

At St. Joseph Hospital's maternity ward, problems developed early in the labor. The physicians identified a breech position for the fetus, which is a potential complication because the baby is positioned to be delivered feet first instead of head first. The breech position increases the probability of the umbilical cord accidentally wrapping around the baby or being squeezed closed during the unusual birthing position. At that time, diagnostic tools were limited, with no electronic monitors or other monitoring devices that are common in Twenty-First Century facilities. Doctors treated patients with manual stethoscopes, blood pressure instruments, observation, and physical examinations.

Breech births at the time were much more serious than in the Twenty-First Century, in which cesarian section, a relatively safe procedure, is available in emergencies. As time passed, Rena's labor proceeded but with difficulty. She worked for hours throughout the day with little progress in moving the baby through the birth canal. After hours of struggling, fiddling and hoping, the medical team decided that the baby could be in peril and they induced labor. At that time, medical practice strove to avoid prolonged labor, especially with a breech condition. The physicians applied the drug Pitocin (Oxytocin) and broke the Amniotic sac.

Finally, the baby appeared but Rena immediately knew something was amiss. She had been through childbirth; she was no novice. She noticed that baby Arlene was not crying after birth. The medical team hovered over the baby and spoke of some problems with the "umbilical cord," mentioning it several times.[1] Rena lay concerned and waiting, her heart racing with anticipation as she heard nearby newborns wailing with new lives. Finally, they presented the five-pound baby girl to her. There was little time for any bonding because the baby struggled to breathe. Her eyes were glazed over, just like those of elderly people with heavy Cataracs. Rena asked the team about the baby's eyes, but they casually dismissed her concerns. She knew something was wrong. Mothers have an innate ability to recognize disorders in their children.

The medical team did not take long to acquiesce to Rena's assertion. The baby was indeed struggling to survive and they moved her to an isolette, an enclosed crib with a high oxygen, sterile environment. In the first three days, Arlene developed jaundice, vomited frequently, and had constant diarrhea. She convulsed often and contracted pneumonia. Rena fell into shock and was sedated, returning her to a hospital bed. As Arlene struggled to survive, Al called on his pastor to baptize the child, anticipating a quick demise. For five days Rena lay in bed trying to recover from the physical effects of a tough labor and the mental anguish of a potentially severely ill newborn. Davina and Amerigo were allowed to visit. When they did, Rena's psychological condition lay firmly in Davina's domain. She focused on maintaining hope in her daughter. Prayers are hope and their visits always incorporated them.

Days passed with Davina holding down the homestead. Davina, with toddler Regina in tow, went about the normal domestic duties. Anxiety was proportional to the number of days with no news. Al only told them what he knew, that there were some complications and the family would be reunited in a few days. When Rena was finally released about ten days after the birth, she arrived at her home and was greeted by Regina and Davina. With no baby in her arms, all Rena could tell her toddler and mother was that Arlene "…cannot come home yet." She then proceeded to the kitchen with her mother where she spewed the details, rendering both women into a slumped state of despondency and tears. The family outlook, which had appeared rosy and bright just a week ago, had plunged into murky gloom.

After a week and a heavy application of penicillin, Arlene beat a pneumonia infection, but the convulsions and gastrointestinal problems remained unabated. The baby could not gain weight. Every time she gained a pound, she relapsed with another malady that shed it off. The medical team tried various combinations of breast milk and special, highly nutritious baby formulations. Nothing worked. The baby continued to struggle and the medical team applied every diagnostic test they knew to discover Arlene's condition. All tests were negative. Her condition was unknown to the Albuquerque medical team and they were out of options. After a month, the hospital released the baby to the Arrigoni family, but her condition remained nearly as critical as the day she was born. She weighed less than a pound above her birth weight. At home, she required twenty-four-hour care to battle a continuing series of ailments ranging from ear infections to convulsions and struggled to hold down food and gain weight. As Rena put it, "Each day was a struggle to defy death."

For months, Davina spent every day with Rena, helping her with the baby and the toddler. Every evening, Amerigo brought gifts before settling in for dinner. Then, they returned home and prepared for the next day and the same routine. Rena regularly visited the local pediatricians, but they were all helpless. They could not diagnose the condition, so they could not treat it. In one of many visits to the family physician for an ear infection, Rena asked the physician what was wrong with her daughter and why she was so often afflicted with ailments. In frustration, the doctor suggested that she ask Arlene. He could not diagnose the condition and it was his way to convey his capitulation. Rena understood the frustration, but she was furious at his callousness. After recovering from that event, she tried another physician the following day. His response was even more insensitive, saying that the child was not normal and "should die," adding that he refused to treat the child's ear infection.

Rena was not stupid. She could see that the child had little hope of living normally, but she also saw the girl as a product of the Lord, deserving the right to exist until the Lord takes her. She lived her beliefs. In her mind, once a child is born it cannot be killed no matter the costs. Arlene's condition was accidental and she was a huge burden to the family, but Rena loved the child and would not abandon her. As long as Arlene lived, Rena committed to making her life as pleasant as possible.

At home, she, Al, Davina and Amerigo prayed nightly, but they wrestled with the meaning of the situation. The Menicuccis had always believed that significant events occur in people's lives to offer opportunities for redirection. They were hard-pressed to find any opportunities in this situation. They were saddled with an incurably sick child that would consume the major resources of the family for the foreseeable future. Amerigo lamented because he believed that Julio Henry was the last disappointment, but that held not a candle to this challenge. It was beyond anything they had experienced and both Al and Rena said so often; they could not recall any retardation cases in Italy. These cases did occur often in the backwoods of Lucca but newborns with Arlene's condition usually succumbed quickly after birth. Breech births often caused injury to the baby and not infrequently resulted in the mother's death. In Italy, infant deaths were not uncommon. In this case, America's superior medical system had saved the baby. Unfortunately, the medical community had little idea of how to treat it.

THE NADIR

Rena and Al were exasperated with the local pediatricians and finally seized on a recommendation to have Arlene examined by the Children's Hospital in Denver, Colorado. The hospital was one of the most medically advanced institutions in the country and specialized in rare childhood disorders. A week later, Al, Rena and Arlene traveled to Denver to meet Dr. Robert Fisher at the hospital. He helped them through the child's admittance process. Once Arlene was secured under the care of the hospital's nurses, Al and Rena settled into their nearby hotel room to set up a temporary home while they waited for the results, expected to consume at least a few days.

Each day they visited the hospital and sat alongside Arlene's crib, comforting and caring for her as she was shuttled to one test after another.

For four days Fisher's team tested, examined, retested and reexamined. The Arrigonis, meanwhile, mostly prayed, as Menicuccis and Arrigonis have done for generations to kindle hope when it appeared to be lost. Finally, on the fifth day, as the Arrigonis entered the child's hospital room, the nurse indicated that Dr. Fisher was ready to present his diagnosis. Discorded emotions coursed through Rena's young body. Initially, exhilaration swept her over; perhaps now, with a diagnosis, they might have found their nadir in what had been boundless agony and suffering. Then dread prevailed as she considered that the results might indicate that their nadir was a permanent condition. Al took Rena's shaking arm and led the couple solemnly to the meeting.

Dr. Fisher was sympathetic but firm. Arlene has "a condition known as galactosemia." Both parents gulped; it sounded sinister. The doctor explained that it was an inherited condition that prevented her body from breaking down the sugar galactose, a major constituent of milk products. He explained that such a condition allows the galactose to accumulate in the body, damaging the liver, brain, kidneys and eyes. A symptom of the disease is cataracts, which Rena noticed in Arlene's eyes immediately following birth. Then came the hammer. Even with appropriate treatment going forward, the child was permanently disabled with no hope of a normal life. She might be expected to live only a few years, he added, seeking to provide some hope of closure for the parents. He further explained that babies born with the condition must be fed only milk-free products throughout life. The critical milk-free period is the initial days following birth, where the baby's diet is carefully controlled, allowing the infant's body to stabilize. Milk products are essentially poisonous to Galactosemia victims.[2]

The news plunged like a dagger into Rena's heart. For many months, she had unwittingly poisoned her child with her breast milk. Many questions rattled in her head. Could her little angel have been saved? Why didn't the Lord provide a warning? They prayed and followed the rules. Had the Lord abandoned them? Then, the stultifying reality settled in with both parents. It was true. They had hit their nadir and it was permanent.

They gathered up Arlene, checked out of their hotel and headed directly to the airport for the trip back to Albuquerque. They said little on the hour-long flight. When they arrived at home, Amerigo and Davina were the first to visit. They sat in horror as the young couple divulged the dispiriting news. The grandparents were witnessing a family ordeal that had no parallel in the history. Al and Amerigo both agreed that mental retardation was not in the blood of either family. But they forgot Aledino Menicucci, Amerigo's brother, who had some inherited disability that led to his early death at twenty-eight years of age. And there was Rena's brother, Julio Henry, who died of suspicious causes about a week after his birth in 1931. Some reports of Julio Henry's symptoms match the general pattern of untreated classic Galactosemia.

Davina comforted her daughter, feeling the anguish as if it were hers. Amerigo, too, was deeply saddened but comforting the family was Davina's job. But he could not prevent doubt from mingling into his soul. The Menicuccis had always believed that opportunities always accompanied significant events in people's lives. The mining accident provided the opportunity for a new direction in America. Dante's crisis led to his full recovery and a robust family. Where were the opportunities in this tribulation? Never had he or Davina been stricken down as that day. The women wept, the men shook their heads in dismay and little Regina hid in her room playing. In the end, they all prayed because it was all they had left.

A ROAD TO NOWHERE

In the following days, the shock of the situation coalesced into the acceptance that, somehow, the family had to adjust to this new situation. Arlene required twenty-four/seven care. She was severely underweight and remained highly susceptible to infections of many types. She convulsed regularly, requiring emergency trips to St. Joseph Hospital, about a fifteen-minute drive away. Each time, the attending physicians calmed the child with tranquilizers and then sent the family on their way home. Arlene struggled to gain weight, vomiting frequently. She had severe bouts of diarrhea followed by constipation. Rena learned the skills of a practical nurse, everything from impacted bowels to spoon feeding to sponging up vomit. Rena slept when Arlene did, which meant she slept little. Al maintained his routine of working and returning home each evening to assist Rena, holding his damaged girl and playing with his healthy toddler.

Every day, Davina and Amerigo attended seven in the morning Mass at Immaculate Conception, followed by special prayers to the Virgin Mary, often lighting a votive candle in her honor. Amerigo prayed to be shown the opportunities from the family's personal disaster. Both individuals drew their deep religious beliefs from personal, life-changing experiences. Gemma Menicucci Morris told the story: "During a trip to Italy when Padre Pio was alive and offering Mass and hearing confessions, Nonno Amerigo shared in our family den the experience he had with Padre Pio. He went to confession and confessed his sins and when he had finished, Padre Pio said, 'What about the other sins, Amerigo?' Nonno was overwhelmed because Padre Pio knew he had forgotten some sins to confess, and they had never met. Later, when they attended Mass, at the elevation of Jesus in the consecration, Padre Pio's hands bled from the stigmata he had received. Davina shook her head in agreement whenever he told the story."

A quick breakfast followed, and then Davina prepared a basket of food and materials that she used at Rena's home every day. Amerigo dutifully transported her to the Arrigoni home each morning and then returned at noon for lunch and again in the evening for dinner with the family. Amerigo spent his days at Super Service Station. Davina assisted Rena as any Italian mother would, providing aid and comfort. Her main job was to prepare meals and care for little Regina. Davina offloaded chores from Rena so that she could concentrate on Arlene, which was a continual struggle. For Davina, it was a six in the morning to seven in the evening job, every day of the year.

After months of this slough, Rena finally hit the wall. Arlene was slowly gaining weight because they had eliminated milk products from her diet, but she remained completely bed-bound. Arlene was becoming a child but with the full dependency of a debilitated newborn. Rena constantly leaned over the crib railing to lift the child, straining the spine and lower back muscles. The repetitive motion finally took its toll and she ruptured a disk in her spine. She collapsed in severe pain. Rena was admitted to St. Joseph Hospital where Dr. Leroy Miller, a neurosurgeon, performed a laminectomy. He removed the damaged parts of the disk that caused her pain. It left her in the hospital for nearly two weeks. During that time, Davina assumed full control of the household with all its attendant duties, including the specialized care of Arlene. It was an all-encompassing job for a young woman but exceedingly difficult for a 60-year-old. Other family members helped during this crisis, notably Louise, Rena's sister and Theresa Domenici Menicucci, her sister-in-law.

As Rena lay recovering in the hospital, she had plenty of time to think and pray. Things were different because the medical team warned her about heavy lifting. She had permanently damaged her spine by repeatedly lifting Arlene and if it happened again, she could disable herself. The message was clear. She needed a different approach. Al had seen it coming and warned her, but Rena was a determined woman, similar to that of her cousin, Teresa Menicucci Clark.[3] Now, she and Al were on the same page. Rena knew she had to pick up her child, but she thought of ways to ease the lifting. Marco Donati, a carpenter and close friend of the family, built a special crib that allowed one side to be lowered so the child could be loaded onto a wheelchair. He modified the home in other ways to facilitate care.

PREGNANCY ELIXIR

Once home, Rena's health quickly improved. With the new setup at home, she managed the child adequately without imperiling her spine. She settled into a daily routine of twenty-four-hour physical care for the child while managing her other daughter and the household. Davina continued to help during the day, and Al worked tirelessly to provide income for the family and assist Rena at other times. Life was a struggle both physically and psychologically. Rena, fully captivated by Arlene, feared that she was neglecting her oldest daughter. She had no time for Home and School Associations, church spaghetti dinners, Christmas Pageants or two-week vacations at Sulphur Springs. They were as tied to their home as the family's Italian ancestors were a century earlier. The situation was heartbreaking for the family as well as for relatives and friends who desperately desired to assist but had nothing to offer.

Rena's mood darkened as she envisioned her healthy daughter growing up in a medically troubled and isolated family. She complained about her own depression with her pediatrician, Dr. Woodward. His solution was unique and non-obvious: Rena should bear another child. It was likely that Arlene would die within a few years, he added, stranding Regina as an only child. At that time, at least two children were recommended per family. It surprised Rena, given their recent experience with Arlene. A second child in that condition could break the family. Woodward assured them that the probability was exceedingly low to start with, but since the couple had already experienced the disease, the probability of a repeat was further reduced.

Unfortunately, Woodward misunderstood both the genetic situation and fundamental statistical theory. Galactosemia appears when the child inherits a defective gene from both parents. In the normal population, the disease occurs roughly at the rate of one in forty thousand births, or about two and a half thousandths of a percent (.0025%). Arlene's condition confirmed that Rena and Al were both unaffected carriers of Galactosemia, and as such, the couple had a twenty-five percent probability of producing another stricken child, ten thousand times higher than the general population. Secondly, a previous occurrence of an event does not alter the probability of that event recurring. In other words, the fact that the couple previously produced a Galactosemic child did not affect the probability of a second one.[4]

Based on their understanding at the time, they agreed with the doctor. A short time later, Rena became pregnant and confident in modern medical care. The physicians carefully applied all their pre-natal skills throughout the pregnancy, including restricting her from milk products. They also prepared a special diet for the baby, which was totally milk-free. They had a special surgical team prepared to assist in her prenatal care and her labor. The team monitored her as she progressed normally through the pregnancy. On 20 December 1960, she produced her third child, a clear-eyed, pink-colored, crying bundle of energy immediately cradled into Rena's breast. Most importantly, Rena prayed as she gazed deeply into the child's eyes as the baby blinked them open, giving thanks to the Lord for what appeared to be a healthy child.

With Davina helping with the Arlene, the Arrigonis' lives stabilized. Arlene remained completely disabled but was gaining a modest amount of weight. The situation existed for about 18 months. Arlene was becoming so heavy that Rena could not handle her and was straining her back with twinges of pain sparking her memory of her own injury. Moreover, she constantly worried that she was depriving her other children of a normal home environment that could affect them emotionally throughout life. The family was isolated from normality. Al could see the situation and agreed that they needed either full-time, in-home help or they had to institutionalize the child.

Rena abhorred the thought of institutionalization and she wanted to exhaust all options before resorting to an institution. All Rena's deterministic skills were now on the line to find someone who would work ten hours a day in their home, nearly every day of the year, to care for a completely helpless four-year-old child. Costs were certainly a concern for the family, as medical bills had ravaged their finances in a time with limited health insurance. Al was a successful professional who continually produced the income needed to support his family. The situation demanded as much as he could produce.

MEXICAN MIRACLE

Both parents spread the word in the community and a number of women were suggested. None worked out. The Italians in the community, in great sympathy with the family, strove to assist fellow paesani (countrymen) and one stepped up. Charlie Mayo, an Italian immigrant and friend of the family, called Rena to report that his severely disabled child had just died and her nurse, a woman from Mexico, was interested in similar work.

Rena interviewed the woman and was immediately impressed at the love that the Mexican, Antonia Ramirez, showed toward Arlene. Antonia gently picked her up, cuddled her and talked softly face-to-face, with the child responding. Rena had her gal. The only problem was that Antonia spoke only Spanish. Unlike her brother Mario, she spoke no Spanish, only English and Italian. The similarities between the languages are many, with some identical words. Rena spoke to Antonia in Italian and Antonia spoke back in Spanish. They communicated more than adequately. Antonia was like a miracle for Rena, freeing her during the day from the constant care required by Arlene. For a year, she basked in her new-found freedom, spending time with her daughters. Over time, Arlene's milk-free diet stabilized her conditions so that emergency episodes such as convulsions were infrequent, greatly lowering the tension level in the home. Arlene was also growing as the food she was ingesting was no longer poisoning her body.

As Antonia passed her first anniversary of working for the family, Rena recognized the problems she was imposing on her family by attempting to treat a severely disabled child in an inappropriate living space. Furthermore, Arlene was gaining weight and could nudge a wheelchair about in open areas. Unfortunately, the Arrigoni home had few open spaces and some hallways were too narrow for a wheelchair. By late 1960, Rena and Al seriously discussed institutionalization for Arlene.

NO HELP FOR THE HELPLESS

As the Arrigonis discussed possible institutions, Rena had her own ideas. She wanted a home where her daughter could be cared for as she and Antonia were doing until the little girl passed to the Lord. The State Hospital and Training Center in Los Lunas, New Mexico was the only public facility available to treat severely impaired children. Unfortunately, the Center was the subject of regular front-page news stories about feckless behavior, ranging from accounting practices to maltreatment of patients. Some of the local churches and other charitable groups offered various levels of assistance to children in Arlene's condition, but no private facility existed for in-patient care over an indefinite period. Families that rejected the state-supplied institutionalized care at Los Lunas or whose applications were rejected due to lack of space were left to fend for themselves.

The situation took a toll on the community and several organizations, such as the National Association for Retarded Children and its New Mexico Charter, the New Mexico Association for Retarded Children, became active. Through the 1950s and well into the 1970s, the groups conducted awareness campaigns, including expert speakers on the care and nurturing of retarded children. They also brought to light some of the issues at the hospital, but the local press discovered most problems.[5]

The Los Lunas facility had become a well-known and infamous subject on the front pages of the local papers over the past decade. One problem was that the hospital had neither the mission nor the facilities to provide long-term care to severely disabled children. Care for these children fell under the Hospital's Training mission, an adjunct to their medical care mission. It broadly applied to people of all ages, but it was staffed and structured to provide specific, short-term training of various types that involved limited in-hospital stays. Originally, the facility's programs only provided specialized vocational training for children with mild or moderate disabilities. The hospital was poorly equipped with neither personnel nor facilities to accommodate severely disabled children who needed constant attention for life. A 1960 hospital brochure stated, "In nearly all cases, the Los Lunas Hospital and Training School admissions are for short-term specified periods for specialized training." State law and political pressure required them to provide a full range of services whether or not they could competently provide them. The government shoved the proverbial square peg in a round hole.

It was fodder for problems. The hospital's mission was too broad for the budget and their overall performance suffered. During the mid-1950s, the hospital was the target of numerous investigations of alleged mismanagement, graft, various illegal accounting schemes, patient abuse, racial discrimination and malpractice. In July 1956, New Mexico Governor John Simms appointed a special council led by Leanard DeLao to investigate the hospital. The damning report suggested sweeping changes in operation and management.

By 1960, when Rena was seriously considering an institution, the Los Lunas facility had restaffed and reformed its operations. Positive reports about the hospital appeared in the local news. Some of the buildings had been remodeled, and others had been expanded. The political shakeup produced some changes, including new leadership. Bed space was increased from their earlier limits and new expert physicians were hired. Whether it was window dressing to buck the press off its backs or whether it had actually improved, the hospital slowly burnished its reputation. The Arrigonis resolved to visit the institution. It was an option that had been hanging over the family for years and had to be seriously considered or rejected. Al arranged a tour of the facility.

OLFACTORY ASSAULT

At the hospital a week later, the Arrigonis looked about the reception area and were impressed with its cleanliness and orderliness; good initial indicators of a properly run organization. Director Francis Russell hosted their visit. Russel had only been on the job for a few months but was brimming with enthusiasm. His published credentials were impressive; Bachelor of Science and Master of Education degrees with broad administrative experience in institutions for retarded children. His presentation to the couple was inspiring, touting his plans for expansion and improvement, along with knowledge of the latest advances for treating severely retarded children. Most important, Russell projected empathy for the couple and all others in similar situations. A heartening opening it was, buoying the couple's demeanor.

The favorable impression lasted as long as it took to enter the wing of the hospital that housed severely retarded children. Stepping inside, Rena's head recoiled in response to a pungent odor of urine that hung heavily in the air. It was similar to the ammonia-based smelling salts that stimulate a punch-drunk prize fighter. The odor offended Rena's Italian feminine spirit. Foul odors are indications of improper cleanliness and health. The assault pivoted to her visual senses; she saw three- and four-year-olds curled in corners of dank rooms, sucking their toes and drooling. Outrage welled within her. These were children of God. How could anyone treat them like this? Then her ears heaped on the offensive. She heard sobbing from children with hydrocephaly, a condition that causes the brain to swell with excess fluids, leaving poorly treated children with grotesquely boated heads that were sometimes larger than their bodies. It produces symptoms similar to severe mental retardation. What struck her was the lack of attendants for these unfortunate souls. Al and Rena were quiet during the tour, collecting and assimilating information.

Russell accompanied them into his office, smiling and asking for comments, demonstrating professional pride for his presentation. Rena sat in numbed silence. After a few moments, Al broke the hush with a simple question for Russell: "If it were your child, would you put him or her here?" Russell stammered and stuttered, trying to find some words to avoid the obvious. But Al pushed and the director eventually stated "No." "Neither will the Arrigonis," Al stated defiantly. Tears welled in Rena's eyes and dripped down her cheeks as hope once again faded.

On the way home, the couple knew that Los Lunas was not for them. They were once again laid low and somber by the prospect that they were truly on their own in caring for Arlene. Al comforted Rena by promising to revise their home and hire whatever help was needed to care for their daughter. Rena knew it would not work. They had already decided that long-term home care was impractical for both Arlene and the family. They needed to convert the entire home into a nursing facility, which was unfair to her other children. When the couple arrived back home, Davina and Amerigo greeted them. Davina could see before the couple exited the vehicle that the tour had flamed out. As Davina heard the tale and witnessed the terrible agony of the couple, her advice was the same one that most Italians took from Italy for times of despair: "Non Devi Mai Pedere la Speranza," (You must never lose hope).

Davina believed the Lord guides those in travail and prayer is the hope to hear his message. Never was faith tested in Amerigo's family like those years. And never did it waiver because Davina was a pillar of spiritual strength that she acquired through her hardships. Gemma Menicucci Morris told the story: "I remember Nonna Davina praying every afternoon. She told me several times that this prayer time was so important to her because she promised God that if He would save her son, Mario, from a lung fungus, she would thank Him every day with prayer. Mario had contracted that fungus in Kansas and was very ill and near death." Mario recovered and Davina dutifully prayed for the remainder of her life.

HE SPEAKS

It was in late 1961 when Rena gathered her resolve. Los Lunas insulted the entirety of her being as an Italian Catholic woman. She saw visions of herself creating a severely-retarded care facility based on Catholic principles of faith, hope and charity, one capable of properly caring for her "beautiful angel," as she often called Arlene. As quickly as those thoughts appeared, she summarily rejected them. She had no experience building such facilities, even if she had the resources. The urges reappeared every time she picked up Arlene, her mind's eye envisioning her child of God under the care of loving attendants.

It was not long before she interpreted the mental urges as the Lord speaking directly to her. The Menicucci family long believed that special events in people's lives open opportunities to serve the Lord in better ways. Rena sensed that she stood at the threshold of a new opportunity. Her dream—creating a special home for Arlene and other families like hers was an extreme longshot, even for accomplished men or a powerful Catholic organization such as the Knights of Colombus. For a woman to contemplate such a feat was profound foolishness. She played it close to her vest, fearing ridicule for radical thinking and embarrassment if she failed.

Over just a few days, with the voice of the Lord continually urging her forward, she played a whim. She dreamed of a home run by Catholic nuns, so she cold-called the Mother Superior of Carmelite Nuns, a cloistered Catholic order based in Albuquerque's South Valley.[6] Rena spoke off-the-cuff, telling her story and laying out her dream of a home that provided loving Catholic care for the most hopeless of children. She explained the pitiful state of public care facilities for families, places where they allowed God's children to rot in dreadful conditions. She asked for advice.

The Mother Superior listened silently and then drew a breath to speak. Rena expected a quick rejection, and she was not disappointed. The Mother Superior sympathized but firmly stated that her order would not allow them to alter their cloistered status to take on such a project, even as worthy as this one was. Furthermore, her order had no experience in child care of any kind. To Rena's astonishment, the nun suggested contacting the

Dominican Nuns who staffed the school and church at St. Therese Little Flower parish on North Fourth Street. "Their order specializes in education and care," she said.

It was like a glowing ember on dry tinder; she was invigorated as her mind churned out images of a real home. She quickly called the Mother Superior and laid out her case. Again, the immediate reaction was negative because her Little Flower nuns already had a teaching mission. The nun was also moved by the obvious community need and the even more obvious need for a Catholic solution. She suggested that Rena call her motherhouse in Kenosha, Wisconsin and talk to Mother General a' Kempis at St. Catherine Hospital. It was Rena's first break. a' Kempis liked the idea and believed it was consistent with their mission. She suggested a meeting in Albuquerque six months hence to discuss the idea. Rena sprang into action preparing for the visit. Rena had no organizational, promotional or business experience; she acted on her instincts, a deep love for her daughter and belief in the Lord's guidance.

She launched a campaign to develop a facility. Her immediate goal was to impress Mother a' Kempis by demonstrating community support. She accumulated names of the most prominent men in town, all of them Catholics who could contribute money to the project and provide professional expertise. She called them one by one and laid out her case. Many family members and others in the community also helped her recruit men. Shortly after, she signed up a half dozen distinguished men, whom she called her board. After a few weeks, Rena called Mother a' Kempis to proudly report that she and her board would meet with her when she visited Albuquerque. At that time, Rena's board contained only men because the U.S. was still patriarchal in social structure, and she knew that she needed them to accomplish her objective.

The meeting with a' Kempis went well. The nun was interested but needed more evidence. Rena's board, which steadily added influential professionals, developed plans for physical structures and operational budgets, all used to update Mother a' Kempis, who remained in constant touch. The nun's intrigue and fascination grew with the steady progress in Albuquerque. Jack Craig, a local landowner and devoted Catholic, greatly bolstered the effort by donating a south-valley property, including a home, to the project, providing a physical place for Rena's facility. It was a boon, but the real problem was that a' Kemis had insufficient nuns to operate a home. Still, Rena and her board relentlessly met, reviewed plans and budgets, surveyed their resources and set goals even without the commitments of the nuns.

As they waited, they considered a facility name. Rena knew the name had to reflect the facility's purpose, which not only conveys Catholic love and charity but also imparts hope to the families. They reviewed many suggestions from board members and the community. None stuck until Rena reasoned it out. She believed Arlene was a child of God, one stricken with a horrid disorder but whose soul remained vibrant. These children were like angels of Heaven, she thought. Then it hit her. Her home would be fit for angels of the Lord. In Italian, Casa Angelica (House of Angels) characterizes it well. It is a home, not a hospital. It is clearly Catholic and reflects the virtues of the Arrigoni family and those of the nuns who operated it. It recognized the sanctity of life by dignifying helpless children. It was brilliant and when she presented it to the board, they resoundingly accepted it. As word spread in the community of the name, it stirred all.

THAT MAN

In 1965, Rena got the break she needed, again based on family help. Rena's sister Louise was married to Bill Stein, a bank officer. One day, a nun walked into the bank and approached a teller. She said she wanted to purchase property where her nuns might reside and work. She needed help from the bank in the real estate effort, a service the bank provided. Although she did not know Bill, she asked to talk to him. The clerk explained that Bill did not handle that type of work, but she insisted on speaking to "that man" as she pointed to Bill working at his desk well back from the teller cages.

Bill, noticing the nun, quickly took charge of the situation and brought her to his desk. She was the Mother Superior of an Italian order of nuns, the Canossian Daughters of Charity, which primarily focused on education but sought a South Valley site for a Novitiate, a training facility for young women contemplating the sisterhood. By creating a Novitiate in America, they could train women without the expense of bringing them to Rome. The Novitiate planned to operate a senior citizen home or "something else." It was the "something else" that Bill heard. Bill quickly secured her credentials and contact information and then called Rena.

Rena pounced on it and called the Mother Superior, Antonietta Colombo, residing at Annunciation Catholic Church. She made an appointment. The two women met and connected immediately, speaking in Italian and reminiscing about the old country. Rena turned quickly to business and presented her speech about a care facility. Sister Colombo loved Rena's idea and agreed to write to Rome for permission to realize Rena's dream as their "something else." Understanding the ways and delays of the Catholic bureaucracy, Rena figured on months of fretting waiting for a response. But it was her best opportunity.

She prayed, as did Al, Davina and Amerigo. Church members included the family in their special intentions during Sunday Masses. Others offered vigil candles to the Virgin Mary, a traditional Catholic practice of seeking divine intervention from a saint. The four elders in the family prayed the rosary at home to maintain hope. Davina had her pulse on her daughter's psychological state, and for the first time in years she noticed that Rena showed growing hope. Davina's goal was to keep hope alive and prayer was the means to do so. Rena said that Davina played a critical role at that time.

Six months passed before Rena received the news that the nuns were "delighted to assume the project." To Rena, it was akin to a miracle directly from the Lord and she operated under that assumption. Her mission was now divinely inspired and powered. Davina and Amerigo were pleased to hear Rena deliver the news as tears of joy flowed down her cheeks. Amerigo was not surprised. He was well aware of the power of the Lord. Mother a' Kempis was disappointed that she could not provide the labor for the project but congratulated Rena on her success.

EXPRESSO MOMENT

The Canossian commitment jolted the board like a triple expresso. Cheers and shouts such as "Let's go!" and "Get moving!" filled the room. By 1965, the project was rolling forward with increasing momentum as the emphasis shifted from concept to reality. Rena commenced converting an ancient home located on the donated property into one that met all of the modern bureaucratic standards for nursing facilities. She was counting on it as the basic structure for Casa Angelica, allowing the nuns to move in expeditiously. She and the board believed the home could be easily modified.

Unfortunately, the building was too deteriorated for restoration. The only way to pass the required codes was to raze it and build a new one. Once again, a roadblock threatened to derail the project. In the board meeting where Rena presented the findings of the inspectors, anguish initially prevailed. The board consisted of distinguished professionals and solid Catholics who were not easily dissuaded. In an audacious response, they drafted plans for a new structure on the land. The fact that they had little money did not deter them.

The process to obtain a state-sanctioned nursing facility was daunting and expensive, but by March of 1966, Rena had already approved a plan for the new seven-thousand-square-foot children's home. Bids were immediately sought, with the low bidder proposing a cost of one hundred and eighty thousand dollars (about one million seven hundred thousand in 2024 dollars). The board at the time had essentially no budget and had been operating on endorphin highs that they always derived from charitable endeavors. They now had a cost goal and sensed they were on the brink of a significant event. Five members immediately volunteered to cosign a loan agreement personally. Within a few weeks, a loan was issued to the Casa Angelica Board to "construct a nursing home for severely retarded children to be operated by the Canossian Daughters of Charity, an order of nuns from Rome, Italy," as was stated on the loan agreement.

Rena was indefatigable, one displaying unbounded energy. She was also a visionary, one who dreams the impossible and leads others in a quest to achieve it. She employed both the vigor and aggressiveness of her Uncle Julio and the smooth sales skills of her father, Amerigo. She brought quality people on board her team, created the vision and fostered it with enthusiasm. Her inborn leadership skills encouraged the members to freely innovate and apply their professional skills as needed. They were all Catholics and solid believers in the necessity of charitable giving as a major aspect of life, and she used every bit of Catholic training in her promotions.

WOMEN RISE

One board member, Ben Raskob, a wealthy cattle rancher, had assisted in developing the Brothers of the Good Shepard Refuge, a Catholic care facility for homeless men in Albuquerque. He served on its advisory board and brought much of his experience to Rena's group. Once on Rena's board, he focused on the essential issue of sustainability: how to fund Casa's day-to-day operations over the long term. He believed that the support might come from the community. Rena knew of a huge and untapped community resource: the women, starting with her family and progressing outward. Many in the Italian colony were distressed as they watched the family struggle and frustrated that they could not help. Now was their chance.

Rena and Ben conceived of a Casa Angelica Auxiliary, one run and operated by women and dedicated to funding its operation. It would be the ongoing "sustainer" for the home. She recruited Anna McCulloch to advise her. Anna had worked on Catholic social programs for decades and had community contacts and organizational skills. She helped Rena organize the Auxiliary's board.

Like a bold field commander, Rena personally led the Auxiliary's recruiting drive in the community, calling family members, friends and just about anyone willing to listen. Rena formed a board of directors for the Auxiliary, led by her sister Louise and Sister-in-law Theresa Domenici Menicucci. They organized the recruiting program. Adele Morelli Davis, daughter of Teodolindo, told the story. Her husband, a military officer, had just been assigned to Kirtland Air Force Base in 1966, and the family was moving into their home. Rena called her. "Adele, I need you to call five Italians in town to support the Auxiliary." Then, she listed the names of the ones to call. Adele protested because she had an infant and was in the throes of a major family relocation. Rena, out of breath, insisted, "I don't care. We have just this one opportunity for Casa, and we need your help." Adele relented as Rena recounted the benefits to the community and their devotion to Catholic Charities. Decades later, Adele said that Rena was one of the most persuasive salespersons she had ever encountered. The community of Catholic women, led by Italians but incorporating many Anglos and Hispanics, responded in force, nearly overwhelming the Auxiliary with labor.

Within a few months, the Auxiliary had an army of women volunteers who went on a spree, conducting fundraisers from Spaghetti dinners to ballroom dances. Emma Dalle Menicucci told the story: "Louise was an auxiliary officer and was in charge of organizing members. She held meetings in her home to organize and direct activities." Charlie Menicucci said it Louise ran it like a military operation and said, "Just about every Italian woman was involved and Louise always had groups of women on call for one job or another." There was something about Casa Angelica, whether its lofty purpose to maintain the sanctity of human life or Rena's love for her child, that set the community afire.

On January 16, 1967, Rena took communion from Archbishop James Davis in the dedication ceremony in the new Casa Angelica facility. Following Mass, Rena stood at the gate to Casa Angelica and helped snip the ceremonial ribbon, opening the facility to the public. In April of 1967, Rena and Al surrendered their precious daughter to the loving care of the nuns. Against astronomical odds, Rena—a determined woman in a man's world—had accomplished what few thought was possible just several years earlier.[7]

THE CASE FOR DIVINE INTERVENTION

Davina and Amerigo were content. They always believed that somehow, Arlene's tragedy would result in benefits. However, the magnitude of Rena's accomplishment astonished even them. The future value of a sustainable Catholic facility that serves the most helpless in the community was incalculable. They were both convinced that the Lord was at work. In those dismal days following Arlene's birth when she was routinely rushed to the hospital clinging to life, hope was routinely dashed. Prayer dutifully restored it.

The Menicucci family generally believed that Rena's sudden conversion from a weary and struggling mother to a brilliant real estate developer was an act of the Holy Spirit. There is a case to be made and the Acts of the Gospels (2: 1-26) describes the doctrine: In the time following Christ's crucifixion, the Apostles lived in isolation, angst and terror, fearing reprisals for association with Jesus. Jesus, seeing this situation, sent the Holy Spirit to rectify the problem. The Holy Spirit—the mysterious third person of a single God—descended on the men, imbuing them with extraordinary courage to boldly evangelize the word of Christ to the world. They suddenly became multilingual and mingled easily among the global population. After her personal Pentecost, Rena became suddenly multilingual, speaking the language of a promoter. She had a clear vision, courage and perseverance to prevail against monumental odds. Like the apostles, she never abandoned hope because she always prayed.

As of today, the nuns of the Canossian Daughters of Charity continue to operate Casa Angelica. While it accepts children of all faiths, it remains a Catholic institution operating according to the highest principles of Christian faith, hope and charity. The Casa Angelica Auxiliary maintains its traditional role as a sustainer. Today, Casa Angelica, operating in its original location, maintains a loving, Catholic home for the most severely disabled children.

SUPREME FAMILY CONTRIBUTION

The contributions from the Arrigoni family extend beyond those of Casa Angelica. The family has no descendants past Rena's and Al's children, eradicating Galactosemia from the bloodline. If, as many Italians believe, family offspring are the ultimate gifts to the future, then the Arrigonis lack of descendants is a monumental gift of avoided tragedy to future generations. The sacrifices from this family not only highlight their virtue and fortitude as human beings but also their deep-seated belief in the Lord Jesus, the one they credited for sustaining them through some of the most devastating times a family can face. The Arrigoni's actions, led by Rena, are possibly the greatest contribution from a Menicucci member in known family history.

See notes 8, 9, 10, 11, 12, 13.

Notes

1. *Arrigoni*, in her book, noted the issue about the umbilical cord at birth, but she never discussed it again. It is possible that a constricted cord could have caused a lack of oxygen to the baby, damaging her brain. If so, Galactosemia was not the only medical condition involved. Also, the child was born with cataracts. This might indicate that Galactosemia had developed in the womb, possibly induced by Rena's consumption of milk products during pregnancy. It may not have mattered whether milk had been restricted from Arlene's diet after birth because she was likely already permanently disabled at birth. Some of the dramatic emergencies with the girl later on might have been prevented had she been fed a milk-free diet following birth.

2. Galactosemia is a rare genetic condition that occurs when the child receives two damaged genes, one from each parent. A parent carrying a single defect is an unaffected carrier and displays no symptoms of the disease. When both parents are unaffected carriers, the chances

of a Galactosemic child is twenty five percent. The chances of the pair producing an unaffected carrier is fifty percent and for a normal birth with no genetic defects, the probability is twenty-five percent. The genetic defect had been in the families' DNAs for decades but was never realized until Arlene. Many generations may pass before the improbable coupling of damaged genes produces a new victim. It is impossible to know about any past incidents of the disease in the family because encounters with Galactosemia were likely expeditiously followed by death. The parents would not have recognized the condition as genetically related, reporting it as an infant death, which occurred routinely in Italy.

In the Twentieth-First Century, Galactosemia remains a serious medical condition. Today, all newborns are tested for Galactosemia following birth. Appropriate dietary restrictions in common practice today would have minimized the damage to Arlene. Cesarean section is the standard method for delivering breech births, eliminating any complications with the cord. Fetuses today can be physically nudged about in the womb to help avoid any pinches to the cord. Had Arlene been born today, she would have likely survived the condition and lived a quasi-normal existence, but one burdened by life-long and expensive medical treatments and careful diets. She might even have become successfully pregnant, producing asymptomatic children. With a family history of the disease, a modern obstetrician carefully screens, controls and monitors the pregnancy using modern diagnostic tools, such as MRIs and genetic tests. *Delnoy, et. al, Berry, Rubio-Gozalbo* and the *Galactosemia Handbook* provide technical details about the malady and how it is treated.

3. Teresa and Rena were both determined and forceful women. Once they had a personal goal, it was difficult to dissuade them from pursuing it. But they approached the goals differently. Rena preferred diplomacy to Teresa's brashness, which included never walking away from a good scrap if she needed to make a point.

4. Davina and/or Amerigo were unaffected Galactosemia carriers. Amerigo's brother Aledino and his son Julio Henry, both of whom died of mysterious ailments, might have suffered from Galactosemia. Duarte Galactosemia is a milder form of the disease but can induce complications, such as nephrites that can reduce lifespans, such as the one of Aladino. However, the causes of death for both children are not known.

5. Information about the Los Lunas facility was derived largely from newspaper reports. *Mateju* presents a copy of the brochure for the

facility indicating that it was not intended for nursing care for permanently disabled children.

6. Cold-calling is a marketing technique where potential customers are called on without being previously introduced. In cold-calling marketing, the success rate is very low, so many are called in order to produce a few customers.

7. History is dominated by men but their success depended on women. Men would not exist at all except for women producing them. The story of Casa Angelica is a testament to the value women provide to the community. *Albright* and *Harney* discuss the role of Italian immigrant women in America.

8. *Spidle* describes the history of medical practice in New Mexico over a century, starting in 1876.

9. *Arrigoni* provides a first-person account of the creation of Casa Angelica.

10. *Giomi* (Ioli) presents a short summary about the Canossian Sisters and the founding of Casa Angelica. Published in December, 1977, Volume IV, Number 11.

11. The story of Casa Angelica is one of the most powerful and enduring tales of any of the early Italians. People discuss it today as if it just happened. Many still marvel at Rena's accomplishments and the robustness of her creation and believe the entire affair was divinely inspired.

12. News reports from the two Albuquerque newspapers provided considerable information for this chapter.

13. Corroborated lore provided information for this chapter.

21

LUCCHESE ATTAIN SIGNIFICANCE (1954–1961)

GROWTH GALORE

In 1954, Albuquerque's Italian colony comprised around three-hundred Italian-surnamed families; about two-thirds were Lucchese. Considering that about three times as many southern Italians as northerners immigrated to America, the large percentage of Lucchese in Albuquerque was remarkable but unsurprising.[1] Lucchese founded Albuquerque's Italian colony and the success of these people in America was not lost on their friends and family in Lucca. Oreste Bachechi, an initial immigrant, was remarkably prescient in his pre-1900 exhortations about Albuquerque. From an economic perspective, the early immigrants could not have picked a better time to immigrate or a better place to land than Albuquerque. In the 1950s and well into the 1960s, Albuquerque was routinely among America's fastest-growing cities per capita. Building permits issued in Albuquerque between 1945 and 1955 rose over seven-hundred percent. Many more new businesses succeeded than failed. The city regularly annexed big blocks of land where homes and businesses sprang from the high desert landscape like desert flowers after a spring rain. Kirtland field comprised Sandia Base and Manzano Base, creating an Air Force Base and opening up civilian employment opportunities. Between 1945 and 1955 Albuquerque's population doubled.

America was a Christian-based country and Albuquerque was heavily Catholic. Moreover, many of the descendants of the early immigrants, some

3rd generation, inherited the zeal and drive that characterized the original immigrants. In other words, they were doing what good, decent Catholic Italians do: produce virtuous and productive people who serve society over generations. The Italians quickly assimilated into Albuquerque's society, selecting to retain certain Italian customs and practices.

Public schools steadily expanded under Superintendent John Milne. The city then had two high schools, four junior highs and 45 elementaries. Nearly sixteen hundred students attended St Mary's school—six hundred 9th-12th grade high-schoolers and nine hundred first-through-eighth grade schoolers. Forty-two hundred students attended the University of New Mexico.

The city had three radio stations (KOB, KGGM, KOAT) and two television stations (KOB and KGGM). In 1956, the city completed the Civic Auditorium, a round structure with a bubble-shaped roof. It drew in some big entertainers, such as Bob Hope and Victor Borge. Frank Sinatra, of northern Italian descent, performed in the arena to a packed house in 1957, including many young, local Italian women who marveled at his handsome, youthful manliness. His silky-smooth crooning all but laid them to faint.

The city maintained eight-hundred miles of roads, two hundred and fifty paved. It constantly proposed bonds for infrastructure and the public generally approved them. Few development projects were denied, but city leaders overwhelmingly defeated a suggested pulp mill facility. Albuquerque's downtown neighborhoods were already plagued with periodic outbreaks of putrid fumes from the human waste processing facility south of the city. A pulp mill, with its infamous reputation for offensive effluents, had no chance.

BOOM TIME

By the middle 1950s, with the Korean War in the mirror, the city, its economy and the Menicucci family were all in the fast growth lane. The war had little effect on Albuquerque, save for those men who had escaped the World War II draft due to age were now called to serve. The scale of the Korean War was a tiny fraction of the world war. Families and businesses grew in concert, with the family enterprises producing adequate resources for both families to live a middle-class lifestyle and royal luxury compared to Colono's life in Italy.

Albuquerque's downtown area remained the heart of the business community, and Super Service Station was in the midst of it. Location and visibility are keys in retailing and the Menicucci brothers capitalized with a constant barrage of advertisements offering one deal or another. Tires—sales and service—were producing major profits for the station. Mario was always quick to explain that gas was a convenience for customers with tiny margins burdened by high labor costs for the islands; it rarely contributed to profit. By the late 1950s, Super Oil and Super Service employed full-time bookkeepers. Mario also purchased a building on Fourth Street directly north of the Super Service Station office. He converted it into a warehouse to store tires and other accessories.

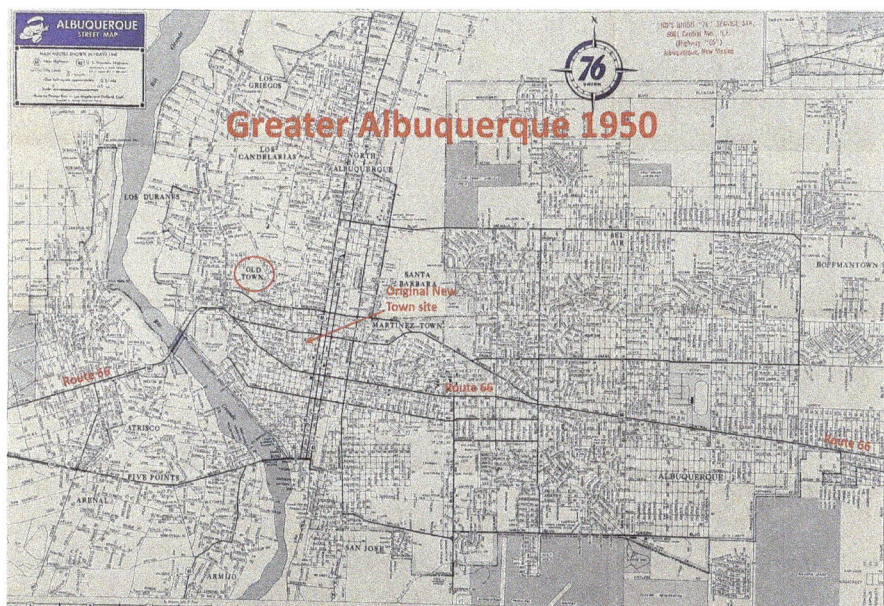

The Greater Albuquerque area in 1950. The phenomenal growth of the city from 1900 is obvious. Route 66 was principally responsible for the rapid development.

When Charlie hired Ralph Green as a mechanic in the mid-1950s, he more than doubled the repair shop's productivity. Ralph performed repairs full-time while Charlie split his time between management and hands-on work. Ralph was a local Hispanic with deep roots in the community. The repair work grew so fast that Mario purchased the building north of the station and Julio connected the two buildings with a hallway. It instantly quadrupled Charlie's available indoor repair stalls from two to eight. No longer would he and his men be forced to repair autos in the winter cold. Nor would they compete with Johnny Matteucci for the stove because they had their own in the new shop.

Dante and Mario developed quickly in their roles as business managers. Dante assumed the mantle of the enterprise leader, taking the job from Julio. He had the right personality, drive and leadership skills for the job. Julio had trained him in his likeness. Julio listed himself in the Albuquerque business directory as a driver for Super Oil, which gave Dante the public notice to proceed upward. Julio used the time to enjoy work that he routinely had done years earlier—delivering products directly to customers. He used the deliveries to take him about town, which could help him identify potential business opportunities. Super Oil had contracts with the Jesuit priests in Jemez to supply oil products to them. Super Service held the contract for all of their automotive repairs.

Julio used his deliveries to Jemez as opportunities for him and his brother to take in a mineral bath or catch a few trout. Julio knew many folks in Jemez, including the man who drove the fishing stream stocking truck. By this time, New Mexico had stocked trout in the state's streams, rivers, and lakes. The stocking driver called and told Julio exactly when and where he planned to stock the streams. With his brother in tow, Julio conveniently arranged Super Oil deliveries to Jemez on the day following stocking. Julio explained, "The trout won't bite when they first put them in the stream because they are shocked. But the next day, they are hungry." These Jemez deliveries with Julio were as close as Amerigo ever got to Super Oil Company. While Julio was overseer of both organizations and spent time at both locations, Amerigo had virtually nothing to do with Super Oil. But if Julio were delivering kerosene in Jemez, then Amerigo was compelled to assist his brother on the delivery and whatever additional Jemez Mountain activity might be appropriate, such as fishing. It was strange to see a two-thousand-gallon fuel tanker truck parked alongside the highway with its operators standing in the Jemez River trout fishing. The brothers were feeling the retirement spirit.

Ward's Trading Post in Jemez Springs was one of several Super Oil Company's customers in Jemez Springs. Other customers included Sulphur Springs and the La Cueva Lodge operated by Leonard Tartaglia. The trading post was directly across from the Los Ojos Bar on state Road 4. Courtesy Jemez Springs Public Library.

Mario, too, was content to do what he learned best—run a retail business. Mario had been schooled by Amerigo, one of the top retailers in Albuquerque. As with Amerigo, customers visited Super Service Station to talk to Mario. During this time, Amerigo focused on customer interaction, while Mario concentrated on learning management. Dante and Mario learned well. In 1957, Standard Oil Company, a major national supplier of oil products, honored Super Oil Company as its top wholesaler. Mario, meanwhile, negotiated a four-hundred-thousand-dollar contract with the state of New Mexico to supply tires for all state vehicles (about four million in 2024 dollars).

Super Service Station in the late 1950s with the employees and owners standing in foreground. By this time, the station had appropriated the nearby property (at right of the station) and converted it into a tire storage area. Courtesy author's collection.

Super Oil Company business office in 1950. Dante had hired Joe Benevidez as a fulltime bookkeeper who worked in the office. Dante employed around eight full-time employees, including himself.

Mario recognized his younger cousin, Charlie's, unique technical role and essentially abdicated the management of the business repair space to him. Mario kept the books for the station, including the repair business, which sometimes led to disputes about purchases for new equipment. Charlie constantly sought to stay abreast of automotive advances because new technology was appearing in automobiles every year. Many new vehicles required special instruments to diagnose problems. Without them, the service mechanic operated blindly. Mario, with limited technical background, was dismayed at the costs of test equipment. He once asked me, "Why does your dad need so much new equipment?" Charlie needed new equipment to service new vehicles. Besides, he was more than compensating for the investment with increased prices for the repair work. It rubbed against Mario's Amerigo-instilled sense of thrift. They believed that you invest in equipment and use it until it wears out. That applied to a lot of tools, such as brooms, but not test equipment for modern vehicles. Automobiles' electrical complexity was rocketing as World War II-developed technology found its way into commercial products. Charlie continuously explained to Mario the need for new equipment to remain competitive.

Dante, like Julio, was involved in the Knights of Columbus, steadily ascending to management positions by organizing organizational fundraising efforts. He also flirted with politics, working with Democrats in his political ward and supporting candidates by hosting political events. Conversely, Mario had a personality like Amerigo's, less ostentatious and aggressive, more reserved and lower key. He picked up American bowling as a hobby, playing on various teams in the city. He joined the Elks Club, as did other family members, but unlike Julio and Dante, he rarely sought organizational or leadership roles. Like Amerigo, he was content to let Julio and Dante gain the spotlight while he quietly ran the station and grew his family.

FELONIOUS NONNA (GRANDMOTHER)

While things in the family businesses were going swimmingly, one odious activity was flourishing right under Julio's nose: narcotics dealing at his home. At least that was the news that Albuquerque's Police Sergeant Alex Nottoli delivered to a suspected scofflaw at his residence one afternoon in 1957. Giulia Grangani Menicucci, Julio's wife, was merrily doing her housework at her new home on San Carlos Road, SW in the Huning Castle Addition. Hearing the front bell, the rotund, sixty-year-old woman waddled to the door, opened it a few inches and mouthed her normal greeting, which she had memorized phonetically. Running the words together, it sounded like: "Sorry, I donna speak English, goo bye." Then, she shut the door and walked away without looking at the visitor. Most people departed. This time, Nottoli, a long-time Lucchese immigrant, held up a letter, pounded on the door and shouted in Italian to open it; "Police business," he said. Once she peered out and saw that it was Alex, whom she knew, she opened the door.[2]

He shoved the letter in her face and facetiously asked if the letter was for her. Giulia looked at it and saw it was from her sister in Italy. She smiled and said yes. It was the package of Canapa seeds that she was expecting from her sister in Italy. She had assumed it was lost in the mail and Alex was delivering it to her. Instead, he delivered bad news. On the face of the letter was written: "Seme di Canapa (Canapa Seeds)." Woefully for Giulia, recent federal laws had outlawed all Cannabis, regardless of its content of hallucinogenic cannabinoids. Canapa was scientifically classified as Cannabis Sativa, although it contains an inconsequential amount of intoxicating ingredients. Canapa is a type of hemp used in craftsmanship throughout Italy. The damning evidence, as Alex saw it, was the letter itself, which had both Giuli's name and the name of the federally illegal contents noted in big lettering and contained seeds. Plus, she admitted the crime by identifying the envelope as intended for her. Giulia was suspected of narcotics trafficking, mail fraud, cultivation with intent to distribute, smuggling and a host of other felonies carrying long prison sentences.

Teresa Menicucci Clark, daughter to Julio, was visiting then and told the story: "That Alex stood there like a big bully, shaking that letter in mama's face and showing off his badge. When Mama finally figured out that she was accused of breaking the law and maybe going to jail, she nearly fainted. She screamed and cried as we got her to the couch. I called Papa and he came right over. When he got there and found out what happened, he laid into Alex: 'She's sixty years old and can't even speak English. She never even leaves the house. How is she going to sell narcotics? What's wrong with you?' Alex tried to explain the law, but his arrogance put everyone off. Alex was from Lucca and Papa told him he was 'disappointed that he thought like that of Lucchese woman.'"

Embarrassed, Alex retreated, but the damage was done. Julio was furious and followed him back to the police station, where he talked directly to the Chief, Paul Shaver. Shaver was an Immaculate Conception parishioner and occasionally added police-style assistance to help usher large congregations; Charlie Menicucci, Julio's son, was chairman of the Usher's Club. Julio served on the church building committee. The two families knew each other and shared the same Catholic life values, including applying common sense before accusing elders of crimes. He always had an open door for Julio.

Julio did not take long to wring out apologies from the city and promises for moderation and common sense in enforcement. Julio agreed to destroy any hemp seeds hanging around the house and to inform his Italian family of the prohibition. No charges were ever filed against Giuli, but the anecdote spread through the community like a forest fire, evoking emotions from outrage to robust laughter. Even today, the tale lives on. Giulia Menicucci was the notorious sexagenarian Italian Nonna accused of dealing narcotics out of her home on San Carlos Road in the Huning Castle Addition, one of Albuquerque's most prestigious neighborhoods.

An unlikely confluence of events led to this absurdity. By 1957, in a matter of six years, sweeping new drug laws outlawed products that had been used for centuries. Giulia's Italian family operated a fabric factory where they used Canapa liberally. She learned various needlecrafts in Italy and was by 1957 an accomplished craftswoman of embroidery and cutwork.[3] She used Canapa fibers, which are exceptionally strong, to fortify heavy-duty embroidered articles, such as potholders. Hemp fibers are, pound-for-pound, many times stronger than mild steel. Giulia had been using hemp since she came to America. It was always readily available. But by 1957, it had disappeared from Albuquerque store shelves. Logically, she wrote to her sister for seeds. She planned to grow some.

Giulia crocheted booties and bibs for each new grandchild as they appeared; pink for the girls and blue for boys. She used Canapa thread to fortify the booties. Courtesy author's collection.

Alex was promoted to sergeant/detective in 1957, just after sweeping federal drug regulations were enacted. It was a big promotion and he sought opportunities to impress his superiors. Part of his job was interfacing with the post office to ferret out drug trafficking. That put him in a position to spot the letter, giving him the unique opportunity to read the Italian-written envelope and surmise Guilia's guilt. His emotional zeal led him to extremes, for which he was disciplined. Italian needlework practice, the new drug laws and Alex's promotion conflated to produce a historically ridiculous event. If it had not been for Alex, it is likely the package would have been delivered without incident.

A Railway Express money truck in 1950 unloads bags of money at Albuquerque National Bank. From left: two federal agents, truck driver, Clyde Tingley, Alex Nottoli, three other police officers. Courtesy Albuquerque Museum, transfer from Albuquerque Public Library, Photographer: Hanna & Hanna.

PERSONALITY CONTRAST

Amerigo was a model of calm professionalism at the station, but the hunting field was a different story. There, his copious enthusiasm overflowed. The family men typically hunted, fished and foraged together and Amerigo was always the one most excited when he viewed huntable game outside the vehicle. Dove season, which started on September 1, excited him because it was the first outing after a long layoff from the previous fall. He could hardly wait to get out of the vehicle and begin shooting. Charlie told the story: "The five of us were driving up to a field near Lemitar loaded with doves. It was opening day and Zio (uncle) was itching to get out. There were hundreds of birds on the fence. Amerigo pushed everyone aside, got out of the car, loaded his gun and fired at an angle. He knocked down twenty-eight and the limit was twenty-five. He picked them up and tried to give some to us so he could keep hunting. Julio stepped up and told Amerigo 'You are over the limit. You're done for the day.'" Amerigo waited in the car sulking and mad as hell but he never did it again, at least not when Julio was there."

SAVING THE PORCINI

While that was typical Amerigo behavior in the field, Julio's might be typified by an event on New Mexico Road 4 south of Jemez Springs around 1960. It was a late, drizzly August afternoon as Julio, Charlie and I were returning from a wonderful mushroom hunting trip. We traveled in Julio's 1950 Desoto Custom 4-Door Sedan. It was more like a small military tank because of its durability and weight. It had plenty of power and its heavy steel frame was advantageous in snow and mud. We had been hunting along Road 4 in the Jemez Mountains high country, where the dirt road becomes nothing more than a wide trail snaking through the forest. We had gathered Porcini by the bushels full, and the car was stuffed with them. Boxes of Porcini filled the trunk, with every nook filled with fungi. Inside, boxes lay on the back seat and floor, leaving me a couple of square feet for sitting. A box-full lay on the front seat between Julio and Charlie. Large Porcini heads, some measuring over a foot in diameter, were tucked along the front and rear dashboards.

It had been a bonanza, and Julio was eager to get home and process them as soon as possible. The weather was hot and muggy, so getting them sliced and on drying racks was essential to produce a good stash of dried mushrooms that could last for years. Driving south out of Jemez Springs along Road 4, their bubbly conversation was abruptly interrupted by a southbound traffic pileup about four miles south of the village. Several arroyos cross the highway in that area, forcing drivers to ford them. In large rain events, which the region had experienced that afternoon, raging waters could scour out the pavement. From a view of the surface waters rushing across the road, it was impossible to know whether pavement was missing underneath, potentially creating a hazard that could stall an automobile as it fords, rendering the passengers in mortal danger of being swept downstream. People feared the crossings and many often waited for hours until the water receded before passing through.

Julio had been through this before but had a load of premier Porcini to process this time. He drove his Desoto in the northbound lane, passing a half dozen cars waiting behind the running water. He and Charlie got out of the vehicle to survey the situation. While Charlie was removing his socks, rolling up his pantlegs to his knee and putting his shoes on his bare feet, Julio grabbed a fishing pole and handed it to him. Charlie waded out into the arroyo as it flowed over the road, using the pole as a probe to confirm the secure pavement in front of him. The flow was only about twenty feet in width, so Charlie only needed to wade about half the distance by leaning forward and extending his long fishing pole to the other bank. Once he had tested the road, he gave the all-clear, got in the car, and Julio plunged through. Water lapped at the bottom of the car doors, but we were out in a few seconds and were speeding along with no other vehicles in front to impede him. More importantly, the Porcini were safe.

Once Julio was through, others followed. Charlie and Julio warned me not to reveal our little adventure to the women. Julio knew the wives would not have approved of the episode, and it was best to avoid the discussion altogether. If Amerigo had been in the vehicle, he would not have agreed to the plan, even after Charlie's assurance. Risk was not part of Amerigo's persona.

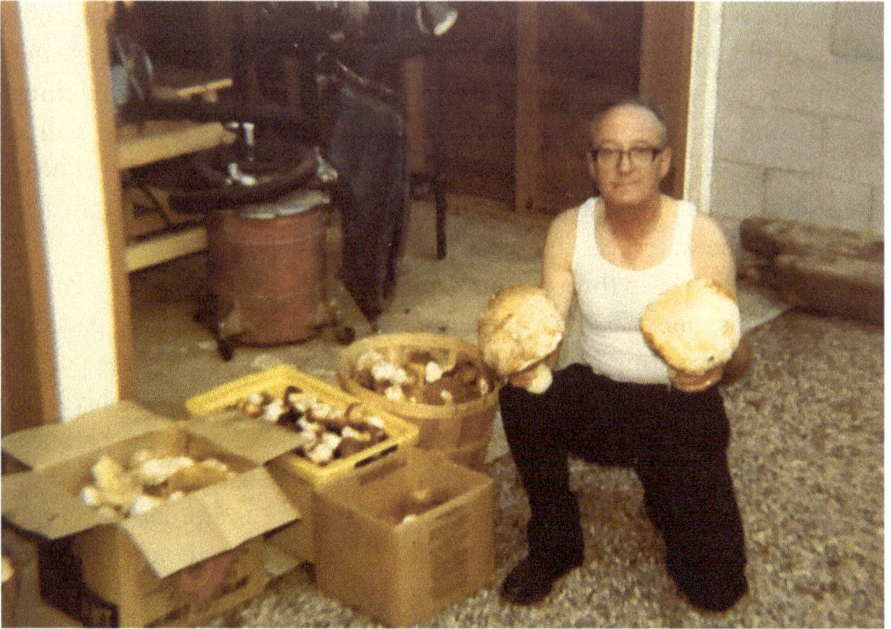

Charlie Menicucci displays some of his prized Porcini catch in the late 1950s. He and other family members spent hours slicing the mushrooms for drying on screens. Courtesy author's collection.

Often Porcini contain some indications of insects, such as worm or ant holes. This one is perfectly clean and was saved to eat fresh in salads, battered and fried or for inclusion in stews or soups. Courtesy author's collection.

A trio of large porcini growing in the Valles Caldera National Preserve. Courtesy author's collection.

BILLION-TO-ONE FLYER

Some hunting excursions ended more regrettably. Gilbert Jojola, one of Dante's drivers, hailed from the nearby Isleta Indian Reservation. Every native Indian reservation in New Mexico contained excellent hunting properties because many native people grew grain and corn. Grain attracts doves and quail, and pheasants favor corn. The Indians closely guarded their land, restricting hunting to tribal members who used their farms for direct sustenance. Tribal members occasionally brought in guests but did so sparingly, according to their customs. Many Indians bristled at the state's game bag limits, arguing that they were too high; the Indians maintained that Americans took more from the field than they needed. Among Albuquerque's hunting community, a reservation hunt was a rare prize for those deemed worthy.

Like a typical native Indian, Gilbert hunted the full range of animals, from finches to bull elk. He was impressed with how the Menicuccis hunted, carefully harvesting as much of the animal as possible, such as the hearts, livers, lungs and gizzards. Gilbert said, "You do just like the

Indians," referring to the Menicucci's routine of carefully harvesting all of the animals. Gilbert relished his work and earned a fine living. In gratitude, he offered a Christmas gift: an invitation for the Menicuccis to hunt quail on his family's property on the reservation south of Albuquerque. He explained that the game populations were getting too high on his fields and needed to be reduced. Dante, of course, jumped on the unusual opportunity, notified the family and set a date—the following Saturday.

That fateful day brought the five family members to the reservation gates, where Gilbert trotted up on a horse and let them pass, locking the gate behind them. He then led them down towards the river, where many grain fields and ample populations of scaled quail thrived. Typical coveys contained thirty to forty birds each. Quail are runners and greatly prefer it to flight. Typically, when a hunter encounters a covey, the birds scatter on the ground. A few flush, but they quickly light back on the ground. The hunter is lucky to get a few clean shots. Then it is on to the next covey.

Gilbert understood the patterns of the birds and their escape routes after they scattered. He knew that with his horse, he could close those routes and drive them back toward the hunters, providing additional shooting opportunities. Charlie and Dante coordinated with Gilbert as they worked up an arroyo gully and were quickly filling out their limits of birds. Gilbert had repositioned himself on a ridge about ten feet above and about a forty-five-degree angle from the men's direction of travel. Gilbert turned to look back towards the hunters as Charlie spied a quail running up a sandy gully and fired a shot. As usual, he killed the quail.

Immediately they heard Gilbert shout. Looking up, he and Dante saw Gilbert falling from his horse while holding his face. "I can't see," he screamed. No blood was around his eyes, but Charlie was Army-trained in field-dressing wounded men. When he pulled up Gilbert's eyelid, he could see a hole about the size of a shotgun shell pellet in the middle of his pupil. Then, it dawned on him that it was a pellet from his gun. Even though Gilbert was not directly in the line of fire, he was close enough that a single pellet ricocheted off a hard surface hidden just below the sand, eluded his normal eyeblinks and entered his pupil with enough force to totally and permanently blind the eye. It was a safe shot from Charlie's perspective because he fired into sand and Gilbert out of sight. Gilbert, too, believed he was safely above and sufficiently behind the target on the ground. Theoretically, it was not an unsafe shot.

They rushed Gilbert to St. Joseph Hospital, about forty minutes away, all the time with him in considerable distress. Charlie felt awful. He was embarrassed; he was an Army Marksman and thrived on precision. Charlie did not see him when he shot, but maybe he should have. Dante, as leader, took the brunt of it, damaging the relationship with his brother. He had lost his best employee and was now obliged to pay for his medical expenses.

Charlie was obsessed with forensics and returned later to the site to reappraise the episode. In reviewing the situation, he concluded that the injury was accidental and resulted from an extraordinary set of conditions that probably could not be duplicated in billions of attempts. The pellet, likely a "flyer" out of the barrel, was already spinning at an angle to the target when it hit a barely hidden rock and ricocheted further out of line. Flyers are lead pellets that are slightly deformed by internal collisions with others as they exit the barrel. The deformation causes the pellet to adopt a curved rather than a straight flight. Flyer pellets spin from the barrel like a sliced golf ball off the tee. Charlie could explain the situation, but it did not improve his disposition and grief. Dante agreed that it was accidental, but he deeply regretted the event.

Gilbert was permanently blinded in the stricken eye, but he believed it was accidental and held no malice toward the family, returning to work at Super Oil a week later. He also worked at Super Service Station with one of Gilbert's brothers, whom Mario hired immediately following the incident. Super Oil covered all of Jojola's medical costs. Dante was so remorseful that he abandoned hunting altogether. He loved game meat and accepted donations from family members like me, but he could not be lured back into the field. Charlie never attempted to hunt on an Indian reservation again and became obsessed with safety in the field, one time banishing me to the truck for walking out of a hunting line by a few feet.[4] After Gilbert's accident, Charlie limited his bird hunting to doves.

BOCCE BALL STRIKES OUT

Second-generation descendants were appearing at the half-century mark for Albuquerque's Italian colony. While respectful of their family traditions, they were piqued by other possibilities. The Bocce ball tradition failed to make the cut as a sport of widespread interest. In the

1930s, the Colombo's Bocce Ball tournaments were front-page stories, on par with other American sports. Bocce is considered a national pastime in Italy, much as golf or bowling are in America. The Italians brought the tradition to Albuquerque with much fanfare. It attracted many as a spectator sport; the players were all Italian male immigrants and recent-generation descendants. The game's uniqueness was its primary attraction. The tenacity with which the Italians played the game was another one. The Colombo put on attractive public events with their tournaments. Over time, the novelty faded and by the 1940s, the public had moved on to other interests. Many in the new generation of Italians were increasingly captivated by American sports, specifically baseball and football. Bowling was the American equivalent of Bocce ball and was more popular. After its heyday, many Italians still played Bocce recreationally during private parties and special events, but it was finished as a local crowd favorite.

A NEW ITALIAN PASTIME

Baseball was a well-established American sport, played daily in nearly every schoolyard in America as well as at the glamorous ballparks, such as Yankee Stadium and Boston's Fenway Park. The game was played competitively in schools, colleges, and many cities, with professional minor league teams. Baseball is as much a cerebral game as it is physical. It is a unique sport in many ways. It was the only one where the manager wore the same uniform as the players. The reason was that the manager was integral to the game, making critical decisions at key points in the contest. The game did not depend on physical size. Small men could compete head-to-head with large ones, widening the potential pool of players. Like most Americans, Italians loved baseball, and many played it, including Pete Domenici, who pitched for a year with the Albuquerque Dukes, the local minor league team. Charlie, Dante and Mario played the game recreationally and some of their children were primed to play in their high schools.

In the middle of the century, professional baseball captured the country and was popularly awarded the moniker "America's Pastime." It was also the Italians' pastime, as many countrymen played in the major leagues. Joe Garagiola played for the St. Louis Cardinals from 1946 through 1954 and was childhood friends with Yogi Berra, of the New York Yankees. Joe

DiMaggio, of the Yanks, was exceptionally popular and routinely made headlines in the Albuquerque papers. Yogi and Joe DiMaggio were part of some of the greatest teams in baseball history. What is more, the great influx of Italian immigration had long ended, and many of the Italians moving into town were first- or second-generation descendants who were as addicted to baseball as the typical American.

Emil Mallegni, an in-law to my maternal grandmother Pia Barsanti Dalle, was an example. He moved to Albuquerque with his family in 1950. Born just outside the gates of Lucca in 1912 and immigrating to America in 1915, he brought a zeal for American sports that he acquired in Chicago, home of the Chicago Cubs and neighbor to the mighty Notre Dame football team in South Bend, Indiana. He and his wife Dena, a cousin to my Maternal grandmother Pia Barsanti Dalle, were fanatics for sporting events at all levels, especially local ones.

After settling into their Albuquerque home near Sixth Street and Marble, one of Emil's first tasks was to purchase season tickets to the Albuquerque Dukes. The couple were seasoned baseball fans, having been trained on the benches at Wrigley Field, home of the "Cubbies," the affectionate moniker that Emil preferred. They knew the best bench seat position to view the game and keep score: behind the plate and towards the first base side. The couple were scrupulous scorekeepers, each independently scoring a play and then deciding which they considered "Mallegni certified." That was the one recorded. Scorekeeping is an intricate, rigorous process for documenting each player's performance and scoring history. From an early age, Emil exuded baseball, and for many years Emil and Dena took me and my closest friend, Ed Matteucci, son of Nello, to the Duke games at Tingly Field, near Tenth Street and Coal, across from the Zoo. The Dukes were the Los Angeles Dodger's Double-A farm club. Kids were admitted to the ballpark for free if they wore a T-shirt with a large Duke logo on it. We watched live baseball dozens of times throughout the summers.

Emil had seen Joe DiMiggio play. He told the story. "DiMaggio was the smoothest player I ever saw. He was a beast in the outfield. He looked slow when he ran because he had such huge strides and was quick like a cat. I saw him hike out after a batted ball into the gap between left and center and he got to the ball before the left fielder had barely started moving." Then, he proudly added with fists on his hips as he grinned, "And he is as Italian as you and me."

FOOTBALL MAKES THE GRADE

Baseball was not the only sport overtaking the country. The other was football, college level. In the 1950s, professional football was only beginning to gain traction with the public and it would be another decade before the masterful Green Bay Coach Vince Lombardi set the professional game into high gear on the national stage. For now, it was all about Notre Dame and the other big-name schools back east. Notre Dame had cemented itself in football history with legendary performances in the 1920s and 1930s, from the Four Horsemen of Notre Dame, George Gipp and Angelo Bertelli, along with famed coach Knute Rockne. Emil pointed out that Rockne was an immigrant, just like him. Epic battles against Michigan State, Southern Cal, Ohio State and Penn State through the 1940s and the 1950s maintained a high national interest in the Catholic school. Even after Rockne left, the Irish continued to produce star line performers, including Johnny Lujack and Paul Horning. Like the Yankees, Notre Dame was mentioned in the Albuquerque press more frequently than the University of New Mexico Lobos.

American football fascinated the Italians for the same reason it fascinated Americans: the game reflected American society's tough, canny resourcefulness. Over the previous half-decade, the immigrant families had seen the United States rescue the planet from two World Wars. Memories of Patton's 3rd Army slicing through the enemy in France and MacArthur gloriously wading ashore to retake the Philippines in 1945 symbolized determination and courage. It is "American grit," as Charlie Menicucci said many times, invoking the image of Marines planting the American flag on Iwo Jima, one of the many the World War II battle that placed the United States Marines on the mantle among the greatest warriors of modern times.

Emil believed that the essence of the American spirit was embodied in American Football. It is a contact sport where physical, body-to-body contact is integral to the game. In contrast to non-contact sports such as basketball, soccer and baseball, where the focus is on the position of the ball relative to a goal, in football the focus is on the individual because major scoring occurs only when a player safely escorts the ball across the goal. The ball differs from most other sports—it is not round but an elongated sphere with pointed ends. It spins and flies through the air like a bullet when it is thrown. A forward pass, in which the ball is thrown downfield to a sprinting player is one of the most exciting plays in all of sports.

The game involves tough guys, people willing to go physically head-to-head with competitors. Football rewards teamwork, hard work, self-sacrifice, and diligence, all prized values in America in the 1950s. Plus, it is a complex game involving intricate and unique offensive or defensive maneuvers. Being a contact sport, injuries add a stochastic element. And, it is fundamentally meritorious. Contests are decided on a fair field in the construct of rigorously enforced rules and regulations. Big-game winners are hailed as heroic champions; losers humbly retreat, hoping for another opportunity. Football reflects America's capitalist market where businesses, operating under a clear set of legal rules, freely compete to provide goods and services to the public. Many other nuances of the game keep the attention and excitement level continually high; for example, the system of downs creates a set of obstacles that must be overcome sequentially to score. The downs system creates a continual series of games embedded within the bigger game. For many, football comprised the basic values of life that most American citizens embraced.

In the 1950s, professional basketball was in its infancy, and the college game was viewed by many as an intriguing, cold season game to fill the dead time between college football and the Major League Baseball season. College basketball teams contained many walk-on student-athletes, and the game was played in thousands of intermural leagues in nearly every school in America, from first grade through college.

GOD'S TEAM

In the post-war years, the Notre Dame Fighting Irish football team became the darling of the Catholic community and a favorite among many Italians. They loved the team itself, but the main attraction was its Catholicism. On the Friday before an important Saturday Notre Dame game, St. Mary's school children were dutifully paraded over to the church thirty minutes before normal dismissal for a Benediction to collectively implore the Lord to look favorable on the Golden-helmeted Fighting Irish players. In Catholicism, a Benediction is a short invocation pleading for divine intervention for an event. Even for lesser important games, Sister Loyola, the principal, burst onto the intercom late in the afternoon on Fridays to lead the school in prayer for the beloved team when it played the following day.

The zeal was not confined to school children and Catholic principals.

Emil and Dena Mallagni lived in Chicago, about fifty miles from the Irish campus in South Bend, Indiana. They resided in south Chicago, which was considered Chicago's Little Italy at the time, and were nearly exclusively Catholic. In their neighborhood, Notre Dame had achieved celestial status. Emil and Dena followed each Notre Dame game, whether broadcast on radio or TV. In the early 1950s, television was in its rudimentary phases of covering sporting events. The public promoted expanding the audience for sports via TV but the professional sports owners and universities viewed it as a threat to stadium ticket revenue. Their problem was not with broadcasts but with the visual content. The TV opponents welcomed radio, which most believed would provide publicity and eventually entice more fans to the stadiums. Listening to a game on the radio is better than nothing but it holds no candle to viewing the event on TV. Television brought the view and audio directly to fans, possibly eliminating the desire for personal attendance. By the early 1950s, Notre Dame had led an effort to televise its games, and just as vigorously, opposition rose. Eventually, common sense, the people's will and huge financial dividends from TV broadcasters quickly scoured out the Luddites. By 1960, TV broadcasts of baseball and college football became regular weekend fare on TV screens across America, including Albuquerque. Notre Dame was a huge draw nationally and the Fighting Irish were televised regularly.

CATHOLIC GAME TIME

Emil explained how tuning into a Notre Dame game contributed directly to the Irish efforts on the field. Seeing his faithful servants supporting this mighty Catholic team, the Lord might be positively inclined toward divine providence in critical game situations. The theory was that the harder one cheers for Notre Dame—whether in stands at Notre Dame Stadium or eating peanuts in front of the TV—the greater the probability of victory. It was a collaborative effort between the Notre Dame football team, the Lord and the fans. Emil equated viewing a Notre Dame game with religious duty.

Emil's unique perspective was powerfully received by many, including me. For some, even today, the scene of the Irish team bursting onto the verdant fields of Notre Dame Stadium on a cool October afternoon induces irrepressible personal emotions and thrills. The couple prepared for games in the style of today's tailgaters. Dena prepared snacks and drinks.

Emil turned the TV on early to ensure it was properly warmed up and tuned in. In those days, there were a host of knobs to operate the TV— everything from contrast to horizontal hold to volume. Careful adjustment of them produced the best possible signal. More importantly, all TV signals were delivered over the air, most into "rabbit ear" antennas on top of the TV set, a box about two cubic feet with a twelve-inch screen. The antenna needed repositioning for each channel and was affected by the location of people in the room. As an electronic expert, Charlie installed an outdoor antenna in his home, which produced a consistently strong signal with no fiddling. Emil was stuck with the rabbit ears. Also, TVs most often failed when the set was turned on. If one discovered the failure early, there was time to find an alternative receiver to watch the game.[5] To Emil, having the TV warmed and ready to watch was essential to allow each play to be clearly viewed. He believed that when you are on a team with the Lord, you do your job properly.

Humbert Pieroni, son of Tony and Pia Sei, was on par with Emil in worship of the team. Pia is the daughter of Pasqualino Sei and Emma Matteucci, Johnny Matteucci's sister. Humbert more than once referred to the Irish as "God's team" when we discussed the Irish's fortunes. Many others did likewise. Humbert and Emil are examples of how many Italians adopted American sports and metastasized their enthusiasm in the community, especially among youth. Emil and Dena had one daughter, Jeanette; Humbert had a son, Christopher, who became a Catholic priest. and a daughter, Allison, a lawyer who married Paul Menicucci, son of Charlie.

ALBUQUERQUE'S BABE

American sports were a good fit for typical Italian Americans, including many among the second and third generations. After World War I, Italian names appeared in many of the box scores for high school sporting events, with some emerging as stellar performers. There were some early adopters. Angelo Petroni was among the original Lucchese immigrants to settle in Albuquerque and the earliest Italian family to embrace athletics. Angelo and Giulia Biancalana had three sons, two noted athletes, Paul (Babe) and John (Red). John was a gifted local semi-pro baseball player with a chiseled physique, handsome face and a robust head full of amber-bronze locs. He was a deputy sheriff and a star center fielder on a regional semi-pro team called "Don Padilla's Grays." He died in his 40s of a heart attack.

Paul was seven years younger than Red, and at Albuquerque High School the Parenti brothers played all three major sports: baseball, basketball and football. Like Red, Paul was naturally athletic and picked up the nickname Babe. He found his way into coaching at St. Mary's High School in 1934 and led the Cougars for nearly four decades. Babe coached all three major sports and track & field. He also taught Freshman-level history. He had no assistant coach; the water boy, a volunteer student who delivered drinks to the players during game timeouts, was his staff. At that time, St. Mary's High School, with six hundred students, was one of the athletic powerhouses in the city. Battles between the Albuquerque High Bulldogs and St. Mary's in the late 1940s and 1950s are the stuff of local sports legend. He coached some fearsome St. Mary's teams, including championship squads in 1949 and 1955. Babe coached more than seven thousand athletes over his coaching career, including some notable Italians, such as John Giannini (1945), son of Johnny, Harold Carazzi (mid-1950s), son of Primo, Dino Giannini (1950), son of Joseph, Gene Franchini (1950) and Jim Franchini (1960s), both sons of Mario, and Larry Bandoni (1951), son of Angelo. Gene Franchini became a New Mexico Supreme Court Justice. All were local sports stars in either baseball or football.

It was not until the late 1950s and early 1960s that some exceptional Italian athletes emerged. Noteworthy performances from Ray Giannini (1958), son of Sixto, Joe Pitti (mid-1960s) and David Marianetti (middle 1960s) were frequently reported in the sports pages of the local papers. Pete Domenici (1950s), son of Chopo, was an early baseball standout who pitched briefly in the Minor Leagues. Richard Matteucci, son of Johnny, set the 100- and 220-yard sprint records at St. Mary's High School that stood for two decades. He went on to run for the University of New Mexico Track and Field team. At a 1963 award ceremony, Babe said that St. Mary's' Marianetti was "among the finest he had ever coached." David went on to play for the University of New Mexico Lobos. Toward the end of his career, Babe was considered the dean of coaches in the city. The sports community sought his opinion on the outcome of games or on proposed New Mexico High School Sports rule changes. He was elected to the Albuquerque Sports Hall of Fame and the New Mexico High School Hall of Honor.

When Babe died on September 11, 1996, Immaculate Church's clergy came to attention. Babe was one of the most beloved men in the city, and the funeral was destined to be huge. Gargantuan might be a better adjective. The church seated around a thousand, including the choir loft. Charlie Menicucci headed the Immaculate Conception Usher's Club and appointed himself head Usher for any important event.[6] Everything had to be right to honor Babe. Charlie was among the team of ushers managing the overflow crowd. According to Charlie, on Saturday, September 14th, "over two thousand people" arrived for the funeral Mass at ten o'clock.

Anticipating the problem, Charlie's ushers reserved pews inside the church for Parenti kin, close friends and dignitaries, including most prominent local politicians and administrators, such as Police and Fire Chiefs and their wives, and Senator Pete Domenici. Microphones on the altar brought the sounds of the Mass to two large loudspeakers sitting on the church's front steps. Between the church's front steps and Sixth Street were hundreds of chairs borrowed from St. Mary's cafeteria for the excess crowd. Inside the church, the seating was tight, everyone elbow-to-elbow. The choir loft held twice its normal capacity, half standing. Men stood in single file along the sides of each aisle in the church, leaving just a narrow corridor for passage. The vestibule was packed full, standing room only. The front doors were blocked open, allowing a glimpse of the ceremony by outsiders. The high funeral mass consumed two hours, including numerous memorial speeches from the many successful professionals and businessmen who played ball for Babe. Billowing clouds of rich, dense incense smoke enveloped the casket and wafted through the church. Holy water, sprinkled with abandon, dotted the casket's pal and the clothing of clergy and nearby congregants.[7] Tears flowed aplenty in the congregation. The Albuquerque Police directed traffic for the event, and the funeral procession was one of the longest in history, stretching many city blocks.[8]

Babe Parenti in his final year before St. Mary's High School closed in 1969. Courtesy Ioli Giomi, taken from Il Giornalino, January 1978, Volume IV, Number 12.

SILENT GIANT

In July 1955, Johnny Matteucci strolled into Super Service Station madly puffing his pipe while crowing about the news. The U.S. Senate had voted unanimously to relieve Renzo Petroni, a local Matteucci family relative, from deportation and awarded him naturalization. It began in 1949 when Renzo visited his uncle Amedeo Matteucci with the intention to naturalize and live in Albuquerque. The Americans had strict immigrant quotas and his temporary visa expired. He tried to extend it but failed. The U.S. Army denied his application because he was not a citizen. Congress had passed a law allowing for additional Italian immigrants, but it only applied to those still in Italy. Finally, he exhausted his options, and 1953 the federal government ordered him out. He was panicked and desperate.

Gino Matteucci in 1951 walking in downtown Albuquerque. At that time, photographers snapped photos of people ambling downtown and later sold the picture to the subject. Courtesy Edward Matteucci.

Renzo did what many in Albuquerque did in times of legal peril—he called Gino Matteucci, Amedeo's son, an esteemed Albuquerque attorney and a first-generation immigrant descendant. Gino orchestrated Renzo's defense, skillfully working both politicians and bureaucrats. It took eighteen months of political manipulation and an act of Congress to save Renzo, which is what Gino delivered.

By 1955, Gino had long since been considered among the most respected men in the colony. Not a single Menicucci voted in an election without checking with Gino on certain candidates, especially judicial positions. I can recall Dante and Mario debating one of Gino's suggestions for a position. Gino was likely the only lawyer in town with no real enemies. His rise to that rank was not accidental but rather an example of the virtue of hard work intelligently performed.

Born in 1908, he was the son of Amedeo and Ancilla Petroni. Gino's father, Amedeo, knew the Menicucci family from Lucca and the relationship carried over to America. The Matteucci family in Italy resided in the economic mid-levels of the lowest third of society, better than the Menicuccis operating at the bottom, but not by much. Amedeo ran a grocery store in Albuquerque, which did well, but the family was middle class, not wealthy. From an early age, Gino took a keen interest in academics, business, government affairs and trades. St. Mary's High School offered no courses in those areas, driving him to Albuquerque High School where he studied typing, accounting and business math. He later matter-of-factly explained that he wanted to be prepared for the future.

Early in Gino's life, one local man attracted his attention. Elfego Baca was building a reputation in town. Baca was born in New Mexico and developed his career as a New Mexico lawman in Socorro, New Mexico, in the late 1800s. He gained his entrance into New Mexico's bar by testifying to a judge that he had read a book on the theory of law. In those days, a law degree was not needed to access the bar, nor was a test for competence. William Keleher, a top Albuquerque attorney, once noted that these were slim qualifications for a lawyer. To Elfego, his ascendency to the bar was another talent in his mix of skills. He operated in a zone between exploitive interlocutors and pernicious gunslingers. Several examples define Elfego. (In the stories about Elfego, all money values are in 2024 dollars.)

In 1896, in one of his first legal cases, a sheep rancher contacted Elfego for relief from a bail bond obligation. One of his employees had been arrested in a bar scrap and jailed. The rancher posted a two-thousand-dollar bond on his behalf but instead of returning to work, the employee bolted to Mexico, leaving the rancher on the hook to service the bond. Elfego took a fee of five-hundred dollars to resolve the case.

Elfego walked about town and found a Mexican laborer. He offered the man twenty dollars for an hour of work, over twice his normal hourly rate, so he readily agreed. The Mexican could not speak English but Elfego taught him just one word to repeat on cue: guilty. Elfego brought the Mexican to court, which satisfied the bond and the money was returned to the rancher. When the judge asked for a plea, Elfego cued the Mexican, who responded "guilty." Elfego convinced the judge to apply a fine instead of jail time. He assessed the man fifty dollars and closed the case. Elfego paid the fine, paid the Mexican twenty-five dollars and walked away with a four-hundred-twenty-five dollar profit. The rancher was aghast. "That is not the right man," he said outside the courtroom. Elfego responded, "What the hell do you care? The case is solved, isn't it?"

Elfego's reputation as a gunman harkened from New Mexico's territorial days where revolvers were a popular means of settling disputes. Early in his career he was sheriff in Socorro, New Mexico and was feuding with some of the local cattlemen over a piece of property. He got into a brawl with a large group of them as he holed up in a barn. He fought them off for over a day, killing and wounding a number of them. He was able to escape unharmed. Later, in Albuquerque, he bragged that there "is at least one Hispano who is not afraid of the American cowboy."

What really characterized Elfego was a fire in 1924 on one of his properties. He submitted an insurance claim for twelve thousand dollars. The adjuster, suspicious and smelling fraud, refused to pay the claim. Early the next morning Elfego called over the adjuster's attorney. As the man sat down, Elfego put his hand on his thirteen-inch-long Colt 45 caliber Peacemaker revolver lying on his desk with the barrel pointed towards the guest. He told the attorney to tell the adjuster: "If I don't have my money by noon today, I will kill him…and I mean it." The attorney both knew that Elfego feared no reprisals for a murder. After all, he had beaten a couple of murder charges already, in one case intimidating the jury by his mere presence. At eleven-thirty in the morning Elfego received a notice that the money had been placed in escrow for him at the bank, which he withdrew at eleven-fifty.

As a pre-teen, Gino relished in Elfego's adventure stories and listened to various renditions of them. Elfego operated a Spanish-language newspaper, La Opinion Publica, where he discussed various topics involving what he saw as a class struggle between Hispanics and Anglos. Gino heard many tales directly from Elfego because the Matteuccis lived only a few blocks from Elfego's office. Gino spent time in his office listening to tales of adventure, all conveyed in heavily accented English. Ed Matteucci, son of Nello and nephew to Gino, told the story: "Gino was attracted to Elfego and spent many afternoons after school in his office listening to stories. Elfego kept a loaded revolver on his desk. Gino spent much time with Elfego, which likely influenced his career decision." Gino learned Spanish from the man, which was easy for an Italian. It was Elfego's innovative spirit that captivated the lad and set him on a course in the legal arena.

In 1926 Gino was awarded a diploma from Albuquerque High School. While most graduates were planning celebrations and perhaps vacations, Gino planned to work over the summer and begin his advanced studies. In June, with the ink barely dry on his diploma, he applied for admission to the University of New Mexico for the fall semester. Amedeo encouraged him and offered to help fund his education. Gino graciously refused because he knew the cost would be a family hardship. His father, Amedeo, and business partner, Michael Palladino, worked their grocery store twelve hours a day, seven days a week. They competed well in Albuquerque's free market, but they were far from wealthy. Instead, he found a job managing the circulation for the *Albuquerque Tribune*'s late edition. Gino studied during the day and weekends and worked evenings managing a cadre of newspaper delivery boys. Naturally, he lived at his family home, where he got fine Italian meals and a pampering Italian mother, all for free. Gino did not accept cash from Amedeo for education but he certainly appreciated the in-kind family contribution to his education with free food and boarding. Even as a teen, Gino displayed the attributes and personal qualities that characterized his life: intelligent thinking, determination and respect.

Gino's work at the *Tribune* sparked his professional career. Most municipal newspapers provided readers with a broad view of the community but often put special emphasis on popular characters. The *Tribune* was no different and Elfego was one of those characters. His name appeared in the local papers a couple of times a week, reporting everything from court rulings to an announcement of a business deal. There was something about Elfego's subtle cleverness that intellectually appealed to Gino. The *Tribune* also helped Gino to understand the political landscape, both locally and nationally. It broadened his vision of possibilities for his future.

By 1931, Gino had decided on law as a career but was uncertain whether it would be in law enforcement or as a legal advisor. In either case, such a career allowed him to help people, a virtue of Catholic life and a growing need in the community. Like many Italians, he believed that each person should work to the level of his or her talent to serve God and society. He played both possibilities. He applied for admission to the Federal Bureau of Investigation's Academy, which trains professional agents. But his second move was outlandish. He applied to Georgetown University Law School in Washington, DC. "I wanted a Catholic school," he said. He realized the high expense, but he planned to do the same as he did with the University of New Mexico and work his way through the program. He searched for work in Washington DC, contacting New Mexico's congressional representative Dennis Chavez for assistance in obtaining a government job. Chavez had just been elected and was pleased to help. He knew the Matteuccis well, as they were the largest Italian family in Albuquerque. Gino's maturity and intelligence impressed Chavez. Gino hoped to land a job that complemented his legal training while he was working to pay for his education. It was a lot to ask, but he was like an angler with two lines in the water and planning to reel in whichever one gets hit first.

A couple of months after Gino's FBI application, he received word of his acceptance to the Academy, and he joyously planned his departure. While he was penning an acceptance letter to the FBI, his joy was interrupted by a letter from Chavez. The letter provided information on how to apply for an opening at the Library of Congress, which was awaiting his application. The situation was upended. A job in Washington DC put him in the proximity of Georgetown University. It was step one in his plan to become a lawyer. In an instant, an outlandish dream was materializing and the FBI career popped like a soap bubble.

He used his savings to relocate to Washington, DC and took a small rental apartment near the Library of Congress. From eight in the morning to four-thirty in the afternoon each day he labored at the national library filing various congressional reports. Like his work at the *Tribune*,

Gino learned the governmental processes of Washington DC. Within a year of his relocation, Georgetown accepted him. In the evenings he attended classes at Georgetown and studied during the weekends. He worked every day from five in the morning to midnight. It took Gino four years to achieve a law degree, normally completed in two by unemployed, full-time students. Gino was both a part-time student and a full-time employee. In 1936, Gino had his degree, but he had already passed the bar exam in New Mexico in 1935. At that time, a degree was not required to sit for the exam. In 1936, he opened an office in the First National Bank building, where he practiced as Albuquerque's first Italian lawyer.

To say that the community respected him is an understatement. Gino's personality projected both confidence and competence. Almost immediately after establishing his practice, he acquired widespread commendations, especially as he worked with some of the most noteworthy lawyers at the time, including William Keleher. He had a wonderfully peculiar way of charging his clients for legal work—family-adjusted fees, which Gino secretly determined as a function of the client's wealth. For an hour of work, Gino might charge a wealthy family member ten dollars an hour (about one hundred in 2024 dollars), whereas a young struggling father might be charged three dollars (about thirty-five in 2024 dollars). Asked why, Gino explained that some people "can't pay as much." Gino's social character blossomed as he headed up various recreational activities at the Italamer Club.

Gino primarily practiced probate and real estate law but had many court cases involving other legal areas. Gino rarely lost a case, not only due to his skill but to his preceding reputation. Ed Matteucci told the story: "Gino was in court cross-examining a witness when the opposing attorney continued to object. Referring to the offending lawyer formally as mister, the judge chastised him for interrupting the proceedings with trivia. Gino stood calmly, reviewing his notes while waiting. Finally, the judge loudly overruled the lawyer, turned to Gino and smiled, 'Go ahead, Gino.' Gino won the case."

In 1937, he worked part-time as the assistant Albuquerque City Attorney. Although he would have earned more in private practice, he believed his service served two purposes. First, it contributed directly to the community, a virtuous goal for Catholics. Second, it allowed him to learn the internal workings of local government, just as he did in Washington, DC.

During the 1940s, Gino added local politics to his growing quiver of legal expertise. He often spoke on behalf of a local Democratic politician seeking office. A typical advertisement highlighted Gino's name in large letters, followed by the topic of discussion. In smaller letters at the bottom was the name of the candidate whom Gino was representing. Gino sought to influence decisions about who was in office but was never sought to be a candidate for an elected position. In the few times he was suggested as a possibility for office, he quietly refused. He believed his greatest value was serving people by providing counsel, a lawyer's primary duty to clients.

HEAR
GINO J. MATTEUCCI
A Prominent Attorney
Speak in Behalf of
ROBERT W. REIDY
ON
KABQ—7:10 Tonight

Clipping from *Albuquerque Journal*, **1954**, inviting the public to hear Gino speak on behalf of a candidate. Gino participated in many political events that advertised him as the speaker instead of the candidate.

THE MAKING OF PETE DOMENICI

Pete Domenici, a generation younger than Gino, was one of the many first-generation Italians influenced by him. Pete was roused by Renzo's case, which was hailed throughout the colony and is still used to regale Matteucci's descendants today. Plus, Gino provided a path to educational success—work. Even those who doubted their ability to afford college education, held out hope of working their way through school, just as Gino did. Pete committed to study law at the University of Denver in 1956, the year after Renzo's case. Gino is primarily responsible for guiding Pete into law school. He likely inspired others to enter the legal field and politics, such as his cousin Rolando, his son Paul, Pete Domenici and later his nephew, Edward, son of Nello. Gino's other son became a medical doctor and military officer.

After passing the bar exam in 1960, Pete headed straight to Gino Matteucci's law firm, where an office awaited him. Gino had several other lawyers working with him in the First National Bank Building downtown. In Pete's eyes, nobody was more qualified as a career advisor than Gino. Pete was bright and interested in civic matters, hoping to practice in that area. Gino had a wide array of experience in law and politics. Pete immediately took cases involving the city, notably land use issues and private property rights disputes; much of it funneled to him by Gino. In 1966, Pete teamed with Harry Kinney and John Gurule to form a People's Party ticket to fill three vacancies on the City Commission. The commission was purposely non-partisan to reduce political pressures from influencing decisions.

The People's Party was well conceived. It was multicultural, incorporating an Italian, a Hispanic and an Anglo. Although each man was listed independently on the ballot, they pledged that they would act in concert to enact their agenda if elected. Their agenda was simple: fix the problems plaguing the city, such as repairing specific roads and fire protection for new subdivisions. Various political heavyweights around town, such as the Kelehers and the labor unions, added their influence with endorsements. At that time, political battles, especially at the local level, centered on issues rather than personalities. Considering Gino's background and close relationship with his protégé, Pete, it is easy to see his fingerprints throughout the campaign. Many years later as Pete gained stature among Senators in Washington DC, he maintained a life-long working relationship with Gino. Gino Matteucci was likely the least known but most influential of Pete's advisors over his political career.

JUST ANOTHER GUY

Although he was wealthy by the end of his career, Gino operated with the humility of any ordinary citizen in Albuquerque. He lived in the same two-thousand square-foot house on Silver Avenue in the Huning Castle Addition for his entire life. He drove the same model cars as his brothers Nello and Larry. When his wife Lydia wanted him to buy her a Cadilac, Gino demurred; he preferred to avoid pretentiousness. They finely agreed that Gino would pay for half of the vehicle if Lydia paid the remainder from her inheritance from her Giacomelli family. He attended Mass regularly and contributed to the church.

Gino is one of the best examples of Albuquerque Italians who cleverly availed themselves of American freedom and free-market capitalism to bolt themselves forward professionally and socially. From his roots—as Italian peasants—to a well-respected lawyer in a great country within a single generation was one of the grandest leaps of personal growth of any of Albuquerque's Italians. In every way, Gino was one of the most exceptional ordinary Albuquerquean.[9]

MANLY GROOMING

Most Italians in the Albuquerque colony were keen on formal appearances at special events. They believed that a wedding or baptism was an occasion to present the very best of the family to the community. For women, it meant new clothing and perhaps some new jewelry. The men required a finely groomed appearance, with mustaches precisely trimmed to provide ideal facial symmetry and a "baby-bottom smooth" shave. Giving away your prized daughter at the altar of God, for example, is no time for parsimony. Many of the barbers in town knew about the Italian male obsession with facial perfection and provided premium cut-and-shave services. Nobody had the technique down better than Marco Jacopetti.

Marco was a trained, upper-class barber from Lucca who immigrated in the 1940s. He understood Italian customs and the cultural significance of proper facial grooming in preparation for important events. He believed that the grooming experience itself should be a memorable part of those events. He knew that although no Italian man admitted it, each enjoyed the physical pleasures of being pampered in a barber chair. It was fine for women to be acknowledged as such in a "beauty salon," but it was not manly. Marco played the situation like a fine instrument. His goal was for a customer to leave his shop with a handsome look and feel like an upper-class Italian man.

Charlie Menicucci and Ted Morelli, son of Teodolindo, told the story of Marco's special-occasion service. Here is the gist of it: Marco began by settling the customer into the barber chair, assisting him in finding maximum comfort by adjusting the foot and backrests. Then, he carefully placed tissue around the neck, protecting the skin from any abrasion from the cotton cape he put over his shoulders, enveloping him in a teepee with a head poking out the top.

A haircut was first. Marco opened his drawer, moving some scissors about to select a specific pair to match a customer's hair. He said that American Indians and Southern Italians had thick hair, requiring a different type of scissor than the thinner ones of the Lucchese men. With his scissors constantly snipping away—whether or not they were cutting—he pruned at a purposefully slow pace, allowing the customers to assimilate the pleasures of personalized attention. Naturally, it was a good time to chat because soon after the trim the customer would be buried under a hot towel.

As an avid angler and hunter, Marco had plenty of whopper stories, including this one reported in the local press: He was lake fishing when he snagged a big Trout. As he was working the trout into the boat, he jerked his head and his upper denture, a single tooth replacement, popped out of his mouth and into the water, sinking out of sight. Marco was angry at the misfortune, but as an angler he was used to the unexpected and kept on fishing. He returned home missing a tooth but toting some impressive lunkers. As his wife was cleaning the fish, opening up their bellies, she discovered Marco's denture in one of them. They called the *Albuquerque Journal*, which sent reporters to the scene to report the incident the next day. Marco had a closet full of similarly tall tales to entertain his customers while they enjoyed a trim.

After several minutes he finished snipping, dusted the customer and reclined the seat to a nearly prone position. Again, he adjusted the rests for maximum comfort. Then he placed a dry towel across his chest, covering his body from neck to waist, arm to arm, protecting all clothing. He grabbed a towel from a steaming pot and held it up like a flag so the customer could see the steam billowing up as it cooled to a comfortable temperature. He meticulously placed it on the face, wrapping it slowly until the entire face was covered. The swirl ended at the customer's nose tip, where Marco fashioned a breathing hole. He gently massaged the towel into the customer's beard stubble, ensuring maximum contact between the towel and beard. It was marvelous theater augmenting the sensual pleasure of facial pampering.

Marco prepared his shaving tools as the customer relaxed, enjoying the humid warmth of the towel. The customer heard Marco mixing the face soap, which generated a unique and pleasantly soothing aroma. His gentle whipping of the lather was mesmerizing and anticipatory as the customer envisioned the hot lather applied to his face. Some even dozed dreamily off. After a few minutes, he discarded the towel from the face. He applied the hot soap liberally with a soft lathering brush, working it into the bearded stubble in every corner of the face with his fingers. Then he placed another steaming towel on the face on top of the soapy beard.

As the customer lay under the second application of towels, he could hear Marco stropping his razors.[10] He had several blades, some for rough cutting and others for finishing. All were high-carbon steel that could be honed to an exquisite sharpness comparable to the best Twenty-First Century commercial razors. After a few minutes of stropping, he pulled off the towel slowly while wiping the face clean. Then he applied a new layer of hot lather, again working it into every corner and crevice with his brush. He then demonstrated his blade's sharpness by pinching a few cut hairs, holding them up high to provide the customer a clear view and slicing off the dangling ends with a swift swipe of his blade, allowing the cut hairs to tumble like confetti onto the floor. "Thatsa sharpa blade," he declared proudly. Impressive and amusing, it was a staple of Marco's premium service.

He then turned the customer's head, positioned the razor in his right hand, swiped away a swath of soap from the customer's face with his left, and wiped the soap on a towel hanging from his pocket. He shaved the uncovered area with short, shallow-angled strokes, which removed enough stubble to serve as a final cut, which it normally was. With just a single pass of the blade, there is always a tiny bit of stubble that could be felt, which ordinarily is inconsequential.

In the premium service, he made a second cut to remove the "inconsequential" stubble to produce that baby-bottom smooth shave in which stubble could not be discerned anywhere on the face. His secret to smoothness was the direction of the cut. A cut against the beard's grain produced an extremely smooth cut because it slightly pulls the hair outward before slicing it off, leaving the stubble to retreat below the skin line and yielding an exquisitely smooth and enduring shave. However, it can induce ingrown hairs, which can become infected. According to Marco, men with thick hair, such as Blacks, southern Italians and Hispanics, could not tolerate reverse-grain shaves because of skin irritation. This was not the case with most northern Italian men with smoother facial features. Whether the final cut was with or against the grain was up to the customer, but for those with the appropriate hair types, he strongly recommended reverse-grain cuts for maximum facial smoothness. When compelled to a with-grain second cut, he cut at various angles and repeated until it was as smooth as possible.

In the final step of premium service, he reapplied the soap. He used his ultra-sharp blade for the final against-grain cut, which was more enjoyable than the first. The beard was so thoroughly saturated with moisture and soap that the blade slipped almost effortlessly through it. When done, the man's face was smooth. And the smoothness could last for twelve hours before any stubble could be detected. He finished with a warm, damp towel wiping the face clean followed by Witch Hazel, lightly smacking in on every part of the face. The sting of the rapidly cooling liquid on the skin and its pungent bouquet provided a delightful finishing touch.

Thirty minutes seemed like hours to the customer as Marco raised the chair into a sitting position. If the man wore a mustache, which many Italians did, he used his tiny scissors to carefully manicure it to perfection, applying wax or glue if needed to create and maintain a specific shape. He also used tiny scissors to trim any extruding hair from a man's nose, ears or eyebrows. After a final touch-up with the comb and a few snips of some wild hairs on the head, he turned the chair around so the customer could approve the final product. With a thumbs up, he removed the customer's apron, whisking it off like a bullfighter's cape and setting it aside. He then carefully dusted the customer and made other adjustments, giving him one final inspection before he gave the go-ahead. Customers for his premium facial service typically rose from the chair refreshed, rubbing their faces and marveling at the smoothness of their skin. Marco charged five dollars (about fifty-seven in 2024 dollars) for his specialty cut.

Marco's single-pass, with-grain cut was his standard shave, costing around a dollar. The shave was as good as any others at a competitive price.

Charlie said that for years, Marco's policy was that customers got a free cut for any nick. He reportedly never had to pay off, although Theresa Domenici Menicucci believed that Marco had drawn blood from the ear of her son during a trim. Her son later confessed that his movements might have caused the accident.

Marco shrewdly sold "family-event preparation" as a manly endeavor. It disguised what it really was—a haircut, facial massage and pampering, a womanly endeavor. Marco understood that women and men enjoy life's same pleasures but labels are important. Marco imported the best high-society, Lucca-style grooming to Albuquerque's Italian colony.

IMMACULATE CEREMONY

In the 1950s and 1960s, the Catholics were a powerful religious presence in Albuquerque. All Masses were said in Latin and high Masses were elaborate affairs.[11] Immaculate's solemn high midnight Masses on major holy days incorporated a large team of participants, starting with six or seven smartly vested ministers: priests, deacons and seminarians. A dozen altar boys, ranging from first-grade through high school seniors, assisted. Only one clergyman performed the ceremony, the celebrant. The pastor always had that job. Whether in the sanctuary or in the procession, the celebrant was flanked by his top two assistants. The trio donned bright white albs topped with brightly colored chasubles, with the backpiece adorned with a large, sparkling embroidered cross. A chasuble is the outermost garment worn by a Catholic celebrant in a Mass. He may also don a cape during processions. A cincture was tied around the waist on top of the alb. Decorative stoles, measuring about four inches wide and seven feet long were draped over the neck of the priest and finished with equal lengths in front. Typically, stoles were decorated with Christian symbols pertinent to the church season and had knots tied at the ends to represent those on the whips used to beat Jesus before his death sentence. Gold thread and gems were integrated into the elaborate embroidery, producing abundant glitters and sparkles with every wearer's movement. At Immaculate Conception, most ceremonial garments were imported from Italy, which is known for its quality silk production.

For major events, a colored-silk cloak, called a cope, was worn over the chasuble, protecting the priest from the elements and by their color, signifying the religious season. He might don a cope during processions.

As on the chasubles, elaborate designs were carefully hand-sewn on it, incorporating gold thread, tiny jewels and creative needlework. A fancy silk cincture adorned with intricate embroidery finished the outfit. The flamboyance of the vestments directly reflected ecclesiastical rank. The garments added color to the ceremony. The jewels and gold thread glistened with every movement of the priests. The intensity and extent of color were directly proportional to the importance of the event.

For important events, altar boys wore black cassocks with colored-silk shoulder capes. The cape was tightly woven fine silk, producing a smooth and shiny cloth that reflected light. Red-silk capes were used for Christmas and elegant gold-silk ones were worn at Easter. Younger altar boys performed simple tasks, such as processing in and out of the church but they sat with their parents during the ceremony. Senior-level boys, seven or eight, served in the sanctuary, the holy area behind the altar rail that comprised the altar and tabernacle. Altar boys had three important jobs: respond to the celebrant in Latin on behalf of the congregation, manage the materials needed by the priest during the Mass and hold a gold paten under the chin of each communicant, catching any host that might miss its mark on a tongue and fall. The paten is a circular polished-gold slightly concave platter with a handle. The host is a wafer of unleavened bread used in Catholic Masses. The issue is that the host was consecrated, meaning it was Christ's actual body. A host could touch humans in two ways: the priest's fingers that he used to hold it and the communicant's tongue. The objective was a clean transfer of the host from the priest's fingers onto the tongue. It was acceptable for the host to touch other objects, but it had to be retrieved expeditiously. The floor was especially off limits because of dirt—undignified for the Lord. Altar boys practiced proper paten-tending. I recall being drilled for an hour after school by Father McGowen, Altar Boy Club supervisor, on paten-tending techniques after I fumbled a catch and showed up with dirty fingernails. We used unconsecrated hosts for practice, which had no sacred properties and were safe for anybody to touch.

Communicants knelt along the altar rail to receive communion and the priest moved along the line distributing hosts. The altar boy followed along with the paten. For most people, the critical transfer went well. But there were some mishaps. Charlie Menicucci told the story about one of them: "Jake Gallegos was holding (the paten) for Fr. Paolo at the ten in the morning. (Mass). He was so old he couldn't feel anything. He grabbed three hosts at a time and dropped all of them on some big fat woman. Jake got one on the paten and the other between his arm and chest. But the third one dropped right between that woman's breasts. She screamed after it went deep in her bra. It was a mess because only the priest could touch the host but he wouldn't reach in her bra. Sister (the school principal) finally came running up and they went to the sacristy where they said they saved the host. I wish I could have seen that recovery." finishing the story with a big grin and wink.

Most altar boys aspired to be Master of Acolytes, the head Altar Boy. They certainly were encouraged to do so. As a completely meritorious system, boys earned lead positions based on documented performance but only high school seniors were eligible.

A seventy-five-member choir completed Immaculate's ceremonial entourage. The church organized the choir as a club headed by a priest, similar to the ushers and altar boys. A choir was a serious church business. Music was essential to the high Mass ceremonies where only the choir sang. Each spring, following the holidays, the choir director accepted membership applications by conducting recitals. All competed for a position that required a long-term commitment to regular practices, personal homework and special training to perform complex historical compositions. Nevertheless, the director always had more applicants than positions, which was limited by the size of the choir loft. The choir often included a locally notable singer or instrumentalist. The choir loft at the rear of the church was designed to produce the illusion of angelic voices raining forth from Heaven. Choir members were attired in seasonally-colored robes with white collars.

For important events, such as Christmas, hundreds of Poinsettias adored the main altars and side altars, choir loft, and small tables throughout the church. At Easter, Lillies, Tulips and Daffodils were the flowers of choice. They and all the other decorations on the altar and sacristy reflected the work of the Altar Society, a women-only organization dedicated to altar and church decorations. Like the other volunteer organizations, the members took pride in their efforts.

Seating for every important ceremony, such as Immaculate's Christmas Midnight Mass, was by reservation only. The best pews were assigned to the families who supported the church most. Italians such as the Bachechis, Vios, Giomis and Domenicis sat up front along with other notables in the community, such as the McCannas and Kelehers.

The ceremony lasted nearly three hours, and afterward, many parishioners toured the Old Town and Huning Castle areas, where people decorated their homes with luminarias, small bags with sand and glowing candles within. According to the Hispanic custom, thousands of these luminarias lining the residential walks presented a welcoming path for the Christ child to come and dwell in the community.

While the Christmas midnight mass was spectacular, the Easter vigil was more so because it celebrated the founding of Christianity and was the only service that integrated the congregation into the ceremony. Although all Catholics were required to attend Sunday Mass, for those who didn't, the minimum qualification to retain church membership was Easter Day Mass. Many once-a-year Catholics flocked to the Easter services, which produced the church's busiest weekend of the year, with all of the Masses heavily attended.

The Easter Saturday night vigil kicked off the celebrations with a full house of people. The church opened its doors at ten in the morning. Upon arriving at the church for the vigil, every adult congregant picked up an unlit stick candle at the door, each with a drip apron to protect hands from molten wax. The church's electric lights were dimmed to the minimum safe level. The altar was sparse and unlit, with a dozen stick candles standing cold. Ushers guided folks to their assigned seats.

While people were seated, the priest, deacons and altar boys gathered in the vestibule at the rear of the church. They prepared to light the Pascal candle, which stood about four feet tall and about two inches in diameter. It was rich in Christian symbolism and a key feature of the ceremony. Once all were seated, the remaining electric space lighting was turned off. The church was entirely dark except for lights from the city seen through the windows. The Immaculate Conception's nave sports high vaulted ceilings, brilliant and colorful stained-glass windows, world-class craftsmanship and artistry built into the structure itself. But in low-light conditions, which dampens human visual acuity for colors, the nave resembled a foreboding subterranean rock cave with bats hanging on the walls.

The congregants faced the rear where about a dozen priests, deacons and altar boys gathered on the front step just outside the church's front doors. There, a priest lit a special fire outside the church, the source of fire for the Pascal candle. By tradition, the fire was started in a small container that resembled a steel dinner plate perched on a short tripod. Carefully piled on the plate was a handful of extremely flammable tinder. The priest blessed the Pascal candle, adorned it with nuggets of incense in the shape of the cross and then turned to the fireplace. Altar boys circled the priest and the tinder to provide protection from the wind. With a snappy blow from a knife on a piece of flint, he knocked a spark into the tinder that immediately burst it afire. After praying over the fire, the priest used a candle taper to transfer the flame to the wick of the Pascal candle. The group moved into the church's vestibule and closed the doors, leaving the original fire outside. Altar boys and ushers extinguished the original fire and removed it from the doorway.

At around ten-thirty in the evening, after the ushers gave the word that all were seated, the priest loudly exhorted from the vestibule: "Dominus Vobiscum" (Peace be with you). In unison, the altar boys responded, "Et cum spiritu tuo," (And with your spirit). The ceremony was officially underway. The priests, deacons and altar boys processed into the church in the following order: Thurifer, cross bearer, pascal-candle bearer, celebrant and his entourage. As the group entered the nave, the Pascal candle provided the only light in the entire church. It was surprisingly bright. I recall seeing shadows of priests projected on the church ceiling, more than twenty feet overhead. The flickering candlelight played on the tumbling incense smoke as it fumed furiously from the solid gold thurifer, billowing upward in continuously varying shapes and undulations. The unique aromatic qualities of the incense added olfactory stimulations, triggering imaginations of a holy place.

When the procession reached the middle of the church, it stopped and the celebrant pointed to the Pascal candle flame, looked around to the congregation and said loudly, "Lumen Christi" (Light of Christ); the altar boys responded, "Deo Gratias." (Thanks to God). That initiated several concurrent activities: Thirty male choir voices, singing acapella, declared in song the good news of Christ rising. Beginning diminutively, the men's voices slowly increased in intensity. Similarly, Immaculate Conceptions' mighty belltower clapped its small bells, slowly integrating its larger ones to increase in magnitude over time.[12] Altar boys lit their candle tapers from the Pascal candle and moved about igniting all the candles in the church. A team of more than a dozen ushers assisted the boys in passing their flames to congregants. Meanwhile, the interior electric space lights were brought on in stages, starting with the spotlights on the tabernacle and then those for the sanctuary. This was followed by floods for the altar, the mosaic, side altars, and the remainder of the building. Meanwhile, the choir intensified its song as the procession made its way to the altar.

In about ten minutes, the procession had dissolved and the priest stood in front of the altar, with the pascal candle at his side. He looked out on a nave flooded with light, color, bells, music, and hundreds of tiny flickering lights among congregants. As the choir finished, the altar ceremony embarked with readings and the Litany of the Saints. Litany in the Catholic tradition is reserved for times of great distress, where the power and influence of multiple saintly entities are implored to sway a situation. Starting with the saint of greatest ecclesiastical importance, it implores each one personally. In Latin, the priest sang out to each saint, and the male choir responded with extended fermata for emphasis. For example, "Sante Petre," (Saint Peter) and its response "Oro pro nobis" (Pray for us), consumed ten seconds or more. The Litany was an eight-minute operatic Drama per Musica (drama for music). Following the litany, baptisms were performed, and the service concluded at around eleven-thirty in the evening.

While the altar was being prepared for the midnight mass, the Immaculate Conception's seventy-five-member choir came into full glory, performing one classic piece after another, including solo performances by high-C sopranos and top-notch bass soloists, all parishioners. The organist, usually the high school music teacher, displayed solo talents. It was an intermission of sorts where congregants were free to move about and refresh themselves. A high mass followed the vigil, with a religiously inspiring and theatrically magnificent production exceeding the one at Christmas.[13]

SYMBOL OF LIGHT

For sheer drama, imagery and symbolism, nothing in the church calendar stood to the Easter Vigil and its Midnight Mass at Immaculate Conception. The Vigil tells the story of the dark times for Jesus' followers following the crucifixion. Many followers saw Jesus as the great messiah who would deliver the Jewish people from the grasp of the Romans. Now, their inspirational leader—a master of marketing and organization, a commander of divine powers, a worker of miracles—hung helplessly from a wooden cross, bleeding to death like any common thug. They apparently had backed the wrong horse and feared reprisals, guilty by association. They pitifully hunkered in dank, dank places, fearing discovery at any moment. The dark church resembled those places; the congregants were those hiding inside. Then, there is a tiny light at first that begins to spread throughout the land. It is the light of the Messiah, Jesus, represented in the Pascal candle. All other candles were lit from its tiny flame, brightening the church. The philosophic symbolism was visceral, powerful and enduring: Jesus brightens the world.

The ceremonies were more than religious rituals. They were theatrical performances, encompassing some of the finest attributes of the great Broadway musicals: the drama of Phantom of the Opera, the hope of West Side Story, the wardrobe, color and pageantry of Lion King, the moralism of Les Misérables and the musical brilliance of The Sound of Music. Unlike the relative recency of Broadway productions, Catholic ceremony was steeped in more than fifteen hundred years of tradition and some of the greatest artistic works in history, including those of Mozart and Verdi. In the Western world, only the Jews and Native Indians could legitimately claim a longer history of religious ceremonial tradition. People came from miles around for a spiritual infusion and the artistic elegance of a grand ceremony impeccably presented.

CATHOLIC YEAR

Catholics revisit the entirety of Christ's life in every church year. The year commences with Advent in Fall, a month to prepare for the arrival of Christ. Christmas and Easter anchor the two most important events in Christianity: Christ's birth and his resurrection. Ordinary time, the period between Easter and Advent recalls how the Apostles applied Christian philosophy to life.

For four weeks before Christmas, Advent services recount the pre-Christian Jews anxiously awaiting the Messiah to deliver them from their travails, Romans among their top concerns. The Old Testament is replete with biblical prophecies of a Messiah but is short on specifics, such as arrival dates. Thus, whether a possible Messiah conforms to any prophecy is subject to interpretation. For Christians, Jesus is the Messiah. Jews continue to wait. Readings from both the New and Old Testament confirm the ecclesiastical confusion in the populace and present hope for a savior. The four-week Advent produces the energy for the Christmas holiday, a joyous celebration of the time Christians believe the Messiah was delivered to the world. Church services between Christmas and Easter chronicle Christ's life, from birth to death to risen savior. This period of the church year highlights the last three years of his life, a period of intense proselytization that ended with his execution. As time passes from Christmas, the tone of the weekly readings becomes more serious, leading to Lent, representing the forty days of Christ's retreat into the desert to prepare for his execution, for which he was certain.

The Easter vigil and the accompanying midnight mass recall the experience of those early Christians, who hid and quaked in fear. The news of Christ's resurrection was like a klieg light flooding a performing stage; the marvelous news enlightened people with hope and renewed spirit. The Catholic Easter Vigil and the Midnight mass celebrated the exact moment Christianity was created. From the perspective of the Catholic congregants, Easter was a springboard to go vigorously forth to serve the Lord by serving the community. As people filed out of church after Easter midnight Mass, there was little rush to the exits. Many folks used the time to socialize, even at two-thirty in the morning. After the Mass, I waited for my father, Charlie, to take me home. I could have walked home, but after five hours of performing, I preferred to wait, observe and ride home with my father, Charlie. I had plenty of company because many altar boys were sons of ushers. Charlie was chairman of the Usher Club, so he stayed on-site late to wind up the operations and prepare for the six o'clock Easter Mass, just a few hours hence.

There was a palpable, impassioned energy among the various chatting groups moving slowly towards the exits. Most discussions centered on some charitable activity in which they were engaged, such as an upcoming Knights of Columbus spaghetti dinner or an ongoing effort to upgrade a building at the Brothers of the Good Shepard Refuge. Catholics typically spent a minimum of ten percent of their time performing charitable work in the community. Many, such as Julio, discussed church matters; he was a prominent member of the Church's building and maintenance committee and served on the finance committee. I often heard him and Pastor Pat Keleher squabbling over some church matter, usually money, with their voices attracting attention. It was an old, stubborn Irishman versus an old, suborn Italian; conflict was inevitable. As Julio explained, it was all to get things right for the Lord.

The women discussed their families and children; the Home and School Association was a popular topic. The association is similar to a parent-teacher organization but with a Catholic school orientation.[14] It involved virtually every parent of a student in one way or another. At that time, St. Mary's was a parish school primarily for parishioner families.

Thus, many of the same people one saw as neighbors, one saw at mass, one saw at school, and one saw at various other charitable events.

The Church was more than a place for worship, it was at the center of life. Ceremony was a key element of church life that spurred and maintained a high level of interest in the Catholic community. It was typical for Immaculate Conception priests to be guests of parishioners, especially those who were heavily involved with the church. Father Landry was a frequent quest of various Menicucci families, but he especially liked Charlie's because there was always an open gallon of wine available.[15]

The exterior view of the front of Immaculate Conception Church built in 1960. A steel fence surrounds the church and school properties. Courtesy author's collection.

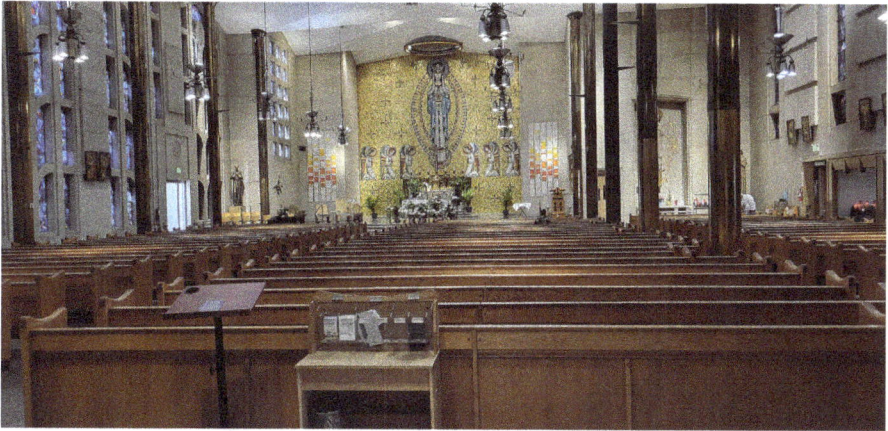

Interior view of the Immaculate Conception Church built in 1960. The large mosaic on the rear wall is its defining feature. The many solid gold articles throughout the church made attractive targets for thieves. Courtesy author's collection.

CORPUS CHRISTI CATHOLICS

From Pentecost (shortly after Easter) to Advent, ordinary time is a rather bland period in the church calendar, especially during summer. The Feast of Corpus Christi was instituted by Pope Urban around 1260 to celebrate the doctrine of Corporeal Presence, the concept that a consecrated wafer of bread is the actual body of Christ. The host is consumed by the faithful during masses. Whether by intent or accident, the event was scheduled in June, adding spice and color to the Catholic calendar during a period of ecclesiastical doldrums. Albuquerque's Catholics embraced it.

The celebration began with mass, in which a large, two-inch diameter host, was consecrated and placed in a Monstrance. A Monstrance is a large vessel, typically constructed of solid gold, designed to display the host while it is transported. It is an elaborate and somewhat gaudy object standing about two feet high containing the host at the center, enclosed in a protective glass container. The host is surrounded by dozens of solid gold, delicately crafted fingerlings extending outward like golden rays emitting from the sun. A stand supports the object and allows a priest to carry it, holding it skyward so that all can see the host.

The Feast of the Corpus Christi had been celebrated for centuries in New Mexico by the Spaniards, but the first public processions in Albuquerque happened in 1945. It produced some of the largest public

Catholic displays in history for two decades. The procession commenced at Sacred Heart Church, on Stover and Fourth Street in south Albuquerque. The Archbishop of Santa Fe presided and led the congregants onto the streets. Thousands of faithful walked behind the archbishop as he proudly held the Monstrance high while leading prayers for the multitude of people following behind. In full regalia, the highest-ordered Knights of Columbus flanked the prelate with swords drawn and pointed upwards, providing security. From Sacred Heart Church, they processed north to Copper Street, where they turned west to the termination point at Robinson Park.

The monstrance was heavy and despite rumors to the contrary, the archbishop received no special infusion of energy from the Lord. He tired and so did the Knights. Altars along the path provided breaks and special prayers. Each was located at about quarter mile marks along the path: at Fourth and Lead, Fourth and Copper and Immaculate Conception Church on Sixth and Copper. The procession ended at Robinson Park, at Eighth and Copper Streets, where the archbishop led a benediction to close the elaborate ceremony. A reception followed at various churches, but the largest was at Immaculate Conception where the school gymnasium was open to all. Volunteers provided food and drinks.

In 1946, a few thousand partook. By 1955, twenty thousand Catholics participated, a huge display of populist strength. All Albuquerque Catholic dioceses participated, including clergy members, church service groups, lay volunteers and Catholic School students. Thousands of dollars were contributed to the event. By the early 1960s, Albuquerque's Fiest was coordinated with the simultaneous celebrations in other Archdiocesan cities, namely Santa Fe. The ceremony consumed several hours and was widely reported by the press, both papers calling it a parade, but the Catholics used its correct name: procession. The Corpus Christi celebration persisted until around 1965, folding in the wake of the Second Vatican Council, which reorganized the church with less emphasis on elaborate High-Church ceremonial tradition. Albuquerque has never witnessed an annual event that more thoroughly energized and organized as many Albuquerque Catholics in a single activity as did the Feast of Corpus Christi.

Archbishop Bryne leads a procession in Old Town for the feast of San Felipe Di Neri. The procession was similar to the Feast of Corpus Christi except much smaller, only involving a few hundred people. The archbishop is not carrying a monstrance because it was not a traditional part of this particular ceremony. Courtesy Albuquerque Museum, gift from Albuquerque National Bank.

The massive belltower had several bells, all fully automated. Every day at noon, its bells echoed through the city announcing time for the Angelus prayers that celebrated Christ's incarnation and his presence in the community. Many people, including some non-Catholics, stopped for a moment of prayer and reflection. Children playing in St. Mary's playground froze and prayed. On a typical day, about three quarters of the populace visibly responded to the bells. Courtesy author's collection.

See note 16.

Notes

1. The defining line between northern and southern Italian is obtuse. In this book I generally use the southern boundary of the Papal States in 1870 as the dividing line. Very roughly that boundary crosses east-west just south of Rome.

2. Two Nottoli families were in town, both from Lucca: Alex J. and Albert J. The two men were brothers. Alex was the oldest, thirteen years older than Albert. Alex had immigrated early in the century and steadily increased in rank at the Albuquerque Police Department.

3. Cutwork is embroidery that is oversewn with various needlework designs, enhancing complexity and refinement for special uses, such as articles used in church ceremonies. Canapa was also used for fly fishing. According to Julio, there were two kinds of fly patterns they had in Italy. One was a hook with Canapa thread binding a pinch of animal fur, making it resemble a furry bug. The other was a hook covered with Canapa thread to mimic a worm. Canapa fibers are extraordinarily strong threads that are pulled from its fibrous stalk. Canapa products, such as pre-spun spools of a colored thread, were available in the late 18th Century Lucca comunes and later in Albuquerque's Italian colony. Giulio scoffed at both and said, "If you want to catch fish (meaning catch many fish), then use real worms."

4. Hunters in the field will walk aside one another as they walk through fields seeking to raise birds that can be shot. As long as each hunter stays in line and shoots forward only, all are protected from shooting themselves.

5. Radios and TVs of the day operated via vacuum tubes, which contained an electric heating element that became red-hot. The element was most prone to failure when electricity heats it rapidly during turn-on causing it to break due to thermal shock.

6. The Ushers club contained only men, especially those with organization, teamwork and security expertise. Many men at the time were World War II military veterans and were well-versed in these fundamental skills. Charlie Menicucci was a prominent club member from the late 1940s, and his skills quickly led him to the position of chair, which he retained for about twenty-five years. He ushered until he died. The club contained about forty men, all commissioned for duty by the pastor in special ceremonies. Four or five ushers managed each service at regular

Sunday masses, which were heavily attended. Daily masses only required one or two. Large events, such as midnight mass or a large funeral, required a dozen or more. Charlie personally oversaw ushers at every large event. It was a rigorous duty. For Easter, his team arrived at nine o'clock in the evening and remained until three in the morning. Charlie returned to the church at five-sthirty to manage the Easter Sunrise mass, which was popular. He stayed through the seven o'clock Mass, which he regularly served on Sundays. He was at Super Service Station at eight the following Monday morning.

7. Holy water is water that has been blessed by a Catholic priest for use in religious ceremonies. A pall is the cloth that is draped over the casket.

8. *Giomi* (Ioli) presents a description of the Parenti family. Published in January, 1978, Volume IV, Number 12.

9. The relationship between Gino Matteucci and Pete Domenici created a confluence of talents at a unique time in history, creating New Mexico's longest-serving and, debatably, one of the most accomplished New Mexico senators. The story of Gino's outsized influence on Pete is a research topic yet to be investigated, with details well beyond the cursory coverage I provide in this chapter.

10. Stropping is a process where a sharp knife blade is dragged along a strip of leather in order to hone the edge. Stropping is the final process of sharpening a blade to the supreme sharpness needed for shaving.

11. In Catholicism, the higher the Mass, the more ceremonial it is. Solemn High Mass is the highest.

12.. Managing the bells and lights was an important task for altar boys, as ceremonies were punctual and perfectly timed. All lighting circuits were on dimmers so the lights could gradually be brought to full brightness. Part of the training for the job was to understand how to choreograph the lights at this most dramatic moment, including instruction on how fast to bring certain lights to full brightness and which others were to be transitioned slowly. It was the highest honor ever bestowed on me in my senior year of high school.

13. The details about the Catholic masses were taken from personal experience, Catholic training at St. Mary's School and the Catholic Missal: *Juergens*. The modern Missal is *Breaking Bread with Mass Propers*.

14. *Menicucci (David)* presents the model for a Catholic Home

and School Association based on pre-Vatican II philosophy. The work was published in 1990 and was essentially obsolete when distributed, but it continues to be printed. It is a historical reference.

15. Priests were often guests of parishioners. Father Landry, a Jesuit from Immaculate Conception, often visited our home for dinner. He enjoyed wine before, during and after dinner. He sometimes enjoyed too much wine and ended up dozing off in the lounge chair unable to be aroused. Emma Dalle Menicucci told the story: "He was sound asleep and snoring. We didn't know what to do, wake him or let him sleep. I left it to Charlie and in the morning, he was gone."

Father Landry enjoyed the ceremonial mass wine. As an altar boy, I remember him saying three daily masses in a row, the six, seven, and eight in the morrning. During the mass, altar boys deliver cruets of water and wine to the priest, who then mixes some of each in the chalice. Most priests mixed a tiny bit of wine into a large amount of water. Typically, the wine cruet was filled for the six o'clock Mass and had enough for three masses. The water cruet was refilled after every mass. Landry did the opposite. He poured all of the wine from the cruet into the chalice and added a few drops of water. When he said the morning masses, the wine cruet (about a cup in volume) had to be refilled for each service. In one case, I was serving the eight o'clock Mass when he was so buzzed that he stumbled as he was leaving the altar, landing flat on his face, blooding up his nose and vestments. The altar boys and ushers rushed to his aid and helped him into the rectory. The next day, complete with two black eyes from the accident, he repeated the act sans the fall. Father Landry loved the Italians because they all loved wine and plenty of it.

16. News reports and personal experience provided considerable information for this chapter.

22

FAMILIES ROOT IN
(1958–1969)

CUSTOMS KEPT AND LOST

By 1960, the Menicuccis and most in the Italian colony were well integrated into Albuquerque's tri-cultural community. The three principal cultures of Albuquerque included Anglos, Hispanics and Native American Indians. Some Italian customs were vigorously guarded, while others were chucked in a single generation. America's range of freedoms altered the immigrants' familial Italian customs.

In 1910 Italy, it was all but impossible for peasants to start businesses because they had no access to capital and no time for anything but day-to-day survival. In America's free market capitalism, one of the easiest tasks for average Americans was to start a business because capital was abundant. Most Italian immigrants had strong entrepreneurial tendencies, including risk-taking, independence, motivation and discipline. Entrepreneurs are disposed to working for themselves, which can grow into a large business. In Italy, these types of folks bristled at the drudgery of peasant life and longed for freedom.

From the moment the Menicuccis stepped on U.S. soil, they had their sights on self-employment. In Italy, each Colono family was essentially a business, although without the profits. It was their passion for self-reliance that led them to Albuquerque. It took a few years before they fully comprehended the expansiveness of American freedoms. Not only could they start businesses, they ran them with little government interference. In

Italy, a bureaucratic labyrinth of taxes, rules and regulations encumbered businesses, especially small ones. In America, the government supported business. In just a single generation in America, the Menicucci brothers owned and operated two burgeoning businesses on land they owned outright. They employed dozens. Profits from the enterprises produced a typical middle-class lifestyle for all family members. The colony embraced the business freedoms, which helps explain why so many immigrants ran businesses in Albuquerque. Julio said, "It (entrepreneurship) is in our (Menicucci) blood."

No American freedom was more universally revered in the colony than voting. The concept of self-government took time to be both understood and appreciated because it was a completely foreign concept to Italians. In America, the people are the government and citizens control it via the ballot box. Through the power of the vote, average citizens could boot out poorly performing leaders and install new ones. The Italian colony took to the concept with enthusiasm and voting became a required duty for family members. Julio was adamant. If I saw him on a voting day, his first words were, "Did you vote?" Among the new traditions that the Italians adopted in Albuquerque, voting was the most important because it engendered patriotic respect for the country. Their love of America was evident in their priority on Independence Day, July 4th. All four Menicucci immigrants believed it was the second most important family holiday after Christmas, the birth of the Lord. Easter, the celebration of the founding event of Christianity, place third. At a July 4th celebration at Charlie's home, Julio said, "This is when we thank those men who fought that king and made this country. If they did not do that, we'd still be living a poor life in Italy." In Italian culture, any secular event that can compete with the Lord was a clear recognition of America's importance in their lives. Albuquerque's Italian immigrants were among the most fervently patriotic Americans in the city.

CULINARY PERSISTENCE

Culinary customs from Italy not only survived but thrived. Italian specialties such as salami, prosciutto, a variety of cheeses, and olive oil were regularly imported by a few immigrants, such as the Matteuccis, specifically for Italians. By the 1950s, these products had spread into the community, with Italian dishes featuring pasta regularly appearing on many Albuquerquean dinner plates. Polenta, a Northern Italian staple, was brought to Albuquerque and infiltrated American diets.

Ravioli was a widely appreciated Italian food used to celebrate Christmas. Customarily, each Italian family gathers at the outset of Advent to prepare ravioli for the family's Christmas Day feast. For the Menicuccis and other Italians, ravioli-making parties typically occurred during Advent.

A few in the Italian community continued to indulge in some Italian specialty foods that never made it to non-Italian plates. The Francini brothers were major suppliers of those foods, such as cardoons, baccala and tripe, all simple, peasant dishes from Italy but with unusual flavors and aromas, which were appreciated by those who acquired tastes for them.

Outdoor activities were popular, especially trout fishing in Jemez. At the time, nearly all of the Italian immigrants had hunted birds in Italy for sustenance. In Albuquerque, they hunted ducks on the Rio Grande River, quail and doves on the outskirts of town and pheasants in the bosque. Bosque is Spanish for forest and refers to the cottonwood forest on the banks of the Rio Grande. Most Italian immigrants had no experience with high-powered rifles and limited experience hunting large animals. In New Mexico, rifle-hunting accidents were frighteningly high. Big game did not attract Julio and Amerigo. Beppe Bandoni, Johnny Giannini, the Bachechis and a few other men embraced it, successfully hunting deer and turkeys in Jemez. It was not until years later that the New Mexico Department of Game and Fish instituted a mandatory hunter training program for all hunters as a prerequisite to purchasing a license. The safety training dramatically reduced hunting accidents, making hunting in New Mexico a relatively safe practice.

ITALIAN INTEGRATION

By 1960, most of Albuquerque's Italians were fully integrated into American society. Some, such as Mario Menicucci, took up American bowling. Other Italians joined the Albuquerque Country Club and played golf, a sport unheard of in Italy. Bricola, a popular Italian card game among immigrants at the Colombo Hall was replaced by Bridge, a similar game but with additional complexity and challenges. By 1960, few Italians and no Menicuccis played Bricola. Mario and his wife adopted Bridge.

By 1960, few Italians fermented their own wine. World War II was the last period of prevalent home fermenting. The liquor industry had flourished since prohibition, and numerous alcoholic beverage dispensaries offered wine at prices below the cost of home fermentation. Large wholesalers such as Southwest Distributing, owned and operated by the Bachechis, amply supplied small retailers, such as Mori's Bar, a small package liquor store on Fourth Street run by Poncho Lommori and the Mint Bar, run by Modesto Dalle. If any fermenting occurred in the city, it was a hobby rather than the production of a family staple.

The Menicuccis bought wine in bulk—four-gallon crates of Petri brand wine at a time. Typically, Julio arranged for bulk sales from Carlo Bachechi, bypassing the retail businesses. Petri wine was a fundamental "table wine," extremely dry, dark red, robust and deep flavor, slightly bitter. Not a sipping wine, it was ideal for mixing with water for use at the basic table beverage at meals. Charlie kept a gallon jug of wine under his chair during meals to facilitate easy refills. Emma Dalle bristled at the ostentatiousness of a large bottle of alcoholic beverage at the table. Julio transferred wine from the gallon containers to quart bottles, each of which was at the center of any meal other than breakfast. Julio and Amerigo preferred brandy and coffee for breakfast drinks. Julio liked a "jigger of Brandy" before big meals "to get your stomach ready for food," as he said frequently. The family purchased as many as fifty cases of Petri brand wine at one time that they distributed to the five families: Julio's, Amerigo's, Mario's, Dante's and Charlie's. He purchased the wine for less than a dollar a gallon (about ten dollars in 2024 dollars). I remember Julio backing up one of Super Oil's one-ton flatbed pickups into our driveway loaded with dozens of cases of wine, which my father, Charlie, and I unloaded and stored in a special, locked wine-vault that my father built inside his garage. Brandy, cheap and abundant, replaced Grappa.

Many Italian immigrants never found a taste for Hispanic foods, but the first generation certainly did. The Menicuccis were all fluent in Spanish and had hired many Hispanics in the businesses who brought information about local customs. All three of the first-generation Menicucci men appreciated indigenous foods, especially red chile and roasted green chile. Davina's and Giulia's recipes often were well-spiced with various spicy-hot products, but it was not until the later years before they incorporated New Mexico chile into their dishes.

Red chiles and green chiles are identical except for age. Green chiles mature to a bright red color, like tomatoes. During maturation, the sugar level increases and the flavor mellows. These red chilis are harvested and dried for later use, similar to mushrooms and herbs. Later, the dried, red pods are deseeded, rehydrated and ground into a powder that forms the basis of red chile sauce. Green chiles are thick-skinned, tart and punctuated by a spicey bite. Roasting them over open coals burns the skin and cooks the flesh. After roasting, the skin is easily removed, and the flavor of the flesh is enhanced with a hint of smoke. After the pod is deseeded, it is ready for immediate use or can be frozen or dried. The Menicuccis, like most of Albuquerque, embraced New Mexico chiles and many over the decades used them regularly in home meals. At our home, roasting and peeling green chiles in the fall became as traditional as making ravioli.

DANTE FLOURISHES

By this time, the Menicucci businesses were under the firm control of the first-generation descendants; Mario handling Super Service, Charlie doing repairs and Dante in command as both Super Oil manager and CEO of the family enterprises. Super Oil grew steadily under Dante's leadership and it anchored the family enterprises with solid, annual profits. Each year brought growth in the businesses and their physical facilities. Dante's organizational zeal was like Julio's but supercharged. He was efficient and a stickler for punctuality. He ran a tight delivery schedule that demanded attention to detail and innovation in the field.

He was all business but always fair with customers and employees. He said, "When people come to work at Super Oil, we take care of them." He meant it. At a time with no employee insurance, the company assumed responsibility. When one of his men was out sick, he typically provided some percentage of their regular pay. If one were injured on the job, he paid all the costs. One time, Ralph Green, Charlie's top mechanic, developed a drinking problem. Charlie's customers found empty miniature bottles of vodka in their autos that had been serviced by Ralph. It created a crisis. Normally, employers immediately fired employees who drank on the job. The Menicuccis never considered the option. Charlie said, "Ralph's family depends on us. We need to help him." Not only did they retain Ralph, they funded four weeks of professional treatment for alcoholism and paid him while he was gone. He returned to Super Service and remained sober.

Dante, like Julio, was a leader in social-political arenas. He steadily grew in the Knights of Colombus ranks and assumed significant volunteer positions at Fatima Church and School, such as heading capital fundraising campaigns. These more than fulfilled his Catholic commitment to charitable work. But he also socialized at the Italamer Club, organizing various events such as dances or benefit dinners. His stature in the Democrat party was growing so rapidly that by 1962, he served as the party's Precinct 36 chairman. He knew he was respected, but he underestimated the extent. Henry Kiker, the Democrat County chairman appointed Dante to the fifteen-member County Executive Committee without consulting him. On July 16, 1962, the *Tribune* reported that Dante had declined the appointment, citing professional obligations at Super Oil Company. The blind appointment indicated Dante's growing presence in the political community. At that time, Dante was one of only a handful of Italians involved in Democrat politics, although most of the colony leaned heavily toward that party. His connection to the party benefited the Menicucci enterprise as many democrats ran the local governments, which ensured friends in high places to assist in times of difficulty. Julio taught him the basic strategy of connecting to government officials, but Dante refined it.

The atmosphere around Super Oil Company reflected many militaristic principles, such as adherence to safety rules, specific schedules and business efficiency. The men performed dangerous tasks and discipline was required to maintain safety. Dante's men enjoyed their work. They bantered, kidded and joked with one another before and after the work day. Dante was careful not to mix the activities. Dante developed teams of long-standing and valuable employees. By the early 1960s, he integrated family members into the company. I drove a three-quarter ton pickup one summer delivering cases of motor oil to Super Oil's cadre of service stations under supply contracts. In those days, working was not optional for young men. The family business was the default option.

Super Oil was never the social drawing card that was Super Service Station. Most of the day, Dante's employees were in the field, leaving only him and his bookkeeper Joe Benevidez, at the office. While a retail business typically thrives on crowds of customers, a wholesale business is a relatively stoic endeavor. And it fitted Dante even better than it did Julio. He provided the overall vision for the enterprises, always looking to the family's future. While Mario and Charlie confined themselves to the station, Dante traveled about frequently, attended meetings with oil company executives and explored new product offerings and business opportunities. When he visited someone, it was usually for business. While he understood the value of personal relations, his intent was professional.

Dante had unique perspectives on life, many of which he inherited from Julio. He could see situations from unique points of view, often jolting listeners. John, son of Mario, told the story: "A Super Oil tanker had just rolled up to the station and the driver was getting ready to dump a load of gas into our tanks. Just then, two cars crashed on the corner and one of them caught fire. The Super Oil driver grabbed the fire extinguisher on board, ran and put out the fire. We all called him a hero. When Dante showed up and heard the story, he looked at the driver, pointed to the extinguished extinguisher and asked, 'Who is going to pay for that fire extinguisher?'" It was not that he was callous about the generous act; he was as altruistic as any Catholic. He just wanted to clarify the consequences for the action. Super Oil had no spare extinguishers, so someone had to buy one. A fuel tanker could not operate legally without an extinguisher, so both a paid driver and the truck would be idle, disrupting the delivery schedule. When it came to business, few were as meticulous as Dante in managing company resources. Super Oil was profitable every year that it operated.

Dante also had a unique ability to answer a direct question on his own, which made one reconsider the validity of the original question. Some at the station reported that an air of tension arose when Dante arrived because it usually meant there was some problem. Charlie said, "He never said what the problem was, just that he was coming over. It made everyone nervous when he took so long to come over." It was Dante's style for good or bad, but it worked to keep the business's profits high and steady.

SUPER BUSINESS

Super Service Station, a retail business, was delighted to be a social drawing card. Good business always correlated positively with the number of people hanging around. Super Service was a gathering place where business and friendly banter were synonymous. In contrast to Super Oil where the employees operated alone and on tight schedules, the station managed a personal-service team. Men waiting for customers to drive up to a gas island and then pounce on it for service, washing the windshield with natural sponges and brushes and wiping them spotlessly clean with lamb-skin chamois. A chamois is very soft leather that is highly absorbent, a perfect tool for producing streak-free windshields and side windows. Chamois produce the best results but require special handling to prevent them from rotting.

Super Service had three key business elements in its favor: Location, Mario and Charlie. The station was located in the heart of downtown and many local residents traded with them due to convenience, but honesty, quality products and outstanding service kept customers coming back. New ones regularly drove up. Often, many who worked downtown left their auto for full servicing while they worked at their downtown job, walking back to pick it up in the afternoon. Such an all-day service might include gasoline fill-up, lubrication, new fanbelts and wipers, engine tune-up, radiator flush, brake adjustment, battery connections cleaned, new tires installed, a full wash and wax job and interior detailing.[1] It kept several men working full time for the day, costing about two hundred dollars (about two thousand in 2024 dollars). The same service in 2024 would cost more than double that amount and consume significantly more time because there is no modern commercial entity that offers the breadth of services comparable to those of Super Service Station. Today, automobile owners must visit several shops over a period of a week to accomplish what Super Service did in a day. Like Amerigo, Mario had an obsession with keeping employees busy. Their logic was simple: when you pay a man to work, he should work.

Mario had fully replaced Amerigo in operating the station and he made all of the routine decisions. Like Amerigo, he was calm and personable, rarely angry. He had natural sales skills that Amerigo honed through the early 1950s. Around 1959, Mario hired Charlie Herrera to "bust tires," which involves separating the tire from the rim so that that innertube, which holds the air, could be extracted and repaired. Large truck tires were too big for the station's hydraulically powered busting machine, so they were done by hand. Ironically, Herrera was a small man, standing about five feet three inches with a modest build, weighing in at about one hundred and forty pounds. He was known at the station as "Little Charlie," to differentiate him from Charlie Menicucci. Herrera grew up in the Espanola Valley in northern New Mexico and prided himself on toughness. He negated his small physical size with exceptionally hard work. Busting truck tires fit the bill and he became the apple of Mario's eye, rapidly advancing at the station. Naturally, Herrera was fluent in Spanish and spoke openly with the Menicuccis. According to Julio, this was unusual. He said, "Norteneos (northern New Mexico Hispanics) only speak it (Spanish) with Hispanos. But he speaks to us."

Around 1961, Mario relinquished the bookkeeping duties to a

hired hand, Lee Nasci, a Lucchese single woman trained in accounting. She spent every hour of every day at the station carefully managing the charge accounts. When customers came in for service, the service manager noted all the dispensed services and products on a daily ledger. It was either a cash sale or charged against an account. Either way, Lee was responsible for transcribing those transactions onto the financial books. At the end of the month, she prepared bills for all charged customers and mailed them. When payments were received, she carefully recorded them, cashed the checks and deposited them. She also prepared a profit-loss statement for the month and updated the balance sheet. Like any good retailer, Mario watched costs closely and strove for high business efficiency.

By the middle 1960s, Mohawk Tires, Super Service's supplier, had a fine reputation and produced various quality tires. Excellent products and good service were the hallmarks of the station. Mario dispatched the station's pickup truck to homes or businesses to replace a tire on the spot, which often led to additional work. Mario spent much of his time dealing directly with customers. Like Amerigo, he loved discussing outdoor activities and bowling, his adopted American sport. The employees enjoyed working for Mario. Most of all, he was big-hearted. Like any good Catholic, he served his church, Our Lady of Fatima, on Lomas Boulevard east of Carlisle. He was a member of the Knights of Columbus and loyally supported charitable events. Yet, like Amerigo, he sought and sought no leadership positions in any of the clubs. He lived his faith in subtle ways, including through the station.

Mario, like Gino Matteucci, gave preference to those who were in need. It was a practice that maddened Dante and Charlie. Charlie told the story: "My, God. He (Mario) sells two hundred and fifty bucks worth of tires to the Lagunas (Native Indians) and then lets them pay them off at five bucks a month. By the time they pay off, they buy more and he does it all over again. We are giving them a free loan." Dante, too, hollered at Mario about the practice; he said: "If you're going to loan money, at least charge them a percent." On the surface, Mario's actions were poor business practices. Mario ignored them because he knew the station was profitable and some people needed help. Ultimately, the costs to Super Service were negligible and Mario continued the practice because it helped people.

The mechanical and electrical repair work was the other half of Super Service's economic engine. Charlie, enjoyed interacting with his customers, often spending time chatting with customers, explaining how he discovered and rectified a problem. His philosophy was that the details are complicated but the fundamentals are simple. He said, "When I tell them all the work that we had to do on their car, they think it was a bargain." In the 1960s, the auto industry's reputation for sleazy operations was mostly attributed to used-car dealers, but auto repair shops were not far behind. Technology was accelerating so rapidly that only well-trained technicians could professionally service the engines. Long gone were the days when tinkerers could openly pass as professionals.

The climate was ripe for corruption. Swindlers concocted one repair scheme after another, ranging from false diagnosis, price gouging and fraudulent parts. Charlie told the story: "Those SOBs steal parts off junk cars, paint them and install them on a customer's car as new. Sometimes they don't even install them right. I get one a week come in here." A lot of the schemers were hit-and-run operators who suddenly appeared, exploited the community and then disappeared to emerge in a different city with the same ploy. Once people identified an honest and competent mechanic, they stuck with him.

As Charlie matured as a repair shop manager, he gained a reputation as an adroit engine diagnostician. John Menicucci told the story: "Charlie had the reputation of being able to repair any vehicle. Stan Sullivan, owner and operator of Sun Drug Company had just bought a new luxury vehicle that developed a turn-signal problem. He returned it to the dealer for warranty service. They tried for days but couldn't correct it. He left the dealer saying that he was bringing it to Charlie and if he fixed it, he would return the working vehicle with Charlie's bill, and the dealer would pay it." Charlie relished in the challenge; it was not unlike the many seemingly intractable technical challenges he faced in MacArthur's Army. "In a few hours he had the problem fixed, and the signals worked normally. Stan paid Super Service but took the bill back to the dealer and got his refund."

JESUIT CONNECTION

Immaculate Conception Church was home to a large Jesuit community and a convent for around thirty Sisters of Charity nuns. The church was the largest in the city at the time, but others in the uptown areas were catching up. All the Menicuccis were not only good Catholics, attending mass and taking sacraments as required, they supported the church as part of their family. It was integrated into life. From Altar Boy to Chairman of the Parish Council, devoted parishioners committed time and talents directly to the parish and its many charitable operations. The church reciprocated by doing business with many of its parishioners. The Menicuccis had long ago captured all of Immaculate's vehicular repair and fuel supply business. Still, the Jesuits steadily produced new sales opportunities from their expanding developments in the Jemez Mountains.

The Menicuccis, all upstanding Catholics, had earned the trust of the Jesuits. By the middle 1960s, the Catholic Church was one of Super Oil's and Super Service's most valued customers as they expanded their operations in the Jemez Mountains. The Bachechi family, in a typical display of Italian generosity, had been donating Jemez Mountain properties to the church, much going directly to the Jesuits. The Jesuits were aggressive businessmen and vigorously developed their properties in and around Jemez Springs, including the Via Coeli Monastery, infamous for its role in the pedophilic scandal in the late 20th and early Twenty-First Centuries. In the 1960s, the Catholic Church was mighty in stature, well-respected in society and business circles. They were excellent customers. The family businesses supplied fuel and service vehicles for every Jesuit-run parish in the city.

The Jesuits met the Menicucci's definition of a "good customer:" One who pays his bill on time. As a youngster, I overheard a conversation between Charlie and Mario about a customer and whether to close his charge account due to his chronic tardiness in payments. Later I asked them why they were treating a good customer so harshly. Charlie responded, "He is not a good customer. He's always here to complain. Then he is late with payment. He is a bad customer. We're better off without him."

RACIAL OBSERVANCES

The Menicucci family and its employees observed and freely discussed racial differences in the community. Jews were observed by many as transfixing on the accuracy of financial transactions. Once, as I was waiting to pay for gas, I was perplexed by a man going over every detail on an invoice for service on his vehicle. As the man demanded details, Mario patiently explained them, calling his cousin Charlie over to help explain the automotive repair charges. After the man left, I asked Mario what that was about. He leaned over and whispered, "Jiudei," a slang term for Jews. It was not derogatory, simply realistic of what he observed. Mario added, "He's a good customer, just a bit finicky about value." As far as the family was concerned, observed traits were idiosyncrasies that every group harbored. But that had nothing to do with business and friendship. To Charlie, the situation was obvious. "The Italians have traits too," he said, "they like lots of wine and are gossipy and vindictive. It don't make 'em bad, just Italian."

The Menicuccis treated every Jewish customer with the same respect as any others. Charlie later explained. "Whenever we worked on Goldberg's car, I knew he'd be back. He just wanted to make sure he got his money's worth. He'd come in claiming the engine sounded unusual. I'd tell him to go talk to Mario while we worked on it. We never did a damn thing except open the hood. After a while, I'd tell him we did some adjustments and take him to listen. Every time he was happy. And he kept coming back." Charlie found the humor in the situation and told the story frequently among bouts of laughter. Business profits had a way of obscuring religious and racial differences. The family courtesy was extended to Sam Ginsburg, a Jewish and wealthy Equitable Life Insurance executive, who lived next door to Charlie for twenty years. They were friends and Sam and his wife joined the Menicuccis on a Jemez Mountain mushroom foraging trip in 1969.

That way of thinking extended to other races. Charlie and Little Charlie often joked that the "pachucos" pushed their cars more than they drove them," a reference to their propensity of impoverished folks to frequently run out of gas because they purchased fuel in small amounts, sometimes a half gallon at a time, due to a shortage of cash. These folks frequently pushed their cars to a filling station. Pachuco is a slightly derogatory Hispanic term referring to impoverished people with few skills. Charlie Herrera hailed from a higher society family in Northern New Mexico. Both appreciated joint humor regarding the frequently observed behavior of another ethnic group.

Pachuco was a word that was applied freely in the community. The students at Washington Junior High referred to St. Mary's students as "St. Mary's fairies." St Mary's students reciprocated with the moniker of "La Washa Pachucos." For years, apparent racially motivated animosity prevailed between the relatively large Anglo and Italian population at St Mary's and the largely Hispanic one at Washington Junior High. Animosity between the races at St Mary's—which enrolled a large percentage of Hispanics—was low, indicating the rub was more based on school pride than racial hatred. Whatever the reason, the principals of the two schools agreed to coordinate dismissal times to avoid problems. Some serious knife cases occurred when students clashed, but the majority of them were typically fist fights, resulting in little real damage beyond pride.

SECOND GENERATION EDUCATION

It was in the mid1960s that second-generation Menicuccis were infiltrating the businesses. John and Mark Menicucci, sons of Mario, started working at the station around eleven years old. One year, John, a year older than Mark, had a hunch that he could earn more mowing lawns than he could at the station. Mark continued to work at the station. After a few weeks, Mark showed his brother that he had earned twenty-eight dollars weekly at Super Service (about two hundred seventy in 2024 dollars). John could barely show more than half that with twice the effort. John promptly returned to the station. Mariangela, daughter to Julio, worked as an assistant to the bookkeeper, Lee Nasci. Mike, son of Dante, worked at Super Oil.

As the youngsters spent more time at the businesses, they learned more about family philosophy. John, son of Mario, told the story: "There were a bunch of Italians going to visit Italy and they stopped by to say goodbye. When they left, I asked Nonno (Amerigo) if he ever thought about going back to Italy. He looked at me like I was crazy and asked, 'Why would I go back to Italy? This is America. This is Heaven. You can't get anything better than this.'" Later, Amerigo dispensed more wisdom. Mark, son of Mario, told the story. "I had taken a business class. I explained to Nonno (Amerigo) about interest rates on borrowed capital and how to calculate business risk. After I was through, he looked at me and said, 'Mark, that is not business risk. Business risk is when you can't borrow money to run your business and you have to go home and tell your wife and children that you have no food for them. That is business risk. What you are talking about, Mark, is opportunity.'"

DOWNTOWN DEGRADATION

Super Service Station in the 1960s was a sprawling campus covering about a quarter of a city block. The station incorporated several buildings that lay adjacent to the original station. Over time, the family bought those neighboring properties and their improvements. Julio built closed walkways to bridge the newly purchased buildings to the old ones. Including the large basement, Super Service properties totaled around twenty thousand square feet of enclosed space. It was so dispersed that walking between the farthest points in the building consumed several minutes. Although profitable, the station's buildings were old and degrading. The station's sprawl evolved from including a hodge-podge of adjacent buildings. A number of non-conforming code issues hovered over the station; every time they took out a construction permit to alter the building, they were forced to bring that part of the structure up to the modern building code—an expensive process.

The electrical system was the worst case. The Grannone Brothers, Charlie and Frankie, sons of John, were electricians and were related to Charlie's family via marriage. (John Grannone was married to Teresa Barsanti, sister to Pia Barsanti Dalle, my maternal grandmother.) The electrical system at the station was ancient and grossly inadequate to support the many new electrical tools and other machinery. The Grannones spent a good portion of each new task trying to decipher the existing system to make repairs. Over the years, as electricians did repairs, they abandoned old, existing wiring and installed new ones in their place. Over time, raceways became clogged with a jumble of wires, with live ones mixed in with abandoned ones. The muddle of wires was confounding and added to repair costs.

The heating system was also a mess. The station used gas-fired stoves instead of coal, but they were inefficient and poorly distributed heat. The plumbing system was equally archaic. The gasoline pumps were old-fashioned. Some work areas were oversized, and others were the opposite. Super Service operated like a modern station with all the latest tools, services and products, but it looked like an old, tired soldier with a drooping, 1920s-era facade.

Many downtown buildings were in worse condition. Albuquerque had a growing jumble of old, crumbling buildings throughout its downtown. Many were so dilapidated that razing was the only option, but property owners hesitated to take any action, fearing investing capital in an area with an uncertain future. Some of the biggest retailers had left downtown for newer uptown areas east of the University of New Mexico.

The slow degradation of downtown real estate led to crime, especially business burglaries. In the 1960s, the Menicuccis possessed some of the city's most advanced equipment and tools. Plus, they had ample windows and doors, but many were out of view from the streets. By around 1965, thieves regularly plundered the station, breaking through the many vulnerable entry points and causing hundreds of dollars in losses of equipment and repairs. The thieves usually entered covertly, but as crime steadily increased, the intrusions became brazen, with raiders driving vehicles up to the front door, smashing it down, gathering up whatever they could in a few minutes and speeding away unchecked. Super Service Station was targeted twice by these raids. The police seemed to be helpless, and for several weeks during a particularly bad spell of intrusions, Charlie slept in his Army cot at the station. He once interrupted a man trying to enter the window. He scared him off with a hammer. From then on, he slept with his loaded 16-gauge shotgun stored under his cot. The intruders wanted Charlie's tools and equipment, and he took the situation personally.

Finally, after months of losses and sleepless nights, Charlie recommended an electronic burglar alarm. Mario agreed and had AAA Alarm Service install the system. They placed microswitches on every operable opening, triggering an alarm signal if any were opened while the system was armed. Strips of foil, each about one-quarter inch wide, were glued to each window in all buildings. These strips were electrical conductors connected to the alarm. If a window was smashed, which breaks the tape, the conduction was interrupted and the alarm bell sounded. Within a few weeks after the alarm was installed, a few failed break-ins convinced the criminal community to move on to other non-alarmed businesses. The damage to Super Service was considerable, weighing on profits for a couple of years.

SUPER RENEWAL

Pete Domenici chaired the City Commission; essentially, he was mayor. He kept Dante and Mario abreast of the public clamoring to renew Albuquerque's urban center. The city had been moving towards some publicly funded renovation, which was quite expensive. A new federal program changed the calculus for the city. Urban Renewal addressed a national problem that plagued Albuquerque and crumbling inner city structures in all states. The federal government provided money to cities through grants, similar in structure to the U.S. Department of Housing and Urban Development Federal Community Development Block Grants. Under the program, the city took large grants but federal rules defined how the money could be applied. Its primary goal was to remodel deteriorating downtowns by relocating businesses from the area, clearing the properties and building modern structures in their places. The community had wide discretion in selecting projects and the Commission was at the heart of the matter. By the last half of the 1960s, Urban Renewal was a topic of discussion at nearly every Commission meeting.[2]

Dante, always with his finger on the political pulse of the city, worked with Pete and managed to put Super Service at the top of the list for relocation. Throughout the late 1950s, the city Police Station, located on Second and Marquette, was old, too small, flooded regularly in summer and was poorly heated. The city was looking for a new location. The commission debated Four possible locations, including the block where Super Service had conducted business for four decades. The Commission chose the Super Service location, and the city commenced formal negotiations with Dante. Of course, this was a big decision and the entire family was involved, but Dante led. The deal was good. He led the family enterprise; he was politically savvy and knew exactly what to do. Julio and Amerigo were consulted out of reverence but by this time were bystanders.

The city appraised the Super Service property and business and presented an offer to the family. Under urban renewal, the family was compensated for the land and the business, essentially covering the entire cost of the relocation. The new property was on the corner of Fourth Street and Lomas Boulevard, just a couple of blocks north of the original station. The price was right and they seized it. Dante performed beautifully. He negotiated the deal himself and obtained unanimous accolades from the family.

Mario and Charlie worked with an architect, Joe Burwinkle, to design a new station. Both men knew exactly what they wanted in their respective areas of operation. The new station offered three gas islands, two bays for lubrication, one for tire service, one for washing and four for the repair work. Mario designed his office in the middle of the sprawling building, where he had a good view of all of the operations. Unlike the old service station, the new one had a smaller footprint, only about eighteen thousand square feet, but was much more efficiently designed. One could walk from the two farthest points in the new station to its opposite point in a half minute. The rear of the station and the large basement stored tires and parts. Charlie claimed about twenty percent of the storage space for his parts, including everything from screws to brake linings. He installed advanced brake servicing equipment, such as a lathe to machine brake disks. He placed his desk in the middle of the action in front of his repair bays, where he spent at least half of his time talking with customers. The station was designed for security, with steel doors on the hidden sides of the building and a modern alarm system that protected the building against theft, fire and flood.

Charlie designed and built a first-class repair shop. He had the latest features, including exhaust removal directly from exhaust pipes, which allowed vehicles to be serviced inside the warm shop while running. The station had four hydraulic lifts and no dangerous grease pit. Charlie was consumed with engineering reliability, so he built a small forensic lab in the storage area to carefully examine parts to determine their cause of failure. He said, "If you know what fails, it makes it easier to diagnose problems." Horace Palladino, who wholesaled auto parts from his business said, "Charlie knew the best manufacturers and those are the ones we stock."[3]

SUPER SERVICE STATION
& TIRE COMPANY INC.
JOSEPH B. BURWINKLE AIA
& ASSOCIATES, ARCHITECTS

Architect's rendering of the new Super Service Station at Fourth Street and Lomas Boulevard built under the Urban Renewal program. No actual pictures of the new station exist. Courtesy author's collection.

Among the first visitors to the new station were Finnish tourists. That day, Amerigo and Julio were in the office of the new facility chatting when the visitor's car pulled up to one of the gas islands. The Super Service attendant went out to help them but could not understand Finnish. Amerigo overheard the driver and passenger speaking Finnish, the language he and Julio learned in the Michigan mines. He immediately went to them and conversed in Finish, translating as needed for the attendant. Once the service was complete, they returned to the office to pay the tab when Julio overheard the conversation and rushed to join Amerigo. The Finns completed their business with the Menicuccis in Finish, astonishing not only the Finns but everyone else at the station.

SUPER JEMEZ MEETING STATION

By the early 1960s, with their boys taking control of the businesses, the two immigrant Menicucci brothers felt their freedom. In 1914, they walked away from the Copper Mines in Michigan and changed jobs, a unique experience in Menicucci family history. Now, a half-century later, they were on the precipice of the second unique generational opportunity. In Italy, all family members worked until the day they died, laboring to the best of their capabilities to their final hours. In America, the Menicucci families had accumulated so much wealth that they would, for the first time in family history, retire from work.

The brothers enjoyed Jemez's recreation, which comprised fishing and mushroom foraging, with a few hot mineral baths interspersed. The Menicuccis were close to the Bachechi family because they bought wine and brandy from them and serviced and supplied their vehicles with gasoline. Victor, son of Oreste, became close friends with the brothers due to his love of outdoor activities and his vehicle, a large Carryall with a positive traction differential that was ideal for mountain outings. Such a differential will direct all the power to the rear wheel with the best traction, which is the opposite of a normal differential. Victor and the Menicuccis had a habit of hanging around the station talking. Mario opened the station at seven each morning and left at five in the afternoon. Charlie arrived at eight in the morning and closed the station at six in the evening. Julio and Amerigo arrived at the station daily around eight o'clock and so did Victor. Super Oil and Super Service operated six days per week. As a retail outlet, Super Service was more inviting as a gathering place than Super Oil. Dante was on the hook to provide large deliveries of oil products to a specific customer at a precise time. There was no time for chatting, a beneficial activity in a retail business.

Every working day, Amerigo arrived at Super Service Station with five large loaves of Italian bread from the Chiordi family's bakery, which he distributed to Charlie, Dante, Julio, Mario and himself. Meanwhile, Victor and the Menicuccis assessed whether to proceed to Jemez that day for fishing, which they did year-round, or mushroom hunting in summer. They often departed for Jemez around ten in the morning and returned before dinner time at six. Victor enjoyed driving and had the peculiar practice of laying his dentures on the middle of the front bench seat while he drove, right next to a tin of Copenhagen snuff and a thermos of coffee, heavily fortified with brandy. If he stopped the vehicle for some reason, he popped his teeth back in, just as many modern athletes do with their mouthguards. He also practiced fuel conservation by turning off the engine at the top of a hill, depressing the clutch and coasting freely down. Just as the vehicle slowed, he engaged the clutch so that the motion of the vehicle cranked the engine to restart it.

The men enjoyed the mountains, but age and infirmity were affecting all; Julio with blood circulation issues and Amerigo with severe sciatica. Victor did not like to walk, so he adopted the role of the personalized chauffeur for the three of them. He aimed to drive the two men as close to the harvesting grounds as possible. The mushroom season was a good test for his carryall in the muddy conditions of the Jemez mountains as he strove to provide Julio and Amerigo the shortest distance to harvest a Porcino. Victor's concept of fishing was similar: drive as close to the stream as possible, toss a salmon-egged hook into the water, rest the pole on a rock and enjoy a cup of fortified coffee and some snuff. Julio and Amerigo, in contrast, hiked and crawled up and down the streams to find hidden and productive fishing holes. They typically caught their limit of trout, while Victor had nothing. Victor could not have cared less because his pleasures were from the Lucchese-style camaraderie and demonstrating his Carryall's capability, along with healthy amounts of wine and tobacco.

A mountain lunch with the three men was an experience in all types of Italian culinary delights, including various types of meat, sausages, olives, garden-fresh tomatoes, many cheeses, bread and olive oil and plenty of wine. Victor supplied the wine from the family business. He always had a bottle of fine wine that was in some way damaged, such as a ripped label, which could not be sold as new. They sold the damaged items at cost and the Italians were often given first right of purchase. Julio and Amerigo's pantries frequently contained bottles of expensive wine they purchased from the Bachechis for a forty percent discount. Victor made sure that the group was well supplied with wine and spirits. It was typical for the threesome to consume a quart of wine during lunch.

QUEST FOR THE RECORD

The trio generated some tomfoolery. One warm July morning, the three men, now all in their late sixties, were in the high mountains of Jemez when they spotted a very large Porcino on the steep side of a hill. None could climb the hill. Julio believed that one always takes a Porcino when it appears, especially one that is potentially record-setting. Such a find had genuine value in the Italian colony by bolstering the family name. The Menicuccis had gained a reputation as accomplished mushroom foragers. In addition, the family discovered and tested two other edible mushroom types, including the Aspen Bolete and the Slippery Jack. A record-sized mushroom would add nicely to the Menicucci brothers' reputations.

Maggiorino Nicola, father-in-law to Dante, held the record: a seventeen-inch diameter Porcino. But he paid the price when he lost his bearings while picking it, became disoriented and wandered through the Jemez wilderness for more than a day before the sheriff and his hound dogs rescued him. Maggiorino had chucked his heavy basket of porcini to lighten his load after he realized he was lost and in for a long walk. But he carried the record-sized mushroom right to the time of his rescue. He was determined to either die with it or display it after rescue. In the colony, the only legitimate proof of a record Porcino was the mushroom itself. He wanted to ensure that he got credited for an important discovery—whether dead or alive.

The three men debated about the mushroom on the hill, trying to estimate the size and assessing the chance of it actually breaking Maggiorino's record. They bantered it about over some snuff and wine, but to Amerigo the decision had long been sealed: they needed that mushroom or they could never forgive themselves. He insisted. It did not take much to sway the others, so they headed back to Albuquerque for help. Charlie told the remainder of the story: "They showed up at two o'clock and I was busier than hell. They wanted me to pick a mushroom. I had to drop everything and rush with them to Jemez. It took me ten minutes to climb up there and it was not even a Porcino. And it wasn't close to Maggiorino's record either. They weren't embarrassed at all, even after I told them how much it cost us. All they cared about was that damn mushroom record." Italians were often irrational when it came to Porcini.[4]

Charlie Menicucci on the telephone at his desk in the new Super Service Station. He spent most of his time talking with customers and directing his mechanics. Courtesy author's collection.

See notes 5, 6.

Notes

1. Batteries at the time involved corrosive liquids that could induce corrosion on its electrical terminals, thus reducing electrical conductivity. A useful service is to clean the connections periodically and tighten the connection to ensure high conductivity. A serviceman of the day also reflooded (add water to) the batteries, if needed.

2. *Albuquerque Urban Renewal Agency* documented the renewal program for Albuquerque in 1962.

3. Charlie was technically oriented, similar to an engineer. As an Army radar man, he was consumed with reliability. He set up a small area of the shop where he did a forensic analysis of every broken part to understand what failed and why it was creating a certain noise. In his laboratory was a workbench with a greasy sheet metal surface and wall shelves chockfull of failed automobile parts, each with its own unique story and lesson. "You can't learn a thing by tossing stuff in the trash bin," he said of his collection.

There were two shelves: one for those failed parts that had been analyzed and the other for the ones queued up for inspection. Like a busy physician, he would call them one by one onto his bench and put them under a large gooseneck lamp with a two-hundred-watt light bulb shielded with a metal dome. His old U.S. Army mug held tools like those used to clean teeth, all ready to scrape away grunge to see some deformity. Four magnifiers of different powers were mounted on gooseneck holders. When Charlie was at his desk, his tools stood at attention like an Army special weapons platoon, ready for action.

Proficient with machine equipment, he made many of his own forensic tools. "See that one?" he said while picking up a hand-fabricated tool that had only been used a couple of times, "Took me an hour to make it just so I could remove a screw on a '46 Ford water pump. But I needed to find out what crapped out." He was like a good university professor— obsessed with immensurable curiosity.

Point to any part on the shelves above his desk and you got a story, as much as you wanted to know or could endure. "That is the fuel pump from old man Jacobson's '39 Ford," he said as he reached for it while turning on his desk light. "That little bushing leaked," he said, pointing to the failure. "Those monkeys"—he always spoke a little derisively about the manufacturers—"should've used a bearing and seal. They were worried about spending an extra dime that would make it last longer. Well, we're busy." Charlie understood the realities of the world but never passed up a chance to suggest a better way, one unencumbered by profit blindness.

Ted Morelli, son of Teodolindo, frequently visited the station to visit Charlie. He said, "Charlie is always doing something interesting in his forensic lab." Ted was among the most highly educated of the first generation of Italian immigrants. He held a Master of Science degree in Engineering from the Massachusetts Institute of Technology and served as an officer in WWII. Only Marchello Giomi, with a doctorate in engineering was more highly educated. Ted spent hours at the station discussing technical issues with Charlie. But their conversations often wandered into politics. Once in the middle of a heated debate between the two, Charlie said to Ted: "Wait. How many votes does a really smart guy get in this country?" Ted soberly answered, "One." Then Charlie asked, "How many votes does a really stupid guy get?" Again, Ted said, "One," wondering what Charlie was up to. Charlie's retort was, "Keep that in mind," which he presented with a full-toothed grin, resulting in raucous laughter from both men and any others eavesdropping.

One of the favorite curse phrases around Super Service Station was "Son of a Bitch." It had many forms and applied to many things. Laments, such as "Why does this have to be a son of a bitch.?" Or, to a bad customer after he left: "Don't let that door hit you on the ass on the way out. Son of a bitch." Proper grammar in cursing was important to some professionals, including Paul Matteucci, son of Gino and a top Albuquerque attorney. He too favored Son of a Bitch as a universal and appropriate cuss phrase, but he made sure that the grammar was correct. While Charlie, Mario and the regular crew were spewing phrases such as, "Look at those son nuva bitches," Paul proudly said it properly: "Look at those sons of bitches." Paul used that grammatically correct cussing until the day he died.

4. Maggiorino's Porcino record has never been matched, as far as it is known.

5. This information in the chapter is based largely on corroborated lore.

6. News reports from the two Albuquerque newspapers provided considerable information for this chapter.

23

ODYSSEY CONCLUDES
(1970–1986)

PRIDEFUL END

In 1970, the Menicucci brothers looked upon their efforts with pride. Both looked forward to celebrating their upcoming fiftieth wedding anniversaries. Julio's family had survived their battles with depression, ones that ravaged him and Dante, but they had generally sidestepped deadly losses. Amerigo's family dodged the mental disorders but had suffered several deadly events, one that took their youngest son, Julio Henry and the decade-long saga with their granddaughter Arlene. They were both mentally exhausted and Davina was physically so. Unfortunately, more drama lay ahead.

Their oldest daughter, Louise, was ill with serious kidney disease that grew steadily more severe. Since 1951, she had suffered from repeated streptococcal infections that were difficult to control. Only two antibiotics were available then: penicillin and prontosil, a sulfa-based drug. Neither one worked for her, probably due to allergies, a common side effect. Her physicians resorted to older treatments, including throat swabs with antiseptics, such as Iodine or Mercurochrome. Charlie was especially close to Louise, his cousin, because they were born at about the same time and had been schooled together. Charlie said of her condition: "She was sick all the time and they kept swabbing her throat. But nothing doing."[1]

Louise commenced with kidney problems in the late 1950s, which the physicians at the time attributed to Strep infections. It was understood that the bacterium often induced nephritis, an inflammation of the Glomerulus, which is the filtering mechanism in the kidney. As a result, her kidney function declined and by the late 1960s, she was on dialysis. The filtration machines at the time worked to a point but did not replace the entire kidney function. Most dialysis patients had some kidney function, and the machine picked up the balance. The patient usually had dialysis only a few times a week. It worked for a while but her body was declining.

Nephritis can cause several symptoms, including a loss of appetite. By late 1969, it was obvious that she had little time left. Adele Morelli Davis told the story: "We (she and her husband) had Louise, Bill, Amerigo and Davina for dinner. Louise sat and nibbled on one chicken wing for the entire meal. During the meal Davina and I went to the kitchen for some food. Davina stood at the sink crying and saying over and over, 'We are going to lose her.' She was right. We could see Louise dying right at the table. It was terrible for all of us."

By January, Louise was hospitalized and constantly on dialysis. Her kidneys had completely ceased functioning. The machine was incapable of keeping her alive and if she did live, she would be tethered to machines. Day after day she skidded further, with new complications developing regularly. By this time in her treatment history and with the medical knowledge of that time, the physicians had exhausted every means to save her. They knew it was fruitless to continue. She was unconscious and in a vegetative state. They advised Bill to authorize the cessation of treatments and allow her to die. She had already been given the Catholic Last Rights and all that was needed was Bill's ok. With a heavy heart, he authorized the removal of the machinery and on February 23, 1970, Louise died peacefully.

The decision did not sit well with some, especially Davina. She and other family members wondered aloud if Bill's decision was premature. Some claimed that she was misdiagnosed at an early stage, in which the medical team provided the wrong treatment. Several family members and friends, all medical professionals of some type, pointed to Loise's skin lesions, which is a sign of Lupus. They believed that she had lupus-induced Nephritis, which causes glomerulus inflammation and permanent damage. They further claimed that misdiagnosis might explain why the treatment failed—the doctors were treating her for the wrong condition. Therefore, they claimed, she might have been saved in the end with proper treatment.

The furor was sufficiently large and boisterous that the physicians ordered an autopsy to resolve the issue. On February 24, 1970, Dr. David Dain performed the autopsy with Dr. Friedenberg, her regular physician, attending. The final diagnosis was clear. She succumbed to chronic glomerulonephritis caused by repeated Strep infections over nineteen years.[2]

FINAL YEARS

Louise's death ravaged Davina and the autopsy results did not help. Adele Morelli Davis told the story: "Davina was on the couch crying day after day for weeks and we couldn't help her. She felt like she died with Louise. She never got over it." Amerigo canceled their 50th wedding anniversary, a customary indication of a distressed family. The couple had lost two of their four children. Amerigo's normally bubbly personality was squelched, replaced with deep-seated mourning. He quit the Jemez trips and spent his time at the station or puttering around the yard. He and Davina had never been so sad, and prayer was their only relief.

The events affected Amerigo's health. Around 1973, he was diagnosed with colon cancer. Fortunately, a surgical procedure removed the cancerous section but his depressed mental state dragged on his health. Within a year, he suffered a mild stroke. He recovered, but his condition put a lid on his outdoor activities, including fishing trips in the local irrigation ditches. Small strokes continued, and his health degraded further with every new one. I saw him at the station during that period, and he was visibly languid with slow reactions. His large, heavy body was depleted. His eyes were sunken, with distortion from his thick eyeglasses adding to his gloomy appearance. He moved slowly and painfully, completely out of character. On April 3, 1979, a heart attack killed him. He died content in his family accomplishments but remained melancholy to the end regarding his lost children.

His funeral mass at Immaculate Conception church attracted a full house. He knew many folks, and they came in crowds to bid their final respects to a friend. The family was saddened, but unlike Louise, who died prematurely, he was an old man who had a long, successful and productive life. In true Italian tradition, his death was both mourned and celebrated. Super Service Station and Super Oil closed on the day of the funeral. Julio was the most downcast of all. Except for his first year in the Michigan mines, he and "his man" had never been separated. To him, it was equivalent to losing a spouse. He sunk into depression again, thinking about his brother, an indispensable half of this team. He knew that the family's success was founded as much on Amerigo's steady management at Super Service as his own leadership in directing the family. With Amerigo gone, Julio stared into a deep void. However, his family—his descendants—were doing well.

After Amerigo died, Davina did not wish to remain in their home. It reminded her too much of the past family struggles. She asked to be transferred to a retirement home. The family visited with her at the home regularly as her physical and mental faculties slowly degraded.

Julio, meanwhile, regressed to his home to live out his final years. He continued to enjoy Jemez with Victor Bachechi, but it was not the same without Amerigo. Victor experienced health problems, and in 1980, Victor died. Julio traveled to Jemez with family members until the early 1980s, when his health degraded, and he spent most of his time at home with Giulia, venturing out only to church and the grocery store.

FINAL MONTHS

Giulia's physical decline became noticeable in 1983 after a series of high blood pressure incidents. She also experienced several bouts of severe gastrointestinal disorders that kept her from her regular duties. Julio hired a Hispanic woman to assist in the home. Giulia taught her Italian cooking as they bantered away in Italian and Spanish. Soon, neither Julio nor Giulia could traverse the stairs to their basement. Charlie visited nightly; I joined them frequently. Our first duty upon arrival in the evening was to retrieve from the basement all of the items that Giulia needed for meals the following day.

In October 1985, Giulia's health seriously declined, and she became bed-bound. On October 30, she experienced a large blood-pressure spike that triggered a massive stroke that killed her. Teresa Menicucci Clark, daughter of Julio, told the story: "Mama was suffering through the day and into the evening. I was holding her hand when she mumbled some prayers, and then she stopped breathing. She looked so content and almost happy." After the funeral, Julio became a bedraggled, elderly man, bearing little physical resemblance to the bold businessman he had been only a decade earlier. He spent much time in his chair at his home, staring, snoozing and living out his last hours.

FINAL WEEKS

It was not much later that Davina experienced an accident in the rest home. On May 8, 1986, her wheelchair brake failed, and she rolled down a hallway and crashed into a set of concrete stairs, lacerating her head and fracturing her skull. They rushed her to the hospital but within a couple of days, she expired.

A few days following Davina's funeral, Julio asked me to put a single luminaria in front of the statue of the Modanna in his grotto and keep it lit. I dutifully complied. Every afternoon, when I returned home from work, I refreshed the candle. I visited him each evening with my father, Charlie, but the visits were somber affairs where our goal was to provide comfort and uplift to a sinking, dying man rather than cheerful banter.

FINAL DAYS

One afternoon in early June 1986, I was sipping wine and talking with Julio. He said, "Now, I'm finished. What is going to happen?" In my thirty-fiver-year-old youth and naivete, I presumed that he meant his life was finished and he feared death. I launched into a long list of reasons not to fear death. He ignored me because I misunderstood him. He was not referring to his life ending but rather to his life's goal being complete. He was now the last one of the four Menicucci immigrants. He had cared for his family, and now his life was finished.

He did not fear death. He stared death face-to-face in the Michigan mines. As an elderly man, he knew that every man's time comes. His angst was Judgement Day. How would the Lord judge his performance in life, and would he enter the eternal kingdom? The luminaria was his final plea to the Madonna to speak to the Lord on his behalf. "The Lord listens to his mama," he always said. It was an astonishing display of humility from a man who could legitimately be characterized as great. During this time, Julio uttered some of the most consequential words about the family's migration to the United States. "In Italy, you work and die. In America, you live. Live." I took the meaning then as I do today: do your job as an honorable Italian man.

FINAL HOURS

On the first week of June 1986, Julio lay dying in his home. Mariangela Menicucci Scanlon, daughter of Julio, called me at about seven on June 4th to inform me that he had passed. I rushed to his home to see him for the last time. I was the first of his grandchildren on the scene; Mariangela, his daughter, was at his side when he took his last breath. We prayed at his bedside and after I exited the back door, I extinguished the candle in the luminaria bag in front of the Madonna. In 1908, his father Raffaello tasked Julio with a mission to implant Menicucci's blood in America. Eight decades later: mission accomplished.

See notes 3, 4.

Notes

1. *Noble* discusses the use of Mercurochrome in treating Strep infections.

2. The report clearly states: "The histological picture of the kidneys is that of in-stage glomerular disease with no normal-appearing glomeruli remaining. Histology is the microscopic examination of tissues and includes review of the patient's medical history. No changes are present histologically to suggest any etiology other than glomerulonephritis. Although the rash on the arm was not examined histologically, the distribution and clinical history are consistent with herpes zoster." Herpes zoster is commonly known as Shingles.

The rash on her arms was due to Shingles, not Lupus. No evidence suggests that Lupus was involved with her condition.

3. The chapter is based largely on corroborated lore.

4. *Ets* presents the biography of an Italian woman named Rosa.

BIBLIOGRAPHY AND REFERENCES

Albright, C. and Moore, *American Women, Italian Style*, Fordham University Press, New York, NY, 2011.

Albuquerque Progress, a periodical published by Albuquerque National Bank reporting on business activity in the city from 1934–1956, available at Genealogical Center, Albuquerque Public Library.

Development of a Community renewal program for Albuquerque, Albuquerque Urban Renewal Agency, 1962.

Allen, Leslie, *Liberty: The statue and the American dream*, The Statue of Liberty-Ellis Island Foundation, 1985.

Alter, George. *New Perspectives of European Marriage in the Nineteenth Century*. Journal of Family History, 16, 1991.

Arrigoni, Rena, *Casa Angelica Arlene's Legacy*, University of New Mexico Press, Albuquerque, NM, 1997.

Artusi, Pellegrino, *Science in the Kitchen and the Art of Eating Well*, University of Toronto Press, Toronto, Canada, 2014, Originally published in 1891, titled *Scienza en Cucina* (Science in the kitchen).

Barry, John, *The Great Influenza*, Viking Press, New York, NY, 2004.

Bateman, N and Selby, P, *History of Kankakee County*, Historical Encyclopedia of Illinois, Middle West Publishing, Chicago, IL, 1906.

Beever, Antony, *The Second World War*, Little, Brown and Company, New York, NY, 1978.

Benedict XVI, Pope, and Sarah, Robert, Cardinal, *From the Depths of Our Hearts: Priesthood, Celibacy and the Crisis of the Catholic Church*, Ignatius Press, February 2020.

Berry, G, *Classic Galactosemia and Clinical Variant Galactosemia*, National Library of Medicine, National Institutes of Health; online. February 4, 2000.

Bertoletti, Fabrizio, *City in Wartime*, published in Iola Giomi's Il Giornalino, Volume V, Number 2, 1978.

Bohme, Federick, *A History of Italians in New Mexico*, PhD dissertation, University of NM, Albuquerque, NM, 1958.

Breaking Bread with Daily Mass Propers, 2019 Roman Catholic Missal, Oregon Catholic Press, Portland, OR. 2018.

Broadcasting-Telecasting Yearbook, Broadcasting Publications, Inc, 1940.

Bruno, Al, *Early Italian Immigrants Were Second-Class Citizens*, La garretta Italiana, March, 2020.

Bryan, Howard, *Albuquerque Remembered*, University of New Mexico Press, 2006.

Bryan, Howard, *Off the Beaten Path*, Albuquerque Tribune, June 30, 1964.

Bryder, L., *The Medical Research Council and treatments for tuberculosis before streptomycin*, Journal of the Royal Society of Medicine, October, 2014.

Catholic New Agency, Washington, DC, various articles.

Catholic News Service, U.S. Conference of Bishops, Washington, DC, various articles.

Clark, Teresa Menicucci, principal consultant, personal communications, Baton Rouge, LA, 2019.

Chavez, Carmen, *Coming of Age During the War: Reminiscences of an Albuquerque Hispana*, NM Historical Review, Volume 70, Number 4, 1995.

Chisum, M., Jacqie, E. and Sandoval, R., *Borderlands: Bataan Death March and POW Camps 36 (with 2018 update)*, part of the El Paso Community College Library Research Guides, 2007.

Churchill, Winston, *The Gathering Storm*, Houghton Mifflin Company, New York, NY, 1948.

Churchill, Winston, *Their Finest Hour*, Houghton Mifflin Company, New York, NY, 1949.

Churchill, Winston, *Triumph and Tragedy*, Houghton Mifflin Company, New York, NY, 1953.

(The) Church of Jesus Christ of Latter-day Saints, *The FamilySearch GEDCOM Specification*, Family History Dept, 15 East South Temple, Salt Lake City, UT, 23 February 2023.

IBID, personal communications, 2022.

Cline, Mary, *Albuquerque. Portrait of a Western City*, Clear Light Publishing, Santa Fe, NM, 2006.

Ciongoli, K., Parini, J., *The Story of Italian Immigration*, Harper Collins, New York, NY, 2002.

Ciotola, Nicholas, *Italians in Albuquerque*, Acadia Publishing, Chicago, IL, 2002.

Collier, Richard, *The Road to Pearl Harbor: 1941*, Atheneum, NY, 1981.

Comer, Nathan, Madow, Leo, and Dixon, James, *Observations of Sensory Deprivation in a Life-Threatening Situations*, Journal of Psychiatry, Published online April 2006, last accessed March 2023.

Courter, Ellis, *Michigan's Copper Country*, Office of Geological Survey, CMG 92-01, Lansing MI, 1992.

Craig, J. and Rimstidt, D., *Gold Production History of the United States*, Ore Geology Reviews, Volume 13, Issue 6, 1988.

Currie, James, *Medical Reports on the Effect of Water, cold and warm, as a Remedy in Fever and Other Diseases*, Royal College of Physicians, Edinburgh, England, 1808.

Danesi, Marcel, *Complete Italian Grammar Review*, Barrons, Hauppauge, NY, 2006.

Davis, Adele Morelli, subject expert consultant, principal consultant, personal communications, Albuquerque, NM, 2022.

Del Frate, Emma, personal communications, Albuquerque, NM, 2023.

Delnoy, B, Coelho, A, and Rubio-Gozalbo, M, *Current and Future Treatments for Classic Galactosemia*. Journal of Personalized Medicine, Feb, 2021.

DeMark, Judith, *Immigrant Experience in NM*, PhD dissertation, University of NM, 1984.

Dewitt, Susan, *Historic Albuquerque Today: An Overview Survey of Historic Buildings and Districts*, Historic Landmarks Survey of Albuquerque, Albuquerque, NM, 1978.

De Sluka, Marco, *The Regions of Italy*, published in Iola Giomi's Il Giornalino, April, 1977, Volume IV, Number 3.

Dickie, John, *Delizia! The Epic History of Italians and Their Food*, Simon & Schuster, New York, NY, 2008.

Doyle, Giuli Scanlon, subject expert consultant, principal consultant, personal communications, Mesa, AZ, 2022.

Doyle, Susan Badger, *German and Italian Prisoners of War in Albuquerque, 1943–1946*, NM Historical Review, Volume 66, Number 3, July, 1991.

Dupont, B, Keeling, D, Weiss, T., *Passenger Fares for Overseas Travel in the 19th and 20th Centuries*, Paper presented at the Annual Meeting of the Economic History Association, Vancouver, BC, Canada, September, 2012.

Durland, Kellogg, *Steerage Impositions*, in The Independent, Vol. LXI, No. 3013, New York, NY, Thursday, August 30, 1906,

Dyreson, D. A. and Dyreson, M. J., *Six Centuries of Settlement*, Fantasma Press, Albuquerque, NM, 1973.

Ellis Island, *The Immigrant Journey*, Ellis Island website, History and Culture section, 2018.

Ellis Island Foundation, The Statue of Liberty, Passenger Search, www.heritage.statueofliberty.org/passenger, last accessed October 2024.

Erkoreka, A. (2010) *The Spanish influenza pandemic in occidental Europe (1918–1920) and victim age*, Influenza and Other Respiratory Viruses 4(2), 2010.

Erkkila, Catherine Boland, *American Railways and the Cultural Landscape of Immigration, Buildings & Landscapes:* Journal of the Vernacular Architecture Forum, Vol. 22, Spring, 2015.

Falagas, M., *The Therapeutic effect of balneotherapy: evaluation of the evidence from randomized controlled trials*, The International Journal of Clinical Practice, June, 2009.

Felice, et. al., *Italy's Growth and Decline, 1861–2011*, CEIS To Vergata, Research Paper Series, Vol. 11, Issue 13, No. 293, October, 2013.

Foner, Eric, *The Story of American Freedom*, W.W. Norton Company, New York, NY, 1998.

Fergusson, Erna, *Albuquerque*, M. Armitage, Albuquerque, NM, 1947.

Galactosemia Handbook, Galactosemia Foundation, Albany, NY, 2022.

Giannini, Armond, personal communications, Albuquerque, NM, 2022.

Giannini, Rita, personal communications, Albuquerque, NM, 2022.

Gilmore, David, *The Pursuit of Italy, A history of a land, its regions and their peoples,* Penguin Books, New York, NY, 2011.

Giomi, Ioli Gradi, *Il Giornalino, Monthly Magazine of the Club Culturale Italiano*, various volumes, Albuquerque Public Library, Special Collections, 1977–1978.

Giomi, Ioli Gradi, *Punta Di Vista E Appunti*, (Viewpoints and Notes), published in Iola Giomi's Il Giornalino, Volume IV, Number 3, April, 1977.

Giomi, Sylvia, personal communications, Albuquerque, NM, 2023.

Gjenvick-Gjonvik Archives, *Stowaways on Steamships Entering USA, A 1911 Report*, last accessed Jan, 2024.

IBID, *2392 Stowaways Reached US Ports During Last Fiscal Year*, in The Nautical Gazette, Inc., Vol 100, No. 2, Whole No. 2578, Saturday, January, 1921, New York, NY, last accessed October 2024.

Grodzinsky, Ewa and Levander, Marta, *History of Body Temperature*, Palgrave Macmillan, London, United Kingdom, 2019.

Goff, Harold, *A History of the Daily Newspapers in Albuquerque*, a typewritten manuscript dated 1937, available at the Genealogical Center at the Albuquerque Public Library.

Grant, R. G., *The Great Depression*, Barrons, Hauppauge, NY, 2003.

Rubio-Gozalbo, et. al., *The natural history of classic galactosemia: Lessons from the GalNet registry*, Orphanet Journal of Rare Diseases, article number 86, 2019.

Goldberg, Ronald, *America in the twenties*, Syracuse University Press, Syracuse, NY, 2003.

Gregory, Desmond, *Napoleon's Italy*, Fairleigh Dickenson University Press, Vancouver, British Columbia, 1967.

Ets, Marie, *Rosa: The Life of an Italian Immigrant*, University of Wisconsin Press, 1999.

Harney, Carol, *The Italian Immigrant Women in North America*, Proceedings of the Tenth Annual Conference of the American Italian Historical Association, Toronto, Canada, October, 1977.

Haskin, Frederic J., *Chapter 8, The Steerage Passenger*. in The Immigrant, an Asset and a Liability, Forgotten Books, New York, NY, 1913.

Historical Studies Branch, *Combat Crew Rotation, World War II and Korean War*, Air University, Maxwell AFB, AL, 1968.

History of Albuquerque, 1870–1976, Chronology of Events; No author or publisher listed. Copy available at the Albuquerque Public Library Genealogy Center, Albuquerque, NM, no date listed.

Hoard, Dorothy, *Historic Transportation Routes on the Pajarito Plateau*, Los Alamos National Laboratory, (contract 24493-001-05 AH, May 2006.

Immaculate Conception Parishioners, *Immaculate Conception Church-Centenial-1883–1983*, Jostens, Albuquerque, NM, 1984.

Heaven, R. and Buxton, S., *Darkness Visible, Awakening Spiritual Light through Darkness Meditation*, Destiny Books, Rochester, Vermont, 2005.

Irving, Minna, *A Human Derelict–The Stowaway*, in The New Age Magazine, Vol. IV, No. 3, March 1906.

Jeansonne, Glen, *Transformation and Reaction: America Between the Wars, 1921–1945*, Waveland Press, Long Grove, IL, 2004.

Juergens, Sylvester, *The New Marian Missal for Daily Mass*, Regina Press, New York, NY, 1961.

Keleher, Michael L., Esq., personal communications, Albuquerque, NM, 2023.

Keleher, William B., Esq., personal communications, Albuquerque, NM, 2023.

Kennedy, Lesley, *At Peak, Most Immigrants Arriving at Ellis Island Were Processed in a Few Hours*, History Channel online, June 2018.

Keynes, John, *The General Theory of Employment, Interest and Money*, Stellar Classics, Laguna Beach, CA, 1936.

Kammer, D., *20th Century Suburban Growth of Albuquerque, New Mexico, 1904–1959*, National Register of Historic Places, August 2000.

Kuhns, Elizabeth, *The Habit, A History of the Clothing of Catholic Nuns*, Doubleday, USA, 2003.

La Bella, Laura, *How Italians Made America Home*, Rosen Publishing Group, New York, NY, 2019.

Langer, William, *An Encyclopedia of World History*, Houghton Mifflin Company, Boston, MA, 1960.

Lankton, Larry, *Cradle to Grave: Life and Death at the Lake Superior Mines*, Oxford press, Oxford, United Kingdom, 1991.

Laskin, David, *Ethnic Minorities at War (USA), in: 1914–1918*, online, International Encyclopedia of the First World War, issued by Freie Universität Berlin, Berlin, Germany, 2014.

Laurino, Maria, *Italian Americans*, WW Norton & Company, Castle House, London, UK, 2015.

La Sorte, Michael, *La Merica*, Temple University Press, Philadelphia, PA, 1985.

Lavender, David, *The Southwest*, University of NM Press, Albuquerque, NM, 1984.

LeDuc, Stephen, *The Ethnic Composition of Underground Labor in a Michigan Copper Township: A Quantitative Portrait, 1870–1920*, Mining History Journal, 2005.

Lewis, Amanda, Jemez Springs Public Library, subject expert reviewer, personal communications, Jemez Springs, NM, 2024.

Lewis, Diane, personal communications, Jemez Springs, NM, 2024.

Lewis, Nancy, *Chasing the Cure in NM*, Museum of New Mexico Press, Santa Fe, NM, 2016.

Lewis, Ronald, *The American Magic, Codes, Ciphers and the defeat of Japan*, Farrar, Straus Giroux, New York, NY, 1982.

Little, Barry, *Italian Wedding Traditions*, Italy magazine, June 2014.

Lord, E., Trenor, J. and Barrows, S. *The Italian in America*, Kessinger Publishing, Whitefish, MT, 2008, originally published in 1905.

Los Angeles Water and Power Associates, *Early Los Angeles Gas Stations*, circa 1926.

Luthy, Shanese, *Untangle Your Roots, There is More Than Census Records and Vital Records*, a presentation at the RootsTech 2023, Salt Lake City, UT, 2023.

Machiavelli, Nicolo, *The Prince*, Banton Books, New York, 2003. Originally published in 1513.

Manchester, William, *American Ceasar*, Little, Brown and Company, New York, NY, 1978.

Mangione, J. and Morreale, B., *La Storia*, Harper Collins, New York, NY, 1982.

Martin, C, *Valle Grande, A History of the Baca Location No. 1*, All Seasons Publishing, Los Alamos, NM, 2003.

Mateju, J., *Yesterday and Today, Brochure for the Los Lunas Hospital and Training School*, Archives of Albuquerque Public Library, Special Collections/Vertical Files, 1960.

Matson, Eva, *It Tolled for New Mexico: New Mexican as Japanese POWs During World War II*, Yucca Tree Press, Yucca Tree Press, Las Cruces, NM, 1994.

Matteucci, Edward, Esq., primary reviewer, subject expert reviewer and principal consultant, Albuquerque, NM, 2022.

McClain, Sally, *Navajo Weapon: The Navajo Code Talkers*, Rio Nuevo Publishers, Tucson, AZ, 1981.

Melosi, Martin, *The Automobile Shapes the City, Automobile in American Life and Society*, online, last accessed May, 2024.

Melzer, Richard, *Sanatoriums of New Mexico*, Arcadia Publishing, Mount Pleasant, SC, 2014.

Menghini, Christina, *Examining Patterns of Italian Immigration to Michigan's Houghton County, 1860–1930*, MS Thesis, Michigan Technical University, 2004.

Menicucci, Ann, personal communications, Albuquerque, NM, 2023.

Menicucci, Barbara Dinegar, MA, primary reviewer, subject expert reviewer and principal consultant, Albuquerque, NM, 2022.

Menicucci, Emma Dalle, primary reviewer, subject expert reviewer and principal consultant, Albuquerque, NM, 2022.

Menicucci, David, *Catholic Home and School Association Guidebook*, National Catholic Educational Association, 1990.

Menicucci, John, principal consultant, personal communications, Albuquerque, NM, 2023.

Menicucci, Mark, personal communications, Albuquerque, NM, 2023.

Menicucci, Theresa Domenici, subject expert consultant, principal consultant, personal communications, Albuquerque, NM, 2023.

Miller, Laura Menicucci, RN, subject expert consultant, personal communications, Albuquerque, NM, 2023.

Morelli, David, primary reviewer, subject expert consultant, principal consultant, personal communications, Forest Grove OR, 2022.

Moreno, Barry, *Italian Americans*, Ivy Press Ltd, Lewes, East Sussex, UK, 2003.

Morris, Gemma Menicucci, personal communications, Albuquerque, NM, 2023.

Morris, Richard, *Encyclopedia of American History*, Harper and Brothers, New York, NY, 1953.

Mueller, Jerome, Roman Catholic Priest, retired, Archdiocese of Santa Fe, subject expert reviewer, personal communications, Jemez Springs, NM, 2024.

National Catholic Register, Denver, CO, various articles.

Neel, Gladys, *History of Albuquerque,* MA Thesis, University of New Mexico, 1928.

Newspapers.com, a paid-membership platform specializing in searches of historical newspapers.

New York Times (Reporter unnamed), *Women in Steerage Grossly Ill Used,* in New York Times, December 14, 1909.

Noble, L., *Case of Streptococcus Septicemia cured by Mercurochrome,* Canadian Medical Association Journal, April 1925.

Norris, F., Eliot, M., *Historic Resource Study Valles Caldera National Preserve,* National Council for Public History, Indianapolis, Indiana, VCNP CR Report R2022-012, NMCRIS Activity No. 153723, 2022.

Office of Price Administration (OPA), *Facts You Should Know, GASOLINE,* United States Government, November 1943.

Palmer, Mo, *Albuquerque Then and Now,* Thunder Bay Press, San Diego, CA, 2006.

Parker, Lewis, *Why Italian Immigrants Came to America,* Rosen Publishing, New York, NY, 2003.

Pedroncelli, Vera, *Los Griegos Remembered,* Dog Ear Publishing, 2024.

Peckinpaugh, Lynne Franchini, personal communications, Albuquerque, NM, 2022.

Perret, Geoffrey, *Old Soldiers Never Die,* Random House, 1996.

Podolsky, David, MD, personal communications, Albuquerque, NM, 2022.

Portale Antenati, Ministero Della Cultura, Direzione Generale Archivi di Italia, https://antenati.cultura.gov.it/, last accessed March 2023. FamilySearch.org provides efficient access to the records, last used, October, 2024.

Prange, Gordon, *Miracle at Midway*, McGraw Hill, New York, NY, 1982.

Puelo, Stephen, *From Italy to Boston's North End: Italian Immigration and Settlement, 1890–1910*, Masters Thesis, University of Massachusetts Boston, Boston, MA, 1994.

Raczynski, Joan, *The Italian Immigrant Experience in America (1870–1920)*, An 11 grade curriculum, internet published for Wilber Cross High School, New Haven Connecticut, unknown date.

Rakestraw, Lawrence, *19th Century Copper Mining*, Isle Royale National Park, 1965.

Riley, Katie Lewis, personal communications, Jemez Springs, NM, 2024.

Roberts, Peter, The New Immigration: A Study of the Industrial Life of Southeastern Europeans in America, MacMillan Company, New York, NY, 1912.

Robinson, Greg, *By Order of the President, FDR and the Internment of Japanese Americans*, Harvard University Press, Cambridge, MA, 1966.

Roos, Dave, *America's First Immigration Law Tried (and Failed) to Deal with Nightmarish Sea Journeys*, History Channel website, March 2019.

Routledge, Joseph, *Jemez Mountains 100 Years Ago*, Butterfly and Bear Press, Jemez Pueblo, NM, 2003.

Rubio-Gozalbo, M, et. al (40 authors), *The natural history of classic galactosemia: lessons from the GalNet registry*, Journal of Rare Diseases, 2019.

Sacks, Lucinda, *Clyde Tingley's New Deal for New Mexico 1925–1938*, Sunstone Press, Santa Fe, NM, 2013.

Sanders, James, *The Education of an urban Minority: Catholics in Chicago, 1833–1965*, Oxford University Press, Oxford, United Kingdom, 1977.

Scanlon, Pat, subject expert consultant, personal communications, Viterbo, Italy, 2023.

Schwaner, Marie Montgomery, personal communications, Albuquerque, NM, 2023.

Schwarz, Katherine, MD, subject area consultant, personal communications, Albuquerque, NM, 2024.

Segel, Robert, *The Browning Model 1917 Water Cooled Machine Gun*, Small Arms Journal, Issue V1N3, volume 1, 17 August 2011.

Sheehan, Michael, *Four Hundred Years of Faith: Seeds of Struggle-Harvest of Faith: Harvest of Faith*, Archdiocese of Santa Fe, Santa Fe, NM, 1998.

Simons, Donna Searight, *Copper miners' lives 100 years ago results (Sic) in bitter labor strike and Christmas Eve tragedy*, Daily Press, Escanaba, MI, December 21, 2013.

Simpson, Albert, *Combat Squadrons of the Air Force World War II*, Office of Air Force History, Headquarters USAF, 1982.

Smith, Adam, *The Wealth of Nations*, Random House, New York, NY, 2003. Originally published in 1776.

Smith, Denis Mack, *Mussolini*, Alfred Knope, Inc, New York, NY, 1982.

Solem, Borge, *The Transatlantic Crossing*, Chapter two: *Steerage Passengers-Emigrants Between Decks,* Norway Heritage website, posted 2007, last accessed October 2024.

Spidle, Jake, *Doctors of Medicine in New Mexico: A History of Health and Medical Practice, 1886–1986*, University of New Mexico Press, Albuquerque, NM, 1986.

Stamm, Roy, *For Me, The Sun*, The Albuquerque Museum, Albuquerque, NM, 1999.

Stahle, Tyler, *Understanding the Genealogical Proof Standard*, FamilySearch Blog, March 9, 2016, last accessed March, 2023.

Stevenson, Noel, *Genealogical Evidence, A guide to the standard of proof relating to the ancestry, heirship and family history*, Aegean Press, Laguna Hills, CA, 1986.

Steinfels, Peter, *A People Adrift, The Crisis in the Roman Catholic Church in America*, Simon & Schuster, New York, NY, 2005.

Stockman, Dan, *As number of US Women religious decline, they look to the future*, Catholic News Service, CatholicPhilly.com, October, 2018, last accessed Mar, 2024.

Strachan, Hew, *The First World War*, Oxford University Press, Oxford, United Kingdom, 2001.

Story, William, *The First World War: a concise global history*, Rowman & Littlefield, 2014.

Summers, W., *Catalog of Thermal Waters in New Mexico*, New Mexico Bureaus of Mines and Mineral Resources, Hydrologic Report 4, 1976.

Swetnam, T., personal communications, Jemez Springs, NM, 2023.

Spurlock, Cindy Tartaglia, subject expert reviewer, personal communications, Cayon, NM, 2023.

Tatangelo, Ann, Genealogist, Angel Research and Genealogical Services, Via Sant' Apollonia, 11 Sora, Frosinone, Italy, subject area consultant, personal communications, 2023.

Tucciarone, J. and Laricia, B., *Italians Swindled to New York: False Promises at the Dawn of Immigration*, The History Press, Charleston, SC, 2021.

Twitchell, Ralph, *The Leading Facts of New Mexican History*, The Torch Press, Cedar Rapids, Iowa, 1917. New Edition, Sunstone Press, 2007.

University of New Mexico oral history project, recorded interviews by Nicholas Ciotola; collection curated at the University of New Mexico Center for Southwest Research, Albuquerque, NM, 2024.

Villanueva, Jari, *History of Bands in World War I*, published online at www.tapsbugler.com, last accessed July 2024.

Wells, Brian, *History of the David Bradley Company*, Belt Pully Magazine, November/December 1999.

Wickersham, George, *Report on the Enforcement of the Prohibition Laws of the United States*, National Commission on Law Observance and Enforcement, January, 1931.

Wills, Gary, *Papal Sin, The Structures of Deceit*, Doubleday, New York, NY, 2000.

Winkler, Rosemary, *Stories of early Albuquerque*, as told in the Albuquerque Genealogical Society Quarterly, Copper Ave. Press, Albuquerque, NM, 2021.

Wolfman, A. and Gorman, A., *Water-borne Typhoid Fever Still a Menace*, American Journal of Public Health 11, no 2, 1931.

Wright, Q., *Mandates Under the League of Nations*, University of Chicago Press, Chicago, IL, 1930.

Maps*

1887 Jemez Springs USGS Reconnaissance Map.
1920 Santa Fe National Forest NM, Prime Meridian, USFS.
1927 Santa Fe National Forest NM, Prime Meridian, USFS.
1938 Central Highway Map, Sandoval County, NM, State Highway Department.
1944 USGS Jemez Springs, NM, Quadrangle, Topographic Map 1:62,500, 15 min series.
1952 USGS Jemez Springs, NM, Quadrangle, Topographic Map 1:62,500, 15 min series.
1966 Jemez Mountain Sportsman's Map, Sante Fe National Forest.

*These maps are available at the University of New Mexico Map and Geographic Information Center (MAGIC) in the Centennial Library on the main campus.

APPENDIX I

IMMIGRANT ITALIANS AND THE ECONOMIC DEVELOPMENT OF JEMEZ

The Jemez Mountains contain bountiful resources, including lumber, game animals, fish, fresh air and tall pines. Historically, the mineral waters powered economic development in the area. People have sought the therapeutic powers of hot mineral bathing for thousands of years. None more so than the Italians. The exact role that the Jemez Mountains played in luring the early Italians to Albuquerque is unknown, but it was certainly a factor. From the earliest days, mountains were the geographical feature that set Albuquerque apart from other desert cities: The Sandia and The Jemez Mountains. Lucchese, loved mountains because they resembled the Apennines in their native land.[1,2]

Italian immigrants were involved with the Jemez mountains from around 1905 when Oreste Bachechi, the earliest Italian immigrant, purchased land north of Soda Dame along New Mexico Highway 4. He later donated many of these properties to the Catholic Church, which built various Catholic facilities along the road. Sulphur Springs was the initial Jemez Mountain attraction. It was located about fifteen miles north of what is now Jemez Springs.

Known colloquially as "The Sulphurs," Sulphur Springs was located on the western side of the Valles Caldera at an elevation of eighty-three hundred feet. Steaming-hot Sulphur-rich waters created natural pools a few feet deep, ideal for bathing. Many people believed in the curative powers of Sulphur, so the Springs created excitement. Investors eyed the Springs as a unique, high-mountain, health resort. But there were no serious developers until after 1876 when U.S. Surveyors determined that Sulphur Springs was outside the boundaries of the Baca Location No. 1. In 1885, after a brief skirmish between a couple of buyers, John Walton controlled the property, built facilities and operated a resort targeting wealthy Santa Feans. He would be the first of many succeeding owners to fail. In 1899, Mariano Otero, an affluent and influential New Mexican family member, bought the property and the mineral rights. He planned to yield a profit by operating the resort and mining Sulphur. W. Timble operated a stagecoach line that shuttled guests from Santa Fe to The Sulphurs. He moved his family on-site where they worked year-round at his mill, producing high-quality Sulphur. Otero's mining problem, like that of Sulphur Springs resort, was its distance to civilization. Although he produced good-quality Sulphur, he struggled to get it to market. Transportation costs dragged on the operation.

Sulphur mill at Sulphur Springs, New Mexico, in the 1920s. Courtesy Jemez Springs Public Library.

In 1901, Otero hired William Meyer to manage the property. He upgraded the facilities and advertised. The resort gained traction with glowing reviews in the Santa Fe New Mexican, the state's largest and most influential newspaper. Unfortunately, Otero died in 1904 and none of his family was interested in mining. The mining operation ceased but the resort remained operational under J. Malette, manager. Again, profits were elusive due to customer saturation and wintertime closures. What was more, the stagecoach service was unreliable. The resort struggled to survive.

In 1909, Joseph Duran purchased a long-term lease on Sulphur Springs and invested thousands of dollars in renovations and upgrades. He advertised frequently in the Albuquerque papers. He contracted for stagecoach services from the rail station at Thronton, a few miles south of Santa Fe. Sulphur Springs was equally accessible for Albuquerqueans because the stage line commenced from the rail depot at Thronton station, a few miles south of Santa Fe. Albuquerque passengers boarded a northbound train for Santa Fe, exited at Thronton station, and boarded the regular twice-a-week stagecoach to Sulphur Springs. Santa Feans did the opposite. The total travel time between either of the cities and Sulphur Springs was twelve hours. The stage left early in the morning, so passengers departed by rail in the afternoon, spent nights at the Depot Hotel at Thronton Station and caught the stage the following morning. In total, the round trip took about two day.[3] Duran failed and the operational costs were fingered as the culprit.

In 1912, Mariano Otero lost all of his Jemez Mountain property, including Sulphur Springs and Jemez Springs, because of a long-standing tax issue: the family had not bothered to pay property taxes. It is unclear who acquired the property after the territorial foreclosure but the most likely owner was Neil Field, an Albuquerque lawyer. During that stretch of years, a number of different proprietors leased and ran the resort. W. Culler acquired the Springs around 1939.

STONE SOLID COMPETITION

In the early 1900s, Sulphur Springs was not the only mineral bath facility in Jemez. About a dozen miles south lay Jemez Springs, owned by Mariano Otero. Jemez Springs produced ample amounts of mineral-rich, steaming-hot spring water. However, the Jemez waters contained no Sulphur, only Sulphates, the fully oxidized form of Sulphur. The waters did not have the characteristic odor of Sulphur, as they did at Sulphur Springs, but they were still desirable. Otero built the first bathhouse in Jemez Springs, called Otero's Bath House. These early facilities were located where the current bathhouse sits. Jemez Springs' greatest advantage was location; much closer to Albuquerque, which contained potential customers. Roads remained an obstacle for most people. New Mexico Road 4 in the early 1900s was a primitive trail suitable only for horse-drawn carriages. Sulphur Springs and Jemez Springs were effectively out of reach for most Albuquerqueans.

Ruins of the original Otero bathhouse at Jemez Springs, New Mexico. The banner—partially obscured—reads: Hot Sulphur Water Baths." The same springs supply the modern bathhouse to the north and outdoor bathing pools to the south, all located across from the Los Ojos Bar in the center of Jemez Springs, New Mexico. Courtesy author's collection.

By the mid-1910s and into the 1920s, as automobiles came onto the market and the Jemez Road improved word of the springs spread in Albuquerque Italian Colony, especially piquing the adventuresome and wealthy folks. Johnny Giannini, Alessandro Matteucci, Oreste Bachechi and the Napoleones were among the first Italians to venture to Jemez Springs regularly by road vehicle.

Around 1916, Charley Clay, a rough and brash Albuquerque ranchman, figured that Jemez Springs' location trumped Sulphur's advantages and he took a lease on the Stone Hotel in Jemez Springs, including the bathhouses. These facilities had operated for some time but barely squeaking by financially. Charley had a different idea. He remodeled the hotel and added a motorized shuttle to transport customers to and from Albuquerque. He saw growth potential in Albuquerque as fertile ground for customers. He invested in a Mitchell, a rugged, high-end vehicle with a 6-cylinder engine and a plush, elegant interior.

Stone Hotel was the first solid competitor to the Sulphur Springs resort, and Charley's stage line opened up Jemez Springs to Albuquerque's consumers. By 1920, Charley had remodeled the Stone Hotel and built a new bathhouse over the hot springs. He traded on his good reputation in Albuquerque by renaming the Stone to Hotel Clay, complete with a jazzy logo. He also traded with many of the Italians in Albuquerque, including Johnny Giannini. It was there that he met Julio and Amerigo.

Charley advertised in Albuquerque and picked up customers as the public was abuzz with excitement about the Jemez Mountains. Moreover, his operation offered essentially the same accommodations as Sulphur Springs. Charley's facility provided both indoor and outdoor bathing. The bathhouses were located in the heart of the Jemez Springs village and were wooden shells constructed over pools of hot, upwelling mineral water, steaming at over 110F. They also provided hot-towel massage therapy and other personal services, such as pedicures. Walk-ins could bathe or receive massages on a pay-as-you-go basis. Lower-cost boarding homes in the area provided simple housing and meals to those in a lower social stratum. Jemez Springs had wide appeal in Albuquerque and many, including many Italians, day-tripped to Jemez Springs for a day of bathing and dining.

In 1921, Charley Clay again stepped-up competition with Sulphur Springs. He announced plans to build a world-class resort, a five-star hotel, by today's rating scale. He located the hotel in the heart of Jemez Springs, right across from the ancient ruins. Called La Esperanza (Hope), it offered twenty-three luxury rooms using the latest in technology, including electric lighting and a fine restaurant. He constructed a beautiful rock-sided structure in the Indian Pueblo style. Charley shuttled his guests to his bathhouses, located about a half mile south of La Esperanza. By 1923, La Esperanza was attracting customers who might have sought out Sulphur Springs. Charley ran his shuttle service more frequently in the warm season to accommodate guests. He had an advantage over Sulphur Springs because he was closer to Albuquerque and he operated year-round.

Super Service Station and Super Oil Company serviced Charley's vehicles and delivered kerosene and gasoline to Charley's operations in Jemez. In addition to Esperanza, the Menicuccis delivered fuel to Ward's Trading Post in Jemez Springs and various Catholic facilities located between Soda Dam and La Cueva. In 1929, Charley cashed in the La Esperanza, selling it to an investing conglomerate. But they kept Charley on board to run the hotel.

CHASING SULPHUR

Italians have a long history of chasing after gold. Carmine Charles Tartaglia (aka Charlie and Carlo), one of the earliest of the Italian immigrants, chased Sulphur. He found it at Sulphur Springs. In the early 1910s, Charles did business in Santa Fe where he learned about the Springs. He and his family frequented the resort. They loved not only the baths but the bounty of the mountains—fish, big game, mushrooms and the serenity of tall pines. The family fell in love with the Jemez Mountains. Charles had an eye for investment, and in 1922, he assumed a multi-year lease to operate the resort. He and his son, Leonard, developed a business plan geared toward Albuquerque instead of Santa Fe. They surmised that a bigger customer base in Albuquerque would enhance revenue. Charley Clay was demonstrating that point in Jemez Springs. Virtually all of Charley's customers were Albuquerqueans and he had plenty of them.

Charles and Leonard were hard-driven Italian businessmen and they saw the situation as a challenge. They invested sweat and money to upgrade the facilities and advertise. For the first six months of operation, Charles offered a horse-drawn stagecoach from Jemez Springs to Sulphur Springs. Other stage lines, including Charley's, were already shuttling visitors from Albuquerque to Jemez Springs but no farther. Charles quickly replaced the stagecoach with his 1922 Oldsmobile model 43A. Called The Four, it seated four passengers comfortably with plush seats. A big-bore four-cylinder engine displacing two hundred and twenty-one cubic inches powered the Oldsmobile. It was one of the best automobiles for the mountains. He ran his shuttle from Sulphur Springs to Albuquerque with stops in Jemez Springs, San Ysidro and Bernalillo. The Tartaglias were going head-to-head with Charley and Charles needed a shuttle to properly cap the Springs' high-class image. A rugged, luxury vehicle was a testament to Charles' emphasis on quality and exemplary service. In this vehicle, he could travel from Albuquerque to Sulphur Springs in about seven hours in fair weather.

Both Charles' and Charley's shuttles operated about twice weekly. Each shuttle carried anyone who paid the passage fee, nine dollars per one-way trip (around one hundred forty in 2024 dollars). Some Albuquerqueans headed directly for a resort. Others camped or stayed with friends in the area. Even the U.S. Postal Service shuttled passengers. The postal truck, likely a Model T Ford, usually had an extra seat or two vacant, depending on the mail load. The Postal Service advertised for travelers to ride in the postal truck for a small fee, a fraction of the shuttle fare. Many people took the offer because it was the cheapest way to get to Jemez without a car. In 1922, most average citizens did not own a vehicle. Those who did usually owned it through their business, as did the Menicuccis later in the decade. Many Italians ventured regularly to Jemez Springs and Sulphur Springs via shuttle.

Automobile shuttles frequently encountered difficulties en route. Weather forecasting had not been developed and every carriage operator looked at the sky, considered the season and decided whether to depart. In the summer season, thunderstorms and flooding were common events during New Mexico's monsoon season. The rains washed out trails, instigated rock slides and created hazardous traveling conditions. The long, sandy stretch of road from Bernalillo to San Ysidro was treacherous, with deep sand on some stretches that bogged down the thin-wheeled, rear-wheel drive automobiles. Horse-drawn coaches were less prone to bogging down in mud, snow or sand than automobiles because horses were pulling the coach instead of propelling itself with the rear wheels. Sometimes, large snow storms trapped people in a coach for a day or two. It was not unusual for a coach to be delayed for half a day due to weather. Even with the travel problems, Jemez Springs was accessible year-round and Sulphur Springs was not.

Charles talked up his new resort in Albuquerque, attracting a few of the wealthier Italians, such as the Bachechis and Palladinos. He had hired a noted chef to run his restaurant. He offered one deal after another and garnered several takers, mostly prominent Albuquerqueans. He advertised routinely in the Albuquerque and Santa Fe papers but like the previous owners, he found an insufficient number of wealthy individuals to support the high costs and logistics of operating the shuttle lines over difficult roads. A ten-day stay at the Sulphur Springs resort costs the equivalent of a vacation trip from Albuquerque to New York City in today's dollars. It was much more expensive than Clay's place but the ambiance was better. Jemez, at sixty-four hundred feet, is home to few conifers. Sulphur Springs, at eighty-three hundred feet elevation was a true mountain resort immersed in huge stands of pine, fir and aspen trees.

Charles' plan was good, and he picked up customers but again, there were some Achilles heals. Charley set prices based on demand and his costs, which were lower than Charles. Charles was forced to keep his prices competitive, which meant his margin was lower than Charley's. Second, Charles had a limited operational window. Snow from late October through the end of April left Sulphur Springs isolated. It operated with a single overseer during the cool period. Whether customers were willing to pay a premium for the advantages of Sulphur Springs was the question. In less than a couple of years, Charles had the answer. He could not compete with Charley.

TRY, TRY, TRY

In spite of the operational difficulties, Sulphur Springs resort, marketing vicariously through its long-standing reputation as a high-society retreat, continued to attract buyers. Around 1926 Neil Field, the proprietor, hired Frenchie Maruin, a professional chef and resort operator to reinvigorate the facility. Like the managers before them, Field and Frenchie spiffed up the grounds and added a few extra features, such as horseback riding for guests. Frenchie was well known for his culinary expertise, so Field used his name in advertisements in Albuquerque. Like Charles, he ran a shuttle, a seven-passenger touring vehicle specially designed for rough mountain roads.

Over the next few years, they continued to struggle when a fire took the facility down. A faulty flue in the kitchen ignited one end of the hotel and spread wildly in the all-wood structure. Screaming and shouting, the manager exhorted the guests to move with extreme dispatch. They all ran for their lives, barefooted in nightclothes and underwear. Then they turned and warmed themselves by a fire that consumed the hotel, leaving nothing but glowing ashes. It was over in less than an hour. A bitter blow it was because Sulphur Springs had little left to compete with Charley Clay in Jemez Springs, whose operation was growing like a weed in May.

Billy and Neil tried to minimize losses and, within a month, advertised that the resort would remain open for bathing. It struggled for years with bathing fees dribbling in, many from Albuquerque's Italian colony who stayed at lodges in Jemez Springs.

CABINS FOR THE MASSES

Through the late 1920s and well into the 1930s, Sulphur Springs resorts struggled to profit, even as the baths themselves remained popular.

As both roads and vehicles improved, demand increased for lower-cost housing near the Sulphur hot springs, which allowed lower-class visitors to use the bathing facilities on a walk-in, pay-as-you-go basis, avoiding the high costs of the resort hotel.

As was typical in American capitalist society, the private sector responded to the need. Art Routledge operated a ranch near what is now the intersection of Forest Service Roads 105 and 106. Road 105 follows the Sulphur Creek to the Springs. He and his family constructed cabins along the creek, which runs adjacent to the road to Sulphur Springs. He rented them to visitors, many of whom bathed at the Springs.

The cabins varied in size but averaged about eight hundred square feet and were mere wooden shells, a frame structure with rustic log sidings. Windows were crude and leaky with barely transparent panes. The cabin had no ceiling; the roof rafters were evident from inside and the walls were uninsulated. A corrugated metal roof shed water but created a nearly ear-ringing racket during a hail storm. A wood stove heated space and cooked food. Each cabin had four or five beds, each with a single mattress. The kitchen consisted of a sink but no running water. Water was taken from a nearby spring and hand-carried to the cabin. Water from the nearby Sulphur Creek, laden with dissolved Sulphur, supplied water for bathing and washing.

Routledge provided food boxes for meat and other foods. It was a wooden cubic container about two feet on a side with a closable top. The box was filled with food. A rope tied to the top of the box was thrown over a tree branch, which allowed the box to be pulled up above the ground. The system was essential to prevent bears from raiding the food. Black bears were common in the area but usually posed no direct threat to humans other than pilfering their food and frightening the children. An odiferous outhouse accompanied each cabin. Mice and rats were the worst problems. They easily invaded cabins, trying to snatch human food. Mouse traps were common features in the cabins and snoozing guests were frequently jolted awake by the snap of a trap. Cleaning and resetting traps were the men's job—safeguarding the family against hazards.

A couple of dozen cabins of various sizes were available for rent. Routledge rented them to hunters even in the late fall and early winter, with frequent sub-zero cold winters in the area. Routledge effectively operated a profitable resort. Not only did he collect rent for his cabins, but he also earned money from selling milk, cream, butter, eggs, and various vegetables that he sold to his tenants. He and his family did well with the property. Many Italian immigrants, including the Menicuccis, were frequent visitors. Some families had standing, year-over-year leases on certain cabins they occupied for long summer periods. The cabins not only provided the Routledge family a good living, they hosted thousands of Sulphur-water bathers who could not afford the resort hotel, including many Italians.

FINAL GASPS

The Routledge cabins did not help Sulphur Springs economically. The Springs made only moderate profits from the bathing facilities. The resort hotel was their main economic engine. In 1939, Neil sold the property and the new owner, W. Culler, rebuilt the hotel and put the resort back into operation. Culler advertised heavily, recanting a litany of curative powers of Sulphur. Some claims were ridiculous, guaranteeing cures for serious diseases and maladies such as rheumatism, sclerosis of the liver and heart disease. Meanwhile, of course, Charley Clay was watching amusingly as his competitors stumbled like two-year-old toddlers. He needed to do little but let Sulphur Springs trip over itself again and again, sending more folks to La Esperanza.

In 1942, Leonard Tartaglia, Charles' son, leased Sulphur Springs and operated it. Again, it failed for the same reasons as before. Leonard got a break when, around that time, Routledge sold his holdings to the Tartaglia family. Cindy Tartaglia Spurlock told the story: "In 1941, an Italian immigrant by the name of Johnny Bonaguidi bought the ranch for his brother-in-law Leonard Tartaglia and his wife Irene Alma. Together they built a cabin rental with twelve cabins on the property. It was the original La Cueva Lodge. They also converted the old Rutledge riding stable into a hopping bar, café and grocery store with a gas pump they owned. It was quite a spot for hunters coming to Jemez. The Tartaglia's descendants are all here today." The Menicuccis supplied gasoline and kerosene to Leonard's business.

What was once a bucolic scene with cattle roaming the grounds was transformed into a prime fall hunting resort, with multiple deer carcasses hanging from cabin front porches. In summer, it was the same vacation spot that Routledge had offered. Tartaglia advertised in Albuquerque about its ideal middle location between the two major hot springs and was a prime location for deer and elk hunting. Elk herds flourished in the area after their successful re-introduction to the state in 1910. For several years, he did exceptionally well.

By 1955, the facilities at Sulphur Springs had degraded due to a lack of maintenance. Culler sputtered along until he, like his predecessors, ran out of money. In 1965, Culler asked Berger Briggs in Albuquerque to list the property. It finally sold in 1970 at a basement bargain price. The entirety of the Sulphur Spring property is now within the boundaries of the Valles Caldera National Preserve, accessible only by hiking. No improvements remain on site.

After Sulphur Springs closed for good, Leonard's lodge catered to hunters. It was not enough to sustain the business; by the 1960s, it was finished. Today's La Cueva Lodge, which operates at the intersection of New Mexico Roads 4 and 126, was built by the Lewis family around 1980. What was the Routledge farm and later the La Cueva Lodge is now private residential property.

JEMEZ LODGES

Charley Clay was not a monopoly, but for a while, it appeared to be so. Customers flocked to his resort and baths in the 1930s and into the 1950s. However, they were offered in a hotel setting. Public demand grew for top-end, high-mountain recreational facilities with rustic façades and luxurious interior accommodations. For these people, recreation was their goal, not bathing. A mountain lodge filled the bill. The Routledge farm was the first vestige of such a lodge, but it was more accurately a farm with the accouterment of rental cabins. Leonard Tartaglia's La Cueva Lodge was the first facility in the area that met the classic definition of a high-mountain lodge.

Around the late 1940s, Seth Seiders, an investor heeding to market demands, built and operated the Lazy Ray Ranch. The Ranch was located about five miles north of Fenton Lake, about a mile north of the Seven Springs Fish Hatchery on the banks of the Cebolla Creek. It was a true dude ranch, with luxury facilities, expert service, recreational activities such as guided hikes and fishing trips, horseback riding and a heated swimming pool. The Cebolla Creek was fishable for many miles above the ranch and guests were guided on horses to the more remote locations with world-class Brown-trout fly-fishing. During hunting season, expert butchers and packers processed and packaged big game animals that customers harvested. The food was excellent, prepared by professional French and Italian chefs. It was popular in Albuquerque and number of Italian families in Albuquerque patronized the ranch, especially the Domenici and Matteucci families. Kathryn Domenici and her husband Robert Domenici and Jeanette Del Frate and her husband Jerry Monahan, spent many weeks a year at Lazy Ray with their close friends, Lydia Giacomelli Matteucci and her husband Gino. Katherine and Lydia became some of the ranch's best spokespersons, bragging about their adventures of luxury.[4,5]

Aside from its outstanding location and amenities, the Ranch was infamous for its Italian Mafia connection. The year of Al Capone's involvement with Lazy Ray is unclear, but it was sometime in the ranch's early days that he selected it as a hideout for his thugs who were running from the law. Capone perceived security in remote mountains. His reasoning was not unlike that of American Army General Grove, who, in the early 1940s, selected Los Alamos as the secret location for the laboratory that developed the atomic bomb. The ranch was well hidden and difficult to reach, especially for inexperienced city-bred lawmen. Plus, there is plenty of cover for an emergency escape, such as from a police raid. Many east-coast Italians, most from southern Italy, had migrated to Rio Rancho, a community to the west of Albuquerque. There were rumors of nefarious mob activity within that group, which as was supposedly linked to the Capote's mob. Unfortunately, there is no physical evidence to examine and the story remains in the realm of amusement rather than historical fact. In 1970, Lazy Ray Ranch closed permanently and the physical facilities were razed. Nothing of the Ranch remains today.

Aspen Grove Lodge was another facility popular with less wealthy Italians, located a few miles west of the La Cueva caves south of New Mexico Road 126. The lodge was ensconced in a dense Aspen grove that, in the fall glowed with a bloom of golden color. It is unknown when the Lodge was built, but it was likely in the late 1940s. The lodge consisted of a single-story four-plex, with each unit able to house a family of six. It was located relatively close to Sulphur Springs and provided excellent trout fishing on the nearby San Antonio River. It rented rooms year-round, but summer was the most popular season, requiring reservations well in advance. The lodge was never advertised, yet it had nearly one hundred percent occupancy throughout the year. The Lodge closed in the 1970s but the building remains.

HISTORY OF JEMEZ NEEDED

This Appendix provides a summary of the economic history of the Jemez Mountains from the perspectives of Italian immigrants. Italians were involved with Jemez from early in the century and they affected economic growth. A much broader and deeper historical story should be told about the area that documents how the early Anglo, Hispanic, native Indian and others contributed to the area's economic development. A great deal of raw information and data exist to support such an effort. Also, many multi-generational descendants live in the area and are excellent sources of anecdotal information. Such a work would contribute significantly to the body of historical knowledge about Northern New Mexico.
See notes 6, 7.

Notes

1. *Summers* discusses the thermal waters in New Mexico. *Norris & Eliot* talk present a comprehensive report on the physical resources of the Valles Caldera National Preserve, on which the Sulphur Springs are located. *Martin* discusses a history of the Valle Grande, the largest valley in the Valles Caldera Preserve, including the mineral waters.

2. *Hoard* presents a history of transportation routes on the east side of the Valles Caldera National Preserve.

3. On June 30, 1964, *Bryan, Albuquerque Tribune* reporter, published an article in his regular column, "Off the Beaten Path," that described the stage line from Thornton Station to Sulphur Springs. The stagecoach trip began at the Thronton Rail Station located near Santa Domingo's pueblo. Passengers boarded it in front of the Depot Hotel. People traveled by rail from Santa Fe or Albuquerque to Thronton, spent the night in the hotel in order to board the stagecoach early the following morning.

According to Bryan, "After breakfast in the morning, the Wason-Timble stagecoach rolled up in front of the hotel, with Carles Wason at the reigns and passengers boarded the four-horse coach for the trip to Sulphur Springs. An hour's drive brought the coach to Pena Blanca and it reached Cochiti Pueblo at ten, where the horses were changed. The stage station at Cochiti was operated by John Morris. The coach, with a fresh team of horses, proceeded up into the mountains through the abandoned town of Allerton, where a sawmill, stores, saloons and houses stood vacant—a few stray burros providing the only signs of life. The coach reached the mining town of Bland at one in the afternoon. Here the horses were changed again and a fresh driver, John Henry, took the reins. Leaving Bland at one in the afternoon, the coach traveled on up the Valle Grande stage station managed by Preston Chalfant, where horses were changed again. Proceeding west, the stage reached its destination at Sulphur Hot Springs at four."

Bryan does not state the specific date of the story, but since Timble was involved, it was likely around 1915. This information is based on information from *Bryan*. ("Off the Beaten Path")

4. *Giomi* (Ioli) presents a description of the Del Frate family. Published in September, 1977, Volume IV, Number 10.

5. Katherine Del Frate Domenici said of Lazy Ray, "It was just like heaven with that stream running through it. You can see the stream from the pool. And the food was just wonderful." She would could go on effusing for ten minutes about Lazy Ray.

5. News reports from the two Albuquerque newspapers provided considerable information for this chapter.

6. Corroborated lore provided material for this chapter.

APPENDIX II

LIST OF ITALIANS LIVING IN ALBUQUERQUE IN 1900, 1925 AND 1950

Following are tables listing all of the Italian surnamed families in Albuquerque at three points in time: 1900, 1925 and 1950. I gathered the information from the Albuquerque directory and the U.S. census records.

There are three columns for each year, including the family surname, Italian origin (north or south) and number of families, all sorted alphabetically by name. For the purposes of this work, the divide between north and south Italy is roughly an east-to-west line running coast-to-costs just south of Rome. I defined a family to be a household with a head, either a man or woman. I counted men living alone as a single family because most of them married and carried their surnames forward. I did not count single women living alone as a family because most of them married into a family with a different surname. Note that Barnett is the legally changed name from Pelletieri. It was the most extreme case of Americanizing an Italian name in the Italian colony.

Some Spanish surnames are similar to Italian. Therefore, any surnames that were not clearly Italian were investigated for their origins. Some names listed in the directories and censuses are misspelled and I corrected them in the table. For example, there is a directory listing for Antonio Domenicci, a misspelling of Domenici. The list has been reviewed by several first-generation Italians. Lastly, although I exercised diligence in extracting names and family information from the source material, the selection process was completely manual, laborious and difficult. Thus, in spite of my assiduousness, the table may contain errors.

ITALIANS LIVING IN ALBUQUERQUE 1900

Surname	Origin	Number of Families
Bachechi	North	1
Berardenelli	South	1
Brattina	North	1
Bruno	South	2
Damiano	South	1
Digneo	South	2
Fracaroli	North	1
Franchini	North	1
Giacomelli	North	1
Giomi	North	2
Gionotti	North	1
Gradi	North	1
Grande	North	2
Lanci	North	2
Masetti	North	1
Matteucci	North	1
Melini	North	2
Napoleone	North	1
Palladino	North	2
Parenti	North	2
Pedroncelli	Unknown	1
Petroni	North	1
Piccinini	North	1
Puchetti	South	1
Rossi	North	2
Tartaglia	South	2
Vaio	North	2
Viviani	North	1
Zanoni	North	1

Northerners: 22, 76%

Southerners: 6, 21%

Unknown: 1, 3%

Total Surnames: 29

Total Families: 40

ITALIANS LIVING IN ALBUQUERQUE 1925

Surname	Origin	Number of Families
Bachechi	North	6
Balduini	North	1
Barnett	North	1
Bandoni	North	2
Barbieri	North	4
Berardinelli	South	3
Bonaguidi	North	3
Caccivillani	South	1
Cappuccilli	Unknown	1
Carboni	North	1
Cimino	South	4
Cinelli	North	1
Corraza	North	1
Cosimati	North	1
Cotignola	North	2
Dalle	North	1
Damiano	South	1
DeAngelo	South	1
Deblassi	North	2
Del Frate	North	3
Dinelli	North	5
Divoti	North	1
Dolzadelli	North	2
Domenicali	North	2
Domenici	North	2
Donati	North	1
Ferrari	North	1
Ferraro	South	2
Fracaroli	North	4

Franchini	North	2
Gionotti	North	1
Gardetti	Unknown	1
Giacomelli	North	2
Giannini	North	7
Giomi	North	3
Giovannini	North	1
Gradi	North	2
Granone	North	3
Granucci	North	1
Landolfi	North	1
Lencioni	North	1
Lommori	North	2
Luchetti	South	1
Luciani	North	1
Marino	South	1
Martino	South	2
Matteucci	North	10
Maurino	South	2
Menicucci	North	2
Monti	North	2
Morelli	North	8
Moretto	North	1
Napoleone	North	6
Nizzi	North	1
Nottoli	North	2
Palladino	North	2
Parenti	North	4
Petroni	North	1
Pieroni	North	1
Puccetti	North	2
Pucci	North	1
Puccini	North	1

Santori	North	1
Schifani	South	1
Scotillo	South	2
Sei	North	2
Speronelli	North	2
Tagliaferro	North	3
Tartaglia	South	5
Tabacchi	North	1
Tobachi	South	1
Tolentino	South	1
Tomasi	North	2
Tomei	North	4
Toti	North	3
Trosello	South	1
Vaio	North	2
Vichi	North	2
Viviani	North	1
Zannini	North	1
Zito	North	1

Northerners: 63, 78%

Southerners: 16, 20%

Unknown: 2, 2%

Total Surnames: 81

Total Families:174

ITALIANS LIVING IN ALBUQUERQUE 1950

Surname	Origin	Number of Families
Arrighetti	North	4
Bachechi	North	7
Baldoni	North	1
Balduini	North	2
Bandoni	North	4
Barbieri	North	3
Barnett	North	1
Bartolucci	North	2
Bonaguidi	North	3
Bossa	North	1
Bottarini	North	1
Buonanni	South	1
Butteri	North	1
Cacciato	South	2
Caccivillani	South	1
Canzoneri	South	1
Capretto	South	1
Caputo	South	1
Carboni	North	1
Carducci	North	1
Caretto	North	1
Carmignani	North	1
Carrara	South	2
Cavalo	South	1
Cesaretti	South	1
Chiado	North	5
Chiordi	North	3
Cicci	South	2
Cimino	South	6

Cinelli	North	3
Cito	South	1
Civerolo	North	2
Corazzi	North	1
Corradini	North	2
Corrazza	North	3
Cosimati	North	2
Covolo	North	3
Dalle	North	1
DeAngelo	South	1
Deblassi	North	9
Degani	North	1
Del Frate	North	10
Denelli	North	1
DeVenzio	South	2
Devoti	North	3
Dinelli	North	4
Domenicali	North	1
Domenici	North	2
Donati	North	2
Fabiani	North	1
Fabizio	South	1
Ferrari	North	1
Ferrero	South	1
Fioretti	North	1
Fracaroli	North	1
Franchini	North	4
Frate	South	1
Frederico	Unknown	1
Galassini	North	5
Giacci	North	2
Giacomelli	North	2
Giannettino	South	1

Giannini	North	6
Gilardi	North	1
Giomi	North	6
Girotti	North	1
Gradi	North	2
Grannini	North	1
Granone	North	1
Granucci	North	2
Guidi	North	1
Jacopetti	North	1
Lancione	South	1
Lencioni	North	1
Limonselli	Unknown	1
Lombardi	North	1
Lommori	North	3
Lonbardelli	North	1
Luciani	North	3
Mainetti	North	1
Mallegni	North	1
Manfredi	North	1
Marchiando	Unknown	1
Marchiori	North	1
Marianetti	North	1
Marino	South	1
Martinelli	North	1
Matteucci	North	14
Medici	North	1
Menicucci	North	3
Mondini	North	1
Mongiello	South	1
Montani	North	2
Monte	North	2
Morelli	North	7

Moretto	North	1
Naccaratto	South	2
Napoleone	North	7
Nicola	North	4
Nizzi	North	4
Nottoli	North	2
Nuccio	Unknown	2
Palermo	South	1
Palladino	North	3
Parenti	North	5
Patino	South	1
Pavioni	North	1
Peloso	South	1
Persichetti	North	1
Pesavento	North	1
Petroni	North	1
Picco	Unknown	1
Pieroni	North	1
Pinello	North	1
Pucci	North	1
Puccini	North	2
Rivoni	Unknown	1
Rizzoli	North	1
Rossi	North	1
Rosso	South	2
Rosssetti	North	1
Ruvolo	South	4
Schifani	South	5
Sei	North	3
Speronelli	North	3
Tabacchi	North	3
Taborelli	Unknown	1
Tagliaferro	North	5

Tartaglia	South	6
Tomei	North	1
Tripodi	North	1
Vaio	North	6
Vincioni	North	2
Zanotti	North	2

Northerners: 98, 81%

Southerners: 16, 13%

Unknown: 7, 6%

Total surnames: 121

Total families: 300

APPENDIX III

FAMILY TREES FOR REFERENCE

Following are the family trees for most of the major characters in the book. The information contained therein has been verified. However, the trees are not comprehensive and are presented for the convenience of the reader in following the story.

Menicucci Family Tree*

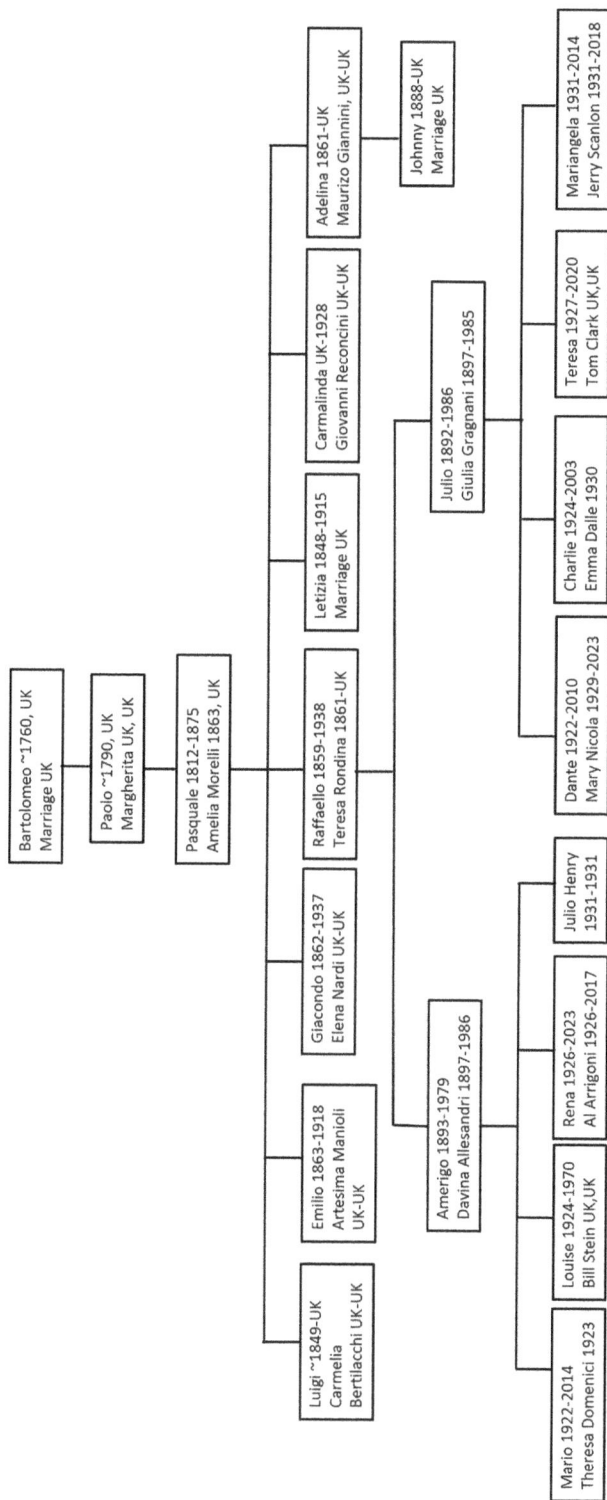

Bartolomeo ~1760, UK
Marriage UK

Paolo ~1790, UK
Margherita UK, UK

Pasquale 1812-1875
Amelia Morelli 1863, UK

Luigi ~1849-UK
Carmelia
Bertilacchi UK-UK

Emilio 1863-1918
Artesima Manioli
UK-UK

Giacondo 1862-1937
Elena Nardi UK-UK

Raffaello 1859-1938
Teresa Rondina 1861-UK

Letizia 1848-1915
Marriage UK

Carmalinda UK-1928
Giovanni Reconcini UK-UK

Adelina 1861-UK
Maurizo Giannini, UK-UK

Johnny 1888-UK
Marriage UK

Amerigo 1893-1979
Davina Allesandri 1897-1986

Julio 1892-1986
Giulia Gragnani 1897-1985

Mario 1922-2014
Theresa Domenici 1923

Louise 1924-1970
Bill Stein UK,UK

Rena 1926-2023
Al Arrigoni 1926-2017

Julio Henry
1931-1931

Dante 1922-2010
Mary Nicola 1929-2023

Charlie 1924-2003
Emma Dalle 1930

Teresa 1927-2020
Tom Clark UK,UK

Mariangela 1931-2014
Jerry Scanlon 1931-2018

*This tree is not comprehensive. It is a reference to individuals involved with the story.
Unknown dates and events are coded as "UK."

Matteucci Family Tree*

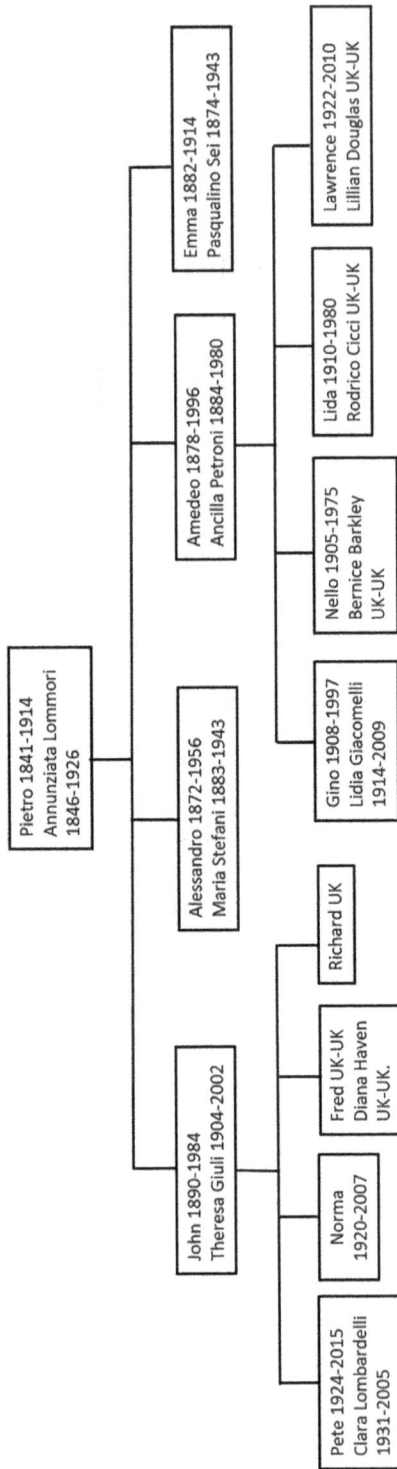

Pietro 1841-1914
Annunziata Lommori
1846-1926

John 1890-1984
Theresa Giuli 1904-2002

Alessandro 1872-1956
Maria Stefani 1883-1943

Amedeo 1878-1996
Ancilla Petroni 1884-1980

Emma 1882-1914
Pasqualino Sei 1874-1943

Pete 1924-2015
Clara Lombardelli
1931-2005

Norma
1920-2007

Fred UK-UK
Diana Haven
UK-UK.

Richard UK

Gino 1908-1997
Lidia Giacomelli
1914-2009

Nello 1905-1975
Bernice Barkley
UK-UK

Lida 1910-1980
Rodrico Cicci UK-UK

Lawrence 1922-2010
Lillian Douglas UK-UK

*This tree is not comprehensive. It is a reference to individuals involved with the story.
Unknown dates and events are coded as "UK."

Menicucci-Morelli Relationship*

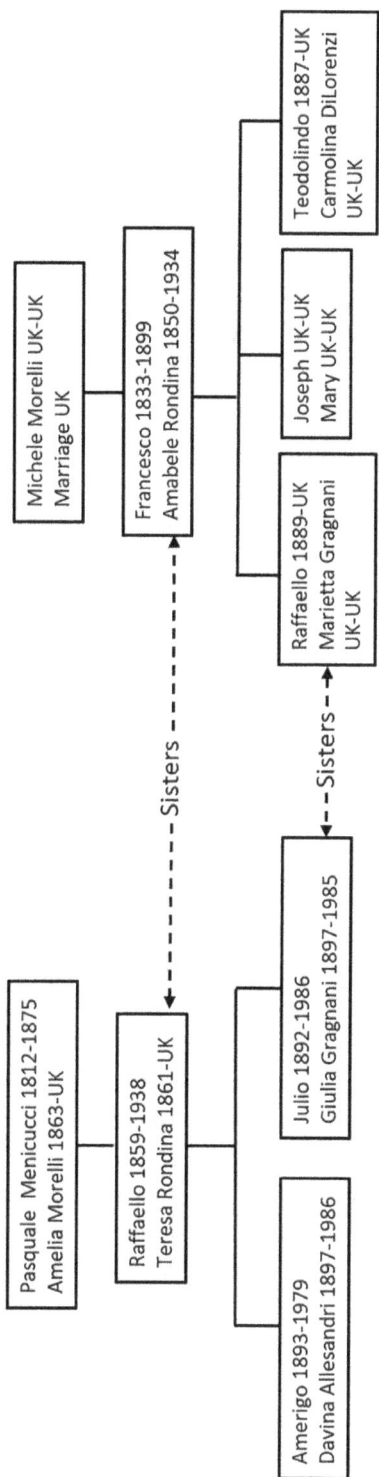

Pasquale Menicucci 1812-1875
Amelia Morelli 1863-UK

Michele Morelli UK-UK
Marriage UK

Raffaello 1859-1938
Teresa Rondina 1861-UK

Francesco 1833-1899
Amabele Rondina 1850-1934

-- Sisters --

Amerigo 1893-1979
Davina Allesandri 1897-1986

Julio 1892-1986
Giulia Gragnani 1897-1985

-- Sisters --

Raffaello 1889-UK
Marietta Gragnani
UK-UK

Joseph UK-UK
Mary UK-UK

Teodolindo 1887-UK
Carmolina DiLorenzi
UK-UK

*This tree is not comprehensive. It is a reference to individuals involved with the story.
Unknown dates and events are coded as "UK."

APPENDIX IV

GUIDANCE AND SUGGESTIONS FOR SEARCHING ITALIAN HISTORICAL RECORDS

Below, I provide an overview of how to search for Italian history. The techniques I discuss are rudimentary and much more detailed information is available. Many publications that provide guidance for conducting historical research are for sale or available in libraries. Experience is the most effective method to learn historical searching.

REQUISITE FUNDAMENTAL TOOLS AND SKILL SETS

Desire: The most important attribute for any investigator is a burning, irrepressible yearning to discover and know historical events. This craving is the basis for novelty required in the search process, including identifying and securing resources, such as computer search tools, libraries and digital repositories. Innovation is needed to address obstacles that arise in the research. A dogged determination to know the truth is a foundational skill.

Clear thought: There is such a labyrinth of information available to the public today that it is easy to become overwhelmed, distracted and inefficient. Clear thinking is the key to negotiating the maze. Whether it is a person or an event that is being sought, it is essential to maintain a focus on the subject of interest. Professional researchers typically identify specific questions to be answered by a search, such as: What was Gino Matteucci's role in mentoring Senator Pete Domenici? With that question as a backdrop, a researcher can easily vet informational sources as worthy of pursuit. It is not uncommon for professional researchers to constantly restate the question they have set out to answer to maintain focus in an investigation.

Discipline: Discipline is a secondary skill that accompanies clarity. It is easy to become sidetracked if interesting information about a different subject is accidentally revealed during a search. Discipline involves pausing sufficiently long to vet the new finding and, if valuable, recording its storage location to retrieve it in the future. But then quickly return to the original search.

Language: Italian civil records are recorded in Italian. Fluency in Italian is not required to search Italian records, but recognition of certain words and phrases is. A fundamental understanding of the structure of the language is useful as well as a good Italian-English dictionary.[1] As many records are inspected and analyzed, proficiency will develop in recognizing the keywords and phrases in the records under inspection. For example, in birth records the words: "...nata una creatura di sesso... (...birth of a child of sex...) are critical because specific data follow. The same basic format is used for marriage and death records, whether or not they are in printed form or completely hand-written.

Cursive Writing: Unfortunately, most Italian records are hand-written in cursive script, rendering it difficult to read even by a fluent reader. Italian cursive writing accomplishes two objectives: it conveys information and presents a work of art by adding superfluous strokes to form letters. The initial letter in the first word of each sentence in an official record was typically heavily dressed with vertical strokes and swirls that had nothing to do with the formation of the letter. For example, an "I" might be interpreted as an "N." It was not until the late 1800s that the Italians began using printed forms for civil records. Thus, only the handwritten entries in the form are those of interest, such as a name or posting date. Before then, each record was entirely recorded in a cursive script that varied in style from one recorder to another. In some cases, even clearly printed records are mostly illegible. As with the language, practice allows the investigator to obtain a working proficiency in reading the cursive writing styles. There are no shortcuts in the self-learning process other than perseverance.

Internet searching: Online search is an essential skill because many historical records are digitized and accessible via the web. Google and Google Scholar, which are readily available, offer Artificial Intelligence search engines and are good tools for searching records. Google Scholar differs from Google in that it focuses on legal cases and scholarly articles. Public and university libraries often provide users with free, high-speed internet access, including the libraries' professional search engines. Internet searching is both an art and science that must be reasonably mastered to wring out the most interesting details from the plethora of online data, including sorting through much false, misleading and bogus information.

One of the keys to effective internet searching is selecting the proper keywords to use in the search engines. Keywords are very much like clues that an investigator provides to an expert hired to find something hidden. It may take several clues to guide the expert into the fertile ground where many sources are unveiled. Often, a Google search will turn up little based on one keyword, but it will render much more when the keyword is altered slightly or paired with another keyword.

Keywords are essential in computer searching. Most people are familiar with typing a word into their smartphone and immediately viewing thousands of results. Phrases can produce more widely varied results. Selecting the proper keywords and key phrases to use in search engines is a good method for identifying relevant information quickly. Selecting keywords is both an art and a science; it is an interactive process with the search engine. The gameshow Password is roughly analogous to how keywords work on a computer search. Contestants take turns attempting to convey a password to another person using only one-word clues. Based on the responses, forthcoming clues are tailored to help elicit the correct word. Similarly, the results from a search can help to spur new ideas for keywords or phrasing for continued searching.

The word password is an example of how keywords work. Suppose that I wish to find out information about the gameshow Password. If I type the word "password" into a search engine, it will respond with thousands of hits related to computer password usage. Even if I type "Password game," the results continue are broadened to include different password games. Only when I add the word "gameshow" to the list of keywords do the results display information relative to my goal.

Key phrases are frequently employed with search engines. They are extremely valuable, with caution. The phrase should be specific because search algorithms will extract what they believe are the appropriate keywords from the question to perform the search. Open-ended questions tend to produce an overabundance of information, much of it unrelated. If a question is too specific, it may omit valuable sources. In almost all instances, a good assumption for an internet searcher is that no matter what has been found, more information exists in cyberspace, and the correct keywords will pull it out of hiding. The researcher should always be mindful that most commercial search engines display paid advertisements as the primary results of a search. Sometimes, an investigator must search deep into the many pages the search provides before useful information emerges.

This short treatise barely covers the fundamentals of the internet. For novices, some online courses on internet searching are available. Local universities and community colleges often offer courses designed to develop skills in internet searching.

Vetting findings: The most important in historical searching is a healthy skepticism of findings. Often, search engines display what their algorithms have determined is the best fit, but it may be completely amiss. A key rule is always to seek additional, independent sources to corroborate a finding. A red flag is when specific information (e.g., a table or graph) reappears in other documents listed in the search. It is not uncommon that a completely incorrect graph can referenced in dozens of documents identified by an internet search. If ten sources are based on the same original material, then the source totals one, not ten.

A researcher should always be skeptical of online documents that list no author, source, or publisher. For them, it is impossible to know whether the author is a PhD, a tenth grader or a computer. Thus, it is impossible to asses quality. Such a source is of limited value because it cannot be verified, lacks credibility and is impossible to reference. It still might render clues in an investigation. The internet is replete with these types of ghost-written documents.

New artificial intelligence-based search engines have quickly come onto the scene and can sometimes falsely provide confidence in the accuracy of the results. Many believe that AI is somehow superior to humans for computer searching. It is, relative to search speed, breadth of examination and sorting capability. And it is a useful tool for researchers. It is still up to the human user to interpret results because even the best algorithms cannot know the investigator's needs.

SEARCHING FOR HISTORICAL INFORMATION

Whether one is a historian, a genealogist or both, Italian civil history is contained in three sources: Civil government records, published reports and books and witnesses' accounts. Each source type is discussed briefly below.

Italian civil records: Civil records are official accounts of civilian activity, such as births, deaths, marriages, tax rolls, property ownership, criminal convictions, etc. These records provide important information about individuals, families and the community, including the dates, times and people involved in various events. Event records contain a plethora of historical information, including the names of witnesses, history of familial lineages, residential locations and baptisms, which can help trace the physical movements of a family within an area and the occupations of its members. When event records are analyzed chronologically over decades, as would be the case if one were searching for the activities of a specific family, a sense of the human constitution of the community can be gleaned. For example, between 1870 and 1890, in the comune of Capannori, the Gianninis were the largest family in the area based on the number of recorded familial civil events. The investigator can construct verified family trees by studying records from specific families.

Italian civil records date back centuries, but with respect to access and ownership, the dividing line is around 1866, when the unified government of Italy mandated that civil records be managed by each comune in each region. Thus, the Italian government manages the modern civil records after 1866, but the Catholic Church manages older ones. A large percentage of the government records have been photographed and are available online. Italian civil records before 1866 are dispersed among the churches in the area, and most have not been photographed or digitized. Searching them must be conducted onsite, with access depending on the whims of the church pastor who owns them. A few clusters of government-managed records prior to 1866 have been digitized. Napolean's ventures in northern Italy produced some records in the Italian archives.

The Mormon Church is responsible for photographing many of the Italian records. The secular Italian government provided the Mormons access to the public records it manages. The older records are in the archives of Catholic churches throughout the country, and Mormons are not Catholic. The Mormons have reportedly been denied access to some Italian Catholic church archives.

Many civic records after 1866 have been photographed and digitized. The Italian government manages the digitized records and are accessible through their official site, the Portali Antenati (Ancestor Portal). However, response times are long, and the site often appears to malfunction or hang. The records can be more quickly accessed through Family Search, the official search platform for the Church of Jesus Christ of Latter-Day Saints (also known as the Mormons).

The Italian records are not digitally indexed, meaning each image is a photo of a page from the Italian record books. Thus, no search engine allows keywords to be used to identify records of interest. The Mormon Church is digitally indexing the records, but the cursive script has hampered progress. New artificial intelligence capabilities will likely complete the indexing for all post-unification records within a decade. Until then, each digitized record must be inspected by eye. Once familiar with the record layouts and key phrases to identify, many records can be quickly perused on a high-speed website. I have reviewed as many as five-thousand records per day while searching for specific names or events. At that review speed, I estimate that I missed about five percent of records of interest.

Notably, among many digitized photographs of record books, there are missing pages, which the photographer accidentally omitted or which did not exist. Sometimes, entire books are missing. In times of duress, such as during wars, records may show inconsistent formats, missing entries or be misfiled.

As is customary, Italian civil records are arranged chronologically based on the posting date, which is usually the first sentence in the record. For example, a birth record on a typed form is usually titled: "Atti Di Nascita" (Birth Acts) and the first sentence in the record is the date, reading such as "L' anno milleottocentonovante due, addi tre di Giugno…. (The year one thousand eight hundred and ninety-two, at three o'clock in June…) The posting date, which is the official record date, always postdates the event date, which is noted in the text of the record. Sometimes, the posting may be as much as a week later than the event date.

The Italian file organization methods are problematic. The civil authorities recorded events in bound books and each record was assigned a unique, chronological identifying number beginning with number one. The number only applies to the specific book in which it is recorded. A new book was initiated if a book was filled with records before the end of the year. The numbering for the new book began anew. Thus, two independent records from the same comune might have the same record numbers and the only difference is the posting date. The books are not clearly marked, and often the numbering systems are confusing. A new book was not always initiated at the beginning of the year. The Italians continued recording in a book until it was filled, even if it contained records from the following year. Thus, some records from a specific year may appear in a book dated a year earlier.

Within the group of Italian civil records, there are three subgroups. The first are the event records, which were described above. The second is the set of supplemental records. These records contain detailed religious and family historical information. They were of interest to the church because they presented the family's history, including previous religious achievements, such as baptisms or other marriages. The identifying numbers on these records differ from those of associated events, and they are stored in various areas called supplements. Occasionally, the event record will reference the associated supplemental record. Supplemental records are almost always written in full cursive script and are difficult to decipher, yet they are rich in history. For example, a wedding event may comprise two records: The official record of the event and the supplemental information about the involved parties. Both records likely have different identifying numbers, were posted on different dates and were recorded in different books.

A third subgroup of records are books containing Italian indexes. These indexes have nothing to do with digitized indexes. Periodically, usually at the end of a decade, the Italian record keepers posted in a separate book a listing of all the people who were involved in a civil event over a specific period (usually a decade). The entries are alphabetized by surname. Adjacent to each name is the date, the event type and a numerical identifier for the associated record. Unfortunately, there is often no reference to the book where the record is stored, causing the confusion described above. It provides a quick means to determine if certain individuals have records within the specified period and record numbers for which to search.

For the purpose and scope of this book relative to Italy, only the civil records for marriages, deaths and births were investigated. No other civil records were sought, such as property ownership or criminal records. Thus, I cannot provide guidance when searching for them. Later in the book, I discuss Albuquerque's history, and these types of civil records were inspected. Some are available online, but others, such as police reports, had to be accessed in person at Albuquerque's City Hall.

Within the United States, civil records include the census and the records, which provide some of the most comprehensive and detailed historical information about people living in a community as well as the commercial activity in the area. Each census reveals personal information unavailable elsewhere, even that which has been retained as family secrets, such as property values, salaries, home addresses, professions, etc. All United States census records are available from 1950 back to their inception in the late 1700s. Information derived from census records is not subject to copyright law and is considered public information.

Likewise, city directories contain listings of residents in a community, including names, addresses and professions. These records are similar to census records in ease of access but contain more errors, such as misspellings of names. Like the census, they are easily accessed through commercial search platforms like Ancestry.com. Fortunately, most records are digitally indexed, allowing researchers to search for records based on keywords or key phrases.

Other civil records of interest to genealogists are the arrival and departure records for ships and planes at United States ports of entry. The Ellis Island website provides direct access to the early 20th-Century records, which are digitally indexed but can also be accessed through search platforms such as Ancestry.com. These records are stored in chronological order depending on the event date, which is often the departure date for the ship. The ship may arrive ten days after the departure, but the date noted on the record reflects its departure. These records provide a great deal of information but can also contain conflicting information, such as the birthplaces, ages and destinations of passengers. Typically, the port authorities in the early 1900s were so busy processing immigrants that they emphasized speed in processing over accuracy.[2]

Published reports and books: Books and magazine articles provided the bulk of fundamental historical information for this book. Knowledge about the historical context for the search greatly aids the researcher in locating and interpreting records. Books provide detailed information about events, including analyses and varying perspectives, all of which give the historical context critical to thoroughly understand the historical record. Libraries provide guidance and professional tools to search for books and articles. Books identified in an out-of-town library can often be accessed via interlibrary loan.

Scholarly articles, including master's and doctoral theses, differ from public articles in that they are usually peer-reviewed for technical accuracy as a condition for publication. Editors and experts usually review public press articles and books as a condition of publication, but self-publishing allows any author to publish material without review. Standard newspaper and newsmagazine reports are typically both accurate and informative. There is much false information online. An investigator's typical mistake is assuming that online searches unveil precise information. Some online information is either entirely wrong or partially so. Family trees are notorious examples. Most published trees are unverified and based solely on lore. Many are completely incorrect, yet they are presented as fact and can easily fool or misdirect a researcher. For example, within the context of this book, I uncovered a half dozen family trees for the Menicucci family and only the accurate one is mine.

Published reports include newspaper and magazine articles, pamphlets, advertisements, public announcements, annotated published pictures, and other similar materials. Several newspaper search engines are free of charge at public and university libraries. However, most provide limited search capabilities, often missing available articles. A professional search tool called Newspapers.com provides comprehensive searching but requires a subscription. This search engine allows the results to be sorted chronologically so the investigator can read about a historic event over time, just as they occurred, rendering a more complete picture of the historical situation. Some small-town newspapers are not included in the Newspapers.com platform.

Witness accounts: Often referred to as lore, witness accounts are the verbal history of events that live in the tales and stories of people in the community. Most people believe lore is the most accurate source of historical information. But lore is hearsay unless it is corroborated by other evidence, such as newspaper reports or other credible witness accounts. Lore can be used as a starting point in an investigation, but it becomes a historical fact only after verifying it. Nevertheless, interviews with knowledgeable people, reviews of personal letters and diaries, and inspections of annotated photos provide useful information and solid evidence for an investigation. Direct quotations from individuals are usually assumed to be accurate, although as I noted in the text, sometimes quotations change over time as stories are verbally passed to new generations.

Inspecting Records: Historical records often contain more information than appears on the surface. Italian records often include additional marks, notes, dates and other information that can provide clues. A good rule of thumb is to inspect and study every part of the record carefully. Clues can be as subtle as the names of witnesses to events, which might indicate they were neighbors or friends or the occupation of certain people.

MANAGING DATA AND INFORMATION

For the following discussion, I use the word data to mean fundamental facts, such as measurements of certain things without any associated interpretation or organization. Information results when an investigator organizes and analyzes data, synthesizes them into information, draws conclusions and documents the work. Published works generally provide information and often supporting data.

Collecting data: Historical searches produce a plethora of data and information that can quickly accumulate into a jumbled pile of discoveries, e.g., book citations, photos, etc. As the pile grows, productivity decreases due to time wasted rummaging for specific details. This concern is heightened when searching Italian digital records because many of them are viewed in short periods, producing many findings. I found that I can attain a rhythmic pace in viewing records, rapidly perusing a page and moving quickly on. I save each interesting source and immediately return to the search. Speed is essential in searching historical digital records because findings are rare; many records are viewed for each discovery.

Organizing the data and information: Once a search is complete, analysis commences and access to specific items among the findings becomes the central need. Efficient access to findings facilitates analysis and documentation when data and information are being assimilated into conclusions. A common aggravating situation is a researcher losing his or her train of thought while writing because data about the topic cannot be found.

A good way to avoid the situation is to apply the typical hierarchical file organizational structure found on most computers. Begin with some organization in mind and create an initial file organizational structure to implement it. Initially, all findings are lumped in a single folder. As the researcher accumulates information and topic areas become obvious, files and subfolders should be created to store information selectively. For example, a high-order file folder may be labeled "Colonial Wars." Subfolders may include "Italian Military Actions" and "Domestic political impact." As the researcher discovers new information, it is immediately archived in the proper subfolder. Periodically, especially in periods of great discovery, an investigator may frequently reorganize the file structure to accommodate new subject areas. A good approach is to organize the data hierarchically on the computer using the normal systems of file folders and subfolders.

File labels: File labels are important to organize and recover information. I recommend that each file name contain two pieces of information: a brief description of contents and critical identifiers. Date and time stamps are normally embedded in computer files. Additional information can be encoded into the title by the investigator. For example, I code the historical date of the contents into each file name. If I save an *Albuquerque Journal* article about a fire event on March 23, 1979, I will name it "Fire Alb 19790323. The 19790323 codes the year, month number and day of the event. This coding scheme is advantageous because it maintains a sequence of numbers that can be automatically sorted in the file folder. For example, suppose five records about fires in Alb, ranging from 1940 through 1990, all with names beginning with "Fire Alb" followed by the date code. With normal sorting of names on the computer, all files with names beginning with "Fire Alb" will be listed chronologically based on the event-date code embedded in the title. If I create a new Fire Alb file with an event date that falls between the dates of the existing files, it will be listed in the correct chronological order on the computer. A file organization such as this allows an investigator to locate files of interest quickly.

File security: Information is critical to a researcher, and its loss can be fatal to a research effort. Regular file backup on a separate device is essential. It is best if the backup device, the one storing backup copies, be located away from the host computer system in a safe location. If the computer and backup device are stored in the same location, a fire or other calamity that affects one will wipe out both, thus negating the backup effort. Many people use cloud services for automatic backup. Dropbox, for example, allows a user to store files on its space, all of which are continuously backed up to the cloud, essentially a larger server that can store a lot of information that can be as quickly retrieved as from a physical backup device. The advantage of this system is that the backups are done automatically for each file, the storage is far away from the home computer, and the records can be accessed from any computer with internet access. The disadvantage is that obtaining the meaningful amount of storage needed for a typical research project will likely require a paid subscription to a service. I recommend that physical devices and cloud storage be used to back up all files in a research project.

Research Notebook: A personal research notebook is a worthy tool even in this age of advanced communications. A notebook can be a common storage area for tidbits of information accumulated along the way and can record an author's thoughts. Many believe that a modern smartphone with audio interpretation can substitute for a notebook, but the act of writing, which requires logical thought and time, can induce clear thinking for the notebook record. The use of both will provide backups in case of losses.

Notes

1. *Danesi* presents the fundamentals of the Italian language.
2. *Luthy*'s presentation discusses records other than census and directories.

APPENDIX V

MENICUCCI DESCENDANTS EMIGRATING FROM AMERICA

As of 2024, only two descendants of the original Menicucci immigrant emigrated from America. One was Nicolas Menicucci, my son. Nicolas migrated for professional reasons. At the time of publication of this book he is a Professor of Theoretical Physics at the Royal Melbourne Institute of Technology. The other is my first cousin, Pat Scanlon, son of Mariangela Menicucci Scanlon. Pat Scanlon and his family now reside permanently in Italy. The story of the circumstances that led him back to the old country is worthy of note. Pat's story is summarized below:

Pat was raised in a Catholic family with an Italian mother who frequently spoke Italian with her parents. She also prepared many Italian meals and adopted many Italian customs for the family. From his earliest days, he was intrigued by Europe; his parents had European roots. It might have been dismissed early on as a passing fascination, but this strange intrigue repeatedly descended upon him. He finished high school with an athletic letter in swimming and went on to the University of New Mexico. He performed academically well and earned acceptance to the university's medical school.

When he sat down to complete the application, he hesitated as he considered his future while his longing for Europe grew. He turned down medical school and instead headed to Europe to visit for a couple of months. Visiting did not satisfy his intrigue, so he sought a job, hoping to remain longer. He landed a job in Florence teaching English. His almost total lack of Italian language skills was an asset that likely helped him to secure the one-year position. English immersion was the preferred pedagogical method of teaching foreign tongues at that time.

The experience in Italy heightened his longing for Italy, but his visa had expired. He returned to Albuquerque and studied Italian at the university. That is where he met his future wife Linda Bartolucci, who had been following her intrigue for Italy and had just completed a long visit to the country. He and Linda were at the head of the class. Pat said, "It was like Italian was in my blood. I seemed to suddenly know Italian words to use in a conversation. Strangely, my pronunciation was better than my vocabulary, giving the impression that I was fluent. People rattled off, and I couldn't understand much."

He and Linda had common interests beyond Italy and later married. They settled in Albuquerque, raising a family of four, all born in Albuquerque. They visited Italy every summer, which drove their interest in the country. Pat had taken a job at Albuquerque Academy as a middle school teacher. After working for a few years, he got the break he needed. The Academy was part of a consortium of English schools throughout the world. A job had opened up for a teacher at one of the consortium's schools in Italy. He applied for the position and was accepted.

He and Linda moved the family permanently to Italy in 2005. Today Linda teaches at the school and is very active in many local parishes and Pat is the Resident Director at School Year Abroad, the same school that brought him back to Italy. Pat explained that "The aroma of the homes in Italy solidified my decision to live here. They were exactly the same as Nonna Giulia's home. The olfactory connections were very powerful." Pat also explains how he reconciles his position in Italy versus what he might have achieved as an American physician. "Of course I could make much more money as a doctor, but the pleasure I have doing a job that I love in this beautiful country more than offsets any monetary difference. Look, in an hour, I can be at the Vatican. I can visit Florence, the home of the Renaissance, on a whim. My children are not only multilingual but mobile between two continents and all the countries in Europe." All of the Scanlons were born in America and have dual citizenship with Italy. He adds, "When Nonno and Zio came to America a century ago, they had no choice. It was their only hope for the future. Now, I have come back to Italy because I do have a choice, which is the great gift that Nonno and Zio gave us."

APPENDIX VI

SCANDALO (SCANDAL) IN ITALIAN CULTURE

The prominence and social potency of "scandalo" in Italian culture is difficult to overstate and explain. The engrained concept begins deep in the bowels of Italian cultural history and centers around the family, which was universally considered the nucleus of life. Life is created, nurtured and groomed for the next generation within the family. For most of human history, procreation was the goal of life. It was certainly the focus of life in the 18th and 19th Century Lucca, where the family originated. Large families provided young people to care for the elderly, mothers to help daughters in child-rearing, and fathers to assist sons in caring for their families. The church encouraged large families ostensibly as a means to serve God but more practically to sustain a healthy civil and parishioner population. It was a self-contained and self-perpetuating system that had operated for centuries.

THE FOUNDATIONS OF SCANDAL IN ITALIAN CULTURE

Most of Albuquerque's Italian colonists were steeped in the culture of large families. With businesses often associated with the family, managing the marriages ensured that only appropriate blood could be injected into the next generation. In 18th and early 19th Century Italy, country folks were essentially immobile, many living their entire lives within a few miles of their birthplace. They knew their neighbors, and by observing them over time, they ascribed certain skills or aptitudes for occupations. Most of the Italian peasants were farmers, who held a range of skills, but others were vintners, grain processors, iron smiths and millwrights, all of which required specific skills. The people believed that some personal skills and traits flowed from one generation to another via the blood (or DNA, in the modern vernacular). Thus, the concept of blood relatives and blood family evolved. Blood relatives are one's parents, grandparents and children. Blood family extends the circle to aunts, uncles and cousins.

A family that specialized in certain skilled trades often produced offspring who adapted easily to the work of that trade, where they excelled and enjoyed it. It was common, for example, to declare "The Puccis know wine" as an indication of the skills of all three Pucci generations within that family: the old, the working and the youngsters. Pucci's family, vintners of some repute, expected to produce offspring with similar skills. They did. Luigi Pucci and his offspring in Albuquerque all worked in the liquor business for decades.

Italians were long-range planners, measuring familial progress over generations. They believed the best approach to success is to manage the bloodlines. Like his sons, Julio held that traits, skills and aptitudes ran in families. Italian marriage became the family's most important event and the father's greatest responsibility. Parents sought control over the selection of mates—either directly or by insinuation—because the union brought new blood into the family to generate the next generation. In the day's vocabulary, new blood brought new traits, so they chose carefully. To the parents, especially the father, desired mates would complement or enhance the family's stature and productivity. Fathers strove to match daughters to men from families in similar trades or professions. Sometimes, they attempted to move the family forward by marrying to the next social level.

Love between the wife and husband was preferred in a marriage, but many parents, especially the older immigrants, prioritized family needs over affection, concluding that since marriage is a lifetime bond under God, the couple will learn to love each other one way or another. Daughters were important, but sons were more important because they carried the family surname; in Amerigo's terms, they carried the "family blood." The female side holds a different surname but it is the paternal name that lives on. Positioning the oldest son in marriage is important to the father's business prospects. A son from a successful farming family might be nicely paired with the daughter of a family that purveyed farming products. In Segromigno, the Menicucci family had for generations only a pool of other peasant families for marriage partners. Families also considered the fecundity of the prospective family. Reproduction was essential to survival; thus, marrying into large families enhances the probability that the marriage will produce children. Julio once told me, "Your job as a man is to take care of your family and children," indicating that producing offspring carrying the family blood should be my objective.

Italian fathers prided themselves in their surname responsibilities, and many sought to retain influence over their offspring concerning the family's name. Many family names had eponymously become business names. Amedeo Matteucci, Luigi Pucci and Frank Franchini are all examples of Italians who used family names for business, uniquely linking the two. Even for others, such as the Menicuccis, the goal was a perfect reputation. Any customer dispute was promptly rectified to the customer's satisfaction. Amerigo's goal was to link the quality and value of service to him personally. Similarly, at Amedeo and Palladino Grocery, Amedeo frequently delivered groceries to talk directly to the customer and ensure complete satisfaction. At his Mint Café, Modesto Dalle built personal relationships with each customer. These men not only operated profitable businesses but they also built friendships with their customers.

Like many Italians, including Amerigo, Julio was also obsessed with the integrity of the family name. As part-time work in the late 1960s, I drove a two-ton flatbed delivery truck for Super Oil. One summer day, I drove the truck back to the warehouse for a refill and reassignment. I saw Julio's auto creep up behind me as I lumbered north on 1st Street. A teenage street rumble was backing up traffic and a line of cars came to a stop. I wanted to impress Julio by getting things going; time was wasted. I honked a couple of times, stuck my teenage head out the window and shouted, "Get outta the way." I was all about demonstrating efficiency to my Nonno (grandfather).

My performance did not impress him. He honked, poked his head out of the window and yelled for me to pull the truck over. He parked in back of me and when I exited, he lit in. I remember his words clearly: "Don't ever honk at people. You might make them mad." He pointed to the door of the truck. "Do you see that name? "Super Oil means you act right." He added, "Don't look out your window at the stop lights because the women might be mad. It is bad for business." He knew the propensities of young men sitting in the high reaches of the truck cabin who could see the legs of women drivers. "You look straight ahead at the lights. Get back to work." The message was crystal clear: People associate Super Service and Super Oil with the Menicucci family. Thus, Menicuccis are responsible for acting properly by following civil law, God's commandments and the rules for common courtesy. Two Menicucci families completely relied on their two businesses for their sustenance. Protecting the family name was not only good for social appearances, it had financial benefits. Most Italians worked in the private sector and many were businessmen. They understood these realities and acted accordingly.

HOW SCANDAL OCCURS

A family's reputation was a prime factor in marital decisions. Families strove to introduce advantageous traits into the bloodline through marriage. They knew that good blood blended with other good blood produced offspring with good blood. In the Twenty-First Century vernacular, they meant that if your child marries someone from a family with similar virtues and beliefs as yours, the likelihood of the marriage producing healthy, productive offspring was high.

That is perfectly sensible but the inverse of the situation scared them. Bad traits can corrupt a bloodline. A family with a generational string of convicted scofflaws might be suspected of harboring a serious imperfection caused by their environmental, heredity, or both. It mattered not. The cautious conclusion is that whatever that family did was wrong, producing flawed offspring. The scandalized family is laden with a metaphorical caution flag that waves at marriage times. Many Italian immigrant fathers strove to a high standard—perfections, as in Jesus Christ. Keeping one's family-slate free from scandal was good for all.

Like people in all parts of the globe, rumor-mongering has been a pastime for as long as people have existed in civilized society. Italians specialize in it, producing a community chatter of fact and fiction that is characterized by the word scandalo, or scandal in English. It has special implications: scandals, true or false, blight a family's prospects for generational quality. Severe consequences, indeed. Most Italian families sought to avoid scandal at all costs and, if they occurred, to quash them as soon as possible. A budding family scandal in 1900 in Italy enveloped a family like political scandals enveloped a U.S. Presidency. Typically, the scandalized party responds by denying, then obfuscating, and covering it up if all else fails. When caught, spin the facts to guard the rear flank in retreat.

Scandal most frequently occurs with a violation of the Catholic faith, where Jesus Christ, a perfect human, is the role model. Perfection was the standard for most Italians, an impossible bar to clear. Fortunately, if one sinned, the offense could be redeemed in the confessional, but it was handled privately. No scandal ensues. A sin made public, such as an illegitimate birth, not only implicated the participants but also the relatives, such as parents who failed to impart moral guidance. Their souls are equally at risk. Scandal in a family often does not die with the death of the participants and, if serious, can sometimes pass through several generations like some inherited disease.

A dramatic incident in Julio's home in the early 1950s is a good example of Giulia and Julio's sensitivity to scandal. Giulia was the least assimilated into American culture as she rigidly adhered to the old Italian customs and language. She never learned English; her total vocabulary at death after living in Albuquerque for sixty years was perhaps seventy-five words. She adhered to strict Italian codes of conduct and dress for public outings, requiring women to have male or parental escorts. Single Italian women lived at home until marriage under the protection of their fathers. After marriage, that care was transferred to her husband. Giulia ran her Albuquerque home in the unmitigated fashion of her grandmother in Italy. Strangely, Juilo never commented on her strict adherence to Italian tradition, ceding total authority of the home to her.

When her oldest daughter, Teresa, around twenty-eight, decided to leave the family home and take an apartment with a female working companion, Giulia exploded with outrage. It rattled through the family as Julio backed up Giulia. Giulia forcefully declared Teresa violated all manner of Italian standards for women's conduct and brought scandal to the family. In 1895 Italy, it was true. A woman leaving home before marriage fomented a major scandal—a genuine problem. In the early 1950s, a couple of young, single working women sharing an apartment as they prepared for marriage was an American custom. It exemplified the earliest indications of the women's movement, which sought freedom from the holds of Patriarchy. Patriarchic society functioned in Italy because so much of life centered on physical labor, demanding men, who were, on average, much stronger than women. Very few women in 1900 Lucca were capable of working the fields. Women, naturally smaller with less strength, were adapted to the critical job of baby producers and homemakers, one of the pillars of Italian life. Women, they observed, were most capable of managing the homestead and nurturing the health and spiritual growth of the family. In this system, one has to lead, and it is designated to the man who is larger, stronger, and the most capable of physically protecting the family. In short, it made common sense.

What made sense in 1900 Italy, made little in 1950s Albuquerque's American-style society. The Albuquerque workforce was more diversified, with many jobs that were agnostic to the sex of the holder. In Italy, women and men were consigned to a specific role adapted to the Italian economic environment and social structure. Albuquerque's prosperity allowed women freedoms that would never have been possible in Italy. Women deviated from their traditional roles, taking many new jobs that were springing into existence. Teresa was moving conservatively with the times.

To Giulia, Teresa was well out of bounds. It did not help that Teresa's two cousins and her younger sister had already married, and all had lived at home until they wed. Giulia pounded on that fact and used it as an argument for proper behavior, meaning staying at home until marriage. From childhood, Teresa was a clear-thinking, loudly-speaking woman of high moral character who had decided to exercise her right to freedom, just like her brothers had. She was an American and worked among other young American women who were models for the freedom she coveted. Teresa was a large, heavy-set Italian woman who never walked away from a good spat, and she was steadfast in her decision. It came to blows.

Julio tried a direct order, declaring as her father that she was prohibited from leaving. Giulia had already tried that, and it had just inflamed Teresa, who was unmoved and continued to pack her belongings into Ellen Ann Ryan's auto. Her workmate was outside the idling vehicle waiting for the victor to emerge. The Ryans lived only a couple of blocks from the Menicuccis in the Huning Castle Addition, and the neighborly connection irritated the situation. Giulia tried shaming her with the ridiculous suggestion that she might appear to be a whore and scandalize the family among neighbors. It was "against God's will," Giulia argued, "you will be living in sin, a scandal." Running in high gear, Teresa responded, "If it's a sin, I'll go confess and say a Hail Mary." Her quick wit infuriated Giulia and left Julio speechless.

Teresa politely bid them farewell as they glumly stood by the front door glaring at her as she processed down the front walk, threw her last bag in the back seat, sat proudly in the passenger seat and slammed the door. She said later, "I want you to know when Ellen Ann drove me away, I thought I just broke jail. We went to Denny's to celebrate." In Julio's empty nest, brooding prevailed. Giulia might have descended into Cardiac arrest had she known that Teresa dined at a restaurant without male escorts. Old

Italian customs lived on unabated in many immigrant Italian families, certainly in Giulia's kitchen.

Italian scandal was genuine, visceral and potent. Successful families managed scandals and minimized damage to their reputations. They were rewarded with respect and favorable mates for their children. Other scandal-plagued families suffered the reciprocal effects, sometimes for decades. Julio and Amerigo had witnessed a scandal in Italy when their aunt, the mother of Johnny Giannini, and her husband had their civil marriage fees waived after Lucca authorities declared them indigent. The scandal of indigency, an indication of improper living, dwelled in the Giannini family for a couple of generations, spanning into their first decade in Albuquerque. Much of Johnni Giannini's antics on the local scene was an attempt to expunge the family scandal by demonstrating wealth and status.

One might assume that by that time, a modern, Twentieth Century culture less dependent on ancient myths and legends might have moderated the fear of scandal. Not so. Fear of scandal endured with vigor in the colony. Scandal was one of the most frequently heard expressions in the Menicucci families and most others. The Italians used scandal as a reason to gossip about other Italians. Hardly a week passed without some scandal or another being adjudicated at the dinner table. Giulia was consumed by scandal, and she influenced Julio, but it did not take much of a scandal to light a fuse under him, especially if the family business was implicated.

The drama that always followed any mental disorder was not confined to the Menicucci family, but all Italians would take similar action to shield the family from the scourge of scandal. In the 1940s, Amerigo was involved with Amedeo Matteucci to quietly slip his wife, Ancilla, out of town for special medical treatment. Ancilla had been treated at Nazareth but with marginal success. The physicians recommended a special treatment center in Colorado Springs, Colorado. Amedeo could not drive her to Colorado himself; someone had to care for Ancilla on the trip. Davina Menicucci, wife to Amerigo, was good friends with Ancilla; she knew Ancilla's Petroni family from Italy. Amedeo feared that the escalation in treatment would attract undue attention from the community. Instead of seeking assistance from family members—there were plenty available to help—he covertly asked Amerigo and Davina to travel with him and Ancilla to Colorado Springs. As far as anyone could tell, they were off on a vacation, a plausible cover story. Amerigo and Davina, understanding the situation, agreed to help. The Matteuccis socialized regularly with

Menicuccis, forming a relationship on par with blood family. The event also demonstrates Amerigo's and Davina's benevolence towards others.

Scandal is an enduring feature of Italian culture, even in the Twenty-First Century. The Italians still enforce an interesting incest law. Incest is not illegal unless it causes a scandal, in which it becomes a felony. They do not define a scandal, leaving it up to the civil authorities to decide whom to prosecute.

During my research for this book, several family members refused to discuss various historical scandals, even though some had occurred over a half century ago. Some agreed to talk about scandals only under anonymity or disguise. In a 2010 interview that I conducted with Mariangela Menicucci Scanlon concerning Dante's illness, she cowered to scandal fears by insisting that our discussion be private, not recorded in in any way, and the source of the information never to be divulged while she was living. Of course, all of the humans involved in those events are now many decades deceased, and many of their acts reside in the public domain. The actions of the people involved in half-century-old scandals have no real bearing on today's descendants other than in their imaginations.

I also encountered several Italian descendants of immigrants who refused access to records of a past prominent family member who has been deceased for a quarter of a century. The fear was that somehow, someway, the information might impugn their family name today. I could not describe several noteworthy early Albuquerque Italians for this book because the living family feared scandal and refused access to historical information. Scandal is so potent it regularly rises from the grave to strike.

VII

TAKING STOCK OF WHAT THEY SOWED THE FOUR IMMIGRANTS REFLECT ON TODAY'S FAMILIES

Throughout this book, I presented a true story on a factual basis and with minimal speculation. In this essay, I take the opposite view and speculate on a question likely of great interest, especially given the less-than-subtle societal changes since the turn of the century. How would the original four immigrants judge the Menicucci family today relative to the original family goals?

Certainly, when the original immigrants died in the middle 1980s, the family was heading in the right direction, but the Italian people measure familial progress in generational terms. Thus, a family name is built over decades, and the success of colonization is measured using the same metrics. Julio's job was to colonize the Menicucci family in America. To him and his brother, this meant creating a family that, over generations, consistently produced morally balanced, productive people who contribute to society to the best of their abilities.

The family has been in Albuquerque for just over a century and is now positioned to produce the fifth generation. If the family colonization was successful, ample evidence should be obvious today. Who better than the immigrants themselves to judge the performance of the family over the past four decades since they left?

Imagine that the four immigrants could return today, just as the people they were in the 1960s and 1970s—the peak of their influence and success—and using that period as their historical reference. Let's envisage them checking out the modern city, politics, church, etc. and performing an audit of the family, with details procured as needed. Suppose we ask them for a report card. How has the family performed relative to your goals? How has the community progressed relative to your expectations?

Naturally, there is no way to accurately know the actions of these people in this hypothetical situation, but their basic personalities and characteristics can suggest some reactions. Given my time with the early family immigrants, I am likely the best person to provide a perspective about their reactions.

THEY SPEAK

Giulia's reaction is the easiest to predict. Giulia marginally assimilated into American culture. She immersed herself in her housework and especially her cooking, but she had little to do with the community outside the home, including within the Italian colony. Her reading was limited to three newspapers, two from Lucca that were sent to her via the US Mail, two weeks late, and the *Albuquerque Journal* and *Tribune*, which she pursued in search of news about other Italians. She rarely watched TV. She was oblivious to many political machinations that contorted the country during the Vietnam War and the Arab Oil Embargo. She was not interested if it did not involve her family in Albuquerque or Italy.

Giulia became famous within the family for her ability to accurately predict the sex of various family babies. She correctly predicted thirteen in a row over about ten years before missing one. But then she went on to correctly get the next three in a row. Her feat is equivalent to having the heads of a fair coin come up ten times in a row, then one tail, followed by three more heads. The odds of such are very low.

Her generational perspective was heavily woven with ancient Italian paternalism regarding the timing of the production of males in the bloodline. She believed that a male first child indicated good fortune. The placement of males in the production line, her family believed, was an indicator of family breadth and generational potential. In Julia's mind, the more males up front, the better. Her examination of the 2024 Menicucci family would center on the birthing order of males and bloodlines introduced by marriage.

Julio would be out of the stops with a furry, demanding to know exactly how many family children were being produced and what good they were doing. Generational progress was his generational focus. "Every generation in America is better than the one before," he said frequently. A family builds generational wealth by working together over generations, typically retaining real property. Amerigo always wholeheartedly agreed. He adamantly refused to define "better," leaving it to be interpreted in the future as appropriate. His simple metric to judge the family's progress: Are Menicuccis today respectful of God and America and producing people who contribute to society to the best of their abilities? He said often, "Some people can only sweep the walk and others, like us, can run a business. So we do." He would seek to know whether the family demonstrated the benefits of "good generational blood," the concept that families develop and hone certain traits or skills that pass over generations.

Davina's perspective would likely differ due to her personal life experiences, some of them quite harsh, and her use of prayer to generate and maintain hope. Prayer was her only salvation in the darkest days a mother can face—the loss of her children and grandchildren. Amerigo learned the power of prayer in a copper mine. For twenty years, the family struggled with one loss after another. Yet, they never lost hope because they prayed.

She and Amerigo were consummate Catholics, among the most loyal Immaculate Conception parishioners. Although their direct involvement with the church operations was limited, they contributed monetarily. Plus, the couple attended seven o'clock Mass every day of the year. I looked forward to serving that mass for a week because Davina and Amerigo waited outside the sacristy for me to exit the sacristy to return to class at St. Mary's. Amerigo stuffed a dime in my pocket and told me to buy some extra milk, adding a pinch of my arm and a wink for emphasis. On Saturdays, they took me to the Little Café, on the corner of Seventh and Tijeras, for breakfast. Every visit, Davina told the waitress, whom she knew by name, to "put a little more food on David's plate. He just served mass." They were proud of my participation in the Catholic church, which they revered. Davina would want to know if Menicucci's descendants are respectful to the Lord, lived virtuous lives and used prayer to generate hope.

Amerigo was a kind, gentle man whose primary concern was the welfare of others. He fiercely embraced the concept of fairness, and he applied it throughout his life. He was a successful retailer because he cared not only for his customers but also for his employees. "We never fire anyone who does his job," he told me. But he had strict work standards: "Men hired to work should work." Above all, he was an extraordinarily honest man. He taught these and other virtues directly to his grandchildren. When asked what principles of living he learned from his grandfather, John, son of Mario, immediately responded: "Honesty, hard work, caring about people and leading a good life." Without question, Amerigo would try to verify that his descendants continued to live by those same principles. He would be pleased.

FAMILY CASE STUDY

The Menicucci family in Albuquerque originated in 1922 with four people. One hundred and two years later, there are nearly two hundred descendants. Nearly all 3rd generation descendants are college-educated, and many have advanced degrees; others opted for trade schools. All are gainfully employed in various professions and jobs, from attorneys to professors, CEOs to specialty craftsmen, religious clerics to American military officers, retail professionals to artists and so on. Many continue to be involved in charitable endeavors, individually or through a religious organization, in keeping with family tradition. Although some have drifted from the Catholic church, most remain Christians and/or adhere to Judeo-Christian ethical principles daily. The family has largely reserved some of the most valued Italian customs, including culinary practices such as the family preparation of Ravioli at Christmas time. Many Menicuccis hunt, fish and gather mushrooms. Some remain religiously fervent, attending Catholic Mass daily. Even the tradition of dying was preserved. On the day that Dante died in 2010, I visited with him. He asked me to join him in prayer, the Holy Mary portion of the Hail Mary prayer, just as Amerigo and Julio employed when they faced death in the mines.

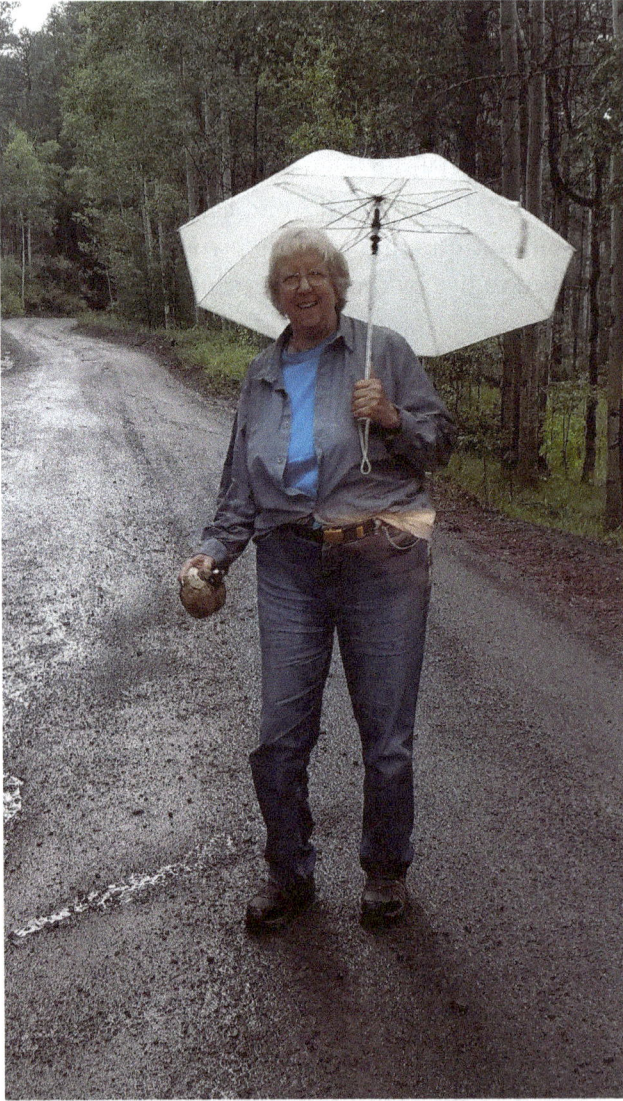

Mushroom hunting remains an activity of great interest to many Italians in America. Barbara Dinegar Menicucci, spouse to author, hunts for Porcini on a rainy August afternoon in the Jemez Mountains in 2022. Courtesy author's collection.

Julio would notice the emergence of at least two notable bloodlines. He first demonstrated an aptitude toward technical matters in the Michigan mines in 1912, and his direct descendants have enhanced and transferred these characteristics to their offspring. Various family members have gained respect and prominence in technical or related fields, beginning with Charlie, his second son. By the late 1980s, Dante had become the local go-to expert in the local press regarding oil price, availability, quality, and delivery technologies. During the years, the country was struggling with price increases following the oil embargo in the 1970s. In December 1982, he introduced Albuquerque to the concept of using a credit card to buy gas at self-service gas islands. It was one of his first clues that the old super service station concept was quickly disintegrating. His skills and proclivities live on in his bloodline, with some of his descendants working in the law and others in manufacturing in the technical sectors. In the direct line below Charlie, son of Julio, descendants include scientists, engineers, medical doctors, researchers, university professors, contractors and technical-trade professionals, to name but a few. Five technical patents have been issued to Charlie's descendants and various others have authored dozens of professional technical articles and other publications, including books.

Another noteworthy bloodline lay in Amerigo's family. Several prominent businesses, employing dozens, were founded and/or operated by Menicucci descendants from Mario, son of Amerigo, employing dozens. Some are family-run in the tradition of Super Service Station and Super Oil. They all concentrate on providing quality professional service, one stating this goal on its front door. In the family tradition, these businesses operate according to Judeo-Christian philosophy, including honesty, fairness and appropriate support to religious organizations. Family members work in various business professions, including consulting, sales and marketing. Julio would recognize and hail the business bloodline developed in Amerigo's family. Amerigo and Julio would both swoon at seeing buildings with the name "Menicucci Insurance" and law office "Calvert Menicucci, P.C.," proudly displayed. Upon learning that the businesses were family-run would leave them in a dead faint. The Lucchese firmly believed they could compete with any others in America's free-market capitalist system, and this generational performance supports the belief.

Identifying these two bloodline characteristics does not obviate that 3rd and 4th generation descendants are now diverging into a wide variety of professional endeavors. Whether and to what extent these traits remain in a bloodline is directly related to descendants. Traits can take generations to develop but can be wiped out in a single generation if descendants produce no offspring. Little "bad blood," as Julio characterized undesirable family traits, has emerged. To date, virtually no Menicuccis, save for Giulia's comical foray with Cannabis trafficking, have been implicated in or convicted of serious crimes, and none has been convicted or incarcerated.

Most of the second and third generations are well educated. While many family members are practicing Catholics or of other faiths, all, even those not attracted to organized religion, appear to live according to basic Judeo-Christian-like virtues and the common-sense rules embodied in the biblical Ten Commandments. Family members are generally gainfully employed and are prominent in charitable activities throughout the community, in both church and secular settings. Each generation of descendants has improved their lifestyle, which is vastly better—based on various metrics—than Raffaello Menicucci's family in 1908. Certainly, all four Menicucci immigrants would beam with pride at the family's generational accomplishments. If the family goal was to bring "good blood" to America, they did.

Many descendants—the second generation through the fourth—are fully committed to American ideals and family-oriented values. Family lore is replete with anecdotes of how American economic freedom lifted the Menicucci family—and many other Italians—from poverty. The extent to which future generations embrace the same fervor for America's unique free-market capitalist system as the immigrants is yet to be known. Standing in judgment today, all four immigrants would bet on the family. True virtue prevails over generations, and in 2024, there is nothing to suggest that much has changed in the family since they departed, and nothing suggests it will not continue. Asked for advice for descendants, Julio and Amerigo would be the ones to speak out: "Tell your children the truth about America. Without it, we would still be poor."

Although the four immigrants would collectively look askance at some of the emerging social customs, especially those regarding sexual practice and violence, from their family-centric viewpoint they would likely today see family descendants—regardless of religious or political affiliation—largely embracing healthy and productive life activities along with keeping traditions of value, such as ravioli.

The Menicuccis and friends assemble ravioli. From left: Emma Dalle Menicucci, Alison Pieroni, wife to Paul Menicucci, and Ed Matteucci, son of Nello. Courtesy author's collection.

Ravioli making during Advent continues an Italian tradition among the descendants of the immigrants. Special Italian-made tools are used in the process, including dough rollers and molds. The recipe for the dough and stuffing was handed down to Emma from her mother Pia Barsanti Dalle, who learned to cook from Emma Giomi Domenici. The ravioli are consumed on Christmas Day.

COMMUNITY'S POOR PERFORMER

Of all the societal changes these people would notice, the condition of the Archdiocese of Santa Fe and that of Immaculate Conception Church, in particular, would induce incredulity and shock. In the middle 1960s, the period of reference for the four immigrants, the Archdiocese of Santa Fe was a regional political and business goliath. It owned thousands of acres of property, and on them operated an array of business interests ranging from health care to education to sacramental administration, employing hundreds of employees. Seventeen catholic churches and many smaller chapels were splayed across the city, about one for every ten thousand citizens. In 1960, the archdiocese, which had created the first school system in New Mexico, controlled a college, four high schools and six elementary schools. In total, they enrolled close to five thousand students, about fourteen percent of the total school enrollment in the city. The Catholics provided low-cost, high-quality private education in the community. It operated a major hospital, a homeless shelter, a home for severely retarded children and a rest home.[1]

In 2024, the Archdiocese of Santa Fe is financially bankrupt. Many people, including some Catholics, feel it is morally bankrupt as well because the crimes that led to the financial disaster were some of the most heinous in society, followed by a decades-long effort to conceal the crimes. Dozens of Catholic priests who had served in the archdiocese for years have been either credibly accused or convicted of sexually abusing male and female children, including rape.

Today, this once mighty giant has ceded to bankruptcy plaintiffs all but the essential real estate and properties to conduct its spiritual and educational mission. It controls eight k-8 schools and no high schools. St. Pius X Catholic High School currently exists but was sold to a private, non-Archdiocesan entity as part of the bankruptcy settlement. Albuquerque's catholic schools today enroll about four thousand students—about the same total as in 1960—but now comprise just over five percent of the total Albuquerque school enrollment, sixty percent less than in 1960. It operates no hospital or college.

Thirty-three churches serve Albuquerque, roughly double the 1960 total, but given the city's population growth, their total presence in the community has shrunk from one for every ten thousand citizens in 1960 to one for every thirty thousand in 2024. Today, the archdiocese struggles to maintain a clerical presence in its remaining churches. Some churches that once had several full-time priests now suffice with visiting priests to perform Sunday Mass.

Many religious orders have withdrawn, most noticeably the teaching nuns, which in 1960 comprised ninety-seven percent of Albuquerque's Catholic school teachers. In 2024, very few nuns remain teaching, and virtually none wait in the wings. As a result, the one-time advantage of Catholic schools—its low-cost, professional labor force—has been replaced by lay people demanding living wages. The net result is substantially higher Catholic school tuition and parish operational costs. In 1960, the St. Mary's grade annual school tuition was about sixty dollars per year per student (about six hundred twenty in 2024 dollars). Today, a Catholic education costs at least ten times that.

Casa Angelica, Brothers of the Good Sheppard Refuge, St. Vincent DePaul and others continue to exist, gratifying the four immigrants. Service to the community is a primary Catholic responsibility, but their operations have been nearly fully secularized. The trends in Albuquerque follow the national ones. In 1960, twenty-six percent of the American population was Catholic; today it has slipped to eighteen percent. Nearly thirty dioceses nationwide are bankrupt, all paying for decades of poor labor practice. Vocations to religious orders have dwindled to a trickle. Modern Catholic religious services have been radically downsized. The Easter and Christmas services, once magnificent performances of spiritualistic uplift and theatric performance, have been replaced by simpler versions, with native tongues traded for the ancient Latin in prayers. In 2023, no Archdiocesan church in greater Albuquerque scheduled a midnight mass at any time of the year.

Modern Albuquerque Catholics rarely publicly demonstrate their faith; gone are the hours-long downtown processions of the Feasts of the Corpus Christi, San Felipe Di Neri and Our Lady of Guadalupe. In 1960, Catholics proudly wore Ash Wednesday cross-of-ashes on their forehead throughout the day. It was a big, thick cross, at least two inches square. At Super Service and Super Oil, every employee except the native Indians wore the cross. I remember dropping by the station on an Ash Wednesday afternoon and looking around, noticing nothing but black crosses on the heads of all the people I could see, including one customer after another who pulled up to the pumps for gas. Today, the same displays are rare. Archdiocesan clerics were widely respected and honored in the community. Today, Catholic churches in Albuquerque are emblazoned with warnings about potential clerical sexual abuse, encouraging parishioners to report suspected crimes, a clear indication that the church hierarchy believes the scourge still lurks in the priesthood.

In 1960, Immaculate Conception stood proudly in downtown Albuquerque with its mammoth sculpted bust of a crucified Christ projecting loudly from its front edifice and its sixty-foot bell tower looming on its south side. Inside, the church was one of religious opulence with solid-gold features throughout, including the sanctuary, tabernacle, support pillars, candle holders, candelabras, altar rails and mass implements, such as chalices and patens. Imported Italian marble slabs formed the altar, and a twenty-foot, Hispanic-designed Mexican-tile mosaic of the Virgin Mary filled the wall behind the altar. A side altar was dedicated to St. Joseph, the second patron saint of the parish after the Blessed Virgin. Four confessionals lined the north wall, and before holy days, all confessionals were manned by priests for several hours at a time.

In 1960, Albuquerque's largest and grandest church regularly opened at five in the morning and remained so until ten in the evening. That atmosphere was one of peace and quiet and served as a sanctuary of hope for Albuquerque's Catholics in distress. On any given midafternoon, the church hosted a couple dozen people praying. Some sat alone, eyes closed, meditating. Others knelt in front of the votive candles at the side altar. Occasionally, one could be seen walking the stations of the cross while praying the rosary. The school was open to the public but rarely experienced an intruder. Parents and others could be seen entering and exiting the school during regular hours. On Sundays, the school was unlocked for special events provided by the nuns and parents, such as donut sales for fundraisers.

In 2024, the church and school remain but lay sequestered behind a six-foot steel fence to keep undesirable people out. Unlike in 1960, when vagrancy was outlawed, tramps today roam Albuquerque's downtown with impunity, sleeping in trash containers at night and invading any building that is open to the public during the day. Many tote guns or knives. Today, those Catholics desperately seeking the sanctuary of hope in Immaculate Conception Church are out of luck unless they time their visit with a service. A full-time, professional security guard regularly patrols the church and school properties, promptly shooing out parishioners following each service.

The Jesuits departed Albuquerque, leaving voids in many Catholic organizations, most notably Immaculate Conception. They reportedly absconded with the church's historical records. A few records may have been turned over to the Archdiocesan archives. Catholic churches have for centuries served as the source of last resort for genealogists investigating familial linkages. In many New Mexico communities, genealogical research before 1900 largely depends on Catholic Church records. Immaculate Conception, the oldest Catholic church in Albuquerque, is not among the record holders.

Today, Immaculate Conception is manned by Archdiocesan priests, most of whom have no historical connection to the parish. The church maintains no archives or library. The school is strong but has about half the students as of 1960 and no high school. As is common with most modern Catholic schools, non-parishioner families comprise the majority of students, along with a growing number of non-Catholics.

The descent of the church would dishearten all four original immigrants. Giulia would refuse to believe it and drop out of the discussion. Once the other three immigrants surmounted their astonishment and absorbed the magnitude of the iniquities, they would surely experience shame and betrayal. Shame on those priests who purported to model the perfection of Christ while covertly engaging in the most despicable criminal behavior in society. Betrayal by the men whom they depended on for guiding their path to God instead acted as agents of Lucifer.

The vast majority of Catholic priests are innocent of the crimes plaguing the church, and many work diligently to restore trust by example. Yet, all Catholic male clerics and brothers bear, and will bear for years to come, the stigma inflicted on the Catholic church by a few miscreants and corrupt management.

THE BLAME FOR SHAME

Based on membership statistics, the American Catholic church reached its zenith in the late 1960s. The seriousness of the declining situation has driven a raging debate that has drawn out some notable scholars. Most appear to agree on two propositions. First, the church is in crisis. Second, the cause of the turmoil shortly followed the Vatican II reformation in the middle 1960s.

Disagreement lies in the proposed solutions, which vary radically. *Wills* and *Steinfels* argue it is the structure of the church that is the culprit, pointing at its stubborn adherence to clerical celibacy and its refusal to ordain females. *Steinfels* takes umbrage with the Vatican itself, recounting historically blunderous decisions that he believes resulted from systemic, organizational deficiency and corruption. Both authors suggest fundamental organizational restructuring to restore order. *Benedict and Sarah* take the opposite approach, blaming the poor execution of the Vatican II reforms and the decline of American morality. They essentially double down on staying the historical course but with more vigorous application.[2]

Several key problems vex the American Catholic church: restoring its reputation, stemming a shrinking customer base and controlling spiraling labor costs resulting from losing its cadre of low-cost clerics, nuns and brothers. The future of the American Catholic church remains undefined, but the damage inflicted from its performance over the past half century will certainly require many generations of reparations and reforms.[3,4]

Notes

1. Sheehan, in 1998, presents a detailed history of the Archdiocese of Santa Fe before the effects of the great sexual abuse scandal that resulted in its economic destruction.

2. *Stienfels, Wills* and *Sara & Benedict* are but a few of the debaters on possible changes in the Roman Catholic Church to meet modern needs.

3. *Stockman* discusses the decline of women in Catholic ministries.

4. Information about the cost of Catholic school education is based on personal knowledge. Other informational sources include the *Catholic New Agency*, the *Catholic News Service* and the *National Catholic Register*.

INDEXES

ITALIAN SURNAME INDEX

Below are indices of the Italians who are discussed in the book. Every Italian who lived in Albuquerque, New Mexico, between 1900 and 1950 is listed in Appendix II.

Bartolomeo 13, 53-54, 74-75

Carmalinda 106

Charlie (son of Julio) 9, 11, 50, 200, 252-253, 285, 305, 310, 331, 344, 348, 351, 355-358, 362-372, 395, 398, 403-415, 420, 422-432, 453, 461-462, 465, 467, 470-76, 478, 481, 483, 495, 498-499, 505-506, 510-537, 541, 617

Dante (son of Julio) 119, 195, 200, 281-282, 288, 297, 300, 311, 331, 342, 347-348, 350-351, 359, 376, 381-382, 396, 401-403, 406, 408, 412-428, 432-433, 440, 462-465, 473-476, 487, 516-521, 525-532, 537, 611, 615, 617

Elena (spouse of Geocondo) 36, 40-46, 67, 72-73

Emilio 48, 61, 64-67, 72-73, 211

Geocondo 35-48, 55, 59, 61, 65-73, 79, 81, 106

Giovanni 74

Julio (Americanized from Giulio) 9, 11, 13, 25, 31, 33, Chapter 2 (35-52), Chapters 4-10 (61-208), Chapter 12 (231-258), Chapters 14-19 (287-434), Chapters 22-23 (513, 542), Appendix VI and VII (604-624)

Julio Henry (son of Amerigo) 248, 250, 431, 438, 440, 456, 537

Letizia 48, 61, 75

Louise (daughter of Amerigo) 200, 252, 413, 441, 450, 453, 537-539

Luigi (son of Geocondo) 48

Luigi (son of Pasquale) 48, 52, 61, 65-68, 73-74,

Mariangela (daughter of Julio) 49, 68-69, 229, 248, 252, 301, 331, 334, 413, 418-419, 426-427, 432, 525, 542, 602, 611

Paolo 13, 54-55, 59, 61, 74-75, 166

Pasquale (son of Geocondo) 66, 68

Pasquale (son of Paolo) 13, 29, 41, 46, 48, 52-53, 56-57, 59, 61, 63-64, 66, 68, 70-77, 81, 106, 137, 162

Raffaello 13, 23, 26, 28-31, 38-48, 52-53, 61, 68-71, 75, 77-82, 105-106, 160, 165, 253, 542, 618

Rena (daughter of Amerigo) 209, 252, 413, 416, Chapter 20 (435-457)

Teresa (daughter of Julio) 68-71, 301, 418, 426, 432, 442, 466, 540

Morelli

Adele 19, 432, 453, 538-539

Amelia (spouse of Pasquale Menicucci) 40, 56, 61

Francesco 70, 138, 167

Raffaello 167, 202

Teodolindo 196, 311, 453, 495, 535

Ted 495, 535

Napoleone

Nick 185, 216, 564

Joseph 216, 564

Tony 216, 564

SUBJECT INDEX

WOPs (With Out Papers) 90
Italy/Italian
    Army 63-64
    Bocce Ball 303-305, 309, 475-476
    Casati act 27
    Census 72, 97, 134, 207, 257, 286, 413, 432-433, 575, 596-597, 601
    Courtship Chapter 9 (159-174), 394
    Explorers 10, 52-53, 303
    Family trees 11-12, 586-589, 594, 598
    Historic records 53, 590-601, 622
    Italian civil registry 11
    Latifando 23-24
    Lucchese 14, 33, 46-48, 56, 83, 91, 97, 104-106, 109, 113, 115, 130, 170,
173, 177-182, 185, 188, 195, 202, 204, 215, 219, 222, 225-229, 244-245, 250,
253, 264, 269, 271, 279, 313, 328, 330, 353, 430, 459, 466, 481, 495, 521, 531,
561, 617
    Mezzadria 14, 23-32, 43-44, 50, 54, 56-57, 63-64, 87, 132, 160, 310
    Mormon Church 594-595
    Ney York Yankees 476-478
    Notre Dame 477-480
    Padrono(e) 23-27, 30-36, 42, 44, 47-48, 52, 54, 56-57, 70, 77-83, 89-97,
105-107, 117, 121
    Papal States 54, 58, 510
    Piedmont 58
    Prayer 36, 45-47, 59, 82, 106, 110-113, 118, 127, 130-131, 151, 157,
160-161, 201-202, 249, 293, 311, 349, 355, 384, 390, 415, 419, 432, 436,
438-443, 447-448, 451, 454, 479, 502-503, 508-509, 539-540, 542, 614-615,
621-622
    Risorgimento 34, 57-58
    Vettore 30, 33, 78-79, 89
    Wedding 26, 49, 165-168, 173, 296-297, 413, 417-424, 428, 494, 537,
539, 596
    Wine 11, 41, 45-51, 94, 104, 115, 124-126, 133, 139, 156, 160-161, 164,
167-170, 180-182, 187, 223, 225, 228-229, 262, 264-265, 295-296, 303, 306-
311, 314, 328, 332, 334-335, 378, 391, 394,395, 424, 427, 506, 512, 515-516,
524, 530-532, 541, 605
Italian Bank 105
Jemez Mountains
    Cabins and resorts 313, 317-319, 326-328, 337, 561-562, 568-571, 622
    Economic development 126, 561-572
    Jemez Springs 227, 316-330, 463, 470, 523, 559, 561-568

LOCATION INDEX

Albuquerque
    Albuquerque Public Library (Genealogy Center) 12, 207, 433
    Country Club 426, 429, 515
    Huning Castle Addition 11, 426, 429-430, 466-467, 494, 501, 609
    Italian colony 10, 21, 174-180, 205, 207, 214, 223, 229, 245, 251, 269,
286, 288, 303, 307, 313-317, 330, 335, 342, 392-394, 420, 453, 459, 475, 487,
493-494, 498, 510, 513-514, 518, 532, 564, 568, 575, 610, 613
    San Carlos Road 11, 429-430, 466-467
    University of New Mexico 12, 20, 263, 350, 460, 478, 482, 489-490, 526,
559, 602
    Urban Renewal 527-529, 534
California
    Antioch 73
    Coloma 64
    San Francisco 64, 68-70, 89, 164, 397
France
    Havre 83-85, 91, 118
Idaho
    Pocatello 61, 65-67, 73
    Weiser 73
Illinois
    Kankakee 109, 114-115, 123-134, 138, 155-157, 162, 166, 169-170, 179
Italy
    Apennines 9, 55, 182, 313-314, 561
    Capannori 15-17, 27-28, 52-53, 55-57, 62, 72, 74, 79, 173, 176, 594
    Comune 14-17, 27-28, 33, 52, 55, 72, 74, 173-174, 181, 510, 594-595
    Frazione 14-17
    Lammari 15, 55, 62, 137
    Lucca Comune 15, 55, 181, 510
    Lucca Province 9, 14-16, 23-24, 26, 28, 47, 50, 52, 55-56, 62, 72, 74, 78-
79, 137, 158, 176
    Milan 58, 64
    Naples 46, 169, 171
    Northern 49, 54-55, 204, 334, 460, 497, 515

www.ingramcontent.com/pod-product-compliance
Lightning Source LLC
Chambersburg PA
CBHW060016030426
42334CB00019B/2068